THE MODERN LAW OF CONTRACT

Seventh Edition

Written by a leading author and lecturer with over thirty years experience teaching and examining contract law, this very popular and well-established textbook has been fully updated and revised for this new edition.

Exploring all recent developments and case decisions in the field of contract law, this volume combines a meticulous examination of authorities and commentaries with a modern contextual approach. Taking into account a variety of theoretical approaches: economic, sociological and empirical, Stone examines a broad range of material.

New features include:

- content that is mapped onto the common undergraduate syllabus and course outlines;
- chapter introductions highlighting the salient features under discussion, with short chapter table of contents to enable easier navigation;
- expanded further reading at the end of each chapter to guide further study and independent research;
- 'For thought' think points throughout the text where students are asked to consider 'what if' scenarios (e.g. what if a particular case had different facts);
- a Companion Website with yearly updates and guidance to useful websites;
- a highly accessible and flexible layout that meets the needs of a broad range of undergraduate students on contract courses.

Clearly written and easy to use, this book enables undergraduate students of contract law to fully engage with the topic and gain a profound understanding of this pivotal area.

THE MODERN LAW OF CONTRACT

Seventh Edition

Richard Stone

Routledge·Cavendish
Taylor & Francis Group
LONDON AND NEW YORK

Fifth edition published 2002 by Cavendish Publishing Limited
Sixth edition published 2005 by Cavendish Publishing Limited

Seventh edition published 2008 by Routledge-Cavendish
2 Park Square, Milton Park, Abingdon, Oxon OX14 4RN
Simultaneously published in the USA and Canada
by Routledge-Cavendish
270 Madison Ave, New York, NY 10016

Routledge-Cavendish is an imprint of the Taylor & Francis Group, an informa business

© 2002, 2005, 2008 Richard Stone

Typeset in Times New Roman and Helvetica Neue by
RefineCatch Limited, Bungay, Suffolk
Printed and bound in Great Britain by
MPG Books Ltd, Bodmin, Cornwall

British Library Cataloguing in Publication Data
A catalogue record for this book is available from the British Library

Library of Congress Cataloging in Publication Data
Stone, Richard, 1951 Mar. 7–
    The modern law of contract / Richard Stone. – 7th ed.
        p. cm.
    Simultaneously published in the USA and Canada.
    Includes bibliographical references and index.
    ISBN 978–0–415–42237–6 (hard cover) – ISBN 978–0–415–42528–5 (paper back)
1. Contracts – England.   2. Contracts – Wales.   I. Title.
    KD1554.Z9S76 2008
    346.4202 – dc22   2007016336

ISBN10: 0–415–42528–X (pbk)
ISBN10: 0–415–42237–X (hbk)

ISBN13: 978–0–415–42528–5 (pbk)
ISBN13: 978–0–415–42237–6 (hbk)

CONTENTS

DETAILED CONTENTS

PREFACE

The aim of this book is to provide a comprehensive but readable account of what I have termed 'the modern law of contract'. By this I mean the law of contract as applied by the English courts at the beginning of the 21st century. This I see as being still rooted in the forms of the classical theory of contract (which is generally accepted as dating from the late 19th century), but with those forms increasingly being stretched to adapt to the modern world. The inadequacies of the classical model which are thus exposed have been the subject of much commentary and analysis, together with suggestions of better models which might be adopted. Understanding the modern law requires an awareness of these critical analyses and this I have attempted to provide throughout the text. What results is not, however, and is not intended to be, a radical re-reading of this area of law. A quick look at the chapter headings will show an overall structure that will be familiar to all contract lecturers. For the purposes of exposition, many familiar authorities have been used. Throughout, however, and in particular through the footnotes, I have tried to indicate ways in which the classical model of contract may be or is being challenged and developed, whether openly or surreptitiously. I hope that the result is a treatment of the law which is easy to follow (to the extent possible given the complexity of some areas) but which is also sufficiently rich to provide a challenge to more discerning readers. At the very least I hope that such readers will be encouraged to think about and explore new lines of thought on a variety of topics.

The previous editions have been well received by students and lecturers, but some changes have been made to this edition as a result of feedback. Each chapter now starts with an outline of the contents, and an overview of the topics covered. Further reading is appended at the end of each chapter (in addition to the full bibliography at the end of the text). At various points, questions 'for thought' are identified. No answers are provided to these. They are intended to stimulate students into thinking about issues for themselves, and developing a critical approach to the law – not simply accepting what judges and commentators say as the only possible answer to any particular question. As a response to the view that assignment and competition law are not covered in undergraduate syllabuses, these sections have been removed. The changes in the gambling laws introduced by the Gambling Act 2005 have led to the removal of the separate chapter on contracts contrary to public policy and its incorporation into the chapter on illegality.

New case law covered in this edition includes *Apple Corps Ltd v Apple Computer, Inc* (formation of contracts by telephone), *Balmoral Group Ltd v Borealis* and *Sterling Hydraulics Ltd v Dichtomatik Ltd* ('battle of the forms' and reasonableness of exclusion clauses), *Laemthong International Lines Company Ltd v Artis (The Laemthong Glory) (No 2)* (privity), *Proform Sports Management Ltd v Proactive Sports Management Ltd* (minors' contracts), *Bairstow Eves London Central Ltd v Adrian Smith* (unfair terms), *Peekay Intermark Ltd v Australia and New Zealand Banking Group Ltd* (misrepresentation), *Halpern v Halpern* (duress), *Yorkshire Bank plc v Tinsley* (undue influence), *Vakante v Addey Stanhope School* and *Wheeler v Quality Deep Trading Ltd* (illegality), and *Jackson v Royal Bank of Scotland* (remoteness of damage).

Readers should note that as regards the use of the terms 'claimant' and 'plaintiff', I have continued the practice of previous editions, which is to use the label which will be found in the report of any particular case (which will depend on when the action was brought). Where the word is used generically, rather than in relation to a particular case, 'claimant' is used.

Finally, my thanks to my publishers, in their new incarnation as Routledge-Cavendish, and in particular Constance Sutherland, for their patience and assistance, and to my wife, Maggie, and the rest of my family for their support during the writing process.

The law is stated, as far as possible, as it stood on 31 March 2007.

Richard Stone
Elston, Newark
July 2007

TABLE OF CASES

TABLE OF STATUTES

TABLE OF INTERNATIONAL INSTRUMENTS

1 INTRODUCTION

CONTENTS

1.1 OVERVIEW

This chapter deals with some preliminary, but fundamental, issues which need discussion before embarking on a detailed consideration of the case law and statutes which make up the English law of contract. The order of treatment is:

■ What is meant by the 'classical' law of contract? This refers to a body of rules, generally developed by nineteenth century cases and the first contract textbook writers. It still has great influence in the modern law of contract.

■ What is the 'subject matter' of contract law? Is it simply a matter of enforcing promises, or is it concerned with regulating markets or facilitating trade? The 'voluntary agreement' seems to be at its heart.

■ Should contracts be looked at as 'discrete', isolated, events, or are they part of a continuing relationship between the parties? The work of Macneil, in particular, suggests that a 'relational' analysis is more satisfactory in many situations.

■ How is 'contract' distinguished from other areas of law involving civil obligations, such as tort and restitution? The 'voluntary exchange' is one of the distinguishing factors.

■ How far is the law of contract governed by general principles, as opposed to specific rules applying to particular types of contract, such as sale of goods, employment, land, credit? It is argued that there is still room for general principles.

■ What techniques for the analysis of contract can be adopted? Consideration is given to:
  □ doctrinal analysis (looking simply at cases and statutes);
  □ socio-economic analysis (drawing on other disciplines to help explain the law); and
  □ empirical research (investigating what happens in practice between contracting parties).

■ International influences on English contract law, including developments towards a European contract law.

1.2 INTRODUCTION

The issues considered in this chapter are principally concerned with identifying what the law of contract is, and its scope. There are a number of possible approaches to this question. It might be asked, for example, what relationships the courts currently regard as being within the scope of the law of contract. Answering this relatively easy question might be of some use, particularly from the practical point of view of deciding how to deal with a dispute between A and B. The task would, however, be essentially descriptive. If we want to go further and analyse the nature of contract or the contractual relationship, we will need to ask why some situations rather than others are dealt with as contractual, and try to find some rational basis for distinguishing between 'contract' and 'non-contract'. This is an issue which has been the subject of regular academic discussion over the last 40 years.[1] Moreover, even texts aimed at practitioners are unable to ignore it. *Chitty on Contracts*, the most well established practitioner's text, has an introductory chapter dealing with the 'nature of contract'. Its more recently published

---

1 See, for example, Macaulay, 1963; Gilmore, 1974; Simpson, 1975a; Macneil, 1978; Atiyah, 1979; Wightman, 1996; Collins, 2003; and Brownsword, 2000.

rival, Furmston's *The Law of Contract*,[2] goes even further, including a lengthy first chapter on 'General Considerations' (written by Professor Roger Brownsword).[3]

Our starting point is the concept of the 'classical law of contract', which many would regard as still the dominant approach, certainly within the decisions of the courts on contractual issues.

1.3 THE CLASSICAL LAW OF CONTRACT

It is generally accepted in modern writings on the English law of contract that during the latter half of the nineteenth century a concept of contract developed, together with an associated body of legal doctrine, which is now referred to as the 'classical law of contract'. This is not necessarily a matter of precise historical accuracy. As Wightman has pointed out,[4] the concept of the classical law can be said to be 'invented' in two senses. First, although based on decisions of the courts, the synthesis of those decisions into a (more or less) coherent body of law was largely the work of the 'treatise writers',[5] whose work decided which cases would be given prominence, and who encouraged the formulation of principles of general application to a wide range of transactions. Second, the recognition of the model of contract law which emerged from the latter part of the nineteenth century as 'classical', with the intention of using that model as the basis for an argument that the requirements of 'modern' contract law were different and that adherence to the classical model was inhibiting its development, is largely the product of the work started by commentators writing in the 1970s.[6]

Whatever the accuracy of the precise historical origins of the classical theory, it is now generally accepted that it is centred around the concept of 'freedom of contract', probably as a reflection of the dominance in the nineteenth century of *laissez-faire* economic attitudes. At a time of the swift industrialisation and increasing commercialisation of society, the best way of allowing wealth to develop was to let those involved in business regulate their own affairs, with the courts simply intervening to settle disputes.

---

2 First published by Butterworths in 1999; 2nd edn, 2003.

3 This chapter was published separately in the title *Contract Law: Themes for the Twenty-first Century*, 2000, London: Butterworths, cited here as 'Brownsword, 2000'. Unfortunately, the pagination is not the same in the two versions of the text. The references here are therefore to paragraph numbers, rather than to pages. Lord Steyn in the Preface to Furmston, 1999, commented that Brownsword's chapter 'examines the grand themes of our contract law in an impressive style. Nothing quite like it has ever been published in English law'.

4 Wightman, 1996, p 49. See also Brownsword, 2000, para 2.2. Chapter 5 of Wightman's book, entitled 'The Invention of Classical Contract' provides a useful summary of the development of the classical theory and its main elements. See also Chapter 1 in Beatson and Friedmann, 1995, especially pp 7–17.

5 For example, Powell, whose first edition appeared in 1790, and Anson, whose *Law of Contract* (designed for students) was first published in 1879.

6 See, in particular, Horwitz, 1974; Gilmore, 1974; Atiyah, 1979. Note that Horwitz's view of the historical development of contract was strongly challenged by Simpson, 1979.

The parties to a contract will be governed by rational self-interest,[7] and giving effect to transactions which result from this will be to the benefit of both the parties and society.

'Freedom of contract' in this context has two main aspects.[8] The first is that it is the individual's choice whether or not to enter into a contract, and if so with whom – in other words, the freedom *to* contract, or 'party freedom'. The second is the freedom to decide on the content of the contractual obligations undertaken, or 'term freedom'. This allows parties to make unwise, and even unfair, bargains – it is their decision, and the courts will not generally intervene to protect them from their own foolishness.

The paradigmatic contract which emerges from the classical theory has the following characteristics:

(a)   It is based on an exchange of promises.

(b)   It is executory. This means that the contract is formed, and obligations under it arise, before either side has performed any part of it.

(c)   It involves an 'exchange', so that each side is giving something in return for the other's promise. It is the existence of this mutuality (given effect through the doctrine of 'consideration')[9] which generally gives rise to enforceability.[10]

(d)   The content of the contractual obligations is determined by deciding what the parties agreed, or what reasonable parties in their position would have agreed, at the time the contract was made. Later developments are of no significance.

(e)   Disputes about a contract can generally be determined by asking what the parties expressly or impliedly agreed (or should be taken to have agreed) in the contract itself. This is sometimes referred to as the 'will theory' of contract.

(f)   The transaction is discrete, rather than being part of a continuing relationship.

(g)   The role of the court is to act as 'umpire' or 'arbiter', giving effect to the parties' agreement. In particular, it has no role in deciding whether or not the transaction is 'fair'.

There is probably also an underlying assumption that the parties are of equal bargaining power.

The type of contract which most closely fits the above paradigm is probably the commercial contract for the sale of goods, where the buyer and seller agree that at some agreed date they will exchange the ownership of goods of a specified type for a specified

---

7   In other words, each party will seek to organise and operate the contract in a way which produces the maximum 'utility' or benefit to that party.

8   Brownsword, 2000, para 2.5. Brownsword also identifies 'sanctity of contract' – the fact that 'parties are to be held to the agreements that they have freely made': ibid, para 2.8. This seems to be a consequence of freedom of contract, rather than an element in it, however. Such a principle might also apply even in the absence of party freedom and term freedom.

9   For which see Chapter 3.

10 This does not, however, take account of the role of the contract under seal, or deed, where no mutuality is required for a promise to be binding. See further on this, Chapter 3, 3.3.

sum of money. In practice, however, most contracts are not of this kind, and attempts to apply to them rules which were designed to be suitable for the paradigmatic case are likely to produce tensions and problems. Nevertheless, the classical theory of contract, and its model of the typical contract, can still be seen to cast its shadow over English law. In the latter part of the twentieth century it was the subject of sustained attack by academic commentators, and many judicial decisions can be seen to have moved, in practice at least, from the strict classical formulations. There is still a reluctance, however, to abandon them, and it is frequently the case that the courts, when involved in a development away from the classical model, will continue to use language which suggests that they are being faithful to it.[11] The challenge for the student of the modern law of contract in England is to reconcile the fact that it is still rooted in classical theory, at least in the way in which its concepts are expressed, while at the same time developing away from it. This is the reason why this book has adopted a format and chapter division which is largely traditional. It is within this traditional framework that the courts continue to consider contract cases. The substance of many of their decisions, however, and virtually all the interventions of Parliament, are taking the law in new directions. The form may be 'classical', but the content is 'modern', and this tension must be kept in mind in considering all that follows.

With this background to the development of the English law of contract in mind, we can now turn to the question of what exactly is meant by the 'law of contract'. What is its scope, and what are its boundaries?

1.4 THE SUBJECT MATTER OF CONTRACT LAW

What is the law of contract about? This is a question to which, perhaps surprisingly, there is no clear, universally accepted answer. There are, however, several candidates for the basis of the legal enforceability of contractual obligations. They can be viewed, for example, as a means of:

(a) enforcing promises; or
(b) regulating the market in the provision of goods and services; or
(c) facilitating exchanges (for example, of goods or services for money).

Any of these individually, or some combination of them, can be put forward as being at the root of the law of contract, but none of them is without difficulty.

As we have seen, the idea of the 'promise' is central to the classical law of contract, and some modern commentators are happy to continue to regard this as its

---

11 A particularly clear example of this is the Court of Appeal's decision in *Williams v Roffey Bros & Nicholls (Contractors) Ltd* [1991] 1 QB 1; [1990] 1 All ER 512, in which lip service was paid to the classical formulation of the doctrine of consideration, while in fact the decision departed significantly from it: see further, Chapter 3, 3.9.8.

distinguishing feature. Burrows, for example, asserts that 'The law of contract is concerned with binding promises. It looks at what constitutes a binding promise and how such a promise is made; at the remedies for breach of such a promise; and at who is entitled to those remedies.'[12] There are, however, severe limitations to an interpretation of contract based on promises. Although some contracts are clearly made by the exchange of promises – for example, 'I promise to build a house for you in accordance with these plans in exchange for your promising to pay me £100,000 on completion of the work' – there are many that do not easily fit this model. In particular, as has been pointed out judicially by Lord Wilberforce, many everyday transactions, such as buying goods in a shop or travelling by bus, do not do so without considerable strain.[13]They can be accommodated at best by taking the view that there is an *implicit* promise involved – for example, that the bus is travelling on the route indicated by its signboard. But in some situations it is difficult to find even a promise of this kind. In the typical shop transaction, a person takes goods to a till and hands over money. The contract has the effect of transferring the ownership of the goods from the seller to the buyer and of the money from the buyer to the seller. What promises are involved in a one-off transaction of this kind, which may well be conducted without any communication between the participants? The only one that can be identified is that the seller is implicitly 'promising' that the goods are of a satisfactory quality. However, since the obligation to supply goods which are satisfactory is imposed by statute and cannot be avoided in a consumer contract,[14] it is not necessary to use the language of 'promises' to explain this aspect of the transaction.

Even in commercial transactions, as the case in which Lord Wilberforce made the statement quoted above itself demonstrated, there are also some situations where contractual rights and liabilities are assumed to exist, but it is difficult to see that there has been any making of promises. The parties in the case which Lord Wilberforce was discussing assumed that stevedores unloading goods from a ship would have the benefit of an exemption clause contained in a contract between the owners of the goods and the carriers. No explicit promise of this kind was made to the stevedores, however. Indeed, in contracts of this type, the identity of the stevedores might well be unknown at the time the contract was entered into. The court resolved this effectively by 'imputing' a promise from the owners to the stevedores, via the agency of the carriers, that they would have the benefit of the clause.[15]

On the other hand, there are clearly some situations where promises *are* at the heart of the contractual obligation. Contracts for the purchase and sale of commodities on the futures market plainly depend on the assumption that promises will be kept or

---

12 Burrows, 1998, p 3: See, also, Fried, 1981.
13 See Lord Wilberforce in *New Zealand Shipping Co Ltd v AM Satterthwaite & Co Ltd, The Eurymedon* [1975] AC 154, p 167; [1974] 1 All ER 1015, pp 1019–20.
14 See Sale of Goods Act 1979, ss 13 and 14, and the Unfair Contract Terms Act 1977, s 6, discussed in Chapter 8, 8.6.11 to 8.6.14, and Chapter 9, at 9.7.19.
15 For further discussion of this case, see Chapter 5, 5.12.1.

that, if broken, compensation will be payable. Another example is the doctrine of promissory estoppel,[16] which is based on the fact that it requires a person who makes a promise to be held to it, even though there is no consideration given for it.

The conclusion must be, therefore, as Brownsword has pointed out, that although it is possible to use 'promise' as a necessary definition of contract, this is only so if we include 'express, implicit and imputed promises'.[17] 'Promise' is not a sufficient condition, however, since there are situations in which clear and explicit promises are not enforced. In general, for example, promises which are neither supported by consideration nor contained in a deed will not be treated as binding on the promisor.[18] In other areas where apparently gratuitous promises have been held to be binding, such as in the case of *Williams v Roffey Bros & Nicholls (Contractors) Ltd*,[19] the courts have been at pains to find 'consideration', even if this has involved 'stretching' this concept so as not to be seen to be departing from the orthodoxy that gratuitous promises are not binding.

Furthermore, there are agreements which appear to have all the hallmarks of the archetypal classical contract – that is, an exchange of promises and consideration – which will nevertheless not be treated as binding. This may arise where there is no 'intention to create legal relations'.[20] This may be because the arrangement has been made in a domestic context.[21] It can also arise, however, in a commercial context where it has been made clear that the agreement is 'binding in honour only'.[22] In both types of case, the courts are giving effect to what they see as being the intentions of the parties. This area, as an element in the formation of the contractual obligation, is discussed at length in Chapter 4. It is another indication, however, that a 'promise' is not in itself sufficient as a basis for identifying contractual obligations.

The second suggested candidate as the basis for modern contract law – market regulation – clearly has some force, in that part of what the courts do in developing and applying the law is to determine the limits of the free market. It does not, however, deal very satisfactorily with the situations where in fact the courts do not intervene to

---

16 See Chapter 3, 3.11.

17 Brownsword, 2000, para 1.11.

18 See, for example, *Foakes v Beer* (1884) 9 App Cas 605 (Chapter 3, 3.13.1 to 3.13.3); and *Atlas Express Ltd v Kafco (Importers and Distributors) Ltd* [1989] QB 833; [1989] 1 All ER 641 (Chapter 12, 12.4.2). The main exception to this principle is to be found in the concept of promissory estoppel: *Central London Property Trust Ltd v High Trees House Ltd* [1947] KB 130; [1956] 1 All ER 256. Even here it should be noted that the gratuitous promise became unenforceable once the conditions which gave rise to its being made had disappeared (that is, the Second World War had come to an end). See further, Chapter 3, 3.11 and 3.13.3.

19 [1991] 1 QB 1; [1990] 1 All ER 512. This case is discussed in detail in Chapter 3, 3.9.8.

20 See Chapter 4.

21 For example, *Balfour v Balfour* [1919] 2 KB 571 – arrangement for a husband to provide financial support for his wife during the marriage (as opposed to following its break-up). See below, Chapter 4, 4.1.

22 For example, *Rose and Frank Co v JR Crompton and Bros Ltd* [1923] 2 KB 261. See below, Chapter 4, 4.4.

'regulate' but simply give effect to what the parties themselves have agreed (or are deemed to have agreed) – even if the result may appear 'unfair' and provide no benefit to the general public.[23] The courts in such a situation will not hold back from enforcing a 'bad bargain'. Nevertheless, some commentators do see market regulation as being at the heart of contract law. Collins, for example, sees the 'social market' as being central to the modern law of contract.[24] He sees three themes – 'concern about unjustifiable domination, the equivalence of exchange, and the need to ensure co-operation' – as forming the core of his interpretation of the law of contract.[25] It might, of course, alternatively be argued that simply enforcing agreed obligations is to the general benefit, because it reduces transaction costs if the parties are aware that a clear agreement will be enforced, no matter that 'injustice' to one of the parties may result. This is the argument that 'certainty' in the law overall is preferable to 'fairness' on the facts of any particular case.

The third candidate identified above as a concept which might be said to be at the centre of contract is 'exchange', and this is at first sight an attractive proposition. Many of the transactions which we think of as involving a contract – for example, the purchase of goods or services – do involve 'exchange'. A person transfers the ownership of goods to another in exchange for the price; work is done in exchange for wages; a company agrees to license the use of a patented process in exchange for royalties. There are, however, situations which do not properly involve an exchange, but which are nevertheless treated as contracts. First, there are those transfers of property which are effected by a formal deed. In this case, provided that the formalities of the deed are properly carried out, the transaction can be entirely gratuitous: nothing is required from the recipient to make the transaction legally binding. Such transactions are regarded as being within the province of contract law, and therefore need to be accommodated within any definitional scheme intended to delineate its scope.

It might, perhaps, be possible to treat transfers by deed as being an example of categorisation error, and to argue that they should be treated as *sui generis* and not part of the general law of contract. This would not solve the problem, however, since there are other situations which do not involve any proper exchange which it would be much more difficult to 'hive off' in this way. As we will see later,[26] in informal contracts,[27] although the law of contract normally requires a degree of 'mutuality', so that something is being provided by each party to the agreement, the value of what is being provided is generally irrelevant. Thus, supposing a rich aunt decides to make her

---

23 As, for example, in *L'Estrange v F Graucob Ltd* [1934] 2 KB 394 – party held to an unread term in a signed contract. See, further, Chapter 9, 9.4.
24 Collins, 2003. See also Collins, 1999.
25 Collins, 2003, p 29. These themes are, in Collins' view, well illustrated by the case of *Schroeder Music Publishing Co Ltd v Macaulay* [1974] 3 All ER 616; [1974] 1 WLR 1308 – which is discussed below, Chapter 15, 15.5.1.
26 Chapter 3, 3.7.
27 That is, those not created by deed.

favourite nephew, who is currently 19 years old, a gift of her Porsche on his 21st birthday. She could commit herself to this transaction by promising that she will transfer the car on the day of his birthday provided that he pays her one penny in exchange. The reality of this transaction is that she is making a gift of the car, and her nephew is providing nothing of real value in exchange. Nevertheless, the courts would treat this as a binding contract (subject to their being satisfied that there was an intention to create legal relations). The application of this approach in a more commercial context can be illustrated by the case of *Chappell & Co Ltd v Nestlé Co Ltd*,[28] where the provision of the wrappers from bars of chocolate was held to be part of the consideration for the supply of a gramophone record. This was the case even though the wrappers were worthless and were thrown away by the company when received. The transaction had the trappings of exchange, but was in essence a gift. Nevertheless, it was treated as contractual.

The reason for this relates to the fact that the courts are generally keen to adopt an approach which complies with the intention of the parties. If the parties, knowing the English law of contract, have used the trappings of exchange to clothe a transaction which is in effect a gift, they have probably done so in order to make their agreement legally enforceable, without the trouble of using a deed. The courts should therefore be prepared to give effect to that intention and treat the transaction as a binding contract.

FOR THOUGHT

Why did Nestlé want people to send in the wrappers? What benefit was there to Nestlé in this promotion? Could this have been sufficient to constitute consideration?

We can, therefore, if we exclude contracts made by deed, argue for 'exchange' as being at the heart of contract. But here, similar to the way in which with the notion of 'promise' we needed to include implied, imputed and constructed promises, we will need to include 'sham' exchanges in order to make the approach work. And if we do that, we may well feel that we have still not really got very near to the essence of what makes a 'contract'.

In the end, we may have to accept that we will not find a straightforward answer to the question of what contract 'is'. As Brownsword points out, finding an 'essential definition' (that is, identifying 'necessary and sufficient' elements) is more difficult than approaching it as a '. . . cluster concept (in which several elements are identified with the usage, but where no single set of these elements can be combined to represent the necessary and sufficient conditions for correct usage)'.[29]

This is accepted, but the view taken here is that, of the various possibilities for

---

28 [1960] AC 87; [1959] 2 All ER 701 – discussed further in Chapter 3, 3.7.1.
29 Brownsword, 2000, para 1.1.

identifying the essence of contract, the concept of the 'voluntary exchange' is the one which comes nearest to doing the job. Although it must be recognised that this cannot be used as a comprehensive and universal definition, it provides a practical basis from which to embark on a discussion of the legal rules which surround the concept of the contract.

The function of contract law is therefore to facilitate exchanges. An important part of this is the allocation of 'risk'. One of the reasons why the parties will put their transaction into the form of a contract is that it provides a mechanism for enforcement of the way in which they have agreed to allocate the risks. In a sale of goods contract, for example, the risk that the goods will be unsatisfactory is placed on the seller.[30] This will be reflected in the price charged. In more complex contracts there may be many more risks which the parties will allocate between them. They may well decide that in certain situations the liability for breach of contract will be excluded or limited;[31] the risk is therefore borne by the other party, who in some circumstances may then be moved to take out separate insurance against that eventuality occurring. The way in which such risks are allocated will again be likely to affect the price of the contract. The manner in which the rules of contract law interact with these allocations of risk will need to be kept in mind at various points in the following chapters.

1.4.1 Voluntary transactions

The approach of this book is, therefore, as indicated in the previous section, that the subject matter of the law of contract comprises transactions under which people, more or less voluntarily, assume obligations towards each other,[32] in connection with the transfer of property (including money) or the provision of services. The transactions are only 'more or less' voluntary, since people have little real choice whether or not to enter into some contracts, for example, contracts to buy food or to obtain work. Even where there is a real choice in this sense, for example, as regards a decision to buy a new CD player, there is likely to be little choice about the terms on which the contract can be made. Large retail organisations are rarely prepared to enter into bargaining with a consumer. Nevertheless, it is only in very rare situations, for example, the compulsory purchase of property by central or local government, that people are forced into a contract which is clearly against their will. Indeed, to the extent that a transaction is not in any way regulated by agreement between the parties, it may be argued that it is not properly categorised as a contract. In *Norweb plc v Dixon*,[33] for example, the view was taken that a supply of electricity to a consumer which was almost entirely regulated, both as to the creation of the relationship and its terms, by the Electricity Act 1989

---

30 Though this is now largely not a matter of choice, but the result of the terms automatically implied by the Sale of Goods Act 1979.
31 See Chapter 9.
32 Or allocate risks between each other.
33 [1995] 3 All ER 952.

could not be regarded as a contract. As a result, money owed by the consumer was not a 'contractual' debt. This decision was followed in *W v Essex CC*[34] in relation to a fostering agreement which was closely regulated by regulations made under the Children Act 1989. As Stuart-Smith LJ in the Court of Appeal commented:[35]

> A contract is essentially an agreement that is freely entered into on terms that are freely negotiated. If there is a statutory obligation to enter into a form of agreement the terms of which are laid down, at any rate in their most important respects, there is no contract.

We may therefore use the definition at the beginning of this paragraph, in terms of voluntary transactions, as a broad indication of the situations with which we are concerned. The rules of contract law help to determine which transactions will be enforced by the courts and on what terms. They also provide a framework of remedies when contracts are broken.

Before leaving this point, it is important to remember that, to the extent that there is a 'general law of contract', it applies to all transactions within its scope. That is, the same general rules will apply to the purchase of a packet of sweets from a local newsagent, as to a multimillion pound deal between large international corporations.

1.5 DISCRETE AND RELATIONAL TRANSACTIONS

As we have seen, the classical theory uses as part of its paradigmatic contract a 'one-off' transaction that is discrete and self-contained. It has been increasingly recognised, however, that many contracts are not of this kind, but have a continuing, or 'relational' aspect. The term 'relational' contracts was coined by Professor Ian Macneil, and his work on this area remains the most influential.[36]

What does 'relational' contract theory mean? One point of possible confusion in Macneil's work is the fact that, as he himself has recognised,[37] he uses 'relational' in two linked but distinct ways. First, he uses it to refer to the fact that all contracts occur in the context of a 'social matrix'. At the minimum, even in relation to a contract which appears to be 'discrete', this matrix will require a common system of communication, a common recognition of a system of order, a mechanism for enforcement and, if we are talking about the majority of contracts, some system of money. In respect of most

---

34 [1999] Fam 90; [1998] 3 All ER 111.

35 [1999] Fam 90, p 113; [1998] 3 All ER 111, p 128.

36 The most accessible route into Macneil's writings is through the collection of extracts from his articles edited by Campbell and published in 2001. This is cited in this book as Campbell, 2001. It should be noted, however, that the extracts omit most of Macneil's footnotes, so that for a full appreciation of his work reference should be made to the original texts (see the comments in the Preface to Campbell, 2001).

37 Macneil, 2000; Campbell, 2001, p 379.

contracts, of course, the social matrix will be much more complex.[38] Macneil's view is that an understanding of this relational aspect of transactions is essential to their proper analysis, whether in terms of law or economics.

The second use of the term 'relational' refers to the fact that many contracts involve a continuing relationship between the parties, which will affect the way in which their contract operates.[39] An obvious example is an employment contract, but it also applies to commercial agreements which, for example, require the supply of goods or services over a period of time. A construction contract will be a 'relational' contract in this sense, as will any lease of property. Macneil gives as one example of a 'quite discrete' transaction 'a cash purchase of gasoline at a station on the New Jersey Turnpike by someone rarely travelling the road'.[40] Such a contract will become less discrete if, for example, payment is by cheque or credit card, or is charged to a business account, or the purchaser has chosen this particular filling station because of a wish to use a 'loyalty' card issued by a particular petrol distributor. Macneil uses the metaphor of the spectrum of contracts, with very 'discrete' contracts at one end, and very 'relational' contracts at the other. Because of the classical theory's focus on the discrete transaction, it has difficulty in coping with the more relational contracts. These may well require the obligations between the parties to be modified over time, to respond to changing circumstances. For example, an employer may need to change the ways in which its employees work to deal with additional orders that have been taken on; or a construction contract may need adjustment to take account of problems with the availability of materials. Classical theory, however, looking at all contracts as if they were discrete, expects everything to be sorted out in the original agreement and has great difficulty dealing with subsequent modifications. In reality, such situations are generally dealt with by co-operation between the parties in the form of negotiation, but classical theory offers little or no scope for the recognition of such a process. The response of the courts faced with trying to apply classical theory to such situations may be to develop 'exceptions', which in form leave the general principle intact, but in fact may serve to undermine it.[41]

This difficulty with dealing with contractual modification leads to a further important insight from Macneil's work concerning the limitations of classical theory. Macneil refers to this as the problem of 'presentiation'.[42] To presentiate is, according

---

38 See, for example, Macneil's analysis of the relational aspects of the sale of bananas in a supermarket: Macneil, 2000; Campbell, 2001, pp 371–72.

39 Macneil has tried to avoid the confusion between the two uses of relational by referring to the second use as dealing with 'intertwined' contracts (see Macneil, 1987). This has not been picked up by other writers as yet, however, and the term 'relational' continues to be used to refer to both aspects of Macneil's theories.

40 Macneil, 1978; Campbell, 2001, p 189.

41 An obvious example of this process is the effect of the development of the doctrine of promissory estoppel in English law in the latter half of the twentieth century on the classical doctrine of consideration: see Chapter 3, 3.11.

42 See, in particular, Macneil, 1974; Campbell, 2001, p 182.

to the *Oxford English Dictionary*, to 'make or render present in place or time, to cause to be perceived or realised as present'.[43] In terms of the law of contract, Macneil uses this to refer to the process whereby, under classical theory, every aspect of the contract is to be determined at the time at which it is formed, so that all future problems with the contract can be answered by simply asking 'what did the parties agree in the contract?' This 'presentiation' works tolerably well with relatively discrete transactions, but the more a contract becomes 'relational', and the longer it lasts, the less likely it is that simply looking to the original agreement will provide satisfactory answers. One response of the English courts to this type of problem has been to make inventive use of the concept of the 'implied term'.[44] This enables the myth of presentiation to be maintained. A better response might be:[45]

> ... to develop an overall structure of contract law of greater applicability than now exists and to merge both the details and the structure of transactional contract law into that overall structure.

Macneil's suggestion is that classical theory's reliance on individual rational self-interest as the governing norm for contractual transactions should be replaced with 10 'common contract norms',[46] which will include 'flexibility'; there are also some separate norms applying according to whether the contract is more or less discrete or relational. The relational norms include 'preservation of the relation' and 'harmonization of relational conflict'.[47] Thus, the resolution of problems which arise in the course of a long-term, or relational, contract forms part of the norms underlying the contract, rather than having to be imposed on it, using tools more suited to discrete transactions.

Macneil's work has been influential on writings about English contract law, but has by no means received universal acceptance.[48] The approach here is to refer to

---

43 Macneil quotes this definition from the first edition of the OED: Macneil, 1974, p 589; Campbell, 2001, p 182. The second edition of the OED (1989) describes the word as 'rare'. The first use recorded is 1659, though in the sense that Macneil uses it, the first example is 1689. Modern examples are largely taken from US law journals.

44 For which see Chapter 8, 8.6.

45 Macneil, 1974; Campbell, 2001, p 187.

46 The 10 norms are: (1) role integrity; (2) reciprocity; (3) implementation of planning; (4) effectuation of consent; (5) flexibility; (6) contractual solidarity; (7) the restitution, reliance and expectation interests; (8) creation and restraint of power; (9) propriety of means; and (10) harmonisation with the social matrix: Macneil, 1982; Campbell, 2001, p 153.

47 Ibid, p 163.

48 For a full review see Vincent-Jones, 2001. Sceptical commentators include Eisenberg, 1995 and McKendrick, 1995b; see also Collins, 1996. Cf Lord Steyn in *Total Gas Marketing Ltd v Arco British Ltd* [1998] 2 Lloyd's Rep 209, p 218: '[This is] a contract of a type sometimes called a relational contract. But there are no special rules of interpretation applicable to such contracts.' Campbell, on the other hand, has argued that Macneil does not pursue the relational analysis far enough (Campbell, 1996).

Macneil's work and how it might relate to the traditional and current approaches to particular issues at the appropriate places throughout the rest of the text. His exposure of the problems of presentation will be found to be particularly helpful at a number of points.

1.6 CONTRACT, TORT AND RESTITUTION

It is generally recognised that there are three main strands to English law relating to civil liability – contract, tort and restitution. To what extent are these distinct, and is there any overlap between them?

As indicated above, the view taken here is that the province of contract law is the facilitation and enforcement of voluntary exchange transactions. The law of tort,[49] on the other hand, is concerned with imposition of standards of behaviour, irrespective of whether the behaviour is linked to a transaction or voluntarily undertaken. There is an overlap, however, in that the performance of a contract can involve a tort, giving rise to the possibility of dual liability. If, for example, during the course of the construction of a building, the negligence of a builder leads to a wall collapsing, injuring a third party, the construction company may be liable in contract for the fact that the wall was defective, and in tort to the injured party for the negligence in its construction. If the person injured is the other party to the contract, then there will be liability in both tort and contract to the same claimant.[50]

The third element in the law of obligations – restitution – has been recognised much more recently as a separate head.[51] The aim of the law of restitution is to prevent 'unjust enrichment'. Thus, where a person has been paid money as a result of a mistake, the law of restitution provides the means by which it may be recovered. There is no need for the situation to involve an exchange transaction, as in contract, or for the behaviour of the person who has been unjustly enriched to fall below an accepted standard, as in tort. Restitution has links with contract, however, in that it is not infrequently used in situations where the parties have been attempting to make a contract, but this has for some reason failed.

The difference between contract, tort and restitution is sometimes said to be based on the nature of the remedies available in relation to each, and in particular the measure of damages. Thus, in contract, the primary measure of damages is the 'expectation' interest, designed to put the claimant into the position as if the contract had been performed satisfactorily (so that benefits to be obtained from the contract, such as lost profits, can be recovered). In tort, on the other hand, the normal measure is to put the

---

49 In discussions of the law of obligations it is not uncommon to use the term 'tort' to mean, in effect, the tort of negligence. It should not be forgotten, however, that tort encompasses a wider area than that, including assault, nuisance, defamation and the interference with others' contractual rights.

50 For a further example see the area of negligent misstatements, dealt with in Chapter 10, 10.4.4.

51 See Chapter 19.

claimant into the position he or she would have been in had the tort not occurred. This will generally be backward looking, compensating for loss and damage caused, but not taking into account lost benefits.[52] In restitution, as indicated above, the object is the return of property and the disgorgement of unjustified benefits. Looking at the differences between the various strands of the law of obligations in terms of the remedies is, however, starting from the wrong end. The basis of liability must be the foundation of the distinction between them, with the remedies which are available being a consequence of that liability. There is no absolute requirement, for example, that contract remedies should be centred on the expectation interest. Indeed, as will be seen in Chapter 18, it is possible in an action for breach of contract to recover damages on any of the three bases just mentioned – that is, expectation, the 'tort' measure (compensating for actual losses, rather than expected benefits)[53] or restitution.

1.7 A LAW OF CONTRACT OR LAW OF CONTRACTS?

Do we have a law of contract or a law of contracts? The premise of a contract text of this kind is that there is a sufficient body of general rules and principles which apply to all (or virtually all) contracts to say that there is a 'law of contract'. The counter-argument can be based on two grounds, both largely relating to developments in the area over the past 100 years.

First, it can be pointed out that there are many specific types of contract which are now the subject of quite detailed statutory regulation. Contracts of employment, consumer credit agreements and contracts for the sale of land, for example, all operate within elaborate statutory frameworks. Even the type of agreement which might be regarded as the archetypal contract – the exchange of goods for money – is governed by the Sale of Goods Act 1979, the Unfair Contract Terms Act 1977 and, if the buyer is a consumer, the Unfair Terms in Consumer Contracts Regulations 1999. This dichotomy is reflected in the format of *Chitty on Contracts*, which appears in two volumes, one devoted to *General Principles*, the other to *Special Contracts*.

The consequences of this can be seen by looking at its effect on the way in which the novice law student learns about the law of contract. This in turn will affect the practitioner's understanding, and will eventually be likely to have an impact on the practical development of contractual doctrine as developed by the courts. The reality is that the contracts falling within 'specialist' areas are often treated for didactic purposes as being best dealt with separately from the general law. The LLB course, therefore, will typically have a Contract Law course, but also separate courses on Employment Law, Land Law, Consumer Law, Commercial Law, etc. The general Contract Law course will not have the time to deal in detail with the statutory regimes governing all the different

---

52 But see *East v Maurer* [1991] 2 All ER 733 for an example of a case where the tort measure took account of a certain type of lost profit. The case is discussed in Chapter 10, 10.4.3.
53 Generally referred to in this context as the 'reliance' interest.

types of contract, and will leave these to be dealt with by the specialist courses. Some of these specialist courses will be optional. The student who does not follow all of them will therefore have an incomplete picture of the rules and principles governing 'contracts'. More importantly, the student will be likely to retain the mental 'pigeon-holing' encouraged by this structure to his or her studies, and therefore be less likely to draw connections between different areas.

One response to this is to say that it does not matter. There is in reality a range of different types of contract, and there is no reason why the rules operating in one area should have any impact in another. A contrary view is to argue that the diversity should be embraced as adding vibrancy to the development of contractual principles. An attempt to adopt an inclusive approach has been put forward by Collins. Noting that the generality of the traditional approach made it 'increasingly irrelevant' to disputes governed by special rules, he puts forward an alternative:[54]

> In order to counter this incoherence and redundancy, the conception of contract law employed here focuses on the social context of market transactions, that is where people seek to acquire property or services by dealing with others.[55] Whilst acknowledging that the law regulates these transactions by classifying them into particular types, this conception of contract law seeks to understand the general principles and social policies which inform and guide the legal classifications and regulation.

This approach is based on the particular analysis of contract adopted by Collins, centred around the regulation of the market. This is not the analysis adopted here but, nevertheless, the discussion does adopt the view that developments in principle which derive from particular types of contract should not be ignored, but regarded as enriching the general law, with the possibility of cross-fertilisation to other areas where appropriate. Just one example will suffice here. There is a long-standing issue as to whether a serious breach of contract can ever have the effect of terminating that contract automatically, or whether there must always be a decision by the 'innocent' party whether or not to treat the contract as repudiated.[56] This has caused particular problems in the area of employment law.[57] One view might be to say that the fact that employment law has special requirements in this area means that a different set of rules should be held to apply to this category of contract. That is not the view adopted here. Nor was it the view of the Court of Appeal, which in *Gunton v Richmond-upon-Thames LBC* held that the rule as to termination was the same in employment contracts as in

---

54 Collins, 2003, p 10.
55 As Collins notes, this has the effect of tending to exclude market transactions establishing 'an economic organization such as a firm, a trade association or a partnership'.
56 This question is considered fully in Chapter 17, 17.6.1.
57 See, for example, *Hill v CA Parsons & Co Ltd* [1972] Ch 305; [1971] 3 All ER 1345; *Sanders v EA Neale* [1974] ICR 565.

other contracts.[58] Although there clearly will be some issues on which particular types of contract need to have special provisions, this should be a situation of last resort. In general, the development of principles in one area should be seen as enlightening and informing their application in other areas, so that there is a continuing dialogue between the demands of special contracts and the development of general principles. To use another analogy, the general principles might be seen as the hub of a spoked wheel, with the special contracts ranged around the rim. The flow of ideas about the development of the law should be in both directions along the spokes; and moreover, an idea originating in one 'special contract' may flow into the hub (general principles) and then out along another spoke to inform the development of a different 'special contract'.

A slightly different divergence can also be observed as having an impact on the development of the law – that is, the difference between the consumer contract and the contract between businesses. There is no doubt that over the past 100 years both Parliament and the courts have seen an increasing need to protect the consumer against unfair and unreasonable terms in contracts drawn up by businesses. The consumer suffers from ignorance (not understanding the effect of the terms being put forward) and lack of bargaining power (there may be no real choice to contracting on the terms put forward). It was for this reason that in the exemption clause area the courts developed strict rules of incorporation and construction, and the doctrine of 'fundamental breach'.[59] In time this was supplemented by parliamentary intervention in the form of the Unfair Contract Terms Act 1977, and European controls through the Unfair Terms in Consumer Contracts Regulations of 1994 and 1999.[60] The governing principle here is that the consumer is the 'weaker party' and therefore needs protection. But is this identification of the consumer for protection an indication that there are two distinct types of contract – the consumer contract and the business contract – or is it simply a question of degree? There may well be, and often are, contracts between businesses where there is also inequality in bargaining power, and one party is significantly weaker than the other. The small business manufacturing a single product which has a major multinational as its sole or dominant purchaser may have no real choice about the terms on which it contracts.

The law has taken notice of this factor in various areas. As regards economic duress, for example, the case of *Atlas Express Ltd v Kafco (Importers and Distributors) Ltd*[61] turned in part on the fact that the defendant company would have been likely to go out of business if it had not agreed to the variation of contract put forward by the national carrier with which it was contracting. Although this is catered for in doctrinal terms by a principle expressed in general terms – that is, whether the party subject to the

---

58 [1981] Ch 448. See also, however, *Boyo v Lambeth LBC* [1995] IRLR 50, and *Cerberus Software Ltd v Rowley* [2001] IRLR 160; see Chapter 17, 17.6.1.
59 See Chapter 9, 9.5.3.
60 SI 1994/3159; SI 1999/2083.
61 [1989] QB 833; [1989] 1 All ER 641 – see Chapter 12, 12.4.2.

alleged duress had any realistic choice about complying[62] – this is a condition which is always most likely to be satisfied by a party which is in the weaker position in the contract. The related concept of undue influence, although frequently used in relation to 'non-business' (that is, consumer) contractors, can also be used in a business or quasi-business context. The defendant in *Lloyds Bank Ltd v Bundy*,[63] for example, was a farmer who had had regular dealings with the bank in relation to his farm business. Nevertheless, Mr Bundy's age and the fact that he, running a small business, had put his trust in the employees of the large corporation (the bank) meant that he was entitled to escape from the agreement which he had made. Even in relation to a piece of legislation clearly in the category of 'consumer protection', the Unfair Contract Terms Act 1977, protection is provided for businesses where the attempt to exclude liability is 'unreasonable'.[64] And the tests of unreasonableness set out in Sched 2 to the Act[65] include the strength of the bargaining position of the business against which the clause is being applied, and the knowledge of the clause: in other words, the same factors as we noted above as justifying special treatment for consumers – ignorance and lack of bargaining power.

The conclusion from all of this is that there is no reason to separate out consumer contracts from business contracts and to hold that they are such different types of agreement that a different set of contractual principles should apply to each. It is quite possible for both to be contained within a general law of contract, which has sufficient flexibility to accommodate a range of differing 'power relationships'.

FOR THOUGHT

What reasons might there be for arguing that the courts should not take account of differences in bargaining power in relation to contracts between businesses? What would be the likely view of those who support the idea that market forces produce the most efficient economy?

1.8 DIFFERENT APPROACHES TO ANALYSING CONTRACT

The approach in this book is, for the most part, to analyse the law of contract within its own terms. In other words, the concentration will be on analysing the relevant cases and

---

62 As suggested by Lord Scarman in *Pao On v Lau Yiu Long* [1980] AC 614, p 635; [1979] 3 All ER 65, p 78 – see Chapter 12, 12.4.2.
63 [1975] QB 326; [1974] 3 All ER 757 – see Chapter 13, 13.5.
64 That is, it does not satisfy the 'requirement of reasonableness' in s 11.
65 Although on its face Sched 2 is only applicable to sale of goods cases, the Court of Appeal has made it clear that it may used more generally – *Overseas Medical Supplies Ltd v Orient Transport Services Ltd* [1999] 2 Lloyd's Rep 273 (Chapter 9, 9.7.16).

statutes, examining how contractual principles have developed through them, and critically appraising the end result. This does not mean that issues of social and political context, or legal history should be ignored. Consideration of such matters is often essential in making any full appraisal of the relevant legal rules. The initial focus, however, is on the law as it has emerged through decisions of the courts and legislation. This is sometimes referred to as 'doctrinal analysis', because it concentrates on legal doctrine.

1.8.1 Economic analysis

Other approaches are, of course, possible. Since contract is intimately linked with the commercial world, it is not surprising that attempts have been made to analyse it in terms of economics. At a basic level, it is clear that particular decisions about the content of the rules of contract can have a broader economic influence. To take a simple example, as regards consumer contracts, it may be thought desirable that producers of goods should be strictly liable for the quality of what they sell. If they are to be liable, however, they may need either to introduce strict quality control procedures, or to take out insurance. The costs of either of these two measures will almost certainly be added to the price of the goods. In economic terms, therefore, the cost of greater consumer protection is higher prices. Economic analysis will also look at 'transaction costs' (which may lead to the conclusion that standard form contracts are more economically efficient than those that are individually negotiated), and 'adjudication costs' (which may suggest that it is more economically efficient to have fixed rules of law, rather than leave it to judges to resolve disputes 'on their merits'). To take an example from the law on exclusion clauses,[66] the decision of the House of Lords in the case of *Photo Production Ltd v Securicor Transport Ltd*,[67] upholding a very widely based clause excluding one of the parties from virtually all liability for breach of contract, might be analysed in economic terms as follows. First, it might be said to be based on an assumption that as between two parties, freely negotiating, they will have allocated responsibilities and risks in the most efficient way, and so will have 'maximised wealth'. Second, the refusal of the court to interfere in a bargain of this kind may discourage others from litigating, and therefore have the overall beneficial economic effect of reducing transaction costs. There have also been attempts to root the foundations of contractual liability in economic theory. Much of this work has originated in the United States.[68] The approach is generally to try to analyse the rules of contract law in terms of their economic efficiency and consequences. It may be argued, for example, that there is a benefit to society in economic terms in allowing and facilitating voluntary exchanges of goods and services.

---

66 For which, see Chapter 9.
67 [1980] AC 827; [1980] 1 All ER 556.
68 See, in particular, Kronman and Posner, 1979; Posner, 1992.

Kronman and Posner use the example of the exchange of goods between A and B.[69] The goods are worth $100 to A, who owns them, but are worth $150 to B (presumably because of the use B can make of them). If A sells the goods to B for $125, this will be an exchange which will 'increase the wealth of society':[70]

> Before the exchange . . . A had a good worth $100 to him and B had $125 in cash, a total of $225. After the exchange, A has $125 in cash and B has a good worth $150 to him, a total of $275. The exchange has increased the wealth of society by $50.

Kronman and Posner use the concept of the 'wealth-maximising' effect of voluntary exchanges as an argument for 'freedom of contract'. This conclusion has been the subject of strong challenges,[71] but the important point here is to note the *technique* rather than the conclusion. There is no doubt that analysing the economic effects of contract law is a valid method of appraisal and can lead to conclusions about how the law should best develop.

1.8.2 Socio-political analysis

A further way of looking at the law of contract is from a socio-political standpoint. In fact, we all have some political assumptions in the background, even if we are looking at contract cases purely within their own terms. It is, for example, impossible to debate the merits of numerous contract principles without some notion of the value or other-wise of the idea of 'freedom of contract', which is, of course, a political concept. Some writers feel, however, that this political/ideological background, be it capitalist, Marxist or whatever, should be made explicit. For example, Collins, in the first edition of *The Law of Contract* stated:[72]

> This book identifies the purpose of the law of contract as the channelling and regulation of market transactions according to ideals of social justice.

A recent collection of writing has been based on feminist analysis.[73] One of the editors suggests that:[74]

---

69 Kronman and Posner, 1979, p 1.

70 Ibid. In this simple example, Kronman and Posner specifically exclude consideration of any adverse effects on third parties. If such effects were to be greater than the increase brought about by A and B's exchange, the transaction would no longer be economically 'efficient'.

71 See, for example, Atiyah, 1986, Chapter 7; Leff, 1974. Macneil argues that adherence to neo-classical economic theory in analysing contract ignores the relational aspect of contract, in that it tends to focus on discrete transactions: see above, 1.5.

72 Collins, 1986. This particular formulation does not appear in later editions of Collins' book, though his overall approach appears to remain the same.

73 Mulcahy and Wheeler, 2005.

74 Ibid, p 1.

Nothing better embodies masculine abstract relations with each other than the model of the discrete contractual transaction with which the majority of the scholarship in the field remains concerned.

By contrast she has a different approach:[75]

My task then is not merely to undermine the understanding of voluntary obligations, suggested by the classical model, that continue to cast a shadow over developments in the field. That task has been undertaken by many others and is well-documented. Instead, I seek to use this critique as a stepping stone to consider how feminist ideas around the notion of an ethic of care can contribute to the ambitious task of persuading lawyers to think differently about why people voluntarily bind themselves to an enforceable agreement with another.

Another approach is to try to identify the ideologies which underpin the decision of the courts on contract issues. Adams and Brownsword, for example,[76] identify three competing ideologies which may be found in the cases. These are: (a) formalism; (b) consumer-welfarism; and (c) market-individualism. Thus, a court may be said to adopt a formalist approach if it feels obliged to follow rules established in earlier cases, even if it does not agree with them, or feels that they do not produce the most satisfactory result on the facts before the court. The case of *Foakes v Beer*[77] may be said to be an example of this type of approach, at least as far as some members of the House of Lords were concerned, in that they felt bound to follow what was regarded as an established rule that part-payment of a debt could never discharge the debtor's liability for the balance, even if the creditor had promised to treat it as so doing. 'Consumer-welfarism', on the other hand, may operate where a court recognises that individuals may be in a weak position as regards dealings with large organisations, and that the rules of contract therefore need to be developed and applied so as to protect them. Examples of this type of approach would include *Carlill v Carbolic Smoke Ball Co*,[78] in which an advertiser was bound by a promise made to consumers who had relied on the advert; or the pre-1977 exclusion clause cases,[79] where the courts devised rules to prevent large organisations from imposing wide clauses exempting them from liability to people who bought their products and services.

The third approach identified by Adams and Brownsword – 'market-individualism' – gives freedom of contract the highest priority and leaves the parties to their bargain, even if it appears to operate harshly on one side. In this situation, the

---

75 Mulcahy and Wheeler, 2005, p 3.
76 Adams and Brownsword, 2004, Chapter 8.
77 (1884) 9 App Cas 605 – discussed in Chapter 3, 3.13.2.
78 [1893] 1 QB 256 – discussed in Chapter 2, 2.7.6.
79 For which, see Chapter 9, 9.3–9.5.

court adopts the role simply of 'referee', determining what obligations the parties must be taken to have agreed to, and then applying them to the situation. A case mentioned above in connection with the economic analysis, *Photo Production Ltd v Securicor Transport Ltd*, is a good example of the court adopting this approach.

1.8.3 Empirical research

Finally, contract may be approached from the bottom rather than the top. In other words, instead of looking at decisions of the appellate courts and the rules which they have developed, the focus could be on how contract law operates in people's day-to-day lives. Does the existence of a particular set of contractual rules affect the way in which people behave? Do businesses have contractual principles in mind when they enter into agreements? When things go wrong, to what extent does the law influence the way in which disputes are resolved? There has been surprisingly little research on these issues, but such as there is suggests that the law of contract is of much less importance to business people than lawyers would like to think.[80] In particular, where parties to a long-standing business relationship find themselves in a dispute, the maintenance of their relationship is likely to be a much stronger influence over the way they resolve their differences than are the strict legal rights between the parties, as determined by the law of contract.

1.8.4 Which approach?

As has been indicated above, the approach taken here is primarily based on looking at legal materials within their own terms. At appropriate points throughout the book, however, aspects of one or more of the alternative approaches outlined above will be referred to, in order to produce a fuller understanding of the way in which the law has developed, or is likely to develop in the future.

1.9 INTERNATIONAL INFLUENCES

The common law of contract has tended to be insular in its outlook, though it has had a very significant international impact. The contract law of North America and much of the Commonwealth still derives many of its basic principles from the 'classical' English law of contract which reached its developed form during the nineteenth century. Moreover, because these were its origins, the law in many of these overseas jurisdictions has continued to look to the decisions of the English courts as providing indicators for its own development. This has been so even when the last formal link, that is, the existence

---

80 See, in relation to the United States, the seminal work of Macaulay, 1963; and, in relation to this country, Beale and Dugdale, 1975; Yates, 1982, pp 16–33 and Lewis, 1982.

of the House of Lords or the Judicial Committee of the Privy Council as the final court of appeal, was severed. Until recently, however, the flow has tended to be in one direction, and English courts have rarely paid much attention to developments in the law of contract in other parts of the common law world. The same has been even more true of civil law jurisdictions where neither has been seen to have any significant influence on the other.

One important exception to this in the past has been in the area of international trade, where the demands of the commercial world for increased certainty, which is most easily achieved by increased uniformity, has led to the creation of international treaties. The most successful development of this kind is the establishment of the Hague-Visby Rules, applying to contracts for the carriage of goods by sea, which have achieved widespread acceptance.[81] The attempt to establish a similar mandatory regime for international sale of goods contracts, by the 1980 Vienna Convention,[82] has been less successful,[83] but the development of standard terms, which parties can choose whether or not to use, has increased the uniformity of contracts in the relevant areas.[84]

In more recent times, that is, the last 10 to 15 years, the position has changed. There has first of all been an increased willingness amongst English judges to recognise that authorities from other parts of the Commonwealth, and in particular from Australia, may be valuable in assisting the development of contractual principles in England. Second, there has been the influence from membership of the European Economic Community, and now the European Union. Most recently, there has been the rapid growth in the ease of international telecommunications followed and assisted by the development of the internet and the world wide web.

All three of these developments are worth examining. As regards the influence of case law from other parts of the Commonwealth, this will be noted where appropriate throughout the rest of the text. The influence of the EU to date can be seen most clearly in the directives which have required implementation into English law. For example, the directive on commercial agents[85] was given effect by the Commercial Agents (Council Directive) Regulations 1993,[86] and that on unfair terms in consumer contracts[87] by the Unfair Terms in Consumer Contracts Regulations 1994[88] (now replaced by the Unfair

---

81 They were enacted into English law by the Carriage of Goods by Sea Act 1971.
82 That is, the United Nations Convention on Contracts for the International Sale of Goods 1980.
83 For conflicting views amongst senior English judges on the merits of mandatory attempts at unification in the commercial area, see the debate between Lord Hobhouse and Lord Steyn, discussed by Brownsword, 2000, paras 7.15 to 7.17.
84 For example, International Chamber of Commerce's INCOTERMS (for international sales) and the Fédération International des Ingénieurs Conseils' Conditions for Works of Civil Engineers (for international construction contracts). See also the Principles for International Commercial Contracts produced by the International Institution for the Unification of Private Law (UNIDROIT).
85 Directive 86/653/EEC.
86 SI 1993/3053 – see Chapter 6, 6.2.2.
87 Directive 93/13/EEC.
88 SI 1994/3159.

Terms in Consumer Contracts Regulations 1999).[89] More recently, the Distance Selling Directive[90] has been implemented by the Consumer Protection (Distance Selling) Regulations 2000.[91] The Directive on electronic contracts[92] has been implemented by the Electronic Commerce (EC Directive) Regulations 2002.[93] There have also been significant effects on employment contracts, particularly in relation to sex discrimination.[94]

To some extent, for example, in the protection of consumers, the European approach merely reflects concerns which exist independently in English law. This is illustrated by the overlap between the Unfair Contract Terms Act 1977 and the Unfair Terms in Consumer Contracts Regulations 1994 and 1999. In other respects, however, the European Directives can lead to concepts novel to English law being incorporated. The most obvious example of this is relates to the concept of 'good faith' in contracting. The English common law has always rejected any attempts to introduce any general obligation to contract 'in good faith'. The attempt by Lord Denning to introduce a concept of 'unconscionability' in *Lloyds Bank Ltd v Bundy*[95] was firmly rejected by his fellow judges,[96] and in *Walford v Miles*,[97] the House of Lords, relying on the traditional English law rule that an 'agreement to agree' is unenforceable,[98] held that there could be no binding obligation to negotiate in good faith. Indeed, Lord Ackner felt that such an approach would be 'repugnant' to the adversarial position of the bargaining parties.[99]

FOR THOUGHT

Is a concept of 'good faith' likely to produce more or less uncertainty in the law? Could this be a reason why the courts oppose its use, particularly in relation to business to business contracts?

Despite this judicial hostility, the concept of 'good faith' does now exist in some parts of English law. Both the Commercial Agents (Council Directive) Regulations

---

89 SI 1999/2083 – see Chapter 9, 9.8.
90 97/7/EC.
91 SI 2000/2334 – discussed in Chapter 2, 2.14.
92 2000/31/EC.
93 SI 2002/2013 – see, further, Chapter 2, 2.12.12.
94 For example, it is as a result of European law that s 3 of the Equal Pay Act 1970 implies into every contract of employment an 'equality clause' aimed at ensuring that men and women receive equal treatment.
95 [1975] QB 326; [1974] 3 All ER 757. See also Chapter 13, 13.5 and 13.9.
96 In particular, by Lord Scarman in *National Westminster Bank v Morgan* [1985] AC 686; [1985] 1 All ER 821. He took a similar line in *Pao On v Lau Yiu Long* [1980] AC 614; [1979] 3 All ER 65.
97 [1992] 2 AC 128; [1992] 1 All ER 453.
98 *Courtney and Fairbairn Ltd v Tolaini Brothers (Hotels) Ltd* [1975] 1 WLR 297; *May and Butcher v R* [1934] 2 KB 17.
99 [1992] 2 AC 128, p 138; [1992] 1 All ER 453, p 460.

1993[100] and the Unfair Terms in Consumer Contracts Regulations 1999,[101] following the wording of the directives on which they are based, impose obligations of 'good faith' on the contracting parties. The reaction of the House of Lords to the introduction of this concept in the first case in which it has been called upon to consider it has been to give it flesh by regarding it as requiring fair and open dealing between the parties:[102]

> Openness requires that the terms should be expressed fully, clearly and legibly, containing no concealed pitfalls or traps . . . Fair dealing requires that a supplier should not, whether deliberately or unconsciously, take advantage of the consumer's necessity, indigence, lack of experience, unfamiliarity with the subject matter of the contract, weak bargaining position . . .

It remains to be seen whether the introduction of 'good faith' in these particular areas will lead to a greater willingness to adopt it more generally. As Brownsword has pointed out,[103] there remains considerable scepticism about the concept[104] and the adoption of a good faith 'requirement', whereby a court would 'aspire simply to follow the shared sense of good faith in the particular contractual setting',[105] is more likely than a good faith 'regime' which would attempt to impose 'the co-operative ground rules'.[106]

The possible practical influence of a 'good faith' approach will be considered further at appropriate places later in the text. The main point here is that a concept which has widespread acceptance in other European jurisdictions has begun to be accepted within English law.

A more wide-reaching attempt to put forward general principles for a European law of contract is contained in the work of the Lando Commission. The approach of this group, which consists of eminent lawyers from a number of European jurisdictions, is rather different from the piecemeal attempts at Europe-wide harmonisation attempted by the institutions of the EU. These have tended to be responses to areas where there is perceived to be a problem. The Lando approach, however, is to try to provide 'a bridge between the civil law and common law by providing rules to reconcile their differing legal philosophies'.[107] To this end it published in 2000 a set of Principles

---

100 SI 1993/3053.

101 SI 1999/2083.

102 *Director General of Fair Trading v First National Bank plc* [2002] UKHL 52; [2002] 1 All ER 97, per Lord Bingham, para 17, p 108. Lord Steyn went further and suggested that the concept should not be limited to procedural fairness: ibid, paras 36–37, p 113. The House was in this case concerned with the UTCCR 1994. For further discussion see Chapter 9, 9.8.2.

103 Brownsword, 2000, Chapter 5.

104 See, for example, Professor Bridge's characterisation of it as 'visceral justice', leading to impressionistic decision-making and undesirable uncertainty in commercial transactions: Bridge, 1999, p 140.

105 Brownsword, 2000, para 5.22.

106 Ibid, para 5.20.

107 Lando and Beale, 2000, p xxiii.

of European Contract Law ('PECL'), together with commentary, divided into nine chapters, and covering most areas of contract, from formation to remedies.[108]

This is an ambitious project, and it is hard to see that it will lead to direct changes in the common law. It may, however, provide a source for Parliament if and when it is looking to reform particular areas, and it is certainly a standard with which the existing common law can be compared, particularly in areas where it appears to operate in a way which is less than satisfactory. To that end, references to the PECL are made at appropriate points throughout the subsequent chapters in order to illuminate the discussion of the existing position.

A further context in which the PECL may well have an influence is in relation to an ongoing project within the European Union to produce a draft of a European Contract Law.[109] An Action Plan issued by the European Commission in 2003[110] proposed the development of a Common Frame of Reference ('CFR') for European Contract Law, and this was followed in 2004 by a communication entitled *European Contract Law and the revision of the acquis: the way forward*.[111] This envisaged a structure for the CFR that would:[112]

> first set out common fundamental principles of contract law, including guidance on when exceptions to such fundamental principles could be required. Secondly, those fundamental principles would be supported by definitions of key concepts. Thirdly, these principles and definitions would be completed by model rules, forming the bulk of the CFR. A distinction between model rules applicable to contracts concluded between businesses or private persons and model rules applicable to contracts concluded between a business and a consumer could be envisaged.

As well as being used by the EU itself in framing legislation, it is also anticipated that the CFR could be used by national legislators:[113]

> when transposing EU directives in the area of contract law into national legislation. They could also draw on the CFR when enacting legislation on areas of contract law which are not regulated at Community level.

The paper also discussed the possible development of an optional instrument on European Contract Law, which would be available for parties to opt in to through a choice of law clause in their contract. The CFR project has been taken forward, and meetings

---

108 Lando and Beale, 2000.
109 A useful collection of essays on this development is to be found in Vogenauer and Weatherill, 2006.
110 COM(2003) 68 final.
111 COM(2004) 651 final.
112 Ibid, para 3.1.3.
113 Ibid, para 2.1.2.

of experts were held in 2005 and 2006.[114] The focus has to date been on the consumer law area, but it is clearly envisaged that the CFR will eventually have a broader scope, and probably be based on a re-drafting of the PECL. Although a final report to the Commission on the CFR was originally scheduled for 2007, it seems unlikely that this deadline will now be met. The Commission issued a *Green Paper on the Review of the Consumer Acquis* in February 2007.[115] To date there does not seem to have been much progress on the broader proposal for a European Contract Law.

The final area identified at the start of this section as contributing to the growing importance of the international context of contract law is the growth in telecommunications and the internet. The influence of these technological advances was seen first in the area of business contracting, dating in particular from the widespread adoption and use of telex machines and then faxes.[116] At its most basic this has required the courts to decide where contracts made by such devices are concluded.[117] Contracting by telex and fax has, however, largely been the preserve of businesses. The same is not the case as regards the most recent telecommunications developments. In particular, the internet is seen as showing the future for much consumer shopping. The ability to access websites offering wide ranges of consumer products, and to order them 'online', is increasing all the time. In such transactions, the ease with which orders may be placed, and payment (by credit card) made, does not relate to the distance between the customer and the supplier. They may be in the same street or on opposite sides of the world. From the point of view of the customer, the information appearing on the screen and the manner in which the transaction proceeds will be the same whatever the location of the supplier. It becomes important therefore, for the sake of developing consumer confidence, that there is clarity as to the law which applies to all such transactions. At the moment, the answer may well depend on the location of the supplier. It is not satisfactory, however, that the customer may be put in the uncertain position of not knowing what set of contractual rules will apply to the transaction. The assumption on the part of the customer may be that it will be the law of his or her own jurisdiction which will be relevant, whereas it may well be that of the jurisdiction where the supplier is located. Although in the short term this may be to the advantage of the supplier, in the long run, if the aim is to attract increasing trade in this form, customers will want rather greater security than this suggests. There will therefore be a strong motivation for making the rules applying to such transactions the same wherever the contract is made. This will, in turn, produce pressure for harmonisation and unification of laws across jurisdictions.

---

114 See, eg, *First Annual Progress Report on European Contract Law and the Acquis Review*, 2005, COM(2005) 456 final.

115 COM(2006) 744 final.

116 See, for example, *Entores v Miles Far East Corp* [1955] 2 QB 327; [1955] 2 All ER 493, discussed in Chapter 2, 2.12.10.

117 As will be seen from the discussion of this topic in Chapter 2, the related question of when such contracts come into existence remains as yet undecided by any clear authority.

1.10 FURTHER READING

Beale, H and Dugdale, T, 'Contracts between businessmen' (1975) 2 Brit J Law & Society 45

Campbell, D (ed), *The Relational Theory of Contract: Selected Works of Ian Macneil*, 2001, London: Sweet & Maxwell

Campbell, D, Collins, H and Wightman, J (eds), *Implicit Dimensions of Contract*, 2003, Oxford: Hart Publishing

Collins, H, *Regulating Contracts*, 1999, Oxford: Oxford University Press

Gilmore, G, *The Death of Contract*, 1974, Columbus: Ohio State University Press

Macaulay, S, 'Non-contractual relations in business' (1963) 28 Am Sociological Rev 35

Mulcahy, L and Wheeler, S, *Feminist Perspectives on Contract Law*, 2005, London: Glasshouse Press

Robertson, A (ed), *The Law of Obligations: Connections and Boundaries*, 2004, London: UCL Press

Smith, S, *Atiyah's Introduction to the Law of Contract*, 6th edn, 2006, Oxford: Clarendon Press

Smith, S, *Contract Theory*, 2004, Oxford: Clarendon Press

Vogenauer, S and Weatherill, S, *The Harmonisation of European Contract Law*, 2006, Oxford: Hart Publishing

2 FORMING THE AGREEMENT

CONTENTS

2.1 OVERVIEW

'Agreement' is central to the English law of contract. In most cases which are adjudicated the courts regard themselves as giving effect to an agreement reached between the parties. The question of whether such an agreement has been formed is therefore a crucial one. This chapter is concerned with the mechanisms which the courts use to decide whether an agreement has been reached. The main areas covered are:

■ Formalities. To what extent does English law use formal mechanisms to decide whether an agreement has been reached? Generally, this will be where a 'deed' is used, or where a statute requires formality in relation to a particular type of contract.

■ More generally there is no requirement of formality. The courts decide whether an agreement has been reached by taking an 'objective' approach, looking at what the parties have said or done as indicators of whether they intended to make an agreement.

■ The most common indicators will be a matching 'offer' and 'acceptance'. The identification of a matching offer and acceptance is the most common way for the courts to find that an agreement has been made.

■ An offer must be distinguished from an invitation to treat, and an acceptance from a counter offer.

■ Particular problems arise in relation to the following:
   □ Unilateral (as opposed to bilateral) contracts. The offer in a unilateral contract (for example, an offer of a reward for the return of property) may be made to the world, and the acceptance may take the form of performing an action (for example, the return of the property).
   □ The 'battle of the forms'. Where parties both try to contract on their own standard terms, and these are inconsistent, which should prevail?
   □ Contracting at a distance. If the contract is made by letter, fax, email, or over the web, when and where does it take effect? Special rules apply to posted acceptances, as opposed to those communicated by telephone or electronically.

■ Revocation of offers. An offer can generally be revoked at any time before it is accepted, provided that the revocation is communicated to the offeree.

■ Certainty. The courts require an agreement to be 'certain', and will not enforce an 'agreement to agree'.

2.2 INTRODUCTION

The main subject matter of this chapter is the means by which the courts decide whether parties have reached an agreement which potentially is one which the courts will enforce. A related question is that of why the law of contract should be engaged to deal with the parties' transaction. There are several potential reasons. First, it might be the case that the courts will simply be responding to the wishes of the parties. In other words, the law is acting in a facilitative way. The parties have intentionally formulated their agreement as a contract, and now wish to make use of the mechanism of the courts to resolve a dispute. They can choose not to use the courts if they wish, and indeed many commercial disputes are settled by alternative methods such as arbitration or mediation. Such methods may make reference to the law of contract as it is thought it would be applied by the courts, but essentially the parties have in such a situation decided to take their dispute out of the formal legal process. Thus, the decision to engage with the law of contract is in the hands of the parties.

Another reason for the courts' involvement may, however, be where there is a dispute as to whether there is a contract at all. This might be because one of the parties disputes the fact of agreement, or wishes to argue that although there is an agreement, it is unenforceable. If the courts become involved, and again there is an element of choice in that one party must initiate an action by issuing a claim form, it will be against the wishes of one of the parties. That party will be arguing that there is no contract, and that therefore the courts should not be involved at all. In this situation, the court is not acting in a purely facilitative way, but is saying to one of the parties that although it thought that it was not entering into a binding contract, in fact it was, and therefore is obliged to submit to the jurisdiction of the court. The extent to which a party can deliberately exclude an agreement from the jurisdiction of the court is considered further in Chapter 4, in connection with the requirement of 'intention to create legal relations'.

A third possibility which now exists is that a third party who claims to be entitled to a benefit under a contract may initiate an action against one or other of the contracting parties.[1] In theory, it is possible for this to arise in a situation where neither of the alleged contracting parties accepts that it has made a binding contract. The court, if it upholds the third party's claim, will in effect be overriding the wishes of the two parties who made the agreement. In doing so, it is likely to be acting to protect the reasonable expectations of the third party. To achieve this, it will hold that the parties have made a binding agreement, even though they dispute that they have done so.

In all these situations, however, the concept of an 'agreement' forms the basis of the court's intervention. As indicated in Chapter 1, this book takes as its subject matter the enforcement of agreements, entered into more or less voluntarily, concerning the transfer of property (permanently or temporarily) or the supply of services. That being so, it becomes important to identify when an agreement has been reached. There are two main ways in which this might be achieved. First, it might be done by identifying certain formal procedures, and deeming the following of those formalities as sufficient to establish that there was an agreement. Second, it might be done by trying to determine whether there was a 'meeting of the minds' of the parties concerned. In practice, English law uses both approaches.

---

1 See the Contracts (Rights of Third Parties) Act 1999, discussed in detail in Chapter 5, 5.5.

2.3   DEEDS AND OTHER FORMALITIES

The formal test of agreement is achieved by the concept of the 'deed'. This is a formal written document, signed and, traditionally, sealed (though this is no longer a requirement since the Law of Property (Miscellaneous Provisions) Act 1989). The existence of a deed will be regarded as indicating that there is an agreement. There are certain contracts where a deed is required (and these situations are considered further in Chapter 3), but the device can be used for any type of contract if the parties so wish. This type of formality should be distinguished from the situations where some special procedure is required *in addition* to the finding of an agreement. In this situation there may be an agreement, but the courts will not enforce it unless certain formalities have been complied with. Three examples will be mentioned here. First, by virtue of s 2(1) of the Law of Property (Miscellaneous Provisions) Act 1989, all contracts involving the sale, or other disposal, of an interest in land must be in writing and signed by the parties. The need for writing in relation to contracts concerning land is of long standing in English law, though prior to 1989 the requirement was only that the contract should be evidenced in writing, and signed by the person against whom it was to be enforced.[2] Although, in practice, the vast majority of such contracts were put into written form, this formulation left open the possibility of a verbal contract being evidenced by, for example, a letter signed by the relevant party. The 1989 amendment of this rule means that the agreement itself must be in writing and signed by both parties. The justification for the stricter rules which apply in relation to this type of contract is that contracts involving land are likely to be both complicated and valuable. Many commercial contracts, however, are also complex and valuable, yet there is no requirement of a written agreement (though, in practice, there is likely to be one). A second type of contract where there is a requirement of a certain degree of formality arises under the Consumer Credit Act 1974, which requires that contracts of hire purchase, and other credit transactions, should be in writing and signed.[3] This is a protective provision, designed to make sure that the individual consumer has written evidence of the agreement, and has the opportunity to see all its terms. A similar protective procedure operates in relation to contracts of employment, though here the requirement is simply that the employee should receive a written statement of terms and conditions within a certain period of starting the job, rather than that the agreement itself should be in writing.[4]

---

2 Law of Property Act 1925, s 40. Cf the Statute of Frauds 1677, which required writing for various agreements, including contracts for the sale of goods to the value of more than £10.

3 In *Wilson v First County Trust Ltd* [2003] UKHL 40; [2003] 4 All ER 97, the Court of Appeal held that the rigid statutory rule which renders a consumer credit totally unenforceable if certain formalities have not been complied with was incompatible with the right to a fair trial under Art 6 of the ECHR. The House of Lords, however, reversed this decision, on the basis that the Human Rights Act 1998 did not apply to the contract in question (which was made prior to 2 October 2000), and because in any case the provisions were compatible with the ECHR.

4 Employment Rights Act 1996, s 1.

A third situation where formality is required was the subject of consideration by the House of Lords in *Actionstrength Ltd v International Glass Engineering*.[5] The case concerned the requirement in s 4 of the Statute of Frauds 1677 that an agreement to guarantee the debt of a third party must, in order to be enforceable, be in writing and signed by the guarantor.

The claimant was a sub-contractor who had worked for the main contractor on a construction contract. When the main contractor became insolvent, the claimant sought to recover under an alleged oral guarantee of payment given by the party for whom the building was being constructed. In the Court of Appeal, it was held that the claimant could not succeed because an oral guarantee was unenforceable by virtue of s 4 of the 1677 Act.

In the House of Lords, the claimant argued that even if the Act applied, the defendant should be estopped from relying on it, on the grounds that it would be unconscionable to do so. The defendant had allowed the claimant to run up the debt owed by the main contractor, knowing that it was relying on the guarantee. It was held that the effect of s 4 could not be overturned by an estoppel, at least not unless there had been a specific assurance that the statute would not be relied on.

The case emphasises the continuing importance of the Statute of Frauds in this area, and the need to ensure that any 'promise to answer for the debt, default or miscarriages of another' is put in writing.

2.4 GENERAL LACK OF FORMAL REQUIREMENT

In most cases, however, English law imposes no formal requirements and looks simply for an agreement between two parties. In other words, the contract does not have to be put into writing, or signed, nor does any particular form of words have to be used. A purely verbal exchange can result in a binding contract. All that is needed is an agreement. This simple assertion, however, masks a considerable problem in identifying precisely what is meant by an agreement. This may seem easy enough: it is simply a question of identifying a 'meeting of the minds' between the parties at a particular point in time. That, however, is easier said than done. By the time two parties to a contract have arrived in court, they are clearly no longer of one mind. They may dispute whether there was ever an agreement between them at all or, while accepting that there was an agreement, they may disagree as to its terms. How are such disputes to be resolved? Clearly, the courts cannot discover as a matter of fact what was actually going on in the minds of the parties at the time of the alleged agreement. Nor are they prepared to rely solely on what the parties now say was in their minds at that time (which would be a 'subjective' approach), even if they are very convincing. Instead, the courts adopt what is primarily an 'objective' approach to deciding whether there was an

---

5 [2003] 2 All ER 615.

agreement and, if so, what its terms were. This means that they look at what was said and done between the parties from the point of view of the 'reasonable person' and try to decide what such a person would have thought was going on.

It has been argued by Collins that this approach means that the courts are not actually looking for agreements between the parties but:

> whether or not the negotiations and conduct have reached such a point that both parties can reasonably suppose that the other is committed to the contract so that it can be relied upon.[6]

In other words it is behaviour justifying 'reasonable reliance' on the other party's commitment that is what the courts are in fact looking for, rather than 'agreement', whether looked at subjectively or objectively.[7] There is, however, not very much to choose between an approach which uses the language of 'objective agreement' as opposed to that of 'reasonable reliance', and certainly little in the way of practical consequence. The former is what is used here, not least because it ties in more comfortably with the language used by the courts, which tends to focus on the presence or absence of 'agreement'. Provided that it is remembered that what is required is objective evidence of such agreement, rather than an actual 'meeting of the minds', this analysis will work satisfactorily, without giving a misleading picture of what is actually happening.

A further complication with regard to 'agreement' arises once parties start to contract over a distance – that is, not face to face. The particular problems relating to contracts made by post or other forms of distance communication are discussed later in this chapter.[8] Suffice it to say here that once this type of contracting is allowed, the idea that at any particular point in time there is a 'consensus ad idem', a 'meeting of the minds', becomes very difficult to sustain.[9] If there is a significant gap in time between an 'offer' and its 'acceptance', the likelihood is that in a significant number of cases the parties will not be ad idem at the point when the courts decide that a contract has been formed.

2.4.1 Promisor, promisee and detached objectivity

Although it is clear that an objective approach to agreement has to be adopted, as has been pointed out by McClintock and Howarth,[10] there are different types of objectivity. There is (a) 'promisor objectivity', where the court tries to decide what the reasonable promisor would have intended; (b) 'promisee objectivity', where the focus is on what the

---

6 Collins, 2003, p 164.
7 Cf the approach of Steyn LJ in *Trentham Ltd v Archital Luxfer* [1993] 1 Lloyd's Rep 25, p 27 – discussed below, 2.11.5).
8 See below, 2.12.6.
9 Cf Gardner, 1992, p 171.
10 McClintock, 1988–91; Howarth, 1984.

reasonable person being made a promise would have thought was intended; and (c) 'detached objectivity', which views what has happened through the eyes of an independent third party. In *Smith v Hughes*,[11] for example, where the dispute was over what type of oats the parties were contracting about, the test was said to be whether the party who wishes to deny the contract acted so that 'a reasonable man would believe that he was assenting to the terms proposed by the other party': in other words, promisee objectivity. As we shall see, however, in subsequent chapters, the courts are not consistent as to which of these types of objectivity they use, changing between one and another as seems most appropriate in a particular case.

The use of the objective approach where there is a dispute as to whether the parties were ever in agreement is discussed further in Chapter 11, 11.6.1.

2.4.2 State of mind

The objective approach must, however, take account of all the evidence. Even if A has acted in a way which would reasonably cause B to assume a particular state of mind as regards an agreement, if B's behaviour, objectively viewed, indicates that such an assumption has not been made by B, the courts will take account of this. *The Hannah Blumenthal*,[12] for example, was a case concerning the sale of a ship, where the point at issue was whether the parties had agreed to abandon their dispute. The behaviour of the buyers was such that it would have been reasonable for the sellers to have believed that the action had been dropped. In fact, the sellers had continued to act (by seeking witnesses, etc) in a way which indicated that they did not think the action had been dropped. This evidence of their actual response to the buyers' behaviour overrode the conclusion which the court might well have reached by applying a test based on an objectively reasonable response.[13]

2.5 THE EXTERNAL SIGNS OF AGREEMENT

As we have seen, the process by which the courts try to decide whether the parties have made an agreement does not necessarily involve looking for actual agreement, but rather for the external signs of agreement. The classical theory of contract relied on a number of specific elements, which were regarded as both necessary and sufficient to identify an agreement which is intended to be legally binding. These were:

(a)   offer;
(b)   acceptance; and
(c)   consideration.

---

11 (1871) LR 6 QB 597. This case is discussed further in Chapter 11, 11.6.1.
12 [1983] 1 All ER 34.
13 See, also, the similar case of *The Leonidas D* [1985] 1 WLR 925.

These three factors, together with an overarching requirement that the court is satisfied that there was an intention to create legal relations, formed the classical basis for the identification of contracts in English law. As far as offer and acceptance are concerned, in the modern law the courts have, as will be noted below, at various times recognised the difficulty of analysing all contractual situations in terms of these concepts. Some attempts have been made to apply a more general test of 'agreement'. These have not been fully developed, but the direction in which English law is moving is perhaps indicated by the Principles of European Contract Law. These suggest that the normal basis for the creation of a contract will be the exchange of offer and acceptance (Arts 2:201 and 2:204). They recognise, however, that not all contracts will be made in this way (Art 2:211). The overall test is simply whether there is 'sufficient agreement' (Art 2:101), with this being determined by whether the terms 'have been sufficiently determined by the parties so that the contract can be enforced' (Art 2:103).

The rest of this chapter explores the current English law approach to offer and acceptance in detail. Consideration is dealt with in Chapter 3 and the intention to create legal relations in Chapter 4.

2.6 HISTORICAL BACKGROUND

The rules of 'offer' and 'acceptance', and their use as the basis for deciding whether there has been an agreement between contracting parties, derives, as with much of the classical law of contract, from late eighteenth and early nineteenth century case law.[14]

2.7 OFFER

An offer may be defined as an indication by one person that he or she is prepared to contract with one or more others, on certain terms, which are fixed, or capable of being fixed, at the time the offer is made. Thus, the statement 'I will sell you 5,000 widgets for £1,000' is an offer, as is the statement 'I will buy from you 5,000 shares in X Ltd, at their closing price on the London Stock Exchange next Friday'. In the former case, the terms are fixed by the offer itself, in the latter they are capable of becoming fixed on Friday, according to the price of the shares at the close of business on the Stock Exchange. The offer may be made by words, conduct or a mixture of the two. The concept applies most easily to a situation such as that given in the above example where there are two parties communicating with each other about a commercial transaction. It fits less easily, as will be seen below, in many other everyday transactions, such as supermarket sales, or those involving the advertisement of goods in a newspaper or magazine. What the

---

14 See, in particular, *Adams v Lindsell* (1818) 1 B & Ald 681; 106 ER 250 – discussed in detail below, 2.12.6.

courts will look for, however, is some behaviour which indicates a willingness to contract on particular terms. Once there is such an indication, all that is then required from the other person is a simple assent to the terms suggested, and a contract will be formed. The 'indication of willingness' referred to above may take a number of forms – for example, the spoken word, a letter, a fax message, an email or an advertisement on a website. As long as it communicates to the potential acceptor or acceptors the basis on which the offeror is prepared to contract, then that is enough. It is not necessary for the offer itself to set out all the terms of the contract. The parties may have been negotiating over a period of time, and the offer may simply refer to terms appearing in earlier communications. That is quite acceptable, provided that it is clear what the terms are.

2.7.1 Distinction from 'invitation to treat'

As we have noted, the objective of looking for 'offer and acceptance' is to decide whether an agreement has been reached. It is important, therefore, that behaviour which may have some of the characteristics of an offer should not be treated as such if, viewed objectively, that was not what was intended. Once a statement or action is categorised as an offer, then the party from whom it emanated has put itself in the position where it can become legally bound simply by the other party accepting. It must be clear, therefore, that the statement or action indicates an intention to be bound, without more. The courts have traditionally approached this issue by drawing a distinction between an offer and an 'invitation to treat'.

Sometimes a person will wish simply to open negotiations, rather than to make an offer which will lead immediately to a contract on acceptance. If I wish to sell my car, for example, I may enquire if you are interested in buying it. This is clearly not an offer. Even if I indicate a price at which I am willing to sell, this may simply be an attempt to discover your interest, rather than committing me to particular terms. The courts refer to such a preliminary communication as an 'invitation to treat' or, even more archaically, as an 'invitation to chaffer'. The distinction between an offer and an invitation to treat is an important one, but is not always easy to draw. Even where the parties appear to have reached agreement on the terms on which they are prepared to contract, the courts may decide that the language they have used is more appropriate to an invitation to treat than an offer.

This was the view taken in *Gibson v Manchester City Council*.[15] Mr Gibson was a tenant of a house owned by Manchester City Council. The Council, which was at the time under the control of Conservative Party members, decided that it wished to give its tenants the opportunity to purchase the houses which they were renting. Mr Gibson wished to take advantage of this opportunity and started negotiations with the Council. He received a letter which indicated a price, and which stated 'The Corporation may

---

15 [1979] 1 All ER 972; [1979] 1 WLR 294.

be prepared to sell the house to you' at that price. It also instructed Mr Gibson, if he wished to make 'a formal application', to complete a form and return it. This Mr Gibson did. At this point, local elections took place, and control of the Council changed from the Conservative Party to the Labour Party. The new Labour Council immediately reversed the policy of the sale of council houses, and refused to proceed with the sale to Mr Gibson. At first instance and in the Court of Appeal,[16] it was held that there was a binding contract, and that Mr Gibson could therefore enforce the sale. Lord Denning argued that it was not necessary to analyse the transaction in terms of offer and acceptance. He suggested that:

> You should look at the correspondence as a whole and at the conduct of the parties and see therefrom whether the parties have come to an agreement on everything that was material. If by their correspondence and their conduct you can see an agreement on all material terms, which was intended thenceforward to be binding, then there is a binding contract in law even though all formalities have not been gone through.[17]

This approach was firmly rejected by the House of Lords. Despite the fact that all terms appeared to have been agreed between the parties, the House of Lords held that there was no contract. The language of the Council's letter to Mr Gibson was not sufficiently definite to amount to an offer. It was simply an invitation to treat. Mr Gibson had made an offer to buy, but that had not been accepted.

FOR THOUGHT

Do you think the House of Lords would have come to the same conclusion if the Council's letter to Mr Gibson had said that it 'is prepared to sell the house' at the specified price, rather than that it 'may be prepared to sell'?

The narrowness of the distinction being drawn can be seen by comparing this case with *Storer v Manchester City Council*,[18] where on very similar facts a contract was held to exist, as Mr Storer had signed and returned a document entitled 'Agreement for Sale'. This document was deemed to be sufficiently definite to amount to an offer from the Council which Mr Storer had accepted. As regards the state of mind of the parties in the two cases, however, it is arguable that there was little difference. In both, each party had indicated a willingness to enter into the transaction, and there was agreement on the price. The fact that the courts focus on the external signs,

---

16 [1978] 2 All ER 583.

17 Ibid, p 586. Ormrod LJ agreed with Lord Denning, but also held that an agreement could be found using the traditional offer and acceptance analysis. Lane LJ dissented.

18 [1974] 3 All ER 824; [1974] 1 WLR 1403.

rather than the underlying agreement, however, led to the result being different in the two cases.

Before leaving these cases, it should noted that there was potentially a political dimension to the decisions in *Storer* and *Gibson*. The question of the sale of council houses was at the time a very controversial political issue, with the Conservative Party strongly in favour and Labour vehemently opposed. In Manchester, the local electors had decided to vote in a Labour Council, and it might have been reasonable to assume that one of the reasons for this was opposition to the previous Conservative Council's approach to the sale of council houses. In such a situation, to decide strongly in favour of enforcing the sale of a council house (particularly since there were, apparently, 'hundreds' of other cases similar to that of Mr Gibson)[19] might have been seen as an intervention by the judges which would have the effect of disregarding the wishes of the electorate. Where the case was clear-cut (as in *Storer*), the courts would be obliged to respect the individual's vested rights; where there was ambiguity, however (as in *Gibson*), there would be an argument for deciding the case in a way which complied with the political decision indicated by the results of the election. There is, of course, no indication in the speeches in the House of Lords of any such political considerations having any effect on their Lordships' opinions. However, it has been strongly argued that judges can be influenced, consciously or unconsciously, by political matters,[20] and it is possible that this may have been a factor tipping the balance against Mr Gibson. In any case, the *Storer* and *Gibson* decisions are good examples of the fact that decisions on the law of contract operate in a social and political context, and their interrelationship with that context should not be ignored.

2.7.2 Self-service displays

Another area of difficulty arises in relation to the display of goods in a shop window, or on the shelves of a supermarket, or other shop where customers serve themselves. We commonly talk of such a situation as one in which the shop has the goods 'on offer'. This is especially true of attractive bargains which may be labelled 'special offer'. Are these 'offers' for the purpose of the law of contract? The issue has been addressed in a number of criminal cases where the offence in question was based on there being a 'sale' or an 'offer for sale'. These cases are taken to establish the position under the law of contract, even though they were decided in a criminal law context. The Court of Appeal has more recently suggested that it is not appropriate to use contractual principles in defining the behaviour which constitutes a criminal offence, in this case relating to an

---

19 See Lord Diplock [1979] 3 All ER 972, p 973; [1979] 1 WLR 294, p 296. *The Guardian* in a front-page story on 9 March 1979, the day after the Lords' ruling, reported that there were 350 other sales that were affected by the Lords' ruling in Manchester alone, with doubts being raised about sales in other local authority areas.

20 See, in particular, Griffith, 1997.

offer to supply drugs.[21] This does not, however, affect the contractual rules deriving from older criminal cases where this was done. The first to consider is *Pharmaceutical Society of Great Britain v Boots Cash Chemists*.[22]

Section 18(1) of the Pharmacy and Poisons Act 1933 made it an offence to sell certain medicines unless 'the sale is effected by, or under the supervision of, a registered pharmacist'. Boots introduced a system under which some of these medicines were made available to customers on a self-service basis. There was no supervision until the customer went to the cashier. At this point, a registered pharmacist would supervise the transaction and could intervene, if necessary. The Pharmaceutical Society claimed that this was an offence under s 18, because, it was argued, the sale was complete when the customer took an article from the shelves and put it into his or her basket. The Court of Appeal disagreed, and held that the sale was made at the cash desk, where the customer made an offer to buy, which could be accepted or rejected by the cashier. The reason for this decision was that it is clearly unacceptable to say that the contract is complete as soon as the goods are put into the basket, because the customer may want to change his or her mind, and it is undoubtedly the intention of all concerned that this should be possible. The display of goods is therefore an invitation to treat and not an offer.

With respect to the Court of Appeal, the conclusion that was reached was not necessary to avoid the problem of the customer becoming committed too soon. It would have been quite possible to have said that the display of goods is an offer, but that the customer does not accept that offer until presenting the goods to the cashier.[23] This analysis would, of course, also have meant that the sale took place at the cash desk and that no offence was committed under s 18. Strictly speaking, therefore, the details of the Court of Appeal's analysis in this case as to what constitutes the offer, and what is the acceptance, may be regarded as *obiter*. It has, however, generally been accepted subsequently that the display of goods within a shop is an invitation to treat and not an offer.

The decision in this case was treated by the Court of Appeal very much as a 'technical' one on the law of contract. There were, however, several other broader issues which were involved in it. First, there is the issue of the degree of supervision necessary to protect the public in relation to the sale of certain types of pharmaceutical product. Second, there was the potential effect on the employment position of pharmacists – the self-service arrangement would probably have the effect of reducing the number of pharmacists which Boots, or other chemists adopting a self-service system, would need to employ. Third, there was the question of whether the law on formation of contracts was to be developed in a way which helped or hindered the growth of the self-service

---

21 *R v Karamjit Singh Dhillon* (2000) *The Times*, 5 April. Cf the earlier comments on the unnecessary use of civil law concepts in a criminal context by Smith, 1972.

22 [1953] 1 QB 401; [1953] 1 All ER 482.

23 As was pointed out at the time by, for example, Williams, 1953. See also Unger, 1953. Montrose, 1955, however, prefers the analysis adopted in the *Boots* case, because it would be 'unfair' to hold the shopkeeper to a mistake in the pricing of goods.

shop. On the first issue Somervell LJ emphasised that the substances concerned were not 'dangerous drugs'.[24] The implication is that the system of control operating under Boots' self-service scheme was sufficient to fulfil the objective of the 1933 Act in protecting the public. The second issue, the effect on pharmacists, was not addressed at all, even though this must have been one of the main reasons for the action being brought by the Pharmaceutical Society. Collins has suggested that the court may not have been impressed 'by the desire of the pharmacists to retain their restrictive practices',[25] but this does not appear from the judgments at all. As regards the final issue, the court noted that the self-service arrangement was a 'convenient' one for the customer.[26] It is also, of course, an efficient one for the shopkeeper, enabling the display of a wide range of goods with a relatively small number of staff. The self-service format has become so dominant in shops of all kinds today that it is important to remember that in the early 1950s it was only gradually being adopted. The decision in the *Boots* case, if it had gone the other way, would have hindered (though probably not halted) its development.[27] The Court of Appeal therefore can be seen by this decision to be making a contribution to the way in which the retail trade developed over the next 10 years.

2.7.3 Shop window displays

The slightly different issue of the shop window display was dealt with in *Fisher v Bell*.[28] The defendant displayed in his shop window a 'flick-knife' with the price attached. He was charged with an offence under s 1(1) of the Restriction of Offensive Weapons Act 1959, namely 'offering for sale' a 'flick-knife'. It was held by the Divisional Court that no offence had been committed, because the display of the knife was an invitation to treat, not an offer.

Lord Parker had no doubt as to the contractual position:

> It is clear that according to the ordinary law of contract the display of an article with a price on it in a shop window is merely an invitation to treat. It is in no sense an offer for sale the acceptance of which constitutes a contract.[29]

No authority was cited for this proposition, but the approach is certainly in line with that taken in the *Boots* case. There has never been any challenge to it, and it must be taken to represent the current law on this point. It was followed in *Mella v Monahan*,[30] where a charge of 'offering for sale' obscene articles, contrary to the

---

24 [1953] 1 QB 401, p 405.
25 Collins, 2003, p 172.
26 [1953] 1 QB 401, p 406; [1953] 1 All ER 482, p 484.
27 This was recognised by Romer LJ, ibid, p 408; p 485.
28 [1961] 1 QB 394; [1960] 3 All ER 731.
29 [1961] 1 QB 394, p 399; [1960] 3 All ER 731, p 733.
30 [1961] Crim LR 175.

Obscene Publications Act 1959, failed because the items were simply displayed in a shop window.

2.7.4 Issues of principle

What are the principles lying behind the decisions in relation to self-service stores and shop window displays? In *Boots*, the court stressed the need for the shopper to be allowed a 'change of mind'. As we have seen, however, that does not necessarily require the offer to be made by the customer, just that the acceptance of the offer should be delayed beyond the point when the shopper may legitimately still be deciding whether to purchase. In any case, the argument cannot apply to the shop window cases. The customer who enters the shop will either say 'I want to buy that item displayed in your window', which could undoubtedly be treated as an acceptance, or 'I am interested in buying that item in your window; can I inspect it?' or 'can you tell me more about it?', which would simply be a stage in negotiation. There is no need, therefore, to protect the *customer* by making the shop window display simply an invitation to treat.

The most likely candidate as an alternative principle on which the decisions are based is freedom of contract. That freedom includes within it the principle that a person can choose with whom to contract – 'party freedom'.[31] On this analysis, the shop transaction needs to be analysed in a way which will allow the shopkeeper to say 'I do not want to do business with you'. This was the view expressed to counsel by Parke B in the nineteenth century case of *Timothy v Simpson*.[32] There are two problems, however, with the modern law of contract allowing such freedom in these situations.

First, such freedom has the potential to be used in a discriminatory way.[33] Certain types of discrimination –on grounds, for example, of race, sex and disability[34] – have as a matter of social policy been made unlawful by statute.[35] To the extent, therefore, that the common law of contract still allows party freedom to operate in these areas, there is a tension between it and the statutory regimes. A shopkeeper who discriminates on impermissible grounds in deciding with whom to contract is not forced by the common law to undertake the contractual obligation, but may face a quasi-tortious action under one of the relevant statutes.

Second, application of the 'party freedom' principle leads to the conclusion that, as far the law of contract is concerned, a shopkeeper is not bound by any price that is attached to goods displayed in the shop or in the window. He or she is entitled to say to

---

31 See Brownsword, 2000, para 2.10.
32 (1834) 6 C & P499, p 500.
33 See Beale, 1995a, p 190; Collins, 2003, p 33; Brownsword, 2000, para 2.15.
34 Race Relations Act 1976; Sex Discrimination Act 1975; Disability Discrimination Act 1995. Other types of discrimination may become unlawful as a result of the effects of the Human Rights Act 1998.
35 Note that the common law did in fact also recognise some restriction on party freedom as regards common carriers and innkeepers – see *Halsbury's Laws*, Vol 5(1), para 441 and Vol 24, para 1113.

the customer seeking to buy the item '. . . that is a mistake. I am afraid the price is different'. Again, however, there is a conflict with the statutory position. Such action on the part of the shopkeeper would almost certainly constitute a criminal offence under s 20 of the Consumer Protection Act 1987. This states that:

> . . . a person shall be guilty of an offence if, in the course of any business of his, he gives (by any means whatever) to any consumers an indication which is misleading as to the price at which any goods, services, accommodation or facilities are available (whether generally or from particular persons).

An indication is 'misleading' if, *inter alia*, it leads the consumer to think that the price is less than in fact it is.[36] Thus, if a shop has a window display indicating that certain special packs of goods are on offer at a low price inside, but in fact none of the special packs are available, an offence will almost certainly have been committed. This was the situation in *Tesco Supermarkets Ltd v Nattrass*,[37] a case concerning s 11 of the Trade Descriptions Act 1968, which was the predecessor to s 20 of the Consumer Protection Act 1987.

In practice, because of their awareness of the statutory position, and their wish to maintain good relationships with their customers, shops and other businesses are unlikely to insist on their strict contractual rights in situations of this kind. That being the case, the question arises as to whether the rule that it is the customer who makes the offer, and the shopkeeper who has the choice whether or not to accept it, is not ripe for reconsideration, so as to avoid the current tension with the statutory controls.

2.7.5 Advertisements

Where goods or services are advertised, does this constitute an offer or an invitation to treat? It would be possible here for the law also to base its principles on 'party freedom': that is, a person putting forward an advertisement should not be taken to be waiving the right as to whom he or she chooses to contract with. In fact, however, the cases in this area show the courts adopting an approach based on pragmatism, rather than on the 'party freedom' principle. The answer to the question 'is this advertisement an offer?' will generally be determined by the context in which the advertisement appears, and the practical consequences of treating it as either an offer or an invitation to treat.

Generally speaking, an advertisement on a hoarding, a newspaper 'display' or a television commercial will not be regarded as an offer. Thus, in *Harris v Nickerson*,[38] the defendant had advertised that an auction of certain furniture was to take place on a certain day. The plaintiff travelled to the auction only to find that the items in which he

---

36 Consumer Protection Act 1987, s 21.
37 [1972] AC 153; [1971] 2 All ER 127. Note that Tesco was found to have a defence under the statute.
38 (1873) LR 8 QB 286; (1873) 42 LJ QB 171.

was interested had, without notice, been withdrawn. He brought an action for breach of contract to recover his expenses in attending the advertised event. His claim was rejected by the Queen's Bench. The advertisement did not give rise to any contract that all the items mentioned would actually be put up for sale. To hold otherwise would, Blackburn J felt, be 'a startling proposition' and 'excessively inconvenient if carried out'. It would amount to saying that 'anyone who advertises a sale by publishing an advertisement becomes responsible to everybody who attends the sale for his cab hire or travelling expenses'.[39] In other words, the practical consequences of treating the advertisement as an offer would be such that it is highly unlikely that this is what the person placing the advert can have intended. Using an approach based on 'promisor objectivity',[40] it is concluded that the advertisement is nothing more than an invitation to treat.

It follows from this that these types of advertisement should be regarded simply as attempts to make the public aware of what is available. Such advertisements will often, in any case, not be specific enough to amount to an offer. Even where goods are clearly identified and a price specified, however, there may still not be an offer. A good example of this situation is another criminal law case, *Partridge v Crittenden*.[41] The defendant put an advertisement in the 'classified' section of a periodical, advertising bramblefinches for sale at 25s each. He was charged under the Protection of Birds Act 1954 with 'offering for sale' a live wild bird, contrary to s 6(1). It was held that he had committed no offence, because the advert was an invitation to treat and not an offer. The court relied heavily on *Fisher v Bell*,[42] and appeared to feel that this kind of advertisement should be treated in the same way as the display of goods with a price attached. To that extent, the case may seem to adopt the 'party freedom' approach implicit in *Fisher v Bell*. Lord Parker, however, pointed out an additional and very practical reason for not treating it as an offer. If it was an offer, this would mean that everyone who replied to the advertisement would be accepting it, and would therefore be entitled to a bramblefinch. Assuming that the advertiser did not have an unlimited supply of bramblefinches, this could not be what he intended. As with *Harris v Nickerson*, this is an analysis based on 'promisor objectivity', looking at what the reasonable advertiser would be taken to have meant by the advert. As a result, the advertisement was properly to be categorised as an invitation to treat. A different approach is taken in the Principles of European Contract Law. Article 2.201(3) provides that:

> A proposal to supply goods or services at stated prices made by a professional supplier in a public advertisement or a catalogue, or by a display of goods, is presumed to be an offer to sell or supply at that price until the stock of goods, or the supplier's capacity to supply the services is exhausted.

39 (1873) LR 8 QB 286, p 288.
40 For which, see 2.4.1, above.
41 [1968] 2 All ER 421.
42 [1961] 1 QB 394; [1960] 3 All ER 731 – discussed above, 2.7.3.

The approach taken by English law does not mean, however, that all newspaper advertisements will be treated as invitations to treat. If the guiding principle is promisor objectivity, rather than party freedom, then provided that the wording is clear and there are no problems of limited supply, there seems to be no reason why such an advertisement should not be an offer. If, for example, the advertiser in *Partridge v Crittenden* had said, '100 bramblefinches for sale. The first 100 replies enclosing 25s will secure a bird', then in all probability this would be construed as an offer. An advertisement of a similar kind was held to be an offer in the American case of *Lefkowitz v Great Minneapolis Surplus Stores*,[43] where the defendants published an advertisement in a newspaper, stating: 'Saturday 9 am sharp; three brand new fur coats, worth to $100. First come first served, $1 each.' The plaintiff was one of the first three customers, but the firm refused to sell him a coat, because it said the offer was only open to women. The court held that the advertisement constituted an offer, which the plaintiff had accepted, and that he was therefore entitled to the coat.

FOR THOUGHT

Would it have made any difference to the court's decision in *Lefkowitz* if the advertisement had indicated that there were just three coats available, but had not said 'first come first served'?

Clearly in this case, the court was rejecting any argument based on party freedom. In this context any such freedom was waived by making such a specific offer to the general public, which did not indicate any intention by the advertiser to put limits on those who were entitled to take advantage of the bargain. The use of such an approach here only serves to highlight the anomaly of the cases on shop sales discussed in the previous section.

2.7.6 *Carlill v Carbolic Smoke Ball Co*

In England, the most famous case of an advertisement constituting an offer is *Carlill v Carbolic Smoke Ball Co*.[44] The manufacturers of a 'smoke ball' published an advertisement at the time of an influenza epidemic, proclaiming the virtues of their smoke ball for curing all kinds of ailments. In addition, they stated that anybody who bought one of their smoke balls, used it as directed, and then caught influenza, would be paid £100. Mrs Carlill, having bought and used a smoke ball, but nevertheless having caught influenza, claimed £100 from the company. The company argued that the advertisement could not be taken to be an offer which could turn into a contract by acceptance. They

43 (1957) 86 NW 2d 689.
44 [1893] 1 QB 256.

claimed that it should be regarded as a 'mere puff' which meant nothing in contractual terms. This is certainly true of many advertising slogans (for example, 'Gillette – the Best a Man Can Get', 'The Best Hard Rock Album in the World . . . Ever!'). A contractual action based on these would be doomed to failure. In the *Carlill* case, however, there was evidence of serious intent on the part of the defendants. The advertisement had stated that '£1,000 is deposited with the Alliance Bank, showing our sincerity in this matter'. The court took the view that the inclusion of this statement meant that reasonable people would treat the offer to pay £100 as one that was intended seriously, so that it could create a binding obligation in appropriate circumstances, such as those which had arisen. In other words, the court adopted an approach based on 'promisee objectivity', rather than the 'promisor objectivity' used in *Partridge v Crittenden*.[45] The defendants raised two further objections. First, they argued that the advertisement was widely distributed, and that this was therefore not an offer made to anybody in particular. The court did not regard this as a problem. Offers of reward (for example, for the return of a lost pet or for information leading to the conviction of a criminal) were generally in the same form, and could be accepted by any person who fulfilled the condition. There was plenty of authority to support this, such as *Williams v Carwardine*.[46] Second, the defendants said that Mrs Carlill should have given them notice of her acceptance. Again, however, the court, by analogy with the reward cases, held that the form of the advertisement could be taken to have waived the need for notification of acceptance, at least prior to the performance of the condition which entitled the plaintiff to claim. As Lindley LJ put it:[47]

> I . . . think that the true view, in a case of this kind, is that the person who makes the offer shows by his language and from the nature of the transaction that he does not expect and does not require notice of the acceptance apart from notice of the performance.

The Smoke Ball Company cannot have expected that everyone who bought a smoke ball would get in touch with them. It was only those who, having used the ball, then contracted influenza who would do so. This case, therefore, is authority for the propositions, first, that an advertisement can constitute an offer to 'the world' (that is, anyone who reads it) and, second, that it may, by the way in which it is stated, waive the need for communication of acceptance prior to a claim under it.

The *Carlill* case has been viewed as giving a surprisingly broad scope to the situations which will fall within the law of contract.[48] Simpson has pointed out that there was much concern at the time about advertisements for dubious 'medicinal'

---

45 See above, 2.7.5.
46 (1833) 5 C & P 566 – see below, 2.12.15.
47 [1893] 1 QB 256, pp 262–63.
48 See, for example, the comments of Collins, 2003, p 4.

products,[49] and this may have influenced the court towards finding liability. Nowadays, it would be expected that such situations would be more likely to be dealt with by legislation,[50] or by an agency such as the Advertising Standards Authority. At the time, however, the consumer protection role had to be taken by the courts, even if this meant stretching contractual principles to provide a remedy.

It should be noted that the offer in *Carlill*, in *Lefkowitz*[51] and the suggested reformulation of the offer in *Partridge v Crittenden*[52] are all offers of a particular kind, known in English law as an offer in a 'unilateral' (as opposed to a 'bilateral') contract. It will be convenient at this point to examine the difference between these two types of contract.

2.8 UNILATERAL AND BILATERAL CONTRACTS

The typical model of the bilateral contract arises where A promises to sell goods to B in return for B promising to pay the purchase price. In this situation, the contract is bilateral, because as soon as these promises have been exchanged, there is a contract to which both are bound. In relation to services, the same applies, so that an agreement between A and B that B will dig A's garden for £20 next Tuesday is a bilateral agreement. Suppose, however, that the arrangement is slightly different, and that A says to B 'If you dig my garden next Tuesday, I will pay you £20'. B makes no commitment, but says, 'I am not sure that I shall be able to, but if I do, I shall be happy to take £20'. This arrangement is not bilateral. A has committed himself to pay the £20 in certain circumstances, but B has made no commitment at all. He is totally free to decide whether or not he wants to dig A's garden or not, and if he wakes up on Tuesday morning and decides that he just does not feel like doing so, there is nothing that A can do about it. If, however, B does decide to go and do the work, that will be regarded as an acceptance of A's offer of £20, and the contract will be formed. Because of its one-sided nature, therefore, this type of arrangement is known as a 'unilateral contract'. Another way of describing them is as 'if' contracts, in that it is always possible to formulate the offer as a statement beginning with the word 'if': for example, 'if you dig my garden, I will pay you £20'. As has been noted above, the arrangements in *Carlill* and *Lefkowitz* were of this type: 'If you use our smoke ball and catch influenza, we will pay you £100'; 'If you are the first person to offer to buy one of these coats, we will sell it to you for $1'.

The distinction between unilateral and bilateral contracts is important in relation to the areas of 'acceptance' and 'consideration', which are discussed further below.

---

49 Simpson, 1985.
50 For example, the Consumer Protection Act 1987.
51 See above, 2.7.5.
52 Ibid.

2.9   TENDERS

Some confusion may arise as to what constitutes an offer when a person or, more probably, a company decides to put work out to tender, or seeks offers for certain goods. This means that potential contractors are invited to submit quotations. The invitation may be issued to the world or to specific parties. Generally speaking, such a request will amount simply to an invitation to treat, and the person making it will be free to accept or reject any of the responses. In *Spencer v Harding*,[53] for example, it was held that the issue of a circular 'offering' stock for sale by tender, was simply a 'proclamation' that the defendants were ready to negotiate for the sale of the goods, and to receive offers for the purchase of them. There was no obligation to sell to the highest bidder, or indeed to any bidder at all. The position will be different if the invitation indicates that the highest bid or, as appropriate, the lowest quotation will definitely be accepted. It will then be regarded as an offer in a unilateral contract. The recipients of the invitation will not be bound to reply, but if they do, the one who submits the lowest quotation will be entitled to insist that the contract is made with them. A similar situation arose in *Blackpool and Fylde Aero Club Ltd v Blackpool Borough Council.*[54] The council had invited tenders for the operation of pleasure flights from an airfield. Tenders were to be placed in a designated box by a specified deadline. The plaintiff complied with this requirement, but due to an oversight on the part of the defendant's employees, the plaintiff's tender was not removed from the box until the day after the deadline, and was accordingly marked as having arrived late. It was therefore ignored in the council's deliberations as to who should be awarded the contract. The plaintiff succeeded in an action against the defendant, who appealed. The Court of Appeal noted that, in this type of situation, the inviter of tenders was in a strong position, as he could dictate the terms on which the tenders were to be made, and the basis on which the selection of the successful one, if any, was to be made. There was nothing explicit in this case which indicated that all tenders meeting the deadline would be considered. Nevertheless:[55]

> ... in the context, a reasonable invitee would understand the invitation to be saying, quite clearly, that if he submitted a timely and conforming tender it would be considered, at least if any other such tender were considered.

By applying this test of 'promisee objectivity' to the circumstances, the court concluded that the defendant was in breach of an implicit unilateral contract, under which it promised that if a tender was received by the specified deadline, it would be given due consideration. The promise was not made explicitly, and indeed the defendant claimed

---

53 (1870) LR 5 CP 561.
54 [1990] 3 All ER 25.
55 Ibid, p 31.

that no such promise was intended,[56] but because it was reasonable for the plaintiff to have assumed that such a promise was implied, the court found that there was a contractual relationship obliging the defendant to consider all tenders fulfilling the terms of the invitation. A person inviting tenders must therefore either explicitly state the terms on which responses will be considered, or be bound by the reasonable expectations of those who put in tenders.

This decision places some limits on the freedom of the party inviting tenders, but limits which can be avoided by careful wording of the tender documentation. Much more stringent controls exist over tendering in a range of public sector contracts as a result of European Directives on the issue, which have been implemented in the UK by various sets of regulations.[57] These Directives are primarily intended to ensure the free working of the European market – and, in particular, to avoid nationals of the same State as the party seeking the tenders having an advantage over those based in other Member States. The controls contained in the Regulations cover such matters as the way in which the tender must be publicised (for example, by being published in the EU's *Official Journal*, as well as any national press), the information that must be provided, and the criteria which must be used to select the successful tender (usually based on either 'the lowest price' or the offer which 'is the most economically advantageous to the contracting authority').[58] Controls of the latter kind are perhaps the most significant, in that they strike most directly at one of the main aspects of the concept of freedom of contract – that is, party freedom. The authority seeking the tenders does not have a free hand to decide with whom it wishes to contract; it must reach its decision in accordance with the Regulations.

There is clearly potential for the approach taken in these Regulations to influence more generally the way in which tendering takes place. It would not be surprising if organisations which are required to use the European procedures in some areas of their activities found it convenient to use the same type of approach even if not constrained to do so by regulation. Such influences on business practice might in turn have an effect on the way in which the courts develop the general legal rules relating to tenders. There is no evidence to date of this happening, but the potential is clearly there.

---

56 Brownsword uses this case as an example of the fact that an analysis of contract based on the making of express promises does not accord with the actual practice of the courts (Brownsword, 2000, para 1.10).

57 For example, the Public Supply Contracts Regulations 1991, SI 1991/2679 (implementing Directive 77/62/EEC, as amended); the Public Works Contracts Regulations 1991, SI 1991/2680 (implementing Directive 71/305/EEC, as amended); the Public Services Contracts Regulations 1993, SI 1993/3228 (implementing Directive 92/50/EEC); the Utilities Contracts Regulations 1996, SI 1996/2911 (implementing Directives 92/13/EEC and 93/38/EEC).

58 See, for example, SI 1991/2679, reg 20; SI 1991/2680, reg 20; SI 1993/3228, reg 21; SI 1996/2911, reg 21.

2.10 AUCTIONS

The Sale of Goods Act 1979 makes it clear that in relation to a sale of goods by auction, the bids constitute offers which are accepted by the fall of the hammer.[59] The same is also the case in relation to any other type of sale by auction.[60] The normal position will be that the auctioneer will be entitled to reject any of the bids made, and will not be obliged to sell to the highest bidder.

There are two situations, however, which require special consideration. The first is where the auction sale is stated, in an advertisement or in information given to a particular bidder, to be 'without reserve'. This situation was first considered in the nineteenth century case of *Warlow v Harrison*.[61] The plaintiff attended an auction of a horse which had been advertised as being 'without reserve'. He then discovered that the owner was being allowed to bid (thus in effect allowing the owner to set a price below which he would not sell). The plaintiff refused to continue bidding and sued the auctioneer. The Court of Exchequer held that on the pleadings as entered, the plaintiff could not succeed, but expressed the view that if the case had been pleaded correctly, he would have been entitled to succeed in an action for breach of contract against the auctioneer:[62]

> We think the auctioneer who puts the property up for sale upon such a condition pledges himself that the sale shall be without reserve; or, in other words, contracts that it shall be so; and that this contract is made with the highest *bona fide* bidder; and, in case of breach of it, that he has a right of action against the auctioneer.

Because of the problem over the pleadings, the ruling in *Warlow v Harrison* was strictly *obiter*, but the principle stated has now been reconsidered and confirmed in *Barry v Heathcote Ball & Co (Commercial Auctions) Ltd*.[63] The claimant attended an auction to bid for two new machines which were being sold by Customs & Excise, who had instructed the auctioneer that the sale was to be 'without reserve'. The claimant had been told this by the auctioneer when viewing the machines. The machines were worth about £14,000 each. When they came up for sale, there were no bids apart from one from the claimant, who bid £200 for each machine. The auctioneer refused to accept this, and withdrew the machines from the sale. They were subsequently sold privately for £750 each. The claimant sued the auctioneer for breach of contract. The trial judge held in his favour, on the basis of there being a collateral contract with the auctioneer to sell to the highest bidder. The claimant was awarded £27,600 damages. On appeal, the

---

59 Sale of Goods Act 1979, s 57.
60 *Payne v Cave* (1789) 3 Term Rep 148.
61 (1859) 1 E & E 309; 29 LJ QB 14.
62 (1859) 1 E & E 309, pp 316–17; 29 LJ QB 14, p 15.
63 [2001] 1 All ER 944; [2000] 1 WLR 1962.

view of the trial judge was confirmed. The Court of Appeal followed the reasoning adopted by the court in *Warlow v Harrison*. An auctioneer who conducts a sale 'without reserve' is making a binding promise to sell to the highest bidder. It made no difference that in *Warlow v Harrison,* the identity of the seller was not disclosed, whereas here it was known. Moreover, the action of the auctioneer in this situation was tantamount to bidding on behalf of the seller, which is prohibited by s 57(4) of the Sale of Goods Act 1979. The claimant was entitled to recover the difference between what he had offered and the market price of the machines. The award of £27,600 damages was therefore also confirmed. This case is useful modern confirmation of the principle set out in *Warlow v Harrison*. In effect, the auctioneer is making an offer in a unilateral contract to all those who attend the auction along the lines of 'If you are the highest bidder for a particular lot, then I promise to accept your bid'. In *Warlow v Harrison,* the whole auction had been advertised as being 'without reserve'. Here the claimant had been told that this was the position as regard the particular lot in which he was interested. This made no difference to the principles to be applied.[64]

The second situation which requires further discussion is where a bidder tries to make a bid the value of which is dependent on a bid made by another bidder. This will only arise in a 'sealed bid' auction of the kind which was involved in *Harvela Investments v Royal Trust of Canada*.[65] In this case, an invitation to two firms to submit sealed bids for a block of shares, together with a commitment to accept the highest offer, was treated as the equivalent of an auction sale. There was an obligation to sell to the highest bidder. This case was complicated, however, by the fact that one of the bids was what was described as a 'referential bid'. That is, it was in the form of 'C$2,100,000 or C$101,000 in excess of any other offer'. The House of Lords held that this bid was invalid and that the owner of the shares was obliged to sell to the other party, who had offered C$2,175,000.[66] It reached this conclusion by trying to identify the intentions of the firm issuing the invitation to bid from the quite detailed instructions issued to each potential bidder. From these, the House deduced that what the sellers had in mind was not a true auction (where a number of bidders make and adjust their bids in response to the bids being made by others) but a 'fixed bidding sale'. Lord Templeman noted three features of the invitation which he regarded as only being consistent with an intention to conduct a fixed bidding sale rather than an auction. First, the sellers specifically undertook to accept the highest bid. As we have seen, however, such an obligation can

---

64 Note that the defendant in this case also queried whether there was any 'consideration' for the promise. As to this the court held that there was, in the form of detriment to the bidder in that his offer can be accepted until withdrawn, and benefit to the auctioneer as the bidding is driven up. For further discussion of the doctrine of consideration, see Chapter 3.

65 [1986] 1 AC 207; [1985] 2 All ER 966.

66 Note that the Court of Appeal, while noting the practical difficulties involved, had come to the opposite conclusion, on the basis that bidders in making 'offers' were entitled to put them in whatever form they chose, in the absence of any express or implied term imposing restrictions: [1985] Ch 103; [1985] 1 All ER 261.

arise in relation to a straightforward auction, by means of a collateral contract with the auctioneer. It is hard to see this as conclusive, therefore. Lord Templeman took it, however, as also implying that the sellers were anxious to ensure that a sale resulted from the exercise. If referential bids were allowed, there was clearly a possibility that this would not happen, because both bidders might submit a referential bid, and it would be impossible to determine who was the highest bidder. The second feature noted by Lord Templeman was that the invitation was issued to two prospective buyers alone. Again, it is difficult to see this as conclusive of the issue. It is quite possible to hold a straightforward auction with only two bidders. The third feature was that the bids were to be confidential and were to remain so until the time for submission of offers had lapsed. This is by far the most convincing reason why it should be assumed that the seller intended a fixed bidding sale rather than an auction. Confidentiality of the amount of a bid is clearly incompatible with an ordinary auction (though as Lord Templeman points out later in his speech, confidential bids combined with a requirement that each bidder states a maximum bid could work as a type of auction).

In the light of all these considerations, the House of Lords concluded that it was a fixed bidding sale that was intended, and that referential bids should therefore be excluded. In effect, the House was here relying on 'promisor objectivity', in that its analysis is focused on what the reasonable 'inviter of bids' must be taken to have intended by the form in which the invitation to bid was framed. In terms of 'offer and acceptance' the inviter was entering into two unilateral contracts with the two bidders to the effect: 'If you submit the highest bid, then we promise to sell the shares to you.'[67]

The result in *Harvela* was clearly of considerable practical importance: if it had gone the other way, it would have made conducting sales by means of confidential bids much more difficult. It may well be, therefore, that considerations of the impact on commercial practice helped to push the House towards the conclusion it reached.[68]

2.11 ACCEPTANCE

The second stage of discovering whether an agreement has been reached under classical contract theory is to look for an acceptance which matches the offer that has been made. No particular formula is required for a valid acceptance. As has been explained above, an offer must be in a form whereby a simple assent to it is sufficient to lead to a contract being formed. It is in many cases, therefore, enough for an acceptance to take the form of the person to whom the offer has been made simply saying 'yes, I agree'. In some situations, however, particularly where there is a course of negotiations between the parties, it may become more difficult to determine precisely the point when the

---

67 This analysis appears most fully in the speech of Lord Diplock: [1986] 1 AC 206, p 224; [1985] 2 All ER 966, p 969. Note that here the offer in the unilateral contract was not implicit, but was explicitly made as part of the invitation to bid: ibid, p 229; p 973.
68 See, for example, Wheeler and Shaw, 1994, pp 229–30.

parties have exchanged a matching offer and acceptance. Unless they do match exactly, so the classical theory requires, there can be no contract. An 'offer' and an 'acceptance' must fit together like two pieces of a jigsaw puzzle. If they are not the same, they will not slot together, and the picture will be incomplete. At times, as we shall see, the English courts have adopted a somewhat flexible approach to the need for a precise equivalence.[69] Nevertheless, once it is decided that there is a match, it is as if the two pieces of the jigsaw had been previously treated with 'superglue', for once in position it will be very hard, if not impossible, to pull them apart.[70]

2.11.1 Distinction from counter offer

Where parties are in negotiation, the response to an offer may be for the offeree to suggest slightly (or even substantially) different terms. Such a response will not, of course, be an acceptance, since it does not match the offer, but will be a 'counter offer'. During lengthy negotiations, many such offers and counter offers may be put on the table. Do they all remain there, available for acceptance at any stage? Or is only the last offer, or counter offer, the one that can be accepted? This issue was addressed in *Hyde v Wrench*.[71] D offered to sell a farm to P for £1,000. P offered £900, which was rejected. P then purported to accept the offer to sell at £1,000. D refused to go through with the transaction, and P brought an action for specific performance. The court held that a rejection of an offer in effect destroyed it. It could not later be accepted. Moreover, a counter offer operated in the same way as a rejection. P's counter offer of £900 there-fore had the effect of rejecting and destroying D's original offer to sell at £1,000. P could not accept it. In effect, P's final communication had to be treated not as an acceptance, but as a further offer to buy at £1,000, which D was free to accept or reject.

The answer to the question posed above, therefore, is that only the last offer submitted survives and is available for acceptance. All earlier offers are destroyed by rejection or counter offer. The courts have not been explicit about the reasons for this rule, but it may well be that it is intended to prevent the 'counter offeror' having the best of both worlds – trying out a low counter offer, while at the same time keeping the original offer available for acceptance.[72]

It should be noted, however, that the courts will not necessarily require exact precision, if it is clear that the parties were in agreement. An example of this approach can be found in the unreported case of *Pars Technology Ltd v City Link Transport Holdings Ltd*,[73] where the parties were negotiating the contractual settlement of an earlier dispute. The defendant offered by letter of 7 February to pay £13,500 plus a

---

69 See, also, Collins, 2003, pp 166–68.
70 Note, however, that a right of cancellation exists under some consumer contracts – discussed below, 2.14.
71 (1840) 3 Beav 334.
72 See Atiyah, 1995, p 76.
73 [1999] EWCA Civ 1822.

refund of the carriage charges of £7.55 plus VAT. The claimant's letter of 12 February in response stated that the defendant's offer to pay £13,507.55 plus VAT was accepted. The defendant later claimed that this was not a valid acceptance, because it stated that VAT was to be paid on the whole amount, rather than just on the carriage charge. The Court of Appeal agreed with the trial judge that the correspondence as a whole had to be considered, and took the view that the claimant had merely been trying to restate the defendant's offer in a different way. The claimant's letter had clearly stated that the defendant's offer made in the letter of 7 February was being accepted. A contract had therefore been concluded on the terms stated in the defendant's offer letter. In essence the court adopted an objective approach based on what the reasonable person receiving the claimant's letter would have taken it to mean. Even though the defendant argued that that was not what he had understood by it, he was bound by the objective view. In fact, this may be an example of the court using 'third party objectivity'[74] – that is, what would the reasonable third party looking at what passed between claimant and defendant have taken to be the outcome. It may also have been that the court was unsympathetic in this case to what it saw as the defendant using a rather technical argument to escape from an arrangement which had clearly been agreed. This is behaviour that it would not wish to encourage, because it wastes court time, and adds unnecessary costs to litigation (bearing in mind that this contract was concerned with the conclusion of an earlier legal dispute). Although it has been confirmed that, even under the new Civil Procedure Rules, normal contractual principles applied to 'offers to settle' and their acceptance,[75] these should not be used in a way which will have the effect of unduly prolonging the settlement of litigation.

2.11.2 Request for information

In some situations, however, it may be quite difficult to determine whether a particular communication is a counter offer or not. If, for example, a person offers to sell a television to another for £100, the potential buyer may ask whether cash is required, or whether a cheque is acceptable. Such an inquiry is not a counter offer. It is not suggesting alternative terms for the contract, but attempting to clarify the way in which the contract will be performed and, in particular, whether a specific type of performance will be acceptable. The effect of an inquiry of this type was considered in *Stevenson, Jaques & Co v McLean*.[76] D wrote to P, offering to sell some iron at a particular price, and saying that the offer would be kept open until the following Monday. On the Monday morning, P replied by telegram, saying: 'Please wire whether you would accept

---

74 See above, 2.4.1.
75 *Scammell v Dicker* [2001] 1 WLR 631; *Pitchmastic plc v Birse Construction Ltd* (2000) *The Times*, 21 June (QBD). Note, however, that there is an *obiter* suggestion in *Scammell v Dicker* that the rules as to the effect of rejection of an offer may not apply to those falling within Pt 36 of the CPR – see, also, Stone, 2001, p 23.
76 (1880) 5 QBD 346.

40 for delivery over two months, or if not, longest limit you could give.' D did not reply, but sold the iron elsewhere. In the meantime, P sent a telegram accepting D's offer. P sued for breach of contract. D argued that P's first telegram was a counter offer, and that therefore the second telegram could not operate as an acceptance of D's offer. The court held that it was necessary to look at both the circumstances in which P's telegram was sent, and the form which it took. As to the first aspect, the market in iron was very uncertain, and it was not unreasonable for P to wish to clarify the position as to delivery. Moreover, as regards the form of the telegram, it did not say 'I offer 40 for delivery over two months', but was put as an inquiry. If it had been in the form of an offer, then *Hyde v Wrench* would have been applied, but since it was clearly only an inquiry, D's original offer still survived, and P was entitled to accept it.

While the distinction being drawn here is clear, it is quite narrow. There is clearly scope in this type of situation for the courts to interpret communications in the way which appears to them best to do justice between the parties.

2.11.3   Battle of the forms

One situation where it may become vital to decide whether a particular communication is a counter offer or not is where there is what is frequently referred to as a 'battle of the forms'. This arises where two companies are in negotiation and, as part of their exchanges, they send each other standard contract forms. If the two sets of forms are incompatible, as is likely to be the case, what is the result? This is a not infrequent occurrence, probably because under the pressure of 'making a deal' the parties' attention is not focussed explicitly on anything other than the most basic elements of the transaction.[77] How should the courts deal with it if a dispute then arises?

One possibility, if the contract is a fairly straightforward one such as a simple sale of goods, is that the court may be able to identify an offer and acceptance at an earlier stage of the negotiations, prior to the exchange of any forms. In such a case the contract may well not incorporate the standard terms of either party – it is likely to consist of simply the basic obligations, with all surrounding issues being determined by the general law of contract rather than any particular terms put forward by the parties. This was the situation in the unreported Court of Appeal case of *Hertford Foods Ltd v Lidl UK GmbH*.[78] The claimant had tried to rely on a *force majeure* clause in its standard terms in order to excuse its non-performance under a sale of goods contract. The Court of Appeal held that, because conflicting standard terms had been exchanged, neither set governed the contract. The court was able, however, to identify a prior oral agreement for the supply of the goods, which contained all the essential terms. The result was that the claimant's *force majeure* clause was of no effect,[79] the claimant was in breach, and the defendant's counterclaim based on that breach was effective.

---

77 Beale and Dugdale, 1975, suggest in addition that contract planning is 'expensive'.
78 20 June 2001. The case is discussed by Ross, 2001.
79 *Force majeure* clauses are discussed in Chapter 16.

What if it is not possible to find an early offer and acceptance of this type? There are then three main possibilities:

(a)   the contract is made on the terms of the party whose form was put forward first;[80]
(b)   the contract is made on the terms of the party whose form was put forward last – the 'last shot' approach;
(c)   there is no contract at all, because the parties are not in agreement, and there is no matching offer and acceptance.

Lord Denning has suggested (in *Butler Machine Tool Co Ltd v Ex-Cell-O Corp (England) Ltd*)[81] that the first possibility might apply where the second set of terms (supplied by the offeree) is so different that the offeree 'ought not to be allowed to take advantage of the difference unless he draws it specifically to the attention of' the other party.[82] Subject to that, he also suggested, in the same case, that the second possibility would apply where the terms proposed were not objected to by the other party. Denning's suggestions are, in fact, very much in line with the approach adopted in Art 19 of the Vienna Convention on International Sale of Goods, § 2–207 of the United States Uniform Commercial Code[83] and Art 2:208 of the Principles of European Contract Law. The Principles also deal with 'conflicting general conditions' in Art 2:209, providing that a contract will generally be formed on the basis of the common conditions. All of these approaches attempt to find a contract wherever possible. In contrast, the strict application of the classical offer and acceptance principles suggests that the third of Denning's possible solutions is the right answer, and that there is no contract at all. Nevertheless, there is a reluctance even in the English courts to come to this conclusion, because it will often be the case that the parties are willing, or indeed keen, to have a contract, and will often have carried on their business as if such a contract had been validly made. If they are then told by the court that they have no contract at all, it may become very difficult to unscramble their respective rights and liabilities.[84]

2.11.4   The traditional view

Because it provides a good example of the way in which the courts have generally tackled the problem of the 'battle of the forms', it is worth looking in a little more detail at the case of *Butler Machine Tool Co Ltd v Ex-Cell-O Corp (England) Ltd*.[85] The

---

80   This appears to have been the approach adopted by the judge at first instance in *Hertford Foods Ltd v Lidl UK GmbH* (2001) unreported, 20 June.
81   [1979] 1 All ER 965; [1979] 1 WLR 401.
82   Ibid, p 968; p 405.
83   Both of these are reproduced in Wheeler and Shaw, 1994, p 208.
84   This sort of situation will often fall to be dealt with by the law of 'quasi-contract' or 'restitution' – for which see Chapter 19.
85   [1979] 1 All ER 965; [1979] 1 WLR 401.

buyers wished to purchase a machine for their business. On 23 May, the sellers offered to sell them one for £75,535, with delivery in 10 months. The offer incorporated the sellers' standard terms, which were said to prevail over any terms in the buyers' order. It also contained a price variation clause, allowing the sellers to increase the price in certain situations. The buyers responded with an order on 27 May. This order incorporated the buyers' terms, which did not include a price variation clause. It also included a tear-off acknowledgment slip, stating: 'We accept your order on the Terms and Conditions stated therein.' The sellers signed and returned this acknowledgment, together with a covering letter, referring back to their terms as set out in their offer of 23 May. There were no further relevant communications. When the sellers delivered the machine, they tried to enforce the price variation clause, but the buyers insisted that they were only obliged to pay £75,535. The trial judge upheld the sellers' claim, but the Court of Appeal reversed this decision. Lord Denning would have liked to do so on the basis that the overall negotiations between the parties indicated that there was a contract, even if it was not possible to identify a clear, matching offer and acceptance. He subsequently developed his argument for this method of identifying a contract in the Court of Appeal in *Gibson v Manchester City Council*,[86] where it was, however, fairly decisively rejected by the House of Lords. In *Butler*, he was also able to find a contract by the traditional 'offer/counter offer' analysis. This was the line taken by the other members of the Court of Appeal. On this basis, the court was unanimous in holding that the buyers' terms should prevail. The sellers' original offer of 23 May was met with a counter offer from the buyers, which, on the basis of *Hyde v Wrench*, destroyed the sellers' original offer. By completing and returning the acknowledgment slip, the sellers were accepting this counter offer, and their covering letter was thought not to be sufficiently specific so as to revive the detailed terms of the offer of 23 May. Although the original terms were referred to in that letter, it was, according to Bridge LJ, in language which was 'equivocal and wholly ineffective to override the plain and unequivocal terms of the printed acknowledgment of order'.[87]

FOR THOUGHT

How might the letter have been worded so that the court would have regarded it as effective to override the acknowledgment?

The *Butler Machine Tool* case confirmed the courts' adherence to the traditional analysis in terms of looking for what objectively appears to be a matching offer and acceptance. It did little to resolve a true 'battle of the forms' such as might have arisen had there been no acknowledgment slip, but simply an exchange of incompatible terms,

---

86 [1978] 2 All ER 583; [1978] 1 WLR 520, CA.
87 [1979] 1 All ER 965, p 971; [1979] 1 WLR 401, p 408.

followed by the manufacture and delivery of the machinery. In such a situation, a court which followed the traditional line would probably be forced to say that there was no contract. Other possibilities might be to argue that delivery, or taking delivery, of the machinery amounted to *acceptance by conduct*, or that the failure to respond to the last offer sent amounted to *acceptance by silence*. These two concepts are considered below. A further suggestion was made subsequently by the Court of Appeal, however, that in certain situations an approach similar to that advocated by Lord Denning might be adopted, and this needs to be noted first.

2.11.5 Subsequent developments

In *Trentham Ltd v Archital Luxfer*,[88] the plaintiffs (Trentham) were the main contractors on a building contract. They entered into negotiations with the defendants (Archital), for sub-contracts to supply and install doors, windows, etc. The work was done, and paid for, but when the plaintiffs tried to recover a contribution from the defendants towards a penalty which the plaintiffs had had to pay under the main contract, the defendants denied that a binding contract had ever been formed. There had been exchanges of letters, and various telephone conversations, but there was no matching offer and acceptance. In particular, there was a dispute as to whose standard terms should govern the contract. The trial judge held that there was a contract, in that the defendants, in carrying out the work, had accepted Trentham's offer – in other words, acceptance by conduct.[89] The defendants appealed. The only full judgment was delivered by Steyn LJ, with whom the other two members of the court agreed. Steyn LJ agreed that there was a contract here. In reaching this conclusion, he started by stating four basic points which he considered relevant to the case:

(a)   The approach to the issue of contract formation is 'objective', and so does not take account of the 'subjective expectations and unexpressed mental reservations of the parties'.[90] In this case, the relevant yardstick was 'the reasonable expectations of sensible businessmen'.[91]

(b)   In the vast majority of cases, the coincidence of offer and acceptance represents the mechanism of contract formation, but 'it is not necessarily so in the case of a contract alleged to have come into existence during and as a result of performance'.[92]

(c)   The fact that a contract is executed (that is, performance has taken place, as

---

88   [1993] 1 Lloyd's Rep 25.

89   As in *Brogden v Metropolitan Railway* (1877) 2 App Cas 666 – discussed further below, 2.12.1.

90   [1993] 1 Lloyd's Rep 25, p 27.

91   Ibid.

92   Ibid, citing *Brogden v Metropolitan Railway* (1887) 2 App Cas 666; *New Zealand Shipping Co Ltd v AM Satterthwaite & Co Ltd* [1975] AC 154 and *Gibson v Manchester City Council* [1979] 1 All ER 965; [1979] 1 WLR 401, none of which provides clear authority for the proposition.

in this case), rather than executory, is of considerable importance – it will almost certainly preclude, for example, an argument that there was no intention to create legal relations, or that the contract is void for vagueness or uncertainty.

(d)   If a contract only comes into existence during and as a result of performance of the transaction, it will frequently be possible to hold that the contract impliedly and retrospectively covers pre-contractual performance.[93]

Applying these points to the case before him, Steyn LJ concluded that the judge had sufficient evidence before him to conclude that there was a binding contract. The parties had clearly intended to enter into a legal relationship. The contemporary exchanges, and the carrying out of what was agreed in those exchanges, support the view that there was a course of dealing which on Trentham's side created a right to performance of the work by Archital, and on Archital's side it created a right to be paid on an agreed basis. Thus, although the trial judge had found that there was offer and acceptance, Steyn LJ was of the view that, in any event:

> ... in this fully executed transaction, a contract came into existence during performance even if it cannot be precisely analysed in terms of offer and acceptance.[94]

Moreover, even if the contract came into existence after part of the work had been carried out and paid for, it impliedly governed pre-contractual performance.

The two main points that this case raises are, first, the potential retrospective effect of a contract. This is of considerable importance in relation to major contracts, in particular construction contracts, where it is common for at least some work to take place before any formal agreement has been reached. This decision clearly recognises that such work will generally be governed by any later agreement that is entered into. The need to use restitutionary remedies will therefore be reduced.[95] The second issue, which is of more importance to the subject matter of this chapter, is the finding that contracts do not necessarily have to be formed by means of a matching offer and acceptance. This unanimous finding by the Court of Appeal is difficult to reconcile, however, with the rejection by the House of Lords in *Gibson* of Lord Denning's similar attempt to weaken the dominance of 'offer and acceptance'. It may, therefore, be significant that in the 14 years since the decision was reached there is no reported case where the argument put forward by Steyn LJ has been adopted. It opened a door to an alternative route to finding a contractual obligation, rather than clearly having challenged the prevailing 'offer and acceptance' orthodoxy, but no other courts seem to

---

93   [1993] 1 Lloyd's Rep 25, p 27, citing *Trollope v Colls v Atomic Power Construction Ltd* [1963] 1 WLR 333.
94   Ibid, pp 29–30.
95   Such remedies are discussed in Chapter 19.

have been prepared to accept even this limited possibility for flexibility. Two recent decisions on 'battle of the forms' cases, for example, show the High Court sticking to a traditional approach.

In *Balmoral Group Ltd v Borealis (UK) Ltd*,[96] there were dealings between the parties over a number of years under which goods were supplied. The purchaser would send an order which made reference to its terms and conditions 'in poor typescript' (as the court put it) at the bottom of the order. The order would be confirmed by the supplier by telephone. The supplier would then send an invoice on which its own terms and conditions were set out. The purchaser's representative would sign these invoices and approve them for payment. The High Court held that, although initially the contract would not have incorporated the supplier's terms and conditions, by the time that the dispute arose the supplier was entitled to assume that the purchaser had agreed to contract on the supplier's terms and conditions, no objection ever having been raised to these. In effect, the purchaser's signature on, and payment of, the invoices indicated an acceptance of the supplier's terms.

By contrast in *Sterling Hydraulics Ltd v Dichtomatik Ltd*,[97] the purchaser's terms prevailed. The purchaser faxed an order to the supplier, stating that it was 'subject to the terms and conditions as set out below and overleaf'. The terms were set out on the second page of the fax. The supplier faxed an acknowledgment, which stated at the bottom of the second page 'Delivery based on our General Terms of Sale'. These 'terms of sale' were not set out in the fax. The goods were delivered by the supplier and accepted by the purchaser. They then turned out to be unsatisfactory, and a dispute arose as to whose terms governed the contract. The supplier argued that its faxed acknowledgment was a counter offer, which was accepted by the purchaser taking delivery. The purchaser argued that the acknowledgment was an acceptance, so that the purchaser's terms governed the contract. The High Court held that the words contained on the acknowledgment were insufficient to indicate that it was intended to be a counter offer, and to displace the purchaser's terms and conditions. The judge felt that the same conclusion would be come to by applying either the traditional offer and acceptance analysis, or the approach suggested by Lord Denning in *Butler Machine Tool v Ex-Cell-O*. The contract was therefore made on the purchaser's terms.

Despite the reference in *Sterling Hydraulics* to Lord Denning's approach, the dominant analysis in these cases is based on finding a matching offer and acceptance, and is therefore very much in line with orthodoxy.

2.12 METHODS OF ACCEPTANCE

We now turn to look in more detail at the issues of acceptance by conduct or by silence. The adoption of an approach to identifying agreement based on a reasonable

---

96 [2006] 2 CLC 220.
97 [2007] 1 Lloyd's Rep 8.

interpretation of behaviour (the 'objective' test) means that there is clearly potential for both these types of behaviour being considered adequate to indicate acceptance. In fact, however, they are not always regarded as providing sufficient evidence of acceptance, and so the relevant case law needs to be analysed carefully.

2.12.1 Acceptance by conduct

In unilateral contracts, the acceptance will always be by conduct – using the smoke ball, digging the garden, etc – though there are some problems as to just what conduct amounts to acceptance. These issues will be considered further later.[98] Can the same apply in bilateral contracts, so that they too can be accepted by conduct? In some everyday situations, this would seem to be the case. In a shop transaction, for example, there may be no exchange of words between the customer and cashier. The customer may simply present the goods selected together with payment, constituting an offer to buy,[99] which will be accepted by the cashier taking the money and, generally, giving a receipt. Can there be acceptance by conduct in more complicated, commercial transactions? This issue was considered in *Brogden v Metropolitan Railway*.[100] The plaintiffs sent the defendants a draft agreement for the supply of a certain quantity of coal per week from 1 January 1872, at £1 per ton. The defendants completed the draft by adding the name of an arbitrator, signed it and returned it to the plaintiffs. This constituted an offer. The plaintiffs' manager, however, simply put the signed agreement into a drawer. There was no communication of acceptance by the plaintiffs. Coal was ordered and delivered on the terms specified in the contract for a period of time, until there was a dispute between the parties. The defendants then argued that there was no contract, because the plaintiffs had never accepted their offer, as contained in the signed agreement. The House of Lords confirmed that it was not enough that the plaintiffs should have decided to accept: there had to be some external manifestation of acceptance. In this case, however, that was supplied by the fact that the plaintiffs had placed orders on the basis of the agreement. The defendants should therefore be taken to be bound by its terms.

This decision confirms that a bilateral contract may be accepted by conduct, and there is no need for a verbal or written indication of acceptance. In *Brogden*, the 'external manifestation' of acceptance (that is, the placing of orders) was also a 'communication' to the other party. What is the position if there is conduct by one party which objectively indicates an intention to accept, but the other party is unaware of it? It is to that issue that we now turn.

---

98 See below, 2.12.13.

99 Assuming that the approach adopted in *Pharmaceutical Society of Great Britain v Boots Cash Chemists* [1953] 1 QB 401; [1953] 1 All ER 482 is followed.

100 (1877) 2 App Cas 666.

2.12.2   Acceptance by silence

In *Brogden v Metropolitan Railway*, as we have just seen, it was held that you cannot accept a contract simply by deciding that you are going to do so. There must be some external evidence which would lead a reasonable person to believe that your intention was to accept. Does that external evidence have to come to the attention of the other potential party to the contract, or is it enough that there was agreement, even if one side was in ignorance of it?

In some cases, the issue will be determined by the form of the offer. In unilateral contracts, for example, it has been recognised since *Carlill v Carbolic Smoke Ball Co* [101] that the offeror may waive the need for communication of acceptance. The court thought that it clearly could not have been intended that everyone who bought a smoke ball in reliance on the company's advertisement should be expected to tell the company of this. It would be perfectly possible, of course, for an offeror to require such notice, but where an offer is made to the world, as in the *Carlill* case, or where a reward is offered for the return of property or the provision of information, the intention to waive such a requirement will easily be found.

2.12.3   Bilateral contracts

In relation to bilateral contracts, the position is different. The leading authority is *Felthouse v Bindley*.[102] An uncle was negotiating to buy a horse from his nephew. The uncle wrote to his nephew offering a particular sum and saying 'If I hear no more about him, I consider the horse mine'. The nephew did not respond, but told an auctioneer to remove this horse from a forthcoming auction. The auctioneer omitted to do so, and the horse was sold to a third party. The uncle sued the auctioneer, and the question arose as to whether the uncle had made a binding contract for the purchase of the horse. It was held that he had not done so, because the nephew had never communicated his intention to accept his uncle's offer. It is true that he had taken an action (removing the horse from the auction) which objectively could be taken to have indicated his intention to accept, but because his uncle knew nothing of this at the time, it was not effective to complete the contract.

This case has long been taken to be authority for the proposition that silence cannot amount to acceptance, at least in bilateral contracts. It is by no means clear that the court intended to go this far. It is uncertain, for example, what the court's attitude would have been had it been the nephew, rather than the uncle, who was trying to enforce the contract. Nevertheless, later courts have taken the principle to be well established. In *The Leonidas D*,[103] for example, Robert Goff J commented:

---

101 [1893] 1 QB 256.
102 (1862) 11 CB(NS) 869; affirmed (1863) 1 NR 401.
103 [1985] 2 All ER 796; [1985] 1 WLR 925.

We have all been brought up to believe it to be axiomatic that acceptance of an offer cannot be inferred from silence, save in the most exceptional circumstances.[104]

No court has challenged the correctness of the general principle said to be established by *Felthouse v Bindley*, though commentators have doubted it.[105] In considering the analogous situation of acceptance of a repudiatory breach of contract, the House of Lords has suggested in *Vitol SA v Norelf Ltd*[106] that silence and inaction can be effective provided that they can be regarded as 'clear and unequivocal' and the other party has notice. If the same approach can be applied to acceptance of an offer, this will presumably fall within the 'exceptional circumstances' referred to by Robert Goff J. In most cases, however, silence by itself will inevitably be equivocal, in that it will be impossible to tell objectively whether the offeree has decided to accept or reject the offer.

The policy which may be said to lie behind the principle is that one potential contracting party should not be able to impose a contract on another by requiring the other to take some action in order not to be bound. It was felt that someone in the position of the nephew in *Felthouse v Bindley* should not be obliged to tell his uncle if he did not want to accept the offer. He should be entitled to do nothing, and not incur contractual obligations simply by inaction.

2.12.4 Inertia selling

During the 1960s, a related problem arose out of the growing practice of what came to be known as 'inertia selling'. The seller in these transactions would send a person who was thought to be a potential buyer a copy of a book, for example, with a covering letter stating that, unless the book was returned within a certain time limit, the recipient would be assumed to want to keep it and would be obliged to pay the purchase price. As we have seen, on the basis of *Felthouse v Bindley*, no binding contract could arise in this way. But, of course, many people were ignorant of their rights under contract law, and were led in this way to pay for items which they did not really want. In order to remedy this, the Unsolicited Goods and Services Act 1971 was passed, which allowed the recipient of unsolicited goods, in circumstances such as those outlined above, to treat them after a specified period of time as an unconditional gift, with all rights of the sender being extinguished. The provisions of this Act, insofar as they deal with goods sent to consumers,[107] have now been replaced by reg 24 of the Consumer Protection (Distance Selling) Regulations 2000.[108] These enable the consumer to treat the goods as

---

104 [1985] 2 All ER 796, p 805; [1985] 1 WLR 925, p 937.
105 See, for example, Miller, 1972.
106 *Vitol SA v Norelf Ltd* [1996] 3 All ER 193 – discussed in more detail below, 17.7.1.
107 That is, where the recipient 'has no reasonable cause to believe that they were sent with a view to their being acquired for the purposes of a business': SI 2000/2334, reg 24(1)(b).
108 SI 2000/2334.

an unconditional gift as soon as they are received. Moreover, reg 24(4) makes it an offence to seek payment for unsolicited goods or services.

2.12.5 Conclusions on 'silence'

The basic rule, therefore, as derived from *Felthouse v Bindley* and reinforced by the Unsolicited Goods and Services Act 1971 and the Consumer Protection (Distance Selling) Regulations 2000, is that acceptance, whether by words or action, must be communicated to the offeror. It is clear, however, from the decision in *Carlill v Carbolic Smoke Ball Co*[109] that, in relation to certain types of unilateral contract, the offeror may waive the need for communication of acceptance. What is not clear is whether this can ever be done in a bilateral contract. While it clearly cannot be used as a means of imposing a contract on an unwilling offeree, there is no authority which specifically precludes the possibility of an offeree choosing to enforce a contract against an offeror who has stated that he will presume acceptance from non-communication. To return to *Felthouse v Bindley*, for example, if the horse had not been sold to a third party, would the nephew have been able to hold his uncle to the promise to buy at the price he had specified? There are two arguments which might be raised against allowing this. The first is that it would run contrary to the principle of mutuality that generally underpins the law of contract. If A can sue B, then B ought to be able to sue A. This principle does not apply universally, however. In relation to contracts with minors, for example, there are situations in which the minor is allowed to enforce a contract, even though the adult with whom he or she has dealt would not be able to do so (see 7.4 below). Moreover, mutuality only operates to a limited extent in unilateral contracts. This objection is not therefore conclusive. The second argument against allowing the silent offeree to sue is a practical one. If there is no outward manifestation of acceptance, how does a court (or anyone else) know that it has occurred? In other words, silence fails the test of unequivocality referred to in *Vitol SA v Norelf Ltd*. The rule would have to require some objective evidence that the offeree had decided to accept. What would not be required, however, would be knowledge of this on the part of the offeror. Thus, again using the facts of *Felthouse v Bindley*, the nephew's removal of the horse from the auction could be regarded as an objective indication of his acceptance of his uncle's offer. The fact that the uncle was unaware of this should not preclude the nephew from enforcing the contract, since the uncle had, by the terms of his offer, waived the need for communication of acceptance. In conclusion, however, it must be stressed that while the above analysis does not directly contradict any existing authority, neither is there any authority which clearly supports it. The issue as to whether an offeror in a bilateral contract can ever be bound if he has waived the need for communication of acceptance remains open.

---

109 [1893] 1 QB 256.

Other jurisdictions adopt a more relaxed approach to the question. The American Second Restatement, for example, provides in s 69 for silence to amount to acceptance in various situations including:

    (b)   Where the offeror has stated or given the offeree reason to understand that assent may be manifested by silence or inaction, and the offeree in remaining silent or inactive intends to accept the offer.

    (c)   Where because of previous dealings or otherwise, it is reasonable that the offeree should notify the offeror if he does not intend to accept.

Application of the principle stated in (b) would be likely to lead to a different result if applied to the facts of *Felthouse v Bindley*. On the other hand, the Principles of European Contract Law provide simply that 'silence or inactivity does not in itself amount to acceptance', thus following the traditional English view.[110]

2.12.6 Acceptance by post

A requirement of communication will not, however, answer all problems. In the modern world communication can take many forms: face-to-face conversations, telephone, letters, faxes, or email. In some of these, there will be a delay between the sending of an acceptance and its coming to the attention of the offeror. The law of contract has to have rules, therefore, to make clear what is meant by 'communication'. The simplest rule would be to say that no communication is effective until it is received and understood by the person to whom it is addressed. This is, in effect, the rule that applies to offers; though, as we shall see, there are some cases which suggest that it may be possible to accept an offer of which you are unaware.[111] These cases are of dubious authority, however, and can only possibly apply in very restricted circumstances. In any case, they simply suggest that in some situations, communication of an offer may not be necessary. Where communication of the offer is required, which is the case in virtually all situations, it is safe to say that communication means that the person to whom the offer is addressed is aware of it. Why should the position be any different as regards acceptances?

The problem first arose in relation to the post, where the delay is likely to be longest. Generally speaking, there will be a delay of at least 12 to 18 hours between the sending of an acceptance by post, and its receipt by the addressee. Does the sender of the acceptance have to wait until it is certain that the letter has arrived before being sure that a contract has been made? The issue was considered in *Adams v Lindsell*.[112]

The defendants sent a letter to the plaintiffs offering wool for sale, and asking for a reply 'in course of post'. The letter was misdirected by the defendants, and arrived

---

110 Article 2.204(2).
111 See below, 2.12.15.
112 (1818) 1 B & Ald 681; 106 ER 250.

later than would normally have been the case. The plaintiffs replied at once accepting, but the defendants, having decided that because of the delay the plaintiffs were not going to accept, had already sold the wool elsewhere. The plaintiffs sued for breach of contract. The court decided that to require a posted acceptance to arrive at its destination before it could be effective would be impractical and inefficient. The acceptor would not be able to take any action on the contract until it had been confirmed that the acceptance had arrived. The court felt that this might result in each side waiting for confirmation of receipt of the last communication *ad infinitum*. This would not promote business efficacy. It would be much better if, as soon as the letter was posted, the acceptor could proceed on the basis that a contract had been made, and take action accordingly. The court, in coming to this conclusion, was thus giving priority to the practicalities of doing business over the question of whether, at the time the contract was formed, the parties were in agreement. It was quite possible that by the time the letter of acceptance was posted, the offeror had had a change of mind and sent a withdrawal of the offer, or made a contract with someone else (as happened in *Adams v Lindsell* itself). Nevertheless, because in the court's view the conduct of business would in general be better served by giving the offeree certainty in this situation, the postal rule was established.[113]

FOR THOUGHT

Does the court's justification for the postal rule still apply, in an era of much more sophisticated and rapid communication? How could the poster of a letter now discover whether or not it has been delivered?

At times the justification of the postal rule has been argued to be based on agency – that is, that the Post Office was acting as agent for the offeror in receiving the acceptance from the offeree. But this analysis was strongly criticised in *Henthorn v Fraser*.[114] The Post Office is more obviously acting as agent for the offeree rather than the offeror and, in any case, if it is acting as agent at all, it would be more accurate to describe it as agent for the physical transfer of the acceptance letter, rather than the communication of its contents.

Gardner, adopting a 'critical legal studies' approach, has suggested that the real reasons for the way in which the postal rule developed are to be found in enthusiasm for the newly established 'penny post' (which began in 1840).[115] He also suggests that the cases on the topic at the end of the late nineteenth century should be looked at in the

---

113 Evans, 1966, disputes whether this was the basis for the decision in *Adams v Lindsell*, and indeed whether the case established the postal rule at all, but concludes (p 561) that of all the reasons put forward justifying it, the one outlined in the text here is the only one which is 'wholly valid'.

114 [1892] 2 Ch 27 – see, in particular, the judgment of Kay LJ. Gardner, 1992, describes the case as 'exploding' the agency analysis.

115 Gardner, 1992.

context of the widespread 'share offers' which were being made at the time. The courts applied the postal rules to stop people escaping from what they felt might be 'bad bargains' for the purchase of shares.[116] Neither of these explanations, however, can deal with the original statement of the rule in 1818, in *Adams v Lindsell*, which was 22 years before the introduction of the penny post, and 60 years before the 'share offer' cases. The arguments based around pragmatism and business efficiency remain the most convincing explanations for the rule's adoption.

2.12.7 Limitations on the postal rule

The rule that comes from *Adams v Lindsell* is thus that a posted acceptance is complete on posting. The offeror is therefore bound to a contract without being aware that this has happened. The same rule was applied to telegrams, where a similar, though shorter, delay in communication would occur.[117] Because the rule is a rather unusual one, however, its limitations must be noted. First, it only applies to acceptances, and not to any other type of communication which may pass between potential contracting parties. Offers, counter offers, revocations of offers, etc, must all be properly communicated, even if sent through the post or by telegram.[118] Second, it only applies where it was reasonable for the acceptance to be sent by post.[119] Clearly, where the offer was made by post, then, in the absence of any indication from the offeror to the contrary, it will certainly be reasonable to reply in the same form, and the postal rule will operate. Wherever the parties are communicating over a distance, it is likely to be reasonable to use the post, even if the offer has been made in some other way. As Lord Herschell put it in *Henthorn v Fraser*:[120]

> Where the circumstances are such that it must have been within the contemplation of the parties that, according to the ordinary usages of mankind, the post might be used as a means of communicating the acceptance of an offer, the acceptance is complete as soon as it is posted.

In this case, the fact that the parties were based in towns some distance apart was held to make the use of the post reasonable, despite the fact that the offer had been hand delivered.

The final limitation that must be noted is that the rule can always be displaced by the offeror. The offer itself may expressly, or possibly impliedly, require the acceptance to take a particular form. In *Quenerduaine v Cole*,[121] for example, it was held that an

---

116 See, for example, *Household Fire and Carriage Accident Insurance Co v Grant* (1879) 4 Ex D 216.
117 *Bruner v Moore* [1904] 1 Ch 305 (exercise of an option).
118 *Byrne v van Tienhoven* (1880) 5 CPD 344.
119 *Henthorn v Fraser* [1892] 2 Ch 27.
120 Ibid, p 33.
121 (1883) 32 WR 185.

offer that was made by telegram impliedly required an equally speedy reply. A reply by post would not therefore take effect on posting. (There seems no reason, however, why it should not take effect on arrival, provided that the offer was still open.) Any implication from the form of the offer should, of course, be looked at alongside the more general rule as to what is reasonable to expect, as set out in *Henthorn v Fraser*. If the offeror wants to be sure that the postal rule will not operate, this should be made explicit in the offer. In *Holwell Securities Ltd v Hughes*,[122] the offer required the acceptance (in fact, the exercise of an option) to be given by 'notice in writing' to the offeror. It was held that this formulation meant that the acceptance would only take effect when actually received by the offeror. The insertion of this phrase is all that is required, therefore, to displace the postal rule. Other language may, of course, be used, provided the intention is clear. The fact that the offeror has this power may be taken as justifying the fact that the postal rule can operate harshly on the offeror. If a party takes the risk of allowing the postal rule to operate, when it is within its power to displace it, then it should not be allowed to complain if it operates to its disadvantage.[123]

If, however, the postal rule is to operate, the fact that the acceptance is complete on posting has been taken to its logical limit. It does not matter that the letter is delayed in the post, the offeror is still bound; in *Household Fire and Carriage Accident Insurance Co v Grant*,[124] it was held that an acceptance that was entirely lost in the post, and never arrived at its destination, was still effective to create a contract.

2.12.8 Acceptance by private courier

The cases that have been discussed in the previous section were all concerned with the service provided by the Post Office. Recently, there has been a growth in the availability of various kinds of private courier service, which might also be used to deliver communications creating a contract. Does the postal rule apply to acceptances sent by such means? There is no authority on this point. There are two possible lines which the law might take. First, it might be argued that the reasons for applying the postal rule in *Adams v Lindsell* apply equally to communications via a private courier. The acceptor gives the letter to a private courier, and thereby puts the acceptance out of his or her control. It would not be conducive to business efficiency to require the acceptor to wait for notification that the acceptance had been received before being able to take any action on the contract. Provided that it was reasonable for the acceptor to use the courier service, the acceptance should take effect as soon as it is given to the courier.

The second line of argument might resist the notion of extending the postal rule beyond its current application. It might well be said that communications have developed dramatically since 1818, when *Adams v Lindsell* was decided. Nowadays, if an acceptor wants to proceed quickly on the basis of a contract, where the acceptance

---

122 [1974] 1 All ER 161; [1974] 1 WLR 155.
123 See the comments of Collins, 2003, p 169.
124 (1879) 4 Ex D 216.

has been given to a private courier, there is no need to wait a long time to receive confirmation that the acceptance has arrived. A telephone call to the offeror will enable the acceptor to find out very quickly whether this has happened or not. If the need for speed is even greater, then the acceptance could be sent by fax or email, with a request for confirmation by phone, fax or email, as soon as it has arrived.

It is difficult to predict which line of argument the courts would find more attractive. If the second approach were accepted, there would be a strong argument for saying that the postal rule itself should be reviewed. As will appear from the following section, there has been no move by the courts in recent years to extend the postal rule to other media, and this may be an indication of an acceptance that in the modern context, the *Adams v Lindsell* approach has much less to recommend it than it did at the time it was decided. Other jurisdictions have managed without such a rule, and the drafters of the Principles of European Contract Law did not feel the need to include anything equivalent to it. They suggest that an acceptance should take effect when it reaches the offeror, in which it includes when it is delivered to the offeror's place of business, mailing address or habitual residence.[125] While there have been no moves in the English courts to overrule *Adams v Lindsell* or the case law flowing from it, it may well be that the tendency will be to limit its scope, and confine it strictly to the area of communications via the Post Office by letter, telegram (as regard international communications) and (probably) telemessage (as regards national communications).

2.12.9 Acceptance by electronic communication

In the modern world, contracts may well be made by much more sophisticated means of communication than the post. Telexes, faxes and email are all widely used, in addition to letters and the telephone, as means of transmitting offers, counter offers, acceptances and rejections. If one of these methods is used for an acceptance, when and where is it effective?

2.12.10 The *Entores* approach

The starting point for the law in this area is the case of *Entores v Miles Far East Corp.*[126] This was concerned with communications by telex machine. The primary issue before the court was the question of where the acceptance took effect, if it was sent from a telex machine in one country and received on a telex machine in another country. The answer to this would affect the position as to which country's law governed the contract.

The leading judgment in the Court of Appeal was given by Lord Denning. His approach was to take as his starting point a very simple form of communication over a

---

125 Articles 1:303(3) and 2:205(1).
126 [1955] 2 QB 327; [1955] 2 All ER 493.

distance (albeit a rather unlikely one in factual terms), that is, two people making a contract by shouting across a river. In this situation, he argued, there would be no contract unless and until the acceptance was heard by the offeror. If, for example, an aeroplane flew overhead just as the acceptor was shouting his or her agreement, so that the offeror could not hear what was being said, there would be no contract. The acceptor would be expected to repeat the acceptance once the noise from the aeroplane had diminished. Taking this as his starting point, he argued by analogy that the same approach should apply to all contracts made by means of communication which are instantaneous or virtually instantaneous (as opposed to post or telegram, where there is a delay). On this basis, regarding telex as falling into the 'instantaneous' category, he held that the acceptance by telex took place where it was received, rather than where it was sent.

The same answer is generally presumed to apply to all other forms of more sophisticated electronic communication which can be said to be more or less instantaneous in their effect. They will all take effect at the place where they are received. It is at least questionable, however, whether Lord Denning's analogy with a face-to-face conversation does really hold up when applied to telexes, faxes and emails. The only true instantaneous types of communication are face to face, by telephone or, possibly, by the kind of electronic message service where both participants are online at the same time. A telex and a fax can sit unread in somebody's in-tray for some time, and an email may not be opened as soon as it arrives. In that respect, they are more analogous to posted communications, which may not be read until some time after they have been delivered to the addressee. This becomes even more important when the time that the acceptance takes effect is the crucial issue.[127] The fact that an extension of the postal rule was rejected in *Entores* is thus more easily explained on the basis of an unwillingness to allow that anomalous approach to be applied more widely, rather than a logical necessity, based on an analysis of the types of communication involved.

There is perhaps a slightly stronger analogy, at least as regards telex or fax, when the question of what happens when there are problems with the communication is considered. As we have seen, Lord Denning took the view that in instantaneous communications it is generally up to the person sending the communication to ensure that his or her message gets through. The sender will in most cases (as with the aeroplane flying overhead) be aware if there is a problem. If, however, the reason for failure to communicate is clearly the responsibility of the recipient, then the position will be different. Thus:[128]

> . . . if the listener on the telephone does not catch the words of acceptance, but nevertheless does not trouble to ask for them to be repeated: or the ink on the teleprinter fails at the receiving end, but the clerk does not ask for the message to

127 As discussed in the next section, 2.12.11.
128 [1955] 2 QB 327, p 333; [1955] 2 All ER 493, p 495.

be repeated: so that the man who sends an acceptance reasonably believes that his message has been received. The offeror in such circumstances is clearly bound, because he will be estopped from saying that he did not receive the message of acceptance.

On the other hand:[129]

> . . . if there should be a case where an offeror without any fault on his part does not receive the message of acceptance – yet the sender of it reasonably concludes that it has got home when it has not – then I think there is no contract.

The expectation is that, as with a personal or telephone conversation, both sender and recipient will know quickly if the communication has failed. That is most likely to be the case with a telex or fax, where the reply may well be received in an office where those working near to the relevant machine will notice if there has been a failed attempt to send a message. They will then, presumably, try to communicate with the sender. This is not the case with email, however, where the intended recipient may have no immediate indication of a failed attempt to communicate, and the sender may well only receive a message saying that the email has not been delivered at some time later. Even as regards telex and fax, there will be no instant response where the message is sent out of office hours, or where the recipient does not notice that an attempt to communicate has been made, or where the relevant machine is not located in an area where a malfunction will be noticed quickly. Even in this respect, therefore, the categorisation of these types of communication as closely analogous to a personal conversation tends to break down. They are 'instantaneous' in the sense that the message is received at the recipient's premises almost immediately, but otherwise are more akin to postal communications than personal or telephone conversations. Once again, the conclusions in *Entores* as to the consequences of telex communication can be seen to be based more on what it is reasonable to expect in a business context than on the analogy with other types of communication which Lord Denning used as the overt basis of his analysis.

Some doubt as to whether the offer and acceptance analysis on the *Entores* model is appropriate, even in relation to instantaneous communication, has been raised by the High Court's decision in *Apple Corps Ltd v Apple Computer, Inc.*[130] A contract had been formed at the end of a long period of negotiation in the course of a transatlantic telephone call. There was some dispute as to who had said exactly what, and when. There was no doubt, however, that a contract had been concluded. The question was whether that contract had been made in England or the United States. The judge took the view that using a traditional 'offer and acceptance' analysis might well be 'extremely forced' and introduce a 'highly random element':[131]

129 [1955] 2 QB 327, p 333; [1955] 2 All ER 493, p 495.
130 [2004] EWHC 768; [2004] IL Pr 34.
131 Ibid, para 42.

The offer and acceptance may well depend on who speaks first and who speaks second, which is likely to be largely a matter of chance in closing an agreement of this sort. It is very arguably a much more satisfactory analysis to say that the contract was made in both places at the same time

The issue of what law was to govern the contract could not, therefore, be determined by answering the question where was the contract formed. Other rules relating to jurisdiction would have to be used to decide this issue.

This was not the only basis on which the judge reached his decision in this case, so his views on this issue cannot be said to be definitively part of the *ratio*. On the other hand they lend support to the view that issues of contract formation need to be decided by pragmatism, and what will work in practice, as much as by the application of strict legal rules.

2.12.11 Time of acceptance

It is important to remember that, as noted above, the court in *Entores* was concerned with the *place* where the contract was made, rather than the *time* at which it was made. This issue may be important in international transactions in deciding which set of legal rules governs the contract. The case provides no direct authority on the issue of the time when a telexed acceptance takes effect. Clearly, the postal rule cannot apply, since that is based on the acceptance taking effect as soon as it is out of the hands of the acceptor, whereas *Entores* requires it to have arrived at the offeror's address.[132] Several other possibilities are feasible. It could take effect only when it is actually read by the person to whom it is addressed; or when it is read by someone on behalf of the addressee (for example, an employee of the addressee); or when it is received on the addressee's telex machine, although not read by anyone; or when the acceptor would reasonably expect it to have been read.

FOR THOUGHT

What do you think Lord Denning's answer to this would have been in *Entores*, taking account of his analogies with face-to-face and telephone conversations?

Two cases subsequent to *Entores* have considered this issue in relation to telexes. In *The Brimnes*,[133] the communication was not an acceptance, but a notice of the withdrawal of a ship from a charterparty. It was held to be effective when it was 'received' on the charterers' telex machine during office hours, although it was not actually read until the

---

132 As noted above (2.12.8), this is the point at which the Principles of European Contract Law suggest that the acceptance should take effect.
133 [1975] QB 929; [1974] 3 All ER 88.

following morning. In *Brinkibon Ltd v Stahag Stahl*,[134] the House of Lords was dealing with a situation virtually identical to that under consideration in *Entores*, and approved the approach taken there. The House refused to indicate whether the same rule should apply in all circumstances, for example, where the message is sent out of office hours, or at night, in the expectation that it will be read at a later time, or where there is some fault with the recipient's machine of which the sender is unaware. As Lord Wilberforce put it:[135]

> No universal rule can cover all such cases: they must be resolved by reference to the intentions of the parties, by sound business practice and in some cases by a judgment where the risks should lie.

This is not particularly helpful, though it goes some way to confirming the suggestion made above that the *Entores* rule is based more on the needs of business practice than logical analysis. Insofar as any general principle can be read into it, it would seem to be the last of those suggested above, that is, that the communication should take effect at the time when the acceptor could reasonably have expected it to be read. It is an approach which has subsequently been adopted in relation to a fax giving notice under a contract.[136] The Wilberforce approach suggests that there may be variations according to the type of communication system being used. There does not seem to be any reason for treating faxes differently from telex, but email, sent to an electronic 'mailbox' which may only be checked once or twice a day, might well be said only to be communicated once the expected time for checking has passed. A similar approach might need to be used in relation to messages left on a telephone answering system: that is, the message should only be regarded as communicated once a reasonable time has elapsed to allow it to be heard by the offeror.

If this line is to be taken, it is clearly to the advantage of the acceptor, in that it allows an acceptance to be treated as effective although the offeror may be unaware of it (as is the case under the postal rule). As with *Adams v Lindsell*, the counter-argument to those who say that this gives the acceptor too much of an advantage would be that the courts have always made it clear that the offeror can specify and insist on a particular mode of acceptance. If actual communication is required, this should be spelt out in the offer. If this is not done, the acceptor must be allowed to proceed on the basis that the acceptance will be read at a time which could reasonably be expected in the normal course of events.

---

134 [1983] 2 AC 34; [1982] 1 All ER 293.
135 Ibid, p 42; p 296.
136 *Mondial Shipping and Chartering BV v Astate Shipping Ltd* [1995] Com LC 1011.

2.12.12 Acceptance in internet transactions

It is likely that in the future an increasing amount of business will be conducted over the internet, either by means of email or, particularly in the case of consumer transactions, via a website. In the latter case, the consumer may be actually receiving a product over the web (for example, downloading a piece of software or a video or music file) or placing an order for goods to be delivered by the post or courier service. How do the principles outlined above apply in these situations?

In relation to email, as has been assumed in the previous discussion, there seems little reason to distinguish between this form of communication and other types of 'instantaneous' communication such as telex or fax. The contract will be formed at the earliest when the acceptance is received by the offeror's email system, and is available to be read. At the latest, it should be regarded as complete once the time has passed at which it would be reasonable to expect the acceptance to have been read. Since most email systems will return an error message to the sender if delivery has not been possible, there is no real need here for any other procedure for acknowledgment of receipt.

As regards contracting via a website, some of the potential problems were indicated by events in September 1999, when a retailer was found to be indicating on its website that televisions were available for the price of £3.[137] This was a mistake: the price should have been £300. However, before it could be rectified, a large number of people had attempted to buy a television at the lower price. The crucial question was whether by responding to the information contained on the website, these people were accepting the retailer's offer, or were themselves making an offer to buy at that price. Given that the purchasers would have had to submit credit card details in order to pay for the goods, and the retailer would presumably have reserved the right not to accept these as satisfactory, the better view would seem to be that the purchasers were making the offer to buy. The advertisement of the televisions would thus be simply an invitation to treat. The seller would be free to accept or reject the offers from the potential purchasers. The contract would be made when the seller had acknowledged to the purchaser that his or her offer was accepted, either by means of a direct response on the website or by a subsequent email.

This area has also been the subject of proposals from the European Commission, which has issued a directive dealing with a range of issues on electronic commerce, including the issue of 'time of acceptance'. The final version of the Directive on Electronic Commerce was adopted in June 2000 (Directive 2000/31/EC). Article 11 provides that:

> Member States shall ensure, except when otherwise agreed by parties who are not consumers, that in cases where the recipient of the service places his order through technological means, the following principles apply:

---

137 See (1999) *The Times*, 21 September.

- the service provider has to acknowledge receipt of the recipient's order without undue delay and by electronic means;[138]
- the order and the acknowledgment of receipt are deemed to be received when the parties to whom they are addressed are able to access them.

These provisions are much vaguer than earlier drafts, which seemed to assume that it is the owner of the website who will be making the offer, and the purchaser who will be accepting it. Since, as we have seen, by far the most likely situation under English law is that the service provider will be seen as making an invitation to treat, with the purchaser making the offer, this would have meant that the requirements of the Directive would have had very little impact. The final draft, however, seems apt to cover the situation where it is the customer who makes the offer. In such a situation, English law in any case requires the offer to be accepted before it is effective, and this will satisfy the need for an acknowledgment of the order. If the offer is made by the website owner, however, and accepted by the customer, the Directive will place an additional requirement on the website owner to acknowledge the acceptance. In all cases, however, the Directive makes the test of when a communication takes place, the point at which it can be accessed by the recipient.

The Directive has been implemented in English law by the Electronic Commerce (EC Directive) Regulations 2002,[139] the relevant sections of which came into force on 31 August 2002.

Regulation 11, entitled 'placing of the order', which deals with the matters covered by Art 11 of the Directive, states as follows:

11 (1) Unless parties who are not consumers have agreed otherwise, where the recipient of the service places his order through technological means, a service provider shall –

 (a) acknowledge receipt of the order to the recipient of the service without undue delay and by electronic means; and

 (b) make available to the recipient of the service appropriate, effective and accessible technical means allowing him to identify and correct input errors prior to the placing of the order.

 (2) For the purposes of paragraph (1)(a) above –

 (a) the order and the acknowledgment of receipt will be deemed to be received when the parties to whom they are addressed are able to access them; and

 (b) the acknowledgment of receipt may take the form of the provision of the service paid for where that service is an information society service.

---

138 But this requirement does not apply where the contract is concluded exclusively by the exchange of email 'or by equivalent individual communications' (Art 11(3)).
139 SI 2002/2013.

(3)   The requirements of paragraph (1) above shall not apply to contracts concluded exclusively by exchange of electronic mail or by equivalent individual communications.

The word 'order' in reg 11(1)(b) (though not necessarily in reg 11(1)(a)) means the contractual offer (reg 12).

The sanctions for non-compliance with reg 11(1)(a) gives a right to the customer to sue the service provider for damages for breach of statutory duty (reg 13). Non-compliance with reg 11(1)(b) gives the customer the right to rescind the contract (reg 15).

The wording of the Regulations seems to confirm the suggestion made above that it will generally be the customer who makes the offer. As noted above, reg 11(1)(b) requires the service provider to make available to the customer 'appropriate, effective and accessible technical means allowing him to identify and correct input errors prior to the placing of an order'. Regulation 12 then provides that 'order' in reg 11(1)(b) means 'the contractual offer'. The service provider will thus be able to argue that any screen which it displays in response to a customer's initial 'order' is simply fulfilling the requirements of reg 11(1)(b), and that reg 12 means that this must be taken as preceding 'the contractual offer'. The 'contractual offer' then becomes customer's clicking of a button confirming that he or she is happy with the terms set out on the page; so, although the Regulations do not on their face purport to affect the rules of offer and acceptance, it is clearly arguable that they do lead to particular conclusions about the stage at which an offer is made.

FOR THOUGHT

> Do the Regulations have any effect on the situation where the website supplier of goods states on its website (as some do) that no contract will be formed until the goods are dispatched to the customer?

2.12.13   Acceptance in unilateral contracts

Particular difficulties arise in connection with acceptances in unilateral contracts. We have already seen that one of the characteristics of the unilateral contract is that the 'acceptance' occurs through the performance of an act, rather than the expression of agreement. It has also been noted that in certain cases, the offeror in a unilateral contract may be taken to have waived the need for communication of the fact of acceptance.[140] Indeed, there may be an argument for saying that a unilateral contract does not really involve an agreement at all, but rather simply a promise which becomes

---

140 For example, *Carlill v Carbolic Smoke Ball Co* [1893] 1 QB 256.

enforceable once a certain condition is fulfilled. This issue will be considered further once certain other difficulties with acceptance in unilateral contracts have been considered.

There is, first, a problem as to when acceptance is complete. Is it when the acceptor starts to perform? Or when performance is complete? If I offer a prize of £100 for the first person to walk from the Town Hall in Leicester to Trafalgar Square in London during the month of February, do you accept this offer when you take your first step away from Leicester, or only when you arrive at Trafalgar Square? An acceptor in a unilateral contract is generally regarded as incurring no obligations until the specified act is completed, so that if you decide to give up halfway to London, I will have no claim against you for breach of contract. This would suggest that acceptance only occurs with complete performance. There are problems with this, however, in relation to the offeror's power to withdraw the offer. As will be seen below, the offeror is generally free to withdraw an offer at any point before it has been accepted. If, in a unilateral contract, acceptance means complete performance, then this means that the offeror would be able to back out at any point before performance was complete. So, to use the example given above, if you have started out to walk from Leicester to London, and have managed two thirds of the distance, I would be entitled to come up to you and say: 'I'm sorry, I have changed my mind. My offer of £100 is withdrawn.' You would have no redress, despite the fact that you might be perfectly willing to continue the walk, because we would not at that stage have a contract. The possibility of withdrawal by notice in this type of contract was given judicial recognition in *Great Northern Railway Co v Witham*,[141] but the court did not on the facts need to decide whether, and in what circumstances, it might be allowed. In an American case, *Petterson v Pattberg*,[142] an Appeals Court took the view that a unilateral offer to allow a reduction on a mortgage if it was paid off before a particular date could be withdrawn at any time before tender of the payment was made. Thus, Petterson had gone to Pattberg's house and announced that he had come to pay off the mortgage, but Pattberg had responded by indicating that the offer was withdrawn. It was held that he was entitled to do so.[143]

Such a result clearly has the potential to operate unfairly, and there have therefore been attempts to argue that partial performance may at least in some circumstances amount to a sufficient indication of acceptance so as to prevent withdrawal by the offeror. In *Errington v Errington*,[144] a father had promised his son and daughter-in-law that if they paid off the mortgage on a house owned by the father, he would transfer it

---

141 (1873) LR 9 CP 16.

142 (1928) 248 NY 86, 161 NE 428.

143 This conclusion has, however, subsequently been described as 'obsolete' (Traynor J, in *Drennan v Star Paving Company* (1958) 51 Cal 2d 409, 333 P 2d 757) because of s 45 of the 2nd Restatement, which states that there is a subsidiary promise in a unilateral offer to keep the offer open for the stated time, or a 'reasonable time', and that partial performance provides consideration for that promise.

144 [1952] 1 All ER 149.

to them. The young couple started to make the required payments, but made no promise that they would continue. This appeared to be, therefore, a unilateral contract. The father died, and his representatives denied that there was any binding agreement in relation to the house. They argued that his offer could be withdrawn, because there had not been full acceptance. The Court of Appeal refused to allow this conclusion. Lord Denning recognised that this was a unilateral contract, but nevertheless held that the offer could not be withdrawn:[145]

> The father's promise was a unilateral contract – a promise of the house in return for their act of paying the instalments. It could not be revoked by him once the couple entered on performance of the act, but it would cease to bind him if they left it incomplete and unperformed.

The reasons behind this conclusion are not made clear, other than that this was a fair result where the young couple had acted in reliance on the father's promise.[146] This approach has clear links with the idea of estoppel, of which as we shall see Lord Denning made inventive use in other areas,[147] but this concept was not raised directly in this case.

The approach taken by Lord Denning in *Errington* received support from the later Court of Appeal decision in *Daulia v Four Millbank Nominees Ltd*.[148] The parties were negotiating over the sale of some properties. The unilateral contract here was that the defendants promised the plaintiffs that if they produced a signed contract plus a banker's draft by 10 am the next morning, the defendants would go ahead with the sale to the plaintiffs. The plaintiffs did what was requested, but the defendants refused to go through with the contract. In the course of his judgment, Goff LJ considered the question of when the offeror in a unilateral contract is entitled to withdraw that offer. He started by confirming that in general the offeror cannot be bound to a unilateral contract until the acceptor has provided full performance of the condition imposed. That general rule is, however, subject to an important qualification, namely:[149]

> . . . that there must be an implied obligation on the part of the offeror not to prevent the condition becoming satisfied, which obligation it seems to me must arise as soon as the offeree starts to perform. Until then, the offeror can revoke the whole thing, but once the offeree has embarked on performance it is too late for the offeror to revoke his offer.

---

145 [1952] 1 All ER 149, p 153.
146 This could be seen as adding support to arguments that the basis of contractual liability is 'reasonable reliance', rather than 'consideration' or 'promise' – see below, 3.4 and 3.15.2.
147 See below, 3.11.
148 [1978] 2 All ER 557.
149 Ibid, p 561.

Goff LJ provided no authority for this proposition,[150] but it received the support of Buckley LJ. It was not, however, part of the *ratio* of the case, since the court decided against the plaintiffs on other grounds. It seems likely, nevertheless, that the approach taken by Denning LJ and Goff LJ in these two cases would be followed in similar circumstances.

A case which might appear to cause difficulties for such a conclusion is the earlier House of Lords' decision in *Luxor (Eastbourne) Ltd v Cooper*.[151] This was a case in which a company wished to sell some cinemas, and Cooper agreed to act as agent and try to provide a purchaser, at a price of not less than £185,000. He was to be paid his commission (£10,000) 'on completion of the sale'. Cooper provided a willing purchaser, but the company withdrew from the sale. The House of Lords refused to imply a term that the principal would not unreasonably prevent the completion of the transaction. The clause referred to payment 'on completion'; since that had not occurred, the agent was not entitled to his commission. This type of arrangement might well be treated as a bilateral contract,[152] but the House of Lords took it to be unilateral. As Lord Russell put it, in this type of estate agency contract:[153]

> No obligation is imposed on the agent to do anything. The contracts are merely promises binding on the principal to pay a sum of money on the happening of a specified event, which involves the rendering of some service by the agent.

The question then became whether any term should be implied into the principal's promise to the effect that the principal would not refuse to complete the sale to a client introduced by the agent. The House of Lords refused to imply any such term, since there was no necessity to do so – necessity being the normal basis for the implication of terms at common law.[154] In effect, therefore, the House was saying that the principal could withdraw his offer at any time before the specified event occurred. Since the sale had not been completed, the event had not occurred, and the agent was not entitled to the commission. The decision could be seen as the House upholding 'party freedom', in that the principal should be entitled to refuse to contract with whomever the agent produces.[155] It may well be, however, that, as Atiyah has argued,[156] an important aspect in reaching this decision was the House's view that risk was inherent in the role of the estate agent. The risk of the principal withdrawing his offer was just one more to put

---

150 Though it is similar to the position taken by the American 2nd Restatement – see fn 140, above.
151 [1941] AC 108; [1941] 1 All ER 33.
152 As, indeed, the Court of Appeal had done – [1939] 4 All ER 411.
153 [1941] AC 108, pp 124–25; [1941] 1 All ER 33, p 44. The issues involved in treating the agency contract as unilateral rather than bilateral are fully discussed in Murdoch, 1975.
154 See Chapter 8, 8.6.4.
155 See, for example, the comments of Lord Wright [1941] AC 108, p 138: 'It would be strange if what was preliminary . . . should control the freedom of the action of the principal in regard to the main transaction . . .'
156 Atiyah, 1986, pp 204–05.

alongside all the others. The rewards of success were great. As Lord Russell pointed out, £10,000 was at the time equivalent to the annual salary of the Lord Chancellor. The risk was therefore worth taking. If that is the case, then it is probably best to view *Luxor v Cooper* as being a case of relevance primarily to the law of agency. Certainly it does not seem to have troubled the Court of Appeal in expressing apparently contradictory views about the possibility of withdrawing unilateral offers in *Errington v Errington* or *Daulia v Four Millbank Nominees*. Even as far as agents are concerned, it is important to remember that *Luxor v Cooper* turned on the precise wording of the promise made by the principal. As later cases have shown,[157] agents are quite able to protect their commission against the kind of withdrawal that took place in *Luxor v Cooper*, by making it payable on the production of a purchaser 'ready, willing and able' to purchase, rather than the completion of a sale.

In conclusion, despite the difficulties raised by *Luxor v Cooper*, it is still suggested that in general, where the offeror knows that the offeree is trying to perform, there will be an implied obligation on the offeror not to withdraw the offer, at least until a reasonable time for performance has been allowed.

2.12.14   Position in 'reward' contracts

It may be significant, however, that in both *Errington* and *Daulia*, the offeror was aware that the other person had embarked upon performance. In such a situation it is relatively easy to conclude that the offeror should be under an obligation not to withdraw – though whether such an obligation arises as an implication of the intention of the parties or is simply imposed by the courts is not clear.[158] On the other hand, where the offer, such as the offer of a reward or prize, is one that is made to the world, it is by no means certain that precisely the same approach should apply. In the case, for example, of the offer of £100 for the return of a lost dog, it seems right that where a person is seen at the opposite end of the street, bringing the dog home, the offeror should not be able to shout out a withdrawal of the reward. But, suppose the offeror has run into financial problems since offering the reward, and cannot now afford to pay it: must the offeror remain committed to keeping the offer open as regards anyone who has started looking for the dog, even if the offeror is unaware of this? It would seem more reasonable that the offeror should be allowed, by giving notice in a reasonable manner (perhaps in the same way in which the offer was made), to withdraw the offer. It is an issue on which there is no English authority, so it is not possible to say with any certainty what the approach of the courts would be, but it is submitted that the fairest rule to all parties would be to hold that the *Errington/Daulia* approach should only apply where the offeror is aware that the other person is trying to perform the condition.

---

157 *Christie, Owen & Davies Ltd v Rapacioli* [1974] 1 QB 781.
158 See the comments of Beale, 1995a, p 205.

2.12.15   Acceptance in ignorance of an offer

It would seem logical that there can be no acceptance of an offer of which the person accepting was ignorant. Some problems have arisen, however, in relation to certain types of unilateral contract. Suppose a reward is offered for the return of a stolen bicycle belonging to A, and posters are displayed advertising this fact. B, who has not seen any of the posters, finds the bicycle, and recognising it, returns it to A, its rightful owner. Can B claim the reward from A? There is one authority which suggests that he might be able to. That is *Gibbons v Proctor*,[159] where a police officer gave information for which a reward had been offered. At the time that he gave the information, the officer was unaware of the reward, though he had learnt of it by the time the information reached the person who had offered the reward. It was held that the officer was entitled to claim the reward. This decision has not been followed in any later case, however, and must be regarded as being of doubtful authority. The better view seems to be that knowledge is necessary for an effective acceptance. This was accepted as being the case, though without any authority being cited, in the criminal law case of *Taylor v Allon*.[160]

A slightly different issue arises where the person performing the act has previously known of the offer, but is acting from different motives. In the Australian case of *R v Clarke*,[161] it was held that a person who had known of the offer, but was at the time acting purely out of consideration for his own danger, should be treated as acting in ignorance of the offer. On the other hand, in *Williams v Carwardine*,[162] it was held that acting out of mixed motives (in this case, to ease one's conscience), while at the same time having the reward in mind, did not preclude a valid acceptance of the offer.

It seems, therefore, that there needs to be at the very least awareness of the offer and, probably, that responding to it must at least be part of the reason for undertaking the relevant actions.

2.12.16   Unilateral contracts and 'agreement'

Having looked at the issues surrounding the question of acceptance in unilateral contracts, we can now return to the question of how well such contracts fit with the concept of an 'agreement'. Is a unilateral contract really anything more than a promise which becomes enforceable on the fulfilment of a condition? Not all such promises are enforceable, of course. A promise by a mother to pay her daughter £500 on her eighteenth birthday is not enforceable. It is only where the promisee does something at the request of the promisor that the relationship becomes 'contractual'. A promise by the Smoke Ball Company to pay Mrs Carlill £100 the next time she caught flu would not

---

159 (1891) 64 LT 594.
160 [1965] 1 QB 304; [1965] 1 All ER 557.
161 (1927) 40 CLR 227.
162 (1833) 5 C & P 566. See also Mitchell and Phillips, 2002.

have been enforceable. It was only because the advertisement was aimed to encourage people to use the company's smoke ball and Mrs Carlill had done so that she became eligible for the reward. This aspect of the unilateral contract derives from the doctrine of 'consideration' which is discussed in Chapter 3. The question here is whether the mere fact that the promisee does something at the request of the promisor means that there is an 'agreement'. Although the promisee is responding to the promisor,[163] in 'reward' or 'advertisement' situations the promisor will know nothing of this until performance is complete. Is it accurate to say that the promisor has an agreement with the promisee in such a situation? The answer is that, as discussed in Chapter 1, we can fit this into the overall 'agreement' framework by accepting that some agreements will be 'implied' or 'imputed'.[164] As long as we are prepared to accept this 'fiction', then the unilateral contract can be treated as falling within the overall classical paradigm of a contract.

Much of the difficulty derives from the insistence by the courts that a unilateral contract must have an offer and acceptance in the same way as a bilateral contract. It might have been better if the courts, recognising that the unilateral contract was not the same as a bilateral contract, had devised a separate set of rules to deal with it. It is arguable that this is what has happened in practice, since a number of cases involving unilateral contracts (for example, *Errington v Errington, Daulia v Four Millbank Nominees, Williams v Carwardine*) seem to involve the courts taking a decision based on pragmatism and 'fairness' rather than formal and logical application of the rules as they apply to bilateral contracts. As such, it is perhaps an area where doctrine has been a hindrance rather than a help to the development of a coherent set of principles.

2.12.17 Cross-offers

A situation similar to the unilateral contract cases on 'accepting' a reward of which one is unaware can arise in a bilateral contract if there are matching 'cross-offers'. Suppose, for example, that two parties send each other a letter offering respectively to buy and to sell certain goods at a certain price. Suppose, also, that the two offers match precisely. Does this create a contract? If what the courts were concerned with was simply a 'meeting of the minds', the answer might well be 'yes'. In *Tinn v Hoffman*,[165] however, it was held that such an exchange does not result in a contract. The case is not conclusive on the general issue, because on the facts there were differences between the two offers. It seems likely, however, that given the general enthusiasm of the courts to look for an 'exchange' of offer and acceptance, rather than simply general agreement, *Tinn v Hoffman* would be followed, and that cross-offers would not be regarded as forming a

---

163 Even this may not be necessary, if *Gibbons v Proctor* (1891) 64 LT 594 is good law – see above, 2.12.15.
164 See Chapter 1, 1.4.
165 (1873) 29 LT 271.

contract. In practice, it is very unlikely that any set of cross-offers would be identical, so the question is probably only of theoretical interest.

2.13   ACCEPTANCE AND THE TERMINATION OF AN OFFER

The general rule is that an offer can be revoked at any point before it is accepted,[166] though, as we have seen, that requires some modification in relation to unilateral contracts. In this section the focus will be entirely on bilateral contracts.

The general rule will apply despite the fact that the offeror may have promised to keep the offer open for a specified time.[167] The reason for this is that before there is an acceptance, there is no contract, and if there is no contract, then the offeror cannot be legally bound to a promise. If the offeree has paid for the time allowance in some way (that is, has given consideration for the promise to keep the offer open), as may well be the case with the exercise of an option, then it will be upheld. In the absence of this, however, there can be no complaint if the offer is withdrawn.

A different approach is taken in the Principles of European Contract Law, which provide that an offer cannot be revoked if it states a fixed time for acceptance (Art 2.202). The Article also envisages the possibility of an 'irrevocable' offer.

FOR THOUGHT

Which approach is preferable, that of the common law, or the PECL? What problems might arise if English law took the view that a person who has promised to keep an offer open for a particular period should always be obliged to keep that promise?

2.13.1   Need for communication

Revocation of an offer must be communicated to be effective. This was implicit in the decision in *Byrne v van Tienhoven*[168] in which the withdrawal of an offer, which was sent by telegram, was held not to take effect until it was received. The *Adams v Lindsell*[169] postal rule does not apply to revocations of offers, but there may still be difficulties as to what exactly amounts to communication and when a revocation takes effect. The issues are much the same as those dealt with in the section on acceptance by electronic communication,[170] and are not discussed again here.

---

166 *Payne v Cave* (1789) 3 Term Rep 148.
167 *Routledge v Grant* (1828) 4 Bing 653; 130 ER 920.
168 (1880) 5 CPD 344.
169 (1818) 1 B & Ald 681; 106 ER 250.
170 See above, 2.12.12.

It is clear, however, that communication of revocation need not come directly from the offeror. Provided that the offeree is fully aware at the time of a purported acceptance that the offeror has decided not to proceed with the contract, the offer will be regarded as having been revoked and no acceptance will be possible. This was the position in *Dickinson v Dodds*,[171] where the plaintiff was told by a third party that the defendant was negotiating with someone else for the sale of properties which he had previously offered to the plaintiff. The defendant had also indicated to the plaintiff that the offer would be kept open for a specified period.

The plaintiff tried to accept the offer within the time limit. The Court of Appeal decided that acceptance was not possible, because the plaintiff knew that the defendant was no longer minded to sell the property to him 'as plainly and clearly as if [the defendant] had told him in so many words, "I withdraw the offer" '.[172] The reasoning of at least some of the judges in this case was clearly influenced by the idea of there needing to be a 'meeting of the minds' in order for there to be a contract. Despite the fact that this approach to identifying agreements no longer has any support, *Dickinson v Dodds* is still regarded as good authority for the more general proposition that an offeree cannot accept an offer where he or she has learnt from a reliable source that the offer has been withdrawn, even where that source was acting without the knowledge of the offeror.

2.13.2 Methods of revocation

As well as being communicated expressly, an offer may be revoked by implication. We have seen that a rejection of an offer, or a counter offer, automatically means that the offer is taken as being no longer available for acceptance.[173] In *Pickfords v Celestica*,[174] the Court of Appeal held that a second offer made to the same offeree will generally have the effect of impliedly revoking the first offer, though this might be otherwise if the offeree had, for example, requested a second offer based on an alternative pricing method, specifically for the purpose of making a choice between the two pricing methods.

An offer may also become incapable of acceptance because of lapse of time. If the offeror has specified a time within which acceptance must be received, any acceptance received outside that time limit cannot create a contract. At best, it will be a fresh offer, which may be accepted or rejected. If no time is specified, the offer will remain open for a reasonable time, which will be a matter of fact in each case. In *Ramsgate Victoria Hotel Co v Montefiore*,[175] it was held that a delay of five months meant that an attempt to accept an offer to buy shares was ineffective.[176]

---

171 (1876) 2 Ch D 463.
172 Ibid, p 472.
173 *Hyde v Wrench* (1840) 3 Beav 334; see above, 2.11.1.
174 [2003] EWCA Civ 1741.
175 (1866) LR 1 Ex 109.
176 See, also, *Manchester Diocesan Council for Education v Commercial and General Investments Ltd* [1969] 3 All ER 1593; [1970] 1 WLR 241.

2.13.3   Revocation and tenders

The ability of an offeror to revoke an offer, even when it has been stated that it will remain open for a specified period, has the potential to cause difficulties in large-scale contracts, where a main contractor may tender for work using a price on the basis of offers received from sub-contractors. What is the position if the main contractor's tender is successful, but the sub-contractor then says that the offer to do the work at the specified price is withdrawn? There is no English authority on this issue,[177] but the application of the principles outlined above would lead to the conclusion that the sub-contractor was entitled to withdraw. Concern about the difficulties that this might cause for contractors led the Law Commission in 1975 to make some provisional proposals that in certain circumstances a promise to keep an offer open for a specified time should be binding, bringing English law into line with what the Law Commission found to be the position in other European jurisdictions (including Scotland) and under the Uniform Commercial Code in the United States.[178] A study of business practice in this country by Lewis, however,[179] found that the problem was not regarded as being as serious as the Law Commission had supposed. Moreover, even where difficulties of this kind arose, informal, rather than legal remedies were seen as being the better option. No further action has been taken on the Law Commission's suggestions.

2.14   RETRACTION OF ACCEPTANCE

As soon as an acceptance takes effect, a contract is made and both parties are bound. It would seem, then, that in the normal course of events, retraction or revocation of an acceptance will be impossible. This general rule has been modified, however, in relation to certain types of consumer contracts, where it has been deemed desirable that the consumer should have a 'cooling-off' period following the formation of the contract, during which a change of mind is permitted. In these cases, a valid contract, in which offer and acceptance have been exchanged, can be set aside purely at the discretion of the consumer contractor. Examples of this type of provision may be found in s 67 of the Consumer Credit Act 1974, ss 5 and 6 of the Timeshare Act 1992, and the Consumer Protection (Cancellation of Contracts Concluded Away From Business Premises) Regulations 1987. A much broader-based exception is now to be found in the Consumer Protection (Distance Selling) Regulations 2000,[180] implementing the European Distance Selling Directive.[181]

---

177 There are some American cases, but they are conflicting: see *James Baird Co v Gimble Bros Inc* (1933) 64 F 2d 344 (2d Cir 1933); *Drennan v Star Paving Company* (1958) 333 P 2d 757.
178 Law Commission Working Paper No 60, 'Firm Offers'.
179 Lewis, 1982.
180 SI 2000/2334.
181 97/7/EC.

The Regulations apply to contracts for the supply of goods or services to a consumer, made under an 'organised distance sales service or service provision scheme',[182] and concluded exclusively by the means of 'distance communication'. This includes contracts made by telephone, post or via the internet. The requirement of an 'organised service' means that the occasional making of contracts without face-to-face contact will not come within the Regulations.

Schedule 1 to the Regulations makes it clear that they cover contracts made by responding to direct mail, catalogues and advertisements in the press which include an order form. The Schedule also refers to 'radio' and 'television (teleshopping)'. This would cover not only the dedicated shopping channels available on cable and satellite television, but also ordinary radio or television adverts which include a telephone number or website address. Adverts or catalogues which require you to go to a shop to conclude your purchase would not, of course, be within the Regulations, because in these transactions there is an element of face-to-face contact. The list in the Schedule is stated to be 'indicative' only, so the courts are free to interpret 'distance communication' to cover situations other than those listed, as might be necessary if retailers develop other means of selling at a distance which have not yet been considered.

A number of contracts are excepted from the Regulations.[183] These include most contracts involving the sale or disposition of interests in land, contracts relating to financial services,[184] sales via an automated vending machine, and auction sales.

In addition to the general exceptions in reg 5, certain other contracts are exempted from the Regulations' 'cancellation' provisions by virtue of reg 6. These include 'timeshare agreements',[185] contracts for the supply of food, etc 'intended for everyday consumption supplied to the consumer's residence or to his workplace by regular roundsmen', and 'contracts for the provision of accommodation, transport, catering or leisure services, where the supplier undertakes . . . to provide these services on a specific date or within a specified period'. This final category means, for example, that booking a train ticket over the internet, a hotel room by telephone or ordering a pizza to be delivered are not within the scope of the cancellation provisions.

Where the contract is within the scope of the Regulations, the cancellation provisions contained in regs 10–12 apply. These mean that the consumer will generally be able to cancel the contract by giving notice within seven working days of receiving goods,[186] or within seven days of the conclusion of a contract for services.[187] If the

182 SI 2000/2334, reg 3(1).
183 SI 2000/2334, reg 5(1).
184 A non-exhaustive list of 'financial services' is given in Sched 2. Contracts for such services do, however, attract cancellation rights under The Financial Services (Distance Marketing) Regulations 2004, SI 2004/2095.
185 It has been noted above that these are covered by separate regulations.
186 Time starts to run on the day after the day of delivery (reg 11(2)).
187 Time starts to run on the day after the conclusion of the contract (reg 12(2)).

supplier has not complied with the requirements for the supply of information contained in reg 8, the period will not start to run until the day after such information is received.[188] If the information is not given within three months, then the cancellation period extends to three months and seven days.[189]

The Regulations also contain provisions as to the manner in which notice can be given, so that, for example, a letter posted to the supplier's last known address is effective on posting, and an email sent to the supplier's last known email address is effective as soon as it is sent.[190]

The effect of these Regulations is that there is now a wide range of consumer contracts where the traditional contractual rule that an acceptance cannot be withdrawn no longer applies. Does this pose a threat to the continuation of the traditional rule? Probably not. The rationale for the Regulations is the avoidance of the risk of consumers being treated unfairly. Although it is possible that a similar approach could be adopted in a business context, in situations of unequal bargaining power, it seems unlikely that this will happen. Indeed, the English courts may well be less likely to consider doing this now that specific provision has been made to protect consumers. The argument would probably be that now that Parliament has intervened to deal with this area, the courts should not rush to depart from established principle in those areas not covered by such intervention. The assumption will be that Parliament intended that the normal rules should continue to apply outside the specified areas.

There is one area, however, where the possibility of withdrawal from a seemingly binding agreement arises under classical contractual doctrine – that is, in relation to situations where the law deems acceptance to take effect at a point in time before that at which it actually comes to the attention of the offeror. The most obvious example of this is the *Adams v Lindsell*[191] postal rule.[192] It may also apply, however, in relation to, for example, acceptances by telex, fax or email, which are received during office hours but not read until some time later, or messages left on a telephone answering machine. As we have seen, the law as yet provides no clear answer to the question of when acceptance takes effect in such cases, but if it is decided that the relevant time is when the acceptance is received on the offeror's machine, rather than when it is read, there is again a delay between acceptance and actual communication, which may lead to the possibility of a retraction. The rest of this section will discuss the issue in relation to posted acceptances, but the principles should surely apply in the same way to any acceptance where there is a delay between the point in time when the law says that the acceptance takes effect (for example, on posting or being printed by the offeror's fax machine) and when it is read by the offeror.

---

188 Regulations 11(3) and 12(3).
189 Regulations 11(4) and 12(4).
190 Regulation 10.
191 (1818) 1 B & Ald 681; 106 ER 250.
192 See above, 2.12.6.

2.14.1 Formalist approach

If a 'formalist' approach is taken to this issue,[193] attempting to apply the established principles 'logically', then the answer must be that no retraction of an acceptance is possible. The general rule that a contract is complete on acceptance should be applied. So even if the acceptor is able, for example, by telephoning the offeror, to indicate that an acceptance which is in the post should be ignored, the offeror should be entitled to say 'Too bad! Your acceptance took effect on posting, and we have a contract. If you fail to go through with it, you will be in breach'.

2.14.2 Purposive approach

This is not the only possible approach, however. It might also be argued that the purpose of the postal rule is to provide a benefit to the acceptor. As we have seen, the main reason for the decision in *Adams v Lindsell* was that such a rule allowed the acceptor to proceed on the basis that a contract had been made, and that this promoted business efficiency. If that is the case, it might be argued that it is a little odd to then apply the rule in a way which is to the acceptor's disadvantage. Moreover, if, as must be the case for there to be any possibility of retraction, we are considering a point in time at which the offeror is as yet unaware of the acceptance, how can there be any harm in allowing the acceptor to withdraw? The offeror cannot in any way have acted on the acceptance, and so can suffer no harm from its retraction. There seems little point in forcing people to go through with a contract, when one party no longer wishes to proceed and the other party is unaware of the fact that there is a contract at all.

2.14.3 Unfairness to offeror

This argument is said by some to be too favourable to the acceptor. The example is given of an acceptance of an offer to buy shares, or goods which have a greatly fluctuating market price. If retraction of acceptance is allowed, then it is said that this gives the acceptor the best of both worlds. The offer can be accepted by posting a letter, which will bind the offeror. Then, if before the acceptance is read, the market price falls below the contract price, the acceptor can avoid what has now become a bad bargain by telephoning a withdrawal.[194] This is regarded as unfair. In an argument which is the converse of the one put forward in the last paragraph, it is said that the postal rule exists for the benefit of the acceptor. It is tipping the scales too far in the acceptor's favour, however, to allow the possibility of retraction as well: a possibility which is not available in any other situation.

---

193 See Chapter 1, 1.8.2.
194 See, for example, Treitel, 2003, p 28. Hudson, 1966, sets out a variety of reasons why Treitel's view on this point should not be accepted.

2.14.4   Guidance from authority

Attempts to argue the case from first principles, then, may lead to different conclusions. Three possibilities have been outlined above, one in favour of allowing retraction, the other two against. This writer's preferred view is the pragmatic one of allowing retraction, but this is by no means widely accepted. Unfortunately, there is little help from case law either.

The only British case to deal with the issue at all is *Countess of Dunmore v Alexander*.[195] This is a Scottish case, which on one reading appears to support the view that a posted acceptance can be retracted by speedier means. The case is not a strong authority, however, since it is not absolutely clear that the court considered that the communication which was withdrawn was an acceptance, rather than an offer. Two cases from other common law jurisdictions suggest the opposite. In *Wenckheim v Arndt*[196] and *Ato Z Bazaars (Pty) Ltd v Minister of Agriculture*,[197] it was held that the attempt to withdraw the acceptance was not effective.[198]

An English court faced with this issue would be free to decide it without any clear guidance from authority. The answer that is given will depend on which of the various possibilities outlined above is the more attractive. It is not unlikely that the court's decision in a particular case will be influenced by what the court sees as the best way to achieve justice between the parties, rather than on any preference based on general principle.

2.15   CERTAINTY IN OFFER AND ACCEPTANCE

Even though the parties may have appeared to make an agreement by the exchange of a matching offer and acceptance, the courts may refuse to enforce it if there appears to be uncertainty about what has been agreed, or if some important aspect of the agreement is left open to be decided later. In *Scammell v Ouston*,[199] for example, the parties had agreed to the supply of a lorry on 'hire purchase terms'. The House of Lords held that in the absence of any other evidence of the details of the hire purchase agreement (duration, number of instalments, etc), this was too vague to be enforceable, and there was therefore no contract.[200]

This does not necessarily mean that all details of a contract must be finally settled in advance. It is not uncommon, for example, in relation to contracts for the supply of

---

195 (1830) 9 Shaw 190.

196 (1861–1902) 1 JR 73 (New Zealand).

197 (1974) (4) SA 392(C) (South Africa).

198 But cf to the contrary, *Dick v United States* (1949) 113 Ct Cl 94; 82 F Supp 326, discussed in Evans, 1966.

199 [1941] AC 251; [1941] 1 All ER 14.

200 Note that the Court of Appeal had agreed with the judge at first instance that there was sufficient information to find a complete and enforceable agreement: [1940] 1 All ER 59.

services for the precise amount to be paid to be left unspecified at the time of the agreement. If a car is left at a garage for repair, it may not be possible to determine at that stage exactly what the repair will cost, because this may depend on what the mechanic finds once work has started. The car owner may well say something along the lines of 'Do the work, but if it looks as though it will cost more than £150, please contact me before going ahead'. It cannot be doubted that there is a contract for repairs up to the value of £150. The court's view of this situation is that there is in effect an agreement that the customer will pay a 'reasonable price' for the work that is done. What is a reasonable price is a question of fact, which can, if necessary, be determined by the courts. This approach now has statutory force by virtue of s 15 of the Supply of Goods and Services Act 1982, which states that:

(1)   Where . . . the consideration for a service is not determined by the contract, left to be determined in a manner agreed by the contract or determined by the course of dealing between the parties, there is an implied term that the party contracting will pay a reasonable charge.

(2)   What is a reasonable charge is a question of fact.

The same rule also operates in relation to goods by virtue of the similar provision contained in s 8(2) and (3) of the Sale of Goods Act 1979.

The possibility of the courts giving specific content to an apparently vague phrase can apply in other areas apart from the price to be paid for goods or services. In *Hillas v Arcos*,[201] for example, there was a contract to supply timber 'of fair specification'. It was held that in the context of the agreement, which was between parties who knew each other and the timber trade well, and taking account of the fact that there had been part performance, the phrase 'fair specification' must be capable of being given a meaning. The contract was therefore enforceable.

2.15.1   Meaningless phrases

The decision in *Scammell v Ouston*[202] might be thought to open the door to an unscrupulous party to include some meaningless phrase in an agreement, which would then allow him to escape from the contract if he wished on the basis of uncertainty. To have such an effect, however, the phrase must relate to some significant aspect of the contract. If it can be deleted and still leave a perfectly workable agreement, the courts will ignore it. This was the position in *Nicolene v Simmonds*,[203] where the contractual documentation contained the statement 'we are in agreement that the usual conditions of acceptance apply'. Since there were no 'usual conditions', it was held that this was

---

201 (1932) 147 LT 503.
202 See above, 2.15.
203 [1963] 1 QB 543; [1953] 1 All ER 822.

simply a meaningless phrase, which could be ignored. There was nothing left open which needed to be determined.

2.15.2 Incomplete agreements

If an agreement leaves undecided, and undeterminable, some important aspect of the contract, then the courts will not enforce it. This can arise where perfectly clear words are used, about the meaning of which there is no dispute, but which do not settle some significant part of the contractual terms. In *May and Butcher v R*,[204] for example, the agreement provided that the price, and the date of payment, under a contract of sale, was to be 'agreed upon from time to time'. The House of Lords held that there was no contract. The parties had not left the price open – when, as we have seen, a 'reasonable price' would have been payable – they had specifically stated that they would agree in the future. The contract contained an arbitration clause, but the House of Lords considered that this was only meant to be used in the event of disputes, and could not be the means of determining basic obligations.

This reluctance to allow for the kind of arrangement which the parties had put into their contract in *May and Butcher v R* can be seen as an example of the English courts' refusal to take account of the ongoing, relational nature of many contracts.[205] Instead, they expect all facets of the contract to be determined at the outset,[206] and very little scope is allowed for the modification and development of obligations over its existence. The practice of the courts thus becomes divorced from the commercial reality of the business relationship of the parties.

The traditional refusal to give effect to an 'agreement to agree' was followed in *Courtney and Fairbairn Ltd v Tolaini Brothers (Hotels) Ltd*.[207] In this case there had been negotiations concerning property development. The plaintiffs, the prospective developers, were in a position to raise finance for the defendants, who were the owners of the property which was to be developed. This they did, in the expectation of being awarded the development contract. In the event, however, this contract was given to another firm, using the finance arranged by the plaintiffs. The plaintiffs argued that they had a contract with the defendants under which it was promised that if the plaintiffs arranged the finance, they would be awarded the development contract. The Court of Appeal disagreed. The letter which was alleged to provide evidence of this contract talked about the 'negotiation of fair and reasonable sums' for the project, based on 'agreed estimates'. This, the court felt, was far too vague to form the basis of determining the price in a major construction contract. Nor could there be a 'contract to negotiate'. Again it would be too uncertain to have binding force:[208]

---

204 [1934] 2 KB 17.
205 For which see Chapter 1, 1.5.
206 That is, they adhere to the myth of 'presentiation' – see Chapter 1, 1.5.
207 [1975] 1 WLR 297.
208 Ibid, p 301.

No court could estimate the damages because no one can tell whether the negotiations would be successful or would fall through; or if successful, what the result would be.

This conclusion was approved by the House of Lords in *Walford v Miles*.[209] The parties had reached agreement on the basic terms of the sale of a business. This was 'subject to contract'. The defendants, the vendors, separately agreed that they would cease negotiations with anyone else. Subsequently, however, they sold to a third party. The plaintiffs sought damages for breach of a collateral contract not to negotiate with anyone else, which they also contended implied a positive obligation on the defendants to negotiate in good faith with them. The House of Lords confirmed that there could not be a 'contract to negotiate'. The positive obligation alleged was therefore ruled out on the basis of the reasons given in *Courtney v Tolaini*. As regards the 'lock-out' agreement not to negotiate with anyone else, this was similarly unenforceable on grounds of uncertainty, since it was for an unspecified time. It was not satisfactory to argue that it should continue for a 'reasonable time'. A reasonable time would only come to an end when negotiations broke down completely; thus, it would indirectly involve an obligation to negotiate in good faith, which the House had already rejected as too uncertain.

This decision has been the subject of considerable academic comment,[210] in part because it can be seen as the House of Lords turning its back on the concept of 'good faith' in contracts,[211] which is commonly part of the law in other jurisdictions.[212] It can be seen as asserting an individualist, adversarial, approach to contract, which emphasises in particular 'party freedom'.[213] In doing so it can be said to be ignoring the reality of business transactions, which commonly do not operate on this basis.

Walford v Miles did, however, leave open the possibility that a 'lock-out' agreement not to negotiate with anyone else, which is sufficiently limited in terms of time, might be enforceable. That this is indeed possible was confirmed by the Court of Appeal in *Pitt v PHH Asset Management Ltd*.[214] The parties were in negotiations over the sale of a property, and the plaintiffs, the prospective purchasers, were concerned that the defendants would accept a higher offer from a third party. An agreement was arrived at under which, in return for the plaintiffs agreeing to exchange contracts within two weeks, the defendants agreed not to consider any further offers within that period. The defendants went back on this agreement and sold to the third party at a price above

209 [1992] 2 AC 128; [1992] 1 All ER 453.
210 See, for example, Brown, 1992; Buckley, 1993; Cumberbatch, 1992; Neill, 1992; Steyn, 1997, p 439. Lord Steyn, a current member of the House of Lords, expresses the hope that if the matter were to be raised again 'with the benefit of fuller argument . . . the concept of good faith would not be rejected out of hand'.
211 See, for example, Brownsword, 2000, para 5.17.
212 See Chapter 1, 1.3.
213 See, for example, Cumberbatch, 1992, p 173.
214 [1993] 4 All ER 961; [1994] 1 WLR 327.

that which the plaintiffs had offered. The Court of Appeal held that in this case, the 'lock-out' agreement was sufficiently specific to be binding, and the plaintiffs' action against the defendants for damages for breach of this agreement was therefore successful.

2.15.3 Obligations distinguished from 'machinery'

The contract will not be regarded as incomplete if it provides a machinery for resolving an aspect which has been left uncertain. As we have seen, in relation to the price, the courts will often be prepared to assume that a 'reasonable price' was intended. They will also be prepared to give effect to an agreement where property is to be valued by an independent valuer, or where the price is to be determined by reference to the prevailing market price. In such situations, the contract provides a mechanism by which the uncertainty can be resolved.

In some cases, however, the courts have been prepared to stretch this principle rather further than might have been expected. In *Sudbrook Trading Estate v Eggleton*,[215] the price for the exercise of an option to purchase was to be determined by two valuers, one to be nominated by each party. One party refused to appoint a valuer, and claimed that the agreement was therefore void for uncertainty. The House of Lords disagreed. The contract was not uncertain in that it provided a clear machinery by which the price was to be determined. This machinery was not, however, itself an essential term of the contract. It was simply a way of establishing a 'fair' price. If the machinery failed, then the court could substitute its own means of determining what was a fair price. This approach was relied on by the Court of Appeal in *Didymi Corp v Atlantic Lines and Navigation Co Inc*.[216] The agreement contained a provision under which the hire under a charter of a ship could in some circumstances be increased 'equitably' by an amount 'to be mutually agreed between the parties'. At first sight, this looks like an 'agreement to agree' which would be unenforceable. The court, however, following the lead given by *Sudbrook Trading Estate v Eggleton*, ruled that the reference to 'mutual agreement' was simply part of the 'inessential machinery' by which the hire was to be determined. The agreement was that the hire should be 'equitable', which meant 'fair and reasonable'. There was therefore no reason why the court should not determine this as a question of fact.[217]

In *Gillatt v Sky Television Ltd*,[218] the Court of Appeal, while not disagreeing with the approach taken in the *Sudbrook Trading Estate* or *Didymi Corp* cases, held on the facts that the valuation clause under consideration was not merely a mechanism for dispute resolution. The clause provided that the claimant was entitled to 55 per cent

---

215 [1982] 3 All ER 1.
216 [1987] 2 Lloyd's Rep 166. See also *Re Malpass* [1985] Ch 42.
217 A similar approach was taken by the Court of Appeal in *Mamidoil-Jetoil Greek Petroleum Co SA v Okta Crude Refinery AD* [2001] EWCA CIV 406; [2001] 2 All ER Comm 193.
218 [2000] 1 All ER Comm 461.

of the open market value of certain shares, 'as determined by an independent chartered accountant'. This provision was distinguishable from the clauses in the earlier authorities, because there was no objective meaning to be given to 'open market value' in that there were different bases on which shares could be valued. The reference to the independent accountant as the determiner of the value was therefore an essential element in that process, and not simply 'machinery'. Moreover, this was not a case where the mechanism for dispute resolution had broken down; under the contract either party could have taken steps towards the appointment of the valuer, but neither had chosen to do so. In these circumstances, the Court of Appeal agreed with the trial judge that the claimant was not entitled to any payment under the contract.

The question of whether a particular valuation provision is 'essential' to the determination of an amount to be made or simply 'machinery' will therefore depend on the precise wording of the clause and the context in which it operates. If it appears that there is no basis for determining the relevant value when essential procedures in the contract have not been followed, then the courts will still be prepared, even in a commercial context, to say that there is no agreement and therefore no binding obligation. The parties should not, therefore, rely on the courts coming to their rescue if they fail to follow the procedures which they have set out in their agreement. In some circumstances they will do so, but the determination of whether particular provisions are 'essential' or simply 'machinery' is sufficiently unpredictable that reliance on the court to intervene is a dangerous option.

The lack of coherence in this distinction suggests that the courts recognise the problems which the classical theory's insistence on 'presentiation' brings,[219] but are reluctant to find a proper method of addressing them. They must adhere to the myth that the parties will have fully determined all future obligations at the moment of contracting, even when this clearly does not accord with the parties' actual intentions or the requirements of business. The result is the unsatisfactory and unhelpful distinction between 'obligations' and 'machinery'.

An incomplete agreement, which is not regarded as creating an enforceable contract, may nevertheless give rise to some legal obligations between the parties under the doctrine of 'restitution'. This is discussed further in Chapter 19.

2.16 FURTHER READING

Evans, DM, 'The Anglo-American mailing rule' (1966) 15 ICLQ 553
Gardner, S, 'Trashing with Trollope: A deconstruction of the postal rules' (1992) 12 OJLS 170
Goodrich, P, 'The posthumous life of the postal rule: requiem and revival of *Adams v Lindsell*', Chapter 4 in Mulcahy, L and Wheeler, S, *Feminist Perspectives on Contract Law*, 2005, London: Glasshouse Press

219 See Chapter 1, 1.5.

Howarth, W, 'The meaning of objectivity in contract' (1984) 100 LQR 205

Hudson, AH, 'Retraction of letters of acceptance' (1966) 82 LQR 169

McClintock, R, 'Objectivity in contract' (1988–91) 6 Auckland UL Rev 317

Mitchell, P and Phillips, J, 'The contractual nexus: is reliance essential?' (2002) 22 OJLS 115

Rawlings, R, 'The battle of the forms' (1979) 42 MLR 715

Steyn, J, 'Contract law: fulfilling the reasonable expectations of honest men' (1997) 113 LQR 433

3 TESTS OF ENFORCEABILITY

CONTENTS

3.1 OVERVIEW

This chapter is concerned with the issue of the enforceability of promises. How does English law decide whether a promise is to be treated as enforceable by the courts? In investigating this question, the following topics will be considered:

- Deeds. These constitute a means of indicating an intention to make an enforceable promise through formal means – that is, putting the promise into a particular type of document.
- Consideration. The doctrine of 'consideration' is one of the hallmarks of English contract law. It means, in effect, that promises do not have to take any particular form, or be put in writing, but will be enforceable if there is mutuality in the agreement – both parties bring something to it. Within this doctrine it will be necessary to consider:
  - What constitutes 'consideration'? Does it have to have a monetary value?
  - What is meant by the requirement that consideration must be 'sufficient', though not necessarily 'adequate'?
  - Can an action already performed (past consideration) be consideration for a new promise? (Generally, it cannot.)
  - When will the performance of an existing duty constitute good consideration? The answer will depend on the type of duty.
- Promissory estoppel. This doctrine allows a promise unsupported by consideration to be enforced – generally in the context of the variation of an existing contract.
- Part payment of debts. Generally, part payment of a debt is not good consideration for the remission of the balance, unless promissory estoppel applies.
- Alternative tests of enforceability. Other jurisdictions use 'reliance' as a test of enforceability alongside consideration. To date, English law has made limited use of this test.

3.2 INTRODUCTION

In the previous chapter, the factors which lead a court to conclude that there was sufficient of an 'agreement' for there to be a binding contract were discussed. In Chapter 4, the overarching concept of an 'intention to create legal relations' will be considered. Three main issues are dealt with in this chapter: (a) deeds, (b) the doctrine of consideration and (c) situations where promises are regarded as enforceable even in the absence of a deed or consideration. The main example of that type of enforceability is to be found in the concept of 'reasonable reliance', which can be seen to be at the root of the so-called 'doctrine of promissory estoppel'.

3.3 DEEDS

The 'deed' is a way of using the physical form in which an agreement is recorded in order to give it enforceability. The agreement is put in writing and, traditionally, 'sealed' by the party or parties to be bound to it. The 'seal' could take the form of a wax seal, a seal 'embossed' onto the document by a special stamp, or simply the attachment of an adhesive paper seal (usually red).[1] Such contracts were also known as 'contracts under seal' (in contrast to 'simple contracts' which use 'consideration' as the test of enforceability).

The formal requirements for making a 'deed' are now contained in s 1 of the Law of Property (Miscellaneous Provisions) Act 1989.[2] There is no longer any requirement that the document should be sealed.[3] The document must, however, make it clear 'on its face' that it is intended to be a deed, and it must be 'validly executed' by the person making it or the parties to it.[4] 'Valid execution' for an individual means that the document must be signed in the presence of a witness who attests to the signature.[5] In addition there is a requirement of delivery – the document must be 'delivered as a deed by [the person executing it] or a person authorised to do so on his behalf'.[6] For a company incorporated under the Companies Acts, the position is governed by s 36A of the Companies Act 1985.[7] The 'execution' of a document by a company can take effect either by the affixing of its common seal,[8] or by being signed by a director and the secretary of the company, or by two directors.[9] For a document executed by a company to be a deed, it simply needs to make clear on its face that this is what is intended by whoever created it.[10] It will take effect as a deed upon delivery, but unless a contrary intention is proved, it is presumed to be delivered upon being executed.[11] In *OTV Birwelco Ltd v Technical and General Guarantee Co Ltd*,[12] it was held that a deed was validly executed within s 36A of the Companies Act 1985 where a company had used its trading name rather than its registered name; nor did it render the deed unenforceable that the seal used was engraved with the trading name rather than the registered name

---

1 Indeed, it was probably sufficient for the document to indicate on its face that it was 'sealed', without the need for any physical 'sealing' – see *First National Securities Ltd v Jones* [1978] Ch 109; Law Commission, Working Paper No 93, paras 4.2–4.3.

2 This followed from the Law Commission Report No 163, *Deeds and Escrows*.

3 Section 1(1)(a); nor is there any limitation on the substances on which a deed may be written. At one time, deeds were traditionally written on parchment rather than paper.

4 Section 1(2).

5 Section 1(3)(a). It may also be signed at the relevant person's direction, but it must still be in his presence and, in this case, in the presence of two witnesses who must each attest the signature: ibid.

6 Section 1(3)(b).

7 As inserted by the Companies Act 1989, s 130(2).

8 Section 36A(2).

9 Section 36A(3). The document should make it clear that it is being executed by the company.

10 Section 36A(5).

11 Ibid.

12 [2002] EWHC 2240 (TCC); [2002] 4 All ER 668.

(contrary to s 350 of the Companies Act 1985). Non-compliance with s 350 rendered the company concerned liable to a fine, but had no automatic effect on the validity of the deed.

If the parties to an agreement have taken the trouble to put it into the form of a deed, following the requirements laid down by s 1 of the 1989 Act (or s 36A of the Companies Act 1985), the courts will assume that it was their intention to create a legally binding agreement, and will not inquire into whether the other main test of enforceability (that is, 'consideration') is present. As will be seen below, the characteristic of the modern doctrine of consideration is that there is mutuality in the arrangement, with something being supplied by both parties to the agreement. This is not necessary in an agreement which is put into the form of a deed. Where, therefore, a transaction is 'one sided' with only one party giving, and the other party receiving all the benefit without providing anything in exchange, the deed is one certain way of making the arrangement enforceable.

Deeds may be used even where the transaction is supported by consideration.[13] This has traditionally been done in relation to complex contracts in the engineering and construction industries. This is probably because, by virtue of the Limitation Act 1980, the period within which an action for breach of an obligation contained in a deed is 12 years,[14] whereas for a 'simple' contract it is only six years.[15] The longer period is clearly an advantage in a contract where problems may not become apparent for a number of years. The practice of 'sealing' a document is also still used, even though it is no longer necessary even for a company. It may in some circumstances serve to make it clear that the document is intended to be a 'deed'. It does not in itself, however, make the transactions concerned any more or less enforceable.

For contracts which are not made in the form of a deed, 'consideration' is generally used as the test of enforceability, and it is to this that we now turn.

3.4 CONSIDERATION OR RELIANCE?

The doctrine of consideration is one of the characteristics of classical English contract law. This provides that no matter how much the parties to a 'simple contract' may wish it to be legally enforceable, it will not be so unless it contains 'consideration'. What does the word mean in this context? It is important to note that it does not have its ordinary, everyday meaning. It is used in a technical sense. Essentially, it refers to what one party to an agreement is giving, or promising, in exchange for what is being given or promised

---

13 The only situation in which a contract must be made by deed to have full effect is a lease of land for more than three years: Law of Property Act 1925, ss 52 and 54(2). Even here the lease will have some effect in equity, and will be enforceable, provided it is in writing (*Walsh v Lonsdale* (1882) 21 Ch D 9), and subject to any intervening third party rights (for example, if the landlord sells the land).
14 Limitation Act 1980, s 8(1).
15 Ibid, s 5.

from the other side. So, for example, in a contract where A is selling B 10 bags of grain for £100, what is the consideration? A is transferring the ownership of the grain to B. In consideration of this, B is paying £100. Or, to look at it the other way round, B is paying A £100. In consideration for this, A is transferring to B the ownership of the grain. From this example it will be seen that there is consideration on both sides of the agreement. It is this mutuality which makes the agreement enforceable. If B simply agreed to pay A £100, or A agreed to give B the grain, there would be no contract. The transaction would be a gift and would not be legally enforceable.

The history of the development of this doctrine is a matter of controversy. Some writers have argued that a study of the history of the English law of contract shows that 'consideration', when first referred to by the judges, meant simply a 'reason' for enforcing a promise.[16] According to this view, such 'reasons' could be wide ranging. It was only in the late eighteenth century at the earliest,[17] and probably not until the production of the first contract textbooks in the second half of the nineteenth century,[18] that the doctrine of consideration came to be regarded as consisting of the fairly rigid set of rules which it is now generally regarded as comprising. The approach here is to deal with the doctrine as it currently appears to be, but to keep in mind that there are alternative tests of contract enforceability. The main alternative is the concept of 'reasonable reliance'. This will be discussed more fully at the end of this chapter,[19] but a brief outline will be given here, in order to put the discussion of consideration in a proper perspective.

The concept of reliance as the basis for enforceability is that it is actions, and reliance on those actions, that creates obligations, rather than an exchange of promises (as under the classical doctrine of consideration). Thus, the window cleaner who, having checked that you want your windows cleaning, then does the work, does so in reliance on the fact that you will pay for what has been done. This is suggested to be a more accurate way of analysing many contractual situations than in terms of the mutual exchanges of promises, which forms the paradigmatic contract under the classical model.[20] Once this principle is accepted, it then opens the door to enforcing agreements where there is nothing that the classical law would recognise as 'consideration', provided that there is 'reasonable reliance'. This is accepted to a greater or lesser extent by many common law jurisdictions,[21] but has only received limited support to date by the English courts – though some recent decisions purportedly based on 'consideration' can be argued to be more accurately concerned with 'reliance'.[22]

---

16 See, for example, Simpson, 1975a, Chapters IV–VII, and in particular p 321; Atiyah, 1986, Chapter 8. This is discussed in more detail below, at 3.15.1.

17 See, for example, *Rann v Hughes* (1778) 7 Term Rep 350n; 4 Bro PC 27.

18 For example, Anson's *Law of Contract*, first published in 1879.

19 See below, 3.15.2.

20 See Chapter 1, 1.2.

21 For example, the United States, Australia, New Zealand and Canada – see below, 3.15.2.

22 For example, *Williams v Roffey Bros & Nicholls (Contractors) Ltd* [1991] 1 QB 1; [1990] 1 All ER 512 – discussed below, 3.9.8

We will return towards the end of the chapter to consider further questions about the theoretical basis of consideration,[23] and whether it is developing in a way which may perhaps have links to its historical origins. At that point it will also be worth looking more generally at the question of whether consideration still retains its dominant position at the heart of the English law of contract, or whether the growth in situations where promises may be enforceable in the absence of consideration means that its role needs further reassessment. In the meantime, in the discussion of consideration in the following sections, the tension between the classical theory and the more modern trends towards reliance-based liability needs to be kept in mind, and will be highlighted at various points.

3.5 BENEFIT AND DETRIMENT

It is sometimes said that consideration requires benefit and detriment. The often quoted, but not particularly helpful, definition of consideration contained in *Currie v Misa*[24] refers to these elements:

> A valuable consideration, in the sense of the law, may consist either in some right, interest, profit or benefit accruing to one party or some forbearance, detriment, loss or responsibility, given, suffered or undertaken by the other.

In other words, what is provided by way of consideration should be a benefit to the person receiving it, or a detriment to the person giving it. Sometimes, both are present. For example, in the contract concerning the sale of grain discussed in the previous section, B is suffering a detriment by paying the £100, and A is gaining a benefit. B is gaining a benefit in receiving the grain, A is suffering a detriment by losing it. In many cases, there will thus be both benefit and detriment involved, but it is not necessary that this should be the case. Benefit to one party, or detriment to the other, will be enough. Suppose that A agrees to transfer the grain, if B pays £100 to charity. In this case, B's consideration in paying the £100 is a detriment to B, but not a benefit to A. Nevertheless, B's act is good consideration, and there is a contract. In theory, it is enough that the recipient of the consideration receives a benefit, without the giver suffering a detriment. It is difficult, however, to think of practical examples of a situation of this kind, given that the traditional rule is that consideration must move from the promisee.

---

23 See below, 3.15.1.
24 (1875) LR 10 Ex 153.

3.6 MUTUAL PROMISES

The discussion so far has been in terms of acts constituting consideration. It is quite clear, however, that a promise to act can in itself be consideration. Lord Dunedin, in *Dunlop Pneumatic Tyre Co Ltd v Selfridge & Co Ltd*,[25] for example, approved the following statement from Pollock, 1902 (emphasis added):

> An act or forbearance of the one party, *or the promise thereof*, is the price for which the promise of the other is bought, and the promise thus given for value is enforceable.

Suppose, then, continuing the example used above, that on Monday, A promises that he will deliver and transfer the ownership of the grain to B on the following Friday; and B promises, again on Monday, that when it is delivered she will pay £100. There is no doubt that there is a contract as soon as these promises have been exchanged, so that if on Tuesday B decides that she does not want the grain, she will be in breach. But where is the consideration? On each side, the giving of the promise is the consideration. A's promise to transfer the grain is consideration for B's promise to pay for it, and vice versa. The problem is that this does not fit easily with the idea of benefit and detriment. A's promise is only a benefit to B, and a detriment to A, if it is enforceable. But it will only be enforceable if it is a benefit or a detriment. The argument is circular, and cannot therefore explain why promises are accepted as good consideration.[26] There is no easy answer to this paradox,[27] but the undoubted acceptance by the courts of promises as good consideration casts some doubt on whether benefit and detriment can truly be said to be essential parts of the definition of consideration. It may be that the concept simply requires the performance of, or the promise to perform, some action which the other party would like to be done. This approach ignores the actual or potential detriment. Alternatively, if it is thought that the idea of benefit and detriment is too well established to be discarded, the test must surely be restated so that consideration is provided where a person performs an act which will be a detriment to him or her or a benefit to the other party, or promises to perform such an act. On this analysis, benefit and detriment are not so much essential elements of consideration, as necessary consequences of its performance.

---

25 [1915] AC 847.
26 Cf Atiyah, 1986, p 191.
27 Though Treitel has suggested that an unenforceable promise may nevertheless constitute a benefit or detriment – Treitel, 1976.

3.7 CONSIDERATION NEED NOT BE 'ADEQUATE' BUT MUST BE 'SUFFICIENT'

The view that the element of 'mutuality' is the most important aspect of the doctrine of consideration is perhaps supported by the fact that the courts will not generally inquire into the 'adequacy' of consideration. 'Adequacy' means the question of whether what is provided by way of consideration corresponds in value to what it is being given for. This is to be distinguished from the question of whether consideration is 'sufficient', in the sense that what is being offered in exchange is recognised by the courts as being in law capable of amounting to consideration. This issue is discussed further below.

Looking first, however, at the question of adequacy, the reluctance of the courts to investigate this means, for example, that if I own a car valued at £20,000, and I agree to sell it to you for £1, the courts will treat this as a binding contract.[28] Your agreement to pay £1 provides sufficient consideration for my transfer of ownership of the car, even though it is totally 'inadequate' in terms of its relationship to the value of the car.

This aspect of consideration was confirmed in *Thomas v Thomas*.[29] The testator, Mr Thomas, before his death, expressed a wish that his wife should have for the rest of her life the house in which they had lived. After his death, his executors made an agreement with Mrs Thomas to this effect, expressed to be 'in consideration' of the testator's wishes. There was also an obligation on Mrs Thomas to pay £1 per year, and to keep the house in repair. It was argued that there was no contract here, because Mrs Thomas had provided no sufficient consideration. The court took the view that the statement that the agreement was 'in consideration' of the testator's wishes was not using 'consideration' in its technical contractual sense, but was expressing the motive for making the agreement. The actual 'consideration' was the payment of £1 and the agreement to keep the house in repair. Either of these was clearly recognised as good consideration, even though the payment of £1 could in no way be regarded as anything approaching a commercial rent for the property.

This approach to the question of 'adequacy' may be seen as flowing from a 'freedom of contract' approach. The parties are regarded as being entitled to make their agreement in whatever form, and on whatever terms they wish. The fact that one of the parties appears to be making a bad bargain is no reason for the court's interference. They are presumed to be able to look after themselves, and it is only if there is some evidence of impropriety that the court will inquire further.[30] The mere fact that there is

---

28 This assumes that there is no evidence of any improper behaviour on the part of the purchaser to induce the sale at such a low price, such as misrepresentation (see Chapter 10), duress (see Chapter 12) or the exercise of 'undue influence' (see Chapter 13).

29 (1842) 2 QB 851.

30 See note 27, above. Campbell has argued that the fact that there appear to be exceptions to the basic principle, in that adequacy *will* be relevant in raising suspicions of, for example, duress or undue influence, means that this basic principle of classical theory is 'metaphysical nonsense': Campbell, 1996, p 44.

an apparent imbalance, even a very large one, in the value of what is being exchanged under the contract, will not in itself be the catalyst for such further inquiry. It might be thought that with the decline of the dominance of 'freedom of contract' during the twentieth century, this aspect of the doctrine of consideration might have also weakened, but there is no evidence of this from the case law.[31]

3.7.1 Economic value

Turning to the question of the 'sufficiency' of consideration (that is, whether what is offered is *capable* of amounting to consideration), in coming to its conclusion in *Thomas v Thomas*, the court pointed out that consideration must be 'something which is of some value in the eye of the law'.[32] This has generally been interpreted to mean that it must have some economic value. Thus, the moral obligation which the executors might have felt, or been under, to comply with the testator's wishes would not have been sufficient. An example of the application of this principle may perhaps be found in the case of *White v Bluett*.[33] A father promised not to enforce a promissory note (that is, a document acknowledging a debt) against his son, provided that the son stopped complaining about the distribution of his father's property. It was held that this was not an enforceable agreement, because the son had not provided any consideration. As Pollock CB explained:[34]

> The son had no right to complain, for the father might make what distribution of his property he liked; and the son's abstaining from what he had no right to do can be no consideration.

The courts have not been consistent in this approach, however. In the American case of *Hamer v Sidway*,[35] a promise not to drink alcohol, smoke tobacco, or swear, was held to be good consideration, and in *Ward v Byham*[36] it was suggested that a promise to ensure that a child was happy could be good consideration.

Even in cases which have a more obvious commercial context, the requirement of economic value does not seem to have been applied very strictly. An example is *Chappell & Co v Nestlé Co Ltd*.[37] This case arose out of a 'special offer' of a familiar kind, from

---

31 See, for example, *Chappell & Co Ltd v Nestlé Co Ltd* [1960] AC 87; [1959] 2 All ER 701 – discussed below, 3.7.1.

32 [1842] 2 QB 851, p 859 (per Patteson J).

33 (1853) 23 LJ Ex 36.

34 Ibid, p 37. If the son did actually comply with his father's request, there is an argument that a 'reliance'-based approach would allow the son to recover (subject only to the question of whether this was a situation where there was an intention to create legal obligations – for which see Chapter 4).

35 (1891) 27 NE 256; 124 NY 538. This case may reflect the greater willingness of United States courts to accept 'reasonable reliance' as a basis for contractual liability – see below, 3.15.2.

36 [1956] 2 All ER 318.

37 [1960] AC 87; [1959] 2 All ER 701.

Nestlé, under which a person who sent in three wrappers from bars of their chocolate could buy a record at a special price. For the purpose of the law of copyright, it was important to decide whether the chocolate wrappers were part of the consideration in the contract to buy the record. The House of Lords decided that they were, despite the fact that it was established that they were thrown away by Nestlé, and were thus of no direct value to them.

The only economic value in the wrappers that it is at all possible to discern is that they represented sales of chocolate bars, which was obviously the point of Nestlé's promotion. This is, however, very indirect, particularly as there was no necessity for the person who bought the chocolate to be the same as the person who sent the wrappers in. In contrast to this decision, the House of Lords held in *Lipkin Gorman v Karpnale Ltd*[38] that gambling chips, given in exchange for money by a gambling club to its customers, did not constitute valuable consideration. The case concerned an attempt to recover £154,693 of stolen money which had been received in good faith by the club from a member of the club. If 'good consideration' for the money had been given by the club, then the money could not be recovered by the true owner. What the club had given for the money were plastic chips which could be used for gambling, or to purchase refreshments in the club. Any chips not lost or spent could be reconverted to cash. This was not regarded by the House of Lords as providing consideration for the money, but simply as a mechanism for enabling bets to be made without using cash. If the contract had been one for the straightforward purchase of the chips, then presumably the transfer of ownership of the chips to the member would have been good consideration, since the club presumably made such a contract when it bought the chips from the manufacturer or wholesaler. The fact that the amount of money paid by the member far exceeded the intrinsic value of the chips (that is, their value as pieces of coloured plastic, rather than as a means of gambling) would have been irrelevant under the principle discussed above relating to the adequacy of consideration. The conclusion that on the facts before the court the chips themselves were not consideration must, therefore, be regarded as being governed by the situation in which they were provided. The contractual relationship between the member and the club is probably best analysed in the way suggested by Lord Goff, who took the view that the transaction involved a unilateral contract under which the club issuing the chips agreed to accept them as bets or, indeed, in payment for other services provided by the club. The case should not be treated as giving any strong support to the view that consideration must have some economic value.

An example of the lengths to which the courts will sometimes go to identify consideration is *De La Bere v Pearson*.[39] The plaintiff had written to a newspaper which invited readers to write in for financial advice. Some of the readers' letters, together with the newspaper's financial editor's advice, were published. The plaintiff received

---

38 [1992] 2 AC 548.
39 [1908] 1 KB 280.

and followed negligently given advice which caused him loss. Since the tort of negligent misstatement was at the time unrecognised, the plaintiff had to frame his action in contract. But where was the consideration for the defendants' apparently gratuitous advice? The purchase of the newspaper was one possibility, but there was no evidence that this was done in order to receive advice. The only other possibility, which was favoured by the court, was that the plaintiff, by submitting a letter, had provided free copy which could be published. This was thought to be sufficient consideration for the provision of the advice, which it would be implied should be given with due care.

FOR THOUGHT

Does this decision mean that those who run phone-in radio programmes where advice may be given should always issue disclaimers, to protect themselves from being sued by dissatisfied recipients of advice?

De La Bere v Pearson is a case which might well be considered to be dealt with better by using 'reasonable reliance' as a basis for liability. If it was reasonable in all the circumstances for the plaintiff to rely on the defendant's advice, and he did so to his detriment, he should be able to recover compensation.[40] Such an approach would be more satisfactory than the technical arguments about consideration in which the court was obliged to indulge in applying the classical theory.

The sufficiency of consideration has recently been considered in a different context in *Edmonds v Lawson*.[41] The Court of Appeal was considering whether there was a contract between a pupil barrister and her chambers in relation to pupillage. The problem was to identify what benefit the pupil would supply to her pupilmaster or to chambers during the pupillage. The court noted that the pupil was not obliged to do anything which was not conducive to her own professional development. Moreover, where work of real value was done by the pupil, whether for the pupilmaster or anyone else, there was a professional obligation to remunerate the pupil. This led the court to the conclusion that there was no contract between the pupil and pupilmaster, because of lack of consideration. It came to a different view, however, as to the relationship between the pupil and her chambers. Chambers have an incentive to attract talented pupils who may compete for tenancies (and thus further the development of the chambers). Even if they do not remain at the chambers (for example, by moving to another set, or working in the employed bar or overseas), there may be advantages in the relationships which will have been established. The conclusion was that:[42]

---

40 This, in effect, would now be likely to be the position under the tort of negligent misstatement – discussed in Chapter 10, 10.4.4.
41 [2000] 2 WLR 1091.
42 Ibid, p 1101.

> On balance, we take the view that pupils such as the claimant provide consideration for the offer made by chambers . . . by agreeing to enter into the close, important and potentially very productive relationship which pupillage involves.

The court was therefore prepared to accept the general benefits to chambers in the operation of a pupillage system as being sufficient to amount to consideration in relation to contracts with individual pupils, without defining with any precision the economic value of such benefits.

As these cases illustrate, the requirement of 'economic value' is not particularly strict. Indeed, in the overall pattern of decisions in this area, it is the case of *White v Bluett* (1853) which looks increasingly out of line. The flexibility which the courts have adopted in this area has led Treitel to refer to the concept of 'invented consideration'.[43] This arises where the courts 'regard an act or forbearance as the consideration for a promise even though it may not have been the object of the promisor to secure it'; or 'regard the possibility of some prejudice to the promisee as a detriment without regard to the question of whether it has in fact been suffered'.[44] This analysis has been strongly criticised by Atiyah as an artificial means of reconciling difficult decisions with 'orthodox' doctrine on the nature of consideration.[45] He argues that if something is treated by the courts as consideration, then it is consideration, and that Treitel's 'invented' consideration is in the end the same thing as ordinary consideration. If some cases do not, as a result, fit with orthodox doctrine, then it is the doctrine which needs adjusting.[46]

As we have seen, the issue of the 'sufficiency' of consideration looks to the type, or characteristics, of the thing which has been done or promised, rather than to its value. In addition to the requirement of economic value, which as we have seen is applied flexibly, there are two other issues which must be considered here. The first is the question of so-called 'past consideration'. The second is whether the performance of, or promise to perform, an existing duty can ever amount to consideration.

3.8   PAST CONSIDERATION IS NO CONSIDERATION

Consideration must be given at the time of the contract or at some point after the contract is made. It is not generally possible to use as consideration some act or forbearance which has taken place prior to the contract. Suppose that I take pity on my poverty-stricken niece and give her my old car. If the following week she wins £10,000 on the football pools, and says she will now give me £500 out of her winnings as payment for the car, is that promise enforceable? English law says no, because I have provided no

---

43 See Treitel, 1976, and also 2003, p 71.
44 Ibid.
45 Atiyah, 1986, p 183.
46 Ibid. Atiyah, of course, argues for a broader concept of consideration anyway, as simply being a 'reason' for the enforcement of a promise or obligation. This is discussed further at 3.15.1.

consideration for it. My transfer of the car was undertaken and completed without any thought of payment, and before my niece made her promise. This is 'past consideration' and so cannot be used to enforce an agreement. A case which applies this basic principle is *Roscorla v Thomas*.[47] The plaintiff had bought a horse from the defendant. The defendant then promised that the horse was 'sound and free from vice', which turned out to be untrue. The plaintiff was unable to sue on this promise, however, since he had provided no consideration for it. The sale was already complete before the promise was made.

A more recent example of the same approach is *Re McArdle*.[48] William McArdle left a house to his sons and daughter. One of the sons was living in the house, and carried out various improvements to it. He then got each of his siblings to sign a document agreeing to contribute to the costs of the work. The document was worded in a way which read as though work was to be done, and that when it was completed, the other members of the family would make their contribution out of their share of William McArdle's estate. If that had been a true representation of the facts, then, of course, it would have constituted a binding contract, but, as Jenkins LJ pointed out:[49]

> The true position was that, as the work had in fact all been done and nothing remained to be done . . . at all, the consideration was a wholly past consideration, and therefore the beneficiaries' agreement for the repayment . . . of the £488 out of the estate was *nudum pactum*, a promise with no consideration to support it.

This being so, the agreements to pay were unenforceable.

3.8.1 The common law exceptions

The doctrine of past consideration is not an absolute one, however. The courts have always recognised certain situations where a promise made subsequent to the performance of an act may nevertheless be enforceable. The rules derived from various cases have now been restated as a threefold test by the Privy Council in *Pao On v Lau Yiu Long*.[50] Lord Scarman, delivering the opinion of the Privy Council, recognised that:[51]

> . . . an act done before the giving of a promise to make a payment or to confer some other benefit can sometimes be consideration for the promise.

For the exception to apply, the following three conditions must be satisfied. First, the act must have been done at the promisor's request. This derives from the case of *Lampleigh*

---

47 (1842) 3 QB 234.
48 [1951] Ch 669; [1951] 1 All ER 905.
49 Ibid, p 678; p 910.
50 [1980] AC 614; [1979] 3 All ER 65.
51 Ibid, p 628; p 74.

THE MODERN LAW OF CONTRACT

v Braithwait,[52] where the defendant had asked the plaintiff to seek a pardon for him in relation to a criminal offence which he had committed. After the plaintiff had made considerable efforts to do this, the defendant promised him £100 for his trouble. It was held that the promise was enforceable. Second, the parties must have understood that the act was to be rewarded either by a payment or the conferment of some other benefit. In *Re Casey's Patents*,[53] the plaintiff had managed certain patents on behalf of the defendants. They then promised him a one-third share in consideration of the work which he had done. It was held that the plaintiff must always have assumed that his work was to be paid for in some way. The defendants' promise was simply a crystallisation of this reasonable expectation and was therefore enforceable.

Third, the payment, or conferment of other benefits, must have been legally enforceable had it been promised in advance. There is little that needs to be said about this. It simply means that the usual requirements for a binding agreement must apply.

The effect of these tests is that consideration will be valid to support a later promise, provided that all along there was an expectation of reward. It is very similar to the situation where goods or services are provided without the exact price being specified. As we have seen, the courts will enforce the payment of a reasonable sum for what has been provided. That is, in effect, also what they are doing in situations falling within the three tests outlined above. It is an example of the courts implementing what they see as having been the intention of the parties, taking an approach based on third party objectivity.[54]

It can also be argued that the whole common law doctrine of 'past consideration' could be dealt with more simply, and with very similar results, by an overall principle of 'reasonable reliance'. Thus, in *Re McArdle*, the son did the work before any promise was made by his siblings. He did not, therefore, act in reliance on their promises. By contrast, in *Lampleigh v Braithwait* and *Re Casey's Patents*, the work was done in reliance on a promise or expectation of payment. The advantage of an analysis on these lines is that it involves one general principle governing all situations, rather than stating a general rule and then making it subject to exceptions. This is not, so far, however, the approach of the English courts, which prefer to adhere to at least the form of classical theory.

3.8.2 Exceptions under statute

Two statutory exceptions to the rule that past consideration is no consideration should be briefly noted. First, s 27 of the Bills of Exchange Act 1882 states that:

> Valuable consideration for a bill [of exchange] may be constituted by (a) any consideration sufficient to support a simple contract, (b) an antecedent debt or liability.

---

52 (1615) Hob 105; 80 ER 255.
53 [1892] 1 Ch 104.
54 For which, see Chapter 2, at 2.4.1.

The inclusion of (b) indicates that an existing debt, which is not generally good consideration for a promise,[55] can be so where it is owed by a person receiving the benefit of a promise contained in a bill of exchange.

The second statutory exception is to be found in s 29(5) of the Limitation Act 1980, which provides that where a person liable or accountable for a debt[56] acknowledges it, the right 'shall be treated as having accrued on and not before the date of the acknowledgment'. The acknowledgment must be in writing and signed by the person making it.[57] The relevance of this provision to the current discussion is that if the acknowledgment is in the form of a promise,[58] it will have the effect of extending the limitation period for recovery of the debt, even though no fresh consideration has been given. The statute is thus in effect allowing 'past consideration' to support a new promise.

3.9 PERFORMANCE OF EXISTING DUTIES

Can the performance of, or the promise to perform, an act which the promisor is already under a legal obligation to carry out, ever amount to consideration? Three possible types of existing obligation may exist, and they need to be considered separately. These are first, where the obligation which is alleged to constitute consideration is already imposed by a separate public duty; second, where the same obligation already exists under a contract with a third party; and, third, where the same obligation already exists under a previous contract with the same party by whom the promise is now being made.

3.9.1 Existing duty imposed by law: public policy

Where the promisee is doing something which is a duty imposed by some public obligation, there is a reluctance to allow this to be used as the basis of a contract. It would clearly be contrary to public policy if, for example, an official with the duty to issue licences to market traders was allowed to make enforceable agreements under which the official received personal payment for issuing such a licence. The possibilities for corruption are obvious. It would be equally unacceptable for the householder whose house is on fire to be bound by a promise of payment in return for putting out the fire made to a member of the fire brigade. The difficulty is in discerning whether the refusal to enforce such a contract is on the basis that it is vitiated as being contrary to public policy,[59] or because the consideration which has been provided is not valid. The case law provides no clear answer. The starting point is *Collins v Godefroy*.[60] In this case, a

---

55 See, eg, *Roger v Comptoir d'Escompte de Paris* (1869) LR 2 CP 393.
56 Or other 'liquidated pecuniary claim'.
57 Limitation Act 1980, s 30(1).
58 It need not be so: *Surrendra Overseas Ltd v Government of Sri Lanka* [1977] 1 WLR 565, p 575.
59 This is discussed further in Chapter 14.
60 (1831) 1 B & Ald 950; 120 ER 241.

promise had been made to pay a witness, who was under an order to attend the court, six guineas for his trouble. It was held that this promise was unenforceable, because there was no consideration for it. This seems to have been on the basis that the duty to attend was 'a duty imposed by law'.

In cases where the possibilities for extortion are less obvious, there has been a greater willingness to regard performance of an existing non-contractual legal duty as being good consideration, though it must be said that the clearest statements to that effect have come from one judge, that is, Lord Denning. In *Ward v Byham*,[61] the duty was that of a mother to look after her illegitimate child. The father promised to make payments, provided that the child was well looked after and happy, and was allowed to decide with whom she should live. Only the looking after of the child could involve the provision of things of 'economic value' sufficient to amount to consideration, but the mother was already obliged to do this. Lord Denning had no doubt that this could, nevertheless, be good consideration:[62]

> I have always thought that a promise to perform an existing duty, or the perform-ance of it, should be regarded as good consideration, because it is a benefit to the person to whom it is given.

The other two members of the Court of Appeal were not as explicit as Lord Denning, and seem to have regarded the whole package of what the father asked for as amount-ing to good consideration. This clearly went beyond the mother's existing obligation, but, as has been pointed out,[63] did not involve anything of economic value. So, on either basis, the decision raises difficulties as regards consideration. Lord Denning returned to the same point in *Williams v Williams*,[64] which concerned a promise by a husband to make regular payments to his wife, who had deserted him, in return for her promise to maintain herself 'out of the said weekly sum or otherwise'. The question arose as to whether this provided any consideration for the husband's promise, since a wife in desertion had no claim on her husband for maintenance, and was in any case bound to support herself. Once again, Lord Denning commented:[65]

> . . . a promise to perform an existing duty is, I think, sufficient consideration to support a promise, so long as there is nothing in the transaction which is contrary to the public interest.

Once again, the other members of the Court of Appeal managed to find in the wife's favour without such an explicit statement. What this quote from Lord Denning makes

---

61 [1956] 2 All ER 318.
62 Ibid, p 319.
63 See above, 3.7.1.
64 [1957] 1 All ER 305.
65 Ibid, p 307.

clear, however, is that he regards the rule against using an existing non-contractual duty as consideration as being based on the requirements of the public interest, which would arise in the examples using government officials of one kind or another. Where this element is not present, however, he is saying that an existing duty of this kind can provide good consideration.

The law on this issue remains uncertain but, in view of the position in relation to duties owed to third parties, and recent developments in relation to duties already owed under a contract with the promisor (that is, in the case of *Williams v Roffey*), it seems likely that Lord Denning's approach would be followed. There does not seem to be any general hostility in English law to the argument that an existing duty can provide good consideration. In other words, performance of, or the promise to perform, an existing 'public' duty imposed by law can be good consideration, provided that there is no conflict with the public interest.[66]

FOR THOUGHT

Is this an area in which a 'reliance'-based approach might provide a better answer? It would still be necessary to exclude situations where public policy suggests that payments should not be enforceable. In other situations where there is a 'duty', the question would still arise as to whether the claimant's actions were undertaken in reliance on the defendant's promise, or simply because they were under a duty. This would be a question of fact, however, rather than law.

3.9.2 Public duty: exceeding the duty

Whatever the correct answer to the above situation, it is clear that if what is promised or done goes beyond the existing duty imposed by law, then it can be regarded as good consideration. This applies whatever the nature of the duty, so that even as regards public officials, consideration may be provided by exceeding their statutory or other legal obligations. The point was confirmed in *Glasbrook Bros v Glamorgan CC*.[67] In the course of a strike at a coal mine, the owners of the mine were concerned that certain workers who had the obligation of keeping the mines safe and in good repair should not be prevented from carrying out their duties. They sought the assistance of the police in this. The police suggested the provision of a mobile group, but the owners insisted that the officers should be billeted on the premises. For this, the owners promised to pay. Subsequently, however, they tried to deny any obligation to pay, claiming that the police were doing no more than fulfilling their legal obligation to keep the peace. It was held

---

66 [1991] 1 QB 1; [1990] 1 All ER 512 – discussed below, at 3.9.8.
67 [1925] AC 270.

by the House of Lords that the provision of the force billeted on the premises went beyond what the police were obliged to do. Viscount Cave LC accepted that if the police were simply taking the steps which they considered necessary to keep the peace, etc, members of the public, who already pay for these police services through taxation, could not be made to pay again. Nevertheless, if, at the request of a member of the public, the police provided services which went beyond what they (the police) reasonably considered necessary, this could provide good consideration for a promise of payment.

This rule is now generally accepted, so that wherever the performance of an act goes beyond the performer's public duty, it will be capable of providing consideration for a promise.

In relation to the police, however, the position is now dealt with largely by statute. Section 25(1) of the Police Act 1996 states that:

> The chief officer of a police force may provide, at the request of any person, special police services at any premises or in any locality in the police area for which the force is maintained, subject to the payment to the police authority of charges on such scales as may be determined by that authority.

In *Harris v Sheffield Utd FC*,[68] which concerned the provision of policing for football matches, the court confirmed the approach taken in *Glasbrook*. Moreover, in applying the predecessor to s 25 of the Police Act 1996,[69] the Court of Appeal held that if a football club decided to hold matches and requested a police presence, such presence could constitute 'special police services' even though it did not go beyond what the police felt was necessary to maintain the peace. A 'request' for a police presence could be implied if police attendance was necessary to enable the club to conduct its matches safely. The football club was therefore held liable to pay for the services provided. It seems, therefore, that the holding of an 'event' to which the public are invited, but which cannot safely be allowed to go ahead without a police presence, will lay the organisers open to paying for 'special services'. To that extent, the position has gone beyond that which applied in *Glasbrook*, in that under the statute the police can receive payment even though they are only doing what they feel is necessary to keep the peace. The Court of Appeal's decision in *Harris* clearly applies to sporting events and entertainments. It is unclear whether it could apply to political rallies or demonstrations, though Balcombe LJ stated that, in his view, political events fell into a different category:[70]

> I do not accept that the cases are *in pari materia* and I do not consider that dismissal of this appeal poses any threat to the political freedoms which the citizen of this country enjoys.

---

68 [1987] 2 All ER 838.
69 That is, Police Act 1964, s 15, which used the same wording as s 25 of the 1996 Act.
70 [1987] 2 All ER 838, p 850.

Nevertheless, the effect of the interpretation of the statutory provisions adopted in *Harris* means that in certain circumstances the police can receive payment for doing no more than carrying out their duty to maintain public order.

3.9.3 Existing contractual duty owed to third party

If a person is already bound to perform a particular act under a contract, can the performance of, or promise to perform, this act amount to good consideration for a contract with someone else? Suppose that A is contractually bound to deliver 5,000 widgets to B by 1 June. B is to use these widgets in producing items which he has contracted to supply to C. C therefore has an interest in A performing the contract for delivery to B on time, and promises A £5,000 if the goods are delivered by 1 June. Can A enforce this payment by C if the goods are delivered to B on the date required? Perhaps somewhat surprisingly, the courts have given a clear positive answer to this question. In other words, they have been quite happy to accept that doing something which forms part, or indeed the whole, of the consideration in one contract can perfectly well also be consideration in another contract.

The starting point is the case of *Shadwell v Shadwell*.[71] An uncle promised his nephew, who was about to get married, the sum of £150 a year until the nephew's annual income as a barrister reached 600 guineas. The uncle paid 12 instalments on this basis, but then he died, and the payments ceased. The nephew sued the uncle's estate for the outstanding instalments, to which the defence was raised that the nephew had provided no consideration. The nephew put forward his going through with the marriage as consideration. At the time, a promise to marry was as between the parties a legally enforceable contract.[72] Nevertheless, the majority of the court had no doubt that performance of this contract could be used as consideration for the uncle's promise, on the basis that that promise was in effect an inducement to the nephew to go through with the marriage. Erle CJ recognised that there was some delicacy involved in categorising the nephew's marriage to the woman of his choice as a 'detriment' to him, but nevertheless considered that in financial terms it might well be. He put the issue in these terms:[73]

> ... do these facts shew a loss sustained by the plaintiff at his uncle's request? When I answer this in the affirmative, I am aware that a man's marriage with the woman of his choice is in one sense a boon, and in that sense the reverse of a loss: yet, as between the plaintiff and the party promising to supply an income to support the marriage, it may well be also a loss. The plaintiff may have made a most material change in his position, and induced the object of his affection to do the same, and may have incurred pecuniary liabilities resulting in embarrassments

---

71 (1860) 9 CBNS 159; 142 ER 62.
72 This is no longer the case as a result of the Law Reform (Miscellaneous Provisions) Act 1970, s 1.
73 (1860) 9 CBNS 159, p 173; 142 ER 62, p 68.

which would be in every sense a loss if the income which had been promised should be withheld.

Moreover, a marriage, while primarily affecting the parties to it, 'may be an object of interest to a near relative, and in that sense a benefit to him'. Thus, not only was going through with the marriage a 'detriment' to the nephew, it was also a 'benefit' to his uncle. On this basis, there was no doubt that it could constitute good consideration for the promise to pay the annuity.

The dissenting judge in *Shadwell*, Byles J, was not convinced that the uncle's promise was made on the basis that it was *in return* for the nephew getting married. There is some force in this view of the facts,[74] and a possible construction of the case is that the majority of the court was 'inventing' consideration, because it felt that the nephew had relied on his uncle's promise. If the nephew had organised his affairs on the basis that he would continue to receive the payment – a reliance reinforced by the fact that payments had been made regularly over 12 years – then it would be unfair to withdraw it.[75] Such an analysis is relevant to the general issue of 'reliance' as an alternative to consideration, as discussed at the end of this chapter. It is, however, the majority view in *Shadwell v Shadwell* that has been accepted by later courts, and the case is therefore taken as authority for the proposition that performance of a contractual obligation owed to a third party can be good consideration to found a contract with another promisor.

3.9.4 Duty to third party: commercial application

The approach taken in *Shadwell v Shadwell* was subsequently applied in a commercial context in *Scotson v Pegg*,[76] where it was held that the delivery of a cargo of coal to the defendant constituted good consideration, even though the plaintiff was already contractually bound to a third party to make such delivery. It was more recently accepted as good law in *New Zealand Shipping Co Ltd v Satterthwaite, The Eurymedon*.[77] Goods were being carried on a ship. The carriers contracted with a firm of stevedores to unload the ship. The consignees of the goods were taken to have promised the stevedores the benefit of an exclusion clause contained in the contract of carriage if the stevedores unloaded the goods. The Privy Council viewed the stevedores' performance of their unloading contract as being good consideration for this promise. As Lord Wilberforce said:[78]

---

74 Which appears to have been accepted by Salmon LJ in *Jones v Padavatton* [1969] 2 All ER 616, p 621.
75 See the comments of Collins, 2003.
76 (1861) 6 H & N 295.
77 [1975] AC 154; [1974] 1 All ER 1015.
78 Ibid, p 168; p 1021.

An agreement to do an act which the promisor is under an existing obligation to a third party to do, may quite well amount to consideration and does so in the present case: the promisee obtains the benefit of a direct obligation which he can enforce.

3.9.5 Performance or promise?

In all three cases so far considered, it has been *performance* of the existing obligation which has constituted the consideration. Can a promise to perform an existing obligation also amount to consideration? Take the example used at the start of this section, where A is bound to deliver goods to B on 1 June, and C promises A £5,000 if he does so. We have seen that if A does deliver by the specified date, he will, on the basis of *Shadwell v Shadwell* and *Scotson v Pegg*, be able to recover the promised £5,000 from C. What if, however, A also promises to C that he will deliver by 1 June? In other words, the contract, instead of being unilateral ('if you deliver to B by 1 June I will pay you £5,000') becomes bilateral? A promises to deliver by 1 June; C promises £5,000. Is A's promise to perform in a way to which he is already committed by his contract with B sufficient consideration for C's promise, so that, if A fails to deliver on time, C, as well as B, may sue A? The reference by Lord Reid in the quotation given above to 'an agreement to do an act' would suggest that a promise is sufficient, though the facts of *The Eurymedon* itself clearly involved a unilateral contract ('if you unload the goods, we promise you the benefit of the exclusion clause'). The issue was, however, addressed more directly by the Privy Council in *Pao On v Lau Yiu Long*,[79] where it was held that such a promise could be good consideration. Citing *The Eurymedon*, Lord Scarman simply stated:[80]

> Their Lordships do not doubt that a promise to perform, or the performance of, a pre-existing contractual obligation to a third party can be valid consideration.

Given the general approach to consideration, under which promises themselves can be good consideration, this decision is entirely consistent. The law on this point is, therefore, straightforward and simple. The fact that what is promised or performed is something which the promisor is already committed to do under a contract with someone else is irrelevant. Provided it has the other characteristics of valid consideration, it will be sufficient to make the new agreement enforceable.

3.9.6 Existing duty to the same promisor

The issue of whether performance of an existing duty owed to the same promisor can be good consideration is the most difficult one in this area. If there is a contract between A and B, and A then promises B additional money for the performance of the

---

79 [1980] AC 614; [1979] 3 All ER 65.
80 Ibid, p 632; p 76.

same contract, is this promise binding? It would seem that the general answer should be 'no'. It is normally considered that once a contract is made, its terms are fixed. Any variation, to be binding, must be mutual, in the sense of both sides offering something additional. If the promise is simply to carry out exactly the same performance for extra money, it is totally one-sided. It would amount to a rewriting of the contract, and so should be unenforceable.[81]

This approach was, until relatively recently, taken to represent English law on this point. The authority was said to be the case of *Stilk v Myrick*.[82] The dispute in this case arose out of a contract between the crew of a ship and its owners. The crew had been employed to sail the ship from London to the Baltic and back. Part way through the voyage, some of the crew deserted. The captain promised that if the rest of the crew sailed the ship back without the missing crew, the wages of the deserters would be divided among those who remained. When the ship returned to London, the owners refused to honour this promise. It was held that the sailors could not recover. The basis for the decision in *Stilk v Myrick* is not without controversy, not least because of the fact that it was reported in two rather different ways in the two published reports (that is, Campbell and Espinasse).[83] There was, for example, some suggestion that this decision was based on public policy, in that there was a risk in this type of situation of the crew 'blackmailing' the captain into promising extra wages to avoid being stranded. This had been the approach taken in the earlier, similar, case of *Harris v Watson*.[84] This issue, and the alternative views of *Stilk v Myrick*, is one to which we shall need to return later. For the moment, however, we will deal with the case in the way in which it has been traditionally treated as part of the 'classical' law of contract. This view of it has been based on the judgment of Lord Ellenborough, as reported by Campbell. He seemed to base his decision on the lack of consideration, rather than public policy. The remaining crew were only promising to do what they were already obliged to do under their existing contract, and this could not be good consideration. The desertion of part of the crew was just part of the normal hazards of the voyage. Campbell's report records Lord Ellenborough's views in the following way:[85]

> There was no consideration for the ulterior pay promised to the mariners who remained with the ship. Before they sailed from London, they had undertaken to do all that they could under all the emergencies of the voyage. They had sold all their services till the voyage should be completed . . . the desertion of a part of the crew is to be considered an emergency of the voyage as much as their death; and

---

81 This illustrates the difficulty which the classical doctrine of consideration has in dealing with relational contracts, where the modification of obligations may well be necessary and expected: see Chapter 1, 1.5.

82 (1809) 2 Camp 317; 170 ER 1168; 6 Esp 129; 170 ER 851.

83 See, for example, Luther, 1999; Gilmore, 1974, pp 22–28.

84 (1791) Peake 102.

85 (1809) 2 Camp 317, p 319; 170 ER 1168, p 1169.

those who remain are bound by the terms of their original contract to exert themselves to the utmost to bring the ship in safely to her destined port.

It might have been otherwise if they had not contracted for the whole voyage, and had been free to leave at the time of the desertion, or if the captain had 'capriciously' dismissed part of the crew (rather than some sailors having deserted). Such circumstances would fall outside the normal hazards of the voyage. Thus, in either of these cases, the remaining crew might not have been compelled by the original contract to proceed with the voyage, and would therefore have provided good consideration by agreeing to do so. On the facts which had actually occurred, however, they had not provided any consideration for the promise of extra money, and so could not recover it.

3.9.7 Going beyond the existing duty

It is implicit in *Stilk v Myrick* that if the crew had gone beyond their existing duty, they would have provided good consideration. In addition to the examples given by Lord Ellenborough, the decision in *Hartley v Ponsonby*[86] suggests that a certain level of desertion may in fact give rise to a situation falling outside the normal hazards of the voyage. In this case, a ship which had started out with a crew of 36 had, at the time that the relevant promise was made to the plaintiff, only 19 left, of whom only four or five were able seamen. In this situation, it was held that the voyage had become so dangerous that it was unreasonable to require the crew to continue. In effect (though the decision does not use this terminology), the original contract with the plaintiff had been 'frustrated',[87] and therefore a fresh contract on the revised (more favourable) terms could be created. The performance of, or promise to perform, actions which are inside an existing duty cannot, however, amount to consideration.

3.9.8 A re-consideration: *Williams v Roffey*[88]

The true basis for the decision in *Stilk v Myrick* is not without dispute, not least because of the differences noted above between the two published reports.[89] Nevertheless, the analysis outlined above (based mainly on Campbell's report) has been accepted and applied, almost without question, in many cases.[90] In 1990, however, a decision of the Court of Appeal cast some doubt on its scope and continued validity. The case was *Williams v Roffey Bros & Nicholls (Contractors) Ltd*,[91] which was concerned with a

---

86 (1857) 7 E & B 872.
87 The doctrine of frustration is fully discussed in Chapter 16.
88 [1991] 1 QB 1; [1990] 1 All ER 512.
89 See, for example, Luther, 1999; Gilmore, 1974, pp 22–28.
90 For example, *North Ocean Shipping Co Ltd v Hyundai Construction Co* [1979] QB 705; [1978] 3 All ER 1170; *Atlas Express v Kafco* [1989] QB 833; [1989] 1 All ER 641.
91 [1991] 1 QB 1; [1990] 1 All ER 512.

contract to refurbish a block of flats. The defendants were the main contractors for this work, and had engaged the plaintiffs as sub-contractors to carry out carpentry work. The agreed price for this was £20,000. Part way through the contract, the plaintiffs got into financial difficulties, at least in part because the contract price for the carpentry work was too low. The defendants were worried that the plaintiffs would not complete the work on time or would stop work altogether. There was a penalty clause in the main contract under which the defendants would have been liable in the event of late completion. The defendants therefore promised to pay the plaintiffs a further £10,300, at a rate of £575 for each flat completed. On this basis, the plaintiffs continued to work on the flats, and completed a further eight. Because, at this stage, it seemed that the defendants were going to default on their promise of additional payments, the plaintiffs then ceased work, and subsequently sued for the additional sums in relation to the eight completed flats. The county court judge found for the plaintiffs, and the defendants appealed. The main issue before the Court of Appeal was whether there was any consideration for the promise to make the additional payments.

The defendants argued that since the plaintiffs, in completing or promising to complete the work on the flats, were only doing something they were already bound to do under the existing contract with the defendants, they provided no new consideration.

In considering these arguments, Glidewell LJ first outlined the benefits (as identified by counsel for the defendants) that accrued to the defendants from the plaintiffs' continuation with the contract. These were:[92]

> . . . (i) seeking to ensure that the plaintiff continued work and did not stop in breach of the sub-contract; (ii) avoiding the penalty for delay; and (iii) avoiding the trouble and expense of engaging other people to complete the carpentry work.

In the view of Glidewell LJ and the rest of the Court of Appeal, this was enough to support the defendant's promise to make the additional payments. In reaching this conclusion, all members of the court were at pains to stress that they were not suggesting that the principle in *Stilk v Myrick* was wrong, but that the present case could be distinguished from it.

FOR THOUGHT

Do you think the Court of Appeal would have come to the same conclusion had it been the carpenters who had sought extra payments from the defendants, as the price for continuing to work on the flats, rather than the defendants taking the initiative in offering the money?

---

92 [1991] 1 QB 1, p 11; [1990] 1 All ER 512, p 518.

3.9.9 *Williams v Roffey*: effect on *Stilk v Myrick* [93]

The basis on which the court distinguished *Williams v Roffey* from *Stilk v Myrick* is not wholly clear from the judgments. Similar benefits to those identified could be said to have been present in *Stilk v Myrick*. For example, as a result of his promise, the captain did not have to seek replacement crew, avoided delays, and made sure the existing crew continued to work.[94] The main reason for distinguishing *Stilk v Myrick* seems in fact to have been related to the alternative, public policy basis for the decision mentioned above. In other words, the court regarded it as significant that there was in *Williams v Roffey* no question of improper pressure having been put on the defendants. Indeed, it was they who suggested the increased payments.

The result is that the position as regards duties owed to the promisor is closely assimilated to the position in relation to duties owed to third parties. Thus, Glidewell LJ summarised the current state of the law as follows:[95]

> . . . (i) if A has entered into a contract with B to do work for, or to supply goods or services to, B in return for payment by B; and (ii) at some stage before A has completely performed his obligations under the contract B has reason to doubt whether A will, or will be able to, complete his side of the bargain; and (iii) B thereupon promises A an additional payment in return for A's promise to perform his contractual obligations on time; and (iv) as a result of giving his promise B obtains in practice a benefit, or obviates a disbenefit; then (v) the benefit to B is capable of being consideration for B's promise, so that the promise will be legally binding.

Williams v Roffey is clearly very significant as regards defining the limits of valid consideration, and undoubtedly has the effect of widening those limits. Promises to perform existing obligations can now amount to consideration, even between contracting parties. Nevertheless, within these wider limits, consideration must still be found, as Russell LJ makes clear:[96]

> Consideration there must . . . be but in my judgment the courts nowadays should be more ready to find its existence so as to reflect the intention of the parties to the contract where the bargaining powers are not unequal and where the finding of consideration reflects the true intention of the parties.

This statement indicates the fact that despite the extensive intervention by Parliament to control various aspects of the contractual relationship in particular situations, where

---

93 For further discussion of the potential implications of *Williams v Roffey*, see Halson, 1990; Hird and Blair, 1996.

94 See, also, *Lee v GEC Plessey Telecommunications* [1993] IRLR 383, discussed below.

95 [1991] 1 QB 1, p 16; [1990] 1 All ER 512, p 521.

96 Ibid, p 18; p 524.

the courts are dealing with a business transaction between parties who are more or less equal, they still adhere to the classical principles of freedom of contract. The starting point is to decide what the parties have agreed, and what their intentions were. Once these have been identified, the courts will as far as possible give effect to them, unless there is a good reason for taking another approach. In *Williams v Roffey*, the courts were faced with what appeared to be a clear arrangement entered into voluntarily, and which in the end has the potential to be for the benefit of both parties. In such a situation, arguments taking a narrow view of the scope of the doctrine of consideration, which might allow one party to escape the effects of a promise, freely given, from which it had gained some advantage, were inappropriate and unnecessary.

The approach taken in *Williams v Roffey* has subsequently been applied in two first instance decisions concerning commercial contracts – that is, *Anangel Atlas Compania Naviera SA v Ishikawajima-Harima Heavy Industries Co Ltd (No 2)* [97] and *Simon Container Machinery Ltd v Emba Machinery AB*.[98] In both cases, the avoidance of the other party withdrawing from a contract was held to be sufficient 'practical benefit' to provide consideration for a new promise designed to keep them 'on board'. In *Lee v GEC Plessey Telecommunications*,[99] *Williams v Roffey* was cited as supporting the view that, in the context of a contract of employment, the employees provide sufficient consideration for an award of enhanced pay or redundancy terms by continuing to work under the contract. The abandoning by the employee of any argument that the pay should be even higher or the terms even more favourable means that 'the employer has secured a benefit and avoided a detriment'.[100] If this is taken at its face value, then it clearly consigns *Stilk v Myrick* to history. The seamen in accepting the offer of additional money and not continuing to bargain for more would be providing sufficient benefit to the employer and suffering sufficient detriment themselves to amount to consideration for the Master's promise. The most recent reference to *Williams v Roffey* in the High Court, however, suggests a more sceptical approach. In *South Caribbean Trading Ltd v Trafigura Beheer BV*,[101] the claimant had only agreed to unload a cargo of oil on the basis that a letter of credit was extended by the defendants. One question was whether the unloading of the oil, which the claimants were already obliged to do, could constitute good consideration for the promise to extend the letter of credit. The judge found the existence of other consideration, but stated, *obiter*, that he would not have treated the promise to unload as good consideration. He noted that this would be contrary to the principle in *Stilk v Myrick*. As regards *Williams v Roffey* he said:[102]

---

97 [1990] 2 Lloyd's Rep 526.
98 [1998] 2 Lloyd's Rep 429.
99 [1993] IRLR 383.
100 Ibid, p 389.
101 [2004] EWHC 2576; [2005] 1 Lloyd's Rep 128.
102 Ibid, para 107.

But for the fact that *Williams v Roffey Bros* was a decision of the Court of Appeal, I would not have followed it. That decision is inconsistent with the long-standing rule that consideration, being the price of the promise sued upon, must move *from* the promisee.

He felt that the Court of Appeal in *Williams v Roffey* had relied too much on analogies with three-party situations, to which different considerations applied. Since, however, as he put it, the case had 'not yet been held by the House of Lords to have been wrongly decided',[103] he would have needed to distinguish it. This he would have done on the basis that the claimants in this case had put pressure, analogous to economic duress, on the defendants to accept the variation in the contract. On that basis the case was different from *Williams v Roffey*. This view may or may not be significant. It is only the opinion of one High Court judge and, as we have seen, other judges have been prepared to follow and apply *Williams v Roffey*. Only the House of Lords will be able to determine whether it was not rightly decided; for the time being, it is binding on the lower courts.

Another response to *Williams v Roffey* and the subsequent cases is to suggest that, despite the fact that the decisions are put in the language of consideration, they are in fact examples of the courts basing contractual liability on reasonable reliance. In other words, the carpenters in *Williams v Roffey* had relied on the promise of extra money in completing the flats, and it was therefore right (in the absence of any suggestion of impropriety on their part in extracting the promise) that they should be able to recover this. The application of this principle to *Stilk v Myrick* would also lead to the seamen being able to recover, on the basis that their continued crewing of the ship was based on the promise of extra payment. The questions then become issues of fact: Was any improper pressure applied? Was there *in fact* any reliance?[104] Such issues are likely to be easier to determine than technical arguments based on what precisely constitutes consideration.

3.9.10   Limitation on *Williams v Roffey*

One limitation on the effect of the decision in *Williams v Roffey* was made clear by the Court of Appeal in *Re Selectmove*.[105] The case concerned an assertion by a company that it had made a binding contract with the Inland Revenue under which it could, effectively, pay off its tax liabilities by instalments. The Inland Revenue argued that this agreement was not binding on them, because the company provided no consideration for the agreement to accept instalments: it was only promising to do something (paying its debts) which it was already obliged to do. The Court of Appeal, while deciding the

---

103 [2004] EWHC 2576; [2005] 1 Lloyd's Rep 128, para 109
104 In other words, could it be shown that, as a matter of fact, the sailors did not rely on the promise, but would have continued to work in any case?
105 [1995] 2 All ER 534; [1995] 1 WLR 474.

case in favour of the Inland Revenue on another point, considered whether *Williams v Roffey* could apply in this situation. The company argued that the arrangement was to the Inland Revenue's 'practical benefit', because it meant that the company could stay in business, and therefore be more likely to meet its debts. The Court of Appeal, however, felt that this would be the case in relation to any agreement to pay by instalments. To treat this as providing consideration would be in direct conflict with the leading House of Lords decision on part payment of debts, that is, *Foakes v Beer*,[106] which had not even been cited in *Williams v Roffey*. The effect of *Foakes v Beer* is that promises relating to the payment of existing debts have to be treated as a separate category from promises concerned with other types of existing contractual obligation. In general, a promise to pay a debt in instalments after the due date (or the payment on the due date of less than was owed) will not amount to consideration for any promise by the creditor (such as to accept such method of payment, or to remit the whole debt where only partial payment was tendered). The reversing of the decision in *Foakes v Beer* was a matter for the House of Lords, or Parliament, and could not be undertaken by the Court of Appeal.

FOR THOUGHT

Would it make a difference in *Selectmove* if a 'reliance' analysis were adopted? The question would be whether the company had altered its position, to its potential detriment, in reliance on the Inland Revenue's promise. It is not clear on the facts that it had done so, and so the result under this analysis might be the same as that achieved by using 'consideration'.

The current position is, therefore, that in relation to a promise to supply goods or services, a renewed promise to perform an existing obligation can be good consideration if the other party will receive a 'practical benefit', but that in relation to debts, a promise to make payment will only be consideration if accompanied by some additional benefit, such as payment early or, perhaps, in a different place.[107]

3.10 CONSIDERATION AND THE VARIATION OF CONTRACTS

The above discussion leads conveniently into a review of the more general issue of the way in which the doctrine of consideration affects the freedom of parties to vary the obligations under a contract which they have entered into. This is an area where

---

106 (1884) 9 App Cas 605. This case is discussed in detail below, at 3.13.2.

107 Note that this restriction does not seem to have been accepted in Australia where, in *Musumeci v Winadell Pty Ltd* (1994) 34 NSWLR 723, Santow J, while noting *Re Selectmove,* applied the *Williams v Roffey* approach to a promise to accept a reduction in the rent payable on a lease.

classical theory has considerable difficulty in coping with the relational aspect of many contracts.[108]

3.10.1   Need for accord and satisfaction

We have already referred to the general principle under classical theory that for a contract to be altered, there must be consideration. To use the language often adopted by the courts, 'accord and satisfaction' must be present: 'accord' meaning agreement and 'satisfaction' essentially consideration. The approach taken in *Stilk v Myrick*,[109] as redefined in *Williams v Roffey*,[110] fits into this general principle. The same approach applies where a contract is brought to an end by mutual agreement. As long as there are outstanding obligations on both sides of the contract, the agreement to terminate will be binding. The foregoing of the existing rights under the contract will amount to good consideration for the promise to release the other party from his or her obligation.

3.10.2   The concept of 'waiver'

Over the years, however, this approach, though still applied where appropriate, has often been found in practice to be too restrictive. Why should parties who are on an equal footing, and who wish to vary obligations under an existing contract, not be allowed to do so, without worrying about the technicality of 'consideration'? Various concepts have been used to allow more flexibility, and to give some force to agreed variations, even where these are not supported by consideration.[111] One such is the concept of 'waiver'. Under this principle, a person who 'waives' (that is, promises not to enforce) certain rights under a contract for a period of time may be stopped from later insisting on performance in accordance with the letter of the contract. So, in *Hartley v Hymans*,[112] a seller requested to be allowed to make late delivery, and the buyer agreed to this. When the seller delivered, the buyer refused to accept. It was held that the seller was entitled to recover damages, despite the fact that delivery was outside the terms of the contract and that the buyer's promise to accept late delivery was unsupported by consideration. The buyer had waived the right to insist on delivery at a particular time and could not go back on that.

Waiver was used by the common law courts, but was then taken over by the chancery courts, and is now almost exclusively an equitable concept. It is important to note that waiver may not be permanent in its effect. The person waiving the rights may do so for a fixed period of time, or may be able to revive the original right by giving

---

108 See Chapter 1, 1.5.
109 (1809) 2 Camp 317; 170 ER 1168; 6 Esp 129; 170 ER 851.
110 [1991] 1 QB 1; [1990] 1 All ER 512.
111 This, it may be suggested, illustrates the weakness of the classical doctrine of consideration: the more the exceptions mount, the less it can really be said to provide a coherent governing principle.
112 [1920] 3 KB 475.

notice. The latter was the case in *Charles Rickards Ltd v Oppenheim*.[113] The contract here was for the building of a car body to fit a Rolls Royce chassis. The suppliers promised the buyer that they could fulfil the contract in 'six or, at the most, seven months'. The precise specification of the work to be done was agreed on 20 August 1947. The latest time for delivery, according to the suppliers' promise, was therefore 20 March 1948. The suppliers failed to meet this deadline, which was held to be a term of the original contract. The buyer, however, did not sue for breach of contract as soon as the date had passed, but continued to seek delivery. This was regarded as the buyer having waived the right to delivery at a particular time.

Although there was continued delay, the buyer would not have been able to refuse delivery if the car had been finished in April, May or June 1948. By the end of June, however, the buyer's patience ran out, and on 29 June 1948 he told the suppliers that unless the car was delivered by 25 July 1948, he would not accept it. The car was not in fact finished until 18 October 1948. The suppliers then sued for non-acceptance, on the basis of the buyer's waiver of the original term specifying a date for delivery. The Court of Appeal, however, did not accept that such a waiver was permanent in its effect. As Lord Denning put it:[114]

> It would be most unreasonable if, having been lenient and having waived the initial expressed time, [the buyer] should thereby have prevented himself from ever thereafter insisting on reasonably quick delivery. In my judgment, he was entitled to give a reasonable notice making time of the essence of the matter.

On the facts, the notice of four weeks given on 29 June 1948 was reasonable and, once it had expired, the buyer – having waited many months for his car – was entitled to cancel the contract. A waiver of rights will, therefore, generally be capable of withdrawal on the giving of reasonable notice.

Looked at in this way, the concept of equitable waiver has clear links with the common law concept of estoppel. This is the rule whereby, if A, a party to an action, has made a statement of fact on which the other party, B, has relied, A will not be allowed to deny that the original statement was untrue.[115] This rule applies only to statements of existing fact, however. In *Jorden v Money*,[116] an attempt was made to apply it to a promise not to enforce a debt. Mrs Jorden had made repeated statements that she would not enforce a bond for £1,200 issued by Money, which she held. On the basis of that assurance, Money married. He then sought a declaration from the courts that the debt had been abandoned. He succeeded at first instance, but the House of

---

113 [1950] 1 KB 616; [1950] 1 All ER 420.
114 Ibid, p 624; p 423.
115 As will be seen from this description, estoppel is based on reliance. Waiver might also be said to be based on the fact that a person relies on the other party's promise not to enforce a particular contractual obligation.
116 (1854) 5 HL 185.

Lords took a different view. Lord Cranworth LC, having stated the general principles of the doctrine of estoppel, continued:[117]

> I think that that doctrine does not apply to a case where the representation is not a representation of fact, but a statement of something which the party intends or does not intend to do.

Whereas the former type of statement (representation of fact) may provide the basis of an enforceable estoppel, the latter type (statement as to future intentions) can only become enforceable by being made part of a contract. Mrs Jorden's statements were of the latter type and, therefore, since they had not been made as part of a contract, were not enforceable. This decision established, therefore, that the doctrine of estoppel in the strict sense had no application to promises. Atiyah has argued forcefully that the orthodox view of *Jorden v Money* misunderstands what lay behind the reason why counsel argued it on the basis of estoppel rather than contract.[118] This was not that there was a lack of consideration for the promise not to enforce the debt. Atiyah argues that the marriage would have provided such consideration, since it was action taken in reliance on the promise (even though not requested by the promisor).[119] The problem was that, at the time, the Statute of Frauds 1677 required such a promise to be evidenced in writing. Since there was no writing available, the plaintiff tried to plead the case in estoppel rather than contract. The court, however, would not allow this to be used as a means of circumventing the requirements of the Statute of Frauds. To do so, as Atiyah points out, would have constituted a significant undermining of the statute – 'for it would have meant that any plaintiff who could show that he had altered his position in reliance on the defendant's promise could ignore the statute and rely on estoppel'.[120]

Nevertheless, even if *Jorden v Money* has been misunderstood (and not all commentators would agree with Atiyah),[121] it has been generally accepted in subsequent cases as establishing that estoppel can only be used in relation to statements of existing fact.[122] This means that simply because action was taken in reliance on a promise, this will not in itself generally render the promise enforceable. To mitigate the practical problems caused by this analysis, particularly where the parties are in agreement about wishing to vary the terms of a contract, in the last 50 years the courts have developed the concept of equitable waiver into a broader doctrine, generally referred to as 'promissory estoppel'.

---

117 Ibid, p 214.
118 See Atiyah, 1986, at pp 234–38. The same point is made by Baker, 1979, p 27.
119 Cf *Shadwell v Shadwell* (1860) 9 CBNS 159; 142 ER 62 – see above, 3.9.3.
120 Atiyah, 1986, p 235.
121 See, for example, Treitel, 2003, p 116.
122 See, for example, *Maddison v Alderson* (1883) 8 App Cas 467; *Argy Trading Development Co Ltd v Lapid* [1977] 1 WLR 444.

3.11 THE DOCTRINE OF PROMISSORY ESTOPPEL

The modern law on this topic, which gives rise to situations in which a contract can in effect be varied without there being consideration, derives from *Central London Property Trust Ltd v High Trees House Ltd*. The plaintiffs were the owners of a block of flats in London, which they rented to the defendants at a rent of £2,500 per annum. Following the outbreak of the Second World War in 1939, the defendants were unable to find suf-ficient tenants to take the flats, because of the large numbers of people leaving London. As a result, the plaintiffs agreed that, in the circumstances, the rent could be reduced by half, to £1,250 per annum. This arrangement continued until after the war ended in 1945, and the difficulty in letting the flats ceased. The plaintiffs then sought to return to the original terms of the agreement, and also queried whether they might not be entitled to claim the other half of the rent for the war years, since the promise to accept less was not supported by any consideration. Denning J, as he then was, confirmed that the plaintiffs were entitled to recover the full rent from the end of the war. Their promise to take less had clearly only been intended to last until that point. On the more general issue, however, on which his views were strictly *obiter*, he considered that the plaintiffs would not be able to recover the balance for the war years. The reason for this was that he thought that there was a general equitable principle whereby:[123]

> A promise intended to be binding, intended to be acted upon, and in fact acted on, is binding so far as its terms properly apply.

His main authority for this view was the 'equitable waiver' case of *Hughes v Metropolitan Railway*.[124] The defendant held a lease of certain houses from the plaintiff. The lease contained a covenant of repair within six months of being given notice. The plaintiff gave such notice. The defendant then suggested that a sale might be arranged, and said that it would defer carrying out any repairs until this had been discussed. Some negoti-ations took place, but they did not result in an agreement for the sale. The plaintiff then served notice to quit, on the basis of the defendant's failure to comply with the original notice to repair. It was held that the plaintiff was not entitled to do this. The effect of the notice had been suspended while the negotiations on the sale were taking place, and time did not start to run again until these had broken down. Lord Cairns stated the general principle in the following famous passage:[125]

> . . . it is the first principle on which all Courts of Equity proceed, that if parties who have entered into definite and distinct terms involving certain legal results –

---

123 [1947] KB 130.
124 Ibid, p 136.
125 (1877) 2 App Cas 439. He also cited *Birmingham and District Land v London and Northwestern Railway Co* (1888) 40 Ch D 268 and *Salisbury (Marquess) v Gilmore* [1942] 2 KB 38. 124 (1877) 2 App Cas 439, p 448.

certain penalties or legal forfeiture – afterwards by their own act or with their own consent enter upon a course of negotiation which has the effect of leading one of the parties to suppose that the strict rights arising under the contract will not be enforced, or will be kept in suspense, or held in abeyance, the person who otherwise might have enforced those rights will not be allowed to enforce them where it would be inequitable having regard to the dealings which have thus taken place between the parties.

Denning J, in *High Trees*, asserted that this general principle supported his view of the relationship between the parties in the case before him. His own statement of the general principle, as set out above, however, raised considerable controversy. First, taken at face value, it seemed to destroy the doctrine of consideration altogether.[126] Second, the application of the 'equitable waiver' approach to the facts of the case (that is, the non-payment of rent) appeared to run counter to the House of Lords' decision in *Foakes v Beer*,[127] which stated that part payment of a debt can never be good satisfaction for the whole. Both of these objections, and their treatment in subsequent case law, must now be considered.

3.12 PROMISSORY ESTOPPEL AND CONSIDERATION

The first point to consider is whether the doctrine of promissory estoppel, as restated and developed by Lord Denning, does strike at the heart of the doctrine of consideration. The argument that it does is based on the fact that Denning, in stating that 'a promise intended to be binding, intended to be acted upon, and in fact acted on, is binding so far as its terms properly apply',[128] was suggesting that all that was needed to make a promise enforceable is that the party to whom it was made has acted in reliance on it. In other words, it espouses a reliance-based theory of the enforceability of contracts. It therefore becomes irrelevant whether the promisee has provided anything in exchange in terms of a benefit to the promisor, or a detriment suffered at the promisor's request. As we have seen, the classical doctrine of consideration requires one or other of these as a condition of making a promise enforceable. If Denning's statement is taken at face value, however, then it would mean that if A promises B £10,000, intending it to be a binding promise, and in reliance on this B decides to go out and buy a car, A would be bound to the promise.[129] The classical doctrine of consideration would hold that B has not provided any consideration, and that A is not therefore bound to pay the £10,000.

---

126 This may well have been his original intention, as he has indicated extra-judicially: Denning, 1979, pp 197–203, 223.
127 (1884) 9 App Cas 605.
128 [1947] KB 130, p 136.
129 A fully fledged reliance-based theory of enforceability would be likely to require B's reliance to be 'reasonable' – and perhaps foreseeable by A. See, further, below, 3.15.2.

The question of whether the doctrine of consideration in its classical form does still survive and, if it does not, the extent to which the doctrine of promissory estoppel has contributed to its demise is one to which we shall return at the end of this chapter. At this stage, however, it is sufficient to note that the broad formulation of 'promissory estoppel' by Denning in *High Trees* has been limited by subsequent decisions. These cases establishing the borderlines of the doctrine can be viewed as supporting the view that it is simply an 'exception' to the general doctrine of consideration and does not strike at its roots.

There are five suggested limitations, of which four certainly apply: the status of the fifth is less clear.

3.12.1 There must be an existing legal relationship

It is suggested that promissory estoppel cannot exist in a vacuum: there must be an existing legal relationship between the parties which is being altered by the promissory estoppel. This was clearly the case in *High Trees* itself. It was concerned with the modification of the existing contractual rights between the landlord and tenants. This limitation may also be said to be exemplified by *Combe v Combe*.[130] In this case, a husband and wife were getting divorced. Between the decree *nisi* and absolute, the husband agreed to pay his wife £100 per annum net of tax. The husband never paid any money, and after seven years his former wife sued on the basis of his promise. Byrne J held that while there was no consideration for the husband's promise, the wife could recover on the basis of the *High Trees* decision. This decision was overturned by a Court of Appeal which included Lord Denning himself.[131] He commented that consideration remained 'a cardinal necessity of the formation of a contract, but not of its modification or discharge'.[132] If this is so, then it severely limits the doctrine's scope as a general challenge to the doctrine of consideration. Promissory estoppel is limited to the modification of existing legal relationships rather than to the establishment of new obligations.[133]

The existing relationship will generally be a contract. It seems, however, that this is not essential. The case of *Durham Fancy Goods Ltd v Michael Jackson (Fancy Goods) Ltd*[134] concerned a bill of exchange drawn by the plaintiffs on the defendants. The plaintiffs made an error by putting on the bill 'Accepted payable . . . For and on behalf of M Jackson (Fancy Goods) Ltd', whereas the proper name of the company was 'Michael Jackson (Fancy Goods) Ltd'. A director of the defendant company signed his

---

130 [1951] 2 KB 215; [1951] 1 All ER 767.
131 Part of the reason for the decision was the fact that promissory estoppel could only be used as a 'shield' rather than as a 'sword': this is discussed further below, 3.12.3.
132 [1951] 2 KB 215, p 220; [1951] 1 All ER 767, p 770.
133 But cf the Australian case of *Waltons Stores (Interstate) Ltd v Maher* (1988) 76 ALR 513, discussed below, 3.15.2.
134 [1968] 2 QB 839; [1968] 2 All ER 987.

name on the bill and returned it,[135] without pointing out the error. When the bill was later dishonoured, the plaintiffs tried to enforce the bill against the director. It was claimed that he was personally liable by virtue of s 108 of the Companies Act 1948, which renders a person who signs a bill liable if the proper name of the company does not appear on the bill. It was held that the director fell within s 108, because 'M Jackson' was not the same as 'Michael Jackson'. The plaintiffs were prevented from recovering from him, however, on the basis that their action in writing the words of acceptance on the bill (including the inaccurate name) amounted to a promise that 'acceptance in that form would be, or would be accepted by them as, a regular acceptance of the bill'.[136] This, in the view of Donaldson J, gave rise to a promissory estoppel, because it would be inequitable to allow the plaintiffs to enforce against the director personally. Such personal liability would not have arisen if the bill had been in the proper form. To the argument that promissory estoppel only arises where there is an existing contractual relationship, Donaldson J commented:[137]

> [T]his does not seem to me to be essential, provided that there is a pre-existing legal relationship which could in certain circumstances give rise to liabilities and penalties. Such a relationship is created by (a) s 108 of the Companies Act 1948, (b) the fact that Mr Jackson was a director of Jacksons and (c) whatever contractual arrangement existed between the plaintiffs and Jacksons which led to the plaintiffs drawing a 90 day bill on Jacksons.

In *Evenden v Guildford City FC*,[138] Lord Denning appeared to go further and, citing *Durham Fancy Goods Ltd v Michael Jackson (Fancy Goods) Ltd*, held that promissory estoppel could apply in a situation where it appears there was no existing legal relationship at all between the parties.[139] He was supported in this view by Browne LJ,[140] who was, however, also prepared to find for the plaintiff on the basis of a contractually binding promise.[141]

---

135 The director's name was, in fact, Michael Jackson, and he was also secretary to the company.

136 [1968] 2 QB 839, at p 848; [1968] 2 All ER 987, p 991.

137 Ibid, p 847; p 991.

138 [1975] QB 917.

139 That is, it was a representation made by a company which was about to become the employer of the plaintiff, to the effect that his new employment would be treated as continuous from that which he was about to leave. This was important for the purpose of redundancy entitlement.

140 [1975] QB 917, p 926.

141 The third member of the Court of Appeal, Brightman J, also found for the plaintiff, on the basis that the statutory presumption of continuous employment under s 9 of the Redundancy Payments Act 1965 could not be rebutted in the light of the statement made by the new employer.

In *The Henrik Sif*,[142] Webster J took the view that the 'legal relationship' necessary as the background to a promissory estoppel could be found where:[143]

> . . . two parties engaged in an exchange of correspondence in which one of them intends the correspondence to have legal effect in circumstances in which the other knows of that first party's intention and makes requests or purports to grant extensions of time which could only be of relevance to the first party if the correspondence between them affected their mutual rights and obligations.

This seems to amount to a kind of 'double-estoppel': the failure to correct a false impression about the parties' legal relationship leading to the context in which a promissory estoppel could operate.

To the extent that these cases suggest that promissory estoppel can apply even where there is no existing contract between the parties (within which consideration will have been provided), they add weight to the suggestion that the doctrine does have the effect of undermining the doctrine of consideration.

3.12.2   There must have been (detrimental) reliance

Under the normal rules for the creation of a contract, obligations may arise as soon as promises have been exchanged. There is no need for either side to have relied on the other's promise in order to be able to enforce it. In relation to promissory estoppel, however, the party trying to enforce the promise must have taken some action on it. This simply means doing something as a result of it, for example, paying the lower rent, as in *High Trees*. In some cases, it has been suggested that the promisee must have suffered a detriment from such reliance, but Lord Denning has consistently denied that this is necessary.

In *WJ Alan & Co v El Nasr*,[144]for example, the dispute concerned a letter of credit, which had been opened in sterling rather than in Kenyan shillings, as specified by the contract. The other party had, however, drawn on this credit in relation to various transactions. The judge rejected the argument that this amounted to a binding waiver of the original terms as to currency, because there was no evidence that the party for whose benefit the waiver would operate had acted 'to their detriment'. Lord Denning in the Court of Appeal refused to accept this as a necessary requirement for either waiver or promissory estoppel:[145]

---

142 [1982] 1 Lloyd's Rep 456.
143 Ibid, p 466. He relied to some extent on the comments of Robert Goff J in the first instance decision in *Amalgamated Investment & Property Co Ltd v Texas Commerce International Bank Ltd* [1981] 2 WLR 554.
144 [1972] 2 All ER 127.
145 [1972] 2 All ER 127, p 140.

I know that it has been suggested in some quarters that there must be detriment. But I can find no support for it in the authorities cited by the judge. The nearest approach to it is the statement of Viscount Simonds in the *Tool Metal* case that the other must have been led to 'alter his position'[146] . . . But that only means that he must have been led to act differently from what he otherwise would have done. And, if you study the cases in which the doctrine has been applied, you will see that all that is required is that the one should have 'acted on the belief induced by the other party'. That is how Lord Cohen put it in the *Tool Metal* case, and is how I would put it myself.

Megaw LJ agreed that there had been a binding waiver, though without dealing with the specific point on 'detriment'. Stephenson LJ left open the question of whether 'any alteration of position' was sufficient, but held that on the facts the party acting on the waiver had suffered a detriment anyway. Despite the fact that there is no absolutely clear authority on the issue, the current general view seems to be that action taken in reliance on the promise is enough, without the need for a specific detriment to be shown.

3.12.3 The doctrine can only be used as a 'shield not a sword'

The third limitation again derives from *Combe v Combe*,[147] the facts of which have been given above.[148] The Court of Appeal, including Lord Denning, thought that the attempt by the wife to use promissory estoppel to enforce her husband's promise was an inappropriate use of the doctrine. Promissory estoppel could not form the basis of a cause of action, and would generally only be available as a defence – 'as a shield, not a sword'.[149]

This limitation is clearly linked to the idea that the doctrine can only be used to modify existing relationships, rather than to create new ones. It does not mean, however, that promissory estoppel can only ever be used by a defendant, and never by a claimant. For example, a landlord might promise to waive an obligation to repair which would otherwise fall on the tenant. Suppose that the landlord subsequently gives the tenant notice to quit for failing to carry out repairs. The tenant could then go to court, as claimant, to challenge the notice. Reliance would be placed on the landlord's promise as having modified the tenant's obligations. The principle stated in *Combe v Combe* would not prevent the tenant from bringing the action against the landlord.[150]

---

146 *Tool Metal Manufacturing Co v Tungsten Electric Co* [1955] 2 All ER 657 – discussed below, 3.12.5.

147 [1951] 2 KB 215; [1951] 1 All ER 767.

148 See above, 3.12.1.

149 [1951] 2 KB 215, p 224; [1951] 1 All ER 767, p 772. This phrase was apparently used by counsel for the defendant and adopted by Birkett LJ.

150 For further discussion of these issues, see Halson, 1999; Thompson, 1983.

3.12.4 It must be inequitable for the promisor to go back on the promise

Promissory estoppel is, as we have seen, derived from the concept of equitable waiver. Thus, as an equitable doctrine, its use is in the discretion of the courts, and even if the other elements for the applicability of it exist, it may still not be applied because it would be inequitable in the circumstances to do so. A clear example of the kind of situation where this would apply is the case of *D and C Builders v Rees*.[151] The plaintiff builders had done work for the defendants and were owed nearly £500. After pressing for payment for some time, the plaintiff agreed to take £300 in satisfaction of the account. Mrs Rees, who knew that the plaintiffs were in financial difficulties, had told them that that was all they were likely to get. Despite their promise to accept the £300 (a promise for which there was no consideration), the builders then sought to recover the balance of the debt. Lord Denning, in the Court of Appeal, held that although there was clearly a promise here of a type which might raise promissory estoppel, the element of intimidation in the defendant's behaviour, knowingly taking advantage of the plaintiffs' circumstances, meant that it was not inequitable to allow the plaintiffs to go back on their promise. The other members of the Court of Appeal did not think it was even necessary to discuss the doctrine.[152]

FOR THOUGHT

What do you think the position would have been in *D and C Builders* if the builders had been aware of Mrs Rees's financial difficulties and had themselves agreed to reduce the bill?

The inequity in *D and C Builders* was fairly obvious. The concept of 'equitability' does not necessarily imply impropriety on the part of the promisee, however. In *The Post Chaser*,[153] the promise was made and withdrawn within a few days. Although the other side had relied on the promise, their position had not in fact been prejudiced by such reliance. It was not, therefore, inequitable to allow the promisor to withdraw the promise.

The question is thus not simply whether the promisee acted in reliance on the promise, but whether there was sufficient reliance to make it inequitable not to enforce the promise. Although Robert Goff J in *The Post Chaser* was clearly supportive of the view noted above that such 'reliance' does not require 'detriment', if there has been detriment, then inequitability may be much easier to establish. In the absence of

---

151 [1966] 2 QB 617; [1965] 3 All ER 837.

152 It may be significant that the contract in this case was at the 'discrete' as opposed to the 'relational' end of Macneil's spectrum of contracts (see Chapter 1, 1.5). There was thus less need for provision for modification of obligations.

153 [1981] 2 Lloyd's Rep 695; [1982] 1 All ER 19.

detriment, the court will probably look at the effect of allowing withdrawal of the promise. Would this have a significant adverse affect on the promisee, because of the way in which he has organised his affairs in the light of the promise? If not, then withdrawal is unlikely to be regarded as 'inequitable'.

3.12.5 The doctrine is only suspensory in its effect

Does the doctrine have a permanent, or only a suspensory effect? This final limitation on promissory estoppel is the one about which there is most uncertainty. There is no doubt that in some circumstances a promissory estoppel will have a purely suspensory effect. In *Hughes v Metropolitan Railway*,[154] for example, the notice of obligation to repair was simply put in abeyance while the negotiations over a possible sale continued. It is also clear that in relation to some sorts of contract, the effect can be to both extinguish some rights and suspend others. This is what happened in *High Trees* itself. The right to receive the full rent during the war years was extinguished by the estoppel, but because the promise was interpreted as having only been intended to be applicable during the war, once that was over, the original terms of the lease automatically revived. So, to that extent, the effect was simply suspensory. Even if the promise is expressed to last indefinitely, it is likely that it will be able to be withdrawn (and thus be only suspensory in effect) by giving appropriate notice. In *Tool Metal Manufacturing Co v Tungsten Electric Co*,[155] for example, there was a promise to accept a reduced royalty in relation to the operation of some patents. It was held that the promisor could withdraw the promise by giving reasonable notice, from which point the original terms of the agreement would come back into operation. The House of Lords in fact held that the initiation of a previous, unsuccessful action to escape from the promise constituted notice of withdrawal.

It is in relation to this type of continuing contract,[156] therefore, that promissory estoppel operates to both extinguish and suspend contractual rights. The obligations to make the higher payments during the period of the operation in both *High Trees* and the *Tool Metal* case were destroyed. The promisor was unable to recover the additional amounts for that period. The original terms were not in themselves extinguished, however, and could be reinstated for the future.

What is not clear is whether the doctrine of promissory estoppel could be used to extinguish, rather than suspend, an obligation which is not a continuing obligation. If, for example, the issue of inequitability had not arisen in *D and C Builders v Rees*,[157] would promissory estoppel have wiped out, or simply postponed, the payment of the balance? It seems clear that if the doctrine is to have any place at all in relation to this type of obligation, it must have the effect of extinguishing the right altogether. It would

---

154 (1877) 2 App Cas 439 – discussed above, 3.11.
155 [1955] 2 All ER 657.
156 A 'relational' contract, in other words – see Chapter 1, 1.5.
157 [1966] 2 QB 617; [1965] 3 All ER 837.

make no sense to say that Rees could rely on D and C Builders' promise to remit the balance of the debt, but that at any time the obligation to pay it could be revived by the giving of notice. It should be remembered, however, that it was only Lord Denning who seriously considered applying promissory estoppel in this situation, and that there has been no other reported case in which the doctrine has been applied to this kind of obligation.

The conclusion must be, however, that it is not true to say that promissory estoppel can *only* operate in a suspensory way. The precise effect of promissory estoppel, in terms of whether it suspends or extinguishes rights, will depend on the nature of the promise, and the type of contract to which it applies. If this is the case, then promissory estoppel is no different in this respect from a contractual modification which is supported by consideration. The precise effect of such a modification also depends on the terms in which it is expressed, and the nature of the contract with which it is concerned. It would have been quite possible, for example, for an agreement of the type considered in *High Trees* to have been entered into on the basis that, during the war, the tenants would undertake additional responsibilities in respect of the maintenance of the property in return for the landlord accepting the reduced rent, thus providing consideration for the landlord's promise. As far as the obligation to pay the rent was concerned, the effect would have been the same as would occur through the application of promissory estoppel. The landlord's right to receive the full rent would have been extinguished during the war, but would have revived once peace had returned.

If this is right, then putting forward the suspensory nature of promissory estoppel as a basis for distinguishing it from the doctrine of consideration (and thus adding weight to the view that it does not 'undermine' consideration) does not look very convincing. In both cases, the issue of the suspension or extinction of rights depends on the nature of the promise and the surrounding circumstances. It does not, therefore, depend on whether or not consideration was given for the promise.

3.13 PROMISSORY ESTOPPEL AND THE PART PAYMENT OF DEBTS

3.13.1 The common law position

The common law position on the part payment of debts is to be found in *Pinnel's Case*,[158] as confirmed by the House of Lords in *Foakes v Beer*.[159] The rule is that part payment of a debt on the date on which it is due can never be satisfaction for the full amount owed.[160] The creditor will still be able to recover the balance of the debt, unless

---

158 (1602) 5 Co Rep 117a; 77 ER 237.
159 (1884) 9 App Cas 605.
160 It seems unlikely that a reliance-based approach would come up with any different general rule on this issue. It is difficult to see that a debtor who has made part payment has 'relied' on a promise to accept this in full satisfaction – unless, perhaps, the debtor has subsequently taken on other commitments on the basis that the original debt has been extinguished.

the debtor can show that some consideration was supplied in return for the creditor's agreement to take the lesser sum. Thus, if payment is made early, or on the day, but at a different place from that specified in the contract, the debt may be discharged. Equally, if the debtor provides goods, or services, instead of cash, this, if accepted by the creditor, will discharge the debt fully, even if the value of what was supplied is less than the total amount owed: 'The gift of a horse, a hawk, or a robe, in satisfaction is good.'[161] Thus, the payment of £5 on the due date could never discharge a debt of £100, but if the debtor offered and the creditor accepted a book worth £5 in satisfaction, the creditor could not then claim the balance of £95. The justification for this rather odd rule is that the book must have been regarded by the creditor as more beneficial than money, otherwise it would not have been accepted, and the court will not inquire further into the creditor's motives.

Two other situations are recognised by the common law as enabling a debt to be discharged, even though it has not been fully paid. The first is where the payment is made by a third party. For example, in *Hirachand Punamchand v Temple*,[162] the debtor's father made a payment in relation to a promissory note which was accepted by the creditor in full settlement of the debt. It was held that the creditor could not subsequently sue the debtor for the balance. This followed a similar view taken in the earlier cases of *Welby v Drake*[163] and *Cooke v Lister*.[164]

Second, if a debtor owes money to several creditors, an agreement may be reached whereby each of them is to receive a proportion of the money owed (a 'composition agreement'). In that situation, none of the creditors will be allowed to sue the debtor to recover the full amount originally owed.[165]

Both of these two situations may be explained on the basis that the creditor should not be allowed to act in a way which would constitute a 'fraud' on the party who has made the part payment, but they do appear to be exceptions to the rule that part payment of a debt must be supported by consideration in order to make it enforceable.[166]

3.13.2 The decision in *Foakes v Beer*

The rule in *Pinnel's Case* was strictly *obiter*, in that the debtor had paid early, and had therefore in any case provided sufficient consideration to discharge the whole debt, but it was confirmed by the House of Lords in *Foakes v Beer*. Dr Foakes owed Mrs Beer a sum of money in relation to a judgment debt. Mrs Beer agreed that Dr Foakes could pay this off in instalments. When he had done so, Mrs Beer sued to recover the interest

---

161 (1602) 5 Co Rep 117a; 77 ER 237.
162 [1911] 2 KB 330.
163 (1825) 1 C & P 557.
164 (1863) CB(NS) 543.
165 *Good v Cheesman* (1831) 2 B & Ald 328.
166 For other possible explanations for these decisions, see Treitel, 2003, pp 128–29.

on the debt, in relation to the delay in the completion of payment resulting from the payment by instalments. The House of Lords held that, even if Mrs Beer had promised to forego the interest (which was by no means certain),[167] it was an unenforceable promise because Dr Foakes had provided no consideration for it. The Court of Appeal has recently confirmed in two cases that this is still the standard position as regards part payment of debts.

The first is *Re Selectmove*,[168] which was discussed above;[169] the second is *Ferguson v Davies*.[170] In the latter case, the plaintiff started a county court action to recover a debt, originally stated at £486.50 but later increased to £1,745.79. The defendant, as part of his 'defence' in relation to these proceedings, sent the plaintiff a cheque for £150, sending letters to the plaintiff and the court indicating that while he admitted liability to this extent, the cheque was sent in full settlement of his dispute. The plaintiff, having sought advice from the county court, presented the cheque for payment, but continued with his action. The trial judge held that by accepting the £150, the plaintiff had compromised his action by a binding 'accord and satisfaction'. The Court of Appeal disagreed. Henry LJ, with whom Aldous LJ agreed, did so on the basis that there was no consideration here for the plaintiff's alleged agreement to abandon his claim. This was not a situation where a claim for a disputed amount was settled by a compromise involving partial payment by the debtor (a common basis for the settlement of legal actions). On the contrary, the defendant had admitted liability for the £150 sent, and so was giving the plaintiff nothing which could amount to consideration for the plaintiff's alleged agreement to forego any further claim. By his own admission, he was bound in law to pay the £150, so this payment merely constituted the settlement of an acknowledged debt, and could not serve as consideration for any other promise. The principles of *Foakes v Beer* and *D and C Builders v Rees*[171] applied, and the plaintiff was free to pursue his claim for the balance which he alleged was owed to him.

It should perhaps be noted that the other member of the Court of Appeal, Evans LJ, with whom Aldous LJ also agreed, decided the case on the different ground that, on the facts, there was no true 'accord', in that the defendant's letters could reasonably be interpreted as not being intended to assert that the £150 was sent as full settlement of all claims by the plaintiff. On the consideration issue, Evans LJ specifically indicated that he was expressing no view. Nevertheless, there is no doubt that, in the light of these latest Court of Appeal decisions, the principles in *Pinnel's Case* and *Foakes v Beer* remain good law in relation to the payment of debts. As Peter Gibson LJ put it in *Re Selectmove*:[172]

---

167 Cf the comments of Gilmore, 1974, at pp 31–32.
168 [1995] 2 All ER 534.
169 See above, 3.9.10.
170 [1997] 1 All ER 315.
171 [1966] 2 QB 617; [1965] 3 All ER 837 – discussed above, 3.12.4.
172 [1995] 2 All ER 531, p 538.

Foakes v Beer was not even referred to in *Williams'* case,[173] and it is in my judgment impossible, consistently with the doctrine of precedent, for this court to extend the principle of *Williams'* case to any circumstances governed by the principle of *Foakes v Beer*. If that extension is to be made, it must be by the House of Lords or, perhaps even more appropriately, by Parliament after consideration by the Law Commission.

3.13.3 The effect of promissory estoppel on *Foakes v Beer*

What is the effect, if any, of the doctrine of promissory estoppel on these principles? In this context, it is important to note that *Foakes v Beer* was decided in 1884, that is, seven years after *Hughes v Metropolitan Railway*.[174] *Hughes* was not even cited in the later case. Given that three of the four members of the House of Lords who delivered speeches in *Foakes v Beer* expressed some unhappiness about the outcome to which they felt that the common law bound them,[175] so that they would gladly have accepted an escape route via the equitable doctrine of waiver if that had been available, it must be assumed that the approach taken in *Hughes* was considered to have no relevance to the situation of part payment of debts. This, then, was a further way in which Lord Denning's decision in *Central London Property Trust Ltd v High Trees House Ltd* broke new ground. The case was concerned, in effect, with the partial payment of a debt (that is, half the rent for the war years). Nevertheless, Denning felt able to apply to it the *Hughes* principle of 'equitable waiver', and it seems now to be generally accepted that this doctrine, in its new guise of 'promissory estoppel', can mitigate the harshness of the rule in *Foakes v Beer*, in appropriate cases.[176] This is not to say that *Foakes v Beer* would definitely be decided differently if it came before the House of Lords again today. That would depend on what exactly Mrs Beer was found to have promised, whether Dr Foakes could be said to have relied on that promise and also on whether promissory estoppel can ever be applied to extinguish a 'one-off' debt as opposed to payment obligations under a continuing contract. This issue has been discussed in the previous section, in considering whether promissory estoppel is only suspensory in its effect. It is, however, probably significant that the issue of promissory estoppel was not discussed in either *Re Selectmove* or *Ferguson v Davies*. This would suggest that the courts remain reluctant to introduce this principle into the area of part payment of simple debts.

---

173 That is, *Williams v Roffey* [1991] 1 QB 1; [1990] 1 All ER 512.

174 (1877) 2 App Cas 439.

175 See (1884) 9 App Cas 605, p 613 (Lord Selborne); p 622 (Lord Blackburn); p 630 (Lord Fitzgerald).

176 Note that an Australian court has gone further: in *Musumeci v Winadell Pty Ltd* (1994) 34 NSWLR 723, Santow J held that, following *Williams v Roffey* [1991] 1 QB 1, a promise to accept a reduced rent could amount to a binding variation of the contract, without the need to rely on promissory estoppel.

3.14   OTHER TYPES OF ESTOPPEL

Before leaving this area, we should also note two other types of estoppel which can have an effect on the operation of a contract. First, there is *estoppel by convention*. This arises where the parties to an agreement have acted on the basis that some provision in the contract has a particular meaning. This type of estoppel will operate to prevent one of the parties later trying to argue that the provision means something different. An example of its use is *Amalgamated Investment and Property Co Ltd* ['AIP'] *v Texas Commerce International Bank Ltd*[177] ('the Bank'). In this case, there was a contract of guarantee between AIP and the Bank. The guarantee was in respect of a loan made by the Bank to a firm called Amalgamated (New Providence) Property Ltd ('ANPP'), which was a subsidiary of AIP. The guarantee contained a promise by AIP to repay money 'owed to you' (that is, the Bank) by ANPP. In fact, ANPP had been lent the money not by the Bank direct, but by a specially created subsidiary of the Bank named 'Portsoken'. When AIP got into financial difficulties and went into liquidation, the liquidator sought a declaration to prevent the Bank using money which it owed to AIP under another transaction in order to discharge ANPP's debt. It was argued that the guarantee was not binding, because it only referred to money owing to the Bank itself, whereas the money had actually been lent by Portsoken. There was no money owed to the Bank by ANPP to which the guarantee could attach. It was held, however, that all parties had acted on the basis that the wording of the guarantee referred to the money lent by Portsoken to ANPP and, on that basis, an estoppel by convention operated to prevent AIP arguing for a different meaning. Therefore, AIP's liquidator could not stop the Bank from using the money owed to AIP in the way it proposed.[178]

A more recent confirmation by the House of Lords of the concept of estoppel by convention is to be found in *Johnson v Gore Wood & Co*.[179] The majority of the House held that the compromise of an action by a company against a firm of solicitors did not preclude the managing director of the company subsequently bringing a personal action against the firm. This was not an 'abuse of process' because the House felt that the earlier negotiations were based on the assumption that a further proceeding by the managing director would be possible. This assumption operated as an 'estoppel by convention'.[180]

The second type of estoppel which needs to be noted is *proprietary estoppel*. This operates in relation to rights in land only. It also differs from promissory estoppel

---

177 [1982] QB 84; [1981] 3 All ER 577.
178 Note that the judgments of the Court of Appeal are not unanimous on the issue of whether the Bank could have sued on the promise in the guarantee (as opposed to using it as a defence to AIP's action): Eveleigh LJ took the view that it could not (see p 126), but Brandon LJ (on the facts, p 132) and Lord Denning MR (as a matter of principle, p 122) thought that it could.
179 [2001] 1 All ER 481.
180 Lord Goff preferred to regard the situation as one involving a 'promissory estoppel' – though this led him to the same conclusion as the majority: see [2001] 1 All ER 481, p 508.

(though both are sometimes confusingly referred to as 'equitable estoppel') in that it may be used to found a cause of action. In other words, it can be used as a sword rather than a shield. An example of its use is *Crabb v Arun District Council*.[181] Mr Crabb owned a plot of land adjacent to a road. He decided to sell half of the plot to the Arun District Council (ADC). The ADC built a road along one edge of the piece of land which it had bought. Mr Crabb was allowed access to this road from a particular point on the land which he had retained. Mr Crabb then decided to sell another portion of this land. On the basis of a promise from the council that he would be allowed another access point onto its road, he sold the piece of land containing the first access point. The ADC, despite the fact that it had initially left a gap in its fencing at an appropriate point, then refused to allow the second access. The result was that the piece of land that Mr Crabb had retained was completely blocked in, without any access from either the original road or the road built by the ADC. Mr Crabb brought an action to compel the ADC to grant him the second access point which had been promised. Although there was no consideration for this promise, Mr Crabb succeeded in his action. The words and actions of the ADC had led Mr Crabb to believe that he would have the second access point, and he had relied on this to his detriment in selling the piece of land containing the first access point. The Court of Appeal therefore allowed him to succeed on the basis of a proprietary estoppel.

3.15 ALTERNATIVE TESTS OF ENFORCEABILITY

As we have seen, the English courts, following classical theory, profess to use the existence of valid consideration as the test for the enforceability of simple contracts. It is said that, in effect, consideration is both necessary and sufficient to make an agreement binding. In particular, a promise unsupported by consideration cannot be enforced. As was noted at the start of this chapter, however,[182] this analysis is not universally accepted, even as an accurate description of what the courts actually do. Indeed, we have already seen that there is a breach in the standard approach via the concept of promissory estoppel, and a probable weakening of it via the case of *Williams v Roffey*.[183]

3.15.1 What does 'consideration' really mean?

One of the leading English sceptics in relation to the traditional analysis of the doctrine of consideration is Professor Atiyah. His views are set out, *inter alia*, in Chapter 8 of his

---

181 [1975] 3 All ER 865.
182 See above, 3.4.
183 [1991] 1 QB 1; [1990] 1 All ER 512.

Essays on Contract, entitled 'Consideration: a re-statement'.[184] Atiyah's view, which is supported by some legal historians,[185] is that 'consideration' originated simply as an indication of the need for a 'reason' for enforcing a promise or obligation, such as the fact that the promisee had given something to the promisor in expectation that the promise would be fulfilled. It became formalised, however, into a rigid set of rules, such as that there must be benefit and detriment, that past consideration is no consideration, that consideration must be of economic value, and that gratuitous promises will not generally be enforced.

In examining how these rules actually operate, however, Atiyah argues that they are not actually followed rigidly by the courts. For example, as regards the need for benefit/detriment, he cites *Chappell v Nestlé*[186] and *Hamer v Sidway*[187] as indicating that this is not necessary for a contract. Nor is it sufficient, in that contracts in which there is clearly benefit or detriment may still not be enforced, as we shall see in later chapters, because of considerations of illegality, duress, or undue influence. In relation to the need for economic value, *Ward v Byham*[188] may be seen as an exception.

Moreover, the unenforceability of gratuitous promises is not applied where promissory estoppel operates. Atiyah argues that promissory estoppel, as expounded in *High Trees*, was a step in the right direction, following a wrong turning taken as a result of the misinterpretation of *Jorden v Money*[189] as an authority for the proposition that a statement of intention cannot give rise to an estoppel. As we have seen,[190] that case was actually decided as it was, according to Atiyah, because of the requirements of the Statute of Frauds 1677, which at the time required that a promise given in consideration of marriage (which was the situation in *Jorden v Money*) had to be proved by writing.

Because there was no writing, the case could not be pleaded in contract and was therefore pleaded as estoppel, but the court refused to allow this to be used as a means of circumventing the requirements of the Statute of Frauds 1677. *High Trees*, which recognised the enforceability of a statement of intention which had been relied on, should have shown the way forward, but was thrown off course by *Combe v Combe*.[191] The real reason for the decision in that case, Atiyah says, was not the fact that the wife was trying to use promissory estoppel as a cause of action, but that justice was not on her side, because she was earning more than her ex-husband. This was a reason (or consideration?) for not enforcing the husband's promise. But, in general, where there has been reasonable reliance on a promise, even if the promisee has not provided what

---

184 Atiyah, 1986: this is in fact a revised version of an inaugural lecture delivered at the Australian National University, Canberra, in 1971 and published by the Australian National University Press in the same year. See also Atiyah, 1978, republished as Chapter 2 in Atiyah, 1986.
185 For example, Simpson, 1975a, Chapters IV–VII, and in particular p 321.
186 [1960] AC 87; [1959] 2 All ER 701 – discussed above, 3.7.1.
187 (1891) 27 NE 256; 124 NY 538 – discussed above, 3.7.1.
188 [1956] 2 All ER 318 – above, 3.9.1.
189 (1854) 5 HL 185.
190 Above, 3.10.2.
191 [1951] 2 KB 215; [1951] 1 All ER 767 – above, 3.12.1; 3.12.3.

we should recognise as 'consideration' in the technical sense, Atiyah is of the view that the promise should be enforceable. This concept of reliance would, he argues, be a more satisfactory way of determining the existence of contractual obligations, as opposed to the formalistic requirement of consideration, with all its technical limitations.

What Atiyah is in effect arguing is that we should return towards the original idea of 'consideration' as meaning a reason for enforcing a promise or acknowledging an obligation. This would be a much more flexible doctrine. The disadvantage, however, is that it would also be rather uncertain and unpredictable, and might depend too much on what the individual judge thinks amounts to a sufficient reason for enforcing a promise on a particular set of facts. One possible basis on which this might be done is by giving a greater status to the requirement of 'intention to create legal relations', to which we shall turn in the next chapter.

3.15.2 'Reliance' as a test of enforceability

It is at this point we must return to the issue raised at the beginning of this chapter,[192] that is, the role of 'reliance' as an alternative to, or replacement for, consideration. One aspect of Atiyah's criticisms is his view that in fact 'reliance' provides a more accurate test of enforceability than the orthodox doctrine of consideration, which takes as its paradigm the mutual exchange of 'binding' promises.[193] Courts enforce promises where the promisee has relied on the promise and it would therefore be unfair to allow the promisor to escape from his or her commitment. This view is, for Atiyah, inaccurate both as a description of the typical contract and in the light of the way in which the courts deal with them. Many common transactions, such as booking holidays, making air reservations and ordering goods are not commonly discussed by the participants in terms of 'promises'.[194] It is actions, and reliance on actions, rather the exchange of promises, which leads to the creation of obligations.[195] On this basis, if you deliver goods to me, on the basis that I will pay you for them, it is your action in transferring the goods to me which creates an enforceable obligation to pay. You have acted to your detriment in reliance on the fact that I will pay for the goods. The same is true of someone, for example, boarding a bus where there is a conductor rather than the obligation to pay on entry. It is unrealistic to talk about my action in terms of its containing an implied promise to pay the fare; rather it is my action in taking advantage of the bus service, and being carried on my journey, which creates the obligation to pay.

---

192 Above, 3.4.

193 This aspect of his theories about contract appears at greatest length in Atiyah, 1986, Chapter 2. Cf also the arguments of Baker concerning 'reasonable expectation' as the basis of contractual liability: Baker, 1979.

194 Ibid, p 23.

195 Atiyah goes on to question whether the law *should* enforce purely executory agreements, where there has been no reliance by either party.

The notion of contractual obligations being based on reliance, rather than a bargained for exchange, is not peculiar to Professor Atiyah.[196] It has a long history in the United States.[197] Indeed, the American Restatement,[198] even in its first version published in 1932, recognised it as part of the law of obligations. In addition to s 75, which contained what we would regard as an orthodox definition of consideration based around the concept of 'bargain', it also included s 90,[199] which reads:

> A promise which the promisor should reasonably expect to induce action or forbearance of a definite and substantial character on the part of the promisee and which does induce such action or forbearance is binding if injustice can be avoided only by the enforcement of the promise.

As will be seen, this provides a test for the enforceability of promises not based on 'consideration' but on 'reliance', and this has remained a central part of the American law of contract. This demonstrates that the English law of contract does not need to make consideration its primary, if not sole, test of enforceability. Recent developments in Australia can be seen as indicating a similar trend away from consideration.

FOR THOUGHT

Would using 'reliance' in place of or alongside consideration as a test of enforceability create greater uncertainty in deciding whether promises are enforceable? Would it be an undesirable development for that reason?

It will be noticed that the language of s 90 of the American Restatement bears a considerable similarity to that used by Lord Denning in developing the doctrine of promissory estoppel.[200] That doctrine can indeed be seen as basing contractual obligations on reasonable reliance. Its limitation as a rival to consideration is, however, as we have seen, the reluctance of the English courts to accept that it can operate to create new obligations rather than to vary existing ones. The Australian courts have been bolder in taking that step, as shown by the case of *Waltons Stores (Interstate) Ltd v*

---

196 A good review of the role of 'reliance' as a test of enforceability is to be found in Collins, 2003, Chapter 5.
197 For example, Fuller and Perdue, 1936.
198 Intended as a 'model' law for potential adoption by the individual States, but also as representing the current law as revealed by the cases.
199 The process by which these two, rather contradictory, sections dealing with the basis of contractual obligations came to co-exist in the same document is entertainingly described by Gilmore, 1974, pp 60–65.
200 See above, 3.11.

Maher.[201] The case concerned the proposed lease of a piece of land as part of a development project. The owners of the land were led to believe that the prospective lessees would proceed with the transaction, and that the necessary exchange of contracts would take place.[202] With that expectation they demolished an existing building on the land, in preparation for the construction of a new building to meet the lessees' requirements. In fact, the lessees had already decided not to proceed with the agreement. They failed to communicate this to the owners, even though they knew that the work on demolishing the building had started. Could the owners claim any compensation?

Although there appeared to be no contract between the parties, the High Court of Australia allowed the owners to succeed on the basis of estoppel. The court felt that the lessees, having 'promised' that the contract would proceed, had acted 'unconscionably' in knowingly allowing the owners to carry on with their work, thereby incurring a detriment. The promise should therefore be enforced. In coming to this conclusion, Mason CJ and Wilson J make specific reference to s 90 of the American Restatement, thus providing the link with the way in which promissory estoppel has been used in that jurisdiction. Brennan J set out a six-point summary of the requirements for this type of estoppel:[203]

(1) the plaintiff assumed or expected that a particular legal relationship exists between the plaintiff and the defendant or that a particular legal relationship will exist between them and, in the latter case, that the defendant is not free to withdraw from the expected legal relationship;

(2) the defendant has induced the plaintiff to adopt that assumption or expectation;

(3) the plaintiff acts or abstains from acting in reliance on the assumption or expectation;

(4) the defendant knew or intended him to do so;

(5) the plaintiff's action or inaction will occasion detriment if the assumption or expectation is not fulfilled; and

(6) the defendant has failed to act to avoid that detriment whether by fulfilling the assumption or expectation or otherwise.

All these conditions were satisfied in the case, and so the owners (the plaintiffs) were entitled to succeed in their action.

Waltons v Maher has the effect of extending promissory estoppel to apply in a situation where it is being used to create a new cause of action. In other words, it

---

201 (1988) 164 CLR 387; 76 ALR 513. This case may be regarded as building on *Legione v Hateley* (1983) 152 CLR 406, where at least some members of the High Court of Australia had first accepted that promissory estoppel should be applicable in Australia to preclude the enforcement of rights, at least between parties to an existing contract.
202 A letter indicating this was sent by the lessees' solicitor.
203 (1988) 164 CLR 387, p 428.

is doing what the Court of Appeal refused to do in *Combe v Combe*.[204] It is thus, in effect, allowing 'detrimental reliance' as an alternative to consideration, provided that such reliance can be said to make it 'unconscionable' for the promisor to renege on the promise.

Subsequent decisions in Australia have accepted the principle applied in *Waltons'* case,[205] and similar developments can be seen in New Zealand[206] and in Canada.[207] Taking into account also s 90 of the American Restatement, it would seem that in the common law world it is increasingly the approach taken by the English courts, in limiting the scope for enforcing agreements on the basis of reliance, that is out of line. It would not be surprising if the concept of promissory estoppel were soon to be developed in England in a way which would bring the law here more into step with the broader approach adopted elsewhere.[208] It seems, however, that any such development will have to be undertaken by the House of Lords. That was the view of the Court of Appeal in *Baird Textile Holdings Ltd v Marks & Spencer plc*.[209] This was a preliminary hearing relating to an application to strike out the claimant's action. The claimant's case was based on Marks & Spencer's termination without notice of a long-standing arrangement under which it bought supplies from the claimant. The court held that the claimant had no realistic chance of arguing either that the arrangement amounted to a contract (because of lack of certainty and of any evidence of an intention to create legal relations) or that Marks & Spencer should be 'estopped' from bringing it to an end without reasonable notice. The court was unanimous in the view that it would be necessary for the House of Lords to develop the law in the way suggested by the claimant.[210] Unless and until this happens, it cannot therefore be said that the doctrine of consideration has as yet been replaced by a reliance-based approach to enforceability, though the areas where 'exceptionally' the latter approach is allowed to be used has significantly increased over the last 50 years.

Before leaving this area, it should be noted that there may be a difference between 'consideration' and 'reliance'-based contracts in the area of remedies. This topic is discussed more fully in Chapter 19, but the issue will be outlined here. The traditional view is that the claimant who successfully argues that a contract has been broken is

---

204 [1951] 2 KB 215; [1951] 1 All ER 767.

205 For example, *The Commonwealth of Australia v Verwayen* (1990) 170 CLR 394; *The Zhi Jiang Kou* [1991] 1 Lloyd's Rep 493.

206 For example, *Burbery Mortgage Finance and Savings Ltd v Hindsbank Holdings Ltd* [1989] 1 NZLR 356.

207 For example, *Gilbert Steel Ltd v University Construction Ltd* (1973) 36 DLR (3d) 496; *Litwin v Pan* (1986) 52 DLR (4th) 459.

208 For the contrary argument that promissory estoppel should be confined to the area with which it was primarily developed to deal, at least in England (that is, the modification of existing contracts), see Halson, 1999.

209 [2001] EWCA 274; [2002] 1 All ER (Comm) 737.

210 Judge LJ, however, appeared rather more sympathetic to the claimant's argument than either of the other members of the court (the Vice-Chancellor, Sir Robert Andrew Morritt or Mance LJ).

entitled to recover damages to compensate for the lost benefits that would have accrued had the contract been performed properly (the 'expectation interest'). This will be the standard (though not universal) approach where the contract is enforceable on the basis of the mutual exchange of consideration. Where contractual obligations are based on 'reliance', however, it is not certain that lost expectations will be compensated. This is reflected in the current wording of s 90 of the American Restatement, which states that 'The remedy granted for breach may be limited as justice requires'. Similarly, in Australia, it has been suggested that what is recoverable as a result of the breach of a promise which has been relied on, but which is not supported by consideration, is damages to compensate the claimant for losses incurred by reliance, rather than the benefits that might have accrued from full performance.[211] If this is the case, then it may be argued that, although reliance may provide an alternative test of the enforceability of a promise, full contractual liability (that is, liability which includes the obligation to compensate for expected benefits) only arises from an agreement based on the exchange of consideration.[212]

3.15.3 'Promise' as a test of enforceability

As has been pointed out earlier in this chapter,[213] there are difficulties in fitting a 'promise' within the normal definition of consideration as involving some detriment to the person providing the consideration or some benefit to the person to whom it is provided. Given, however, that (again as noted above) much of the classical law of contract is centred on the notion that an exchange of promises makes both enforceable, even while both are executory, it is not surprising to find that there have been attempts to argue that 'promises' rather than reliance should be regarded as providing the badge of enforceability. This involves arguing that the reason for enforcing a promise is the fact that the promisor has used this form of discourse. Thus, the focus is on what the promisor has done, rather than (as with the consideration and reliance analyses) on what the promisee has done in response to the promise. The fullest modern attempt to present this argument is to be found in the work of Charles Fried.[214]

Drawing on the work of earlier philosophers,[215] Fried argues that there is a moral obligation to keep a promise, independent of reliance by the promisee, or of utilitarian arguments about the benefits that may flow from promise-keeping. Rather,

---

211 *The Commonwealth of Australia v Verwayen* (1990) 170 CLR 394.

212 For an argument that the gap as far as remedies is concerned is less than might appear at first sight, see Collins, 2003, pp 89–90. Collins points out that a finding of an estoppel can lead to a requirement to complete a promised obligation in situations where the normal contractual remedy would only be damages.

213 Above, 3.6.

214 See Fried, 1981. For an argument for the enforcement of gratuitous promises based on an economic analysis, see Posner, 1977.

215 For example, Immanuel Kant.

the obligation to keep a promise 'is grounded in respect for individual autonomy and trust'.[216] More fully:[217]

> An individual is morally bound to keep his promises because he has intentionally invoked a convention whose function is to give grounds – moral grounds – for another to expect the promised performance. To renege is to abuse a confidence that he was free to invite or not, and which he intentionally did invite.

Part of Fried's argument for putting 'promise' at the centre of contract is that the doctrine of consideration is inadequate as a test of enforceability. He suggests that two principle elements of the doctrine are mutually inconsistent. One says that the law is not concerned with the adequacy of consideration.[218] This appears to support the idea that 'the free arrangements of rational persons should be respected'.[219] The second principle is that only where something is given in exchange for a promise should the promise be enforceable. This means that 'the free arrangements of rational persons',[220] which might include the making of binding gratuitous promises, can be frustrated by the doctrine of consideration. His conclusion is that an analysis based on promise provides a more coherent basis for enforceability. He recognises, however, that his approach does not accord with Anglo-American contract law as it currently operates: 'There are too many gaps in the common law enforcement of promises to permit so bold a statement.'[221] This mismatch between theory and reality has formed the basis of the criticisms of Fried's approach, with Professor Atiyah as one of the strongest sceptics.[222] Atiyah suggests that the gaps in the extent to which promises are actually enforced by the courts means that it is preferable to view promises as being '*prima facie* binding rather than absolutely and conclusively binding'.[223] He continues:[224]

> Exchanges of benefits are likely to be in the interests of those who make them, and there is therefore a strong *prima facie* case for upholding them. Promises are likely to be relied upon and those who rely would suffer loss from breach: these too are *prima facie* good reasons for upholding the binding nature of a promise.

It is only fair to note, however, that Fried is aware of the limitations of his thesis.

---

216 Fried, 1981, p 16.
217 Ibid.
218 See above, 3.7.
219 Fried, 1981, p 35.
220 Ibid.
221 Ibid, pp 37–38.
222 See Atiyah, 1986, Chapter 6.
223 Ibid, p 148.
224 Ibid.

His conclusion, however, is that, although there are many gaps in the common law enforcement of promises:[225]

> . . . the doctrine of consideration offers no coherent alternative basis for the force of contracts . . . Along the way to this conclusion I have made or implied a number of qualifications to my thesis. The promise must be freely made and not unfair . . . It must also have been made rationally, deliberately. The promisor must have been serious enough that subsequent legal enforcement was an aspect of what he should have contemplated at the time he promised.

Put like this, it is clear that any analysis of contract based on Fried's approach will need to put considerable weight on the question of whether the promisor *intended* (or, at least, should have realised that others would assume from his words and actions that he was intending) to bind himself legally. As we saw above,[226] this is also an issue in relation to attempts to give a broad definition to 'consideration'.

The idea of a law of contract focussed on 'intention' as the primary test of enforceability rather than consideration or reliance is a possible one. The Principles of European Contract Law use such a test. Article 2.101 which deals with the conditions for the conclusion of a contract states:

(1) A contract is concluded if:
    (a) the parties intend to be legally bound; and
    (b) they reach a sufficient agreement without any further requirement.
(2) A contract need not be concluded or evidenced in writing nor is it subject to any other requirement as to form. The contract may be proved by any means, including witnesses.

Such an approach does not, of course, necessarily get rid of the problems or issues discussed in this chapter. It is still necessary to determine when there is an intention to be bound, and this will have to be determined from the words and actions of the parties, as is made clear by Art 2.102: 'The intention of a party to be bound by a contract is to be understood from the party's statements or conduct as they were reasonably understood by the other party.' The focus will be on what was meant by the parties' words and actions, but it seems likely that whether there was 'mutuality' in the agreement, and whether one party 'relied' on the other will become relevant in deciding whether they implied an intention to make a binding contract. 'Intention' will be the central issue, and the approach should avoid some of the formal rigidity of the traditional 'consideration-based' focus of the common law, but it will not increase certainty, and it will not be likely to make the job of the courts any easier.

---

225 Fried, 1981, p 38.
226 Above, 3.15.1.

Of course, even within the common law, the question of whether there was an intention to create legal relations is regarded as important. Discussion of the role played by this concept is the subject matter of the next chapter.

3.16 FURTHER READING

Adams, J and Brownsword, R, 'Contract, consideration and the critical path' (1990) 53 MLR 536

Atiyah, PS, 'Contracts, promises and the law of obligations' (1978) 94 LQR 340

Atiyah, PS, 'Consideration: a re-statement', Chapter 8 in Atiyah, PS, *Essays on Contract*, 1986, Oxford, Clarendon Press

Campbell, D, 'The relational constitution of the discrete contract', Chapter 3 in Campbell, D and Vincent-Jones, P (eds), *Contract and Economic Organisation*, 1996, Aldershot: Dartmouth

Fried, C, *Contract as Promise*, 1981, Cambridge, Mass: Harvard University Press

Halson, R, 'Sailors, sub-contractors and consideration' (1990) 106 LQR 183

Halson, R, 'The offensive limits of promissory estoppel' (1999) LMCLQ 256

Hird, NJ and Blair, A, 'Minding your own business – *Williams v Roffey* revisited' [1996] JBL 254

O'Sullivan, J, 'In defence of *Foakes v Beer*' [1996] CLJ 219

Thompson, MP, 'Representation to expectation: estoppel as a cause of action' (1983) 42 CLJ 257

Treitel, GH, 'Consideration: a critical analysis of Professor Atiyah's fundamental restatement' (1976) 50 Australian LJ 439

4 INTENTION TO CREATE LEGAL RELATIONS

CONTENTS

4.1 OVERVIEW

There may be situations where, despite the identification of an agreement and consideration, the courts feel that an agreement should not be enforced because the parties did not intend that it should create legal relations. The main approach is based on two presumptions:

■ If the agreement is a 'domestic' agreement the courts will presume that it is not intended to be legally binding. It will be up to the party wishing to enforce to overturn that presumption.
■ If the agreement is 'commercial' the courts will presume that it is intended to be legally binding. It will be up to the party wishing to escape from the agreement to prove that the presumption should be overturned.

The most frequent issues relate to the categorisation of the agreement (as domestic or commercial), and the evidence that is necessary to overturn the presumption.

There is also statutory control of the situation in relation to agreements between trade unions and employers, which are generally treated as unenforceable.

4.2 INTRODUCTION

In addition to the tests of the existence of a contract dealt with in the previous chapters, the courts will also sometimes inquire whether, despite the fact that offer, acceptance and consideration can be identified, the parties did really intend to create a legally binding relationship. In line with the traditional approach that the courts regard themselves simply as 'referees' or 'umpires' giving effect to the parties' intentions, it is only where the parties themselves have entered into an agreement which they intend to be legally binding that the courts will treat it as a contract. As with other tests of the parties' intentions, the courts take an objective approach, looking at what they have said and done and the context in which they have been dealing with each other. This was confirmed recently in *Edmonds v Lawson*,[1] where Lord Bingham said:[2]

> Whether the parties intended to enter into legally binding relations is an issue to be determined objectively and not by inquiring into their respective states of mind.

Collins has suggested that this 'objective' approach may well not coincide with reality:[3]

> In cases where the issue is litigated, it seems likely that one party intended a legal agreement and the other wanted the agreement to be merely morally binding. This contradiction removes any possibility of justifying the limits of contracts on the basis of the joint intent of the parties. We are forced to the conclusion that the courts must rely upon hidden policy considerations when determining the intentions of the parties.

We are not, however, in fact 'forced' to this conclusion. In many cases, rather than the parties having different intentions, they may not, at the time of entering into their agreement, have thought about the issue at all.[4] In such a situation, the courts will adopt the approach, which they also adopt in other areas where there is later

---

1 [2000] 2 WLR 1091.
2 Ibid, p 1099.
3 Collins, 2003, pp 104–05.
4 See, for example, the comments by Upjohn LJ in *Coward v Motor Insurers' Bureau* [1962] 1 All ER 531, p 536, and by Lord Cross in *Albert v Motor Insurers' Bureau* [1971] 2 All ER 1345, pp 1369–70.

disagreement as to the parties' intentions at the time of contracting,[5] of asking what the reasonable person in the position of the parties would have been likely to intend. This is the way in which the issue is dealt with in the proposed Principles of European Contract Law, Art 2.102 of which simply states that:[6]

> The intention of a party to be legally bound by contract is to be determined from the party's statements or conduct as they were reasonably to be understood by the other party.

Although this approach may be used as a device to bring 'policy' considerations into the law, it is also capable of acting as a means of coming to an 'objective' view in an area where the parties' evidence as to their respective states of mind is in conflict.

Another way of approaching the issue of 'intention' would be through formal requirements. It would be possible to require, for example, that an agreement, to be legally binding, must be in writing, and have within it a clause confirming that it is intended to be legally binding. In one particular situation, relating to the enforceability of collective agreements between trade unions and employers, this is precisely what has been required.[7] As has been explained in earlier chapters, however, generally the English law of contract does not require formalities. Verbal agreements are enforceable, and no particular forms of words are required. It can be argued, however, that the requirements of offer, acceptance and consideration, discussed in Chapters 2 and 3, may be regarded in themselves as indications of an intention to enter into a legally binding contract. If the parties have taken the trouble to specify their obligations in a way which makes them clear and unambiguous (as required by 'offer and acceptance'), and the agreement has the element of mutuality required by the doctrine of consideration, this may reassure a court that legal enforceability was intended. If, for example, a transaction which would otherwise appear as a gift has consideration introduced artificially, this may well be strong evidence of an intention to make a contract. The transfer of the ownership of a valuable painting, worth £50,000, which involves the recipient giving the supplier £1 in exchange would fall into this category. There would be no point in the recipient giving the money unless the intention is to make the transaction of transfer into a contract, and the parties into 'seller' and 'buyer'. The introduction of consideration is in this case therefore evidence of an intention to create legal relations. Taking this approach to its logical conclusion, some have argued that there is no need for a separate heading of intention,[8] and this point will be discussed below.[9]

The generally accepted view, however, is that, although this analysis has some force, there are nevertheless some agreements which may have all the other characteristics of a

---

5 See Chapter 2, 2.4.1.
6 Lando and Beale, 2000.
7 See Trade Union and Labour Relations (Consolidation) Act 1992, s 179 – discussed, further, below, 4.5.
8 For example, Hepple, 1970.
9 See 4.6.

contract, but which are clearly not meant to be treated as legally binding. If the parties to an apparently binding commercial agreement specifically state that it is not to have legal consequences, surely the courts should pay attention to this? Certain domestic arrangements may also raise difficulties. If, for example, there is an agreement between a man and a woman that he will cook a meal for them both, in return for her providing the wine to go with it, this may involve an offer, acceptance and consideration, but no one would expect it to be regarded as legally binding. If she failed to turn up, he would not be able to sue for the cost of preparing the meal. Given, however, that no formalities are required, and that offer, acceptance and consideration can be identified, how are those agreements which are intended to be binding to be distinguished from those which are not? The evidence of the parties themselves is likely to be unreliable, so some other means of determining the issue must be found.

In fact, as we have noted above, English law operates on the basis of an 'objective' approach, based on what a reasonable person in the position of the parties would have been likely to have intended. This approach is assisted by the 'presumptions' as to intention, which differ according to whether the agreement is to be regarded as 'domestic' or 'commercial'. These two categories of agreement must therefore be looked at separately.[10]

4.3 DOMESTIC AGREEMENTS

The leading case in this category is *Balfour v Balfour*.[11] This involved an agreement between husband and wife, resulting from her inability (due to illness) to return with him to his place of work, in Ceylon. He agreed to pay her £30 per month while they were apart. Later, the marriage broke up and the wife sued the husband for his failure to make the promised payments. The Court of Appeal held that her action must fail. Two members of the court centred their decision on the lack of any consideration supplied by the wife. Atkin LJ, however, stressed that even if there were consideration, domestic arrangements of this kind are clearly not intended by the parties to be legally binding. He used the example of the husband who agrees to provide money for his wife in return for her 'maintenance of the household and children'.[12] If this was a contract, then each would be able to sue the other for failure to fulfil the promised obligation. As regards this possibility, Lord Atkin commented:[13]

---

10 Unger (1983, pp 60–66), from a 'critical legal studies' perspective, suggests that the division between 'family' and 'commercial' agreements can be explained by the conflict between the principle of freedom to contract, and the counter-principle 'that the freedom to choose the contract partner will not be allowed to work in ways that subvert the communal aspects of social life'.
11 [1919] 2 KB 571.
12 Ibid, p 579.
13 Ibid.

All I can say is that the small courts of this country would have to be multiplied one hundredfold if these arrangements were held to result in legal obligations. They are not sued upon, not because the parties are reluctant to enforce their legal rights when the agreement is broken, but because the parties, in the inception never intended that they should be sued upon. Agreements such as these are outside the realm of contracts altogether.

The onus was on the wife to establish a contract and she had failed to do so.

Lord Atkin's judgment is the one which has received most attention in subsequent case law, and has been taken as establishing the position that in relation to domestic agreements there is a presumption that they are not intended to be legally binding.

There are two points to be noted here. First, the notion of the 'domestic' agreement should probably be taken as relating more to the subject matter than to the relationship between the parties. If, for example, a woman agrees to sell her car to her brother for £1,500, there seems little reason to deny this agreement the status of a contract, and it should be presumed to be binding unless there is evidence to the contrary. A recent decision of the High Court, however, has cast some doubt on this. It suggests that there may be situations which fall into a sort of 'halfway house' between domestic and commercial, and that in this case the burden of overturning the presumption may be affected. In *Sadler v Reynolds*,[14] the alleged contract was between a journalist and a businessman. The journalist wanted to ghostwrite the autobiography of the businessman, who had had a 'rags to riches' life, involving more than one spell in prison. The two had become friendly, meeting socially, and the journalist alleged that there had been an oral contract for him to write the autobiography. The judge, Elizabeth Slade QC, suggested that the agreement fell 'somewhere between an obviously commercial transaction and a social exchange'.[15] The onus was on the journalist to prove that there was an intention to create legal relations, 'albeit that the onus [was] a less heavy one than that which would be required to establish such an intent in the context of a purely social relationship'. The judge clearly viewed the nature of the relationship as more significant than the nature of the agreement, since at first sight an agreement to write a book would appear to be 'commercial', so that the burden of proving that it was not binding should have fallen on the businessman. The judge held, however, that it was up to the journalist to prove that it *was* binding. It follows that, as the cases seem to suggest, social arrangements between friends who are not related, or household agreements between a couple living together, but not married, should come into the category of 'domestic', and therefore be presumed not to be binding. An example of an agreement between friends is *Coward v Motor Insurers' Bureau*,[16] where

---

14 [2005] EWHC 309.
15 Ibid, para 56.
16 [1963] 1 QB 259; [1962] 1 All ER 531.

an agreement between workmates to share the cost of transport to work was held not be legally binding.[17]

The second point to note is that, since the rule is simply based on a presumption, it will always be possible for that presumption to be rebutted (as indeed was the case in *Sadler v Reynolds*). In *Merritt v Merritt*,[18] for example, an arrangement between husband and wife similar to that agreed in *Balfour v Balfour*, but here made in the context of the break-up of the marriage, was held to be legally binding. Lord Denning distinguished *Balfour v Balfour* in the following terms:[19]

> The parties there [that is, in *Balfour v Balfour*] were living together in amity. In such cases, their domestic arrangements are ordinarily not intended to create legal relations. It is altogether different when the parties are not living in amity but are separated, or about to separate. They then bargain keenly. They do not rely on honourable understandings. They want everything cut and dried. It may safely be presumed that they intend to create legal relations.

The context in which the agreement was made was such therefore that although it prima facie concerned a domestic matter, the support of a wife by her husband, the presumption that it was not intended to be binding was rebutted.

What will be the position in relation to agreements other than between spouses? The same principles apply, as is shown by *Simpkins v Pays*.[20] This involved an agreement which is of relevance to the increasing numbers of people involved in national lottery 'syndicates'. The plaintiff, the defendant and the defendant's granddaughter lived in the same house. They regularly entered a newspaper 'fashion' competition, which required the listing of eight items in order of merit. Each of the three women made a listing, and the three entries were submitted on one form. There was no fixed arrangement as to who paid the entry fee or the postage, but the form was submitted in the defendant's name. When one of the lines won £750, which was paid to the defendant, the plaintiff sued to recover a third share of this. The judge held that there was, on the evidence, an agreement to 'go shares' if one of the lines won,[21] and that this was intended to be legally binding. His reasons for coming to this conclusion are not very clear, but seem to relate to the fact that there was a 'mutuality in the arrangement between the parties'. Having heard the evidence of the parties, he felt that their agreement went beyond the 'sort of rough and ready statement' made in family associations

---

17 Cf *Albert v Motor Insurers' Bureau* [1971] 2 All ER 1345, where, in relation to a very similar situation, Lord Cross (who alone dealt with the issue in the House of Lords) took the view that there was an intention to enter into a contract (despite the fact that it was unlikely that either party would have considered taking legal action to enforce it).
18 [1970] 2 All ER 760.
19 Ibid, pp 761–62. See also *Darke v Strout* [2003] EWCA Civ 176.
20 [1955] 3 All ER 10.
21 Ibid, p 12.

which would not be intended to be binding.[22] There was a clear understanding as to what would happen in the event of a win, and this agreement was meant to be enforceable.

If you are invited to take part in a lottery syndicate, should you insist that there is a written agreement as to how the prize is to be divided in the event of a win?

The fact that all the surrounding circumstances may need to be considered was again stressed by Devlin J in *Parker v Clark*.[23] Here a young couple (the plaintiffs) agreed to live with older relatives (the defendants) and help look after them. In exchange, the plaintiffs were promised that the defendants' house and contents would be left to them. The arrangement did not work out, and the plaintiffs, having moved out, sued for damages. Devlin J noted that:[24]

> . . . a proposal between relatives to share a house, and a promise to make a bequest of it, may very well amount to no more than a family arrangement . . . which the courts will not enforce.

On the other hand, it was possible for such an arrangement to be legally binding:[25]

> The question must, of course, depend on the intention of the parties, to be inferred from the language they use and from the circumstances in which they use it.

In this case, the fact that the plaintiffs had sold their own house in order to move in with the defendants suggested that this was intended to be a binding agreement. The presumption that there is no intention in domestic agreements was again held to be rebutted.

Do you think the outcome would have been different if the plaintiffs had simply been renting a house, and had terminated the tenancy, prior to moving in with the defendants?

---

22 [1955] 3 All ER 10.
23 [1960] 1 All ER 93.
24 Ibid, p 100.
25 Ibid.

Although the cases so far considered may suggest that it is relatively easy to see on which side of the dividing line an arrangement between relatives should fall, in some cases the decision may be very finely balanced. This is demonstrated by *Jones v Padavatton*,[26] where the four judges who considered the facts were divided 2:2 as to whether or not they indicated an intention to create legal relations. In this case, the alleged contract was between a mother and daughter. The mother, who lived in the West Indies, promised her daughter, who was at the time working in the United States, that if she (the daughter) would go to England to study for the Bar, she (the mother) would pay her $200 per month. The daughter agreed to this arrangement, which began in February 1962. In 1964, the mother bought a house in which the daughter was to live, supporting herself by letting out some of the rooms. This replaced the previous arrangement of monthly payments. In 1967, with her daughter still unsuccessful in the Bar examinations, the mother sought possession of the house. The daughter's defence was based on there being a contract between herself and her mother. The trial judge was convinced by the daughter's evidence to this effect, and held that there was a contract. On appeal, this view was supported by Salmon LJ, who felt that, among other things, neither party could have 'intended that if, after the daughter had been in London, say, for six months, the mother dishonoured her promise and left her daughter destitute, the daughter would have no legal redress'.[27] The other two members of the Court of Appeal disagreed. Fenton Atkinson LJ noted the vagueness of the arrangements, and the fact that in cross-examination the daughter had admitted that she had refused to see her mother when the latter had come to the house in London because 'a normal mother doesn't sue her daughter in court'.[28] In conclusion, his view was that:[29]

> At the time when the first arrangements were made, the mother and daughter were, and always had been, to use the daughter's own words, 'very close'. I am satisfied that neither party at that time intended to enter into a legally binding contract, either then or later when the house was bought. The daughter was prepared to trust the mother to honour her promise of support, just as the mother no doubt trusted the daughter to study for the Bar with diligence, and to get through her examinations as early as she could.

There was, therefore, never any contract between them, and the mother was entitled to succeed.[30]

---

26 [1969] 2 All ER 616.
27 Ibid, p 622. He found, however, that the contract could not have been intended to last for more than five years, and so on that basis the mother was entitled to succeed in her action for possession.
28 Ibid, p 625.
29 Ibid.
30 Danckwerts LJ delivered a judgment to the same effect, relying primarily on *Balfour v Balfour* [1919] 2 KB 571.

This case perhaps serves to illustrate the importance of deciding whether the initial presumption is for or against there being a legal relationship. If there had been a presumption in favour of intention to create legal relations in *Jones v Padavatton*, which the mother had to rebut, it is not inconceivable that the result would have gone the other way. The fact that it was a 'domestic agreement' meant that the presumption went against there being an intention to be legally bound, and thus made it easier for the mother to succeed in her argument.

Finally, it should be noted that the question of whether or not, if the agreement is broken, the innocent party would in practice go to the courts to enforce it should not be regarded as being conclusive as to whether there was an intention to create legal relations. There are many minor commercial agreements (for example, the arrangement for newspapers to be delivered by a local newsagent) where the parties would be unlikely to consider it to be worth involving the courts to remedy a breach. Nevertheless, such agreements are clearly intended by the parties to affect their legal relations and to create binding obligations.[31] Moreover, even in relation to substantial commercial transactions, research has shown that parties often prefer to settle disputes in ways which do not involve recourse to lawyers.[32] This does not mean that they do not intend their agreements to be legally binding. As noted in *Jones v Padavatton*,[33] the fact that the parties would not be expected to sue each other may be relevant if such expectation is based on the relationship between the parties (for example, mother and daughter), but even then it cannot be conclusive.

4.4 COMMERCIAL AGREEMENTS

If the agreement is not a 'domestic' one, then it will be regarded as 'commercial'. This means the presumption is that the agreement is intended to be legally binding. It was confirmed in *Edmonds v Lawson*[34] that this could include an agreement which was primarily educational – as with the agreement between a pupil barrister and her chambers. The trouble taken by the chambers in selecting pupils and the importance to the pupil of obtaining a pupillage suggested that the arrangement was not intended to be binding in honour only. The fact that the relationship was also governed by the Bar Council's regulations, and that it was unlikely in practice that a chambers would sue a pupil who defaulted, did not prevent it from being intended to be legally binding.

---

31 That is, in the example just given, on the part of the newsagent to deliver papers each day, and on the part of the customer to settle the bill at regular intervals. See also the comments of Lord Cross in *Albert v Motor Insurers' Bureau* [1971] 2 All ER 1345, p 1370, and Salmon LJ in *Jones v Padavatton* [1969] 2 All ER 616, p 622.

32 See, for example, Macaulay, 1963; Beale and Dugdale, 1975; Lewis, 1982.

33 [1969] 2 All ER 616.

34 [2000] 2 WLR 1091.

In *Edwards v Skyways*,[35] Megaw J emphasised that there will be a heavy onus on a party to an ostensibly commercial agreement who wishes to argue that the presumption has been rebutted. In that case, the plaintiff was a pilot who had been made redundant. As part of the arrangements for this, he was offered and accepted a payment which was stated to be '*ex gratia*'. The company then found that the terms which had been offered would be more expensive for it than it had realised, and denied that there was any legal obligation to make the payment. The judge held that '*ex gratia*' did not mean 'not legally binding', but simply recognised that, prior to the offer being made, there had been no obligation to make such a payment. Once it had been made, however, and accepted as part of the redundancy arrangement, it was capable of being legally binding and there was no evidence to overturn the presumption that this should be the case.

A similar reluctance to overturn the presumption is shown by the House of Lords decision in *Esso Petroleum Ltd v Commissioners of Customs and Excise*.[36] This concerned a 'special offer' of a common type, under which garage owners offered a free 'World Cup Coin' to every purchaser of four gallons of petrol. The coins could be collected to make a set, but had minimal intrinsic value. Promotional advertising will often be considered as a 'mere puff', and not intended to be legally binding. As discussed earlier, in relation to offer and acceptance, however, the case of *Carlill v Carbolic Smoke Ball Co*[37] shows that in appropriate circumstances it can be found to be intended to create a legal relationship, on the basis of a unilateral contract. Similarly, in the *Esso* case, the majority of the House of Lords held that there was a unilateral contract under which the garage proprietor was saying 'If you will buy four gallons of my petrol, I will give you one of these coins'. The minority (Viscount Dilhorne and Lord Russell) felt that there was, however, no intention to create legal relations. As Viscount Dilhorne put it, if this arrangement was held to be a contract:[38]

> . . . it would seem to exclude the possibility of any dealer ever making a free gift to any of his customers, however negligible its value, to promote his sales.

Moreover, he did 'not consider that the offer of a gift of a free coin is properly to be regarded as a business matter'. The majority, however, viewed what was being done as clearly a 'commercial' transaction. As Lord Simon commented:[39]

> Esso and the garage proprietors put the material out for their commercial advantage, and designed it to attract the custom of motorists. The whole transaction took place in the setting of business relations . . . The coins may have been themselves of little intrinsic value; but all the evidence suggests that Esso contemplated

35 [1964] 1 WLR 349.
36 [1976] 1 All ER 117.
37 [1893] 1 QB 256 – see above, 2.7.6.
38 [1976] 1 All ER 117, pp 120–21.
39 Ibid, p 121.

that they would be attractive to motorists and that there would be a large commercial advantage to themselves from the scheme, an advantage in which the garage proprietors would share.

The decision thus emphasises the difficulty faced by a commercial organisation in avoiding legal liabilities in connection with any transaction which it enters into with a view to commercial advantage. The advantage here was indirect (neither Esso nor the garages benefited directly from the exchange of the coins for petrol), but was nevertheless sufficient (that is, in terms of the likely increased sales of petrol which would result) to bring the presumption of an intention to create legal relations into play.

FOR THOUGHT

If a newspaper publisher advertises that a particular DVD will be available as a 'free gift' inside the paper on a particular day does the decision in *Esso v Commissioners of Customs and Excise* mean that you could sue the newspaper publisher (as opposed to the newsagent) if the DVD was missing?

It is possible, however, by using sufficiently explicit wording, to rebut the presumption even in relation to a clearly commercial agreement. This is commonly done in relation to agreements relating to the sale of land which are generally stated to be 'subject to contract', even where a price has been agreed between the parties. This is intended to ensure that they are not binding until fully considered written contracts have been exchanged.[40]

An example of a similarly explicit attempt to exclude 'intention to create legal relations' is to be found in *Rose and Frank Co v Crompton Bros*.[41] This case was concerned with a continuing agency arrangement between two companies. The agreement contained within it an 'Honourable Pledge Clause', which specifically stated that it was not entered into as 'a formal or legal agreement', but was 'only a definite expression and record of the purpose and intention' of the parties. The parties 'honourably pledged' themselves to the agreement in the confidence 'that it will be carried through by each of the . . . parties with mutual loyalty and friendly co-operation'.[42] The Court of Appeal held that this should not be regarded as creating a legally binding agreement. To hold otherwise would be to frustrate the clear intentions of the parties:[43]

I can see no reason why, even in business matters, the parties should not intend to rely on each other's good faith and honour, and to exclude all idea of settling

---

40 Note also the formalities required for this type of contract by the Law of Property (Miscellaneous Provisions) Act 1989, s 2(1). See also the comments of Atiyah, 2006, pp 101–103.
41 [1925] AC 445.
42 Ibid, p 451.
43 [1923] 2 KB 261, p 288 (*per* Scrutton LJ).

disputes by any outside intervention . . . If they clearly express such an intention, I can see no reason in public policy why effect should not be given to their intention.

The House of Lords agreed with the Court of Appeal that the overall agency arrangement was not legally binding, and could therefore be terminated without notice. In relation to particular orders placed under the agreement, however, they preferred the dissenting view of Lord Atkin in the Court of Appeal that such orders were enforceable contracts of sale. The 'honour clause' applied only to the general framework agreement, and not to specific orders made under it. Once again, therefore, the presumption of legal enforceability prevails in relation to commercial dealings, and the rejection of this by the parties is interpreted strictly so as to apply only in the limited circumstances to which the rejection most clearly applies.

'Honour clauses' have long been included on football pools' coupons, with the effect that the promoter is under no contractual obligation to pay winnings to a person who has submitted a coupon with a winning line ('the punter').[44] It has now been confirmed by the Court of Appeal that such a clause must be taken to apply also to any agreement between the punter and a collector of coupons who then forwards them to the promoter. In *Halloway v Cuozzo*,[45] the collector had failed to forward the plaintiff's coupon, which contained a winning line. The Court of Appeal held that the collector had no contractual liability towards the punter. Moreover, the lack of intention to create legal relations also prevented the creation of a duty of care, so that there was no liability in the tort of negligence either.

Public policy arguments may also influence a decision as to whether there is intention to create legal relations. In *Robinson v HM Customs & Excise*,[46] the claimant was an informer for the Customs and Excise. He tried to bring a contractual claim for the payment of reasonable remuneration and expenses. It was held, however, that there was no intention to create legal relations in respect of the supply of information by the claimant. The payments were discretionary and dependent on results (for example, arrests, seizures of illicit goods) and there were reasons of public policy why the court could not become involved in inquiring into these matters.

4.5   COLLECTIVE AGREEMENTS

Some problems of intention to create legal relations have arisen in the area of 'collective agreements'. By this is meant agreements between trade unions and employers, or employers' organisations, as to the terms and conditions of work of particular groups

---

44 *Jones v Vernons Pools* [1938] 2 All ER 626; *Appleson v H Littlewood Ltd* [1939] 1 All ER 464.
45 (1999) unreported, 9 February, CA.
46 (2000) *The Times*, 28 April.

of employees. Each employee will have a binding contract of employment with the employer, but some of the terms of this agreement (for example, as to rates of pay) may specifically be stated to be subject to the current collective agreement between employer and trade union. What is the status of the collective agreement itself? It is clearly made in a commercial or business context, and therefore it would seem that there should be a presumption of legal enforceability.

The issue was considered by the High Court in *Ford Motor Co Ltd v AEF*.[47] Ford was seeking an injunction restraining the trade union from calling strike action by its members. Part of Ford's argument depended on establishing that the collective agreements which it had reached with the AEF were legally binding. In deciding this issue, Geoffrey Lane J took the view that it was necessary to look at the general context in which such agreements were made. An objective view of whether they were intended to be enforceable should take account of not only the wording of the agreements themselves and their nature, but also 'the climate of opinion voiced and evidence by the extra-judicial authorities'[48] (here, he had in mind the *Donovan Report* on industrial relations which had recently been published,[49] and academic writing on the issue). Taking these matters into account:[50]

> Agreements such as these, composed largely of optimistic aspirations, presenting grave practical problems of enforcement and reached against a background of opinion adverse to enforceability, are, in my judgment, not contracts in the legal sense and are not enforceable at law.

To make them legally binding would require 'clear and express provisions' to that effect.

This judgment seems to draw on a much wider range of factors than the other cases in this area in order to determine the issue. It is probably the case, however, that such an approach was a result of the particular sensitive context (that is, industrial relations) rather than being indicative of the way in which the issue should be dealt with more generally. The *Ford* decision should not, therefore, be regarded as indicating any general departure from the presumption of legal enforceability which attaches to agreements in the commercial area. As far as collective agreements themselves are concerned, the matter is now dealt with by statute. Section 179 of the Trade Union and Labour Relations (Consolidation) Act 1992 provides that collective agreements are 'conclusively presumed not to have been intended by the parties to be' legally enforceable. The only exception is where the agreement is in writing, and expressly stated to be legally enforceable. We thus have here a presumption against legal enforceability which is even stronger than that which operates in relation to domestic agreements. It cannot be rebutted by taking account of verbal statements, or by looking at the context, but

---

47 [1969] 2 QB 303.
48 Ibid, pp 329–30.
49 Cmnd 3623, 1968.
50 [1969] 2 QB 303, pp 330–31.

only by a clear intention committed to writing. This, therefore, is one of the few occasions in which English law requires formality in the making of an agreement if it is to be legally enforceable.

4.6 IS A REQUIREMENT OF INTENTION NECESSARY?

At the beginning of this chapter, reference was made to the argument that the insistence on a requirement of intention, in addition to the other elements of validly formed contract (offer, acceptance, consideration), is unnecessary. This view has been taken by, for example, Williston in the United States,[51] and Hepple in the UK.[52] Hepple argues that the problems with this area derive largely from a failure to take account of the particular approach to consideration adopted by Lord Atkin in *Balfour v Balfour*.[53] He points out that, in defining consideration in terms of 'mutual promises' or as 'a benefit received by one party or a loss suffered by the other', Lord Atkin failed to add that the benefit or loss, or indeed the mutual promises, 'must be received as the price for the other'. Hepple argues that many domestic agreements may involve mutual promises, 'and yet not be . . . contract[s] because the promise of the one party is not given as the price for the other'.[54] In other words, the concept of the *bargain* is central to the test of enforceability of contracts under English law and the vital elements in the identification of a bargain are offer, acceptance and consideration. These three elements should be treated *together* as indicating a *bargain*. Thus, an analysis which tries to separate out *agreement* (that is, offer and acceptance) from consideration is missing the point of why the courts started looking for evidence of these three elements in the first place:[55]

> This separation of agreement from consideration . . . has resulted in a funda-
> mental point being overlooked. This is that the common law recognised at an
> early stage that usually parties do not define their intention to enter into legal
> relations. Consequently, the fact that they have cast their agreement into the form
> of bargain (offer, acceptance, consideration) provides an extremely practical test
> of that intention. This test of bargain renders superfluous any *additional* proof of
> intention.

Accordingly, Hepple regards the courts as falling into error in trying to identify an additional element of intention in cases such as *Ford Motor Co Ltd v AEF*.[56] This only results 'in the use of unnecessary legal fictions'.

---

51 Williston, 1990.
52 See Hepple, 1970.
53 [1919] 2 KB 571.
54 Hepple, 1970, p 128.
55 Ibid.
56 [1969] 1 WLR 339.

The argument may be justified as according with the principle that the intention of the parties must be decided objectively. In other words, can the party who claims that he or she thought that the agreement was intended to be enforceable be said to have acted reasonably in this assumption?[57] The presumption would be that as long as offer, acceptance and consideration were present, and no specific statement had been made about enforceability, then it would be intended to be legally binding. Social and domestic agreements could still be excluded from enforceability either because no reasonable person expects them to be legally binding, and therefore an assumption that they are would be unreasonable, or because what is given in exchange in such agreements is not generally to be regarded as good consideration. In either case, no 'bargain' is created.

This line of argument is in effect introducing a rule of formality into the formation of contracts. The formal requirements become not writing, or signature, but 'offer', 'acceptance' and 'consideration'. The parties who go through the process of making an agreement which contains these elements will, in the absence of specific and explicit evidence to the contrary, be deemed to have made a 'bargain' and therefore a binding agreement. Although this has some attractions, it is submitted that it does not truly represent the English common law approach to contracts. This is based not only in relation to formation, but in many other areas as well, on the basis that the court is trying to give effect to the intention of the parties. This is the overriding concept, and the evidence which may go towards establishing whether any intention to create a legal relationship existed and, if so, what it was intended to be is subsidiary. For that reason, the courts legitimately remain concerned to establish the existence or absence of intention, even if other indicators of a binding agreement are present. The existence of the presumption of enforceability in commercial agreements does not contradict such an approach. It simply allows it to operate in a way which is efficient, and does not encourage the parties to an agreement to become involved in unnecessary disputes as to their supposed intentions.

4.7 FURTHER READING

Allen, D, 'The gentleman's agreement in legal theory and in modern practice' [2000] Anglo-American Law Review 204

Brown, I, 'The letter of comfort: placebo or promise?' [1990] JBL 281

Freeman, M, 'Contracting in the haven: *Balfour v Balfour* revisited', in Halson, R (ed), *Exploring the Boundaries of Contract*, 1996, London: Dartmouth

Hedley, S, 'Keeping contract in its Place: *Balfour v Balfour* and the enforceability of informal agreements' (1985) OJLS 391

Hepple, B, 'Intention to create legal relations' (1970) CLJ 122

Unger, R, *The Critical Legal Studies Movement*, 1983, Cambridge, Mass: Harvard University Press, pp 60–66

---

57 Cf Principles of European Contract Law, Art 2.102.

5 PRIVITY

CONTENTS

5.1 OVERVIEW

The doctrine of privity states that only those who are parties to a contract can have rights or liabilities under it. The doctrine is well established in English law, but also has a number of exceptions to it. In particular, the Contracts (Rights of Third Parties) Act 1999 means that there are many situations where the parties can choose to sidestep the doctrine. The order of treatment here is:

- The origins of the doctrine. What are the reasons underlying the doctrine, and how did it develop in English law?
- The Contracts Rights of (Third Parties) Act 1999. This is a major exception to the doctrine. It allows the parties to a contract to create benefits which are legally enforceable by a third party. Similar rights appear in the Principles of European Contract Law.
- Common law devices to evade the doctrine. These include:
  - Damages on behalf of another. In some situations the courts allow a party to a contract to recover damages for a loss suffered by a third party as a result of a breach of contract.
  - The trust of a promise. This device has been used to create third party rights, but has recently fallen into disuse – and has probably been superseded by the 1999 Act.
  - Collateral contracts. In some situations the courts will find that there is in fact a 'collateral contract' with a third party, sitting alongside the main contract.
  - Tort of negligence. A third party to a contract has sometimes been allowed to use the tort of negligence to recover damages from a party in breach, but recovery for pure economic loss is very restricted.
- Statutory exceptions. There are some specific contracts (for example, certain types of insurance contract) where statutes give rights to third parties.
- Privity and exclusion clauses. Parties quite often purport to give the benefits of an exclusion clause to third parties, and the courts have in some cases used agency concepts to enable these to be enforceable or to modify tortious liability. The 1999 Act reduces the need for these devices to be used.
- Imposing burdens:
  - Restrictive covenants are used in land law to impose burdens on third party occupiers of land. Limited use of this approach has been made outside the land law context.
  - The tort of interference with contractual rights can be used to obtain an injunction to stop a third party encouraging a breach of contract.

5.2   THE RATIONALE FOR THE DOCTRINE

The doctrine of privity has long been regarded as one of the fundamental characteristics of the English law of contract although, as will be seen later in this chapter, the courts have recognised a number of exceptions to it and sanctioned a variety of devices for avoiding its effect. In addition, Parliament has given parties the opportunity to avoid a significant part of the doctrine by virtue of the Contracts (Rights of Third Parties) Act 1999.

The essence of the doctrine of privity is the idea that only those who are parties to a contract can have rights or liabilities under it. Since the paradigm of the classical contract is a two-party bargain, it follows that only those two parties whose dealings led to the creation of it will be regarded as being able to enforce it or be sued under it. Even the classical law, however, allowed for the possibility in certain circumstances for there to be multiparty contracts, for example, between members of a club or those entering a competition.[1] It seems, therefore, that the doctrine cannot simply be based on a rule that a contract can only ever have two parties.

A related argument, and one that, as we shall see, has often been put forward by the courts, is that the doctrine of privity is based on the doctrine of consideration and, in particular, the rule that consideration must move from the promisee. This possibility is discussed in more detail below.

Whatever the technical arguments put forward, what, if any, are the policy reasons for the doctrine? What is it meant to achieve? There are two aspects to the doctrine which need to be considered separately. First, there is the rule that the burden of a contract should not be placed on a third party. At first sight this seems like a rule that is clearly justifiable. To use an unlikely but striking example from Collins: 'It would plainly be a serious invasion of the liberty of the individual . . . if the parties to a contract agreed that a third person should run a marathon.'[2] To make such an agreement enforceable, at least without the consent of the third party, would be an unjustifiable intrusion into personal freedom. There are other situations, however, where the answer may not be so clear-cut.

Suppose, for example, that Anne owns a famous painting. Brian, the owner of a gallery, makes a contract with Anne for the loan of the painting for a special exhibition for three months. Brian spends a large amount of time and money promoting this exhibition, with Anne's painting being the central attraction. A week before the exhibition is to open Anne sells the painting to Claire. Should Claire be obliged to allow the painting to be used in Brian's exhibition? The doctrine of privity would say 'no'. Claire is not a party to the contract between Brian and Anne, and so cannot be affected by obligations arising out of it. Brian is left with a remedy in damages against Anne, which

---

1 See, for example, *Clarke v Dunraven* [1897] AC 59 – this is discussed further below, 5.3.2.
2 Collins, 2003, p 303.

may well be inadequate to recompense him,[3] and will not really make up for the fact that his exhibition has lost its central exhibit. It is not clear why it would be unfair or unreasonable in such a situation to require Claire to honour Anne's commitment to lend the painting to Brian, particularly if Claire is aware of the commitment at the time when she buys the painting from Anne. As we shall see later in this chapter, the courts have struggled to find the best solution to this type of situation – wishing in some cases to require the third party to bear the burden of the obligation, while at the same time not undertaking a direct attack on the doctrine of privity.

Other problems relating to the imposition of burdens can arise where, for example, the two companies which are parties to a contract wish to avoid being sued in tort by individual employees of either firm in relation to actions undertaken in relation to the contract. Here the burden is the purported removal of a right to sue. Once again, the general doctrine of privity would say that the employees cannot be bound by this agreement, and in many cases that may be the just and fair result. If, however, the contracting parties have made other arrangements (for example, by insurance) which would provide satisfactory protection for the employees, and these arrangements have been approved by the employees' representatives, is there any real reason why the individual's right to take legal action should not be curtailed?

Even in the area of the imposition of burdens, therefore, the rule that only a party can be affected by a contract is not necessarily appropriately applied in all situations. When we turn to the conferring of benefits, there seems to be even less justification for a strict doctrine of privity. If A and B have agreed that C should have a benefit under their contract, why should C not be able to enforce this? Suppose, for example, that Alison promises Bernard that she will pay £1,000 to Oxfam if Bernard gives up smoking for a year. This is a contract which (subject to the question of intention to create legal relations)[4] is clearly enforceable by Bernard. However, the charity which is to benefit will not at common law be allowed to enforce, because it is not a party to the agreement. Treitel argues that the answer may lie with the doctrine of consideration:[5]

> A system of law which does not give a gratuitous promisee a right to enforce a promise may well be reluctant to give this right to a gratuitous beneficiary who is not even a promisee.

This argument is open to the objection, however, that what is really contrary to the doctrine of consideration is that a promise for which no consideration has been given should be enforceable.[6] In the example used above, consideration has been given for

---

3 It is quite likely on the facts as given that only 'reliance' damages would be recoverable, the likely profits from the exhibition being too speculative: *Anglia Television Ltd v Reed* [1972] 1 QB 60. See the discussion of this case and related issues below, Chapter 18, 18.4.2.

4 See above, Chapter 4.

5 Treitel, 2003, p 588.

6 Cf Flannigan, 1987, p 577.

Alison's promise by Bernard. There could be no objection to Bernard seeking to enforce it (though his remedies might be limited).[7] If the charity were given a right to sue, Alison would be under no greater obligation than she already is as regards Bernard. She can obviously only be required to pay the money once, and there seems little reason why the charity should not be able to sue her directly for it. The justification becomes even less in a situation where the third party has acted in reliance on the promise; as we have seen in Chapter 3, reliance is increasingly used by the courts as the basis for enforcing promises between two parties and there seems little reason why this should not also apply in a tripartite relationship.

It seems, therefore, that the rationale for the doctrine of privity is by no means clear and unanswerable. Moreover, there are several reasons why the doctrine may be said to be out of tune with the modern English law of contract. First, there is the weakening of the doctrine of consideration identified in the previous chapter. The concept of what constitutes consideration has been expanded by cases such as *Williams v Roffey*,[8] and this means that it may be easier to regard third parties as having provided consideration. More importantly, there is the growth of the area of 'estoppel', with the associated idea of 'reliance' as a basis for the enforceability of promises attaining increasing importance. This would suggest that where a third party has relied on a promise made in a contract between two other parties, there may be good reason to regard the promise as enforceable by the third party.[9]

The second major reason why privity is out of tune with the modern law is that it does not accord with the reality of many commercial contracts. As Adams and Brownsword have pointed out,[10] many commercial transactions (such as those surrounding construction contracts) do not simply involve two parties entering into an agreement. They involve 'multiple linked contracts' which can be regarded as 'networks',[11] to which the traditional approach of the doctrine of privity is simply inappropriate and unhelpful. Adams and Brownsword have suggested that a 'network' of contracts, with a more relaxed approach to third party rights, would have the following characteristics:[12]

(i) there is a principal contract (or, there are a number of principal contracts) within the set giving the set an overall objective;

(ii) other contracts (secondary and tertiary contracts, and so on) are entered

7 It is difficult to see what 'losses' he could recover for in an action for damages; he will undoubtedly have saved money through not smoking, and his health may well have improved. It is not a situation where an order for specific performance would normally be regarded as appropriate – on this, see Chapter 18, 18.7.3.

8 [1991] 1 QB 1; [1990] 1 All ER 512.

9 Cf the comments to this effect by Steyn LJ in *Darlington Borough Council v Wiltshier Northern Ltd* [1995] 3 All ER 895, p 904.

10 Adams and Brownsword, 1990b.

11 Ibid, p 27.

12 Ibid. See also Adams and Brownsword, 1995, p 149.

into, an object of each of which is, directly or indirectly, to further the attainment of this overall objective; and

(iii) the network of contractors expands until a sufficiency of contractors are obligated, whether to the parties to the principal contract, or to other contractors in the set, to attain the overall objective.

As well as construction contracts, Adams and Brownsword suggest that contracts for the carriage of goods and 'many credit and financing arrangements' fit this pattern. Within such a network, the interlocking obligations of contracts designed to achieve an overall objective is far from the classical paradigm of the two-party exchange of mutual promises or obligations and calls for a different regime from that which the traditional doctrine of privity has provided.

The doctrine has therefore been ripe for reform for some time.[13] Any attempt to do so, however, will be faced with the question of to what extent the boundaries should be extended. As the Law Commission recognized, in its working paper on the subject published in 1991,[14] contracts can have far-reaching effects. It used the example of a contract between a building company and a highway authority for the construction of a new road. The road may be intended for the benefit of all road users, but it would surely not be acceptable for them all to have a right of action, for example, in the event of delay in completion of the project.[15] It is this problem that Collins suggests provides the best rationale for having a doctrine of privity:[16]

> The most significant justification for the doctrine of privity thus boils down to the simple point that the law of contract must draw a line at some point to set the limits to the range of liability to third parties.

In other words, the doctrine is there to avoid there being indeterminate liability to an indeterminate number of people.[17] But this does not, of course, mean that the boundaries of liability have to be set as narrowly as they have been under the traditional doctrine. A view can be taken as to the appropriate situations in which third parties should have rights (or even obligations) under a contract; provided that the limits are clearly defined, this should not cause problems for the law, and might be more effective in meeting the intentions of all concerned.[18]

The fact that the strict doctrine of privity as applied by the English courts is not

---

13 See, for example, the 1937 recommendations of the Law Revision Committee (Sixth Interim Report, 1937, Cmnd 5449).

14 In its Consultation Paper No 121, *Privity of Contract: Contracts for the Benefit of Third Parties*, 1991.

15 Ibid, paras 2.19, 5.9.

16 See Collins, 2003, p 317.

17 See Cardozo CJ, *Ultramares Corp v Touche* (1931) 174 NE 441, p 444.

18 The concept of the 'network contract', as defined by Adams and Brownsword and outlined above, would be one way of providing an extended limit without running the risk of indeterminate liability.

necessary is illustrated by the fact that, although many common law jurisdictions have adopted it, a more relaxed view has long been taken in the United States.[19] Civil law jurisdictions have also not found it necessary to be as narrow as the English courts in determining who may enforce a contract. Provision for third party enforcement is also to be found in the Principles of European Contract Law,[20] and this is dealt with in more detail below.[21]

It is the way in which the traditional doctrine deals with the conferring of benefits which has attracted the most criticism and it is this area in which, following recommendations to this effect from the Law Commission,[22] there has now been legislative intervention. The effect of the Contracts (Rights of Third Parties) Act 1999 is discussed in detail later in this chapter, and we shall try to assess there whether the reform meets the objections that have been raised. Since the Act has not replaced the common law, however, we shall start by looking at the development of the common law doctrine.

5.3   DEVELOPMENT OF THE DOCTRINE

There were some decisions dating from the seventeenth century which allowed a third party beneficiary to enforce a promise, but these pre-dated the strict formulation of the doctrine of consideration. The modern law is generally taken to derive from the case of *Tweddle v Atkinson*.[23] This concerned an agreement reached between the fathers of a couple who were about to get married, under which the father of the bride was to pay £200 and the father of the groom £100, to the bridegroom, William Tweddle, the plaintiff. William sought to enforce his father-in-law's promise, but it was held that he could not. The main justification appears to have been that it was necessary for there to be mutuality of obligations as between those enforcing a contract and having it enforced against them. As Crompton J put it:[24]

> It would be a monstrous proposition to say that a person was a party to the contract for the purpose of suing upon it for his own advantage, and not a party to it for the purpose of being sued.

It is not clear why this proposition should be thought to justify the strong epithet 'monstrous'. There are other situations in the law of contract where there is not mutuality of this kind and yet obligations are enforced. In certain situations, unilateral contracts will

---

19 *Lawrence v Fox*, 20 NY 268 (1859). For a short overview of the US law on third party rights, see the Law Commission Consultation Paper 121, pp 151–55.

20 Article 6.110.

21 See 5.6.

22 Report No 242, *Privity of Contract: Contracts for the Benefit of Third Parties*, 1996, Cmnd 3329 – following on from Consultation Paper No 121, published in 1991.

23 (1861) 1 B & S 393; 121 ER 762.

24 (1861) 1 B & S 393, p 398; 121 ER 762, p 764.

lack mutuality, as will some contracts made by minors. A better reason for the decision would seem to be that William Tweddle was not the person to whom the promise was made, even though it was intended for his benefit.[25] If he had been, it will be noted that it would have been quite possible for the court to have found that he had provided consideration for the promise. The agreement was clearly made in consideration of William's marriage and, as we saw in the last chapter (in *Shadwell v Shadwell*,[26] decided just a year before *Tweddle v Atkinson*), going through with a marriage ceremony can be good consideration for a promise of payment. This again indicates that the doctrine of privity is properly regarded as separate from, though closely linked to, the doctrine of consideration.

5.3.1 Affirmation by the House of Lords

Tweddle v Atkinson was a decision of the court of Queen's Bench, but the principle it was taken to have been based on was reaffirmed by the House of Lords in a commercial context in *Dunlop Pneumatic Tyre Co Ltd v Selfridge & Co Ltd*.[27] This concerned an attempt by Dunlop to control the price at which their tyres were sold to the public. They had a contract with Dew & Co, who were wholesalers in motor accessories, that in selling the tyres to retailers they would require the retailer to undertake to observe Dunlop's list price. Selfridge & Co entered into such an agreement with Dew & Co. Dunlop subsequently sought an injunction and damages in relation to alleged breaches of this agreement. The House of Lords held that they could not succeed. The following passage from the speech of Viscount Haldane LC indicates the approach taken:[28]

> My Lords, in the law of England, certain principles are fundamental. One is that only a person who is a party to a contract can sue on it. Our law knows nothing of a *jus quaesitum tertio* arising by way of contract. Such a right may be conferred by way of property, as, for example, under a trust, but it cannot be conferred on a stranger to a contract as a right to enforce the contract *in personam*. A second principle is that if a person with whom a contract not under seal has been made is to be able to enforce it, consideration must have been given by him to the promisor or to some other person at the promisor's request.

On both grounds, Dunlop were doomed to failure. They were not parties to the agreement between Dew and Selfridge and, moreover, had provided no consideration for Selfridge's promise not to sell below the list price. Note also that although this was not raised as an issue in the case, Dunlop could not, of course, rely on the terms of their contract with Dew, because Selfridge were not a party to this contract.

---

25 Cf the comments of Collins on 'autonomy' as a rationale for privity (Collins, 2003, p 314).
26 (1860) 9 CBNS 159; 142 ER 62.
27 [1915] AC 847.
28 Ibid, p 853.

FOR THOUGHT

Could Dunlop have recovered any compensation from Dew? Were they in breach of their contracts with Dunlop?

The doctrine of privity is not one for which the courts have shown any great affection,[29] but it was again reaffirmed by the House of Lords in 1968 in the case of *Beswick v Beswick*.[30] A nephew had bought his uncle's coal merchant's business, and had promised as part of the deal to pay his uncle £6.50 a week and then, when his uncle died, to pay his aunt (if she survived) £5 a week. After his uncle's death, the nephew refused to make the payments to his aunt, and she sued. In the Court of Appeal, Lord Denning tried to open up a broad exception to the doctrine of privity by relying on s 56(1) of the Law of Property Act 1925, which states that:

> A person may take an immediate or other interest in land or other property, or the benefit of any condition, right of entry, covenant or agreement over or respecting land or other property, although he may not be named as a party to the conveyance or other instrument.

Lord Denning's view (with which Danckwerts LJ agreed) was that this in effect abolished the doctrine of privity in relation to written contracts, and therefore allowed Mrs Beswick to sue her nephew on the promise made to her husband for her benefit.[31] The House of Lords rejected this argument, deciding that the history and context of s 56 meant that it should be interpreted as not intended to apply to a straightforward contractual situation such as that in *Beswick v Beswick*, although the exact scope of the section remains uncertain.[32] The case, therefore, fell to be dealt with under common law principles. The House accepted what Lord Reid referred to as the 'commonly held' view that where a contract between A and B contains an obligation to pay money to a third party, X, 'such a contract confers no right on X and X could not sue for the [money]'. In other words, the traditional doctrine of privity applied and Mrs Beswick was therefore

---

29 See, for example, the comments of Lord Scarman in *Woodar Investment Development Ltd v Wimpey Construction (UK) Ltd* [1980] 1 All ER 571, p 591; and by Steyn LJ in *Darlington Borough Council v Wiltshier Northern Ltd* [1995] 3 All ER 895, pp 903–04: '. . .there is no doctrinal, logical or policy reason why the law should deny the effectiveness of a contract for the benefit of a third party where that is the expressed intention of the parties.' See, also, *Smith and Snipes Hall Farm Ltd v River Douglas Catchment Board* [1949] 2 KB 500; *Drive Yourself Hire Co (London) Ltd v Strutt* [1954] 1 QB 250.

30 [1968] AC 58.

31 Cf the *dicta* of Lord Denning in *Smith and Snipes Hall Farm Ltd v River Douglas Catchment Board* [1949] 2 KB 500, and *Drive Yourself Hire Company (London) Ltd v Strutt* [1954] 1 QB 250.

32 It recently received a full consideration in *Amsprop Trading Ltd v Harris Distribution Ltd* [1997] 2 All ER 990.

prevented from suing in her personal capacity. The House of Lords agreed, however, that as the administratrix of her husband's estate, she could take his place as a party to the contract with the nephew, and thus obtain an order for specific performance of the obligations contained in it. Thus, while affirming the doctrine of privity, the House of Lords found a way to achieve what was clearly a just result.

5.3.2 A special case: multiparty contracts

There is one situation which does not fit neatly within the doctrine of privity, and which should be noted before moving on to consider the more general attempts which have been made to avoid the effects of the doctrine. This is the situation of the 'multiparty' contract.

As we have seen, the typical model of a contract is based on a two-party relationship. Nevertheless, there are situations which are clearly governed by contract but which do not fall into this pattern. Where a group of people each contract with one body, for example, on joining a sports club, and agree to abide by the body's rules, can one member enforce those rules against another? Or is the only contract between each member and the club itself? The issue was considered in *Clarke v Dunraven*.[33] The case concerned the participants in a race organised by a yacht club. There was a collision during the race, as a result of which the plaintiff's yacht sank.[34] The plaintiff sued the defendant, claiming damages based on provisions in the club rules. The defendant denied that there was any contractual relationship between him and the plaintiff. The House of Lords held that there was. The committee of the club had, in effect, made an offer to prospective entrants to the race to the effect that, if they wanted to take part in the race, they would have to abide by the conditions which the committee had laid down. One of the conditions must be deemed to be that (in the words of Lord Esher, in the Court of Appeal):[35]

> . . . if you do sail [for a prize in a race], you must enter into an obligation with the owners of the yachts who are competing, which they at the same time enter into similarly with you, that if by a breach of any of our rules you do damage or injury to the owner of a competing yacht, you shall be liable to make good the damage you have so done.

There was, in other words, an obligation under a unilateral contract with the club's committee to enter into a contract with every other competitor. Applying this approach, the House of Lords held that there was a contract between all the competitors, which they had each entered into when they entered the race. The plaintiff was

---

33 [1897] AC 59.
34 It should be noted that under the modern law, this situation would be much more likely to be dealt with by the tort of negligence.
35 [1895] P 248, p 255.

therefore entitled to succeed in his action, based on the obligation contained in the regulations governing the race to pay for damage caused by a breach of the rules of racing. Thus, in the example given above, each member of the sports club is in a contractual relationship, based on the rules of the club, with every other member. This analysis avoids any problems of privity, but creates difficulties as regards offer and acceptance. Who exactly is making the offer and acceptance as between the first and last individuals to join? Any attempt to find a way around this, such as making the club the agent for the receipt of both offer and acceptance, is bound to look very artificial.

Although the approach taken in *Clarke v Dunraven* has the potential to be applied to many situations involving clubs or competitions, it was not adopted by the Court of Appeal in *Ellesmere v Wallace*,[36] which concerned the recovery of entrance fees for a horse race.

5.4 EVADING THE DOCTRINE

The current position as regards the doctrine of privity is that, its status having been confirmed by *Beswick v Beswick*, there has not in recent years been any direct challenge in the courts to either aspect of the doctrine (that is, the conferring of benefits or the imposition of obligations). There have, however, been various attempts to evade the effects of the doctrine, some of which have been more successful than others. The whole area must, however, now be reconsidered in the light of the Contracts (Rights of Third Parties) Act 1999. This has fundamentally changed the position in relation to the conferring of benefits, but has not altered the common law as regards imposing burdens. The order of treatment will therefore be to look first at the Act; then at the various devices which have been used previously by the courts to confer benefits, and which may still be relevant in situations to which the Act does not apply; and, finally, at the common law rules relating to the imposition of burdens.[37]

5.5 THE CONTRACTS (RIGHTS OF THIRD PARTIES) ACT 1999

The Act received the Royal Assent on 11 November 1999, and applies to contracts made on or after 11 May 2000. It also applies to contracts made between these two dates if the contract specifically states that the Act is to apply.[38]

The Act is based on the 1996 Law Commission Report No 242, *Privity of*

---

36 [1929] 2 Ch 1. Since the fees went towards the prize for winning the race, to have found otherwise might have rendered the agreement unenforceable as a gaming and wagering contract within s 18 of the Gaming Act 1845. *Clarke v Dunraven* does not appear to have been cited in the case.

37 Note, also, that some aspects of the law of agency, in particular, the concept of the 'undisclosed principal', can be regarded as exceptions to privity: these are considered further in Chapter 6.

38 Section 10(2), (3).

Contract: Contracts for the Benefit of Third Parties.[39] In one respect, therefore, this may appear as a speedy response to an identified need for law reform. It should not be forgotten, however, that, over 60 years ago, a similar reform was recommended by the Law Revision Committee.[40]

5.5.1 The main effect

The simplest reform would have been to say that third parties should be able to sue whenever a contract happens to benefit them. For reasons which were noted earlier,[41] the Law Commission rejected this as being unacceptably wide, and opening the floodgates to litigation. It should only be where the contracting parties *intend* to confer a benefit on the third party that the right of action should arise. Even this would go too far, however. The Law Commission in its Consultation Paper which preceded the Report gave the example of a contract between a building company and a highway authority for the construction of a new road.[42] Although it is one of the objects of the contract, and therefore one of the intentions of the parties, that the road will potentially benefit all road users, it would not be acceptable to allow all such users to have a right of action, for example, in the event of delay in completion of the project. The range of potential third party claimants should be narrowed to those on whom the parties to the contract intend to confer an *enforceable legal obligation*.[43]

This objective is put into effect by s 1 of the Act, which states:

(1) . . . a person who is not a party to a contract (a 'third party') may in his own right enforce a term of the contract if:
  (a) the contract expressly provides that he may; or
  (b) subject to sub-s (2), the term purports to confer a benefit on him.
(2) Sub-section (1)(b) does not apply if on a proper construction of the contract it appears that the parties did not intend the term to be enforceable by the third party.

Sub-sections (1)(b) and (2) therefore operate to create a rebuttable presumption that if a contract appears to confer a benefit on a third party, such a benefit is intended to be legally enforceable by that third party. A court faced with a promisor who denies that such legal enforceability was intended will have to decide what the 'proper construction' of the contract is. This will presumably mean applying an objective test of what reasonable contracting parties would have thought was meant by the term or terms in question.

---

39 Cmnd 3329.
40 Sixth Interim Report, 1937, Cmd 5449.
41 Above, 5.2.
42 Consultation Paper 121, paras 2.19, 5.9.
43 Report No 242.

This analysis was adopted by the first reported case on the Act, *Nisshin Shipping Co Ltd v Cleaves & Co Ltd*,[44] and confirmed by the Court of Appeal in *Laemthong International Lines Company Ltd v Artis (The Laemthong Glory) (No 2)*.[45] The latter case concerned a letter of indemnity ('LOI') issued by the receiver of goods to the charterer of the ship from which they had been unloaded. The ship was subsequently seized because another party alleged that it had a better claim to the goods. The ship-owner sought to enforce the indemnity against the receiver. The Court of Appeal noted that one clause in the LOI referred to indemnifying the charterer's 'agents', and took the view that the shipowner could come within this. A further clause referred to providing indemnity in the event of the ship being arrested, and that benefit was one which could only benefit the shipowner. The clauses of the LOI therefore did purport to confer a benefit on the shipowner. Once this was established, the wording of the Act had the effect that the burden of proof was on the promisor (in this case the receiver) to show that there was no intention to give an enforceable right to the third party. The receivers tried to argue that the situation was analogous with the chain of contracts which exists, for example, when goods are sold from manufacturer, to wholesaler, to retailer, or as between a main contractor and sub-contractor in construction contracts, and which the Law Commission in its report which led to the 1999 Act had suggested should not be taken as creating third party rights. In this case the charterer had issued its own LOI to the shipowner, but the court rejected the analogy with the 'chain' contracts. The situations referred to by the Law Commission were ones where established commercial practice made it unlikely that third party rights would be intended. There was no comparable established practice in relation to LOIs. The receivers had failed to prove that the clauses were not intended to provide an enforceable benefit, and the shipowner was entitled to rely on them.

The fact that the burden of proof shifts in this way once a benefit is established means that care will need to be taken in drafting contracts. If the parties do not want a third party to be able to enforce any benefits under the contract, they will be well advised to say so in specific terms.[46]

The intended third party beneficiary need not be in existence at the time of the contract, but must be expressly identified in the contract by name, or as a member of a class, or as answering a particular description.[47] Thus, unborn children, future spouses and companies which have not at the time been incorporated all have the potential to benefit. A contract between the partners of the firm, for example, that each of their spouses will in certain circumstances receive benefits from partnership property will apply both to the spouses of those already married and any future spouses of those who at the time are single.

44 [2003] EWHC 2602; [2004] 1 Lloyd's Rep 38.
45 [2005] 1 Lloyd's Rep 688.
46 It has been claimed that the Act has led to a 'proliferation' of clauses to this effect: Beale, Bishop and Furmston, 2001, p 1183.
47 Section 1(3).

If the above conditions are satisfied, the third party will be able to enforce the term of the contract (subject to any other relevant terms of the contract)[48] in exactly the same way as a party to the contract, obtaining damages, injunctions or specific performance in the normal way.[49] If the term is an exclusion clause, the third party will be able to take advantage of the exclusion or limitation.[50]

An important issue which arises once third party rights are recognised in this way is the extent to which the parties to the contract should be free to change, or even cancel, their agreement. In other words, does the third party have a legal right as soon as the contract is made, or only at some later stage? Normally, of course, the parties to an agreement can change it in any way they wish, provided there is consideration for any such change.[51] Clearly, however, the right under s 1 would be of limited effect if the parties could at any time withdraw the promised benefit. At the same time, it would probably be restricting the normal freedom of the parties too greatly to prevent all possibility of such change. The Act deals with this situation by s 2.

The balance of s 2 lies in favour of the freedom of the contracting parties. Section 2(3) provides that they can include a clause in their agreement which removes the need for any consent by the third party to a variation, or which lays down different procedures for consent from those contained in the Act. If no such clause is included, however, the provisions of s 2(1) will operate. This provides that the parties may not rescind or vary the contract so as to extinguish or alter the third party's rights under it if one of three conditions is satisfied. These are that:

(a)   the third party has communicated to the promisor (by words or conduct) his assent to the relevant term (the 'postal rule' (see 2.12.6 above) does not apply here – s 2(2)); or

(b)   the third party has relied on the term and the promisor is aware of this; or

(c)   the third party has relied on the term and the promisor could reasonably be expected to have foreseen that the third party would do so.

Where the situation is that the third party has relied on the promise, that reliance does not have to be detrimental. If, for example, T (the third party) has been promised £1,000 by A under a contract between A and B, the fact that T has, in reliance on that promise, bought goods at a bargain price, or has acquired shares that have subsequently doubled in value, will be enough to prevent A and B from cancelling the promise, provided that

---

48 Section 1(4).
49 Section 1(5).
50 Section 1(6).
51 See above, 3.9.6 and 3.10.1.

A knew or could reasonably be expected to have known that T had acted in reliance on the promise.

It is important to remember that these provisions relating to the ability of the parties to change the contract do not set out the requirements for the third party's right to arise. As soon as a contract is made which satisfies the requirement of s 1 of the Act, the third party acquires legal rights under it and may enforce the relevant term without having either assented to or relied on the promise. The significance of the provisions in s 2 is simply that once one of the events specified there has occurred, the promise may not be withdrawn or varied.

5.5.3 Defences

The availability of defences is dealt with by s 3 of the Act. Unless the parties to the contract have agreed otherwise in the contract,[52] the promisor can raise against the third party any defences (including 'set-offs') that could have been raised against the promisee (that is, the other party to the contract). Thus, if the promisee has induced the contract by misrepresentation or duress, the promisor can use that as a defence to the action by the third party. Similarly, if goods are to be supplied by A to B, with B promising to pay the price to be paid to T, B could raise against T the fact that the goods were not of satisfactory quality under s 14 of the Sale of Goods Act 1979. The main contracting parties may also agree that a set-off arising between them from unrelated dealings may nevertheless be used by the promisor against the third party. The Explanatory Notes to the Act suggest that this could arise where:

> P1 and P2 contract that P1 will pay P3 if P2 transfers his car to P1. P2 owes money under a wholly unrelated contract. P1 and P2 agree to an express term in the contract which provides that P1 can raise against a claim by P3 any matter which would have given P1 a defence or set-off to a claim by P2.

The promisor may also rely on defences, set-offs or counterclaims against the third party which arise from previous dealings between the promisor and the third party.[53] Thus, if T has induced A to contract with B on the basis of a misrepresentation, A can rely on that as a defence to an action by T, whether or not it would have been available against B. Similarly, if A and B contract that A is to pay £1,000 to T, but T already owes A £500, that can be set off by A against any claim by T.

The effect of s 7(2) should also be noted in this context, since it provides additional protection for the promisor. If the third party is taking action for negligent performance of an obligation under the contract, s 2(2) of the Unfair Contract Terms Act 1977 (which restricts the ability of a party to limit liability for loss or damage, other

---

52 Section 3(5).
53 Section 3(4).

than death or personal injury, caused by the party's negligence)[54] cannot be used to restrict the promisor's ability to rely on an exclusion clause.

Section 3(6) deals with the converse situation to those covered by s 3(2)–(5), that is, where the third party seeks to rely on a term of the contract (the most obvious example being an exclusion clause) in an action brought against him. The sub-section provides that the third party will only be able to enforce the term if he could have done so if he had been a party to the contract.

5.5.4   Protection from double liability

The right of the promisee to enforce the contract is specifically preserved by s 4. In order that the promisor does not face being liable to both the promisee and the third party, however, s 5 provides that where the promisee has recovered compensation from the promisor in relation to a term falling within s 1 of the Act, this must be taken into account in any award subsequently made to the third party. The converse situation is not specifically dealt with, but it must be presumed that the courts would not allow the promisee to recover where compensation has already been paid to the third party by the promisor.

5.5.5   Exceptions

Section 6 excludes certain types of contract from the provisions of the Act. These include:

(a)   contracts on a bill of exchange, promissory note or other negotiable instrument;[55]
(b)   contracts binding on a company and its members under s 14 of the Companies Act 1985;[56]
(c)   terms of a contract of employment, as against an employee;[57] and
(d)   contracts for the carriage of goods by sea,[58] or, if subject to an international transport convention, by road, rail or air.[59]

In relation to carriage contracts, however, the exception does not apply to reliance by a third party on an exclusion or limitation of liability contained in such a contract. The

---

54 See Chapter 9, 9.7.
55 Section 6(1).
56 Section 6(2).
57 Section 6(3) – the same applies to 'workers' contracts' as against a worker (including a home worker), or a term of a relevant contract against an agency worker. Relevant definitions of employee and worker are those to be found in s 54 of the Minimum Wage Act 1998. For home worker, see s 35(2) of that Act, and for 'agency worker' see s 34. A 'relevant contract' is one dealing with work falling within s 34(1)(a) of the 1998 Act.
58 As defined in s 6(6).
59 For the appropriate convention, depending on the mode of transport, see s 6(8).

'Himalaya' exclusion clause of the type considered in *The Eurymedon*[60] could therefore now apply for the benefit of the stevedores without the need to rely on agency.

5.5.6 Effect of the Act

The Contracts (Rights of Third Parties) Act 1999 has the potential to lead to significant changes in the way in which contracts can be enforced by third parties. For example, if applied to the facts of *Beswick v Beswick*,[61] the term in the contract between old Mr Beswick and his nephew purported to confer a benefit on Mrs Beswick, thus falling within s 1(1)(b) of the Act. It is likely that the court would construe this term as being intended to confer a legally enforceable benefit on her under s 1(2). She would therefore be able to sue the nephew in her personal capacity rather than only in her (fortuitous) capacity as administratrix of her husband's estate. Similarly, in the commercial context, in a case like *Woodar v Wimpey*,[62] there was a promise to pay part of the purchase price of a plot of land to a third party. The contract specifically identified the third party, and purported to confer a benefit on it. Again, assuming that the court construed this as being intended to confer a legally enforceable benefit, the third party could sue directly for the breach of the promise to pay. Other possible effects of the Act will be noted in discussing the cases dealt with in the rest of this chapter.

FOR THOUGHT

Would the Act have made a difference to the outcome of *Dunlop v Selfridge*, discussed above at 5.3.1? Did the contract between Selfridge and Dew purport to confer a benefit on Dunlop?

Not all commentators have welcomed the Act. Stevens, for example, has argued that the reform was unnecessary, given the developments in remedies available to the promisee.[63] Moreover, the Act runs the risk of creating uncertainty and has left the law in an 'incoherent state' doctrinally.[64] It must be remembered, however, that the main contracting parties are still in control. They can decide that the provisions of the new Act should not apply, and there will be nothing that the third party can do about it. They also have the freedom to change their minds, subject to the provisions restricting variation or cancellation. Where, however, the parties have decided that they wish to confer a benefit on a third party, and have put that clearly into their contract, the courts will be

---

60 [1975] AC 154 – see below, 5.12.1.
61 [1968] AC 58 – see above, 5.3.1.
62 [1980] 1 WLR 277 – see below, 5.7.
63 Stevens, 2004, p 15.
64 Ibid.

able to enforce their wishes directly, rather than having to rely on the range of, at times, rather strained devices which they have used in the past.

The extent to which these devices can be safely consigned to history is, however, not yet clear. Section 7(1) of the Act specifically states that the Act 'does not affect any right or remedy of a third party that exists or is available apart from this Act'. Moreover, as we have seen, the Act does not apply to all contracts. It is therefore still necessary to consider the ways in which the doctrine of privity was circumvented prior to May 2000, since some of this law may well prove to be of continued relevance. Before these are looked at, however, the suggested law relating to this area contained in the Principles of European Contract Law will be noted.

5.6 THE PRINCIPLES OF EUROPEAN CONTRACT LAW

The Principles deal with the issue of third party rights in Art 6.110. The provisions are in fact very similar to those contained in the 1999 Act which have just been discussed.

Paragraph 1 of the Article provides that a third party can enforce a contractual obligation where:

> . . . its right to do so has been expressly agreed between the promisor and the promisee, or when such agreement is to be inferred from the purpose of the contract or the circumstances of the case.

Thus, as with the 1999 Act, the intention to confer an enforceable benefit on the third party may be either express or implied. The Article also makes it clear that the third party need not be identified at the time of the contract.[65]

As regards the possibility of varying or removing the right, this is dealt with by para 3 of the Article. This gives the promisee (but not the promisor) the power to deprive the third party of the right to performance other than in two circumstances. These are, first, where the promisee has previously given notice to the third party that the right has been made irrevocable or, second, where the promisor or the promisee has been notified by the third party that the latter has accepted the right. This second condition clearly corresponds to the idea of the third party's 'assent', as used in s 2(1) of the 1999 Act.

The provisions of Art 6.110 are much less detailed than the 1999 Act, but the general approach is identical.

We now turn to consider the devices which the common law has used to avoid the effects of the doctrine of privity.

---

65 Cf 1999 Act, s 1(3).

5.7 DAMAGES ON BEHALF OF ANOTHER

It has been argued in some cases that where a contract is made by one person for the benefit of another, the contracting party should, in the event of breach, be able to recover damages to compensate the potential beneficiary's loss. This was the approach taken by Lord Denning in *Jackson v Horizon Holidays*.[66] Mr Jackson had booked a holiday for himself and his family, which turned out to be a disaster. The hotel for which the booking was made was not completed when the Jacksons arrived, and the alternative offered was of a very poor standard. The facilities did not match what had been promised, and the family found the food distasteful. There was no doubt that the defendants were in breach of contract. The trial judge awarded £1,100 damages, but the defendants appealed against this as being excessive. The Court of Appeal upheld the award, with Lord Denning holding that Mr Jackson was entitled to recover damages on behalf of the rest of his family. In particular, Lord Denning relied on the following quotation from Lush LJ in *Lloyd's v Harper*:[67]

> I consider it to be an established rule of law that where a contract is made with A for the benefit of B, A can sue on the contract for the benefit of B, and recover all that B could have recovered if the contract had been made with B himself.

Lord Denning felt that this indicated that where one person made a contract which was intended to benefit others, such as the father booking a family holiday, a host making a restaurant reservation for dinner or a vicar arranging a coach trip for the choir, and there was a breach of contract, the father, the host or the vicar should not only be able to recover lost expenses, but:[68]

> . . . he should be able to recover for the discomfort, vexation and upset which the whole party have suffered by reason of the breach of contract, recompensing them accordingly out of what he recovers.

This would have had the potential of opening up a large hole in the doctrine of privity, since all that a third party beneficiary would need to do would be to persuade the contracting party to sue in order to obtain the promised benefit or appropriate compensation. In *Woodar Investment Development Ltd v Wimpey Construction (UK) Ltd*,[69] the House of Lords rejected the idea that it was possible generally to circumvent the doctrine of privity in this way. The decision in *Jackson* was accepted as being right, either (according to Lord Wilberforce) because it related to a special situation of a kind which perhaps calls for special treatment, such as ordering a meal in a restaurant, or hiring a

---

66 [1975] 3 All ER 92; [1975] 1 WLR 1468.
67 (1880) 16 Ch D 290, p 321.
68 [1975] 3 All ER 92, p 96; [1975] 1 WLR 1468, p 1473.
69 [1980] 1 All ER 571; [1980] 1 WLR 277.

taxi for a group, or, more generally, because, as James LJ had held in the Court of Appeal, Mr Jackson's damages could justifiably be increased to take account of the fact that the discomfort of the rest of the family was part of his loss, in that it contributed to his own bad experience. This did not constitute, however, any significant exception to the doctrine of privity, and the more general basis on which Lord Denning had upheld the award of damages was specifically rejected. Lord Denning was held to have used the quotation from *Lloyd's v Harper* on which he relied out of context. As Lord Russell pointed out, Lush LJ was clearly concerned with the relationship between principal and agent, and it is to this situation alone that his statement should be taken to refer.

Despite this strong rejection of any general right to claim damages on behalf of a third party, in 1993 the House of Lords seemed to open the door again to claims of this kind. *Linden Gardens Ltd v Lenesta Sludge Disposals Ltd*[70] concerned a building contract between a property company, P, and a construction company, C, in relation to a development containing shops, offices and flats. Before the building work was complete, P assigned its interests to T. The assignment was made without C's consent, and therefore was not effective to create a contractual relationship between T and C. Defects in the construction work were later discovered. The defective work had taken place after the assignment of the contract. P sued C, but it was argued that P had suffered no loss, because at the time of C's breach of contract, the property had already been assigned to T. The House of Lords, however, drawing on an analogy for the carriage of goods, where a consignor of goods is allowed to sue on the carriage contract even though ownership of the goods has been transferred to a third party,[71] held that this was a situation where a party to a contract was entitled to recover damages on behalf of another. Here, C knew that P was not going to occupy the premises itself, and therefore could foresee that any breaches would adversely impact on whoever acquired the premises from P. This exception seemed to indicate a retreat from *Woodar v Wimpey*. It was applied by the Court of Appeal in the subsequent cases of *Darlington BC v Wiltshier Northern Ltd*[72] and *Alfred McAlpine Construction Ltd v Panatown Ltd*.[73] The second of these cases was appealed to the House of Lords,[74] however, which gave the opportunity for the House to reconsider the way in which the Court of Appeal had been developing the exception established in the *Linden Gardens* case.

The facts of the *Panatown* case were that M, a building contractor, entered into a contract with P to construct an office building and car park on land owned by U, a

---

70 [1993] 3 All ER 417.

71 *Dunlop v Lambert* (1839) 6 Cl & F 600; 7 ER 824, as interpreted in *The Albazero* [1976] 3 All ER 129. The House held that the limitation of *Dunlop v Lambert* laid down in *The Albazero* was confined to contracts for the carriage of goods under a bill of lading. Under such a contract it is established by statute that the consignee will be able to sue the carrier directly – the Carriage of Goods by Sea Act 1992.

72 [1995] 3 All ER 895; [1995] 1 WLR 68.

73 [1998] EGCS 19; [1998] CLC 636.

74 [2001] AC 518. Reported as *Panatown Ltd v Alfred McAlpine Construction Ltd* [2000] 4 All ER 97.

company within the same group of companies as P. The reason for this arrangement was that it (legitimately) avoided the payment of VAT. In addition to the main contract between P and M, there was also a 'duty of care deed' ('DCD') executed between U and M which gave U a right to sue M for negligent performance of its duties under the building contract. The DCD was expressed to be assignable to U's successors in title. When there were problems of alleged defective work and delay, P initiated arbitration proceedings under its contract with M. M sought to argue as a preliminary point that since P had no proprietary interest in the site, it had suffered no loss. It was this issue that the House of Lords had to consider.

The House was divided 3:2 on whether P was entitled to recover. There were two bases on which P argued that it should be able to do so. The first, so-called 'narrow ground', was based on *Dunlop v Lambert*,[75] as interpreted in *The Albazero*.[76] This principle was stated by Lord Diplock in *The Albazero* as follows:[77]

> . . . in a commercial contract concerning goods where it is in the contemplation of the parties that the proprietary interests in the goods may be transferred from one owner to another after the contract has been entered into and before the breach which causes the loss or damage to the goods, an original party to the contract, if such be the intention of them both, is to be treated in law as having entered into the contract for the benefit of all persons who have or may acquire an interest in the goods before they are lost or damaged, and is entitled to recover by way of damages for breach of contract the actual loss sustained by those for whose benefit the contract is entered into.

Where this principle applies, the party recovering the damages is required to account for them to the third party who has suffered the loss. As we have seen, the House of Lords in the *Linden Gardens* case extended this approach from contracts concerning goods to those involving real property. Moreover, the Court of Appeal in *Darlington BC v Wiltshier Northern Ltd* held that it could apply even where the third party owned the property from the beginning, rather than it being transferred after the contract had been entered into. The justification for this principle, as an exception to the normal rule that a contracting party can only recover for his or her own loss, is that it should apply where otherwise the liability of the defaulting party would disappear into a legal 'black hole' – in that privity would prevent the third party from suing, and the contracting party would only be able to recover nominal damages.[78]

---

75 (1839) 6 Cl & F 600; 7 ER 824 – though doubts were expressed as to whether this case had been properly understood by later courts – see, in particular, the speech of Lord Clyde.

76 [1976] 3 All ER 129.

77 Ibid, p 137.

78 See Steyn LJ in *Darlington BC v Wiltshier Northern Ltd* [1995] 1 WLR 68, p 79. Whether this 'black hole' actually exists has been a matter of debate amongst academic commentators: see, for example, Wallace, 1999, Unberath, 1999, Treitel, 1998.

The 'broader ground' argued by P was based on the speech of Lord Griffiths in the *Linden Gardens* case. This amounted to a more direct challenge to the assumption that a contracting party in this type of situation should only be able to recover nominal damages. Lord Griffiths gave an everyday example to show why that assumption should not always apply:[79]

> To take a common example, the matrimonial home is owned by the wife and the couple's remaining assets are owned by the husband and he is the sole earner. The house requires a new roof and the husband places a contract with the builder to carry out the work ... The builder fails to replace the roof properly and the husband has to call in and pay another builder to complete the work. Is it to be said that the husband has suffered no damage because he does not own the property? Such a result would in my view be absurd and the answer is that the husband has suffered loss because he did not receive the bargain for which he had contracted with the first builder and the measure of damages is the cost of securing the performance of that bargain by completing the roof repairs properly by the second builder.

Under this ground, P argued that the defective work by M caused loss to P, not just to U, because it had not received what it had contracted for. It should therefore be entitled to substantial damages related to the cost of remedying the defective work. It seems that if this ground applies, there is not necessarily any obligation on the successful claimant to use any damages recovered to remedy the defects – but the views of the Lords in *Panatown* were divided on this issue.

The majority of their Lordships in *Panatown* found that P should not be able to succeed because of the existence of the DCD. The fact that it had been specifically provided that the third party (U) should have a remedy against the builder (M) meant that there was no 'black hole' and therefore no need to apply the exception to the normal rule, even though the remedy available under the DCD was more limited than that which would be available in an action for breach of contract. In coming to this conclusion, the majority confirmed the existence of the 'narrow ground' exception, but expressed scepticism about whether the 'broader ground' was part of English law. The minority (Lords Goff and Millett) would have allowed P to recover on either ground.

The speeches in the *Panatown* case, while providing much fuel for further discussion, have not really helped to clarify the law in this area. Because the majority decision is based on the existence of the DCD, any comments on the more general principles will be able to be distinguished in a later case where no such deed exists. This leaves open the possibility that the views of the minority, that the 'broader ground' provides the better basis for the development of the law in this area, may still be adopted, despite the fact that the majority did not regard it with favour.

---

79 [1994] 1 AC 85, p 96; [1993] 3 All ER 417, p 421.

It is possible, of course, that the availability of the power to confer rights directly on a third party under the Contracts (Rights of Third Parties) Act 1999 means that there will be less need to expand the situations where a contracting party can recover damages on behalf of a third party. Indeed, the fact that the parties can now make this specific provision for third party rights might lead the courts to return to a more restrictive line in this area, as suggested by *Woodar v Wimpey*. However, as Lord Goff pointed out in his speech in *Panatown*, the issue of what damages a contracting party can recover can be argued to be logically separate from the doctrine of privity.[80] If that approach is followed, then the existence of the 1999 Act, which is concerned with privity rather than damages, should not necessarily prevent further developments. Much will depend on how those in the relevant industries, in particular the construction industry, formulate their contracts in the future, and whether they decide to take advantage of the facility in the 1999 Act to give enforceable rights to third parties. If they do not, as some commentators have suggested,[81] this may leave the door open for further case law to develop the common law rules.

5.8 THE TRUST OF A PROMISE

The Chancery courts developed the concept of the 'trust' to deal with the situation where property was given to one person (the 'trustee') to look after and deal with for the benefit of another (the 'beneficiary'). Whereas the common law regarded the trustee as the legal owner of the property, and therefore as having a free hand to deal with it, in equity, it was held that the trustee had to take account of the claims of the beneficiary and, moreover, the beneficiary could take action to compel the trustee to act in the beneficiary's interest. This tripartite trust arrangement has obvious possibilities for the development of a way round the doctrine of privity, and this was successfully attempted in *Les Affréteurs Réunis SA v Leopold Walford (London) Ltd*.[82] A contract for the hire of a ship (a 'time charterparty') included a clause promising a commission to the broker (Walford) who had arranged the contract. Walford was not a party to the contract, but was held by the House of Lords to be able to sue to recover the commission, on the basis that the charterers, to whom the promise had been made, were trustees of this promise. The House of Lords was thus ruling that the trust concept could apply to a promise to pay money, as well as to a situation where property was transferred into the hands of the trustee. This opened up a potentially substantial exception to the doctrine of privity. Later case law has, however, made the finding of the existence of a trust subject to some fairly strict requirements which have limited the usefulness of the device. There must have been a definite intention to create a trust and, in looking for

---

80 [2000] 4 All ER 97, pp 119–20. See also Harris, Campbell and Halson, 2002, pp 80–81.
81 See, for example, Beale, Bishop and Furmston, 2001, p 1182.
82 [1919] AC 801.

this, the court will expect to find a clear intention to benefit the third party, which is intended to be irrevocable.

5.8.1 Intention to create a trust

The intention to create a trust will be easiest to find where the parties actually say that that is what they are doing. The courts are much more reluctant to imply an intention which is not made explicit. Two cases can be contrasted. *Re Flavell*[83] concerned a partner in a firm of solicitors. When he retired, his partners agreed to pay him an annuity. It was also agreed that when Flavell died, the annuity would be paid to his personal representatives, to be applied for the benefit of his widow and children. After Flavell's death, his creditors wanted the annuity to be regarded as part of the general assets of the estate, and therefore available to them. The High Court held, and the Court of Appeal confirmed, however, that the words used in setting up the annuity had created a trust in Mrs Flavell's favour. She therefore had a prior claim over the creditors.

Sixty years later, in *Re Schebsman*,[84] a different conclusion was reached. Schebsman was the employee of a company. On his retirement, the company agreed to pay him £5,500 in instalments over six years. If he died within that period, certain sums were to be payable to his widow. Schebsman did die within the six years, shortly after having been declared bankrupt. The trustee in bankruptcy claimed that the payments to Mrs Schebsman were made on the basis of a trust, and therefore should, under the provisions of the relevant bankruptcy legislation, form part of Schebsman's estate and go to pay off his creditors. The Court of Appeal held that the contract between Schebsman and the company was simply that payments should be made direct to Mrs Schebsman. Mr Schebsman would have had no rights over them. But it was a straightforward contract between Mr Schebsman and the company, not a trust. Mrs Schebsman had no right to enforce this contract, but equally the trustee in bankruptcy had no claim. As the company was willing to pay Mrs Schebsman, effectively she won.

The distinction between *Flavell* and *Schebsman* is clearly a fine one. It may well have been important that, in *Flavell*, the payment was to be made to the personal representatives, rather than direct to Mrs Flavell. This indicated an arrangement more akin to a trust than a straightforward contract.

5.8.2 Need for a clear intention to benefit the third party rather than the promisee

If the contract is intended to benefit the promisee, then, even if it might incidentally benefit a third party, there will be no trust. Thus, in the Canadian case of *Vandepitte v*

---

83 (1883) 25 Ch D 89.
84 [1944] Ch 83.

Preferred Accident Insurance,[85] a father took a policy of car insurance which was stated to be 'available to any person while legally operating the car'. His daughter drove the car with his permission, and injured the plaintiff. The plaintiff sued the daughter and won. The relevant Canadian legislation provided that this judgment could be enforced against the daughter's insurer. However, the daughter had no insurance contract. The plaintiff argued that the father was the trustee of a promise made by his insurance company for the benefit of his daughter. This argument was rejected by the Privy Council on the basis that the father, in making the contract with the insurers, was doing so for his own benefit, not his daughter's. There was no clear intention that she was to benefit, and therefore the trust argument failed.

5.8.3 Intention to benefit must be irrevocable

Whereas the parties to a contract are generally free to change it by mutual agreement,[86] a trust, once established, is regarded by the courts as irrevocable because it creates rights for the third party beneficiary which the trustee and the promisor are not entitled to change.[87] This requirement has perhaps been the biggest obstacle to the development of the concept of the 'trust of a promise'. For example, in *Re Sinclair's Life Policy*,[88] a policy of life insurance was taken out for the benefit of the insured's godson. There was a clear intention in this case to benefit the third party. The policy, however, contained a provision enabling the policy to be surrendered for the benefit of the insured. It was not, therefore, irrevocable, and so could not be the subject of a trust.

This was an additional reason for the decision in *Re Schebsman*.[89] The court was not prepared to concede that parties to a contract had given up their right to consensual variation. As Du Parcq LJ put it:[90]

> I have little doubt that in the present case both parties . . . intended to keep alive their common law right to vary consensually the terms of the obligation undertaken by the company, and if circumstances had changed in the debtor's lifetime injustice might have been done by holding that a trust had been created and that those terms were accordingly unalterable.

An element of discretion as regards who is to benefit will not, however, be fatal to a

---

85 [1933] AC 70.

86 Though, of course, as has been noted above, the Contracts (Rights of Third Parties) Act 1999 in some circumstances prevents the parties from changing an agreement to benefit a third party: above, 5.5.2.

87 But note that Atiyah has pointed out that 'the concept of the revocable trust is by no means unknown to the law' (Atiyah, 1995, p 371), so that the courts' insistence on 'irrevocability' in these circumstances is perhaps indicative of a more general reluctance to use the trust device in this context.

88 [1938] 1 Ch 799.

89 [1944] Ch 83.

90 Ibid, p 104.

trust. In *Re Webb*,[91] insurance policies were taken out by a father in favour of his children. The policies allowed him to exercise options which would vary the benefits. This was held not to be fatal to a trust. Similarly, in *Re Flavell*,[92] where there was a discretion to pay to the widow or daughters, the trust was upheld. So, the existence of a discretion will only defeat the trust if it enables the benefit to be diverted away from the beneficiaries altogether.

5.8.4 Effects of a trust

If a trust is found to exist, the third party can sue but must join the promisee as a party. The third party is entitled to any money paid or payable under the contract: the promisee has no rights to it, unless the trust fails for some reason.

5.8.5 Conclusion on trust device

The trust of a promise is a true exception to the doctrine of privity. The restrictions outlined above mean, however, that it has limited application. Indeed, it was not even considered in *Beswick v Beswick*.[93] The principle has never been denied, however, and if an appropriate case arose again, no doubt the courts would apply it.[94] On the other hand, the situations where the trust device has been used are ones in which the parties could now generally achieve their objective much more easily by using the provisions of the Contracts (Rights of Third Parties) Act 1999.

5.9 COLLATERAL CONTRACTS

A collateral contract generally takes the form of a unilateral contract under which one party says 'if you enter into contract X, I will promise you Y'. The consideration for the promise is the entering into contract X. It is quite possible for such an agreement to be made between the two parties to contract X.[95] In a three-party situation, however, the construction of a collateral contract can be a means of evading the doctrine of privity. In *Shanklin Pier v Detel Products*,[96] the plaintiffs, who were the owners of a pier, were promised by the defendants, who were paint manufacturers, that the defendants' paint, if used to re-paint the pier, would last for seven years. As a result, the plaintiffs

---

91 Ch 255; [1941] 1 All ER 321.
92 (1883) 25 Ch D 89.
93 [1968] AC 58; [1967] 2 All ER 1197.
94 See, for example, the comments of Dillon and Waite LJJ in *Darlington BC v Wiltshier Northern* [1995] 3 All ER 895, pp 902–03, 908.
95 See, for example, *Esso Petroleum Co v Mardon* [1976] QB 801; [1976] 2 All ER 5, discussed in Chapter 8, 8.4.2.
96 [1951] 2 KB 854; [1951] 2 All ER 471.

instructed the firm of painters who had undertaken the re-painting to purchase and use the defendants' paint. This they did, but the paint only lasted three months. At first sight, the plaintiffs appeared to have no remedy, since they had provided no consideration for the promise given by the defendants (the paint manufacturers). The only contract which the defendants had made was to sell paint to the painters, and the plaintiffs were not a party to that agreement. It was held, however, that the plaintiffs could recover on the basis of a collateral contract. The consideration for the promise as to the paint's durability was the instruction by the plaintiffs to their painters to purchase the paint from the defendants.

FOR THOUGHT

What would have been the position if the pier owners had relied on promotional material published by the paint manufacturers, rather than direct communication with them? Would the manufacturers have been making a promise in these circumstances?

In this case, there was a particular 'main' contract in prospect, that is, the purchase of the paint to re-paint the pier. This will usually be the case, but the device can be used even where there is no such contract specified at the time of the promise. In *Wells (Merstham) Ltd v Buckland Sand and Silica Co Ltd*,[97] the plaintiffs, who were chrysanthemum growers, bought sand produced by the defendants from a third party on the basis of the defendants' assurances as to its iron oxide content. These assurances turned out to be unreliable, and the plaintiffs sued the defendants for the resulting loss on the basis of a collateral contract. The court held that although at the time the assurance was given there was no specific main contact in contemplation, this did not matter as long as it could be said to be made *animo contrahendi*, that is, with a view to a contract being made shortly. The plaintiffs were entitled to succeed.

The collateral contract device is not, of course, a true exception to the doctrine of privity (in the way that the trust is), because in the end the claimant and defendant are found to be the parties to a contract, albeit a collateral one. The way in which it has been used by the courts at times, however, has been clearly as a means of avoiding the doctrine of privity, in that they have not been over-scrupulous in investigating whether the parties themselves thought that they were entering into a contract of the kind alleged or had any intention of doing so. It may well be that in the light of the Contracts (Rights of Third Parties) Act 1999, the courts will in future be less willing to find a collateral contract, given that the parties will now usually be able to achieve their objective of benefiting a third party more directly.

97 [1965] 2 QB 170; [1964] 1 All ER 41.

5.10   THE TORT OF NEGLIGENCE

Where a contract is performed negligently and this causes loss to a third party, can the third party bring an action in the tort of negligence? In certain circumstances, the answer is clearly 'yes', particularly where the negligent performance has caused physical harm to the third party or his or her property. Suppose that A Ltd and B Ltd enter into a contract under which B Ltd is to transport goods owned by A Ltd from Leicester to London. B Ltd loads the goods negligently, and in the course of the journey they fall from B's lorry and injure C or damage C's car. The negligent performance by B Ltd of the contract with A Ltd will render it liable for any damage to A Ltd's goods; B Ltd will also, however, be liable in the tort of negligence for the foreseeable losses suffered by C. This is not really any exception to the doctrine of privity, because C's remedy has no relation to the fact that A Ltd and B Ltd have made a contract. The answer as far as C is concerned would be the same if B Ltd was transporting its own goods.

What if, however, there is a contractual relationship between C and A relating to the goods? Suppose, for example, the goods belong to C and that A Ltd has a contractual obligation to transport them to C's premises. A Ltd contracts with B Ltd to move the goods. Again, B Ltd loads the goods negligently, and the goods are damaged in transit. In this situation, C may well be able to sue A Ltd for breach of contract and A Ltd, in turn, may be able to sue B Ltd. But can C sue B Ltd directly in tort? The answer would appear to be yes, provided that C was actually the owner of the goods at the time. B Ltd would normally owe a tortious duty of care towards C in relation to the goods.[98] The answer will be otherwise, however, if C, while having rights in relation to the goods, is not the owner. In *The Aliakmon*,[99] there was a contract for the carriage of goods by sea. The goods had been sold by A to C, and A had engaged B to transport the goods. The goods were damaged in transit by B's negligence. At the relevant time, the goods remained in A's ownership, though the 'risk'[100] as between A and C had passed under their contract to C. It was held by the House of Lords that C could not recover from B in negligence. The main reason for this was that there was well established authority that a person could not generally claim for losses in relation to property as regards which he or she did not at the relevant time have ownership or a possessory title. The House was also cognisant of the fact that the contract was stated to be subject to an international carriage convention[101] under which the liability of the

---

98 The existence of the duty will be established, of course, on the normal tortious principles as laid down in *Caparo Industries plc v Dickman* [1990] 2 AC 605. Generally, where it is foreseeable that a negligent act will result in physical harm, there will be a duty, but note *The Nicholas H* [1996] AC 211, in which it was held that in the particular circumstances of the case it was not 'just and reasonable' to impose a duty even where foreseeable physical harm had occurred.

99 [1986] AC 785.

100 That is, who would bear the cost of any damage to the goods. This meant, in effect, that C was liable to pay A the full price for the goods even if they were damaged in transit.

101 That is the Hague Convention.

carrier was restricted, and felt that this restriction should not be allowed to be circumvented by giving C a right of action against B. It is possible, therefore, that in a situation where this consideration did not apply, the court might be prepared to allow a person such as C, holding nascent rather than actual ownership rights, a remedy, but there is no case law as yet to support this.

So far we have been concerned with cases of physical damage. Are there any situations in which the third party could sue for pure economic loss caused by negligence? The situations in which the law of tort has been prepared to allow recovery for economic loss have generally been very limited, but in *Junior Books Ltd v Veitchi Co Ltd*,[102] the House of Lords appeared to open up the area in a way which also constituted a potentially large exception to the doctrine of privity. The dispute concerned a floor which had been defectively laid and subsequently cracked. The floor was laid by a sub-contractor, who had been nominated by the owner of the building. The only contracts, however, were between the owner and the main contractor (who was engaged to construct the building), and the main contractor and the sub-contractor. There was no contract between the owner and the sub-contractor, and the only loss caused by the sub-contractor's negligence was economic; there was no physical damage to any of the owner's property. Nevertheless, the House of Lords held that the sub-contractor did owe a duty of care to the owner, and that it could be liable in damages for the negligent manner in which it had laid the floor. As a result, the owner was put into the position it would have been in if the contract had been performed, which is not normally the objective of tortious, as opposed to contractual, damages. If this case had been followed, then the possibilities for using tort as a way around privity of contract would be greatly expanded. The decision in *Junior Books* is now, however, considered to be highly anomalous, to be confined to its own facts, and not to be treated as laying down any principle of general application.[103] The House of Lords has not, however, ever taken the step of saying that it was wrongly decided on its own facts. It is possible, therefore, that if the same or a closely analogous situation arose in the future, the *Junior Books* approach could be applied again. The fact that the parties could now create a direct liability between the owner and the sub-contractor by virtue of the 1999 Act means that such a development is now even less likely than it was. In any case, *Junior Books* has not produced the major exception to privity that it once appeared to have done.

There is a further group of cases where the tort of negligence does extend to pure economic loss, and has the potential to provide remedies to third parties where there has been a defective performance of a contract. These are concerned with the negligent carrying out of professional duties, often in the form of giving advice or opinions. The principles derive from *Hedley Byrne & Co v Heller & Partners*[104] as now restated in

---

102 [1983] 1 AC 520.

103 *D and F Estates Ltd v Church Commissioners for England* [1989] AC 177. See also the criticisms in *Simaan General Contracting Co v Pilkington Glass Ltd (No 2)* [1988] QB 758.

104 [1963] 2 All ER 575. This case is discussed further in Chapter 10, in connection with the law relating to negligent misstatements which induce a contract: 10.4.4.

Caparo Industries plc v Dickman.[105] Thus, in *Smith v Eric S Bush,*[106] the defendant surveyor had given a negligent valuation of a house which he had surveyed for a mortgage lender. This caused losses to the plaintiff, who had borrowed money from the mortgage lender in order to buy the house, and who had relied on the survey. There was no contractual relationship between the defendant and the plaintiff, though each of them had a contract with the mortgage lender. It was held that in the circumstances there was a duty of care owed by the surveyor to the plaintiff. It was clear that the surveyor was aware that the valuation was likely to be relied upon by the plaintiff as well as the mortgage lender.

A similar result was arrived at in *White v Jones.*[107] Here the defendant solicitor had failed to carry out his client's instructions to draw up a will. As a result, the intended beneficiaries of the client were disappointed, and sued the solicitor for negligence. In this case there was a contract between the defendant and the client for the production of the will, but there was no contractual relationship between either of them and the disappointed beneficiaries. It was clear, however, that the contract for the will was intended to benefit the beneficiaries. The House of Lords was therefore prepared to find a duty of care owed by the solicitor to the beneficiaries. It was a significant factor in this conclusion that the estate of the client would not have been able to recover any substantial damages against the solicitor for breach of contract, because it had not suffered any loss. A similar conclusion was reached in a subsequent 'disappointed beneficiary' case, *Carr-Glynn v Frearsons,*[108] so this appears to have become an established way of circumventing the doctrine of privity and allowing a third party to obtain the intended benefit of a contract. It seems likely that it should be regarded as limited to the particular circumstances of the negligent creation of a will where, once the testator has died, there is no other way of holding the solicitor to account for the negligence. Where the contracting party has a remedy in contract, the courts are always going to be very reluctant to give a tortious remedy to a third party.[109] It is probably also significant that the majority of cases in which the courts have been prepared to use the tort of negligence to give the third party a remedy have been situations involving a 'non-business' claimant. Where the three parties concerned are involved in a network of contractual business relationships, the courts will be much more reluctant to intervene, since they will not wish to interfere with agreements as to liability that may have been carefully negotiated, in particular where such liabilities have been distributed on an understanding as to where the insurance obligations are to lie.

---

105 [1990] 2 AC 605.
106 [1990] 1 AC 831.
107 [1995] 2 AC 207; cf also *Ross v Caunters* [1980] Ch 287.
108 [1998] 4 All ER 225.
109 Cf *Goodwill v Pregnancy Advisory Service* [1996] 1 WLR 1397, concerning a failed vasectomy, where the partner of the supposedly sterilised man became pregnant. She was not able to sue in tort, but the man would have had an action in contract.

Finally, it is important to remember that even in those limited cases where tort provides a remedy, it is always going to be for the consequences of a *negligent act or omission*, and not simply for non-performance. A simple refusal to perform the contract will never give the third party a remedy in tort.[110]

There is, therefore, some scope for the use of the tort of negligence as a means of avoiding the effects of privity, but, as has been indicated, the circumstances in which this will apply are strictly limited.

There are two other situations where the law of tort may have an impact on situations involving the doctrine of privity: these are where an exclusion clause purports to exclude a third party's liability; and where a third party is accused of interfering with the contractual position as between contracting parties. These are dealt with below at 5.12 and 5.14, respectively.

5.11 STATUTORY EXCEPTIONS

In a number of situations, there has been statutory intervention to mitigate the effects of the doctrine of privity. These are generally connected with insurance, and the need to make sure that the intended beneficiary under an insurance contract is enabled to enforce his or her rights. Examples include the Third Parties (Rights against Insurers) Act 1930, s 11 of the Married Women's Property Act 1882, s 148(7) of the Road Traffic Act 1988, and the Carriage of Goods by Sea Act 1992. These statutory exceptions are not affected by the Contracts (Rights of Third Parties) Act 1999.

5.12 PRIVITY AND EXCLUSION CLAUSES

One particular situation where the parties to a contract may wish to confer a benefit on a third party is in relation to exclusion clauses. Where some part of the contract is to be performed by employees or sub-contractors of one of the parties, that party may wish to extend the benefit of a clause excluding liability to such people. The doctrine of privity stands in the way of this, however. The problem generally arises where some loss or damage has been caused by negligence. If it is the negligence of an employee of a contracting party, then that party may well be protected, as far as breach of contract or vicarious liability in tort is concerned, by an exclusion clause. The employee will not be protected, however, and the injured party may decide to take action directly against him or her in tort, perhaps relying on the fact that the employer may well feel obliged to make good any damages awarded. In *Adler v Dickson*,[111] for example, Mrs Adler was a

---

110 In this context, the failure of the solicitor in *White v Jones* to draw up the contract must be regarded as a 'negligent omission' rather than a deliberate refusal to perform.

111 [1955] 1 QB 158; [1954] 3 All ER 397.

passenger on a cruise. She was injured when she fell from the ship's gangplank, which had been negligently left unsecured. Her contract was with the shipping company, but she sued the master and boatswain personally, alleging negligence. The contract contained a very broadly-drawn exemption clause. The Court of Appeal held, however, that this only protected the company itself and not its employees, who were not parties to the contract with Mrs Adler. Since in this case the company had made clear that it would reimburse any damages awarded against its employees, the decision had the effect of negating the benefit of the exclusion clause as regards the contracting party (that is, the company) as well. On the facts, this was probably justifiable, in that the clause had not purported to protect the employees.

If, however, a clause is specifically worded to have this effect, and there is evidence that both parties intended that it should do so, the *Adler v Dickson* approach may have the effect of frustrating their intentions. The courts have therefore sought ways to avoid applying the doctrine of privity in such situations. One possibility, where the claimant has specifically promised not to sue the third party, is for the promisee to intervene to seek a stay of the action. This was recognised as a possibility in *Gore v Van der Lann*,[112] where the plaintiff was injured boarding a bus and sued the bus conductor, rather than the corporation which ran the bus service. On the facts, however, there was no evidence of any contractual obligation on the part of the corporation to reimburse the conductor, and therefore no grounds for granting a stay of the action. A stay was granted on this basis, however, in *Snelling v Snelling*,[113] though this was not an exemption clause case. The plaintiff, the director of a company, had agreed with his fellow directors that if any of them resigned, they would forfeit the balance of a loan which each of them had made to the company. The plaintiff resigned, and sued to recover his loan from the company. The company was not a party to the agreement between the directors, but it was held that they could intervene to stop the plaintiff's action. Ormrod J held that it was a necessary implication of the agreement to forfeit the loan that the plaintiff would not sue the company for its recovery:[114]

> In my judgment, therefore, the second and third defendants have made out an unambiguous case and have shown that the interests of justice required that the plaintiff be not permitted to recover against the defendant company. It follows that this is a proper case in which to grant a stay of all further proceedings in the plaintiff's action against the company.

This principle could therefore be applied in an appropriate case to prevent an action against a third party who was purportedly protected by an exclusion clause, and therefore indirectly to give the third party the benefit of that clause. Its limitation, however,

---

112 [1967] 2 QB 31; [1967] 1 All ER 360.
113 [1973] 1 QB 87; [1972] 1 All ER 79.
114 Ibid, p 98; p 89.

is that it is dependent on the existence of a specific promise (express or implied), and also on the willingness of the promisee to intervene on the third party's behalf. Other attempts to avoid the effects of privity in this type of situation have been more broadly based.

FOR THOUGHT

Would the Contracts (Rights of Third Parties) Act 1999 be likely to make a difference to the outcome in *Adler v Dickson* or the other cases in the above section?

5.12.1 Vicarious immunity

In *Elder, Dempster & Co v Paterson, Zochonis & Co*,[115] the House of Lords allowed shipowners to take the benefit of an exclusion clause (which was stated to apply to them) contained in a contract between the charterers of the ship and the owner of goods being carried on it. The *ratio* of the decision is not very clear, but one possible basis for it was a principle of 'vicarious immunity', under which those who perform contracts on behalf of a contracting party can take the benefit of exclusion clauses contained in that contract. This analysis, which would constitute a major exception to the doctrine of privity, was, however, subsequently rejected by the House of Lords in *Scruttons Ltd v Midland Silicones Ltd*.[116] The House ruled that the third party stevedores in this case were unable to rely on an exclusion clause contained in a contract of carriage to which they were not parties. It recognised, however, that it might be possible in some situations for a contracting party to be regarded as the agent of someone who was involved in the performance of the contract, for the purpose of bringing them into a contractual nexus with the other party. Lord Reid identified four requirements which would need to be satisfied:[117]

> I can see a possibility of success of the agency argument if [first] the bill of lading makes it clear that the stevedore is intended to be protected by the provisions in it which limit liability; [secondly] the bill of lading makes it clear that the carrier . . . is also contracting as agent for the stevedore that these provisions should apply to the stevedore; [thirdly] the carrier has authority from the stevedore to do that, or perhaps later ratification by the stevedore would suffice; and [fourthly] that any difficulties about consideration moving from the stevedore were overcome.

---

115 [1924] AC 523.
116 [1962] AC 446; [1962] 1 All ER 1.
117 Ibid, p 474; p 10.

THE MODERN LAW OF CONTRACT

This possibility was developed by the Privy Council in *New Zealand Shipping Co v Satterthwaite & Co, The Eurymedon*,[118] in which Lord Reid's four conditions were found to be fulfilled. The case again concerned the liability of stevedores for the negligent unloading of a cargo. The contract of carriage contained a very detailed exclusion clause,[119] which, among other things, specifically stated that the carrier was to be regarded as acting as agent for any independent contractors carrying out any part of the contract, and that such contractors would have the benefit of the exclusion clause. The majority of the Privy Council found this sufficient to enable them to construct a contract between the owner of the goods and the stevedores. It was in the form of a unilateral contract, under which the owners said 'if you agree to unload these goods, we will give you the benefit of the exclusion clause'. The carriers acted as the stevedores' agents for the receipt of this offer. The consideration provided was the unloading of the goods. The stevedores were, of course, bound to do this anyway under their contract with the carriers, but, as discussed in Chapter 3, the performance of an existing contractual duty owed to a third party is generally regarded as perfectly good consideration.[120]

There is no doubt that the contract constructed in *The Eurymedon* was a 'fiction' in the sense that it is highly unlikely that any of the parties intended precisely such an arrangement as the Privy Council found to have existed. On the other hand, the result is clearly commercially convenient, since it is the clear desire and expectation of all concerned in contracts of this kind that third parties who perform part of the contract should be able to take the benefit of any relevant exclusion clause. The decision has not, however, opened up a major exception to the doctrine of privity: indeed, like the collateral contract device, it is not really an exception at all, since the individual who initially looks like a non-contracting third party is found to be a party to a contract after all. The approach taken in *The Eurymedon* was applied again by the Privy Council in *The New York Star*,[121] and must now be regarded as an established principle which can be applied wherever the wording of the clause and the relationships between the various parties make it appropriate.

In *The Mahkutai*,[122] however, the Privy Council, while recognising the general acceptance of *The Eurymedon* principles in relation to exemption clauses and third parties, refused to apply them on the facts. In this case, shipowners, who were not party to a contract for the carriage of goods entered into by a charterer of their ship, sought to rely on an exclusive jurisdiction clause contained in the bill of lading. The Privy Council noted, however, that the wording of the relevant clause limited its extension to sub-contractors to the benefit of 'exceptions, limitations, provisions, conditions and

---

118 [1975] AC 154; [1974] 1 All ER 1015.
119 Commonly known as a 'Himalaya' clause, after the ship involved in *Adler v Dickson* [1955] 1 QB 158; [1954] 3 All ER 397.
120 See Chapter 3, 3.9.3.
121 [1981] 1 WLR 138.
122 [1996] AC 650.

liberties'. The Privy Council interpreted this as being limited to terms 'inserted in the bill for the carrier's protection . . . It cannot therefore extend to a *mutual* agreement, such as an exclusive jurisdiction clause'.[123] In reaching this conclusion, the Privy Council also noted the very technical nature of *The Eurymedon* analysis, involving fine points of contract and agency. It considered whether the time might have come to take a further step, and to recognise the situations currently dealt with by this principle as involving 'a fully-fledged exception to the doctrine of privity of contract',[124] thus escaping from the technicalities. It concluded, however, that it was not appropriate in the present case to take such a step. Nevertheless, the question has been raised, and there would seem to be a clear invitation to counsel in subsequent cases to try to argue for a general exception to privity, rather than relying on the technical analysis in terms of agency and consideration.[125] The enactment of the Contracts (Rights of Third Parties) Act 1999 makes it much less likely, however, that this invitation will need to be taken up. The benefit of an exclusion clause can now be given to a third party quite straightforwardly, and the further development of the common law is therefore likely to prove unnecessary.

5.12.2   Modification of the duty of care

An alternative way of giving negligent third parties the benefit of an exclusion clause has been recognised in some cases. This treats the contract as part of the context in which the negligence occurs, and therefore relevant to defining the defendant's duty of care. In *Southern Water Authority v Carey*,[126] the negligence of sub-contractors had caused the loss. The main contract contained an exclusion clause purporting to extend to the sub-contractors, and stating that the main contractor contracted on their behalf. The agency argument, based on *The Eurymedon* failed, however, because of the rule of agency that the principal (in this case the sub-contractors) for whom an agent acts must be identifiable at the time of the contract. That was not the case here. The judge nevertheless decided in favour of the sub-contractors, on the basis that the existence of the exclusion clause negated any duty of care owed by the sub-contractors to the plaintiff. In the absence of a duty of care, the tortious action must fail. The validity of this approach was subsequently confirmed by the Court of Appeal in *Norwich City Council v Harvey*.[127] Once again, the case concerned the negligence of sub-contractors, who in this case had set fire to the plaintiff's premises. The main contract, however, contained a clause placing the burden of insuring against fire on the plaintiff. In this

---

123 [1996] AC 650, p 666 (emphasis added).
124 Ibid, p 665.
125 Cf the approach of the Supreme Court of Canada in *London Drugs Ltd v Kuenhe & Nagel International Ltd* (1992) 97 DLR (4th) 261.
126 [1985] 2 All ER 1077.
127 [1989] 1 All ER 1180.

context, the Court of Appeal took the view that the sub-contractors were not in breach of any duty of care. As May LJ put it:[128]

> I do not think that the mere fact that there is not strict privity between the employer and the sub-contractor should prevent the latter from relying on the clear basis on which all the parties contracted in relation to damage to the employer's building caused by fire, even when due to the negligence of the contractors or sub-contractors.

5.13 IMPOSING BURDENS: RESTRICTIVE COVENANTS

The exceptions and evasions of the doctrine of privity which we have looked at so far have all been concerned with the recovery of a benefit by a third party. In this section we are concerned with the possibility of imposing a restriction on a third party's behaviour.

In land transactions, the seller of a piece of land will often wish to restrict the use to which the purchaser can put the land, particularly if the seller is retaining ownership of adjacent land. Of course, as between the original seller and purchaser, this can be achieved by contract. But what about someone who buys from the original purchaser? Can that person be made subject to the restriction? In *Tulk v Moxhay*,[129] it was held that this could be the case in relation to land, provided that certain conditions were satisfied, in particular, that the original seller still had an interest to protect (for example, continued ownership of the adjacent land).

5.13.1 Application outside land law

Land law has subsequently developed a complicated set of rules dealing with the enforceability of such 'restrictive covenants'. Outside the land law area, however, the courts have been reluctant to extend this exception to the privity doctrine. In *Taddy v Sterious*,[130] the court refused to apply it to an attempt to restrict the price at which the plaintiff's goods were sold by a third party. The plaintiffs had attached a notice to the packets of tobacco which they manufactured indicating that it was supplied to retailers on condition that it was not sold below the stipulated price. Acceptance of the goods was deemed to be acceptance of these conditions, and where the goods were bought from a wholesaler, the wholesaler was deemed to be the agent of the manufacturer. Despite this elaborate attempt to create an obligation which attached to the goods, in the same way as a covenant may attach to land, it was held that the defendant,

---

128 [1989] 1 All ER 1180, p 1187.
129 (1848) 2 Ph 774; 41 ER 1143.
130 [1904] 1 Ch 354.

who bought the goods from a wholesaler with full knowledge of the conditions, was nevertheless not bound by them. There have, however, been some cases concerned with shipping contracts where an approach analogous to the restrictive covenant has been used to bind a third party. In *De Mattos v Gibson*,[131] for example, the plaintiff had chartered a ship from its owner, C. C had then mortgaged the ship to G, who had notice of the charter. When C ran into financial difficulties, G proposed to sell the ship. The plaintiff successfully obtained an injunction restraining G from acting in a way which was inconsistent with the charter. Knight Bruce LJ said that where a person had acquired property from another with knowledge of a prior binding contract as to the use of the property made with a third party:[132]

> . . . the acquirer shall not, to the material damage of the third person, in opposition to the contract and inconsistently with it, use and employ the property in a manner not allowable to the giver or seller.

Moreover, he considered that the rule applied in the same way to both land and personal property. The same line was taken by the Privy Council in *Lord Strathcona SS Co v Dominion Coal Co*.[133] The plaintiffs had chartered a ship which had subsequently been sold. It was held that the new owner, the defendant, could be restrained by injunction from using the ship in a way which would prevent the operation of the charter contract made by the previous owner. It was regarded as significant, however, that the new owner had been aware of the existence of the charter at the time that the ship was bought.

5.13.2   The current position

The further development of this exception to privity was halted by the refusal of Diplock J (as he then was) in *Port Line Ltd v Ben Line Ltd*[134] to accept the earlier decisions as being correctly based on equitable principles analogous to the law relating to 'restrictive covenants'. He took the view that these cases could be more properly viewed as falling within the area where the law of tort could provide a remedy,[135] rather than as examples of a more general exception to the doctrine of privity. This analysis was apparently accepted for the following 20 years, but in 1979 Browne-Wilkinson J indicated that there might still be some life in the equitable, restrictive covenant approach outside the area of land law. In *Swiss Bank Corp v Lloyds Bank Ltd*,[136] a loan had been made to buy shares. The lender argued that the borrower was contractually bound to repay the loan and interest out of the proceeds of any dealings with the

---

131   (1859) 4 D & J 276; 45 ER 108.
132   Ibid, p 282; p 110.
133   [1926] AC 108.
134   [1958] 2 QB 146; [1958] 1 All ER 787.
135   See below, 5.14.
136   [1979] Ch 548; [1979] 2 All ER 853.

shares. This was said to be a specifically enforceable obligation. The shares were also subject to a charge by Lloyds Bank (presumably they had been put up as security for a loan). The lender alleged that Lloyds' rights over the shares were subject to the rights of the lender as set out in the original contract of loan. Browne-Wilkinson J held that the obligation to repay the loan out of dealings with the shares was specifically enforceable. This meant that the lender held an equitable interest in the shares, and that Lloyds' rights were subject to this obligation. The Court of Appeal and the House of Lords held that there was no specifically enforceable obligation of the kind alleged, but did not disagree with the judge's analysis of the relationship between the parties if there had been. It seems, therefore, that the equitable approach will still be available in certain appropriate cases. What will be needed is to show that the contract which is alleged to bind the third party has created an equitable interest in property falling within the scope of the contract. The third party will not then be allowed to act in a way which adversely affects this equitable interest. Nevertheless, although this demonstrates the theoretical availability of the 'restrictive covenant' approach in relation to personal property, the tortious action considered in the next section is more likely to work in practice.

5.14 THE ROLE OF THE LAW OF TORT

The cases and principles discussed in this section are in many ways the proper concern of the law of tort. However, this is an area (of which there are several) in which the rigid division drawn between tort and contract is unhelpful. The particular tortious action which we need to consider is that of 'wrongful interference with contractual rights'. A person who knowingly and intentionally brings about a breach of contract between two others thereby commits a tort. Moreover, an injunction will generally be obtainable to prevent the interferer acting in this way. To this extent, it can be said that a third party is bound by the provisions of a contract between two other people.

The existence of this tort was recognised and applied in *Lumley v Gye*.[137] Lumley had engaged a singer, Johanna Wagner, to sing at a series of concerts at his theatre.[138] It was a provision of this contract that she should not sing elsewhere. The defendant, who knew of this, persuaded Ms Wagner to sing at his theatre. Lumley first obtained an injunction against Ms Wagner preventing her from breaking her contract in this way. Her response was to leave the jurisdiction, and to refuse to sing at either theatre. Lumley then sued Gye, and it was held that he would be entitled to recover damages if Gye had intentionally interfered with his contract with Wagner.[139] This remedy has also been held to be available where goods are sold subject to a restriction on their disposal.

---

137 (1853) 2 El & Bl 216; 118 ER 749.

138 The full story, together with a reconsideration of the legal issues raised by the case, can be found in Waddams, 2001.

139 Though when the action was re-heard on this basis the decision went against Lumley – see Waddams, 2001.

In *BMTA v Salvadori*,[140] the purchaser of a new car agreed not to sell it for a year without first offering it to the plaintiff. The defendant bought the car with knowledge of this restriction, and with the intention of evading its effects, and was again held liable in tort. This would be the way, therefore, in which, in the example given at the beginning of this chapter, the gallery owner might be able to recover compensation from the new owner of the painting.[141]

As has been noted above, this is an alternative way of analysing the outcome in cases such as *De Mattos v Gibson* and *Lord Strathcona SS Co v Dominion Coal Co*. It is, however, more limited than the 'restrictive covenant' approach. Such covenants may, in certain circumstances, bind even those who are unaware of them. The tort of interference with contract, on the other hand, requires knowledge on the part of the tortfeasor. It is only where he or she is aware of the other contract, and the fact that rights under it may be affected, that the tortious remedy will be available to restrain, or provide compensation for, the interference.

5.15 FURTHER READING

Adams, J and Brownsword, R, 'Privity and the concept of a network contract' (1990) 10 Legal Studies 12
Adams, J, Beyleveld, D and Brownsword, R, 'Privity of contract – the benefits and burdens of law reform' (1997) 60 MLR 238
Burrows, A, 'The Contracts (Rights of Third Parties) Act and its implications for commercial contracts' [2000] LMCLQ 540
Flannigan, R, 'Privity – the end of an era (error)' (1987) 103 LQR 564
Law Commission, *Privity of Contract: Contracts for the benefit of third parties'*, Consultation Paper No 121, 1991
Law Revision Committee, Sixth Interim Report, 1937, Cmd 5449
Smith, SA, 'Contracts for the benefit of third parties: in defence of the Third-Party Rule' (1997) OJLS 643
Waddams, S, 'Johanna Wagner and the rival opera houses' (2001) 117 LQR 431

---

140 [1949] Ch 556.
141 See above, 5.2. It still does not give the gallery owner the right to insist on the painting being displayed – but the threat of legal action against the new owner might be enough to secure this outcome. It is more likely to do so than the existence of the contractual action for damages against the original owner.

6 AGENCY

CONTENTS

6.1 OVERVIEW

This chapter deals with a situation where, in contrast to the normal position under the English law of contract, three parties are involved, rather than two. This involves the concept of agency. To some extent this concept operates as an exception to the standard doctrine of privity discussed in the previous chapter. The issues which will be considered are:

■   Definition of agency. Agency needs to be distinguished from other concepts, such as sale or employment, and labels are not always relevant. The category of 'commercial agent' needs to be noted.

■ Agency and privity. How does the concept of agency interact with the doctrine of privity?

■ Creation of agency. Agency can be created expressly, impliedly or through the operation of law.

■ Powers of an agent. It is important to know when the agent is acting with authority – this can be express, implied, or ostensible.

■ Ratification. This deals with the possibility of a principal being able to take over a contract which was made without actual authority.

■ Duties of agent and principal. What are the obligations which arise out of the agent–principal relationship?

■ Third party's position. What are the rights and liabilities of principal and agent towards the third party?

■ Termination. How does an agency relationship come to an end, and what are the consequences of this?

6.2 DEFINITION OF AGENCY

The concept of the agent is a useful one in the law of contract, but it is not all that easy to define.[1] For our purposes, we may take it as referring to the situation where one person (the agent) has the power to bring another person (the principal) into a contractual relationship with a third party.[2]

It is important to remember that to describe someone as an agent is to identify a *relationship* and not a *job*.[3] Thus, although many agents will be appointed and described as such, many other 'agents' have this status simply from the responsibilities which arise out of their employment. The shop assistant who deals with customers is in that situation acting as agent for the owner of the shop. The company director who makes a contract on behalf of an incorporated company is equally acting as an agent. The company has a separate legal personality, but of course cannot itself physically make contracts. It has to act through human agents.

It quickly becomes apparent that the concept of agency is of vital importance in all areas of commercial activity. Without it, dealings would become cumbersome, expensive and impractical.

The Principles of European Contract Law deal with agency in Arts 3.101 to

---

1 See, for example, Stone, 1996, Chapter 1.
2 Throughout this chapter, the 'third party' will be used to refer to a person who deals with an agent.
3 As such, an agency contract is likely to be at the relational end of Macneil's discrete/relational spectrum: see Chapter 1, 1.5. The need for trust and co-operation which this implies is perhaps reflected in the 'good faith' obligations discussed below.

3.304.[4] Much of what is contained in these Articles is very close to the relevant common law principles, but where there are differences these are identified in the notes at the end of this chapter. The main areas of difference relate to the rights and liabilities of the 'undisclosed principal', and the right of the agent to delegate to a sub-agent.

6.2.1 Relevance of labels

Because the central core of agency is the relationship that it denotes, the labels used by the parties are of only minor significance. If a person is described as an 'agent', this may well indicate that he or she has authority to bind his or her principal, but it does not necessarily do so. The point was considered in *Lamb & Sons v Goring Brick Co.*[5] GBC were manufacturers of bricks and other building materials. Lamb & Sons were builders' merchants. An agreement was made under which Lamb were appointed 'sole selling agents' of GBC's bricks and other materials. Following a change of ownership of GBC, it became important to establish the exact effect of this agreement. The Court of Appeal held that it did not create a relationship of agency. The arrangement was that GBC sold its bricks to Lamb, and that Lamb then sold them on to others. In a true agency relationship, Lamb, as agent, would simply have brought GBC into a contractual relationship with the purchasers, and would not themselves have bought and sold the bricks.

It was confirmed by the Court of Appeal in *AMB Imballagi Plastici SRL v Pacflex Ltd*[6] that a similar arrangement, where one party found potential customers, but the transactions involved sale by the supplier to the 'agent', and then sale by the 'agent' to the customer, did not fall within the scope of the Commercial Agents (Council Directive) Regulations 1993.[7] In *Mercantile International Group plc v Chuan Soon Huat Industrial Group plc*,[8] on the other hand, the Court of Appeal considered an arrangement whereby the agent made contracts for the sale of goods in the name of the principal,[9] but earned its remuneration by paying the principal for the goods, and then charging a higher price from the 'third party'. It was held that this was a situation of agency.[10]

---

4 The Articles do not deal with the internal relationship between principal and agent – only with their relationship with a third party.
5 [1932] 1 KB 710.
6 [1999] 2 All ER Comm 249.
7 See 6.2.2 below.
8 [2002] 1 All ER Comm 788.
9 The contracts with the third parties made it clear that the agent was contracting as such.
10 The method of remuneration did not amount to 'commission', however, so that the arrangement did not fall within the compensation provisions of the Commercial Agents (Council Directive) Regulations 1993.

Is a car dealer which advertises itself as being a 'sole selling agent' in a particular town for a particular make of car likely to be an 'agent' of the car manufacturer under the above definition?

6.2.2 Commercial agents

This chapter is concerned with the common law rules applying to agency. It should be noted, however, that a particular category of commercial agency is now governed additionally by Regulations deriving from a European directive. These are the Commercial Agents (Council Directive) Regulations 1993. They apply to independent commercial agents who have continuing authority to negotiate the sale or purchase of goods.[11] They do not apply to agents who are also employees, or company directors, or partners. Nor do they cover an agent engaged for a particular transaction. The details of these Regulations are beyond the scope of this book. This chapter simply notes, at the relevant points, the areas where the provisions of the Regulations differ significantly from the common law rules. For a full discussion of the Regulations, reference should be made to a specialist agency or commercial law text.[12]

6.3 AGENCY AND PRIVITY

In some situations, agency operates as an exception to the doctrine of privity. This is particularly so where the agent contracts on behalf of an undisclosed principal. In other words, the third party thinks that he or she is contracting with the agent in person, whereas in fact there is a principal standing behind the agent, who will step in and take over the contract.[13] This, as far as the third party is concerned, is an exception to the general principle that only those who are parties to a contract can have rights and liabilities under it. Moreover, the concept of agency can be used to circumvent the restrictions of privity. In *New Zealand Shipping Co Ltd v AM Satterthwaite & Co Ltd, The Eurymedon*,[14] for example, the carriers were deemed to be the agents of the stevedores

---

11 The European Court of Justice has held (on a reference from the Court of Appeal) that the provisions of the Regulations apply whenever an agent operates within the EU, even if the principal is situated outside: *Ingmar GB Ltd v Eaton Leonard Technologies Ltd*, Case 381/98 [2001] 1 All ER Comm 329.
12 For example, Reynolds, 2005; Stone, 1996.
13 This concept is not accepted in the Principles of European Contract Law. By virtue of Arts 3:301–3:303, the 'agent' in this situation is termed an 'intermediary', and generally no rights or liabilities are created between the third party and the intermediary's undisclosed principal. The only exception to this is in the situation of the intermediary's insolvency, or fundamental non-performance.
14 [1975] AC 154; [1974] 1 All ER 1015; see 5.12.1 above.

in order to create a contract between the stevedores and the owners, and thus give the stevedores the protection of an exclusion clause set out in the contract between the owners and the carriers.

6.4 CREATION OF AGENCY

Agency can be created in a variety of ways. The three principal ones are express agreement, implied agreement and operation of law.

As regards express agreement, the agent may be appointed generally, to make contracts on behalf of the principal in a range of situations, or simply to act in connection with one particular project. Subject to the limitations indicated by *Lamb & Sons v Goring Brick Co*,[15] there are no particular problems with this way of creating agency. No special formalities are required, and the agreement does not even need to constitute a contract. Even where the agent has the power to make agreements which have to be in writing (such as contracts for the sale of land), the appointment does not have to be in writing.

The one exception to this is where the agent is to have power to execute a deed, for example, a conveyance of land. In that situation, the agency itself must be created by deed, generally known as a power of attorney.

As regards implied agreements to create agency, the courts here profess to be looking for the intentions of the parties, and if they think that they intended to create an agency relationship, then that will be given effect. As is usual in contract law, the intention will be determined by an objective consideration of what the parties have said or done. This type of pragmatic approach to the implication of agency may be seen in *Heatons Transport (St Helens) Ltd v Transport and General Workers Union*,[16] where shop stewards were deemed to be agents of the union, and thus rendered the union responsible for their (the shop stewards') unlawful continuance of industrial action.

Agency can also be imposed by law, irrespective of the intentions of the parties in three ways: by statute, by necessity or from cohabitation.

An example of agency created by statute is to be found in s 56(2) of the Consumer Credit Act 1974. The effect of this section is to make a dealer who negotiates with a customer to arrange a credit transaction (such as a hire purchase arrangement) the agent of the finance company for the purpose of such negotiations. This reversed the common law position as stated in *Branwhite v Worcester Works Finance*,[17] which made the dealer the agent of the customer.

Agency of necessity arises chiefly in relation to shipping contracts. Thus, if a cargo is in danger of perishing, the master of the ship will have the power to sell it or

---

15 [1932] 1 KB 710; see above, 6.2.1.
16 [1973] AC 15; [1972] 3 All ER 101.
17 [1969] 1 AC 552; [1968] 3 All ER 104.

even jettison it.[18] Similarly, if the ship itself is in urgent need of repair, the master may incur expenses towards this, or even sell the ship to raise the money to carry out the work.[19] The Court of Appeal's decision in *Industrie Chimiche Italia Centrale and Cerealfin SA v Alexander G Tsavliris Maritime Co, The Choko Star*[20] emphasised the exceptional nature of agency of necessity, and the fact that it would only arise where the 'agent' was unable to receive instructions from the 'principal'. Modern communications make it rare that such instructions will be unobtainable, and thus the scope for this type of agency seems to be greatly reduced.

Agency from cohabitation is presumed wherever a man and woman are living together in a household (not, for example, as managers of a hotel – *Debenham v Mellon*),[21] whether or not they are married. It will entitle the woman to pledge the man's credit in order to purchase 'necessaries'.[22] In *Miss Gray Ltd v Earl Cathcart*,[23] the presumption was said to be rebuttable by the issue of an express warning to traders; by the fact that the woman was already adequately supplied, or had a sufficient allowance, or had been specifically forbidden to pledge the man's credit; or if the order was extravagant. Given these limitations, the practical application of this type of agency seems as limited as it is outdated in social terms.

6.5 POWERS OF AN AGENT

The power that an agent has to bind the principal depends on the agent's authority. There are three types of authority to be considered: express, implied and ostensible.

As regards express authority, the limits of the agent's authority may well be expressly established by the agreement between the principal and agent. This may occur when the relationship is first established, or may change over time. The principal will generally be entitled at any time to alter the agent's authority, provided that this does not conflict with any contractual agreement between them. The third party will be bound by the limits of the agent's express authority, as long as he or she is aware of them. If the third party does not know of certain limitations and contracts outside them, then issues of implied or ostensible authority, or ratification, may arise. This will also be the case if the agreement between principal and agent is silent, or unclear, as to the extent of the agent's authority.

Implied authority derives either from the type of work which the agent is doing, or the place where the agent is working.[24] The first category will be referred to here as

---

18 *The Gratitudine* (1801) 3 Ch Rob 240; 165 ER 450.
19 *Gunn v Roberts* (1874) LR 9 CP 331.
20 [1990] 1 Lloyd's Rep 516.
21 (1880) 6 App Cas 24.
22 Compare the position in relation to minors' contracts in Chapter 7, 7.4.
23 (1922) 38 TLR 562.
24 The concept is recognised by Art 3:201(2) of the Principles of European Contract Law.

'usual authority', that is, the authority 'usually' attaching to a particular job. The second category will be labelled 'customary' authority, in that it will arise out of the customs of a particular place of business.

A classic, though not unproblematic, example of usual authority is to be found in *Watteau v Fenwick*.[25] The defendant owned a beerhouse and employed a manager, who had authority to buy goods for the business. The manager was under express instructions, however, not to buy cigars, as these would be supplied by the defendant. The manager bought cigars on credit from the plaintiff. The plaintiff sued the defendant for the price of the cigars. It was held that since the plaintiff was unaware of the express limitation, and since it was within the usual authority of a manager of a beerhouse to order goods of this type, the defendant was liable.

The decision may be contrasted with *Daun v Simmins*,[26] in which it was held that the manager of a 'tied' public house would normally only have authority to buy spirits from a particular source. The supplier in this case could not rely on an implied usual authority in order to sue the principal.

The main issue here is therefore one of fact. What exactly is the usual authority of this particular type of agent, and was the third party aware of any express limits on it?

The controversial aspect of *Watteau v Fenwick* is that the third party was unaware that he was dealing with an agent, and it is not at all clear that the usual authority should be allowed to operate in the situation of an undisclosed principal.[27] A more recent example of the application of the general principle that an agent will have implied authority to perform such duties as may reasonably be associated with the agent's job title is to be found in the Court of Appeal decision in *SMC Electronics Ltd v Akhter Computers Ltd*.[28] An employee of Akhter, whose job title was 'Director PSU Sales', entered into a commission agreement with SMC under which SMC would introduce business relating to the supply of PSUs (power supply units), in return for a share in the profits. It was held that, although the employee (who was not a 'director' of the company) did not have specific authority to make this contract, such authority could be implied from his job title.

Customary authority operates to authorise the agent to act according to the usages or customs of a particular place or market. Thus, in *Scott v Godfrey*,[29] a custom of the Stock Exchange allowed a stockbroker to act as agent for several principals at once in buying shares from one seller, thus bringing each principal into a separate contractual relationship with the seller.

The third type of authority, 'ostensible' authority, involves the principal having, by words or action, led the third party to believe that the agent has authority, when

---

25 [1893] 1 QB 346.
26 (1871) 41 LT 483.
27 See *Rhodian River Shipping Co SA v Halla Maritime Corp* [1984] 1 Lloyd's Rep 373, where Bingham LJ describes *Watteau v Fenwick* as 'a somewhat puzzling case' (p 378).
28 [2001] 1 BCLC 433.
29 [1901] 2 KB 726.

in fact the agent does not. It is also sometimes referred to as 'apparent authority' or 'agency by estoppel'.[30]

The requirements for its existence were set out in *Rama Corp Ltd v Proved Tin and General Investments Ltd*.[31] Slade J said that ostensible authority was a kind of estoppel, and that therefore what was needed was: (a) a representation; (b) a reliance on the representation; and (c) an alteration of position resulting from such reliance. The precise nature of the representation required was expanded on by Diplock LJ in *Freeman and Lockyer v Buckhurst Properties (Mangal) Ltd* in the following passage:[32]

> . . . 'ostensible' authority . . . is a legal relationship between the principal and the contractor created by a representation, *made by the principal to the contractor*, intended to be and in fact acted upon by the contractor, that the agent has authority to enter on behalf of the principal into a contract of a kind within the scope of the 'apparent' authority so as to render the principal liable to perform any obligations imposed upon him by such a contract.

Moreover, the agent 'must not purport to make the agreement as principal himself'.

The 'representation' may come from conduct rather than a statement. In *Summers v Solomon*,[33] for example, it came from the conduct of the principal in allowing the agent to buy goods for his jewellery business. When the agent was dismissed, the ostensible authority created by this conduct survived, and a third party who was unaware of the termination of the agency was allowed to recover from the principal the price of jewellery with which the agent had absconded. Similarly, in *Lloyd v Grace, Smith & Co*,[34] the representation came from the fact that a firm of solicitors had allowed a clerk to carry out conveyancing work without supervision. The firm was liable when the clerk acted fraudulently in relation to the third party.

As the quotation by Diplock LJ given above makes clear, the representation must emanate from the principal, not the agent. This was confirmed in *Armagas Ltd v Mundogas SA, The Ocean Frost*,[35] where the agent, a chartering manager, falsely represented that he had authority for a particular transaction involving the sale and lease back of a ship. The third party could not enforce the transaction against the principal, since the principal had not made any representation of authority. This principle has, however, been weakened by the subsequent Court of Appeal decisions in *City Trust v Levy*[36] and *First Energy (UK) Ltd v Hungarian International Bank Ltd*,[37] which suggest

30 The concept of the 'apparent agent' with authority derived from representations (verbal or by conduct) of the principal is recognised by Art 3:201(3) of the Principles of European Contract Law.
31 [1952] 2 QB 147; [1954] 1 All ER 554.
32 [1964] 2 QB 480, p 503; [1964] 1 All ER 630, p 644 (emphasis added).
33 (1857) 7 E & B 879; 119 ER 1474.
34 [1912] AC 716.
35 [1986] AC 717; [1986] 2 All ER 385.
36 [1988] 3 All ER 418 – reported with *United Bank of Kuwait v Hamoud*. See also Stone, 1993.
37 [1993] 2 Lloyd's Rep 195. See also Brown, 1995.

that authority to enter into a transaction can be distinguished from authority to communicate that the principal has given approval for such a transaction. The latter type of ostensible authority may exist even where the former does not. If this is so, the agent has only to claim that approval has been given in order to bind his or her principal to a contract with the third party.

The other two requirements for ostensible authority noted by Slade J are more easily dealt with. That of reliance simply means that the third party will not be able to plead ostensible authority if he or she was not aware of the representation, or did not actually believe that the agent had authority, or ought to have known that the agent's authority was limited.[38] The requirement of an 'alteration of position' will be satisfied in the context in which we are discussing agency by the fact that the third party has entered into a contract.

6.6 RATIFICATION

Where an agent enters into an unauthorised contract, the principal may be happy to adopt it. This can be done by the process of ratification.[39] For ratification to be available, however, the agent must purport to act on behalf of a principal, the principal must be in existence at the time of the contract, and the principal must have capacity.

Because the agent must purport to be acting of behalf of another, ratification is not available where the principal is undisclosed. The third party must know that there is, or is supposed to be, a principal in the background. If the third party thinks that the agent is acting on his or her own account, no later ratification will be possible. In *Keighley Maxted & Co v Durant,*[40] the agent had made a contract at a higher price than that which his principal had authorised. The principal later purported to ratify this unauthorised act. The House of Lords held that he could not, because the agent had not disclosed to the third party that he was acting on behalf of someone else.

FOR THOUGHT

Why is an undisclosed principal not allowed to ratify a contract? What disadvantage to the third party would there be if this was allowed?

---

38 See *Overbrooke Estates Ltd v Glencombe Properties Ltd* [1974] 3 All ER 511 – discussed further in Chapter 10, 10.5.

39 This process is recognised by Art 3:207 of the Principles of European Contract Law. The Principles also provide a procedure whereby a third party can seek clarification of an agent's authority – with the right to treat the agent's actions as authorised if this clarification is not forthcoming 'without delay': Art 3:208.

40 [1901] AC 240.

Provided, however, that the agent mentions the principal, it does not matter that the agent is in fact intending to act independently. In *Re Tiedemann and Ledermann Frères*,[41] the agent acted in the principal's name in relation to a sale which he in fact intended to be for his own benefit. The third party then tried to rescind the contract on the basis of the misrepresentation as to whom he was contracting with. The principal, however, ratified the contract, and this prevented the third party from rescinding it.

The second requirement for ratification, that is, that the principal is in existence at the time of ratification, arises mainly in relation to contracts made on behalf of new companies which are being formed. In *Kelner v Baxter*,[42] it was held that if the company was not in existence (in that it had not been incorporated) at the time of the contract, it could not later ratify the agreement. The purported 'agents', the promoters of the company, were therefore personally liable. Such personal liability is now imposed by statute, by virtue of s 36C of the Companies Act 1985.

The final requirement is that the principal must have capacity. There are in theory two aspects to this rule. The first is that the principal must have capacity to make the transaction at the time of the contract. This has most obvious relevance to minors, who might want to ratify after reaching majority. It could also apply to contracts made outside the powers of a company. Both these situations have now been affected by statutory provisions, however, namely ss 1–3 of the Minors' Contracts Act 1987[43] and s 36 of the Companies Act 1985, which means that this aspect of the rule is of little practical significance.

The second aspect is that the principal must have capacity at the time of ratification. This was applied in *Grover and Grover Ltd v Matthews*.[44] A contract of fire insurance was purported to be ratified after a fire had destroyed the property which was the subject of the insurance. It was held that this was ineffective, because at the time of the purported ratification the principal could not have made the contract himself (because the property no longer existed). 'Capacity' is thus being given a rather broader meaning than usual, to cover the issue as to whether the principal would have in practice been able to make the contract in question.

Ratification is retrospective in its effect, and the original contract must be treated as if it had been authorised from the start.[45] This was confirmed by the Court of Appeal in *Presentaciones Musicales SA v Secunda*.[46] The implications of this rule are clear from the decision in *Bolton Partners v Lambert*.[47] Bolton Partners owned a factory, which Lambert offered to buy. This offer was accepted by the managing director, though in fact he had no authority to do this. On 13 January, there was a disagreement, and Lambert

---

41 [1899] 2 QB 66.
42 (1866) LR 2 CP 174.
43 See Chapter 7, 7.4.
44 [1910] 2 KB 401.
45 This is also the effect of ratification under the Principles of European Contract Law: Art 3:207(2).
46 [1994] Ch 271.
47 (1889) 41 Ch D 295.

withdrew his offer. On 17 January, Bolton Partners started proceedings for breach of contract. On 28 January, the Board of Directors of Bolton Partners ratified the actions of the managing director. Lambert argued that this ratification came too late, but the Court of Appeal held that it had retrospectively validated the original contract, and that Lambert's attempt to withdraw was therefore ineffective.

Despite the considerable leeway granted by this decision, it has subsequently been held that the ratification must take place within a reasonable time of the acceptance, and certainly before the contract has been performed.[48] Moreover, if the contract has been specifically stated to be 'subject to ratification', a withdrawal prior to ratification will be effective.[49]

6.7 DUTIES OF AGENT AND PRINCIPAL

This section considers the duties which exist as between principal and agent, as opposed to between principal or agent and the third party.

6.7.1 Duties of agent

An agent has a duty to carry out instructions, to act with due care and skill, and to act personally rather than through another. In addition, the agent has various fiduciary duties.

As regards the duty to carry out instructions, an agent is obliged to do anything which the agreement creating the agency binds him or her to do. In *Fraser v Furman Productions Ltd*,[50] an agent failed to take out an insurance policy on behalf of some employers, who, as a result, were liable to compensate an injured employee. The agent was held liable to reimburse the employer.

An agent is also under a duty not to exceed the authority granted by the principal. We have already considered the issue of authority as it affects the third party. At this point, we are looking at the express and implied authority as between principal and agent. Express authority needs no discussion. Implied authority will arise from the relationship, and will include authority to take all actions necessarily incidental to the purposes for which the agent has been engaged. The authority as between principal and agent may not be identical with that between agent and third party, as is shown by the following quotation from *Waugh v HB Clifford & Sons*.[51] Brightman J said that if, in a defamation action, the defendant's solicitor offered £100,000 in settlement:[52]

---

48 *Metropolitan Asylums Board Managers v Kingham & Sons* (1890) 6 TLR 217.
49 *Watson v Davies* (1931) 1 Ch 455.
50 [1967] 1 WLR 898.
51 [1982] 1 Ch 374; [1982] 1 All ER 1095.
52 Ibid, p 387; p 1105. Note that 'implied authority' is here used to refer to the authority as between principal and agent.

It would in my view be officious on the part of the plaintiff's solicitor to demand to be satisfied as to the authority of the defendant's solicitor to make the offer. It is perfectly clear that the defendant's solicitor has *ostensible* authority to compromise the action on behalf of his client, notwithstanding the large sum involved . . . But it does not follow that the defendant's solicitor would have implied authority to agree to damages on that scale without the agreement of his client. In the light of the solicitor's knowledge of his client's cash position it might be quite unreasonable and indeed grossly negligent for the solicitor to commit his client to such a burden without first inquiring if it were acceptable . . . It follows in my view that a solicitor (or counsel) may in a particular case have ostensible authority vis à vis the opposing litigant where he has no implied authority vis à vis his client.

Thus, an agent may be able to bind the principal to a contract with the third party, but at the same time be in breach of the duty to carry out instructions.

The second general duty is to act with care and skill. The degree of care and skill required of an agent will depend on the circumstances. The agent must act with the skill which an agent in his or her position would normally possess. Thus, a solicitor or accountant must act with the skill to be expected of someone qualified in that profession. The standard is one of 'reasonable care' in that context. If the agent is not acting for reward, then this duty will be applied less strictly.

There is generally a duty of 'non-delegation'. In other words, the agent is normally expected to act personally on behalf of the principal. Delegation of the agent's responsibilities will only be permissible where this has been authorised, expressly or impliedly, by the principal.[53] Such delegation will not create any privity between the sub-agent and principal, unless this is specifically provided for. This was the case in *De Bussche v Alt*,[54] so that the sub-agent was, unusually, held directly liable to the principal. Since the sub-agent had made a secret profit[55] from dealing with the principal's property, he was liable to account to the principal for this.

The final area of duties derives from the fact that an agent is treated as a fiduciary. The duties of a fiduciary were said by Millett LJ, in *Bristol & West Building Society v Mothew*, to include the following obligations:[56]

The fiduciary must act in good faith; he must not make a profit out of his trust; he must not place himself in a position where his duty and his interest may conflict; he may not act for his own benefit or the benefit of a third person without the informed consent of his principal.

---

53 *De Bussche v Alt* (1878) 8 Ch D 286. The Principles of European Contract Law, on the other hand, provide that delegation is presumed to be authorised in relation to tasks which 'are not of a personal character and which it is not reasonable to expect the agent to carry out itself': Art 3:206.

54 Ibid.

55 For which, see below.

56 [1996] 4 All ER 698, p 712.

This is not a comprehensive list. The duty not to make a profit will apply also to profiting from information acquired as an agent. Moreover, in *Henderson v Merrett Syndicates Ltd*, Lord Browne-Wilkinson suggested that the fiduciary duties of an agent are not static but may change with circumstances.[57] To the list given by Millett LJ we might also add the duty to account for transactions undertaken for the principal. These duties will now be considered in turn.

The agent must not put him or herself into a position where there is a conflict between the duties owed to the principal and the agent's own interests.[58] In *Armstrong v Jackson*, a stockbroker sold his own shares to a client. This was held to involve a conflict of interest:[59]

> As vendor it is to his interest to sell his own shares at the highest price. As broker, it is his clear duty to the principal to buy at the lowest price and to give unbiased and independent advice . . . as to the time when and the price at which shares shall be bought.

As a result, the principal was entitled to rescind the contract, and this was available irrespective of any of the normal bars to rescission for misrepresentation.[60]

The agent will not be liable, however, if the principal is fully aware of the position.[61] In *Harrods Ltd v Lemon*,[62] one department of the plaintiffs' business was acting as estate agents for the defendant, Mrs Lemon, and another department as surveyors for a person who was seeking to buy her house. There was a clear conflict of interest, but Mrs Lemon continued with the contract with full knowledge of the facts. Harrods were therefore entitled to their commission on the estate agency contract.

An agent who makes a secret profit out of his or her position will be liable to account for this to the principal.[63] A recent example of the application of this principle is to be found in *Allwood v Clifford*.[64] The claimant, Allwood, was expecting octuplets and engaged Clifford to negotiate with the *News of the World* in relation to her story. Clifford, in the course of his dealings with the newspaper, arranged that his consultancy firm would receive £15,000 from the newspaper for providing public relations advice and consultancy in relation to the newspaper's part in breaking the story. Allwood claimed that Clifford should account to her for this money, since he had obtained it while acting as her agent. The court held that unless the principal had given full informed consent to the arrangement with the third party, the burden of proof of

---

57 [1995] 2 AC 145; [1994] 3 All ER 506.
58 Compare the Principles of European Contract Law, Art 3:205, which allows the principal to avoid a contract with a third party where there is an undisclosed conflict of interest.
59 [1917] 2 KB 822.
60 See Chapter 10, 10.4.1.
61 This is also the position under the Principles of European Contract Law: Art 3:205(3).
62 [1931] 2 KB 157.
63 As in *De Bussche v Alt*, above.
64 [2002] EMLR 3.

which lay on the agent, the agent could not retain a payment in this situation.[65] No such consent had been given, and Clifford was obliged to pay the £15,000 to Allwood. The fact that Clifford had acted honestly and in good faith, and that there had been no conflict of interest, was irrelevant.

Equally, the agent must not take a 'bribe'. This was defined in *Industries and General Mortgage Co v Lewis*[66] as involving: (a) a payment made, or to be made, to the agent by the third party; (b) knowledge by the third party that the agent is acting as an agent; and (c) failure by the third party to disclose the payment to the agent to the principal.

If these three conditions are satisfied, the payment will be treated as a bribe. There is no need to show any fraudulent intent on the part of anyone involved.

The effects of a bribe being given are that the agent may be dismissed, and the principal may sue the agent and the third party in tort for any loss caused by the bribe. Alternatively, the principal may recover the amount of the bribe from the agent, or from the third party, if not yet paid.[67] Moreover, in *Attorney General for Hong Kong v Reid*,[68] the Privy Council held that a principal was able to 'trace' money given as a bribe into other property which may have been purchased with it, and to recover the full value of the relevant property at the time when the agent is compelled to disgorge the bribe. If the bribe is paid over, the principal is still entitled to set aside the transaction to which it related.[69]

Commercial agents covered by the Commercial Agents (Council Directive) Regulations 1993 are also under a general duty to act 'dutifully and in good faith', and to perform various specific duties, such as to supply the principal with 'all the necessary information available to him'.

6.7.2 Duties of the principal

The main duty of the principal is to pay the agent for the work that has been done. The agent's right to be paid will exist wherever this can be either expressly or impliedly taken to arise from the agency agreement. Where there is a written agreement, the courts will look at this very carefully in deciding whether the agent is entitled to payment. Thus, in *Taylor v Brewer*,[70] the agreement referred to the principal paying 'such remuneration . . . as shall be deemed right'. It was held that this did not entitle the agent to reasonable remuneration, or indeed to any payment at all. It was entirely at the discretion of the

---

65 Applying the approach laid down in *Anangel Atlas Compania Naviera SA v Ishikawajima-Harima Heavy Industries Co Ltd* [1990] 1 Lloyd's Rep 167, where on the facts it was held that consent to the arrangement had been given.
66 [1949] 2 All ER 573.
67 *Mahesan v Malaysia Government Officers' Co-operative Housing Society Ltd* [1979] AC 374; [1979] 2 All ER 405.
68 [1994] AC 324; [1994] 1 All ER 1.
69 *Logicrose Ltd v Southend United Football Club Ltd* [1988] 1 WLR 1256.
70 (1813) 1 M & S 290; 105 ER 108.

principal. Similarly, in *John Meacock v Abrahams*,[71] the fact that the contract provided for payment in certain circumstances (which had not arisen) precluded the agent from claiming on a *quantum meruit* basis.

If it is decided that the agreement does allow for payment, when will it be earned? As would be expected, this will be when the agent has done what he or she has been employed to do. The difficulty arises, however, in deciding in some cases whether this has occurred. In one of the leading cases, for example, *Luxor (Eastbourne) Ltd v Cooper*,[72] a company wished to sell some cinemas and Cooper agreed to try to provide a purchaser. He was to be paid 'on completion of the sale'. Cooper provided a willing purchaser, but the company withdrew from the sale. The House of Lords refused to imply a term that the principal would not unreasonably prevent the completion of the transaction. The clause referred to payment 'on completion'; since that had not occurred, the agent was not entitled to his commission. The way around this is for the agent to insist that the commission should be earned by providing someone 'ready, willing and able' to purchase. This was held to be effective to entitle the agent to his commission in *Christie Owen and Davies v Rapacioli*[73] and, more recently, in *FDP Savills Land and Property Ltd v Kibble*.[74]

Here again, the approach is to look very carefully at the wording of the agreement, and to apply it strictly.

In relation to commercial agents falling within the Commercial Agents (Council Directive) Regulations 1993, the principal has an obligation to act 'dutifully and in good faith'. The Regulations also give the agent a more general right than exists under the common law to reasonable remuneration for work done, and a right to receive information on a range of issues relating to the agency, including the basis on which commission has been calculated.

6.8 THIRD PARTY AND PRINCIPAL

This section looks at the rights and liabilities as between third party and principal. Where the principal is 'disclosed' (that is, the third party knows who the principal is, or at least is aware that the agent is acting for a principal), the basic rule is that the agent will drop out of the transaction. The third party will be able to sue the principal and vice versa. Where the principal is undisclosed, however, the position is more complex.

As has been noted above, the fact that an undisclosed principal is allowed to take over a contract from an agent runs counter to the general doctrine of privity.[75] It means

71 [1956] 3 All ER 660.
72 [1941] AC 108; [1941] 1 All ER 33.
73 [1974] QB 781; [1974] 2 All ER 311.
74 [1998] EGCS 170.
75 As noted above, the Principles of European Contract Law do not recognise the rights of an undisclosed principal to take over a contract, other than in the case of insolvency or fundamental non-performance by the agent (who in this situation is termed an 'intermediary'): Art 3: above, note 14a.

that the third party will find that he or she has rights against, and liabilities towards, a person with whom there was no intention to contract, and of whom the third party had no knowledge at the time of the contract. This rather unusual concept has been limited by two requirements: first, the terms of the contract should be consistent with an agency relationship and, second, no personal considerations should militate against allowing the principal to take over the contract.

In relation to the first of these requirements, if an undisclosed principal is going to step in, this must be consistent with the terms of the contract. In *Humble v Hunter*,[76] for example, the alleged 'agent' who had entered into a charter of a boat was described in the documentation as 'owner'. It was held that this designation was inconsistent with his acting as an agent, and so the court refused to allow an alleged undisclosed principal to take over the contract. In *Fred Drughorn Ltd v Rederiaktiebolaget Transatlantic*,[77] however, the description of a party as 'charterer' rather than 'owner' was held not to preclude an undisclosed principal from stepping into the agent's place.

FOR THOUGHT

> Would the description of a party to a contract as 'landlord' of a property prevent an undisclosed principal from enforcing the contract?

If the character of the person with whom he or she is contracting is an important consideration for the third party, an undisclosed principal may be prevented from suing on the contract. For example, in *Collins v Associated Greyhound Racecourses*,[78] the Court of Appeal held that the identity of the underwriters of shares in a new company was crucial, because the company needed to be sure that they were 'responsible persons'. If the underwriters failed, then the company would be in financial difficulties. There was no scope in this situation for an undisclosed principal.

The concerns need not relate to financial solvency. In *Said v Butt*,[79] a person had arranged for someone else to buy him a ticket for the first night of a play, when he knew that the manager would not have sold him one. It was held that since at first nights the manager traditionally exercises control over the audience, the 'principal' should not be allowed to use the ticket acquired by his 'agent'. On the other hand, if the contract is not of a type to which personal considerations are relevant, the fact that there is personal animosity between the principal and third party will not be a bar to their being brought together by an agent without the third party's knowledge. This was

---

76 [1848] 12 QB 310.
77 [1919] AC 203.
78 [1930] 1 Ch 1.
79 [1920] 3 KB 497.

the case in *Dyster v Randall*,[80] which concerned the sale of a piece of land. The personal considerations were held to be immaterial to this contract.

6.8.1 Liability of the principal

The third party will, of course, have rights against the principal (whether disclosed or undisclosed) in the same way as any other contracting party. Problems may arise, however, where payment to the third party is to be made via the agent. If the principal pays the agent, but the agent fails to pass this on, can the third party still sue the principal? In *Armstrong v Stokes*,[81] it was held that if the third party was unaware that the other party was dealing as agent, and the principal paid the agent in good faith while the third party was still giving credit to the agent, the third party could not then recover from the principal. This case suggests then that the third party cannot recover from the principal if the principal has paid the agent. The court, however, clearly limited its views to the facts before it, and did not express an opinion as to what the situation would be if either the principal was disclosed, or the principal had a set-off against the agent.

The first situation was considered by the Court of Appeal in *Irvine v Watson*,[82] in which it was held that even though a disclosed principal had paid the agent, the third party could still recover from the principal. The only exception would be where the third party had acted in such a way as to lead the principal to believe that the agent had paid the third party.

The second situation (set-off by the principal against the agent) does not seem to have been judicially considered. The reverse situation (set-off between agent and third party) was considered in *Cooke v Eshelby*.[83] The House of Lords held that the third party could not plead a set-off against the agent in an action by the principal unless the principal had acted so as to induce the third party to believe that the agent was contracting as principal. By analogy, it would seem to follow that in an action by the third party against the principal, the principal would not be able to rely on a set-off against the agent.

6.9 THIRD PARTY AND AGENT

This section looks at the rights and liabilities as between third party and agent. The general rule, as has been stated above, is that the agent drops out, and has no liability under, or power to enforce, the contract between the principal and third party. In some situations, however, the third party may be able to sue the agent. The dominant issue is

---

80 [1926] Ch 932.
81 (1872) LR 7 QB 598.
82 [1880] 5 QBD 414.
83 (1887) 12 App Cas 271.

the intention of the parties. According to Brandon J in *The Swan*, this is to be determined from the nature of the contract, its terms and the surrounding circumstances.

The test is objective, based on:[84]

> . . . what two reasonable businessmen making a contract of that nature, in those terms, and in those surrounding circumstances, must be taken to have intended.

Relevant factors may include the way in which the agent has signed the contract. If the signature indicates that it is signed on behalf of someone else, this will suggest that the agent is not liable. Custom or trade usage may also suggest that the agent may have some liability or rights under the contract.

In *The Swan*, the relevant surrounding circumstances included the fact that the agent was also the owner of the boat, which was chartered to a company of which the agent was the major shareholder. The company, via the agent, ordered repair work to be done by the third party. It was held that since the repairers knew that the agent was also the owner, it was natural for them to assume that he would accept personal liability for the repairs.

What is the situation where there is in fact no principal? There are two situations to consider here. First, it may be that the agent is in fact the principal, and is just pretending to be an agent. In this situation, the agent will certainly be liable on any contract, and will also be able to enforce, unless the third party would thereby be prejudiced (for example, if there were personal considerations involved).[85]

Second, the principal may not be in existence, for example, because it is a company which has not yet been formed. The position is now largely governed by statute: s 36C(1) of the Companies Act 1985 states:

> A contract which purports to be made by or on behalf of a company at a time when the company has not been formed has effect, subject to any agreement to the contrary, as one made with the person purporting to act for the company or as agent for it, and he is personally liable on the contract accordingly.

This is very clear as regards the agent's *liability*. It is not specific as to whether the agent would also be able to enforce against the third party. The Court of Appeal in *Phonogram Ltd v Lane*,[86] however, indicated a willingness to interpret the section broadly, in line with its purpose, and this suggested that the agent would be allowed to sue the third party in such a situation. That was also the view taken by the majority of the Court of Appeal in *Braymist Ltd v Wise Finance Co Ltd*,[87] though with the caveat that the third party may have a right to escape from the contract if the identity of the other

---

84 [1968] 1 Lloyd's Rep 5, p 12.
85 Compare the situation of enforcement by an undisclosed principal, discussed above, 6.8.1.
86 [1982] QB 938; [1981] 3 All ER 182.
87 [2002] 2 All ER 333.

contracting party is important. Earlier decisions, such as *Newborne v Sensolid (Great Britain) Ltd*,[88] which turned on narrow interpretations of the precise form of signature used, must now be regarded as of dubious authority.

If the third party can sue either the principal or the agent, at what stage does a choice have to be made as to whom to pursue? Judgment cannot be enforced against both, but what if, for example, the principal is sued, but turns out to be unable to pay? Can the third party at that stage act against the agent?

The rules are not very clear, but s 3 of the Civil Liability (Contribution) Act 1978 has established that (contrary to the previous position) obtaining judgment against one party is not an automatic bar to suing the other. The test in all cases now seems to be whether the third party has 'elected' to sue one party or the other. The case of *Clarkson Booker Ltd v Andjel*[89] said that this was a question of fact, not law. What was required was a 'truly unequivocal act' taken with 'full knowledge of all the facts'.[90] Clearly, a choice exercised at a time when the third party was unaware that the selected defendant was insolvent would not be taken with 'full knowledge'. Otherwise, however, the court seemed to feel that the institution of proceedings would raise a prima facie case of election. It is not an area, however, about which it is possible to state any propositions with any degree of certainty.

It may be possible for the third party to take action against the agent on the basis of a collateral contract. This will be particularly appropriate with regard to pre-contractual statements or promises which the agent may have made. An example is *Andrews v Hopkinson*,[91] where a dealer told the plaintiff that a car being acquired on hire purchase terms was 'a good little bus. I would stake my life on it'. When the car later turned out to be seriously defective, the plaintiff was allowed to recover on the basis of a collateral contract.

The final way in which the agent may be liable to a third party is for breach of the implied warranty of authority. Any agent who purports to act as such impliedly warrants that he or she has the required authority to enter into the contract. If this turns out to be untrue, the third party may sue. The remedy is less satisfactory than that available in an action for breach of contract, however, in that recovery will be limited to whatever the third party would have been able to obtain from the principal. If the principal is insolvent, this may be very little.

The remedy exists, however, irrespective of whether the warranty is fraudulent, negligent or innocent.[92] It has even been held to be available where, unknown to the agent, the principal had become certifiably insane, and therefore the agent's authority is automatically terminated.[93]

---

88 [1954] 1 QB 45.
89 [1964] 2 QB 775; [1964] 3 All ER 260.
90 Ibid, p 792; p 266.
91 [1957] 1 QB 229; [1956] 3 All ER 422.
92 *Collen v Wright* (1857) 8 E & B 647; 120 ER 421.
93 *Yonge v Toynbee* [1910] 1 KB 215.

In *Penn v Bristol & West Building Society*,[94] it was held by the Court of Appeal that a third party could sue on a breach of the warranty of authority even though the loss resulted from the third party contracting with someone other than the principal. A bank had lent money to a prospective purchaser of a house, relying on a solicitor's representation that he was acting for both the current owners (who were husband and wife). In fact, he had no authority to act for the wife. When the sale was subsequently, at the wife's instigation, declared null and void, it was held that the bank could recover from the solicitor its losses resulting from lending money to the purchaser, on the basis of the solicitor's breach of the implied warranty of authority.

6.10 TERMINATION OF AGENCY

Agency may be brought to an end either by the act of the parties, or by operation of law.

Where the agency was created by agreement, it will be determinable in the same way. A continuing agency may also be determined by giving such period of notice as is specified in any agreement or, failing that, reasonable notice. Finally, if either party acts in a way which is inconsistent with the continuation of the agency, it will be terminated – though, of course, this may well give rise to rights of action for breach of contract. As regards termination by operation of law, if an agency is for a particular transaction, the relationship will terminate when that transaction is completed. If it is for a specified period, it will cease at the end of that period.

Agency may also be terminated by subsequent events. These may be physical, as where, for example, the subject matter is destroyed, or the principal or agent dies, or becomes insane. Alternatively, they may be legal, as where the principal or agent becomes bankrupt, or the relationship becomes illegal (for example, if the principal becomes an enemy alien).[95]

The effects of termination are that, as far as principal and agent are concerned, rights vested at the time of the termination will subsist, but no new rights can be created, at least once the agent has notice of the termination.

In relation to the third party, again rights accrued against either principal or agent will remain. New rights against the principal will only arise on the basis of ostensible authority. Otherwise, the agent will be liable, either directly on the contract or for breach of the implied warranty of authority.

There are special provisions as to termination provided by the Commercial Agents (Council Directive) Regulations 1993 in relation to commercial agents falling within the scope of the Regulations. These cover such matters as the minimum periods of notice which must be given, and the rights of the agent to compensation when an

---

94 [1997] 3 All ER 470.

95 In some of these situations the agency contract will be deemed to be 'frustrated', and the doctrine of frustration (as discussed in Chapter 16) will apply.

agreement is terminated. It was held in *Hackett v Advanced Medical Computer Systems Ltd*[96] that no particular formality was required for giving notice under the Regulations.

Several cases have considered the rights to compensation for the termination of a commercial agency, which was one of the main areas with which the European Directive on which the Regulations are based was concerned. The aim was to ensure that commercial agents were not treated unfairly, and to harmonise the provisions in this area. The compensation provisions will apparently apply whatever the reason for the termination of the agency, even if it results from the expiry of a fixed-term contract.[97] The compensation provisions do not, however, apply to a sub-agent of a commercial agent as against that agent's principal. The only rights of the sub-agent are against the commercial agent. That was the view of the Court of Appeal in *Stuart Light v Ty Europe Ltd*.[98]

The amount of compensation to which the agent will be entitled is dealt with in reg 17. Two approaches are recognised – 'compensation' and 'indemnity' – which correspond to the principles operating in this area in France and Germany respectively. The parties are free to choose which method should be adopted, but if they fail to do so then the 'compensation' provisions will apply. Both approaches introduce a new notion into English law, which is that where the agent has participated in building up the business, the agent has an interest in the business which should be protected. This differs from the normal approach to damages for breach of contract, which is the method which the common law uses to compensate an agent whose contract has been terminated.[99]

Under the Regulations, the agent is entitled to compensation for 'damage' suffered as a result of the termination. Two types of damage are specified. The first is damage incurred where the termination has deprived the agent of commission. This will depend on an estimation of the work on which the agent would have been expected to earn commission over the remainder of the contract.[100] The second type of damage is that arising from the agent's costs and expenses incurred in the performance of the agency contract.[101]

The entitlement to payment on the indemnity basis, if this is what has been provided for in the contract, will arise where the agent has either brought in new customers, or has significantly increased the volume of the principal's business, and the principal continues to derive 'substantial benefits' from this. The payment of an indemnity may take account of the fact that the agent has lost commission on the

---

96 [1999] CLC 160.
97 *Stuart Light v Ty Europe Ltd* [2003] EWCA Civ 1238, *obiter*, following the line taken by the High Court in *Tigana Ltd v Decoro Ltd* [2003] EWHC 23; [2003] ECC 23.
98 [2003] EWCA Civ 1238.
99 See Chapter 18 for the common law approach to damages.
100 Or until it was terminated by proper notice. This head of damages corresponds most closely to the common law concept of 'expectation' damages – see 18.4.1.
101 This corresponds most closely to the common law concept of 'reliance' damages – see 18.4.2.

new business which has been brought in. If circumstances exist where an indemnity is appropriate, the amount is governed by reg 17(4), which limits the amount of the indemnity to a figure based on the agent's average annual earnings over the preceding five years.[102] The maximum amount of the indemnity will be the equivalent of one year's remuneration.

In operating these provisions, it is still unclear how far English courts should have regard to the principles operating under French and German law in deciding how they should be applied. In *Page v Combined Shipping and Trading*,[103] the Court of Appeal appeared, *obiter*, to suggest that common law principles could be applied to the 'compensation' provisions. In *Moore v Piretta*,[104] however, the judge had no doubt that, in applying the 'indemnity' provisions, account had to be taken of the way in which these operated under German law. The Scottish cases of *Roy v MR Pearlman Ltd*[105] and *King v Tunnock*[106] have shown the appeal courts in that jurisdiction looking to French law in applying the 'compensation' provisions. However, in the subsequent English decision of *Barret McKenzie & Co Ltd v Escada (UK) Ltd*,[107] the High Court did not accept the *King v Tunnock* approach (which was based on a two year 'tariff') and seemed to advocate a separate 'English' way of dealing with these issues. This was also the view taken in *Tigana Ltd v Decoro Ltd*.[108] Davis J set out 14 factors which would be relevant in deciding the level of compensation,[109] but felt that if the Regulations had intended the compensation calculations to be determined by the French approach, they should have said so. Instead, he was of the view that:[110]

> The court has to make its assessment of the compensation (if any) to be paid under reg 17 having regard to the 'balance sheet' . . . of relevant considerations, by reference to the circumstances of each case.

This approach, while having the merits of flexibility, leaves an undesirable degree of uncertainty around the consequences of termination of a commercial agent's contract. The matter awaits clarification by the appeal courts.[111]

---

102 Or over the entire period of the agency, if less than five years.
103 [1997] 3 All ER 656.
104 [1999] 1 All ER 174.
105 1999 SC 459.
106 2000 SC 424.
107 [2001] ECC 50.
108 [2003] EWHC 23; [2003] ECC 23.
109 Ibid, para 89.
110 Ibid, para 100.
111 For discussion of the way in which the compensation provisions might be expected to work, see Saintier, 1997.

6.11 FURTHER READING

Brown, I, 'The agent's apparent authority: paradigm or paradox' [1995] JBL 353

Reynolds, F, *Bowstead and Reynolds on Agency*, 18th edn, 2005, London: Sweet & Maxwell

Saintier, S, 'New developments in agency law' [1997] JBL 77

Stone, R, 'Usual or ostensible authority: one concept or two?' [1993] JBL 325

Stone, R, *Law of Agency*, 1996, London: Cavendish

7 CAPACITY

CONTENTS

7.1 OVERVIEW

In certain situations the courts will refuse to enforce a contract because one of the parties is deemed to lack the capacity to make the contract. This chapter focuses on the following aspects of this topic:

■ The fact that those under the age of 18 are generally regarded as lacking the capacity to make binding contracts.
■ The exceptions to the general rule based on:
□ contracts for 'necessary goods or services';
□ beneficial contracts of service;
□ other contracts related to earning a living;
□ contracts involving long-term obligations, which are voidable, rather than void.

■ The effects of entering into a contract with a minor:

   ☐ executory contracts are unenforceable; executed contracts will stand;

   ☐ the adult party may be able to recover property under the Minors' Contracts Act 1987, even in relation to void contracts;

   ☐ the obligations of a minor to make payment for necessary goods and services received – obligation only to pay a 'reasonable price' for goods (Sale of Goods Act 1979).

■ Minors' liability in tort. In general the courts will not allow a tortious action to be used as a means of indirectly enforcing a contract, even where the minor has lied about his or her age.

■ Mental disability and intoxication. Similar rules apply where a contracting party suffers from a mental disability or intoxication, provided the other party is aware of the incapacity.

7.2 REASONS FOR LIMITATIONS ON CAPACITY

It has been seen that the idea of 'agreement' plays a central role in the classical law of contract. Much of the law is based on the presumption that parties enter into agreements of their own free will,[1] and that therefore the courts' primary concern can be to determine, and then give effect to, what the parties themselves have agreed. There are certain situations, however, where, despite the fact that an agreement has apparently been made, the courts have felt the need to intervene so as to deny or limit its effect as a contract. One of these situations arises where, for some reason, one of the contracting parties is felt to need protection. It is in this context that the rules relating to 'capacity' can come into operation.[2] In order to make a valid, enforceable contract, both parties must be regarded as having capacity in law to enter into such an agreement. The reason for intervention on the basis of 'lack of capacity' may relate to the need to protect the contracting partly from him or herself,[3] or to the need to ensure that a contracting party is not being 'exploited' because of his or her mental state.[4] Three aspects of this topic are considered in this chapter, namely minors' contracts, mental disability and intoxication.

There are other problems of 'capacity' which relate to the question of whether one party has the power or authority to make the contract, or is acting *ultra vires*. This sort of problem can arise in connection with agency arrangements, and that aspect has been considered in Chapter 6. It can also arise in relation to the ability of incorporated bodies to make particular contracts, although the position as regards companies

---

1 See also Chapters 12 and 13, which deal with contracts entered following 'duress' or 'undue influence'.

2 An alternative analysis might be based on the lack of 'consent' by the minor or other 'incapacitated' party. The difficulties with this approach have been noted by Collins, 1999, pp 116–17.

3 This would appear to be the primary motivation in relation to minors' contracts.

4 Such a state resulting from, for example, illness or intoxication.

was radically changed by the amendments to the Companies Act 1985 made by the Companies Act 1989, with the result that issues of capacity are now much less likely to arise in this context. It may still be an issue in relation to other incorporated bodies. This type of incapacity is not considered here, since it is regarded as more appropriately the concern of texts on company law. The issue is one of the scope of the powers of the incorporated body, which will vary from case to case, rather than the application of general contractual principles to a particular type of contract or situation.

7.3 MINORS' CONTRACTS[5]

Those who have not reached the age of 18[6] are regarded in English law as 'minors' and, as such, have limited capacity to enter into contracts. The choice of age for this purpose is inevitably somewhat arbitrary, but follows the general law as to the age at which a person attains 'majority' for many purposes of the law.[7] It indicates that the object of the rules is largely paternalistic – that is, it is intended to protect minors from the consequences of their own actions. If they were concerned with the question of whether the minor had genuinely consented to the agreement and understood its consequences, there would be an argument for an approach based on an inquiry into the individual minor's capacity, rather than having a general rule. Even within the paternalistic approach, the result is somewhat unsophisticated, since different age groups might be thought to need different types of protection. Children under the age of 10, for example, are unlikely to appreciate what is involved in undertaking legal obligations, and might at first sight appear to be in need of the greatest protection. In practice, however, they are less likely to be the target of unscrupulous adult contractors than teenagers, who may well have money combined with an over-estimation of their under-standing of the way the world works.[8] A simple age 'cut-off' for contractual capacity is therefore probably the best compromise.

---

5 Traditionally, contracts made by those below the age of majority were called 'infants' contracts'. By the second half of the twentieth century this was no longer in line with modern usage, particularly when the 'infant' concerned could be 19 or 20. The change to the more modern 'minors' contracts' was effected by the Family Law Reform Act 1969, s 12; the Sale of Goods Act 1979, s 3; and the Minors' Contracts Act 1987.

6 See the Family Law Reform Act 1969, which reduced the age of majority from 21 to 18.

7 Though, of course, a person can leave school, get married and consent to sexual intercourse at the age of 16.

8 One of the most obvious ways in which teenagers might engage in contracts is via the internet. In practice, the scope for this is limited by the fact that those under 18 may find it difficult to obtain a credit card.

Should the cut-off be lower than 18, given the other responsibilities (employment, marriage, parenthood) which may well be undertaken under that age? Would it be better to have an absolute rule of incapacity for very young children, and a presumption of incapacity of those between, for example, 8 and 18?

One result of the current approach is that the law can sometimes appear to operate harshly against those who contract with minors. In particular, the adult party who is unaware that the other contracting party is a minor may still find the contract unenforceable.

The law starts from the presumption that all minors' contracts are either void or voidable. There are two main exceptions to this, namely contracts for 'necessaries', and 'beneficial contracts of service'. Such contracts may be fully enforceable. In addition, certain contracts which involve a minor obtaining an interest in property which involves continuous or recurring obligations may be voidable. The scope of these various categories will be considered next, before moving on to the consequences of entering into a contract with a minor.

7.3.1 Contracts for necessaries

The first major exception to the rule as to unenforceability relates to contracts for 'necessaries'. The reasoning here is that a total rule of unenforceability would act to the minor's disadvantage. If traders knew that any contract with a minor would involve the risk of the minor deciding not to honour it, they would be reluctant to enter into such contracts at all. As a consequence, the minor might have difficulty acquiring the basic requirements of everyday life, such as food or clothing. In reality, of course, the majority of transactions of this type take place on the basis of the simultaneous exchange of goods and payment, where there is little or no risk to the trader. In relation to more complicated transactions, and particularly those which do not involve payment on the spot, the question of whether the contract concerns 'necessaries' will still be important.

7.3.2 The definition of 'necessaries'

The concept of necessaries, which covers both goods and services, was explained in some detail in *Chapple v Cooper*,[9] where it was held that a widow who was a minor was liable in contract for the cost of her husband's funeral. According to Alderson B in this case, 'necessaries' include not only things which are absolutely necessary for survival, but also all those which are required for a reasonable existence. Food and clothing are

---

9 (1844) 3 M & W 252.

obviously covered, but so are medical assistance and education. Once the goods or services are of a kind which can be put in the general category of 'necessaries', there is then a further question as to whether they are appropriate to the particular minor. Whether a silk dress can count as a necessary will depend on the minor's normal standard of living. Items of 'mere luxury', however (as opposed to 'luxurious articles of utility'), will not be regarded as necessaries, nor will articles bought as gifts for others normally be so regarded.[10] The approach of the common law is confirmed as far as goods are concerned by s 3 of the Sale of Goods Act (SGA) 1979, which states:

> . . . 'necessaries' means goods suitable to the condition in life of the minor and to his actual requirements at the time of sale and delivery.

As will be noted, this adds to the test stated above the question of whether the minor is already adequately supplied with goods of this kind. The same limitation almost certainly applies to services. Its application in relation to goods is illustrated by *Nash v Inman*.[11] The plaintiff was a tailor; the defendant, who was an undergraduate at Cambridge University, had ordered 11 fancy waistcoats. When the plaintiff sued for payment, the defendant pleaded lack of capacity. The plaintiff argued that the waistcoats were in the category of necessaries. There was no doubt that they were among the class of things (that is, clothing) capable of being necessaries. It was up to the plaintiff to prove, however, that the defendant was not already adequately supplied with items of this kind, which he was unable to do. It should be noted that this case made it clear that the trader who is ignorant of the minor's situation will not be protected. The decision is made by looking at matters entirely from the minor's point of view.

7.3.3 Beneficial contracts of service

People who are under the age of majority, and in particular those who are over the age of compulsory full-time education (that is, those who are 16 or above), must have the possibility of being able to earn a living.[12] Consequently, the law recognises that contracts of employment, training or apprenticeship may be enforceable. The contract, taken as a whole, must not, however, be oppressive. *De Francesco v Barnum*,[13] for example, concerned a girl of 14 who entered into a contract with the plaintiff as an apprentice dancer. The contract was to last for seven years. During its operation, the

---

10 *Ryder v Wombwell* (1868) LR 4 Exch 32.

11 [1908] 2 KB 1.

12 For those under 16 (see Education Act 1996, s 558), there are statutory controls over the basis and extent to which they can be lawfully employed – see the Children and Young Persons Act 1933 and the Children and Young Persons Act 1963 (both prospectively amended by the Employment of Children Act 1973). See, also, the Working Time Regulations 1998, SI 1998/1833, relating to the working time of adolescents.

13 (1889) 45 Ch D 430.

girl was forbidden to marry, and could not accept any professional engagements without the plaintiff's consent, but, on the other hand, was not guaranteed work by the plaintiff. The plaintiff could decide to terminate the agreement virtually at his discretion. The Court of Appeal held that the stipulations were of an extraordinary and unusual character, which gave the plaintiff inordinate power without any corresponding obligation. The agreement was, as a whole, not beneficial, and was thus unenforceable.

The inclusion of some disadvantageous terms, however, will not necessarily be fatal. In *Clements v London and NW Railway*,[14] C was employed as a porter. Under his contract he agreed to forgo his rights under the Employers' Liability Act 1880. Instead, he agreed to join an insurance scheme to which the employer contributed. The Court of Appeal held that although the insurance scheme had some disadvantages (for example, lower rates of compensation), it also had wider coverage than the Act in terms of the types of accident included. On balance, the court was not prepared to say that the contract of employment as a whole was disadvantageous.

7.3.4 Other contracts related to work

The rules about beneficial contracts of service extend to contracts related to the way in which the minor earns a living. Thus, in *Doyle v White City Stadium*,[15] a contract between a boxer and the British Boxing Board of Control, under which the boxer received a licence in return for agreeing to abide by the Board's rules, was held to be enforceable, despite the fact that in this particular case the rules operated to the boxer's disadvantage, in that they led to his forfeiting his 'purse' for a fight because he had been disqualified (whereas he would have still received it if he had simply been defeated). This decision was relied on in *Chaplin v Leslie Frewin*,[16] in which the court upheld a contract relating to the production of the minor's autobiography (he was the son of Charlie Chaplin). The contract enabled the minor to earn money, and to make a start as an author, and for that reason was to be regarded as beneficial.[17]

The contract must, however, in some way contribute to the minors' ability to earn a living. This was the view of the High Court in *Proform Sports Management Ltd v Proactive Sports Management Ltd*,[18] a case involving the footballer, Wayne Rooney. In 2000, when he was 15, Rooney entered into a representation agreement with an agent (the claimant). In 2002, Rooney terminated that agreement and entered into an agreement with another agent (the defendant). The claimant sued the defendant for the tort of interference with contractual relations. In order to decide whether the tort had been

---

14 [1894] 2 QB 482.
15 [1935] 1 KB 110.
16 [1966] Ch 71; [1965] 3 All ER 764.
17 Note that Lord Denning took a different view on the basis that it was not in the minor's benefit 'that he should exploit his discreditable conduct for money': ibid, p 88; p 769.
18 [2007] 1 All ER 542.

committed, it was necessary to determine whether the 2000 agreement was enforceable. It was held that that agreement was not a contract for necessary services. It simply provided for representation services, and did not involve finding Rooney work. Rooney was already registered with Everton Football Club at the time, which subsequently employed him. The 2000 agreement was therefore voidable, and there was no liability in tort for inducing or facilitating the breach of a voidable contract. This decision essentially treats contracts related to work, as opposed to employment contracts, as a type of contract for services.

FOR THOUGHT

> Do you think the court would have taken a different view if Rooney had not been registered to Everton at the time of the contract, and the agent had been involved in finding a club prepared to take him on?

Trading contracts will not be enforced. In *Mercantile Union Guarantee v Ball*,[19] the court refused to enforce a hire purchase contract made by a minor who ran a haulage business. The minor businessperson is therefore at a considerable disadvantage, as compared with the minor employee. Once the age of the minor is known to others with whom he or she wishes to trade, it is unlikely that any contracts will be forthcoming. The reason for this is in line with the general paternalistic approach taken in this area, in that it is felt undesirable that the minor should enter into contracts carrying the high financial risks which will often be involved in business agreements. On the other hand, it poses severe restrictions on the teenage entrepreneur who wishes to set up a business producing and dealing in, for example, computer software.

7.3.5 Voidable contracts

Certain contracts are regarded as being valid, unless the minor repudiates them, either during minority or within a reasonable time of becoming 18. These are, in general, contracts which involve the minor obtaining an interest in property which involves continuous or recurring obligations. So this rule applies, for example, to contracts involving obligations of shareholding, such as the duty to pay 'calls';[20] partnership agreements;[21] marriage settlements;[22] and contracts relating to interests in land, such as leases.[23] In relation to the last category, it should be noted that s 1(6) of the Law of

---

19 [1937] 2 KB 498.
20 That is, a demand to pay money due in relation to a share price payable by instalments: *Dublin and Wicklow Railway v Black* (1852) 8 Ex 181.
21 *Goode v Harrison* (1821) 5 B & Ald 147.
22 *Edwards v Carter* [1893] AC 360.
23 *Davies v Beynon-Harris* (1931) 47 TLR 424.

Property Act 1925 prevents a minor from holding a legal estate in land. The interests concerned will therefore always be equitable.

The repudiation of one of the above contracts during minority is always possible. What constitutes the period after reaching 18 for which this right subsists is not easy to determine. The House of Lords in *Edwards v Carter* simply felt that repudiation must occur within a 'reasonable' time and that, in the particular case, a period of four years and eight months was too long to be reasonable. It is likely to be regarded as a question of fact in each case as to what is acceptable, and it does not seem possible to lay down any clear rules on this point.

7.4 EFFECTS OF ENTERING INTO A CONTRACT WITH A MINOR

What are the consequences of entering into a contract with a minor? For example, can property transferred be recovered if the contract is void? And, if the contract is for necessaries, is the minor obliged to pay the full contract price? The answers to these questions will be discussed as they operate in relation to void, voidable and enforceable contracts.

7.4.1 Void contracts

The first point to note is that, since the passage of the Minors' Contracts Act (MCA) 1987,[24] it is possible for a void contract to be ratified (expressly or impliedly) on the minor's attaining majority. If this is done, the contract will take effect as normal, with full enforceability on both sides.

If the contract remains void at the time when a dispute arises, the position is more complicated. The Infants Relief Act 1874 declared most such contracts to be 'absolutely void', but this was an inaccurate representation of reality, and has been repealed by the MCA 1987. The position now is that a contract which has been fully executed will be effective to transfer the ownership of any money or other property which has changed hands under it. A minor who purchases non-necessary goods for cash is not entitled to demand to be allowed to return them. If the minor has performed, it seems that he or she will be able to claim damages (though not specific performance) from the adult party. Money or property transferred will only be recoverable by the minor, however, if there has been a total failure of consideration.[25] If the adult party has performed, in whole or in part, then, if it is services that have been provided, the adult is without a remedy. If property has been transferred, the common law said that it was irrecoverable, but the position has been altered by s 3 of the MCA 1987. This empowers the court, 'if it is just and equitable to do so', to require the minor to return to the adult

---

24 Repealing s 2 of the Infants' Relief Act 1874.
25 *Valentini v Canali* (1889) 24 QBD 166.

any property transferred, or any property representing it. This is a broad discretion, and the court is given no guidance as to how it should be exercised, but it does provide the opportunity to prevent a minor taking advantage of the situation, and gaining unjust enrichment. Not all such cases are covered, however. As has been noted, the section has no application where it is non-necessary services that have been provided; nor will it provide a remedy where goods, or the proceeds of their sale, have been consumed by the minor.

7.4.2 Voidable contracts

If a minor repudiates a voidable contract, this will not affect obligations which have already fallen due and have been performed. Money or property transferred by the minor will be irrecoverable, unless there has been a total failure of consideration.[26] The position as regards liabilities which have fallen due, but have not been performed at the time of the repudiation, is less clear. The point was considered, *obiter*, in *North Western Rail Co v McMichael*.[27] Parke B took the view that a call on shares which had become due was of no effect once repudiation had taken place. In other words, the repudiation was, to that extent, retrospective.

7.4.3 Enforceable contracts

Where a minor has received necessary goods and services, what is the obligation as regards payment? As far as goods are concerned, the position is governed by s 3(2) of the SGA 1979, which states that:

> Where necessaries are sold and delivered to a minor . . . he must pay a reasonable price for them.

Two points emerge from this. First, the liability only arises after delivery. The fact that ownership has passed under the SGA 1979 rules for 'passing of property' is irrelevant.[28] Second, the liability is only to pay a reasonable price, which is not necessarily the contract price. This was also the line taken on this issue by Fletcher Moulton LJ in *Nash v Inman*.[29]

It seems, however, that the position may be different as regards necessary services. The relevant authority is *Roberts v Gray*.[30] The defendant was an aspiring billiards player who made a contract to go on a world tour with the plaintiff, who was a leading player. The defendant, however, backed out before the tour began. The Court of Appeal

---

26 *Corpe v Overton* (1833) 10 Bing 252.
27 (1850) 5 Ex 114.
28 See Sale of Goods Act 1979, ss 16–18.
29 [1908] 2 KB 1 – discussed above, 7.3.2.
30 [1913] 1 KB 520.

regarded this as a quasi-educational contract and therefore within the scope of a contract for necessaries. The defendant argued that, nevertheless, no damages should be payable, because he had received nothing under the contract. By analogy with contracts for necessary goods, only where services had actually been supplied should a liability to pay for them arise. The Court of Appeal refused to accept this. Hamilton LJ commented:[31]

> I am unable to appreciate why a contract which is in itself binding, because it is a contract for necessaries not qualified by unreasonable terms, can cease to be binding because it is still executory.

Damages were awarded to the extent of the plaintiff's full losses in organising the abortive tour. In effect, then, the minor was made liable on the agreement itself, rather than for what had been received under the agreement. This is also the approach taken to beneficial contracts of service. Thus, it seems to be only in relation to contracts for the supply of necessary goods that there can be no recovery on an executory contract.

7.5 MINORS' LIABILITY IN TORT

Although it is perfectly possible for a minor to be liable in tort, there being no age limit in relation to tortious liability, the courts will not allow such an action to be used as a means of indirectly enforcing an otherwise unenforceable contract. It is for this reason that it has been held that a minor who has misrepresented his or her age in order to obtain a loan,[32] or non-necessary goods,[33] cannot be sued in deceit. In other situations, it may be more difficult to decide exactly when indirect enforcement of the contract would result from a successful tortious action.

FOR THOUGHT

Why should a minor who deliberately misrepresents his or her age in order to make a contract be immune from liability on the contract? A teenager who obtains goods by deception may be criminally liable – why should there not also be civil liability in this situation?

The first case to consider is *Jennings v Rundall*.[34] The defendant was a minor who had hired a horse for a short journey. In fact it was taken on a long journey, and suffered

---

31 [1913] 1 KB 520, p 530.
32 *Leslie Ltd v Sheill* [1914] 3 KB 607.
33 *Stocks v Wilson* [1913] 2 KB 235.
34 (1799) 8 Term Rep 335.

injury as a result of this overriding. The plaintiff's action in tort failed on the basis that this was in substance an action for breach of contract, which would not have been sustainable because of the defendant's minority.

This must be contrasted with *Burnard v Haggis*.[35] This again concerned the hire of a horse to a minor. The defendant had said that he did not require a horse for jumping, and indeed was specifically told by the owner that he would not let the particular horse out 'for jumping or larking'.[36] The price charged was apparently the lower fee appropriate for riding, rather than the higher amount which would have been charged for jumping.[37] The defendant lent the horse to a friend who used it for jumping with the result that the horse fell and was killed. The defendant was held liable in tort to the owner. The distinction between this case and *Jennings v Rundall* appears from the judgment of Willis J, who commented that the act of riding the mare into the place where she was killed was as much a trespass as if:[38]

> . . . without any hiring at all, the defendant had gone into a field and taken the mare out and killed her. It was a bare trespass, not within the object and purpose of the hiring.

Thus, the test is the 'object and purpose' of the contract. Did the tortious act occur as part of the performance of the 'object and purpose'? If so, there will be no liability. So, in *Jennings v Rundall*, the object and purpose was riding the horse on a journey. In *Burnard v Haggis*, however, jumping was outside the object and purpose, and the defendant was therefore liable.

This approach has been confirmed by later cases. Thus, in *Fawcett v Smethurst*,[39] the taking of a hired car on a longer journey than indicated at the time of hire was still within the contract's 'object and purpose'. However, in *Ballett v Mingay*,[40] the defendant, who had hired a microphone and amplifier and was found to have lent them to a friend, was held to be altogether outside the scope of the contract, and the defendant was therefore liable in tort.

Insofar as there is immunity, it extends not only to torts committed in the course of a contract but, as noted above, also to fraud which induces a contract. Thus, fraudulent misrepresentation of the minor's age does not stop the minor from pleading lack of capacity, and avoiding the contract. Nor does it give the adult party a right to bring an action in tort for deceit. Where property had been transferred as a result of such fraud, equity had developed remedies in certain situations to allow the adult party to recover it.[41]

---

35 (1863) 14 CBNS 45; 143 ER 360.
36 Ibid, p 46; p 361.
37 Ibid.
38 Ibid, p 53; p 364.
39 (1914) 84 LJKB 473.
40 [1943] KB 281; [1943] 1 All ER 143.
41 *Stocks v Wilson* [1913] 2 KB 235.

Although this equitable remedy is still available in theory, the enactment of the more general provision relating to restitution in s 3 of the MCA 1987 means that it is of virtually no practical importance, and so is not discussed further here.

7.6 MENTAL DISABILITY

The law also provides protection for those who make contracts while under some mental disability. There are, of course, degrees of mental disability, unlike the position in relation to minors, where the person is either under 18 or over 18. English contract law recognises three categories. First, there are those whose mental state is such that their affairs are under the control of the court, by virtue of the Mental Capacity Act 2005. Since the court effectively takes over the individual's power to make contracts, any contracts purported to be made personally by the individual will be unenforceable against him or her. Second, there are those whose mental state is such that, although they are not under the control of the court, they are unable to appreciate the nature of the transaction they are entering into. Contracts made by people in such a condition will be enforceable against them (even if the contract may in some sense be regarded as 'unfair'), unless it is proved that the other party was aware of the incapacity. This was the view taken in *Imperial Loan Co v Stone*.[42] In New Zealand, some authorities suggested that a contract with such people might be unenforceable, even if the other party was unaware of the disability, if the contract could said to be 'unfair'.[43] This line of authority was rejected by the Privy Council in *Hart v O'Connor*,[44] which involved the sale of property at significantly less than the market value. It was there held that *Imperial Loan Co Ltd v Stone* still represented the true position under the common law. In other words, for the agreement to be set aside on the basis of the mental disability, it must be shown that this disability was apparent to the other party at the time of the contract. Lord Brightman summed up the position as follows:[45]

> . . . the validity of a contract entered into by a lunatic [*sic*] who is *ostensibly* sane is to be judged by the same standards as a contract made by a person of sound mind, and is not voidable by the lunatic or his representatives by reason of 'unfairness' unless such unfairness amounts to equitable fraud which would have enabled the complaining party to avoid the contract even if he had been sane.[46]

---

42 [1892] 1 QB 599.

43 See, for example, *Archer v Cutler* [1980] 1 NZLR 386.

44 [1985] 2 All ER 880. This involved the sale of property at significantly less than the market value.

45 Ibid, p 894, emphasis added.

46 On the facts, the sale at an undervalue, and the surrounding circumstances, did not reveal any evidence of 'equitable fraud'. See also the rules relating to contracts made with 'poor and ignorant' persons: *Cresswell v Potter* [1978] 1 WLR 255 – discussed in Chapter 13, 13.9.

The third category consists of those people who are capable of understanding the transaction, but who are, as a result of some mental disability, more susceptible to entering into a disadvantageous contract. Contracts made by such people are binding, unless affected by the rules relating to 'undue influence', which are discussed in Chapter 13 below.

The only exception to the above rules relates to contracts for necessaries. The Mental Capacity Act 2005 applies the same rule to contracts for necessary goods and services as the SGA 1979 applies to minors. Thus, a person who lacks capacity to contract for the supply of such goods and services must pay a reasonable price for them if they are supplied.[47] 'Necessary' means suitable to a person's condition in life and to his or her actual requirements at the time when the goods or services are supplied.[48] These rules will apply to people in both of the first two categories listed above.

7.7 INTOXICATION

Those who, as a result of drunkenness, whether voluntary or involuntary, are 'incompetent to contract' are, by virtue of s 3 of the SGA 1979, liable to pay a reasonable price for necessary goods 'sold and delivered'. 'Incompetent to contract' presumably means 'unable to understand the nature of the transaction'.[49] Beyond this, there appears to be little authority on contracts made by those who are intoxicated. It is assumed, however, that similar rules apply as in the case of incapacity through mental disability. This means, amongst other things, that, in contrast to the position in relation to minors, there must be an awareness of the incapacity on the part of the other party before the contract will be unenforceable.[50]

Such cases as there are on this topic are concerned with intoxication through the consumption of alcohol. There seems no reason why the same rules should not apply to a person who is incapacitated through drug taking.

7.8 FURTHER READING

Collins, H, *Regulating Contracts*, 1999, Oxford: Oxford University Press, pp 116–117
Hudson, AH, 'Mental incapacity revisited', [1986] *Conveyancer and Property Lawyer* 178

---

47 Mental Capacity Act 2005, s 7.
48 Ibid.
49 See *Gore v Gibson* (1843) 13 M & W 623.
50 Ibid.

8 THE CONTENTS OF THE CONTRACT

CONTENTS

8.1 OVERVIEW

This chapter deals with ways in which a court decides on the precise obligations that are contained in a contract. In doing this, the following issues become relevant:

■ Is a pre-contractual statement intended to be a term of the contract? This involves distinguishing between representations and terms, and identifying the factors, such as the importance of the issue, which help the courts to make a decision.
■ Remedies for pre-contractual statements. Where a statement is not part of the main contract, the party to whom it was made may nevertheless have a remedy on the basis of a collateral contract, or for misrepresentation.
■ Express terms. The courts need to consider:
  □ If a term has been put forward in writing, but not in a signed document, has it actually been incorporated into the contract;

- ☐ The precise meaning of a term – this will generally only arise where the term is ambiguous. The court will not generally accept oral evidence as explaining a written term (though there are exceptions). In business contracts the courts will tend to adopt a 'purposive' interpretation, taking account of the commercial context.
- ■ Implied terms. There are two main bases on which terms may be implied:
  - ☐ Common law. Courts will normally only imply terms which are 'necessary', or which fill a clear gap in a contract of a common type (for example, landlord and tenant);
  - ☐ Statute. The main examples of statutorily implied terms are those contained in the Sale of Goods Act 1979, relating mainly to the quality of goods.
- ■ Statutory controls. In relation to consumer contracts, all the terms of an agreement must comply with the requirements of the Unfair Terms in Consumer Contracts Regulations 1999.

8.2 INTRODUCTION

This chapter is concerned with the situation where the parties have fulfilled all the requirements for making a valid contract, as described in Chapters 2 to 4. It may then become necessary to determine exactly what the obligations are under the contract. Problems may arise in a number of ways. There may, perhaps, have been a lengthy period of pre-contractual negotiation, and it may not be clear which, if any, of the statements which were made at that stage were intended to form part of the contract. The contract may be in writing, and yet one of the parties may allege that it does not truly represent their intentions. In this case the job of the court will be to 'construe' the contract in order to decide what the language which it contains should be taken to mean. The task of 'interpreting' or 'constructing' the contract is likely to be influenced by the surrounding circumstances, including the relative bargaining power of the parties.[1] Such a contextual approach would be easier if the courts adopted a 'relational' approach to construction.[2] This would enable them to take a broad view of the commercial and personal factors surrounding the agreement, both at the time it was made and as it has developed. Under the classical theory, the courts are limited to matters which may help them to decide what they think that the parties actually meant at the time the agreement was made.

The process of construing a written contract can also, in some circumstances, be constrained by statutory regulation.[3]

---

1 This is particularly the case with 'consumer' contracts, or where clauses purporting to limit or exclude liability are concerned.
2 For which, see Chapter 1, 1.5.
3 See, in particular, the Unfair Terms in Consumer Contracts Regulations 1999, SI 1999/2083 – discussed below, 8.7.

In other situations, the contract may be purely verbal, in which case there may be a dispute as to what was said or promised, and by whom. The problems here are likely to be mainly evidential and so outside the scope of this book. Nevertheless, issues of construction may arise here in a similar way to written contracts.

Some of the problems in deciding what the terms of a contract are may be resolved by the rules which the courts have developed to enable terms to be implied into a contract. Moreover, in certain situations, terms will be implied by statute, irrespective of the wishes or intentions of the parties.

The order of treatment adopted here is to look first at the question of pre-contractual statements, and the remedies that may be available for them. Second, the approach to express terms and their interpretation will be discussed. Finally, the rules relating to the implication of terms, both at common law and by statute, will be considered.

8.3 DISTINCTION BETWEEN REPRESENTATIONS AND TERMS

The importance of identifying those pre-contractual statements which do not form part of the contract arises from the question of the remedies that will be available in each case. If a statement amounts to a promise which forms part of a contract, then a person who breaks it will be liable for the full range of contractual remedies discussed in Chapter 18. In particular, the claimant will normally be entitled to damages which will compensate for any profits that may have been lost as a result of the broken promise. A statement which is not a term, however, and which turns out to be untrue, or which contains a promise which is broken, may still give rise to a remedy, but on a different and often more restricted basis. This is discussed in the next section (see below, 8.4) on remedies for pre-contractual statements.

Where there have been statements made prior to a contract, and there is then a dispute as to whether or not they were intended to form part of the contract, how do the courts resolve the issue? The courts' professed approach is (as in many other areas of contract law) to try to determine the intentions of the parties. Did they intend the statement to be contractually binding? In looking at this, the courts generally adopt an approach based on 'detached objectivity',[4] that is, asking what the reasonable third party would have taken the parties to have intended.[5]

In trying to identify the answer to this, there are a number of matters which will be considered. For example, the importance apparently attached to the statement by the claimant may be very significant, as in *Bannerman v White*.[6] A buyer of hops had been assured that sulphur had not been used in their production. He had made it clear that

---

4 See Chapter 2, 2.4.1.

5 Which, of course, may not in the end correspond to what either party *really* intended – see, further, Chapter 11, 11.6.1.

6 (1861) 10 CBNS 844; 142 ER 685.

he would not be interested in buying them if it had. When it turned out that sulphur had been used, he was entitled to reject them for breach of contract. The undertaking that no sulphur had been used was a 'preliminary stipulation'.[7] If it had not been given, the purchaser would not have bothered to inquire about the price and would not have continued to negotiate towards a contract. Evidence, such as was given in this case, that the truth of a pre-contractual statement is a pre-condition of any binding agreement being reached will strongly support the view that it was intended to form part of the contract.[8]

In this case, there was, in effect, a guarantee by the seller that sulphur had not been used, breach of which entitled the buyer to reject the goods. Even where the matter is of importance to the recipient of the statement, however, the maker will not be taken to have intended to guarantee its truth if it has been made clear that the truth should be verified independently. In *Ecay v Godfrey*,[9] for example, the seller of a boat made statements as to its condition, but also advised the buyer to have it surveyed. In this situation, it was clear that the seller could not be taken to have intended his statements to have formed part of the contract. The same principle will apply where such verification would normally be expected, even if it has not been actively encouraged. This will normally be the position, for example, in relation to the sale of real property, where a purchaser will generally be expected to commission an independent survey, rather than relying on the statements of the seller.[10]

It would be possible, of course, to engage in a full scale inquiry in each case as to the evidence of the parties' intentions. This would be time-consuming, however, and therefore not a very efficient way of proceeding. In practice, in situations where it is not clear that the pre-contractual statement amounted to a precondition for making the contract, the courts have developed three rather more specific tests which they use as a means of determining whether it should be regarded as creating a contractual obligation. These tests tend to operate as presumptions of an intention as to whether the statement is part of the contract, which may, of course, be rebutted by other evidence suggesting the contrary intention. The tests focus on (a) whether the contract was put into written form, (b) whether the claimant was relying on the skill and knowledge of the defendant, and (c) the lapse of time between the statement and the contract.

---

7 (1861) 10 CBNS 844, p 860; 142 ER 685, p 692.
8 For a further example of this approach, see *Couchman v Hill* [1947] KB 554 – heifer warranted to be 'unserved' (that is, not in calf). The buyer had indicated that he would not bid for it if it was in calf. The apparently contrary decision in *Hopkins v Tanqueray* (1854) 15 CB 130 probably turns on the particular rules accepted to apply to the market where the sale took place.
9 (1947) 80 Lloyd's LR 286.
10 Note, however, that this particular situation may be affected by the current proposals for the sale of domestic property under which the seller would be expected to provide a survey as part of a 'seller's pack'.

8.3.1   Was the contract put into written form?

As we saw in Chapter 2, there is generally no need for a contract to be put into writing in order for it to be a valid agreement. On the other hand, if the parties have taken the trouble to commit their contract to writing, the courts will be reluctant to find that it does not contain all the terms that were important to either party. Moreover, if a written contract has been signed, the party who has done so may find it virtually impossible to depart from its express provisions.[11] This is often referred to as the 'parol evidence rule', by virtue of which the courts will be reluctant to accept oral evidence in order to add to the terms in what appears to be a complete written contract. The rule and the exceptions to it are further discussed, later in this chapter, in the context of the identification of the express terms of a contract. This was part of the reason for the rejection of an alleged term (relating to the age of a motorcycle) in *Routledge v McKay*.[12] The purchaser of the motorcycle had prepared a 'written memorandum' at the time of the sale, but this was silent as to the age of the machine. The Court of Appeal was not prepared to say that this definitely precluded any term other than those specified in the memorandum, being part of the contract, but commented that:[13]

> . . . as a matter of construction, it would be difficult to say that such an agreement was consistent with a warranty being given at the same time so as to be intended to form part of the bargain then made.

The rule is not an absolute one, however, and if the party can show that the term which was not included was of the utmost importance, then the courts may be prepared to allow it to be added. This is most likely to be the case where the written contract is in a standard form, rather than the result of individual negotiation. An example is *Evans & Son Ltd v Andrea Merzario Ltd*.[14] The plaintiffs had made a contract for the transport of machinery by sea. They had made it clear to the defendants that it was of great importance that the machinery should not be carried on deck. The defendants had given an oral assurance that the plaintiffs' machinery would be carried below deck. The printed standard conditions for the contract, however, allowed for freight to be carried on deck. The plaintiffs' machinery was carried on deck and was lost overboard. It was held by the Court of Appeal that in this case the verbal assurance took precedence over the written conditions. The statement that the plaintiffs' goods would be carried below deck was a contractual term, and the plaintiffs were entitled to succeed.

---

11 *L'Estrange v Graucob* [1934] 2 KB 394. This case is discussed further in the context of exclusion clauses, in Chapter 9, 9.4.
12 [1954] 1 All ER 855; [1954] 1 WLR 615.
13 Ibid, p 859; p 622, per Lord Evershed MR.
14 [1976] 2 All ER 930; [1976] 1 WLR 1078.

8.3.2 Was the claimant relying on the skill and knowledge of the defendant?

If there is an imbalance of skill and knowledge relating to the subject matter of the contract as between the claimant and defendant, this will be relevant in deciding whether an oral pre-contractual statement should be treated as a contractual term. The fact that the defendant is in a better position to be able to guarantee the truth of a statement will lend weight to its being regarded as part of the contract. If, on the other hand, it is the claimant who is the expert, then the reverse will be true.

Two cases concerning contracts for the sale of cars conveniently illustrate the two sides of this test. The first case to consider (though the later in time) is *Dick Bentley Productions Ltd v Harold Smith (Motors) Ltd*.[15] The plaintiff had bought a car from the defendants, relying on a pre-contractual statement as to its mileage, which later turned out to be untrue. The Court of Appeal held that the test to be applied was that of whether an intelligent bystander would reasonably infer from what was said or done that the statement was intended to be contractual (that is, 'detached objectivity').[16] Applying this test, the court came to the conclusion that the statement as to the mileage was a term of the contract, on the basis that the defendant was a car dealer who should be taken to have better knowledge of such matters than the plaintiff, who was not involved in the motor trade. In reaching this decision, the court distinguished the earlier case of *Oscar Chess Ltd v Williams*.[17] Here, the defendant was a private individual who had sold a car to a garage. The relevant pre-contractual statement was that the defendant had innocently told the garage that the date of the car was 1948, when in fact it had been first registered in 1939. The garage sued for breach of contract, but the Court of Appeal held that, on the basis of the fact that the plaintiffs here had the greater skill and knowledge of such matters, the statement should not be regarded as a term. The intelligent bystander, looking at all the circumstances, would not say that the seller intended to guarantee the age of the car. The seller was in no position to do so, since all he could rely on were the car's registration documents, and he had no means of determining whether they were accurate. The purchaser, on the other hand, being in the motor trade could, for example, have taken the engine and chassis numbers and checked with the manufacturer.

It is possible for a private seller of a car to be liable for a false statement as to its age, as is shown by *Beale v Taylor*[18] (discussed below, 8.6.11). Treitel sees this as inconsistent with *Oscar Chess v Williams* (which was not cited in *Beale v Taylor*). But, as Halson points out, the seller in this case, while not in the motor trade, was in a better position than the buyer to know the age of the car, and in that respect the balance of knowledge was in favour of the seller.[19] It is also the case that *Beale v Taylor* turned on

---

15 [1965] 2 All ER 65.
16 For which, see Chapter 2, 2.3.1.
17 [1957] 1 All ER 325; [1957] 1 WLR 370.
18 [1967] 3 All ER 253.
19 Halson, 2001, p 289

the interpretation and application of s 13 of the Sale of Goods Act 1893 (implied term as to compliance with description). This section was not mentioned in *Oscar Chess v Williams*, for reasons which are unclear.[20]

It should be noted that a case such as *Bentley v Harold Smith*, if the facts recurred, would be more likely nowadays to be dealt with as a negligent misrepresentation under s 2(1) of the Misrepresentation Act 1967. The remedy in damages for misrepresentations provided by this section was not, of course, available at the time.[21]

Other cases where the greater skill and knowledge of the defendant has been relevant in giving contractual status to a pre-contractual statement include *Birch v Paramount Estates Ltd*[22] (developer stating that a house would be as good as the show house), *Schawel v Reade*[23] (owner selling a horse which he stated was 'perfectly sound') and *Harling v Eddy*[24] (owner selling a heifer stating that there was 'nothing wrong' with her).

8.3.3   Was there a significant lapse of time between the statement and the contract?

The courts generally consider that the closer in time that the statement was made to the conclusion of the contract, the more likely it is that it was a matter of importance to the claimant, and should therefore be treated as a contractual term. It is certainly true that if there is no significant gap, the statement may well be treated as being intended to be part of the contract, particularly if the agreement is not put into writing. It is by no means clear, however, that the mere existence of a delay should be regarded as in itself reducing the significance of the statement. Such delay may well have been caused by matters irrelevant to the statement, and the claimant may have felt that having settled the issue which the statement concerned, there was no need to re-state it at the time of the contract. Nevertheless, whatever the true significance of the delay, it is undoubtedly the case that as far as the courts are concerned it will weaken the claimant's case.

An example of the application of this test is the case of *Routledge v McKay*.[25] This concerned the sale of a motorbike. The defendant, who was selling the bike, had told the plaintiff that the date of the bike was 1942. In fact, it dated from 1930. A week elapsed between the defendant's statement and the making of the contract of sale (which was put into writing). It was held by the Court of Appeal that the defendant's statement was not a term of the contract. The decision may appear a little harsh, but it may be significant that application of both the other tests outlined above would have gone in favour of the defendant. Thus, the written agreement made no mention of the

---

20 See Atiyah, Adams and MacQueen, 2005, p 150.
21 The Misrepresentation Act 1967 is dealt with in detail in Chapter 10.
22 (1956) 16 EG 396.
23 [1913] 2 IR 64.
24 [1951] 2 KB 739; [1951] 2 All ER 212.
25 [1954] 1 All ER 855; [1954] 1 WLR 615.

age of the bike, and neither party had any special skill or knowledge. Both were private individuals, and the defendant in making the statement had innocently relied on false information contained in the bike's registration document.[26]

> If a week was too long to allow incorporation of the statement, how much shorter would the period have had to be to make the court take a different view of this aspect of *Routledge v McKay?* Would a gap of more than a day be too long?

As this last case shows, it must be remembered that none of the tests discussed here is automatically conclusive of the issue. All may need to be considered and, if they point in different directions, weighed against each other. The ultimate question is whether the statement, viewed objectively, was intended to form part of the contract. All the other tests are simply matters which may provide guidance to the court in determining this issue.[27]

8.3.4 Pre-contractual statements under the Principles of European Contract Law

The suggested approach to the incorporation of a pre-contractual statement under the Principles is set out in Art 6.101. This provides that the main question is whether the party to whom the statement was made reasonably understood it to give rise to contractual obligation, taking into account:

(a)   the apparent importance of the statement to (the party to whom it was made);
(b)   whether the party was making the statement in the course of a business; and
(c)   the relative expertise of the parties.

There is a clear overlap with the approach of the English courts here, though the number of matters to be taken into account is narrower. On the other hand, they specifically make the fact that a statement was made in the course of a business something which will tend towards a statement being regarded as part of the contract.

Paragraphs 2 and 3 of the Article deal with the responsibility of a 'professional supplier' for statements about the quality or use of goods and services in advertising and marketing information. Where the statement is made by the supplier directly,

---

26 In that respect, the case was therefore virtually identical to *Oscar Chess Ltd v Williams* [1957] 1 All ER 325; [1957] 1 WLR 370.

27 Of course, in reaching a conclusion on this issue, judges may well be influenced, consciously or unconsciously, by the question of where they feel that responsibility 'ought' to lie. This issue then ceases to be purely factual.

it will be treated as giving rise to a contractual obligation unless 'the other party knew or could not have been unaware that the statement was incorrect'. Where the statement is purported to be made on behalf of the supplier, 'or by a person in earlier links of the business chain', it will again give rise to a contractual obligation, unless the supplier 'did not know and had no reason to know of the information or undertaking'.

This goes considerably further than English law, and brings advertising material much more clearly within the scope of contractual obligations.

8.4 REMEDIES FOR PRE-CONTRACTUAL STATEMENTS

This section is concerned with the situation where the answer to the question raised in the previous section is that the statement is not a term of the contract. What remedies, if any, are available to a person who has made a contract in reliance on such a statement? Although it may be argued that discussion of this issue is out of place in this chapter (since, by definition, such statements are not part of the 'contents of the contract'), it is nevertheless helpful to consider them briefly at this stage, in order to understand fully the importance of deciding whether a statement is part of the contract or not. It is only by considering the consequences of that decision that its significance can be properly appreciated.

There are three possible forms of action which must be considered: the action for misrepresentation, for breach of a collateral contract, and for the tort of negligent misstatement.

8.4.1 Misrepresentation

The common law and equity recognised two remedies for misrepresentation. Provided that there were no complicating factors, such as the involvement of third party rights, rescission of the contract was the main remedy for all types of misrepresentation. If the misrepresentation was made fraudulently, there was, in addition, the possibility of an action in tort for deceit, which would provide for the recovery of damages.[28] Both these remedies are still available in appropriate cases. In addition, however, there is now the possibility of an action for damages for so-called 'negligent misrepresentation' under s 2 of the Misrepresentation Act 1967.

For any of these remedies to be available, the statement must have been a representation in the strict sense. That is, it must have been a statement of existing fact, or (probably) of law,[29] not a statement of opinion,[30] or a promise to act in a particular way in the future. Thus, for example, a statement by a seller of a computer system that

---

28 *Derry v Peek* (1889) 14 App Cas 337.
29 See 10.3.2 below.
30 *Bisset v Wilkinson* [1927] AC 177.

a 24 hour service facility will be provided is not a 'representation', but a promise. A statement that the system is ideal for a small business may well be a statement of opinion rather than fact.[31] However, a statement that the firm has already sold 1,000 similar systems, or that it has a team of six service engineers, are representations which, if untrue, may give the other party a remedy.

The statement must have induced the contract.[32] This rule, together with other aspects of the law relating to misrepresentations, is discussed in more detail in Chapter 10.

8.4.2 Collateral contract

We have already encountered the concept of the collateral contract as a means of evading the doctrine of privity by bringing apparent third parties into a contractual relationship, as in *Shanklin Pier v Detel Products*.[33] As noted there, however, the collateral contract can also be used between parties who themselves subsequently enter into a main contract. The collateral contract will take the form of one party expressly, or impliedly, saying to the other 'if you enter into the main contract, I will promise you X'. It can thus provide a remedy for pre-contractual statements which have not been incorporated into the main contract. It has the advantage over the remedies for misrepresentation in that it is not limited to statements of existing fact. A promise to act in a particular way is clearly covered. Continuing the computer contract example used above, a statement that 'we will answer all service calls within six hours' could not be a misrepresentation, but could found an action for breach of a collateral contract. A statement of fact, or even opinion, may also give rise to a collateral contract, if it can be said that the maker of the statement was guaranteeing its truth.

An example of the use of a collateral contract in a two-party situation is *City of Westminster Properties v Mudd*.[34] A tenant had been in the practice of sleeping in the shop which he rented. When the lease was renewed, the landlord tried to insert a clause stating that the premises should not be used for lodging, dwelling or sleeping. The tenant objected, but was assured orally that if he signed the lease, he would be allowed to sleep there. In fact, probably due to an oversight, the new clause was omitted, but a provision containing an obligation only to use the premises for the purposes of trade remained. The landlord subsequently tried to rely on this clause to forfeit the lease, claiming that the tenant was in breach of it through sleeping on the premises. It was held that the tenant could rely on a collateral contract giving him the right to sleep on the premises which, in effect, overrode the clause in the lease itself.

---

31 Unless it is based on facts which the maker of the statement knows to be untrue: *Smith v Land and House Property Corp* (1884) 28 Ch D 7.
32 *JEB Fasteners v Marks, Bloom & Co* [1983] 1 All ER 583.
33 [1951] 2 KB 854; [1951] 2 All ER 471.
34 [1959] Ch 129; [1958] 2 All ER 733.

In *Esso Petroleum Co Ltd v Mardon*,[35] a representative of Esso had given a prospective tenant of a petrol station an estimate of the potential throughput, which was put at 200,000 gallons a year. This failed to take account of the fact that the local planning authority had required the petrol pumps to be sited on a side street, invisible from the main road. The tenant was dubious as to the accuracy of the estimate, but accepted it as being based on Esso's superior knowledge of the petrol retailing business. He entered into a lease, but the throughput never exceeded 78,000 gallons a year. It was held by the Court of Appeal that the tenant was entitled to recover damages from Esso on the basis of a collateral contract. Although the estimate was an expression of opinion, rather than a statement of fact, or a promise as to the throughput which would be achieved, it contained the implied promise that it was made with reasonable care and skill. As Lord Denning commented:

> They [Esso] knew the facts. They knew the traffic in the town. They knew the throughput of comparable stations. They had much experience and expertise at their disposal. They were in a much better position than Mr Mardon to make a forecast. It seems to me that if such a person makes a forecast – intending that the other should act on it and he does act on it – it can well be interpreted as a warranty that the forecast is sound and reliable in the sense that they made it with reasonable care and skill.

The consideration for the promise that the estimate was made with due care and skill was Mr Mardon's agreement to enter into the lease. A contract collateral to the lease was thus created, and Mr Mardon was entitled to recover damages for Esso's breach of this contract.

8.4.3 Limitations of the 'collateral contract'

As will be seen from these examples, the collateral contract is a very flexible device. Its disadvantage, compared to the action for misrepresentation, is that it will only provide a remedy in damages, and will not allow the claimant the possibility of rescinding the main contract. Moreover, the level of damages which can be awarded is more restricted than in the case of actions for deceit, or under s 2(1) of the Misrepresentation Act 1967.[36]

---

35 [1976] QB 801; [1976] 2 All ER 5. Note that Lord Denning also used the collateral contract analysis to find the defendants liable in *Evans & Son Ltd v Andrea Merzario Ltd* [1976] 1 WLR 1078, whereas (as noted above, at 8.3.1) the other members of the Court of Appeal found that the pre-contractual promise had been incorporated into the main contract. This shows that the approaches taken to finding liability for pre-contractual statements are not necessarily mutually exclusive.

36 See Chapter 10. The actions for deceit and under s 2(1) of the 1967 Act allow for recovery of *all* losses caused by the misrepresentation; in relation to a collateral contract, only losses which were in the reasonable contemplation of the parties at the time of the contract will be recoverable.

8.4.4 Negligent misstatement

In 1963, the House of Lords confirmed that the tortious action for negligence could provide a remedy for negligent misstatements which have resulted in purely economic loss.[37] The development of the law in this area over the past 40 years or so has been complicated, as the courts have tried to decide exactly when a duty of care as regards such statements can be said to arise. The subsequent trend, as shown by cases such as *Caparo Industries plc v Dickman*,[38] has been to limit strictly the number of 'special relationships' which can give rise to such a duty, though this has been softened to some extent by the later decisions in *Henderson v Merrett Syndicates Ltd*[39] and *White v Jones*.[40] There is little doubt, however, that a duty of this kind may arise between parties who subsequently enter into a contract. The possibility was recognised in *Esso v Mardon*, for example. In practice, however, the existence of the remedies under s 2(1) of the Misrepresentation Act 1967 means that it is not very likely to be needed in this situation.[41] The action under the 1967 Act has the advantage that the burden of proof as regards negligence is on the defendant (who effectively has to disprove it), and that more extensive damages are available. The only situation where it might be necessary for a party to a contract to look to the common law negligence action is where the statement is not a representation in the strict sense, and it is also impossible to construct a collateral contract.[42]

8.4.5 Conclusion on pre-contractual statements

As we have seen, there is a variety of actions which may be available in relation to pre-contractual statements. There is nothing to stop a claimant relying on more than one, as was pointed out by Lord Denning in *Esso v Mardon*.[43] In an unusually frank (for a judge) recognition of the way in which lawyers manipulate legal concepts to achieve their desired result, he explained how, at a time when no damages were available for a non-fraudulent misrepresentation, other alternatives would be sought:[44]

> In order to escape from that rule, the pleader used to allege – I often did it myself – that the misrepresentation was fraudulent, or alternatively a collateral warranty. At

---

37 *Hedley Byrne & Co v Heller & Partners* [1964] AC 465; [1963] 2 All ER 575.
38 [1990] 1 All ER 568.
39 [1995] 2 AC 145; [1994] 3 All ER 506.
40 [1995] 2 AC 207; [1995] 1 All ER 691. See also the speech of Lord Steyn in *Williams v Nature Life Ltd* [1998] 1 WLR 830, p 837, accepting 'assumption of responsibility' as the test for the existence of a duty. The approach taken in *White v Jones* to the identification of a duty of care was also applied by the Court of Appeal in *Gorham v British Telecommunications plc* [2000] 4 All ER 867.
41 See Chapter 10, 10.4.6.
42 The tortious remedy is discussed further in Chapter 10, 10.4.4.
43 [1976] QB 801; [1976] 2 All ER 5.
44 Ibid, p 817; p 13.

the trial we nearly always succeeded on collateral warranty. We had to reckon, of course, with the *dictum* of Lord Moulton that 'such collateral contracts must from their nature be very rare'.[45] But more often than not the court elevated the innocent misrepresentation into a collateral warranty; and thereby did justice . . . Besides that experience, there have been many cases since I have sat in this court where we have readily held a representation . . . to be a warranty sounding in damages.

Nowadays, since damages for negligent misrepresentations are now available, the decision as to which action will be the most appropriate to press will depend mainly on the type of statement (is it a statement of fact?) and on the remedy which is being sought (is rescission of the contract required, or will damages be adequate?). If the statement cannot be constructed as being of fact, then collateral contract may be the best remedy to pursue. On the other hand, if rescission rather than damages is what is important, the contractual action for misrepresentation is the only one which will provide this.

8.5 EXPRESS TERMS

In this section, we are concerned with terms that have without doubt been put forward by one or other party as a term of the agreement. There may be disputes, however, as to whether the clause has been incorporated into the contract, as to its proper meaning, and as to the consequences of breaking it. In dealing with all these questions, the approach of the courts will again be professed to be that they are trying to determine the parties' intention, from an objective viewpoint. The focus under classical theory is on the time of the original agreement, with later developments being ignored.[46]

8.5.1 Incorporation

We have already discussed the rules which the courts adopt to decide whether pre-contractual statements should be regarded as having been incorporated into a contract. The situation under consideration here is slightly different, and will generally arise in relation to written contracts in a standard form which have not been signed. One party may object that a particular clause should not be regarded as being included in the contract, because they were unaware of it for some reason, and would have objected to it. The rules that operate in this area have mainly developed in relation to the incorporation of exclusion clauses, and detailed discussion of them will be left until Chapter 9. In appropriate cases, they can apply to other types of clause, however, as is shown by the case of *Interfoto Picture Library v Stiletto Visual Programmes*.[47]

---

45 In *Heilbut, Symons & Co v Buckleton* [1913] AC 30, p 47.
46 Whereas a 'relational' approach would allow later developments to be considered – see Macneil, 1978, and Chapter 1, 1.5.
47 [1988] QB 433; [1988] 1 All ER 348.

The defendants were an advertising agency. They needed some photographs for a presentation. On 5 March 1984, they contacted the plaintiffs, who ran a library of photographic transparencies, to see if they might have anything suitable. The plaintiffs sent round a packet of 47 transparencies, together with a delivery note. The transparencies were, however, apparently overlooked and not used. They were eventually returned on 2 April, that is, nearly a month after they had been received. The plaintiffs then claimed the sum of £3,783 from the defendants as a 'holding charge' for the transparencies. This was calculated in accordance with the terms laid down in the delivery note, which stated that, in relation to transparencies not returned within 14 days of receipt, a charge of £5 per day plus VAT would be made in respect of each transparency. The issue before the court was thus whether the terms of the delivery note formed part of a contract between the parties and, if so, whether the plaintiffs could enforce these terms against the defendants. The Court of Appeal held that the clause could not be enforced. It did so by reference to the case law on exclusion clauses and when they are deemed to have been incorporated into a contract. In particular, the court relied on *Parker v South Eastern Railway Co*,[48] and *Thornton v Shoe Lane Parking*.[49] *Parker* established the principle that, in order to rely on an exclusion clause in an unsigned contract, the defendant had to have taken reasonable steps to bring it to the attention of the claimant. *Thornton* added the gloss that the more unusual and onerous the clause, the more the defendant had to do to draw it to the claimant's attention. The court saw no reason why this approach should not apply to the case before it. The clause was particularly, and unusually, onerous in its effect. The plaintiffs had done nothing to draw it to the defendants' attention. It should be regarded as not having been incorporated into the contract.

The approach taken in the *Interfoto* case is an unusual one in relation to a commercial agreement. This aspect of the rule of incorporation has tended to be used mainly as a means of protecting consumers, particularly in relation to exclusion clauses. Where parties are contracting at arm's length, in a business context, it would more commonly be the case that the court would expect each party to take care over the obligations to which it was committing itself. If they agree to unfavourable terms, then that is their own fault. It is perhaps significant that the *Interfoto* decision has not so far led to many similar reported decisions. An example of a similar approach is to be found in *AEG (UK) Ltd v Logic Resource Ltd*,[50] but the majority Court of Appeal decision is strictly *obiter*, since it found that the clause was also unreasonable under the statutory test contained in the Unfair Contract Terms Act 1977.[51] Indeed, given the statutory control of exclusion and other clauses by this Act and the Unfair Terms in Consumer

---

48 (1877) 2 CPD 416.
49 [1971] 2 QB 163; [1971] 1 All ER 686.
50 [1996] CLC 265 – the case is discussed in detail by Bradgate, 1997.
51 See Chapter 9, 9.7.

Contracts Regulations 1999,[52] there would seem to be little need to develop further a restrictive rule for incorporation under the common law.[53]

A move towards a relaxed approach towards incorporation is perhaps exemplified by the Court of Appeal decision in *O'Brien v Mirror Group Newspapers*,[54] which was concerned with a consumer contract. The claim concerned a 'scratch card' game operated by the defendants, Mirror Newspapers. The claimant had obtained one of the scratch cards from a newspaper, from which it appeared that he would win £50,000 if this was the prize on a particular day, which could be discovered by ringing a particular telephone number. He rang the number and was told that the prize amount was £50,000, so he thought that he had won that amount. It then transpired that, because of an error, a large number of winning cards had been produced. The defendants therefore relied on Rule 5 of the rules applying to the competition, which they claimed allowed them to draw lots between all the holders of the 'winning' cards to decide who won the £50,000. The claimant was not successful in this draw, and sued, claiming that Rule 5 had not been incorporated into his contract with the defendants. The rules of the competition had been published in a number of newspapers, but did not appear every day. The Sunday paper from which the claimant had obtained his card stated 'FULL RULES AND HOW TO CLAIM SEE DAILY MIRROR'. The paper from which he obtained the number to ring to see if his card had 'won' stated 'Normal Mirror Group rules apply'. The claimant argued that this was insufficient for the rules to be incorporated into his contract.

The Court of Appeal agreed with the trial judge that a contract was made by an offer contained in the newspaper on the day the claimant telephoned the defendants, which the claimant accepted by making the telephone call. The trial judge thought that the claimant, who admitted buying a number of the relevant newspapers, must have seen the rules, or at least have been aware that there were rules applying to the competition. He did not feel that Rule 5 was sufficiently unusual or onerous that the defendants ought to have done more to bring it to the attention of those who might play the scratch card game. The Court of Appeal agreed. As Hale LJ put it:[55]

> The offer and therefore the contract clearly incorporated the term 'Normal Mirror Group rules apply'. The words were there to be read and it makes no difference whether or not the claimant actually read or paid attention to them.

> The question, therefore, is whether those words, in the circumstances, were enough to incorporate the Rules, including Rule 5, into the contract.

---

52 Also discussed in Chapter 9, 9.8.
53 As Hobhouse LJ pointed out in his dissent in *AEG (UK) Ltd v Logic Resource Ltd*, the *Interfoto* approach, unless strictly controlled, runs the risk of 'distorting the contractual relationship between the parties and the ordinary mechanisms of making contracts'.
54 [2001] EWCA Civ 1279; [2002] CLC 33.
55 Ibid, para 19.

Applying the approach taken in the *Interfoto* case, the test was whether the rules could be said to have been fairly and reasonably brought to the notice of the claimant. This depends on the nature of the contract and the nature of the term. In the view of Hale LJ, although Rule 5 did turn an apparent winner into a loser, it could not by any normal use of language be called 'onerous' or 'outlandish'. It did not impose any extra burden upon the claimant, unlike the clause in *Interfoto*. It did not seek to absolve the defendant from liability for personal injuries negligently caused, unlike the clause in *Thornton v Shoe Lane Parking*; it merely deprived the claimant of a windfall for which he had done very little in return. He bought two newspapers and made a call to a premium rate number, which would have cost him a matter of pennies, not pounds. Nor was there any evidence that this type of rule was 'unusual' in this sort of competition. In any event, as Hale LJ concluded:[56]

> The words 'onerous or unusual' are not terms of art. They are simply one way of putting the general proposition that reasonable steps must be taken to draw the particular term in question to the notice of those who are to be bound by it and that more is required in relation to certain terms than to others depending on their effect. In the particular context of this particular game, I consider that the defendants did just enough to bring the Rules to the claimant's attention. There was a clear reference to rules on the face of the card he used. There was a clear reference to rules in the paper containing the offer of a telephone prize. There was evidence that those rules could be discovered either from the newspaper offices or from back issues of the paper. The claimant had been able to discover them when the problem arose.

Although the court had sympathy with the claimant, he was bound by the terms of the competition, and his claim failed. It would seem then that even in consumer contracts, there is no necessary requirement to take special steps to draw attention to a clause which may have the effect of disappointing the expectations of the unwary contractor.

FOR THOUGHT

What do you think the position would be if the consumer, unlike Mr O'Brien, had paid a significant sum for what he or she was expecting to obtain under the contract? Would the courts adopt a different approach?

8.5.2 Construction

Even where there is no dispute as to whether a clause is incorporated, the parties may disagree as to what it was intended to mean. It will be necessary to try to construe the

---

56 [2001] EWCA Civ 1279; [2002] CLC 33, para 23.

clause in order to give effect to it. The courts will adopt the approach of trying to assess objectively what the parties must be taken to have intended. If the contract is in the form of a written document, this will generally be regarded as very strong evidence of the parties' intentions. The 'parol evidence rule' will apply, with the effect that it will not normally be open to one of the parties to argue that some part of the written document should be disregarded, or interpreted in a way which is not consistent with its most obvious meaning. The Law Commission has doubted whether there is such a rule of law as the 'parol evidence rule' – regarding it as being essentially a circular statement, to the effect that when it is proved that a written document was intended to set out all the express terms of an agreement, other evidence of what was intended will not be admissible.[57] Nevertheless, as the Commission itself recognised, since the 'rule' has regularly been referred to by writers and judges, it provides a convenient shorthand for the approach to constructing contracts to which it applies.[58] The rule, whatever its precise status, thus makes it very important for the parties to ensure that any written document forming part of the contract is clear and explicit as to the obligations which are being imposed on each side. The parol evidence rule is not, however, unchallengeable, and there are certain established exceptions to it.

Exceptions to the parol evidence rule include:

(a) *Ambiguity*

Where a word or phrase contained in the written document is ambiguous, other evidence may be given as to what was actually intended, as in *Robertson v Jackson*.[59] The phrase in question was 'turn to deliver' in relation to the unloading of goods at a particular port. The contract did not on its face give any indication of when the ship's 'turn to deliver' would arise. The court was prepared to allow oral evidence as to the custom applying in that port. This exception must now be considered in the light of the overall approach to construction taken in recent cases, such as *Investors Compensation Scheme Ltd v West Bromwich Building Society*,[60] discussed in the next section.

(b) *Written agreement incomplete*

If either or both of the parties can show that the written agreement was not intended to contain all the terms of the contract, then oral or other extrinsic evidence may be used to fill it out. In *Allen v Pink*,[61] for example, the written document relating to the sale of a horse was little more than a receipt. It stated the price and the names of the parties, but contained no other terms. In the

---

57 See Law Commission Report No 154, 1986, para 2.7.
58 See also Wedderburn, 1959. Treitel does not accept the Commission's analysis of the rule as being 'circular' – see Treitel, 2003, pp 193–94.
59 (1845) 2 CB 412.
60 [1998] 1 All ER 98.
61 (1838) 4 M & W 140.

circumstances, the court was prepared to allow evidence of an oral promise as to the horse's behaviour in harness. This case was fairly clear. It will be more difficult where the written agreement contains some terms. The court will have to consider objectively whether it appears to be complete, or whether it is more likely that the parties intended it to be supplemented by other obligations. The insertion of a clause to the effect that 'this document contains all the terms of the contract' will presumably make it difficult to rebut the presumption that it is complete, and that any other evidence of additional terms should be excluded.[62]

(c) *Custom*
Sometimes, a particular word or phrase is used in a particular trade, market or locality, in a way which does not accord with its obvious meaning. In *Smith v Wilson*,[63] evidence was allowed to establish a local custom to the effect that the phrase '1,000 rabbits' meant '1,200 rabbits'. Custom may also be used to fill out an aspect of the contract on which the written document is silent. In *Hutton v Warren*,[64] a custom as to allowances to be given to an outgoing tenant for seeds and labour used in the last year of the tenancy was held to be incorporated into a lease which contained no such provision. Parke B commented that:[65]

> It has long been settled that, in commercial transactions, extrinsic evidence of custom and usage is admissible to annex incidents to written contracts in matters with respect to which they are silent.

This use of custom overlaps with the use of custom to imply terms; this is discussed further below. Custom may not be used, however, where it is clearly contradicted by the terms of the contract. Where, for example, a charter provided that the expenses of discharging a cargo should be borne by the charterer, it was not possible to override this by showing a custom that the expenses should be borne by the owner of the ship.[66]

(d) *Starting or finishing date*
Extrinsic evidence may be used to establish the date on which a contract is intended to start to operate. In *Pym v Campbell*,[67] evidence was allowed as to an oral provision that the contract should not start to operate prior to the approval of a third party.

---

62 This is certainly the position as regards an 'entire agreement' clause, which has the effect of preventing reliance on any alleged collateral contract: *The Inntrepreneur Pub Co (GL) v East Crown Ltd* [2000] 2 Lloyd's Rep 611.
63 (1832) 3 B & Ad 728.
64 (1836) 1 M & W 466; 150 ER 517.
65 (1836) 1 M & W 466, p 475; 150 ER 517, p 521.
66 *Palgrave, Brown & Son Ltd v SS Turid (Owners)* [1922] 1 AC 397.
67 (1856) 2 E & B 370.

(e)   *Other exceptions*

Where it can be argued that a written document was intended simply to record earlier oral agreements, but fails to do so accurately, extrinsic evidence may be allowed to prove this, and thus to 'rectify' the written document.[68] The parol evidence rule may also be circumvented by showing the existence of a collateral contract. An example of this is the decision in *City of Westminster Properties v Mudd*[69] which has been discussed above.[70] This is perhaps not a true exception, since it concerns not the interpretation of one contract, but rather a decision as to the priority between two inconsistent contracts. Finally, as we have seen earlier,[71] a pre-contractual statement may become part of the contract if the courts feel that it related to something of great importance to one or other of the parties. This is perhaps best exemplified by the case of *Evans v Andrea Merzario*,[72] where the statement that the cargo would be carried below deck was held to override the provision in the written contract allowing it to be carried on deck.

8.5.3   'Purposive' or 'commercial' interpretation [73]

The approach of the courts to determining the meaning of an express term of a contract has been modified in recent years. Traditionally, it was said, particularly in relation to commercial agreements, that the courts used to apply a 'literal' approach,[74] subject only to the *contra proferentem* rule that any ambiguity would be interpreted against the person who put the clause forward.[75] The assumption was that contracting parties had an obligation to use the correct language to achieve their objectives, and that if they happened to have used words which bore a different meaning, the court would not look behind those words to discover their 'real' intentions.

This approach has now been clearly rejected. In *Prenn v Simmonds*,[76] Lord Wilberforce recognised that agreements may need to be placed in context to be properly understood:[77]

---

68 The remedy of 'rectification' is discussed further in Chapter 11, 11.8.2.
69 [1959] Ch 129; [1958] 2 All ER 733.
70 At 8.4.2.
71 See 8.2 and 8.3 above.
72 [1976] 2 All ER 930; [1976] 1 WLR 1078.
73 See McMeel, 1998; Gee, 2001. McMeel argues that the modern approach is better categorised as 'commercial' rather than 'purposive'. He points to the decision in *Deutsche Genossenschaftsbank v Burnhope* [1996] 1 Lloyd's Rep 113 as illustrating the problems with 'unfocused purposive construction': McMeel, 1998, p 392.
74 Whether it is possible, in fact, ever to adopt a strict 'literal' approach, without paying any attention to the cultural background or other context in which language is used, is of course a matter open to debate.
75 The *contra proferentem* rule is discussed further in Chapter 9, in relation to exclusion clauses: 9.5.1.
76 [1971] 3 All ER 237.
77 Ibid, p 239.

The time has long passed when agreements, even those under seal, were isolated from the matrix of facts in which they were set and interpreted purely on internal linguistic considerations.

Similarly, in *Reardon Smith Line v Hansen-Tangen*,[78] Lord Wilberforce again referred to the need for the court to place itself in the same 'factual matrix' to that of the parties when they made the contract.[79]

The modern approach has now been set out fully by Lord Hoffmann in *Investors Compensation Scheme Ltd v West Bromwich Building Society*.[80] He commented that 'almost all the old intellectual baggage of "legal" interpretation has been discarded' in favour of an approach which generally relies on 'the common sense principles by which any serious utterance would be interpreted in ordinary life'.[81] He then identified five relevant principles. First, he defined the overall approach in these terms:[82]

> Interpretation is the ascertainment of the meaning which the document would convey to a reasonable person having all the background knowledge which would reasonably have been available to the parties in the situation they were in at the time of the contract.

Second, Lord Wilberforce's 'factual matrix' should be extended to include 'absolutely anything which would have affected the way in which the language of the document would have been understood by the reasonable man'. Third, and as a restriction on the second principle, prior negotiations and expressions of subjective intent may only be used in an action for 'rectification'. Lord Hoffmann did not go into detail as to the reasons for this restriction, but Lord Wilberforce in *Prenn v Simmonds* dismissed such evidence as simply being 'unhelpful'.[83] Statements made during negotiations will frequently be made in a situation where the parties' positions are changing and are therefore not good evidence of the 'final' agreement. Moreover, statements about one party's objective may be 'dangerous', since there is no guarantee that this objective is accepted by the other side.[84] This does not, however, preclude consideration of evidence of the 'genesis' and the objectively determined 'aim' of the transaction.[85]

Lord Hoffmann's fourth principle is that 'the meaning which a document . . .

---

78 [1976] 2 Lloyd's Rep 621; [1976] 1 WLR 989.
79 Ibid, p 625; p 997.
80 [1998] 1 All ER 98.
81 Ibid, p 114.
82 Ibid.
83 [1971] 3 All ER 237, p 240.
84 [1971] 3 All ER 237, p 241. See also the comments of the Court of Appeal in *P & S Platt Ltd v Crouch* [2004] EWCA Civ 1110; [2004] 1 P & CR 18, at paras 39 and 52–57 – applying the restrictive approach to a case concerned with s 62 of the Law of Property Act 1925. For discussion of this case, see Warwick, 2003.
85 Ibid.

would convey to a reasonable man is not the same thing as the meaning of its words'. This is because the background may enable the reasonable person not only to resolve any ambiguity as to the meaning, but to conclude that the parties must have used the wrong words or syntax.[86] As McMeel points out,[87] when Mrs Malaprop refers to a headstrong 'allegory' on the banks of the Nile,[88] no reasonable person would misunderstand her, because the context or 'background' makes it clear that she is intending to refer to an 'alligator'.[89]

The fifth and final principle identified by Lord Hoffmann recognises that, although there is a proper reluctance to accept that, particularly in formal documents, people have made linguistic mistakes, on the other hand:[90]

> . . . if one would nevertheless conclude from the background that something must have gone wrong with the language, the law does not require judges to attribute to the parties an intention which they plainly could not have had.

The same point had been made previously by Lord Diplock:[91]

> . . . if detailed semantic and syntactical analysis of words in a commercial contract are going to lead to a conclusion that flouts business common sense, it must be made to yield to business common sense.[92]

The approach embodied in Lord Hoffmann's five principles has the laudable aim of trying to ensure as far as possible that the agreed aims of contracting parties are not thwarted by an over-literal or blinkered approach by the courts. The court must pay attention to the surrounding context and, so far as it can be identified, the objective purpose of the agreement in deciding what the words of a written contract should be taken to 'mean'.[93]

---

86 Lord Hoffmann here cites *Mannai Investment Co Ltd v Eagle Star Life Assurance Co Ltd* [1997] AC 749, where a tenant giving notice to terminate a lease which was stated to expire on *12* January was held to be effective, even though under the lease the date for termination would have been *13* January.

87 McMeel, 1998, p 390 – adopting and adapting an example used by Lord Hoffmann in *Mannai Investment Co Ltd v Eagle Star Life Assurance Co Ltd* [1997] AC 749, p 774.

88 Sheridan, *The Rivals*, Act III, Scene 3.

89 Although as McMeel (pedantically?) points out (McMeel, 1998, p 390), the creature would in fact be a 'crocodile' if it was on the Nile, since alligators are found in the Americas, rather than Africa.

90 [1998] 1 All ER 98, p 115.

91 In *Antaios Cia Naveria SA v Salen Redierna B, The Antaios* [1985] AC 191, p 201; [1984] 3 All ER 229, p 233.

92 A similar approach is to be found in *Schuler AG v Wickman Machine Tool Sales Ltd* [1974] AC 235; [1973] 2 All ER 39, in considering the question of whether a term is a 'condition' giving the right to repudiate for breach. See Chapter 17, 17.6.5.

93 For a discussion of issues of 'reasonable expectation', 'fairness' and 'good faith' which may be implicit in Lord Hoffmann's approach, see Brownsword, 2003.

It should not be thought, however, that these principles are necessarily easy to apply to actual cases. In the case of *Bank of Credit and Commerce International SA v Ali*,[94] the House of Lords was considering an agreement by employees as part of a redundancy arrangement that they would not pursue any further legal claims against their employers. It was later established, in other litigation,[95] that former employees of the company could claim 'stigma damages' as a result of their innocent association with an organisation that had been found to be carrying out its business in a corrupt and dishonest manner. The question in the present case was whether the agreement entered into by the claimants precluded them from pursuing an action for 'stigma damages'. The majority of the House of Lords held that, on its proper construction, the agreement should not be taken to cover a form of action which had not even been recognised as possible at the time the agreement was made. In coming to this conclusion, Lord Bingham, who gave the leading speech, referred specifically and approvingly to Lord Hoffmann's summary of the relevant principles in *Investors Compensation Scheme Ltd v West Bromwich Building Society*.[96] Lord Hoffmann himself, however, was in a minority of one in the House of Lords in holding that the agreement should, on its proper construction, be held to preclude any action by the claimants.[97] Both the majority and the minority purported, therefore, to be operating on the same principles, and to be taking into account the context of the agreement. Nevertheless, they came to different conclusions. This suggests that the process of interpreting contracts will continue to be a matter where there will be much scope for the particular opinions of individual judges, and that the modern 'contextual' approach will not be likely to lead to an increase in certainty, at least in the short term.

8.5.4 Interpretation under the Principles of European Contract Law

The approach suggested by the Principles of European Contract Law in relation to interpretation is contained in Chapter 5 of the draft. The general approach is to attempt to give effect to the intention of the parties, whether or not this accords with the literal meaning of the words used.[98] In this the Principles are taking a similar approach to that currently adopted by the English courts, as outlined in the previous section. In determining the parties' intentions, if the intention of one party can be established, and the other party could not have been unaware of that intention, then the first party's intention will prevail.[99] If it is not possible to establish the parties' subjective intentions, then

---

94 [2001] 1 All ER 961.
95 *Malik v BCCI SA* [1998] AC 20; [1997] 3 All ER 1.
96 [1998] 1 All ER 98.
97 Indeed, he saw the approach of the majority as involving an 'artificial' approach to construction, out of line with modern trends.
98 Article 5.101(1).
99 Article 5.101(2).

the contract is to be given the meaning that 'reasonable persons of the same kind as the parties would give to it in the same circumstances'.[100]

Article 5.102 sets out some of the circumstances which should, in particular, be taken into account in interpreting the contract. These include preliminary negotiations, and the conduct of the parties, 'even subsequent to the conclusion of the contract'. In contrast, English law does not, as we have seen in the previous section, generally take account of preliminary negotiations, or of subsequent words or conduct, in interpreting an agreement. 'Good faith and fair dealing' are also to be considered, which again are not commonly part of the English law approach.[101] Otherwise, the matters set out in Art 5.102 are predictable, and include the circumstances in which the contract was concluded, the nature and purpose of the contract, previous interpretation and practice by the parties, the meaning given to terms and expression in the 'branch of activity concerned' and the previous interpretation of similar clauses. Finally, 'usages' (presumably meaning 'customs') should be considered.

The *contra proferentem* rule is to be applied to a contract term which has not been individually negotiated,[102] and, where there is a conflict between individually negotiated terms and other terms, preference should be given to those individually negotiated.[103] Thus, the Principles operate to control to a limited extent standard term contracts. Terms are to be interpreted in the light of the whole contract.[104]

Finally, an interpretation which renders a contract lawful is, unsurprisingly, to be preferred to one that would not.[105] Article 5.107 suggests the approach to be taken where there are linguistic discrepancies between different language versions of a contract.

Overall, therefore, the Principles suggest an approach similar to that currently adopted by the English courts, but drawing on an even wider range of circumstances when trying to determine the parties' intentions, and placing the contract 'in context'. The availability of the criterion of 'good faith and fair dealing' would give a broad discretion not generally available to English courts.

8.5.5 Conditions, warranties and innominate terms

Not all terms within a contract are of equal importance. In a contract for the provision of a service, for example, terms specifying the dates on which the service is to be provided and the date for payment will be likely to be more important than, for example, a term requiring the supplier of the service to submit an annual account of the work done. The consequence of breach of one of the first two terms is probably going

---

100 Article 5.101(3).
101 See Chapter 1, 1.9.
102 Article 5.103.
103 Article 5.104.
104 Article 5.105.
105 Article 5.106.

to be more serious than the latter, and may indeed result in the contract as a whole being terminated. The parties may attempt to give effect to such differences in the status of various contractual provisions by the way in which their agreement is drafted in respect of its 'express terms'. There is, in fact, a generally accepted hierarchy of terms, with 'conditions' being more important than 'warranties'. Use of these labels may well indicate an intention by the parties as to the relative status of the terms concerned, though any presumption to this effect may be rebutted by other evidence.[106]

As indicated above, the distinction between the status of terms is of most importance when the consequences of a breach are being considered. Breach of 'condition' may well lead to the other party having the right to treat the contract as being at an end as well as suing for damages. Breach of 'warranty' will probably only entitle the other party to claim damages. If no labels are used, and the term is difficult to classify, it may be regarded as an 'innominate' term, in relation to which the consequences of the particular breach which has occurred may determine whether the party not in breach has a right to bring it to an end.[107] The context in which the breach occurred will be important, as will its effect on the rest of the contract. The details of the rules which the courts apply in this area are, however, left until Chapter 17, which is concerned specifically with the issues of performance and breach. It is important, however, that the parties should have such issues in mind when drafting their agreement, so that if they wish they can include express terms dealing with the consequences of a breach of any particular obligation. They may also wish to agree in advance the amount of damages that will be recoverable in such circumstances. The principles governing such clauses, known as 'liquidated damages' clauses, are discussed in Chapter 18.

8.6 IMPLIED TERMS

The express terms of an agreement may not tell the complete story, because in certain situations a term or terms may be 'implied' into a contract, although neither party has made reference to it at the time of the agreement. This may arise from one or other of the parties to the agreement claiming that, although a particular term has not been set out explicitly either in words or writing, it should nevertheless be part of the contract. In addition, in some situations, a term will be implied because Parliament has by statute required that all contracts of a particular type should contain such a term.

The order of treatment here will be to look first at terms implied by the courts, which can be further divided into terms implied by custom, terms implied in fact, and terms implied by law. Terms implied by statute will then be considered.[108]

---

106 *Schuler AG v Wickman Tool Sales Ltd* [1974] AC 235; [1973] 2 All ER 39 – see below, 17.6.5.
107 *Hong Kong Fir Shipping Co v Kawasaki Kisen Kaisha Ltd* [1962] 2 QB 26; [1962] 1 All ER 474 – see below, 17.6.7.
108 For a useful discussion of the justifications for the use of implied terms, see Collins, 2003, pp 245–46.

8.6.1 Terms implied by the courts

The general approach of the courts is that they are reluctant to imply terms. The parties are generally expected to take the trouble to set out the provisions of their agreement in full. A contract in which certain terms are implicit clearly gives great opportunities for dispute, and the courts have been reluctant to give any encouragement to parties to try to escape from contractual obligations on the basis of some term which was not stated, but which is now alleged to be of great significance. There are certain situations, however, where this reluctance is overcome, and terms are implied. When the courts do this, they run the risk of suggesting that all contractual issues can be resolved by deciding what the parties must have agreed at the time of the contract – that is, the myth of 'presentation'.[109] A 'relational' approach would recognise that not all issues can be solved in that way, in particular where a contract or a contractual relationship develops over time. This would allow a more flexible approach to the implication of terms to deal with particular situations.

The first basis on which the courts, applying the classical approach, will imply terms is where the implication of the term derives from a local or trade custom.

8.6.2 Terms implied by custom

Provided that there is sufficient evidence to establish the custom, the courts will be prepared to interpret the contract in the light of it. An early example is *Hutton v Warren*,[110] which has been discussed above, in connection with the parol evidence rule. As will be remembered, a tenant claimed to be entitled, on quitting his tenancy, to an allowance for seed and labour. There was nothing in the lease to this effect, but the court accepted that this was a well established local custom, and implied a term. A different kind of implication was suggested in *British Crane and Hire Corp Ltd v Ipswich Plant Hire Ltd*.[111] This concerned a contract for the hire of an earth-moving machine, together with a driver, and the issue was who was responsible for the cost of pulling it out of marshy land in which it had become stuck. One of the factors which the Court of Appeal regarded as relevant was that there was evidence that it was normal practice in the trade for liability to be placed on the hirer, rather than the owner, in such circumstances. Lord Denning commented:[112]

> The [hirers] themselves knew that firms in the plant hiring trade always imposed conditions in regard to the hiring of plant: and that their conditions were on much the same lines.

---

109 For which, see Chapter 1, 1.5.
110 (1836) 1 M & W 466; 150 ER 517.
111 [1975] QB 303.
112 Ibid, p 310.

This, together with the fact that the hirers had previously contracted with the owners on such terms, led to the implication that liability should rest with the hirer. The issue is thus primarily one of fact. The person wishing to rely on the custom must produce convincing factual evidence of its existence and general acceptance. Assuming that there is sufficient evidence, the courts will imply a term to give it effect.

Such implication will not be possible, however, if the contract contains an express term which is inconsistent with the custom. In that case, the express term will prevail over the custom. In *Les Affréteurs Réunis SA v Leopold Walford (London) Ltd*,[113] there was evidence of a custom that a broker's commission was payable only in relation to hire which had been earned under a charter. The contract, however, provided that commission was payable on the signing of the charter. This specific term was held to indicate the parties' intention in relation to this issue. There was therefore no room for a term implied from custom.

> **FOR THOUGHT**
>
> If a party to a contract is unaware of a custom which may affect its interpretation, is it fair to allow that custom to operate? Should it only apply where both parties are aware of it?

8.6.3 Terms implied in fact

The approach here is based on the attempt to determine the true intention of the parties. The courts will imply a term if they consider that it represents the true intention of the parties on a particular issue. In other words, the term is implied not as a matter of law, but on the basis that, as a matter of fact, this is what the parties had agreed, though the agreement was implicit rather than explicit. The courts will not easily, however, be convinced that such implication should take place. It is certainly not sufficient that a particular clause would appear to be 'reasonable'. Nor will a term be implied to deal with an eventuality which the parties had not anticipated. If they had not expected a particular circumstance to happen, they cannot be said to have intended that a particular term would apply to the situation. This was the view of the Court of Appeal in *Crest Homes (South West) Ltd v Gloucestershire CC*,[114] where in a construction contract the local planning authority unexpectedly imposed conditions which entailed additional expense and a loss of profit for the builder. The court was not prepared to imply a term that the defendant (which had performed its side of the bargain in accordance with the original contract) should bear any liability for these costs. This shows the court being unwilling to use the concept of the implied term to

---

113 [1919] AC 801.
114 (1999) unreported, 22 June, CA.

deal with 'relational' aspect of contracts – which may require the modification of obligations to deal with changed circumstances.[115]

8.6.4 The *Moorcock* test

The starting point for the law in this area is the case of *The Moorcock*.[116] This concerned a contract which involved the plaintiff's ship mooring at the defendant's wharf in the Thames. The Thames being a tidal river, at low tide the ship, as both parties knew would be the case, settled on the river bed. Unfortunately, the ship was damaged because of a ridge of hard ground beneath the mud of the river bed. There was no express term in the contract as to the suitability of the river bed for mooring a ship there. Nevertheless, it was held by the Court of Appeal that such a term could, and should, be implied. The reason for this was that without such a provision, the contract would have effectively been unworkable. It was implicit in the contract for the mooring of the ship that it would have to rest on the bottom of the river. Both parties must have contracted on the basis that it was safe to do so. On this basis, the court felt that it must have been the parties' intention that the owners of the wharf should warrant that the river bed was suitable for the purpose of the contract. Bowen LJ explained this reasoning as follows:

> Both parties knew that the jetty was let for the purpose of profit, and knew that it could only be used by the ship taking the ground and lying on the ground. They must have known, both of them, that unless the ground was safe the ship would be simply buying an opportunity of danger and buying no convenience at all, and that all consideration would fail unless the ground was safe. In fact, the business of the jetty could not be carried on unless, I do not say the ground was safe, it was supposed to be safe.

Note that the test being applied here is a stringent one. It is not based on the reasonable expectation of the owner of the ship, but rather on what is necessary in order to make the contract work at all. The fact that a contract might work better with a particular term implied would not be sufficient. *The Moorcock* can thus be characterised as having established a test of 'necessity' in relation to the implication of terms.[117]

8.6.5 The 'officious bystander' test

The reason why necessity is a good test for the implication of terms is that it must be regarded as a sure guide as to what the parties intended. If a contract will not work

---

115 See Macneil, 1978, and Chapter 1, 1.5.
116 (1889) 14 PD 64.
117 Collins, however, points out (2003, p 240) that, to the extent that this is based on identifying the objectives of the contract, the process may prove difficult because the parties may often disagree as to those objectives.

without the inclusion of a particular term, it is a reasonable assumption that the parties intended that term to be included. The courts have been prepared, however, to consider other tests of intention. One of the most commonly used is the test of the 'officious bystander'. This derives from the case of *Shirlaw v Southern Foundries*.[118] MacKinnon LJ suggested that a term may be implied where it is so obvious that it 'goes without saying', so that:[119]

> . . . if, while the parties were making their bargain, an officious bystander were to suggest some express provision for it in the agreement, they would testily suppress him with a common 'Oh, of course!'.

The test is again a strict one, in that there will be relatively few provisions of such obviousness that they will satisfy the 'officious bystander' test. Moreover, it is not a particularly easy one to apply, as is perhaps shown by the fact that in *Shirlaw's* case itself, there was considerable disagreement between members of the Court of Appeal and House of Lords as to what terms, if any, should be implied into a contract appointing the managing director of a company. Nor is it well suited to complex commercial transactions, in relation to which it may be difficult to formulate an appropriate question for the officious bystander to ask. A final difficulty is that in relation to terms other than those which are 'necessary' in the *Moorcock* sense, it may be difficult for a court, after the event, to establish what the parties, at the time of the contract, would have agreed. If the matter is before the court, they are by definition in dispute, and identifying an obligation (which will inevitably favour one side of the agreement) to which they would clearly have said 'yes, of course that is included' may be very difficult.[120] Overall, the *Moorcock* test is probably the more satisfactory of the two.

The operation of both the *Moorcock* and the 'officious bystander' tests was considered by Gatehouse J in *Ashmore v Corp of Lloyd's (No 2)*.[121] The case arose out the problems of Lloyd's 'names' who had made substantial losses out of insurance contracts. The plaintiffs were arguing that Lloyd's had a duty to alert names about matters of which Lloyd's became aware which might seriously affect their interests. One basis for the action was that the duty should be based on an implied term in the names' contracts with Lloyd's. Gatehouse J, however, was unable to find that either of the tests outlined above helped the plaintiffs. Looking first at the *Moorcock* test of business efficacy, many thousands of people had been or were names with Lloyd's under the same contractual arrangements as the plaintiffs. It could not be said that these contracts would not work without the suggested implied term.

118 [1939] 2 KB 206.
119 Ibid, p 227.
120 Cf the comments of Collins (2003, p 240) on the fact that it is unlikely in many situations that the parties would be in agreement – the matter may indeed have been left out of the contract 'for fear of failure to reach agreement'.
121 [1992] 2 Lloyd's Rep 620.

As to the officious bystander, Gatehouse J found the suggested question too complicated to be answered by a simple 'yes'. The question was set out in this way by the plaintiffs:[122]

> If, at the Rota meeting to admit a new Member, an officious bystander inter-rupted the proceedings and said, 'You Lloyd's are asking this applicant to engage in a high risk business and, in effect, entrust his entire personal fortune to an underwriting agent approved by you with whom he is not to interfere, and whom you know he relies upon and is by the system you impose forced to rely on: [Question] what if something professionally discreditable is or becomes known to Lloyd's about the underwriting agent which might prejudice the member's underwriting interests, other than matters which in Lloyd's reasonable opinion are not capable of being seriously prejudicial to the member's underwriting inter-ests, would you Lloyd's be obliged to take reasonable steps to alert the applicant, if thought necessary, in confidence, and tell the underwriting agent within a reasonable time thereafter what you have done?' Surely, the answer would be 'of course'.

On the contrary, the response of Lloyd's to such a complex question, thought Gatehouse J, would have been to refer the question to their lawyers, following which the most likely answer would have been an uncompromising 'no'.

Similarly, in *Wilson v Best Travel Ltd*,[123] the court refused to imply a term into a contract between a tour operator and holidaymaker that a hotel would be reasonably safe. Applying the officious bystander test, the judge did not think the tour operator would have said 'of course' to an inquiry as to whether such a term was included, given that the hotel was not under the operator's control.

These cases illustrate the reluctance of the courts to imply a term, and that the tests to be satisfied are applied quite strictly. There are, however, two recent examples of the courts being prepared to imply terms on the basis of what they thought that the parties must have intended. The first is *Griggs Group Ltd v Evans*,[124] which is an example of the use of the 'officious bystander' test to imply a term. The dispute was over whether the defendant retained the copyright in a logo which he had produced for the claimant, other than in relation to its use at the point of sale in the United Kingdom. The claimant alleged that it had acquired worldwide copyright in the contract under which the logo was produced. The contract was silent on the issue, so a term needed to be implied. Both the High Court and the Court of Appeal found in favour of the claimant. Jacob LJ commented:[125]

---

122 [1992] 2 Lloyd's Rep 620, p 623.
123 [1993] 1 All ER 353.
124 [2005] FSR 31.
125 Ibid, para 19.

> If an officious bystander had asked at the time of the contract whether Mr Evans [the defendant] was going to retain the rights in the combined logo which could be used against the client by Mr Evans (or anyone to whom he sold the rights) anywhere in the world, other than in respect of point of sale material in the UK, the answer would surely have been 'of course not'. Mr Evans had no conceivable further interest in the work being created – indeed he surely would never have had the job at all if there had been a debate about this and he had asserted that that was to be the basis of his work.

In other words, in this case the 'officious bystander' test was conclusive, and led to the implication of a term which gave the claimant all the copyright in the work.

The second case is *Equitable Life Assurance Society v Hyman*,[126] where a more general approach to implication was adopted. The issue was whether the life assurance society could decide to reduce the level of bonuses which certain of its policyholders would receive, in contravention of past practice and the expectations of the policy-holders. The articles of association of the society, which governed the society's powers in relation to bonuses, gave the directors a very broad discretion which seemed to allow them to make the reductions. The House of Lords, however, held that a term should be implied into the articles to the effect that the society could not exercise its discretion under the articles so as to defeat the reasonable expectations of the parties, which included an expectation that the directors would not exercise their discretion in a way that prejudiced the rights of a particular group of policyholders. Lord Steyn confirmed that this term could be implied on the basis of the 'necessity': 'In my judgment an implication precluding the use of directors' discretion in this way is strictly necessary.'[127] Despite these protestations, the case seems to be an example of a rather more relaxed approach to the implication of a term 'in fact' than has been the case previously. Whether this is an indication of a general trend towards the more frequent implication of terms on this basis remains to be seen.[128]

8.6.6 Terms implied by law

The distinction between terms implied in fact and terms implied by law was well explained by Lord Denning in *Shell UK Ltd v Lostock Garage Ltd*.[129] The case

---

126 [2000] 3 All ER 961.
127 Ibid, p 971.
128 Collins suggests (2003, pp 245–46) that neither the 'necessity' test nor the 'model contract' approach properly explain the reasons for implying terms. He suggests that the courts are in fact trying to achieve 'a fair and practical allocation of risks between the parties'. To the extent that he sees this as being based on the court's view of the 'reasonable expectations of the parties', the decision in *Equitable Life Assurance v Hyman* may be seen as recognising more explicitly than previously the true basis on which the courts decide that a term should be implied.
129 [1977] 1 All ER 481.

concerned a contract under which a garage owner agreed to buy petrol exclusively from Shell. Subsequently, at a time when there was a petrol 'price war', the garage owner discovered that Shell was supplying other petrol stations in the area at a lower price. This was having a disastrous effect on his business. The garage owner was arguing that a term should be implied to the effect that Shell would not discriminate against him in the terms on which it supplied the petrol. The majority of the Court of Appeal (Bridge LJ dissenting) held that no such term could be implied. In coming to this conclusion, Lord Denning emphasised the difference between terms implied in fact, and those implied by law. As regards the first category, as we have seen, this involves deciding what the parties themselves would have put into the contract had they addressed themselves to the issue. Lord Denning thought that the required term could not be implied on this basis, because it was highly unlikely that Shell would have agreed to the inclusion of such a term if this had been requested by the garage owner. Terms implied by law, however, do not depend on determining the intention of the parties. The court in this case will impose the term on them, whether they would have agreed to it or not.

Two conditions need to be satisfied before this can be done, however. First, the contract has to be of a sufficiently common type (for example, seller–buyer, owner–hirer, employer–employee, landlord–tenant) that it is possible to identify the typical obligations of such a contract. Second, the matter to which the implied term relates must be one which the parties have not in any way addressed in their contract. There must be a clear gap to be filled. In *Shell v Lostock Garage*, the garage owner failed on the first test. Lord Denning was not prepared to hold that exclusive dealing contracts of this kind were sufficiently common that typical terms could be identified.

In *Scally v Southern Health and Social Services Board*,[130] Lord Bridge similarly referred to the distinction:

> . . . between the search for an implied term necessary to give business efficacy to a particular contract and the search, based on wider considerations, for a term which the law will imply as a necessary incident of a definable category of contractual relationship.

8.6.7   *Liverpool City Council v Irwin*

This type of implication of terms derives from the House of Lords' decision in *Liverpool City Council v Irwin*.[131] The contract in this case was a tenancy agreement in relation to a block of flats. The agreement said nothing about who was to be responsible for the maintenance of the common parts of the block and, in particular, the lifts and rubbish chutes. The tenants argued that a term should be implied that the City Council was responsible. It would clearly not have been possible to imply such a term using the

---

130 [1991] 4 All ER 563, p 571.
131 [1977] AC 239.

Moorcock or the 'officious bystander' test. It would have been quite possible to have a workable tenancy agreement in which, for example, the responsibility for the common parts was shared among all the tenants of the block. An officious bystander suggesting that a term should be included imposing liability on the landlord alone would have been unlikely to have been considered to be stating the obvious, at least as far as the City Council was concerned. The House of Lords nevertheless decided that it was possible to imply a term to the effect that the landlord should take reasonable steps to keep the common parts in repair. What the House was in effect doing was to say that:

(a) the agreement was incomplete, in that it was mainly concerned with the tenant's obligations, and contained very little about those of the landlord;
(b) it was an agreement of a type that was sufficiently common that the court could decide that certain terms would normally be expected to be found in it;
(c) the term implied was one which the House thought was reasonable in relation to the normal expectations of the obligations as between landlord and tenant.

Despite the fact that Lord Wilberforce insisted on referring to the test as one of 'necessity' rather than 'reasonableness', it is clear that in practice it is the latter word which indicates the approach being taken, once the preconditions for any implication in law have been met. In other words, if it is established that the agreement is one of 'common occurrence', and that it is 'incomplete', the courts will themselves decide what term should be implied in order to make the contract work 'reasonably' – meaning here 'as would commonly be expected in relation to a contract of this type'.[132]

An example of a term implied by law into an employment contract is to be found in *Malik v BCCI*.[133] The employee had worked for the Bank of Credit and Commerce International which collapsed in 1991, amidst allegations that the bank had operated in a corrupt and dishonest manner. The employee claimed that having worked for BCCI had adversely affected his future employment prospects. On a trial of a preliminary issue as to whether the employee had any cause of action, it was confirmed by the House of Lords that there should be implied into contracts of employment a mutual obligation of 'trust and confidence'. This obligation can be excluded or modified by the parties, but otherwise will operate as a 'default' clause in all contracts of employment. In this case, the implied term had not been amended by the parties, and was held to include the obligation that the employer should not:[134]

> Without reasonable and proper cause, conduct itself in a manner calculated and likely to destroy or seriously damage the relationship of confidence and trust between employer and employee.

---

132 Such an approach is likely to be most useful in respect of 'relational' contracts – see Macneil, 1978, and Chapter 1, 1.5.
133 [1998] AC 20; [1997] 3 All ER 1.
134 Ibid, p 34.

Thus, the employee did have the basis for a cause of action against his former employer for the damage caused by the way it was alleged the business had been run.

The possibility of implying a term in law was also raised in *Ashmore v Corp of Lloyd's (No 2)* [135] as an alternative to implication in fact. The plaintiff argued that there were many contracts in identical terms between 'names' and Lloyd's, and that therefore this was an appropriate situation in which to use the *Liverpool City Council v Irwin* approach. Gatehouse J disagreed. What was important was not the number of contracts; rather, there needed to be a broad category or type of relationship, even though within that type the detailed terms might vary on particular points. The fact that in this case each contract was in identical terms did not create a category, or genus, of contracts for which typical terms could be found. The plaintiff's attempt to imply a term by this means failed once again.

There are two reasons why it may be appropriate for Parliament to enact that certain provisions should be implied into all contracts of a particular type. One relates to efficiency. If it is virtually universal practice for certain terms to be used in particular contractual relationships, there is no need for the parties to state them specifically every time. In terms of economic analysis, there is a saving in 'transaction costs'. Rather than having to agree an appropriate wording on each occasion, the parties can rely on the statutory formulation as representing their obligations. In such a situation, however, there should be the possibility of the parties being able to agree to depart from the statutory wording, if they so wish.

The second reason why terms might need to be implied by statute is for the protection of one of the parties. It may be thought that a particular type of contractual relationship is likely to involve inequality of bargaining power, so that, unless protective provisions are implied, the weaker party may be forced into a very disadvantageous bargain. If this is the reason for the implication, then it may well be that the obligation to include the term should be absolute, without any possibility of it being excluded or amended in particular contracts.

Examples of both of these bases for implying terms by statute can be found in the history of the implied terms as to quality under the Sale of Goods Acts. The original Sale of Goods Act (SGA) 1893 was intended to represent a codification of current commercial law and practice. Thus, the implied terms as to quality, contained in ss 13–15, were those which merchants of the time would have expected to appear in any contract for the sale of goods. This was an example of the first ground for implying terms, that is, business efficiency. In line with this approach, s 55 of the SGA 1893 allowed the parties to agree to different terms as to quality, or to exclude them altogether, if they so wished. By the time of the enactment of the revised version of the SGA in 1979, however, the

---

135 [1992] 2 Lloyd's Rep 620.

atmosphere had changed. The provisions as to quality had come to be regarded as important elements in the law of consumer protection. Their role was therefore at least in part to provide protection for the weaker party in a sale of goods contract. As a result, the Unfair Contract Terms Act (UCTA) 1977 made it impossible in situations where the contract is made between a business and consumer for the business to exclude the implied terms.[136] Even as between business parties, the exclusion will be subject to a test of 'reasonableness'. The terms implied by the Supply of Goods and Services Act 1982 also seem to be based on principles of protection, rather than the avoidance of transaction costs.

A further example of a term implied on the grounds of protection is to be found in the Equal Pay Act 1970. Section 3 implies into every employment contract an 'equality clause' which has the effect of ensuring that, as between men and women employed on 'like work', there is equal treatment in relation to all terms of their contracts.

The implication of terms on this basis runs counter to the normal philosophy of classical English contract law, which is to make the intentions of the parties paramount. Here, the clause is imposed on the parties, whether they like it or not. Even if they expressly agree that it is not to operate, the courts will still give effect to it. This is an area where there is clearly a tension between the 'classical' and 'modern' law.

8.6.9 Implied terms under the Sale of Goods Act [137]

Various terms are implied into all sale of goods contracts by virtue of ss 12–15 of the SGA 1979. Similar provisions are to be found in the Supply of Goods and Services Act 1982, but these are not discussed here.

The implied terms under the SGA 1979 are all labelled as 'conditions' or 'warranties'. Breach of a condition will generally give the innocent party the right to repudiate the contract as well as claiming damages, whereas breach of warranty will only give a right to damages.[138]

8.6.10 Title

Section 12 of the SGA 1979 is concerned with 'title' in the sense of the 'right to sell'. There is an implied condition in every sale of goods contract that the seller has this right 'at the time when property is to pass'. The condition will be broken if the goods belong to someone else, or if they cannot be sold without infringing another's rights, for example, in a trade mark.[139] A breach of this condition will be regarded as constituting

136 See the UCTA 1977, s 6 – discussed further in Chapter 9, at 9.7.19.
137 The discussion of these terms is in outline only. For a full treatment see, for example, Atiyah, Adams and MacQueen, 2005, or Bridge, 1998.
138 For further discussion of the distinction between 'conditions' and 'warranties', see Chapter 17, 17.4.3.
139 *Niblett v Confectioners' Materials* [1921] 3 KB 387.

a 'total failure of consideration'. This has the potential to allow the purchaser to recover any money paid, even though use has been made of the goods transferred. In *Rowland v Divall*,[140] the plaintiff car dealer had bought a car from the defendant. The car had previously been stolen, but neither party was aware of this at the time. The plaintiff resold the car to a third party, from whom it was reclaimed, some months later, by the true owner's insurance company. The plaintiff had to repay the purchase price to the third party, and then sought to recover what he had paid to the defendant. Despite the fact of the lapse of time, and the consequent reduction in the value of the car, which was demonstrated by the fact that the insurance company had in fact sold it back to the plaintiff at much less than the original contract price, the plaintiff was allowed to recover what he had paid to the defendant in full, on the basis of a total failure of consideration. The use that the plaintiff had made of the car was irrelevant. The essence of a sale of goods contract is not the use of the goods, but the transfer of ownership. The breach of s 12 meant that ownership had never been transferred, and the plaintiff was therefore entitled to recover all his money.

In *Rowland v Divall*, the plaintiff was a dealer who was primarily interested in the ability to resell the car. The same principle, however, applies to a private purchaser. In *Butterworth v Kingsway Motors*,[141] the plaintiff had bought a car which, unknown to him, was subject to a hire purchase agreement, and was reclaimed by the finance company nearly a year later. The plaintiff was allowed to recover the full purchase price from the defendant, notwithstanding the fact that the defendant was equally ignorant of the defect in title. The plaintiff thus had almost a year's free use of the car. This decision has been the subject of considerable criticism,[142] but has not as yet been overruled.

Section 12 also contains an implied warranty of quiet possession, and freedom from encumbrances.

8.6.11 Description

Section 13 says that where goods are sold by description, there is an implied condition that they will match the description. The description may come from the seller or the buyer, and can apply to specific as well as generic goods.[143] Section 13(3) makes it clear that selection by the buyer, as in a self-service shop, does not prevent the sale being by description. Virtually all sales will, as a result, be sales by description, unless the buyer indicates a particular article which he or she wishes to buy, without describing it in any

---

140 [1923] 2 KB 500.

141 [1954] 1 WLR 1286.

142 For example, Atiyah, Adams and MacQueen, 2005, pp 114–19; Bridge, 1998, pp 395–97.

143 *Varley v Whipp* [1900] 1 QB 513. Where particular items are identified at the time of the contract (for example, 'my Chippendale table') they will be 'specific goods': SGA 1979, s 61. Where goods of a specified type are to be sold (for example, 10 tons of wheat), without any particular items being identified, they will be 'generic goods'.

way, and the article itself has no label or packaging containing a description. There must, however, be some reliance on the description by the buyer in order for s 13 to apply. *Harlingdon and Leinster Enterprises v Christopher Hull Fine Art Ltd*[144] concerned the sale of a painting which turned out not to be by the artist to whom it was attributed in the catalogue. It was found as a matter of fact that the buyer had not relied on this attribution, and therefore this was not a sale by description.[145]

It is important to distinguish statements as to *quality* from statements of description. To describe a car as 'new' is description; to say that it has 'good acceleration' is a statement of quality, and not within s 13. Statements in advertisements can, however, be regarded as part of the description, even if the goods have subsequently been inspected. In *Beale v Taylor*,[146] a car was advertised as a 1961 model. In fact, it was made of two halves welded together, only one of the halves dating from 1961. It was held that there was a breach of s 13.

Note that s 13 applies to private sales as well as those in the course of a business.

8.6.12 Satisfactory quality

Where a sale of goods contract is made in the course of business, s 14(2) implies a term of 'satisfactory quality'. The scope of the phrase 'in the course of business', which also applies to the implied term under s 14(3), was considered by the Court of Appeal in *Stevenson v Rogers*.[147] The case concerned the sale by a fisherman of his fishing boat. The court noted that the original wording of the relevant section in the Sale of Goods Act 1893 had limited liability to where the seller dealt 'in goods of that description'. This limitation had been removed, however, and did not appear in s 14 of the 1979 Act. The fact, therefore, that the fisherman was not regularly in the business of selling fishing boats did not prevent this being a sale 'in the course of business', so that the implied term under s 14(2) applied. In coming to this conclusion, the court held that the narrower interpretation of 'the course of a business' used by the Court of Appeal in *R and B Customs Brokers v UDT*[148] in relation to the UCTA 1977 should not be used in this context.[149]

Where the requirement of 'satisfactory quality' applies, this means, according to s 14(2A), that the goods must:

> . . . meet the standard that a reasonable person would regard as satisfactory, taking account of any description of the goods, the price (if relevant) and all other relevant circumstances.

---

144 [1990] 1 All ER 737.
145 It was significant in this case that the seller professed no specialist knowledge, whereas the buyer was an 'expert' in paintings of the relevant type.
146 [1967] 3 All ER 253. See also 8.3.2, and note 18, above.
147 [1999] 1 All ER 613.
148 [1988] 1 All ER 847.
149 For discussion of this case, see Chapter 9, 9.7.3.

This test of satisfactory quality was substituted for the previous test of 'merchantable quality' by the Sale and Supply of Goods Act 1994. The previous case law on s 14(2) is therefore only of limited assistance in the interpretation of this section. Section 14(2B), however, indicates some of the factors which will be relevant in applying the new test. These include the state and condition of the goods, and in particular their:

(a) fitness for all the purposes for which goods of the kind in question are commonly supplied;
(b) appearance and finish;
(c) freedom from minor defects;
(d) safety; and
(e) durability.

The test of 'merchantable quality' had centred on the issue now dealt with in (a) above. By virtue of the decision in *Aswan Engineering Establishment Co v Lupdine Ltd*,[150] however, goods which were fit for just *one* of the purposes for which they were commonly used would be merchantable. The new wording contained in (a) above means that the fitness of the goods for *all* such purposes will be relevant to the test of whether they are of satisfactory quality.

The test refers to the expectations of a 'reasonable person' as to the quality of the goods. This was considered in *Bramhill v Edwards*.[151] The contract was for the purchase of a motor home that had been imported from the USA. The particular vehicle, which the buyer had inspected before purchase, was two inches wider than the maximum prescribed in the relevant United Kingdom regulations. There was evidence that the licensing authorities and insurers were 'turning a blind eye' to this issue, and that it was not causing significant problems for owners of such vehicles, many of which had been imported. The trial judge held that a reasonable person would have found the vehicle unsatisfactory. The Court of Appeal disagreed. The reasonable person should be taken to be aware of the relevant background facts – in this case, the significant number of imports, and the tolerant attitude of the authorities. On this basis, there was no breach of s 14(2).

Defects which have been brought to the buyer's attention prior to the contract, or which should have been revealed by any inspection actually undertaken by the buyer, will not make the goods of unsatisfactory quality (s 14(2C)). (This was a further basis on which the seller in *Bramhill v Edwards* succeeded.)

There seems no reason to doubt that the new test will, like the test of merchantability, include the containers in which the goods are supplied, and may also include instructions for use. If the goods are supplied in bulk, extraneous items which are concealed within them may render the goods unsatisfactory. In *Wilson v Rickett*

---

150 [1987] 1 WLR 1.
151 [2004] 2 Lloyd's Rep 653

Cockerell Co,[152] the presence of detonators in a bag of coal was held to make the coal unmerchantable.

If the buyer is a consumer, then, as a result of additions made by the Sale and Supply of Goods to Consumers Regulations 2002,[153] an additional circumstance needs to be taken into account in relation to the test of satisfactory quality. Section 14(2D) states that:

> . . . if the buyer deals as consumer . . . the relevant circumstances mentioned in subsection (2A) above include any public statements on the specific characteristics of the goods made about them by the seller, the producer or his representative, particularly in advertising or on labelling.

This means that, for the first time, statements made in national advertising and emanating from the manufacturer ('producer') rather than the seller can affect the seller's obligation to sell goods of 'satisfactory quality'. There is some protection for the seller in the new s 14(2E) in relation to statements of which the seller was not aware, which have been withdrawn or corrected, or which could not have influenced the consumer's decision to buy the goods. The scope of 'satisfactory quality' in consumer contracts is nevertheless significantly expanded by this amendment.

Finally, it is important to note that the test of satisfactory quality does not relate to the particular use that the buyer has in mind (for which see s 14(3), below) but to the general standard of the goods. This is confirmed by the recent Court of Appeal decision in *Jewson Ltd v Boyhan*,[154] which is discussed below (see 8.6.14).

8.6.13 Fitness for a particular purpose

If the buyer wants the goods for a particular purpose, and the seller is aware of this, then by virtue of s 14(3) there will, in all sales in the course of a business, be an implied term that the goods will be reasonably fit for that purpose, unless:

> . . . the circumstances show that the buyer does not rely, or that it is unreasonable for him to rely on the skill and judgment of the seller.

The section can apply even though the goods only have one purpose, in which case the seller will be taken to have notice of it,[155] but it will usually be more appropriate to use

---

152 [1954] 1 QB 598.
153 SI 2002/3045 – the Regulations came into force on 31 March 2003. They were intended to give effect to the European Directive on Certain Aspects of the Sale of Consumer Goods and Associated Guarantees (1999/44/EC). In addition to amending the definition of satisfactory quality, as indicated in the text, the Regulations provide for additional remedies for consumers, including a right to demand free repair, or a reduction in price for goods which are unsatisfactory.
154 [2003] EWCA Civ 1930.
155 *Priest v Last* [1903] 2 KB 148.

s 14(2) in such circumstances. Section 14(3) may need to be relied on, however, if there is something special about the circumstances in which the goods are to be used. In *Griffiths v Peter Conway*,[156] the plaintiff contracted dermatitis from wearing a Harris Tweed coat. This was brought about by the fact that the plaintiff had an unusually sensitive skin. On the facts, this was not something which the seller knew, and so the claim under s 14(3) failed. If the seller had been aware, however, then the action under this section would have been the appropriate one, despite the fact that the coat had only one 'purpose', that is, to be worn.

FOR THOUGHT

> For thought: Would it have made any difference if a significant proportion of people were sensitive to Harris Tweed and the seller of the coat was aware of that fact?

The same approach was used by the House of Lords in *Slater v Finning Ltd*.[157] A camshaft supplied by the defendant failed when used in an engine fitted to the plaintiff's fishing boat. Replacement camshafts supplied by the defendant also failed. The plaintiff sold the engine, with its latest replacement camshaft, and it was fitted to another fishing boat in which it was apparently used without problem. The judge found that the problem of the failure of the camshafts must have been caused by some unexplained idiosyncrasy of the plaintiff's fishing boat. There was therefore no breach of the implied condition of fitness for purpose. This conclusion was confirmed by the House of Lords, which also made clear that where the problem arose from an abnormal or unusual situation not known to the seller, it was irrelevant for the purposes of s 14(3) whether or not this situation was known to the buyer.

A claim will not succeed under s 14(3) where the problems arise from the buyer's misunderstanding of instructions supplied with the goods. This was the view taken in *Wormell v RHM Agriculture (East) Ltd*.[158] This decision appears to accept, however, that defective instructions could lead to goods being found to be not fit for a particular purpose.

Once it is clear that the seller knew of the particular purpose, the burden is on the seller to show that there was no, or unreasonable, reliance. This is a hard test to satisfy, since the courts tend to favour the buyer, and have made it clear that partial reliance is sufficient to found an action.[159]

---

156 [1939] 1 All ER 685.
157 [1996] 3 All ER 398.
158 [1987] 3 All ER 75.
159 *Ashington Piggeries v Christopher Hill* [1972] AC 441.

8.6.14 Relationship between s 14(2) and s 14(3)

In *Jewson Ltd v Boyhan*,[160] the Court of Appeal emphasised the need to distinguish carefully between s 14(2) (satisfactory quality) and s 14(3) (fitness for a particular purpose). The defendant had supplied electric boilers for a flat conversion project. The boilers had the effect of reducing the energy efficiency rating of the flats and therefore made the flats more difficult to sell. The trial judge found the defendants in breach of both s 14(2) and s 14(3).

In allowing the defendant's appeal, the Court of Appeal held that s 14(2) was concerned with the intrinsic quality of what was supplied. Here the question under s 14(2) was whether the boilers were satisfactory as boilers for flats, ignoring the particular circumstances which gave rise to the problems in this case. The answer was 'yes', so there was no breach of s 14(2). As regards s 14(3), the important issue was whether the claimant had reasonably relied on the defendant's skill and judgment in supplying the boilers. The answer was yes, as regards the intrinsic quality of the boilers for heating flats, but no as regards their suitability for these particular flats. On this issue, the defendant had insufficient information for it to be reasonable for the claimant to rely on them for this purpose. The defendant was therefore not liable under s 14(3) either.

8.6.15 Sale by sample

Where there is a sale by sample there is an implied condition, by virtue of s 15:

   (a)   that the bulk will correspond with the sample in quality;
   (b)   [repealed];
   (c)   that the goods will be free from any defect, making their quality unsatisfactory, which would not be apparent on reasonable examination of the sample.

This section does not seem to have given rise to any serious difficulties in application.

8.6.16 Implied terms under the Principles of European Contract Law

The Article of the Principles dealing with implied terms is very short.[161] It states that:

   . . . a contract may contain implied terms which stem from:
   (a)   the intention of the parties;
   (b)   the nature and purpose of the contract; and
   (c)   good faith and fair dealing.

---

160 [2003] EWCA Civ 1930.
161 Article 6.102.

This is very broad, and would allow courts to operate all the approaches adopted by the common law, and outlined above. Moreover, the final category would give the court power to imply terms which are 'fair and reasonable' in the circumstances, in a way which has never been explicitly allowed under English law.

8.7 STATUTORY CONTROLS

As we have seen, the contents of the contract may be subject to statutory control, in that terms may be implied, and exclusion of such terms may be prohibited, by statute (for example, the SGA 1979; the UCTA 1977). There is now, however, a broader control of the contents of certain types of consumer contract, which results from the Unfair Terms in Consumer Contracts Regulations 1999.[162] These Regulations prohibit a wider range of contractual clauses than simply the exclusion clauses affected by the UCTA 1977. The Regulations thus represent a further inroad into the traditional common law principle that the intention of the parties is paramount. Since, however, they relate most closely to the type of control contained in the UCTA 1977, and overlap to a considerable extent with that Act, full discussion of these Regulations is left to Chapter 9. It is important to remember, however, that all clauses in consumer contracts, other than those which are 'individually negotiated', or relate either to the definition of the main subject matter of the contract or to the question of price or remuneration,[163] are subject to a test of 'fairness'. They will be regarded as 'unfair' if they 'cause a significant imbalance in the parties' rights and obligations arising under the contract, to the detriment of the consumer'.[164] This constitutes a very powerful control over the contents of consumer contracts. It enables the courts to abandon almost entirely any pretence that regulation is based on the intentions of the parties. What is 'fair' to the consumer will be the test, which may well be decided by considering the consumer's reasonable expectations. This statutory framework means that the divide between the construction of contracts between businesses, and those between consumers, which has always existed, has grown considerably. Depending on how the Regulations are applied, and what further controls may be introduced, in future it may be necessary to deal with the contents of consumer and non-consumer contracts entirely separately.

Indeed, if the Law Commission's proposals to replace the Regulations with a broadly based Unfair Contract Terms Act are accepted,[165] most terms in contracts entered into by small businesses (that is, those with under 10 employees) with other businesses, as well as those made by consumers, will be subject to a test of 'reasonableness'. This will further erode the idea that the substance of the agreement is for the

---

162 SI 1999/2083.

163 Ibid, reg 6.

164 Ibid, reg 5(1).

165 See Law Commission, *Unfair Terms in Contracts*, Law Com No 292, Scot Law Com No 199, Cm 6464, 2005.

parties to determine, and that the courts simply aim to give effect to their intentions. These proposals are discussed in more detail in Chapter 9, at 9.10.

8.8 FURTHER READING

Brownsword, R, 'After *Investors*: interpretation, expectation and the implicit dimension of the "new contextualism" ', Chapter 4 in Campbell, D, Collins H, and Wightman, J (eds), *Implicit Dimensions of Contract*, 2003, Oxford: Hart Publishing

Gee, S, 'The interpretation of commercial contracts' (2001) 117 LQR 358

Law Commission, Report No 154, *Law of Contract: the Parol Evidence Rule*, 1986, Cmnd 9700

McKendrick, E, 'The interpretation of contracts: Lord Hoffman's re-statement' in Worthington, S (ed), *Commercial Law and Commercial Practice*, 2003, Oxford: Hart, 139

McMeel, G, 'The rise of commercial construction in contract law' [1998] LMCLQ 382

Mitchell, C, 'Leading a life of its own? The roles of reasonable expectation in contract law' (2003) 23 OJLS 639

Peden, E, and Carter, JW, 'Incorporation of terms by signature: L'Estrange Rules!' (2005) 21 JCL 96

Phang, A, 'Implied terms, business efficacy and the officious bystander – a modern history' [1998b] JBL 1.

Staughton, C, 'How do the courts interpret commercial contracts?' [1999] CLJ 303

Wedderburn, KW, 'Collateral Contracts' [1959] CLJ 58

9 CLAUSES EXCLUDING OR LIMITING LIABILITY

CONTENTS

9.1 OVERVIEW

This chapter deals with the situations where parties attempt to exclude or limit their liability for breach of contract by including exclusion or exemption clauses in the contract. It is an area governed by both common law and statute. The statutory provisions were developed in the latter half of the twentieth century and tend to have a consumer focus. The common law rules were developed earlier to deal with imbalances in bargaining power between the parties. The common law is looked at first, here, followed by the statutory rules:

- Common law
  - Rule of incorporation. Was the clause part of the contract? Was appropriate notice of it given to the other party?
  - Rule of construction. Does the wording of the clause make it clear that it covers the breach that has occurred?
- Statute
  - Unfair Contract Terms Act (UCTA) 1977. The statute makes some exclusion clauses void (for example, clauses which attempt to exclude liability for death or personal injury caused by negligence). Many other clauses are subject to a test of 'reasonableness'. Case law on the Act has tended to allow businesses more freedom to exclude liability when contracting with each other than in contracts with consumers.
  - Unfair Terms in Consumer Contracts Regulations (UTCCR) 1999. These regulations derive from a European directive. They impose a requirement of 'fairness' on most terms in consumer contracts. 'Good faith' is part of the test of fairness.
  - There is overlap between UCTA and UTCCR which at times makes it difficult to determine which should apply.
- Principles of European Contract Law. These contain provisions which largely adopt a similar approach to that of the UTCCR.
- Proposals for reform. The Law Commission has recommended that the law should be simplified by combining the UCTA and the UTCCR into one statute.

9.2 INTRODUCTION

It will very often be the case that a contract will include a clause excluding or limiting the liability of one of the parties in the event of certain types of breach. The exclusion may be total, or may limit the party's liability to a specified sum of money. There is nothing inherently objectionable about a clause of this kind. Provided that it has been included as a result of a clear voluntary agreement between the parties, it may simply indicate their decision as to where certain risks involved in the transaction should fall. If the contract involves the carriage of goods, for example, it may have been agreed that the owner should be responsible for insuring the goods while in transit. In that situation, it may be perfectly reasonable for the carrier to have very restricted liability for damage to the goods while they are being carried. The inclusion of the clause is simply an example of good contractual planning.[1]

It is also the case that it may be difficult at times to distinguish between a clause that limits liability and one that simply determines the obligations under the contract. Suppose, for example, that there is a contract for the regular servicing of a piece of

---

1 See, for example, Yates, 1982, pp 11–33. For an analysis of exclusion clauses based around the allocation of risks, see von Mehren, 1982.

machinery. The owner, O, is anxious that any replacement parts should be those made by the original manufacturer of the machine, M Ltd; the servicer, S, cannot guarantee that such parts will always be available. The situation might be dealt with in two ways. A clause might be inserted to say: 'S will use parts manufactured by M Ltd when available, but may substitute equivalent parts if necessary to complete a service within a reasonable time.' This would appear to define S's obligations under the contract. Alternatively, the clause might say: 'S will use parts manufactured by M Ltd, but will not be liable for any loss arising from the use of equivalent parts, if this is necessary to complete a service within a reasonable time.' Here the clause is put in the form of a limitation of S's liability, but in effect it produces the same result as the previous version of the clause. It is generally possible to rewrite any clause which on its face appears to limit liability for a breach of contract into one which defines the contracting parties' obligations.[2] If this is so, is there any need to treat 'exclusion clauses' as a special type of clause?[3] Could not all clauses simply be subject to the standard rules of incorporation and interpretation which were discussed in Chapter 8? This has not been the traditional approach of the courts, though the distinction between the two types of clause is blurred in relation to the statutory controls which now apply.[4] The courts, however, have tended to view clauses which attempt to limit liability as a separate category, and have developed particular rules to deal with them.

Part of the reason for this is that many exclusion clauses are not simply the product of good contractual planning between parties bargaining on equal terms. They appear in standard form contracts, which the other party has little choice as to whether to accept or not, and may give the party relying on them a very broad exemption from liability, both in tort and in contract.[5] When such inequitable clauses began to appear with some frequency in the nineteenth century, the courts devised ways of limiting their effectiveness. While the techniques adopted, as will be seen below, for the most part consisted of 'heightened' application of those used more generally for the purposes of constructing and interpreting contracts,[6] the courts clearly viewed exclusion clauses as a particular type of clause needing special treatment. This separation of exclusion clauses from the general run of contractual provisions, and in particular the distinction drawn between clauses which exclude liability and those that define obligations, is understandable in the context of a general approach based on 'freedom of contract'. If the courts were saying on the one hand that parties should be free to determine their own contractual obligations, and that the question of whether the obligations undertaken were

---

2 The task is more difficult if the clause relates simply to consequential losses resulting from a breach, or is designed to put a financial 'cap' on liability, rather than removing it altogether.

3 This argument has been put by, for example, Coote, 1964, Chapter 1, and Yates, 1982, pp 123–33.

4 That is, the Unfair Contract Terms Act 1977 and the Unfair Terms in Consumer Contracts Regulations 1999 – see below, 9.6.

5 Note that it is quite possible for an exclusion clause in a contract to restrict tortious liabilities, particularly for negligence occurring in the performance of the contract.

6 In particular, the rules relating to 'incorporation' and 'construction'. The doctrine of fundamental breach, while it lasted, was a technique developed more particularly to deal with exclusion clauses.

'fair' or 'reasonable' was generally irrelevant, it would cause problems if, on the other hand, they were seen to be interfering in this contractual freedom. By treating exclusion clauses as distinct from clauses defining obligations, such interference could be seen as limited and designed to tackle a particular type of situation tangential to the central issue of the freedom of the parties to determine their obligations towards each other.

In the twentieth century, the fact that contracts at times needed regulation to achieve 'fairness' was acknowledged more directly and, moreover, Parliament intervened to add a statutory layer of controls on top of the common law rules (that is, the Unfair Contract Terms Act (UCTA) 1977 and the Unfair Terms in Consumer Contracts Regulations (UTCCR) 1999).[7] These controls are not limited to clauses which are stated as excluding liability, but do extend to some extent to provisions which purport to define obligations. It may be that we are therefore moving towards a situation where the law of contract controls 'unfair' terms of whatever type, rather than having special rules for exclusion clauses. At the moment, however, the body of case law directed at exclusion clauses is still of sufficient importance to merit separate treatment. Despite the statutory interventions, the common law remains very important, not least because its rules apply to all contracts, whereas the UCTA 1977 and the UTCCR 1999 apply only in certain situations.

9.3 COMMON LAW RULES

The approach of the courts to exclusion clauses has not traditionally been to assess them on their merits. In other words, they have not said 'we think this clause is unreasonable in its scope, or unfair in its operation, and therefore we will not give effect to it'. As has been noted above, such an approach would have run too directly counter to the general ideas of 'freedom of contract' which were particularly important to the courts of the nineteenth century. So, instead, the courts developed and adapted formal rules relating to the determination of the contents of the contract, and the scope of the clauses contained in it, which were used to limit the scope of exclusion clauses. The main rules which are used are those of 'incorporation' and 'construction', though we will also need to note the so-called 'doctrine of fundamental breach'.

9.4 INCORPORATION

A clause cannot be effective to exclude liability if it is not part of the contract. The ways in which the courts determine the contents of a contract have been considered in the previous chapter. The rules discussed there, including the parol evidence rule and its exceptions, are also relevant to the decision as to whether an exclusion clause is part of

---

7 Below, 9.7 and 9.8.

the contract. It will almost always be the case that an exclusion clause will be in writing – though there is no principle which prevents a party stating an exclusion orally, as with any other contractual term. The first question will be, therefore, whether that written term can be regarded as part of the contract. The courts have generally been concerned to limit the effect of exclusion clauses (particularly as regards consumers), and they have, therefore, in this context applied fairly strict rules as to the incorporation of terms. The rules are based on the general principle that a party must have had reasonable notice of the exclusion clause at the time of the contract in order for it to be effective. If, however, the contract containing the clause has been signed by the claimant, there will be little that the courts can do. In *L'Estrange v Graucob*,[8] for example, the clause was in small print, and very difficult to read, but because the contract had been signed, the clause was held to have been incorporated. Scrutton LJ made it clear that in such cases questions of 'notice' were irrelevant:

> In cases in which the contract is contained in a railway ticket or other unsigned document, it is necessary to prove that an alleged party was aware, or ought to have been aware, of its terms and conditions. These cases have no application when the document has been signed. When a document containing contractual terms is signed, then, in the absence of fraud, or, I will add, misrepresentation, the party signing it is bound, and it is wholly immaterial whether he has read the document or not . . .

This rule has been applied strictly by English courts.[9] The main exceptions relate to the situations referred to by Scrutton LJ in the above quotation – that is, where the signature has been induced by fraud or misrepresentation.[10] An example of the application of this principle is to be found in *Curtis v Chemical Cleaning and Dyeing Co Ltd*.[11] The plaintiff had taken a dress for cleaning. She was asked to sign a receipt containing a widely-worded exemption clause. On querying this, she was told by the assistant that the clause meant that the defendants would not accept liability for damage to the beads and sequins with which the dress was trimmed. When it was returned, the dress had a stain

---

8 [1934] 2 KB 394.

9 It has been strongly criticised by Spencer, who has argued that the rule was based on a misapplication of the parol evidence rule (see 8.3.1) and the defence of *non est factum* (see 11.9): Spencer, 1973. He suggests that the claimant should not be bound by the clause where 'he did not mean to consent to the disputed term, and although he appeared to consent to it, the other party either caused or connived at his mistake': ibid, p 121. The Ontario Court of Appeal took a less strict view than the English courts in *Tilden Rent-a-Car Co v Clendenning* (1978) 83 DLR (3d) 400, refusing to apply *L'Estrange v Graucob* where the contract was made in a 'hurried, informal manner' and it was clear to the other party that the signatory had not read the contract. See also *Trigg v MI Movers International Transport Services Ltd* (1991) 84 DLR (4th) 504, applying the *Tilden* decision without reference to *L'Estrange v Graucob*.

10 For the law relating to the general effect of these on contractual obligations, see Chapter 10.

11 [1951] 1 KB 805.

on it. The defendants relied on the exclusion clause, but the Court of Appeal held that the misrepresentation (albeit innocent) by the assistant of the scope of the clause overrode the fact that the plaintiff had signed the document.

A further possibility of challenge to a signature lies in the plea of *non est factum*, which is an argument that the party signing made a fundamental mistake about the nature of the document. This plea is rarely successful, however.[12] In general, when a person has signed the document, it is taken as conclusive evidence that the person has agreed to the contract and all its terms.[13]

Where the contract has not been signed, the court will be concerned with such matters as the time at which the clause was put forward, the steps which were taken to draw attention to it, the nature of the clause, and the type of document in which it was contained. These matters will now be considered in turn.

9.4.1 Relevance of time

If a contract containing the clause has not been signed, then the *time* at which it is put forward will be important. If it is not put forward until after the contract has been made, then it clearly cannot be incorporated. All the main terms of the contract must be settled at the time of acceptance. This is, in effect, the same rule as was applied in *Roscorla v Thomas*,[14] preventing a promise made after the agreement from being enforced, because no fresh consideration was given for it. In the same way, the promise by one party to give the other the benefit of an exclusion clause will be unenforceable if made after the formation of the contract. Thus, in *Olley v Marlborough Court Hotel*,[15] the plaintiff made the contract for the use of a hotel room at the reception desk. A clause purporting to exclude liability for lost luggage was displayed in the room itself. It was held that this came too late to be incorporated into the contract.[16] The position might have been different if the plaintiff had been a regular user of the hotel, and therefore as a result of a long and consistent 'course of dealing' could be said to have had prior notice of the clause.[17] The defendant might then be entitled to assume that the plaintiff had previously read the clause even if this was not in fact the case.

---

12 It is discussed further in Chapter 11, at 11.9.
13 Collins (2003, p 234) has suggested that a distinction should perhaps be drawn between agreeing to the contractual obligation in general terms and agreeing to the particular provisions. As regards the latter, he suggests that the rules as to 'notice' dealt with in the next section should apply. There is no English case law to support such an approach, sensible though it might be.
14 (1842) 3 QB 234 – see above, 3.8.
15 [1949] 1 KB 532. Note that the liability of a hotel owner for the loss of guests' property is now affected by the Hotel Proprietors Act 1956.
16 Cf also *Thornton v Shoe Lane Parking* [1971] 2 QB 163; [1971] 1 All 686 – ticket from a machine – below, 9.4.3; and *Chapelton v Barry UDC* [1940] 1 KB 532; [1940] 1 All ER 356 – below, 9.4.4.
17 Cf in an non-exclusion clause context, *British Crane and Hire Corp Ltd v Ipswich Plant Hire Ltd* [1975] QB 303 – discussed in Chapter 8, 8.6.2.

Incorporation by a 'course of dealing' was considered in *Kendall (Henry) & Sons v Lillico (William) & Sons Ltd.*[18] Here the contract was between buyers and sellers of animal feed. They had regularly contracted with each other on three or four occasions each month over a period of three years. On each occasion, a 'sold note' had been issued by the seller, which put responsibility for latent defects in the feed on the buyer. The buyer tried to argue that it did not know of this clause in the sold note. However, the House of Lords held that it was bound. A reasonable seller would assume that the buyer, having received more than 100 of these notes containing the clause, and having raised no objection to it, was agreeing to contract on the basis that it was part of the contract. Regularity is important, however, and *Kendall v Lillico* was distinguished in *Hollier v Rambler Motors*,[19] where there had only been three or four contracts over a period of five years. It was held that an exclusion clause contained in an invoice given to the plaintiff after the conclusion of an oral contract for car repairs was not incorporated into the contract. Inconsistency of procedure may also prevent incorporation. In *McCutcheon v MacBrayne*,[20] the plaintiff's agent had regularly shipped goods on the defendant's ship. On some occasions, he was required to sign a 'risk note' containing an exclusion clause, on other occasions the contract was purely oral. The agent arranged for the carriage of the plaintiff's car which was lost as a result of the negligent navigation of the ship. No risk note had been signed, and the House of Lords refused to accept that the exclusion clause could be incorporated from the agent's previous dealings. There was no consistent course of conduct sufficient to allow such an argument to succeed.

9.4.2 Requirement of 'reasonable notice'

More commonly, the clause will be presented as part of a set of standard terms, which the other party will be given or referred to at the time of making the contract. In that situation, the test is whether 'reasonable notice' of the clause has been given. This test was stated in *Parker v South Eastern Railway*,[21] where a clause was contained on a cloakroom ticket, given in exchange for the deposit of a bag. The front of the ticket, which contained a number and date, also said 'See back'. On the other side of the ticket were various clauses, including one excluding liability for goods exceeding the value of £10. The plaintiff's bag, worth £24.50, had been lost. The jury had found that the plaintiff had not read the ticket, nor was he under any obligation to do so. On that basis, the judge had directed that judgment should be given for the plaintiff. The Court of Appeal, however, ordered a new trial, on the basis that the

---

18 [1969] 2 AC 31 – on appeal from *Hardwick Game Farm v Suffolk Agricultural Poultry Producers Association.*
19 [1972] 2 QB 71; [1972] 1 All ER 399.
20 [1964] 1 WLR 125.
21 (1877) 2 CPD 416.

proper test was whether the defendants had given reasonable notice of the conditions contained on the ticket. The relevant principle was stated by Mellish LJ in the following terms:[22]

> I am of the opinion, therefore, that the proper direction to leave to the jury in these cases is that if the person receiving the ticket did not see or know that there was any writing on the ticket, he is not bound by the conditions; that if he knew there was writing, and knew or believed that the writing contained conditions, then he is bound by the conditions; that if he knew there was writing on the ticket, but did not know or believe that the writing contained conditions, nevertheless he would be bound, if the delivering of the ticket to him in such a manner that he could see there was writing upon it, was, in the opinion of the jury, reasonable notice that the writing contained conditions.

The question of what constitutes reasonable notice is, therefore a question of fact. The standard to be applied is what is reasonable as regards the ordinary adult individual, capable of reading English.[23] Thus, in *Thompson v London, Midland and Scottish Railway*,[24] the fact that the plaintiff was illiterate did not help her. The position might be different, however, if the defendant had actual knowledge of the plaintiff's inability to read the terms and conditions. In such a case, the giving of reasonable notice might require rather more of the party wishing to rely on the clause. In *Thompson*, the Court of Appeal in addition held that stating on a ticket 'Issued subject to the conditions and regulations in the company's timetables and notices' was sufficient to draw the other party's attention to the existence of the terms, and thereby to incorporate them into the contract. This was so even though the timetable containing the relevant clause was not available for free, but had to be purchased from the company. This is perhaps at the limits of what could amount to reasonable notice,[25] but the principle remains that the contractual document itself does not need to set out the exclusion clause if it gives reasonable notice of the existence of the clause, and indicates where it can be read. What is reasonable will, of course, depend on all the circumstances. In *Thompson*, for example, the court placed some stress on the fact that the ticket was for a specially advertised excursion, at a particularly low price, and not for a regular service. There is some suggestion in the judgments, though the point is not made very clearly, that a different standard of notice might be required in relation to full-priced regular services. The point seems to be that special conditions, including the possibility of limited liability, were reasonably to be expected in relation to a cheap excursion, whereas there would not be the same level of expectation in relation to regular services.

---

22 (1877) 2 CPD 416, p 423. The principle is stated in terms of the correct direction to a jury, since at that time it was common for civil cases to be heard before a jury.

23 Ibid.

24 [1930] 1 KB 41.

25 Indeed, Treitel (2003, p 218) suggests that the notice might not nowadays be regarded as sufficient.

FOR THOUGHT

Do you think the outcome of *Thompson* would (should) have been the same if the plaintiff had been blind, and carried a white stick?

9.4.3   Incorporation and unusual exclusions

The *Thompson* decision is clearly helpful to the defendant. More recently, the courts have adopted an approach which requires an assessment of the nature of the clause alongside the amount of notice given. Thus, the more unusual or more onerous the exclusion clause, the greater the notice that will be expected to be given. In *Spurling v Bradshaw*,[26] for example, Lord Denning commented that:[27]

> Some exclusion clauses I have seen would need to be printed in red ink on the face of the document with a red hand pointing to it before the notice could be held to be sufficient.

In *Thornton v Shoe Lane Parking Ltd*,[28] this approach was applied, so that a clause displayed on a notice inside a car park, containing extensive exclusions, was held not to be incorporated into a contract which was made by the purchase of a ticket from a machine. The Court of Appeal did not decide definitively the point at which the contract was made, but it was probably when the customer accepted the car park owner's offer by driving up to the barrier, thus causing the machine to issue a ticket. If that was the case, then, applying the same principle as in *Olley v Marlborough Court Hotel*,[29] any conditions or reference to conditions contained on the ticket came too late – the contract was already made. It was not feasible, as would (at least theoretically) be possible if dealing with a human 'ticket issuer', for the recipient to inquire further about the conditions, or to reject the ticket. Even if the ticket could be a valid means of giving notice, however, or if the customer could be required to be put on inquiry by a notice at the entrance stating 'All cars parked at owner's risk', there was an issue about the degree of notice required. The exclusion clause in this case was very widely drawn, and purported to cover negligently caused personal injuries (which the plaintiff had in fact suffered). As a result, the court felt that the defendant needed to take more specific action to bring it to the attention of customers. In the view of Megaw LJ:[30]

---

26 [1956] 2 All ER 121.
27 Ibid, p 125.
28 [1971] 2 QB 163; [1971] 1 All ER 686.
29 [1949] 1 KB 532; [1949] 1 All ER 127 – above, 9.4.1.
30 [1971] 2 QB 163, p 173; [1971] 1 All ER 686, p 692.

> . . . before it can be said that a condition of that sort, restrictive of statutory rights [that is, under the Occupiers' Liability Act 1957], has been fairly excluded there must be some clear indication which would lead an ordinary sensible person to realise, at or before the time of making the contract, that a term of that sort, relating to personal injury, was sought to be included.

In cases such as this, therefore, the nature and scope of the attempted exclusion becomes a relevant factor in relation to incorporation. The issue is not solely procedural, but is affected by the substance of the clause. We have seen that the same approach may be used in relation to other types of clause. Thus, in Chapter 8, it was noted that the same rule operated in *Interfoto Picture Library v Stiletto Visual Programmes*[31] to prevent the incorporation of a clause which was not an exclusion clause, but which was nevertheless exceptional, and unusually onerous. Bradgate has argued that these cases, together with the Court of Appeal decision in *AEG (UK) Ltd v Logic Resource Ltd*,[32] have, in effect, created a common law test of the 'reasonableness' of exclusion clauses.[33] It is not clear, however, that they do go that far. If the person relying on the clause in each case had specifically drawn the other party's attention to it, so that actual notice was given, it seems likely that the courts would have held it to be incorporated and enforceable. The same would be likely to be true if the contract containing the clause had been signed.[34] It is only where there is reliance on 'reasonable notice', rather than actual knowledge, that the courts feel the need to consider the nature of the clause, and whether it is unusual. It is then still the reasonableness of the notice, rather than the reasonableness of the clause itself, that is the issue. The need for a common law test of substantive reasonableness is also unclear (as Bradgate recognises) given the statutory tests contained in the UCTA 1977, and the UTCCR 1999.[35] In the *AEG* case, for example, the Court of Appeal also held the clause to be unreasonable under the 1977 Act. The existence of these statutory protections for the 'vulnerable' contracting party makes it less likely that the courts will expand the approach taken in *Thornton*, etc., into a more general test of the reasonableness of exclusion clauses.

9.4.4 Need for a 'contractual' document

In order to be effectively incorporated, the exclusion clause must generally be contained, or referred to, in something which can be regarded as a contractual document. This is the aspect of the rule that reasonable notice must be given. Notice is unlikely to be regarded as reasonable if the clause appears in something which would not be

---

31 [1988] QB 433; [1988] 1 All ER 348 – see 8.5.1.
32 [1996] CLC 265.
33 Bradgate, 1997.
34 On the basis of *L'Estrange v Graucob* [1934] 2 KB 394 – above, 9.4.
35 Both of which are discussed below, 9.7 and 9.8.

expected to contain contractual terms. Thus, in *Chapelton v Barry UDC*,[36] the plaintiff wished to hire a deckchair. He took a chair from a pile near a notice indicating the price and duration of hire, and requesting hirers to obtain a ticket from the attendant. The plaintiff did so, but when he used the chair it collapsed, causing him injury. It was accepted that the collapse of the chair was due to the negligence of the defendant (Barry UDC), but the council argued that it was protected by a statement on the ticket that 'The council will not be liable for any accident or damage arising from hire of chair'. It was held by the Court of Appeal, however, that the ticket was a mere receipt. It was not a document on which the customer would expect to find contractual terms, and the exclusion clause printed on it was therefore not incorporated. The purpose of the ticket was simply to provide evidence for the hirer that he had discharged his obligation to pay for the chair. It was, the court felt, distinguishable from, for example, a railway ticket 'which contains upon it the terms upon which a railway company agrees to carry the passenger'. The test of which category the document should fall into will, presumably, depend on what information, terms, etc., the court thinks that a reasonable person would expect to find on it. In fact, in this case, the ticket was in any case provided too late, as it was held that the contract was formed when the deckchair was first taken for use, whereas the ticket was not handed over until after this had been done.[37]

9.5 CONSTRUCTION

Once it has been decided that a clause has been incorporated into the contract, the next issue is whether it covers the breach that has occurred. In other words, the wording of the clause must be examined to see if it is apt to apply to the situation which has arisen. This is the called the rule of 'construction', but might equally well be called the rule of 'interpretation'. The clause is being 'constructed' or 'interpreted' to determine its scope.

9.5.1 *Contra proferentem* rule

The rules of construction, like the rules for incorporation, are of general application, and can be used in relation to all clauses within a contract, not just exclusion clauses. The more general issues have been discussed in Chapter 8.[38] There has been much case law, however, involving the proper interpretation of exclusion clauses. In this context, the courts have traditionally taken a stricter approach to construction than elsewhere. The rule of construction has been used as a means of limiting the effect of exclusion clauses, and a person wishing to avoid liability has been required to be very precise in the use of language to achieve that aim. One aspect of this is the *contra proferentem*

---

36 [1940] 1 KB 532; [1940] 1 All ER 356.
37 Thus applying the same principle as in *Olley v Marlborough Court Hotel* [1949] 1 KB 532; [1949] 1 All ER 127 – above, 9.4.1.
38 Above, 8.5.2.

rule, whereby an exclusion clause is interpreted against the person putting it forward. Thus, in *Andrews v Singer,* [39] a clause excluding liability in relation to implied terms was ruled ineffective to exclude liability for breach of an express term. Similarly, in *Wallis, Son and Wells v Pratt,* [40] it was held that a clause stating that the suppliers of goods gave no 'warranty' in relation to them did not protect them from being liable for a breach of 'condition'.[41] Moreover, if there is ambiguity in the language used, this will be construed in the claimant's favour. Thus, it has been held that a reference in an insurance contract to excess 'loads' did not apply where a car was carrying more *passengers* than the number which it was constructed to carry.[42] It has also been held that the phrase 'consequential losses' does not cover direct losses flowing naturally from the breach, such as lost profits.[43]

Particular difficulty can arise where the defendant seeks to exclude liability for negligence in the performance of a contract. The principles to be applied here were set out by the Privy Council in *Canada Steamship Lines Ltd v The King*.[44] The court was dealing with Canadian law, but the principles have been taken as applying to English law as well.[45] They were stated by Lord Morton as follows:

(1) If the clause contains language which expressly exempts the person in whose favour it is made (hereafter called 'the *proferens*') from the consequence of the negligence of his own servants, effect must be given to that provision . . .

(2) If there is no express reference to negligence, the court must consider whether the words used are wide enough, in their ordinary meaning, to cover negligence on the part of the servants of the *proferens* . . .

(3) If the words used are wide enough for the above purpose, the court must then consider whether the 'head of damage may be based on some ground other than negligence' . . . The 'other' ground must not be so fanciful or remote that the *proferens* cannot be supposed to have desired protection against it; but subject to this qualification . . . the existence of a possible head of damage other than negligence is fatal to the *proferens* even if the

---

39 [1934] 1 KB 17.
40 [1910] 2 KB 1003.
41 For the distinction between warranties and conditions, see 8.5.5.
42 *Houghton v Trafalgar Insurance* [1954] 1 QB 247.
43 *Hotel Services Ltd v Hilton International Hotels (UK) Ltd* [2000] 1 All ER Comm 750, CA. This was in the context of a clause referring to 'indirect and consequential' losses. The court recognised that in other contexts 'consequential' loss could be interpreted to cover direct losses: here, however, it should be interpreted together with 'indirect' and taken to refer only to losses falling within the second limb of the remoteness rule in *Hadley v Baxendale* (1854) 9 Exch 341; 156 ER 145 – for which see Chapter 18, 18.5.2.
44 [1952] AC 192, p 208.
45 For recent confirmation of this, see, for example, *EE Caledonia Ltd v Orbit Valve plc* [1994] 1 WLR 1515; *Shell Chemical v P & O Tankers* [1995] 1 Lloyd's Rep 297; *Toomey v Eagle Star Insurance* [1995] 2 Lloyd's Rep 88 and *Monarch Airlines Ltd v London Luton Airport Ltd* [1997] CLC 698.

words used are *prima facie* wide enough to cover negligence on the part of his servants.

This approach is stated in terms of excluding liability for the acts of the defendant's servants, but it will apply equally to the situation where the defendant is potentially directly liable for negligence.

As the first principle makes clear, if the drafter of a contract wishes to ensure that negligence liability is covered, the safest way is to say so explicitly. The use of the word 'negligence' is obviously sufficient, but synonyms may also be enough. In *Monarch Airlines Ltd v London Luton Airport Ltd*,[46] for example, it was held that the phrase 'act, omission, neglect or default' was clearly intended to cover negligence.

This is relatively straightforward. It is when the drafter of the contract decides to use general words such as 'any loss howsoever caused' that difficulties start to arise.[47] In that situation, the second and third principles stated by Lord Morton come into play. A distinction then needs to be drawn between the situations where the defendant is liable only for negligence and where there is some other possible basis for liability. In the latter situation, the defendant will need to use words which specifically cover negligence in order to avoid liability. General words which purport to cover 'all liabilities' may well not be enough. If, for example, a bailee is strictly liable for the safety of the bailor's goods, a general clause excluding liability will be taken to attach to the strict liability, and not to liability for negligence. Similarly, in *White v John Warwick*,[48] in a contract for the hire of a bicycle, a clause exempting the owners from liability for personal injuries was held to cover only breach of strict contractual liability as to the condition of the bicycle, and not injuries resulting from negligence in the fitting of the saddle.[49]

The position is different, however, if the only basis of liability which exists is negligence liability. Then the implication of Lord Morton's second principle is that general words may be sufficient.[50] In *Alderslade v Hendon Laundry*,[51] the plaintiff had not received certain handkerchiefs which he had left with the defendant laundry. A clause in the contract stated 'The maximum amount allowed for lost or damaged articles is 20 times the charge made for laundering'. Lord Greene MR took the view that as regards loss (as opposed to damage), the laundry could not be regarded as undertaking a strict obligation, but only to take reasonable care of items (that is, not to be

---

46 [1997] CLC 698.
47 It is not clear why the drafters of contracts do not explicitly refer to negligence. Maybe there is a feeling that the other party might be put off by such an explicit recognition of the possibility that their proposed contracting partner will not take reasonable care in the performance of the contract.
48 [1953] 2 All ER 1021.
49 Excluding liability for negligence giving rise to personal injury is now in any case prohibited by s 2 of the UCTA 1977: below, 9.7.5.
50 *Joseph Travers & Sons Ltd v Cooper* [1915] KB 73.
51 [1945] KB 189; [1945] 1 All ER 244.

negligent). On that basis, the clause was apt to cover negligence liability. Salmon LJ in *Hollier v Rambler Motors*,[52] however, in discussing this case, took the view that it was the perception of the customer that was important:[53]

> I think that the ordinary sensible housewife, or indeed anyone else who sends washing to the laundry, who saw that clause must have appreciated that almost always goods are lost or damaged because of the laundry's negligence, and, therefore, this clause could apply only to limit the liability of the laundry, when they were in fault or negligent.

This must be regarded as having modified the approach taken by the Court of Appeal in *Alderslade* itself. The position thus now seems to be that where the reasonable claimant would read a clause as covering negligence, the courts will be prepared to allow exclusion without any specific reference to negligence, or the use of a general phrase clearly including negligence.[54] In the end, it is a matter of attempting to assess the intentions and reasonable expectations of the parties. Thus, in *Hollier v Rambler Motors*,[55] the plaintiff's car was at the defendant's premises when it was damaged by fire, caused by the defendant's negligence. There was a clause in the contract which stated 'The company is not responsible for damage caused by fire to customers' cars on the premises'. In the Court of Appeal, the view was taken that customers would assume that this clause related to fires which arose without negligence on the part of the defendant (though as a matter of law there would in fact be no liability in such a case). The clause was not, in effect, an exclusion of liability, but simply a 'warning' that the defendant was not, as a matter of law, liable for non-negligent fire damage. If the defendant wanted to exclude liability for negligence, this should have been done explicitly. Even where the only possible liability is for negligence, therefore, it is still better to use specific rather than general words.

The position as regards exclusion of liability for negligence was significantly affected by the UCTA 1977,[56] and this may mean that, at least as far as consumers are concerned, the above rules will be of less significance. Clauses purporting to exclude negligence are either void (if relating to death or personal injury) or subject to a requirement of 'reasonableness'. In the consumer context the courts may well be reluctant to find that attempts to exclude liability for failing to take reasonable care in the performance of a contract are 'reasonable', even where the negligence is the fault of the defendant's employee rather than the defendant personally. In the commercial

---

52 [1972] 2 QB 71; [1972] 1 All ER 399. This case has been criticised by Barendt, 1972.

53 Ibid, p 79; p 405.

54 Cf *Rutter v Palmer* [1922] 2 KB 87 – garage in possession of the plaintiff's car with a view to selling it; clause stating 'Customers' cars are driven by your staff at customers' sole risk' was wide enough to cover negligence by the driver.

55 [1972] 2 QB 71; [1972] 1 All ER 399. Note that this case has been criticised by Barendt, 1972.

56 Below, 9.7.5.

sphere, however, as has been indicated above, the courts still make regular reference to Lord Morton's principles in the *Canada Steamship* case.[57]

9.5.2   Relaxation of the rule of construction

More generally, the existence of stricter statutory controls over exclusion clauses has encouraged the courts to take the line that there is no need for the rule of construction to be used in an artificial way to limit their scope. The consumer and the standard form contract are dealt with by the UCTA 1977 (and now also by the UTCCR 1999).[58] Businesses negotiating at arm's length should be expected to look after themselves. If they enter into contracts containing exclusion clauses, they must be presumed to know what they are doing. Thus, on three occasions since the passage of the UCTA 1977, the House of Lords has criticised an approach to the interpretation of exclusion clauses in commercial contracts, which involves straining their plain meaning in order to limit their effect. In *Photo Production Ltd v Securicor Transport Ltd*,[59] Lord Wilberforce commented that in the light of parliamentary intervention to protect consumers (by means of the UCTA 1977):[60]

> . . . in commercial matters generally, when the parties are not of unequal bargaining power, and when risks are normally borne by insurance, not only is the case for judicial intervention undemonstrated, but there is everything to be said, and this seems to have been Parliament's intention, for leaving the parties free to apportion the risks as they think fit and for respecting their decisions.

Lord Diplock, agreeing with Lord Wilberforce, commented that:[61]

> In commercial contracts negotiated between businessmen capable of looking after their own interests and of deciding how risks inherent in the performance of various kinds of contract can be most economically borne (generally by insurance), it is, in my view, wrong to place a strained construction on words in an exclusion clause which are clear and fairly susceptible of one meaning only . . .

Similarly, in *Ailsa Craig Fishing Co Ltd v Malvern Fishing Co Ltd*,[62] Lord Wilberforce

---

57 See, for example, *EE Caledonia Ltd v Orbit Valve plc* [1994] 1 WLR 1515; *Shell Chemical v P & O Tankers* [1995] 1 Lloyd's Rep 297; *Toomey v Eagle Star Insurance* [1995] 2 Lloyd's Rep 88; and *Monarch Airlines Ltd v London Luton Airport Ltd* [1997] CLC 698.
58 Below, 9.7 and 9.8.
59 [1980] AC 827; [1980] 1 All ER 556.
60 Ibid, p 843; p 561.
61 Ibid, p 851; p 568.
62 [1983] 1 All ER 101.

again expressed the view (particularly in relation to clauses limiting liability, rather than excluding it altogether) that:[63]

> . . . one must not strive to create ambiguities by strained construction, as I think the appellants have striven to do. The relevant words must be given, if possible, their natural, plain meaning.

Lord Fraser agreed that limitation clauses need not:[64]

> . . . be judged by the specially exacting standards which are applied to exclusion and indemnity clauses . . . It is enough . . . that the clause must be clear and unambiguous.

Finally, in *George Mitchell (Chesterhall) Ltd v Finney Lock Seeds Ltd*,[65] Lord Bridge reaffirmed the need for straightforward interpretation:[66]

> The relevant condition, read as a whole, unambiguously limits the appellants' liability to replacement of the seeds or refund of the price. It is only possible to read an ambiguity into it by the process of strained construction which was deprecated by Lord Diplock in the *Photo Production* case . . . and by Lord Wilberforce in the *Ailsa Craig* case.

The interpretation of exclusion clauses in commercial agreements should now also take into account the approach of Lord Hoffmann in *Investors Compensation Scheme Ltd v West Bromwich Building Society*,[67] as discussed in Chapter 8.[68] That this is the correct approach was confirmed by the Court of Appeal in *Keele University v Price Waterhouse*.[69]

FOR THOUGHT

Is it right that all commercial agreements should be approached in this way? Doesn't the fact that the parties to a business contract may be of very different bargaining strength mean that in some circumstances a strict approach to interpretation would be justified?

---

63 [1983] 1 All ER 101, p 104.
64 Ibid, pp 105–06.
65 [1983] 2 AC 803; [1983] 2 All ER 737.
66 Ibid, pp 814–15; p 742.
67 [1998] 1 All ER 98.
68 Above, 8.5.3.
69 [2004] EWCA Civ 583; [2004] PNLR 43. This case is also an example of the court deciding not to consider the 'reasonableness' test under the UCTA 1977 because, on its true construction, the clause did not cover the loss for which the claimant sought to recover.

9.5.3 Fundamental breach

At one time, the view was taken by some courts, and in particular the Court of Appeal, that some breaches of contract are so serious that no exclusion clause can cover them. This was expressed in the so-called doctrine of fundamental breach. This doctrine found its origins in shipping law, where there is strong authority that if a ship 'deviates' from its agreed route, there can be no exclusion of liability in relation to events which occur after the deviation, even though the deviation was not the cause of any loss which occurs.[70] Applied more generally to the law of contract, it took two forms. One was that there are certain terms within the contract which are so fundamental that there cannot be exclusion for breach of them. Such would be the situation where the contract stipulated for the supply of peas, and beans were provided instead.[71] The supplier in such a case has departed so far from the basic contractual obligation that some courts felt that it could not be justifiable to allow him to exclude liability. To do so would appear to make a mockery of the whole idea of a contractual obligation. If, for example, a person who has contracted to sell potatoes supplies the same weight of coal, it surely ought not to be permissible to allow reliance on a broadly written exclusion clause which states 'the supplier may substitute any other goods for those specified in the contract'. The rules of incorporation and construction do not have any necessary effect on such a clause. The answer appeared to be to treat the promise to supply potatoes as a 'fundamental term'. Any breach of this term would provide a remedy to the other party irrespective of an exclusion clause.

Stated in this form the doctrine had close links with the 'deviation' principle in shipping law, which similarly is concerned with the breach of a specific obligation regarded as being central to the contract. The second form of the doctrine of fundamental breach was different in that it looked not at the particular term which had been broken, but at the overall effects of the breach which had occurred. If the breach was so serious that it could be said to have destroyed the whole contract, then again, exclusion of liability should not be possible. Two cases illustrate these two aspects of the doctrine: *Karsales v Wallis*[72] and *Harbutt's Plasticine Ltd v Wayne Tank and Pump Co Ltd*.[73] In *Karsales v Wallis*, the contract was for the supply of a Buick car, which the plaintiff had inspected and found to be in good condition. When delivered (late at night), however, it had to be towed, because it was incapable of self-propulsion. Amongst other things, the cylinder head had been removed, the valves had been burnt out, and two of the pistons had been broken. The defendant purported to rely on a clause of the agreement which stated:

---

70 See, for example, *Joseph Thorley Ltd v Orchis SS Co Ltd* [1907] 1 KB 41.
71 *Chanter v Hopkins* (1838) 3 M & W 252. See also *The Bow Cedar* [1980] 2 Lloyd's Rep 601 – contract for ground nut oil; goods supplied 50 per cent ground nut oil, 50 per cent soya bean oil.
72 [1956] 2 All ER 866.
73 [1970] 1 QB 447; [1970] 1 All ER 225.

No condition or warranty that the vehicle is roadworthy, or as to its age, condition or fitness for purpose is given by the owner or implied herein.

The county judge held for the defendant, but the Court of Appeal reversed this. The majority of the court (Lord Denning reached the same conclusion, but on slightly different grounds) held that what had been delivered was not, in effect, a 'car'. The defendant's 'performance' was totally different from that which had been contemplated by the contract (that is, the supply of a motor vehicle in working order). There was, therefore, a breach of a fundamental term of the agreement, and the exclusion clause had no application.

In *Harbutt's Plasticine*, the contract involved the supply of pipework in the plaintiff's factory. The type of piping used was unsuitable, and resulted in a fire which destroyed the whole of the plaintiff's factory. The obligation to supply piping that was fit for its purpose could clearly have been broken in various ways, not all of which would have led to serious damage to the plaintiff's premises. In this case, however, the consequences of the defendant's failure to meet its obligation in this respect were so serious that the Court of Appeal regarded it as a 'fundamental breach' of the contract, precluding any reliance on an exclusion clause.

These two Court of Appeal decisions illustrate that a 'fundamental breach' could occur either through the breach of a particularly important term, or through a breach which had the consequences of destroying the whole basis of the contract.

In arriving at its decision in *Harbutt's Plasticine*, however, the Court of Appeal had to deal with the views expressed by the House of Lords in *Suisse Atlantique Société d'Armemente SA v Rotterdamsche Kolen Centrale NV*.[74] The case concerned a charter which included provisions whereby, if there were delays, the charterers' liability was limited to paying $1,000 per day 'demurrage'. The owners attempted to argue that the charterers' breach was so serious that the demurrage clause should not apply, and that they should be able to recover their full losses. The House of Lords rejected this and, in so doing, expressed strong disapproval of the argument that there was a substantive rule of law which meant that certain types of breach automatically prevented reliance on an exclusion clause. As Viscount Dilhorne commented:[75]

> In my view, it is not right to say that the law prohibits and nullifies a clause exempting or limiting liability for a fundamental breach or breach of a fundamental term. Such a rule of law would involve a restriction on freedom of contract and in the older cases I can find no trace of it.

As this quotation illustrates, the House was of the opinion that the parties should generally be allowed to determine their obligations and the effect of exclusion clauses in their contract. If there was a breach which appeared fundamental, then it was a

---

74 [1967] 1 AC 361; [1966] 2 All ER 61.
75 Ibid, p 392; p 67.

question of trying to determine the parties' intentions as to whether such a breach was intended to be covered by any exclusion clause. Of course, as Lord Wilberforce noted,[76] 'the courts are entitled to insist, as they do, that the more radical the breach, the clearer must be the language if it is to be covered', but the question is one of the proper construction of the clause, and not a rule of law.

In *Harbutt's Plasticine*, the Court of Appeal attempted to distinguish *Suisse Atlantique* on the basis that in that case the parties had continued with the charter even after the alleged fundamental breach. The Court of Appeal therefore argued that the principles outlined by the House of Lords in *Suisse Atlantique* should apply only where there was an affirmation of the contract by the parties following the breach, and not where the breach itself brought the contract to an end. In the latter type of situation, there should be no possibility of reliance on an exclusion clause. The difficulty with this argument was that it is a well-established principle in contract law that a breach never in itself brings a contract to an end.[77] The party not in breach always has the option (if the breach is a serious one) of either accepting the breach and terminating the contract or affirming the contract and simply suing for damages. Suppose, for example, there is a contract for the sale of components which are to be supplied with certain fixing holes drilled in them. If, when delivered, the fixing holes are not there, this will amount to a breach of 'condition' by virtue of s 13 of the Sale of Goods Act 1979.[78] The buyer will have the right to accept the breach, reject the goods and sue for damages. Alternatively, however, the buyer may affirm the contract, accept the goods, and simply sue for the cost of having the holes drilled, and any other consequential losses. The Court of Appeal in *Harbutt's Plasticine* took the view that this did not apply to certain fundamental breaches of contract, which themselves brought the contract to an end, without the need for acceptance by the party not in breach. This view, was, however, firmly rejected by the House of Lords in *Photo Production Ltd v Securicor Transport Ltd*,[79] which overruled *Harbutt's Plasticine*, and finally disposed of the argument that certain types of fundamental breach could never be covered by an exclusion clause.[80]

The facts of the *Photo Production* case were as follows. The plaintiffs owned a factory, and engaged the defendants to provide security services, which included a night patrol. Unfortunately, one of the guards employed by the defendants to carry out these duties started a fire on the premises which got out of control, and destroyed the entire factory. Thus, rather than protecting the plaintiffs' property as they had been contracted to do, the defendants could be said to have achieved the exact opposite. The contract, however, contained a very broadly-worded exclusion clause, which, on its face,

---

76 [1967] 1 AC 361, p 432; [1966] 2 All ER 61, p 92.
77 This rule is discussed further in Chapter 17, 17.6.1.
78 See 8.6.11.
79 [1980] AC 827; [1980] 1 All ER 556.
80 See also s 9 of the UCTA 1977, which confirms the position that exclusion clauses always survive a breach of contract, and can be given effect (subject to the other restrictions contained in the Act) whether or not the contract has been terminated as result of the breach.

seemed to cover even the very serious breach of the agreement which had occurred. The Court of Appeal took the view that this could not protect the defendants. There had been a fundamental breach, and the exclusion clause was ineffective. The House of Lords, however, took this opportunity to state its position with no possible ambiguity. It ruled that there was no rule of law that a fundamental breach of contract prevented an exclusion clause from being effective. The so-called doctrine of fundamental breach was in fact no more than an aspect of the doctrine of construction. Of course, it was the case that the more serious the breach of contract, the clearer the words would need to be which would exclude liability for it. But, if two businesses had negotiated an agreement containing a clause which on its plain wording covered such a breach, there was no reason why the courts should not give effect to it. In the present case, the House, while noting the breadth of the exclusion clause, also noted that the plaintiffs were paying a very low rate for the defendants' services. It was therefore not unreasonable that the defendants should have a low level of liability. The *ratio* of the case was not, however, that the clause such as that under consideration could be enforced because it was reasonable in all the circumstances, but because on its true construction it covered the breach.

The decision in *Photo Productions* is a strong affirmation of the 'freedom of contract' approach to commercial agreements, and a rejection of an 'interventionist' role for the courts.

9.5.4 The current position

The demise of the doctrine of fundamental breach as a rule of law (and there has been no attempt to revive it since the *Photo Production* decision) has to some extent simplified the law in this area. It may still be difficult to decide in particular cases, however, what to do where a breach effectively negates the whole purpose of the contract. It is a matter of looking at the precise wording of the exclusion clause and trying to determine the intentions of the parties in relation to it. The likelihood of exclusion being effective will decrease with the seriousness of the breach, but it is now always a question of balance, rather than the application of a firm rule.

In considering where the balance is likely to be struck, some of the older case law may still be relevant in indicating the types of situation where the courts will require considerable convincing that the parties really did intend that a serious breach was intended to be covered by the exclusion clause. Some of the cases referred to above, such as *Karsales v Wallis*[81] and *Harbutt's Plasticine Ltd v Wayne Tank and Pump Co Ltd*,[82] may be relevant in this context. A decision to similar effect is *Pinnock Bros v Lewis and Peat Ltd*,[83] where the contract was for the supply of copra cake to be used as cattle feed. The cake was contaminated with castor beans, and the cattle became ill.

---

81 [1956] 2 All ER 866.
82 [1970] 1 QB 447; [1970] 1 All ER 225.
83 [1923] 1 KB 690.

There was an exclusion clause expressed to cover liabilities for 'defects' in the goods. The court refused to apply the clause, holding that what was supplied was so contaminated that it could not be called 'copra cake' at all. On its proper construction, therefore, the clause referring to 'defects' was not apt to cover the situation.[84] In *Glynn v Margetson & Co*,[85] a bill of lading relating to a contract for the carriage of a cargo of oranges from Malaga to Liverpool contained a clause allowing considerable freedom (referring to most of Europe and the 'the coasts of Africa') in the route which could be taken 'for the purposes of delivering . . . cargo . . . or for any other purposes whatsoever'. The ship, having loaded the oranges, went to a port some 350 miles in the opposite direction from Liverpool to collect another load before proceeding to Liverpool. The oranges had deteriorated on arrival as a result of the prolonged voyage. The detour made here was strictly within the terms of the bill of lading,[86] but the House of Lords nevertheless held the carrier liable. It took the view that the clause in the bill of lading could not have been intended to allow the carrier to act in a way which was inconsistent with the 'main purpose' of the contract, that is, to deliver the cargo from Malaga to Liverpool. Finally, in *Gibaud v Great Eastern Railway Co*,[87] the contract was for the storage of a bicycle in the cloakroom at a railway station. It was in fact left in the booking hall, from which it was stolen. The owner had been given a ticket which limited the railway's liability to £5. The Court of Appeal considered the argument that the defendant could not rely on the clause because the bicycle had not been kept in the cloakroom. It accepted, following *Lilley v Doubleday*,[88] that where the bailee of goods had undertaken to store them in a particular warehouse but in fact stored them elsewhere, the benefit of an exclusion clause would be lost. The principle was that:[89]

> . . . if you undertake to do a thing in a certain way, or to keep a thing in a certain place, with certain conditions protecting it, and have broken the contract by not doing the thing contracted for in the way contracted for, or not keeping the article in the place where you have contracted to keep it, you cannot rely on the conditions which were only intended to protect you if you carried out the contract in the way in which you had contracted to do it.

On the facts, however, it was held that there was no binding obligation to store the bicycle in the cloakroom, so that the railway company was able to take the benefit of the clause.

The courts are also likely to be reluctant to find that a clause allows a defendant to

---

84 Note that the facts of this case would now fall within the scope of s 6 of the UCTA 1977 – see below, 9.7.19.
85 [1893] AC 351.
86 So this was not a 'deviation' case in the strict sense – see above, 9.5.3.
87 [1921] 2 KB 426.
88 (1881) 7 QBD 510.
89 [1921] 2 KB 426, p 435.

escape liability where there has been a deliberate breach of contract. Thus, in *Sze Hai Tong Bank Ltd v Rambler Cycle Co Ltd*,[90] the carrier delivered goods to a person who was known to have no authority to receive them,[91] and this resulted in a loss to the owner. The carrier attempted to rely on a clause in the bill of lading which stated that its liability ended once the goods were 'discharged' from the ship. The Privy Council held, however, that the clause could not have been intended to cover the carrier if the goods had simply been handed over to a passer-by. It must have been intended only to cover an authorised discharge, and not a deliberate delivery to an unauthorised recipient.[92]

9.6 STATUTORY CONTROLS

In many situations, the common law controls discussed in the previous sections have effectively been superseded by statutory controls contained in the Unfair Contract Terms Act (UCTA) 1977 and the Unfair Terms in Consumer Contracts Regulations (UTCCR) 1999.[93] Although the issues of incorporation and construction may still be important, it is likely that the statutory provisions will determine the outcome of the case where the clause (a) is contained in a consumer contract, or (b) forms part of the defendant's written standard terms, or (c) purports to exclude liability for the defendant's negligence. Despite the fact that, strictly speaking, the common law rules are logically prior to any consideration of the statutory provisions – so that if a clause is not incorporated or does not cover the breach it can have no effect at all, and the statutory provisions are irrelevant – in practice, they will often be considered first.

That this is not necessarily the case, however, is demonstrated by the Court of Appeal decision in *Keele University v Price Waterhouse*,[94] where, having interpreted an exclusion clause in a way that meant that it did not cover the loss for which the claimant was seeking compensation, the court declined to consider the UCTA 1977, treating the question of reasonableness under that Act as 'moot'.[95]

The Law Commission has put forward proposals which would result in the UCTA 1977 and the UTCCR 1999 being replaced by a new single piece of legislation.[96] These proposals are discussed below, at 9.10.

---

90 [1959] AC 576.
91 The person was in fact the buyer of the goods, but the seller had not authorised delivery as was required by the contract. The buyer defaulted on payment for the goods.
92 The court also felt that the interpretation contended for by the carrier would fall foul of the 'main purpose' rule, as applied in *Glynn v Margetson & Co* [1893] AC 351, above.
93 SI 1999/2083.
94 [2004] EWCA Civ 583; [2004] PNLR 43.
95 Ibid, para 29.
96 *Unfair Terms in Contracts*, Law Com No 292, Scot Law Com No 199, Cm 6464, 2005.

9.7   UNFAIR CONTRACT TERMS ACT 1977

The UCTA 1977 has had a very significant effect on the law relating to exclusion clauses. Where it applies, it has to a large extent replaced the common law rules. It must be remembered, however, that the UCTA 1977 does not apply to all contracts. The first point for discussion here is therefore the precise scope of the Act.

9.7.1   Scope of the UCTA 1977

There are certain contracts, listed in Sched 1, which are not within the scope of ss 2–4 (which are the main protective provisions) at all. These include:[97]

(a)   contracts of insurance;
(b)   contracts concerning the creation or transfer of interests in land: this includes continuing covenants under a lease: *Electricity Supply Nominees v IAF Group*;[98]
(c)   contracts concerning the creation or transfer of intellectual property rights (copyright, patent, etc);
(d)   contracts relating to the formation, dissolution, or constitution of a company, partnership, or unincorporated association;
(e)   contracts relating to the creation or transfer of securities.

The UCTA 1977 also has only limited application in relation to various types of shipping contract, including carriage of goods by sea.[99] In relation to contracts of employment, s 2(1) and (2) (which deal with exclusion of liability for negligence) do not apply other than in favour of an employee. It was suggested in *Brigden v American Express*[100] that an employee could potentially use s 3 of the Act against terms put forward by an employer (though on the facts the claim failed). This was specifically disapproved by the Court of Appeal in *Commerzbank AG v Keen*.[101] The Court held that an employee did not contract with his or her employee 'as a consumer', and that the terms of employment were not standard terms of the employer's *business* (which in this case was the business of banking).

It is always advisable to check the provisions of Sched 1 in relation to contracts falling into the above categories.

---

97 UCTA 1977, Sched 2, para 1.
98 [1993] 3 All ER 372.
99 Contracts of marine salvage or towage, any charterparty of a ship or hovercraft, and any contract for the carriage of goods by ship or hovercraft are subject to s 2(1) (which deals with death or personal injury caused by negligence), but not to the other provisions of s 2, or ss 3, 4 or 7: UCTA 1977, Sched 1, para 2.
100 [2000] IRLR 94.
101 [2006] EWCA Civ 1536; [2006] 2 CLC 844.

9.7.2 'Business' liability

The next limitation on the scope of the UCTA 1977 which must be noted appears in s 1(3). This states that ss 2 to 7 apply only to:

> . . . business liability, that is, liability for breach of obligations or duties arising (a) from things done or to be done in the course of a business . . . or (b) from the occupation of premises used for the business purposes of the occupier.[102]

In general, therefore, the non-business contractor is free to include exclusion clauses, without their being controlled by the UCTA 1977.[103] In many situations, the test of whether obligations arise in the course of a 'business' will not give rise to problems, but it is perhaps unfortunate that the Act does not contain a comprehensive definition of what is meant by 'business'.

9.7.3 Meaning of 'business'

Section 14 states that ' "business" includes a profession and the activities of any government department or local or public authority'. This leaves open the position of organisations such as charities or universities, which may engage in business activities, but might not be thought to be contracting 'in the course of a business'.[104] The protective policy of the UCTA 1977 would suggest that such situations ought to be covered. The phrase 'in the course of a business' has, however, been interpreted fairly restrictively in relation to its use in another context within the Act. Section 12 uses it as part of the definition of whether a person 'deals as a consumer' for the purposes of buying goods, which is an important consideration in relation to the application of s 6. In *R and B Customs Brokers v UDT*,[105] the plaintiff was a private company involved in the export business. A car was bought by the company for the personal and business use of the directors. It was held by the Court of Appeal that it was not bought 'in the course of a business', because the plaintiff's business was not that of buying and selling cars. If this approach is taken in relation to s 1(3), it would mean, for example, that a university which provides car parking facilities on its site in return for payment, or a charity which makes money by organising a 'car boot' sale and selling 'pitches', would not be covered by the UCTA 1977. It is difficult to see, however, why the other contracting party should be any less protected in such a situation than if dealing with a commercial

---

102 But note that where access is obtained to premises for recreational or educational purposes, any liability for loss or damage from the dangerous state of the premises is not 'business liability' unless granting access for such purposes falls within the business purposes of the occupier: UCTA, s 1(3)(b) as amended by the Occupiers' Liability Act 1984.

103 Though the scope of s 6, which deals with sale of goods contracts, is wider – see 9.7.19, below.

104 Though a publicly funded University might be treated as a 'public authority', as it is in the Freedom of Information Act 2000 (and, probably, for the purposes of the Human Rights Act 1998).

105 [1998] 1 All ER 847.

organisation, which might well be in no better position to meet financial liabilities, or to insure against them, than the university or charity.

Some doubt about the correctness of the decision in *R and B Customs Brokers* was expressed by the Court of Appeal in *Stevenson v Rogers* [106] in considering whether a sale was 'in the course of business' for the purposes of s 14 of the Sale of Goods Act 1979. It was suggested there that the earlier decision should be confined to its particular facts, that is, the interpretation of s 12 of the UCTA 1977, and not necessarily applied elsewhere. The court therefore refused to apply the same approach in interpreting the Sale of Goods Act 1979. It would be difficult (though not impossible), however, to argue that within one statute the same phrase has been used with different meanings. Moreover, in *Feldarol Foundry plc v Hermes Leasing (London) Ltd*,[107] which involved the purchase of a car by an aluminium foundry for the use of its managing director, the Court of Appeal, without much reluctance, held that it was bound by the approach taken in *R and B Customs Brokers*. It remains the case therefore that, pending a decision to the contrary by the House of Lords, the interpretation of 'in the course of a business', where that phrase is used in the UCTA 1977, should follow the approach taken in *R and B Customs Brokers*.

9.7.4 Disclaimers

The final issue in relation to the scope of the UCTA 1977 concerns the types of clause which are covered. As was noted at the start of this chapter, in drawing up a contract, it is possible to attempt to avoid liabilities in a number of ways. The most obvious is by an exclusion clause which states that in the event of a breach there will be no liability, or that it will be limited to a particular sum. It is also possible, however, to attempt to achieve the same objective by clauses which define the obligations arising under the contract restrictively ('disclaimers'), or make the enforcement of a liability subject to restrictive conditions (for example, 'all claims must be made within 48 hours of the conclusion of the contract'). Section 13 makes it clear that all clauses of this kind which have the effect of excluding or restricting liability are generally caught by the Act's provisions. It states:

(1) To the extent that this Part of the Act prevents the exclusion or restriction of any liability, it also prevents:
  (a) making the liability or its enforcement subject to restrictive or onerous conditions;
  (b) excluding or restricting any right or remedy in respect of the liability, or subjecting a person to any prejudice in consequence of his pursuing any such right or remedy;
  (c) excluding or restricting rules of evidence and procedure; and (to that

---

106 [1999] 1 All ER 613 – discussed above, 8.6.12.
107 [2004] EWCA Civ 747; (2004) 101 LSG 32.

extent) ss 2 and 5–7 also prevent excluding or restricting liability by reference to terms and notices which exclude or restrict the relevant obligation or duty.

(2) But an agreement in writing to submit present or future differences to arbitration is not to be treated under this Part of this Act as excluding or restricting any liability.

It should be noted that the final words of s 13(1), which deal with avoiding liability by the definition of contractual obligations,[108] do not apply to s 3 or 4. As will be seen below, the terms of s 3, which is concerned primarily with non-negligent contractual liability, are themselves wide enough to cover clauses which define obligations. Section 4 is concerned with one particular type of clause, the indemnity clause, so that there is probably no need for the provisions of s 13 to apply.

In *Smith v Eric S Bush*,[109] the House of Lords confirmed that s 13 extends s 2 of the UCTA 1977 to a clause which is in the form of a disclaimer, which in this case was given by a surveyor providing a valuation of a property to the plaintiff, via a building society. The valuation was stated to be given without any acceptance of responsibility as to its accuracy. This was held to be an 'exclusion clause' within the scope of the UCTA 1977, and to fall foul of its requirement of 'reasonableness'.[110] Similarly, in *Stewart Gill v Horatio Myer & Co Ltd*,[111] the Court of Appeal held that a clause restricting a right of set-off or counterclaim could be regarded as an exclusion clause, and therefore within the scope of the UCTA 1977.

9.7.5 Exclusion of negligence under the UCTA 1977

Section 2 of the UCTA 1977 is concerned with clauses which attempt to exclude business liability for 'negligence', which is defined for the purposes of the Act in s 1(1) to cover the breach:

(a) of any obligation, arising from the express or implied terms of a contract, to take reasonable care or exercise reasonable skill in the performance of the contract;

(b) of any common law duty to take reasonable care or exercise reasonable skill (but not any stricter duty);

(c) of the common duty of care imposed by the Occupiers' Liability Act 1957.

Thus, it applies to negligent performance of a contract (sub-s (a)); the tort of negligence

---

108 These words have been criticised by Yates (1982, pp 75–81) in relation to their application to s 6 of the UCTA 1977 (for which, see below, 9.7.19), and more generally in terms of logical inconsistency.
109 [1990] AC 831; [1989] 2 All ER 514.
110 For which see below, 9.7.10.
111 [1992] 2 All ER 257.

independent of any contract (sub-s (b)); and the statutory duty of care imposed on occupiers towards lawful visitors (sub-s (c)).

Section 2 states:

(1) A person cannot by reference to any contract term or to a notice given to persons generally or to particular persons exclude or restrict his liability for death or personal injury resulting from negligence.

(2) In the case of other loss or damage, a person cannot so exclude or restrict his liability for negligence except in so far as the term or notice satisfies the requirement of reasonableness.

(3) Where a contract term or notice purports to exclude or restrict liability for negligence a person's agreement to or awareness of it is not of itself to be taken as indicating his voluntary acceptance of such a risk.

The level of control imposed by s 2 thus depends on the consequences of the negligence. To the extent that the exclusion clause attempts to limit liability for death or personal injury resulting from negligence, it will be totally ineffective (s 2(1)). As regards any other types of loss or damage, the clause will be effective to the extent that the clause satisfies the 'requirement of reasonableness' set out in s 11 of the UCTA 1977.[112] It is not clear what the approach of the courts will be towards a clause which attempts to exclude or limit liability for all loss or damage (including death or personal injury) resulting from negligence by the use of a general phrase such as 'no liability for any loss, injury or damage, howsoever caused'. Clearly, the clause will not be effective in relation to death or personal injuries resulting from negligence. However, this does not mean that the clause is totally without effect. The Act does not invalidate a clause altogether simply because it attempts to exclude liability for personal injuries. It may be arguable, however, that the overall breadth of the clause makes it unreasonable even in relation to the other losses. The answer to this will depend on the precise interpretation of the requirement of reasonableness, and we will return to this issue in the context of that discussion.

9.7.6 Standard terms and consumer contracts

Whereas s 2 is only concerned with the exclusion of negligence liability, s 3 covers all types of liability arising under a contract, including strict liability, but is limited in the types of contract which it affects. It states:

(1) This section applies as between contracting parties where one of them deals as a consumer, or on the other's written standard terms of business.

(2) As against that party, the other cannot by reference to any contract term:

---

112 This is discussed further, below, 9.7.10.

> (a) when himself in breach of contract, exclude or restrict any liability of his in respect of the breach; or
>
> (b) claim to be entitled:
>
> (i) to render a contractual performance substantially different from that which was reasonably expected of him; or
>
> (ii) in respect of the whole or any part of his contractual obligation, to render no performance at all, except in so far as (in all of the cases mentioned above in this sub-section) the contract term satisfies the requirement of reasonableness.

The section is thus directed at situations where there is inequality of bargaining power, and the claimant may have effectively been forced to accept a wide-ranging exclusion clause, which may appear to operate unfairly. The section operates in relation to two types of contract. First, it covers contracts where the claimant 'deals as a consumer'. The definition of 'dealing as a consumer' is to be found in s 12. A party 'deals as a consumer' if:

> (a) he neither makes the contract in the course of a business nor holds himself out as doing so; and
>
> (b) the other party does make the contract in the course of a business; and
>
> (c) in the case of a contract governed by the law of sale of goods or hire purchase, or by s 7 of this Act, the goods passing under or in pursuance of the contract are of a type ordinarily supplied for private use or consumption.

9.7.7 Meaning of 'in the course of a business'

The scope of the phrase 'in the course of a business' as defined in *R and B Customs Brokers v UDT*[113] has been discussed above.[114] As we have seen, it means that it is not simply the private individual who can claim to deal 'as a consumer'. Businesses will apparently be able to do so in relation to contracts which do not form a regular part of their business. Despite the doubts as to whether this was what Parliament intended, and the refusal of the Court of Appeal to follow this interpretation in relation to the same phrase where used in the Sale of Goods Act 1979,[115] the *R and B Customs Brokers* approach remains the governing authority in relation to the UCTA 1977. Where the contract is concerned with the supply of goods, however, a business will only be treated as dealing as a consumer where the goods are of a type 'ordinarily supplied for private use or consumption'. In *R and B Customs Brokers*, this was satisfied because the subject matter of the contract was a car. It will have the effect, however, of meaning that many business purchases will not be considered 'consumer contracts' even if the business

---

113 [1988] 1 All ER 847.
114 Above, 9.7.3.
115 In *Stevenson v Rogers* [1999] 1 All ER 613 – discussed further above, 8.6.12.

does not generally deal in the goods concerned. A business buyer which purchases an industrial floor cleaner, for example, will not be dealing as a consumer, even though the buyer does not regularly buy and sell floor cleaners, and wants the machine simply to clean the office floors. If, however, the buyer is an individual, this restriction does not apply. This is a consequence of the modification of s 12 of the UCTA 1977 by the Sale and Supply of Goods to Consumers Regulations 2002.[116] Regulation 14 inserted a new sub-s (1A) into s 12, the effect of which is that where the contract is one for the supply of goods and the consumer is an individual, it is no longer necessary for the goods to be 'of a type ordinarily supplied for private use or consumption' in order for the consumer to obtain the full protection of ss 6 and 7 of the UCTA 1977. Whatever the type of goods supplied, there will be no possibility of excluding liability for the implied terms as to description and quality under ss 13–15 of the Sale of Goods Act 1979, or the equivalent statutory implied terms in hire or hire purchase or other contracts involving the supply of goods. The owner of a large number of messy dogs who buys an industrial grade floor cleaner will now be treated as 'dealing as a consumer'. There was no obvious reason why such buyers should not be treated as 'dealing as a consumer' and the change is to be welcomed.

A person claiming to deal as a consumer does not have to prove this: the burden of proof is on the party claiming that a person is not dealing as a consumer.[117]

FOR THOUGHT

Is a University which buys computers for the use of its staff or students buying 'in the course of business' or as a consumer?

9.7.8 Standard terms of business

The second type of contract which is covered by s 3 is one which is made on the basis of the defendant's 'written standard terms of business'. This phrase is not further defined, but it is to be assumed that the individual negotiation of some of the terms of the agreement will not prevent them from being 'standard'. In *St Albans City and District Council v International Computers Ltd*,[118] the Court of Appeal rejected an argument that the terms were not 'standard' because the contract had been preceded by negotiation. The exclusion clause itself will, however, presumably have to be part of the standard package. Regularity of use will suggest that terms are 'standard', but it is not necessary that they are *always* used by the party wishing to rely on them.[119] If the terms are those of a trade association which are simply adopted by the mutual agreement of

---

116 SI 2002/3045. The Regulations came into force on 31 March 2003.
117 Section 12(3).
118 [1996] 4 All ER 481.
119 *Chester Grosvenor Hotel v Alfred McAlpine Management Ltd* (1991) 56 BLR 115.

both parties, then presumably these will still be treated as 'standard terms' if they are regularly used by the party whom the clause concerned would benefit.

It is important to remember that this provision is not concerned directly with inequalities in bargaining power. It is likely in practice (because of the way in which the requirement of reasonableness operates) to benefit the weaker party more frequently, but there is no reason in theory why it should not be relied on by a large corporation which happens to have made a contract on the basis of the standard terms of a much smaller and less powerful business. It is also important to note that this category is unlikely to be needed to be used by the private individual, despite the fact that many contracts between individuals and businesses are made on the standard terms of the business. The reason for this is, of course, that the private individual will contract 'as a consumer', and will therefore be within the other category covered by s 3.

9.7.9   Effect of s 3

The effect of s 3 is that, in relation to any contract within its scope, any attempt to exclude or restrict liability by the non-consumer, or the party putting forward the standard terms, will be subject to the requirement of reasonableness (s 3(2)(a)). Moreover, s 3(2)(b) goes on to make it clear that this extends also to any contractual term by virtue of which such a party claims to be entitled:

(i)   to render a contractual performance substantially different from that which was reasonably to be expected of him; or

(ii)   in respect of the whole or any part of his contractual obligation, to render no performance at all . . .

The point of the provisions in s 3(2)(b) is similar to that of s 13. It is trying to anticipate attempts to exclude liability indirectly by the use of clauses which define a party's obligations very restrictively. It would apply, for example, to a clause such as that used in *Karsales v Wallis*[120] purporting to allow the supplier of a 'car' to deliver something which was incapable of self-propulsion (though such a clause would probably also fall foul of the special provisions relating to sale of goods contracts), or to a clause allowing a party who had agreed to provide a cleaning service each month to miss several months in a row without penalty.[121] Such clauses are permissible, but only to the extent that they satisfy the requirement of reasonableness. This enables a court to distinguish clauses which are genuine and legitimate attempts to set out the parties' contractual obligations from those which are being used to escape any substantial liability at all. The test of

---

120 [1956] 2 All ER 866 – see above, 9.5.3.

121 Cf *Watford Electronics Ltd v Sanderson CFL Ltd* [2001] EWCA Civ 317; [2001] 1 All ER Comm 696, where the Court of Appeal took the view that an 'entire agreement' clause, which constituted an 'acknowledgment of non-reliance' as regards pre-contractual representations was not caught by s 3.

legitimacy, as indicated by s 3(2)(b)(i) above, is likely to be the reasonable expectation of the other party.

The precise scope of s 3(2)(b) was considered by the Court of Appeal in *Paragon Finance plc v Staunton*.[122] The claimant argued that a clause allowing the provider of a mortgage complete freedom to vary the interest payable should be regarded as subject to s 3(2)(b); in other words, if the clause could be used to permit the lender to charge an unexpectedly high interest rate, this would constitute 'a contractual performance different from that which was reasonably expected of him', and the clause could be declared 'unreasonable' under the UCTA 1977. The Court of Appeal rejected the claim, holding that the power to set the interest rate was not 'performance' of the contract in the sense meant by s 3(2)(b). In reaching this conclusion, the court distinguished both *Timeload Ltd v British Telecommunications plc*[123] (power to terminate arbitrarily a contract for the use of a particular telephone number) and *Zockoll Group Ltd v Mercury Communications Ltd*[124] (power to withdraw a particular telephone number without giving reasons), where the court had held that the terms concerned did potentially fall within the scope of s 3(2)(b). Both of those cases involved a positive obligation to provide something under the contract, which was not the case as regards the setting of the interest rate in *Paragon v Staunton*.

The overall effect of s 3 is that, because the vast majority of exclusion clauses will be in either a consumer contract or one which is on standard terms, there will be very few situations in which an exclusion clause is not at least subject to the requirement of reasonableness. It gives the appeal courts the opportunity to indicate the acceptable limits of exclusion of liability, though as will be seen (see 9.7.10–9.7.15 below), it is not one which they have shown any great willingness to take.

9.7.10 The requirement of reasonableness

The test to be applied to determine whether a clause meets the requirement of reasonableness is set out in s 11 of the UCTA 1977. The central element of the test is stated in s 11(1) as being whether the clause was:

> . . . a fair and reasonable one to be included having regard to the circumstances which were, or ought reasonably to have been, known to or in the contemplation of the parties when the contract was made.

This very general test imposes no very significant restrictions on the exercise of a court's discretion in relation to a clause, and therefore makes things difficult for the parties in terms of contractual planning. It will be very difficult to predict whether a

---

122 [2002] 2 All ER 248.
123 [1995] EMLR 459.
124 [1999] EMLR 385.

particular clause is likely to fall foul of this test. A few guidelines to its operation can be found, however, both within the UCTA 1977 itself and from case law.

9.7.11 Interpretation of reasonableness

Starting with the wording of s 11, it is clear that the point at which the clause should be assessed is when the contract was created, and that the test is directed at the clause itself, not at any particular application of it. It is submitted that *obiter* statements to the contrary by the Court of Appeal in *Overseas Medical Supplies Ltd v Orient Transport Services Ltd*[125] (see 9.7.16 below) should be regarded with caution, as running against the clear wording of s 11. Thus, the issue should be whether the clause is one which, at the time at which the parties made the contract, could be regarded as fair and reasonable. Subsequent events should not be relevant in deciding this issue. In particular, the actual breach which has occurred and for which the clause is claimed to provide exclusion or limitation of liability should not, in theory, be considered. The strict reading of the section makes it clear that it is quite possible for a court to feel that it would be reasonable for the defendant to have excluded liability for the particular breach which has occurred, but that the clause is too widely worded to be reasonable, and should therefore fail. This is in line with a policy which aims to discourage the use of unnecessarily wide clauses, rather than simply trying to provide a just solution to individual disputes. The Court of Appeal in *Stewart Gill Ltd v Horatio Myer & Co Ltd*[126] confirmed that it is the reasonableness of a clause as a whole, rather than the part of it which is being relied on in the particular case, which must be considered. Where, however, a clause contains two separate exclusions or limitations, and in particular if they are in two sub-clauses, it is appropriate to consider the reasonableness of each sub-clause individually.[127]

Where the clause is one which attempts to limit liability to a specific sum of money, rather than excluding it altogether, s 11(4) directs the court to take into account, in assessing the reasonableness of the clause:

(a) the resources which [the defendant] could expect to be available to him for the purpose of meeting the liability should it arise; and

(b) how far it was open to him to cover himself by insurance.

This recognises that it may be quite reasonable for a contracting party who is impecunious, or is engaging in a particularly risky activity, to put a financial ceiling on liability.

Finally, s 11(5) states that:

---

125 [1999] 2 Lloyd's Rep 273.
126 [1992] QB 600.
127 *Watford Electronics Ltd v Sanderson CFL Ltd* [2001] EWCA Civ 317; [2001] 1 All ER Comm 696.

It is for those claiming that a contract term or notice satisfies the requirement of reasonableness to show that it does.

This makes it clear that the burden of proof as regards reasonableness lies on the party seeking to rely on the clause.

9.7.12 Guidelines in Sched 2

The only other part of the UCTA 1977 which provides guidance on the operation of the reasonableness test is Sched 2. The role of the Schedule is indicated by s 11(2):

> In determining for the purposes of s 6 or 7 above whether a contract term satisfies the requirement of reasonableness, regard shall be had in particular to the matters specified in Sched 2 to this Act; but this sub-section does not prevent the court or arbitrator from holding, in accordance with any rule of law, that a term which purports to exclude or restrict any relevant liability is not a term of the contract.

Strictly speaking, therefore, the 'guidelines' which it contains are to be used only in relation to exclusion clauses which attempt to limit liability for breach of the statutorily implied terms under sale of goods and hire purchase contracts. In practice, however, the considerations set out are likely to be regarded as relevant whenever reasonableness is in issue.[128] There are five factors listed, covering the following areas:

(a) The relative strength of the bargaining position of the parties – in particular, did the plaintiff have any option about contracting with the defendant, or were there other means by which the plaintiff's requirements could have been met?

(b) Whether the plaintiff received an inducement (for example, a discount) to agree to the term; could the same contract have been made with other persons without the exclusion clause?

(c) Whether the plaintiff knew or ought reasonably to have known of the existence and extent of the term. (Note that there is a clear overlap here with the common law requirement of incorporation.)

(d) Whether at the time of contract it was reasonable to expect that compliance would be practicable with any condition which, if not complied with, leads to the exclusion or restriction of liability.

(e) Whether goods were manufactured, processed or adapted to the special order of the customer. (Note that this consideration is specifically linked to contracts for the supply of goods: put into general terms it would require the court to consider whether the contract was specially negotiated to meet the claimant's requirements.)

---

128 See, for example, *Overseas Medical Supplies Ltd v Orient Transport Services Ltd* [1999] 2 Lloyd's Rep 273 – discussed below, 9.7.16.

The weight to be given to any of these considerations is left entirely to the discretion of the court. Moreover, since they are only 'guidelines', there is no obligation to look at them at all. It is unlikely, for example, that the Court of Appeal would overturn a judge's decision on the reasonableness issue simply because one of the above guidelines had not been considered, even in relation to a contract for the supply of goods. The list is not exhaustive, and other matters may be taken into consideration if the court feels that this is appropriate.

9.7.13 Judicial approach to 'reasonableness' – pre-UCTA 1977

As far as the case law on 'reasonableness' is concerned, there are two House of Lords decisions which are worth noting, one applying a test of reasonableness which pre-dated the UCTA 1977, the other dealing with the UCTA 1977 itself.

The first case is *George Mitchell (Chesterhall) Ltd v Finney Lock Seeds Ltd*.[129] This concerned a contract for the sale of cabbage seed which turned out not to match its description, with the result that the entire crop failed and the purchaser suffered a loss of £63,000. The contract contained an exclusion clause, limiting the liability of the seller to the price of the seed, which was under £200. The clause was subject to the test of reasonableness (now superseded by the UCTA 1977) contained in s 55(4) of the Sale of Goods Act 1979,[130] which required the court to decide whether it was fair and reasonable to allow reliance on the clause. The trial judge and the Court of Appeal held that the clause did not on its true construction cover the breach. The House of Lords differed on the construction issue, holding that the wording was apt to cover the breach, and so had to go on to consider the question of reasonableness. The House emphasised that it was best on this issue, wherever possible, for the appeal courts to accept the judgment of the trial judge, who had the benefit of hearing all the witnesses.[131] Since that was not possible here, however, the House went on to determine the 'reasonableness' issue itself. It approached it as an exercise in 'balancing' various factors against each other. On the one hand, the clause was a common one in the trade, and had never been objected to by the National Union of Farmers. Moreover, the magnitude of the damage in proportion to the price of the goods sold also weighed in the defendants' favour. Lord Bridge, however, found three matters to put into the other side of the balance. First, the fact that the wrong seed was supplied was due to negligence (albeit of the defendants' sister company, rather than the defendants themselves). Second, the trial judge had found that the defendants would have been able to take out insurance against crop failure, without needing to increase the price of the seeds significantly. Third, and in Lord Bridge's view most importantly, there was evidence from a number of witnesses (including the chairman of the defendants) that it was general practice in

---

129 [1983] 2 AC 803; [1983] 2 All ER 737.
130 As set out in the 1979 Act, Sched 1, para 11.
131 Cf the comments of the Court of Appeal to the same effect in *Phillips Products Ltd v Hyland* [1987] 2 All ER 620.

the trade not to rely on this clause in cases like the one which the House was consider-ing, but to negotiate more substantial compensation. As Lord Bridge put it:[132]

> This evidence indicates a clear recognition by seedsmen in general, and the [defendants] in particular, that reliance on the limitation of liability imposed by the relevant condition would not be fair and reasonable.

This indicates that where the courts are dealing with a common type of contract within a particular area of business activity, the practices of the trade or business are likely to be of considerable relevance. In addition, the fact that all the circumstances must be considered, and that the appeal courts are reluctant to interfere with decisions of the trial judge, means that it is not necessarily the case that, because a particular exclusion clause has been found unreasonable in one situation, it will be precluded from use in others. This element of uncertainty will pull in two directions. It will make those who wish to include exclusion clauses cautious, and may encourage them to word clauses narrowly and precisely. On the other hand, the claimant who wishes to challenge a clause may well be deterred by the fact that the outcome of such a challenge will be very unpredictable.

9.7.14   The UCTA 1977 in the House of Lords

The second House of Lords case which has discussed the concept of 'reasonableness' is *Smith v Eric S Bush*.[133] The case concerned a 'disclaimer' of liability for negligence put forward by a surveyor carrying out a valuation of a property for a building society, which was relied on by the purchaser of the property. Having decided that this dis-claimer did constitute an exclusion clause, by virtue of s 13 of the UCTA 1977,[134] the House then had to consider whether it satisfied the requirement of reasonableness. The factors which were considered relevant to this issue were set out most clearly in the speech of Lord Griffiths. He thought that there were four matters which should *always* be considered in deciding this issue. They were as follows.

(a)   Were the parties of equal bargaining power? (This also appears in the guidelines in Sched 2 to the UCTA 1977.)
(b)   In the case of advice, would it have been reasonably practicable to obtain the advice from an alternative source, taking into account considerations of costs and time? In this case, although the purchaser could have obtained another survey, it was relevant that the house was 'at the bottom end of the market', which made it less reasonable to expect the purchaser to pay for a second opinion.
(c)   How difficult is the task being undertaken for which liability is being excluded?

---

132 [1983] 2 AC 803, p 817; [1983] 2 All ER 737, p 744.
133 [1990] 1 AC 831; [1989] 2 All ER 514.
134 See above, 9.7.4.

The more difficult or dangerous the undertaking, the more reasonable it is to exclude liability.

(d) What are the practical consequences of the decision on reasonableness? For example, if the risk is one against which a defendant could quite easily have insured, but which will have very serious effects on a claimant who is required to bear the loss, this will suggest that exclusion is unreasonable. It might be otherwise if a finding of liability would 'open the floodgates' to claims.

With these considerations in mind and, in addition, the fact that this was an individual private house purchase, not a deal in relation to commercial property, the House decided that the disclaimer of liability did not meet the requirement of reasonableness.

9.7.15 Inequality of bargaining power

It is clear from the Sched 2 guidelines and the points made by the House of Lords in *Smith v Bush* that inequality of bargaining power is an important factor in deciding on the question of 'reasonableness'. The existence of inequality does not, however, automatically render any exclusion unreasonable. This was illustrated by *Snookes v Jani-King (GB) Ltd*.[135] A clause in a franchise agreement stated that any proceedings relating to the agreement should 'be brought in a court of competent jurisdiction in London'. The claimant started proceedings in Swansea, and the defendants applied to strike out the claim on the basis that the Swansea court did not have jurisdiction. The claimant pleaded that the clause requiring claims to be brought in London was an unfair term under the UCTA 1977. The judge accepted that the clause was contained within the defendants' written standard terms, and so potentially fell within s 3 of UCTA. He held, however, that the defendants had proved that the clause satisfied the test of reasonableness, taking into account the factors listed in Sched 2. Although the defendants were in the stronger bargaining position, this did not make the clause automatically unreasonable. The claimant had had plenty of time to object to the clause before signing the agreement and, since the claimant was based in Birmingham, a requirement to take action in London was not unduly onerous. It was not relevant that the defendants had not raised the clause in defending actions brought by other claimants. Overall the clause was reasonable.

9.7.16 'Reasonableness' in the Court of Appeal

Several Court of Appeal decisions have involved a consideration of the test of reasonableness. Two of these, *Phillips Products Ltd v Hyland*[136] and *Thompson v T Lohan (Plant Hire) Ltd*,[137] involved differing interpretations of the same clause, but did not

---

135 [2006] ILPr 19.
136 [1987] 2 All ER 620.
137 [1987] 2 All ER 631.

add significantly to the guidelines on how the test should be applied as indicated by the *George Mitchell v Finney Lock Seeds* and *Smith v Bush* decisions.

In *Phillips Products Ltd v Hyland*, however, Slade LJ noted, and followed, the injunction from Lord Bridge in *George Mitchell* that appeal courts should be very reluctant to interfere with the trial judge on this issue. Lord Bridge, having pointed out that the test of reasonableness involves a balancing of considerations, commented that:[138]

> There will sometimes be room for a legitimate difference of judicial opinion as to what the answer should be, where it will be impossible to say that one view is demonstrably wrong, and the other demonstrably right. It must follow, in my view, that, when asked to review such a decision on appeal, the appellate court should treat the original decision with the utmost respect and refrain from inter-ference with it unless satisfied that it proceeded on some erroneous principle or was plainly and obviously wrong.

With this in mind, Slade LJ concentrated his consideration of the first instance judg-ment on the issue of whether the judge had directed himself to the correct issues. Given that he appeared to have done so, and that his conclusion was not 'plainly or obviously wrong', the court did not feel it appropriate to interfere. It also followed from this approach, however, that:[139]

> . . . our conclusion on the particular facts of this case should not be treated as a binding precedent in other cases where similar clauses fall to be considered but the evidence of the surrounding circumstances may be very different.

Subsequent Court of Appeal decisions have, however, given some further guidance as to factors which are relevant in applying the test. In *Schenkers Ltd v Overland Shoes Ltd*,[140] the clause was contained in the standard trading conditions of the British International Freight Association (BIFA). The Court of Appeal felt that it was rele-vant, particularly where the parties were of equal bargaining power, that the clause was one which was in common use and well known in the trade. It could therefore be taken to reflect a general view as to what was reasonable in the trade concerned. Although in *George Mitchell v Finney Lock* it had been found that there was an expectation in the trade that an exclusion clause which was in common use would not in practice be relied on, that had not been shown to be the case here. Although there was 'no ready or frequent resort to the clause', there was no evidence of a recognition in the trade that the clause was unreasonable.

The second case is *Overseas Medical Supplies Ltd v Orient Transport Services*

---

138 [1983] 2 AC 803, p 816; [1983] 2 All ER 737, p 743.
139 [1987] 2 All ER 620, p 630.
140 [1998] 1 Lloyd's Rep 498.

Ltd,[141] which was also concerned with a clause (though a different one) contained in BIFA's standard trading conditions. The trial judge in this case held that the clause was unreasonable, and this was upheld by the Court of Appeal. In coming to that conclusion, Potter LJ outlined various factors which are relevant to the decision on reasonableness.[142] He pointed to eight relevant issues, namely: (1) the way in which the relevant conditions came into being (for example, whether they are part of the standard conditions used in a particular trade); (2) the guidelines in Sched 2 to the UCTA 1977 (even where the contract is not concerned with sale of goods, and is not a consumer transaction); (3) in relation to equality of bargaining position, the question of whether the customer was obliged to use the services of the supplier and how far it would have been practical or convenient to go elsewhere; (4) the clause must be viewed as a whole, rather than taking any particular part of it in isolation. It must also be viewed 'against a breach of contract which is the subject matter of the present case' (but see the comment on this below); (5) the reality of the consent of the customer to the supplier's clause; (6) in cases of limitation, the size of the limit in comparison with other limits in widely used standard terms; (7) the availability of insurance (though this is by no means a decisive factor); (8) the presence of a term allowing for an option to contract without the limitation clause but with an increase in price.

All of these factors are sensible ones for the court to consider. In relation to the second sentence of (4) above, however, which derives from *AEG Ltd v Logic Resource Ltd*,[143] it seems to be incompatible with the wording of s 11 of the UCTA 1977 which, as we have seen,[144] states that the test is whether the clause was a reasonable one to include in the contract having regard to the parties' state of knowledge at that time. The nature of the breach which has actually occurred ought therefore not to be relevant to the assessment of the reasonableness of the clause. The statement to the contrary by Potter LJ is clearly *obiter*, and it is submitted that it should not be relied upon pending further clarification by the appellate courts.

In both *Schenkers Ltd v Overland Shoes Ltd* and *Overseas Medical Supplies Ltd v Orient Transport Services Ltd*, the Court of Appeal again emphasised that the appeal courts should be reluctant to interfere with a decision on this issue by the trial judge, and in both cases upheld the first instance decision. Appealing decisions on 'reasonableness' may often turn out to be a fruitless exercise. In *Watford Electronics Ltd v Sanderson CFL Ltd*,[145] however, the Court of Appeal did intervene to find that a clause which the trial judge had regarded as unreasonable was in fact reasonable. Intervention was justified because the judge had misdirected himself on the proper basis for applying the reasonableness test; it was not therefore simply a disagreement on the result of applying the proper test, where intervention would presumably not

---

141 [1999] 2 Lloyd's Rep 273.
142 Ibid, p 277.
143 [1996] CLC 265, CA.
144 See above, 9.7.11.
145 [2001] EWCA Civ 317; [2001] 1 All ER Comm 696.

generally be appropriate. The contract was for the supply of computer software. It turned out not to function properly and caused the purchaser substantial losses. The supplier had included a clause excluding its liability for indirect and consequential losses, and limiting any compensation to a refund of the purchase price. In deciding that these provisions were not unreasonable, the court took account of the fact that there had been considerable negotiation and the purchaser had, as a result, gained the inclusion of a 'best endeavours' clause; there was no significant difference in bargaining power between the parties; and the purchaser had used similar limitation clauses in its own contracts, thus indicating that it was aware of the fact that such clauses were used to allocate liabilities. Chadwick LJ concluded:[146]

> Where experienced businessmen representing substantial companies of equal bargaining power negotiate an agreement, they may be taken to have had regard to the matters known to them. They should in my view be taken to be the best judge of the commercial fairness of the agreement which they have made; including the fairness of each of the terms in that agreement. They should be taken to be the best judge on the question whether the terms of the agreement are reasonable. The court should not assume that either is likely to commit his company to an agreement which he thinks is unfair, or which he thinks includes unreasonable terms. Unless satisfied that one party has, in effect, taken unfair advantage of the other – or that a term is so unreasonable that it cannot properly have been understood or considered – the court should not interfere.

This suggests a very 'hands-off' approach to the supervision of exclusion clauses in business contracts. A similar view was taken by the Court of Appeal in *Granville Oil & Chemicals Ltd v Davis Turner & Co Ltd*[147] in considering whether cl 30(B) of the British International Freight Association Standard Trading Conditions met the requirement of 'reasonableness' under s 11 of the UCTA 1977. The clause required that if written notice of legal action is not given within nine months of the event giving rise to it, then the other party is discharged from liability. The judge had found that this clause was unreasonable, because he held that it could be used in relation to a situation where fraud was involved, and where the defendant had fraudulently concealed facts giving rise to the claim. The Court of Appeal disagreed. It held that the clause should not be interpreted to cover fraudulent behaviour, and that it was therefore reasonable. The most interesting aspect of the judgment, however, is probably the final paragraph of the judgment of Tuckey LJ, in which he again confirmed the reluctance of the appeal courts to interfere in commercial agreements. He commented:

> I am pleased to reach this decision. The 1977 Act obviously plays a very important role in protecting vulnerable consumers from the effects of draconian contract

---

146 [2001] EWCA Civ 317; [2001] 1 All ER Comm 696, para 55.
147 [2003] EWCA Civ 570; [2003] 2 Lloyd's Rep 356.

terms. But I am less enthusiastic about its intrusion into contracts between commercial parties of equal bargaining strength, who should generally be considered capable of being able to make contracts of their choosing and expect to be bound by their terms.

There seems to be a general view at Court of Appeal level that intervention in commercial agreements on the basis of the UCTA 1977 should be a rare event. Two recent cases show that trial judges are nevertheless prepared to hold a clause unreasonable when they think that it is necessary to do so.

The Court of Appeal line was largely followed by the trial judge in *obiter* statements in *Sterling Hydraulics Ltd v Dichtomatik Ltd*.[148] The exclusion clause in a supply contract limited the supplier's liability to the contract price. This was reasonable given that the supplier was unaware of the precise purpose for which the product was to be used. A provision requiring claims based on hidden defects to be notified within a week of discovering the defect was, however, found to be unreasonable. An even more interventionist approach was taken in *Balmoral Group Ltd v Borealis (UK) Ltd*.[149] The contract was again one for the supply of goods, but the clause in this case had the effect of removing all liability on the part of the supplier for defects in the goods. The trial judge noted the comments in the *Granville Oil* case about the need to allow business parties to allocate their own risks, but held that this blanket exclusion of liability, judged at the time of the contract when the outcome of any breach would be uncertain, did not satisfy the requirement of reasonableness.

FOR THOUGHT

How should the courts decide when, exceptionally, to intervene in business contracts? Should they be looking primarily at the balance of power between the parties, or is it the scope of the clause that should be the determining factor in relation to 'reasonableness'?

9.7.17 Indemnities

Section 4 deals with 'indemnities'. It states:

(1)   A person dealing as a consumer cannot by reference to any contract term be made to indemnify another person (whether a party to the contract or not) in respect of liability that may be incurred by the other for negligence or breach of contract, except in so far as the contract term satisfies the requirement of reasonableness.

---

148 [2007] 1 Lloyd's Rep 8.
149 [2006] CLC 220.

(2) This section applies whether the liability in question:

    (a) is directly that of the person to be indemnified or is incurred by him vicariously;

    (b) is to the person dealing as consumer or to someone else.

The section is designed to deal with attempts to impose liability on a person dealing as a consumer by way of an obligation to indemnify another for liability for negligence or breach of contract. This can only be done insofar as the clause satisfies the requirement of reasonableness.

This might be attempted where, for example, a consumer sues in tort an individual employee who has acted negligently in the course of employment. The employee may well be entitled to be indemnified by his or her employer, and the employer may in return have provided for an indemnity in the contract with the consumer. By virtue of s 4, this will only be enforceable if it satisfies the requirement of reasonableness.[150]

9.7.18 Guarantees of consumer goods

Section 5 is concerned with guarantees given by the manufacturers of consumer goods. It states:

(1) In the case of goods of a type ordinarily supplied for private use or consumption, where loss or damage:

    (a) arises from the goods proving defective while in consumer use; and

    (b) results from the negligence of a person concerned in the manufacture or distribution of the goods, liability for the loss or damage cannot be excluded or restricted by reference to any contract term or notice contained in or operating by reference to a guarantee of the goods.

(2) For these purposes:

    (a) goods are to be regarded as 'in consumer use' when a person is using them, or has them in his possession for use, otherwise than exclusively for the purposes of a business; and

    (b) anything in writing is a guarantee if it contains or purports to contain some promise or assurance (however worded or presented) that defects will be made good by complete or partial replacement, or by repair, monetary compensation or otherwise.

(3) This section does not apply as between the parties to a contract under or in pursuance of which possession or ownership of the goods passed.

The type of situation to which this section is directed is where a 'guarantee' provided by the manufacturer of goods, for example, tries to limit a consumer's rights, by giving, for

---

150 The clause, if dealing with negligence, however, may well be caught anyway by s 2: cf *Phillips Products Ltd v Hyland* [1987] 2 All ER 620.

example, a right to replacement, but denying any other liability. Where the goods have proved defective while 'in consumer use',[151] and this results from the negligence of the defendant, then the limitation of liability will be ineffective (s 5(1)).

Note that this section does not apply to guarantees given by a seller, or hirer, of goods.[152] The effect of such provisions in these contracts is covered by ss 6 and 7 of the UCTA 1977, which are discussed below.

9.7.19 Exclusions in contracts for the supply of goods

Exclusion of the implied terms in sale of goods contracts under the Sale of Goods Act (SGA) 1979[153] and their equivalent in hire purchase contracts under the Supply of Goods (Implied Terms) Act 1973 is governed by s 6 of the UCTA 1977. There is a total prohibition on the exclusion or restriction of liability for breach of the implied term as to title (s 12 of the 1979 Act and s 8 of the 1973 Act) whatever the status of the parties to the contract. An individually negotiated provision in a contract between two businesses dealing on equal terms which attempts to limit liability for breach of this implied term will nevertheless be treated as ineffective. Equally, although the Act is normally concerned only with 'business liability', s 6(4) of the UCTA 1977 extends the scope of s 6(1) to non-business contracts. If a contract between two private individuals contains an attempt to exclude s 12 of the 1979 Act or s 8 of the 1973 Act, this will also be ineffective. The broad scope of this provision can only be justified on the basis that the implied term as to title in contracts for the supply of goods is so fundamental that any attempt to exclude liability in relation to it cannot be countenanced.

As regards the implied terms as to quality, there can be no exclusion of liability under s 13 (description), s 14 (satisfactory quality, fitness for particular purpose) or s 15 (sample) of the SGA 1979, or under the equivalent provisions in ss 9–11 of the 1973 Act, as against a person dealing as a consumer. Where the buyer contracts other than as a consumer, however, liability for breach of these sections may be excluded, provided the clause satisfies the 'requirement of reasonableness' under s 11.[154] A person contracts 'as a consumer' when he or she does not contract 'in the course of a business'.[155] The narrow definition of 'course of a business' adopted in *R and B Customs Brokers v UDT*[156] will apply. This significantly reduces the situations in which exclusion of the implied terms will be permissible. As noted above,[157] the Court of Appeal has adopted a narrower test of 'course of a business' in relation to the question of when the implied

---

151 That is, other than exclusively for the purposes of a business: s 5(2)(a).
152 Section 5(3).
153 For which see Chapter 8, 8.6.9–8.6.14.
154 See above, 9.7.10.
155 UCTA 1977, s 12. See the discussion above, 9.7.3.
156 [1998] 1 All ER 847. See above, 9.7.3.
157 See 9.7.3.

terms under s 14 of the SGA should be included in a contract.[158] The test of reasonableness also applies to an attempt to exclude the implied term as to description by a non-business supplier.[159]

Terms similar to those implied by the SGA 1979 into sale of goods contracts are implied into other contracts under which the possession or ownership of goods passes by the Supply of Goods and Services Act 1982. This covers contracts of hire, and contracts for the supply or work and materials.[160] Section 7 of the UCTA 1977 applies similar restrictions on exclusion of liability for breach of these terms as are contained in s 6 in relation to sale of goods and hire purchase contracts. There can be no exclusion of liability for breach of an implied term as to title arising under s 2(1) of the 1982 Act. Where s 2(1) does not apply, any implied term as to the right to transfer ownership, possession or to guarantee quiet possession can only be excluded insofar as it satisfies the requirement of reasonableness.[161] As regards implied terms as to description, quality, fitness for purpose, or compliance with sample, the position is the same as under s 6 – that is, liability cannot be restricted as against as person dealing as a consumer; otherwise, any clause must satisfy the requirement of reasonableness.[162]

9.7.20   Exclusion of liability for misrepresentation

There are special provisions in s 8 of the UCTA 1977 in relation to liability for misrepresentations. These are dealt with in Chapter 10.[163]

9.8   UNFAIR TERMS IN CONSUMER CONTRACTS REGULATIONS 1999 [164]

From 1 July 1995, certain contracts have been subject to regulations deriving from the European Directive on Unfair Terms in Consumer Contracts.[165] The first set of regulations was issued in 1994, but a revised set replaced these in 1999. The current regulations are the UTCCR 1999.

9.8.1   Application of the Regulations

The application of the Regulations is in some respects narrower than the UCTA 1977, but in other respects broader. It is narrower in that they apply only to contracts between

---

158 *Stevenson v Rogers* [1999] QB 1028; [1999] 1 All ER 613.
159 UCTA 1977, s 6(4). The other implied terms as to quality only apply to sales in the course of a business.
160 For example, under a contract to build a wall, the ownership of the bricks will pass.
161 Section 7(3A) and (4).
162 Section 7(2) and (3).
163 See 10.5.
164 SI 1999/2083.
165 Directive 93/13/EC.

a seller or supplier of goods or services and a 'consumer'. A consumer is defined in the Regulations as being 'a natural person . . . acting for purposes which are outside his trade, business or profession' (reg 3(1)). As we have seen, most of the provisions of the UCTA 1977 apply to contracts between businesses, even though they may do so in a way different from consumer contracts. Moreover, the case of *R and B Customs Brokers v UDT*[166] shows that, in some circumstances, a 'business' can be treated as a consumer. The UTCCR 1999, however, do not apply to contracts between businesses, and only natural persons can be consumers under them.[167]

The UTCCR 1999 are broader than the UCTA 1977 in that they potentially apply to all types of contract term, not just exclusion clauses. They do not, however, apply to any clause which is 'individually negotiated'.[168] The purpose of the UTCCR 1999 is to regulate standard form consumer contracts. In relation to these the courts now have general power of supervision to ensure that provisions are 'fair'. Freedom of contract in relation to the content of consumer contracts has been significantly curtailed.[169]

Apart from these general provisions as to the application of the Regulations, reg 4 also excludes from their scope terms which are included in a contract to comply with or reflect any UK statutory or regulatory provisions, or the provisions of any international conventions to which the Member States of the European Community, or the Community itself, are party.

9.8.2 Terms attacked

Regulation 8(1) provides that any 'unfair term' in a consumer contract 'shall not be binding on the consumer'. The test of 'unfairness' is contained in reg 5(1), and covers:

> . . . any term which contrary to the requirement of good faith . . . causes a significant imbalance in the parties' rights and obligations under the contract to the detriment of the consumer.

This definition, with its reference to 'good faith', reveals the European origins of the Regulations. English consumer law has no general concept of 'good faith', and so when the Regulations first came into force, it was unpredictable how the courts might treat this definition. It was to be expected that they would concentrate on the questions of 'imbalance' and 'detriment' which are more familiar. The 1994 Regulations contained a Schedule setting out some factors which the court should have regard to in assessing the issue of good faith. These were:

---

166 [1998] 1 All ER 847. See above, 9.7.3.
167 The point was confirmed by the European Court of Justice in *Cape SNC v Idealservice Srl* [2001] ECR I–9049; [2002] All ER (EC) 657.
168 Regulation 5(1).
169 Although the Regulations only have limited application to terms dealing with main subject matter and the price: reg 6(2) – see below.

(a)   the strength of the bargaining position of the parties;

(b)   whether the consumer had an inducement to agree to the term;

(c)   whether the goods or services were sold or supplied to the special order of the consumer; and

(d)   the extent to which the seller or supplier has dealt fairly and equitably with the consumer.

This list has not been reproduced in the 1999 Regulations. It is hard to believe, however, that the factors listed will not in practice be among those that a court will consider in assessing 'good faith'.

The first reported case on the 1994 Regulations, *Director General of Fair Trading v First National Bank plc*,[170] concerned a term in a loan agreement issued by a bank. This provided that if the consumer defaulted on an instalment, the full amount of the loan became payable. This is not unusual, but the term to which exception was taken, and about which the Director General received complaints, was to the effect that interest on the outstanding debt would remain payable even after a judgment of the court. Thus, a court might order the consumer to pay off the debt by specified instalments, but the effect of the contract was that interest would continue to accrue at the contractual rate while the instalments were being paid. The Court of Appeal concluded that the term created 'unfair surprise' and did not meet the requirement of 'good faith'. The House of Lords disagreed. Lord Bingham, with whom the other members of the House agreed, in interpreting what was reg 4(1) and is now reg 5(1), dealt with the requirements of 'significant imbalance' and 'good faith' separately. As regards the first factor he stated that:[171]

> The requirement of significant imbalance is met if a term is so weighted in favour of the supplier as to tilt the parties' rights and obligations under the contract significantly in his favour. This may be by the granting to the supplier of a beneficial option or discretion or power, or by the imposing on the consumer of a disadvantageous burden or risk or duty.

This test is concerned with the substance of the agreement, and requires consideration of the contract as a whole. 'Good faith', on the other hand, as far as Lord Bingham is concerned, seems to be more concerned with procedural fairness:[172]

> The requirement of good faith in this context is one of fair and open dealing. Openness requires that the terms should be expressed fully, clearly and legibly, containing no concealed pitfalls or traps. Appropriate prominence should be given to terms which might operate disadvantageously to the customer. Fair dealing

---

170 [2002] UKHL 52; [2002] 1 All ER 97.

171 Ibid, para 17; p 107.

172 Ibid, para 17; p 108.

requires that a supplier should not, whether deliberately or unconsciously, take advantage of the consumer's necessity, indigence, lack of experience, unfamiliarity with the subject matter of the contract, weak bargaining position, or any other factors listed in or analogous to those listed in Schedule 2 to the Regulations.

The test in reg 5(1) is therefore a composite one, 'covering both the making and the substance of the contract'.

Lord Steyn, while agreeing with Lord Bingham, took the view that 'good faith' was concerned with substance as well as procedure, and will therefore overlap with the test of 'significant imbalance':[173]

> The examples given in Schedule 3 convincingly demonstrate that the argument of the bank that good faith is predominantly concerned with procedural defects in negotiating procedures cannot be sustained. Any purely procedural or even predominantly procedural interpretation of good faith must be rejected.

It is submitted that Lord Steyn's approach is preferable and more in accordance with the wording of the Regulation, which makes 'significant imbalance' an element within an overall test of 'good faith'. The other members of the House, however, in concurring with Lord Bingham, expressed no specific view on the issue, so it must be taken that his analysis reflects the view of the majority. In practice, given that substantive issues are clearly raised by the 'significant imbalance' test, it probably does not matter in relation to these Regulations that 'good faith' is treated as primarily a procedural requirement. In other contexts, however, it might be important to give 'good faith' a role in considering the substantive effect of contractual provisions, rather than simply the procedures surrounding their adoption.

Applying the tests of 'significant imbalance' and 'good faith' to the clause before it, the House was unanimous that it did not contravene the Regulations. The provision for interest to be payable after judgment was not in itself unusual. The problems were created by the legislative framework, which restricted the power of the court to award interest when giving a creditor time to pay a debt by instalments, rather than by the contractual provision itself. It was the powers and procedures relating to the making of orders that needed to be addressed, in order to avoid any future unfairness.[174]

The 1999 Regulations contain another type of guidance for the courts, which was also in the 1994 Regulations (in Sched 3, as referred to by Lord Steyn in the passage quoted above). This is contained in Sched 2 to the 1999 Regulations and consists of an 'indicative and illustrative' list of terms which may be regarded as unfair. The inclusion

---

173 [2002] UKHL 52, paras 36–37; [2002] 1 All ER 97, p 113.
174 In particular, there was a need to draw attention to the courts' powers under the Consumer Credit Act 1974, ss 129 and 136, which would allow it in appropriate circumstances to amend contractual provisions when making a 'time order' for the payment of a debt. This would allow the court to incorporate the recovery of interest into the calculation of instalment payments.

of a term on the list does not necessarily mean that *any* clause of that type will be unfair: it will depend on the context in which it is put forward. Nor, on the other hand, is the list exhaustive. A clause of a type which does not appear in it may nevertheless be found to be unfair. The list contained in the Schedule is lengthy, and there is not space to reproduce it in full here. It contains some provisions which are familiar from the controls imposed by the UCTA 1977, such as clauses restricting liability for death or personal injury, or allowing the seller or supplier to provide inadequate performance, or a different product or service from that contracted for. Other provisions reflect the common law rules relating to exclusion clauses, such as the restriction on clauses with which the consumer had no real opportunity of becoming acquainted before the contract. In general, the list is concerned with clauses which allow the seller or supplier to impose on the consumer, for example, by allowing the seller or supplier to cancel the contract without notice, or giving the seller or supplier exclusive rights of interpretation, or requiring the consumer to pay disproportionately high compensation for a breach.

The assessment of whether a particular clause is unfair must take account of the nature of the goods or services supplied, and all the surrounding circumstances.[175]

FOR THOUGHT

Is the test of 'unfairness' under the UTCCR significantly different from the test of 'reasonableness' under UCTA? Does it simply lead the courts to the same conclusions by a slightly different route, or are there situations where a clause might be found to be 'unfair' but not 'unreasonable', or vice versa?

The UTCCR 1999 do not apply to simply bad bargains. Regulation 6(2) provides that clauses which define the main subject matter of the contract, or concern the adequacy of the price or remuneration for goods or services supplied, will not be assessed, provided they meet the criterion of intelligibility.[176] The consumer who has agreed to pay over the odds for goods or services will not be helped by these Regulations. This limitation applies only to terms which fall within the strict wording of reg 6(2). It does not apply to terms which are simply an important part of the agreement: *Director General of Fair Trading v First National Bank plc*.[177] The House of Lords here noted with approval the distinction drawn by Chitty between 'terms which express the substance of the bargain and "incidental" (if important) terms which surround them'.[178] Applying this approach, it held that a term in a credit agreement relating to interest payable after a judgment had been obtained against the debtor was 'ancillary' and not

---

175 Regulation 6(1).
176 See below, 9.8.3.
177 [2002] UKHL 52; [2002] 1 All ER 97.
178 Ibid, para 11; p 105, quoting Chitty, 2004, para 15.025.

'concerned with the adequacy of the bank's remuneration as against the services supplied'.[179] On that basis, it was not within the scope of reg 6(2)[180] and the fairness of the clause had to be considered.

The approach taken in this case suggests that the courts will take a narrow view of what is within the scope of reg 6(2). In general, provisions which deal with the consequences of breach are almost certainly going to be treated as ancillary. On the particular facts of *Director General of Fair Trading v First National Bank plc*, there was, nevertheless, some argument for not treating the provisions as to the payment of interest following a court judgment in this way. This is because in a loan agreement the main consideration provided by the debtor is the payment of interest. Provisions as to such payment (for example, the rate at which such interest is to be paid) should therefore be regarded as dealing with the 'adequacy of the remuneration' received by the creditor and therefore not subject to review in terms of 'fairness' under the 1999 Regulations. The decision in *First National Bank plc*, however, shows that this does not extend to provisions relating to the payment of interest following default by the debtor. Terms as to the level of interest in consumer credit agreements are nevertheless reviewable, not under the 1999 Regulations, but under the Consumer Credit Act itself, which gives the court the power to intervene if the terms of the agreement are 'extortionate'.[181] This includes the power to rewrite the agreement to make it fair to the debtor.

A similarly narrow approach to the scope of reg 6(2) was taken in *Bairstow Eves London Central Limited v Smith*.[182] The High Court held that a provision whereby an estate agent's commission doubled from 1.5 per cent to 3 per cent in the event of late payment fell within the scope of the fairness provisions of the Regulations (and was found to be unfair). This was so, even though the format of the provision was to state that the standard commission was 3 per cent with a reduction for early payment.

9.8.3 The requirement of 'plain, intelligible language'

Regulation 7 requires that the seller or supplier should ensure that the terms of the contract are expressed in 'plain, intelligible language': if there is doubt about the meaning of a term, the interpretation most favourable to the consumer will prevail. The latter part of this regulation simply gives statutory effect to the common law *contra proferentem* rule.[183] The requirement to use plain, intelligible language goes further, however, and clearly strikes against the use of complex, though unambiguous, legal jargon. There is no apparent sanction for a failure to meet this standard, however. It

---

179 [2002] UKHL 52; [2002] 1 All ER 97.
180 Note that the House of Lords was in fact considering the 1994 version of the Regulations, where the relevant regulation (though worded identically to reg 6(2) in the 1999 Regulations) was reg 4(2).
181 Consumer Credit Act 1974, ss 137–139.
182 [2004] EWHC 263.
183 See above, 9.5.1.

does not of itself render the term unfair, though presumably it could be a factor in such an assessment. The weight that is given to it will have to await the view of the courts.

9.8.4 General supervision

The Office of Fair Trading (OFT) is given a general supervisory role under reg 10. The power previously lay with the Director General of Fair Trading. As a result of the Enterprise Act 2002, however, all powers previously exercised by the Director General are now in the hands of the OFT itself. The supervisory role includes the power to receive complaints and to seek injunctions restraining the use of unfair terms.[184] The 1999 Regulations also contain a new power to require traders to produce copies of their standard contracts in order to facilitate the consideration of a complaint, or to monitor compliance with any undertaking or court order relating to the continuing use of an unfair term.[185] The supervision powers have been extensively used through the agency of the OFT's Unfair Contract Terms Unit. This has led to many cases (several hundred each year) in which terms investigated by the Unit have been modified or abandoned.[186] Thus, although the number of legal actions under the Regulations have been small, their effect has been felt through this less formal enforcement action and has been significant.

These supervision and enforcement powers may also be exercised, subject to supervision by the OFT, by the 'qualifying bodies' listed in Sched 1 to the Regulations. These include various statutory regulators (that is, data protection, gas, electricity, water, telecommunications), local authority trading standards departments and the Consumers Association. The OFT also has a power (though not a duty) to disseminate information and advice about the operation of the Regulations.

The first reported case under the Regulations, *Director General of Fair Trading v First National Bank plc*, noted above, involved an application for an injunction, following complaints by consumers, and a consequent exchange of correspondence between the Director General and the bank.

9.9 THE PRINCIPLES OF EUROPEAN CONTRACT LAW

The Principles of European Contract Law contain a number of provisions dealing with the control of unfairness within contracts. The most general is in Art 1.201 which imposes a duty on all contracting parties to act 'in accordance with good faith and fair dealing', and provides that this duty is not to be excluded or limited. More specifically, Art 4.110 deals with terms which have not been individually negotiated. It adopts the

---

184 Regulation 12.
185 Regulation 13.
186 See Bright, 2000; Wilkinson, 2000; and the Office of Fair Trading's own bulletins.

language of the European Directive on Unfair Terms in Consumer Contracts,[187] and is very similar to reg 6 of the UTCCR 1999. It refers to a term being unfair where, contrary to good faith and fair dealing, it causes a 'significant imbalance' in the rights and obligations of the parties. As with reg 6, it does not apply to terms defining the subject matter of the contract, or the adequacy of value of each party's obligations in relation to those of the other party. The main difference between this provision and reg 6 of the UTCCR 1999 is that Art 4.110 applies to all contracts, not just to consumer contracts.

A limitation on the power to exclude remedies is contained in Art 4.118. This applies to the right to avoid a term falling within Art 4.110, and also attempts to exclude remedies for 'fraud, threats and excessive benefit and unfair advantage-taking'.[188]

Finally, there is a provision relating to the exclusion or restriction of remedies for non-performance (rather than defective performance) in Art 8.109. This allows such exclusion or restriction, unless it would be contrary to good faith and fair dealing.

These provisions would give the courts wide control over not only exclusion clauses, but all contractual terms, other than those forming part of the central obligations of the contract. The approach currently operating in England in relation to consumer contracts would extend to all agreements, including commercial agreements. The whole scheme of controls would operate within the general principles of 'good faith and fair dealing', concepts with which, as we have seen in *Director General of Fair Trading v First National Bank plc*,[189] the English courts are just starting to come to terms.

9.10 PROPOSALS FOR REFORM

As has been noted earlier, there is a significant overlap between the controls over exclusion clauses contained in the UCTA 1977 and the UTCCR 1999. In addition, 'UCTA is a complex statute',[190] making it difficult to understand, particularly for the non-lawyer reader, and parts of the UTCCR 1999 are expressed in language which is 'alien to English and Scots readers, lawyers and non-lawyers alike'.[191] There is also the fact that the current legislation, in concentrating primarily on protection for consumers, ignores the fact the small business contractors may well be in just as disadvantageous a position as regards bargaining power as the individual consumer. Concerns about these issues led to the Department of Trade and Industry asking the Law Commission and the Scottish Law Commission, in 2001, to review the legislation. That review has now been completed, and the results and recommendations, together with a draft Bill, were

---

187 Directive 93/13/EC.
188 As controlled by Arts 4.107–4.109.
189 [2001] UKHL 52; [2002] 1 All ER 97 – above, 9.8.2.
190 *Unfair Terms in Contracts*, Law Com No 292, Scot Law Com No 199, Cm 6464, 2005, para 1.14.
191 Ibid, para 1.15.

published in the Law Commission's Report, *Unfair Contract Terms*.[192] The Report was published in February 2005, but it is not clear as yet how quickly, if at all, the Government may act to give the proposals legislative effect.

The Report is substantial and is worthy of careful study, but the following are the main points which emerge from the recommendations:

(a)   Both the UCTA 1977 and the UTCCR 1999 will be replaced by a new 'Unfair Contract Terms Act'.

(b)   Only 'natural persons' should be regarded as 'consumers', and then only when acting for purposes unrelated to any business which he or she may run. This will have the effect of reversing the decision in *R and B Customs Brokers v UDT*.[193] The current position under the UTCCR 1999 will be of general application.

(c)   Terms which are currently automatically ineffective to exclude liability by virtue of the UCTA 1977 (for example, under s 2(1)) will continue to be ineffective under the new Act.

(d)   All terms in consumer contracts, whether or not negotiated, should be subject to a test of reasonableness. The only exception applies to 'core' terms (for example, price), which are defined in much the same way as under the UTCCR 1999.[194] Even these terms must be 'transparent' (that is, clear and comprehensible) and in line with the consumer's reasonable expectations in order to be valid.

(e)   The test of reasonableness to be applied is whether the clause was a fair and reasonable one to include in the contract (as under the UCTA 1977). Factors to be considered should include:
- whether the clause is transparent;
- its substance and effect;
- the circumstances in existence at the time it was made.

Lack of transparency could in itself render a clause unfair. Guidelines for 'reasonableness' (similar to those in Sched 2 to the UCTA 1977) will be included in the new Act.

(f)   The *contra proferentem* rule will be given statutory force.

(g)   An Indicative List, similar to that included in the UTCCR 1999, will be part of the new Act. Examples of unfair clauses will be included in the Explanatory Notes published with the Act.

(h)   The burden of proof of 'fairness and reasonableness' in a consumer contract will rest on the party seeking to rely on the clause.

(i)   In business to business contracts, *exclusion clauses* (but not other terms) which are contained in written standard terms will continue to be subject to the 'fair and reasonable test', as under s 3 of the UCTA 1977. The effect of ss 2(1) and 2(2) of

---

192 *Unfair Terms in Contracts*, Law Com No 292, Scot Law Com No 199, Cm 6464, 2005, para 1.14.
193 [1988] 1 All ER 847 – see above, 9.7.3
194 See above, 9.8.2.

the UCTA 1977 will also be preserved. The burden of proof will again rest on the party seeking to rely on the clause.

(j) The requirement of reasonableness imposed on attempts to exclude liability for the statutory implied terms as to description, quality and fitness for purpose in relation to business to business contracts will no longer apply. If such exclusions are contained in written standard terms, however, they will continue to be caught by the replacement for s 3 of the UCTA 1977.

(k) A new category of contract – 'small business contracts' (SBCs) will be created. These will involve a business contractor which has nine or fewer employees. The other contractor will be a business (it may be another small business).

(l) In SBCs with a value of less than £500,000, *any* terms, other than core terms, which have been put forward as part of the other party's written standard terms will be subject to the test of fairness and reasonableness. The burden of proof, however, will here rest on the party *challenging* the term.

There are, of course, other more detailed provisions in the Law Commission's proposals, but the above highlights the main changes from the current position. If enacted, these proposals should have the effect of leading to greater clarity. In particular, it will be helpful that there is one piece of legislation dealing with the area rather than two. The actual process of deciding when clauses are 'fair and reasonable' will not, however, become any easier. It will also be interesting to see the courts' reaction to the extended power to challenge clauses given to small businesses. As we have seen, in general the courts have tended to be unsympathetic to claims of 'unreasonableness' in business to business contracts. It is likely that a similar approach will be adopted where both parties are small businesses. If there is a genuine imbalance in bargaining power, however, the new provisions will provide the opportunity for greater intervention.

9.11 FURTHER READING

Barendt, E, 'Exclusion clauses: incorporation and interpretation' (1972) 35 MLR 644

Bradgate, R, 'Unreasonable standard terms' (1997) 60 MLR 582

Coote, B, *Exception Clauses*, 1964, London: Sweet & Maxwell

Law Commission, *Unfair Terms in Contracts*, Law Com No 292, Cm 6464, 2005

Spencer, J, 'Signature, consent and the rule in *L'Estrange v Graucob*' (1973) 32 CLJ 104

von Mehren, A, 'General limits on the use of contract', 1982, Vol vii, *International Encyclopaedia of Comparative Law*, The Hague: Mohr/Nijhoff

Yates, D, *Exclusion Clauses in Contracts*, 2nd edn, 1982, London: Sweet & Maxwell

10 MISREPRESENTATION

CONTENTS

10.1 OVERVIEW

The concept of misrepresentation is concerned with pre-contractual statements, which induce a contract, but turn out to be false. There are other remedies for some false statements of this kind, such as collateral contracts, but a claimant will often wish to rely on the remedies for misrepresentation. The following issues are important in deciding if a remedy is available on this basis:

- Definition. A misrepresentation must be
  - made by one party to the other;
  - a statement of existing fact or law;
  - generally in the form of a positive statement, rather than silence. There are, however, a number of exceptions to this principle – for example, when circumstances change between the making of the statement and the making of the contract;
  - something which in part, at least, induces the other party to make the contract.

■ Remedies for misrepresentation

  ☐ Rescission of the contract. This is the main remedy which is available for all types of misrepresentation, even if wholly innocent. Certain bars, such as lapse of time, or the intervention of third party rights, will prevent rescission being available.

  ☐ Damages at common law. Damages are only available at common law if the maker of the statement has acted fraudulently, or been negligent in one of the limited situations where there is a duty of care (under the *Hedley Byrne v Heller* principle).

  ☐ Damages under the Misrepresentation Act 1967, s 2(1). This is the most powerful remedy available, providing damages unless the maker of the misrepresentation can prove that there were reasonable grounds for him or her to believe in the truth of the statement.

■ Exclusion of liability for misrepresentation

  ☐ Exclusion of liability is governed by s 3 of the Misrepresentation Act 1967, which requires such clauses to satisfy the 'requirement of reasonableness'.

  ☐ 'Entire agreement' clauses may prevent contractual liability for pre-contractual statements, but cannot circumvent s 3 of the 1967 Act.

10.2 INTRODUCTION

This chapter and the next three deal with problems which may arise out of behaviour that takes place prior to a contract being formed. A party to a contract may, after a valid agreement has apparently been concluded, nevertheless decide that it has turned out not to be quite what was anticipated, or that the behaviour of the other party means that it should not be enforced. This may be the result of false information, a mistake as to some aspect of what was agreed, the imposition of threats, or the application of improper pressure. These situations are dealt with by the English law of contract by rules which are traditionally grouped under the headings 'misrepresentation', 'mistake', 'duress' and 'undue influence'. In such a situation, the party who is unhappy with the agreement may wish to escape from it altogether, or to seek compensation of some kind. This chapter discusses the rules relating to 'misrepresentation' which allow for such an eventuality. The other areas are covered in the subsequent chapters.

An issue central to the consideration of these areas is the level of responsibility placed on parties during negotiations. The Principles of European Contract Law, for example, in addition to the general, and non-excludable, duty to deal in 'good faith',[1] deal specifically with negotiations in Art 2.301. This is headed 'Negotiations contrary to good faith' and contains the following three paragraphs:

---

1 Article 1.201: see above, 9.9.

(1)   A party is free to negotiate and is not liable for failure to reach an agreement.

(2)   However, a party who has negotiated or broken off negotiations contrary to good faith and fair dealing is liable for the losses caused to the other party.

(3)   It is contrary to good faith and fair dealing, in particular, for a party to enter into or continue negotiations with no real intention of reaching an agreement with the other party.

The Article recognises that negotiation is an important part of contractual dealings, but that such negotiations do not always lead to a contract. There is nothing inherently wrong in negotiations breaking down. Parties should be allowed to explore the possibilities of making an agreement without the need to feel under any obligation to end up in a contract with each other. This view is also that taken by English contract law. The Principles go further, however, and in para 3 make a party who, in negotiating, is not genuinely trying to reach an agreement liable for any losses which such behaviour may cause to the other party. This positive obligation is not recognised by English law and 'time-wasters' are free to back away from a contract without penalty. Similarly, para 2 of the Article, which is probably the most significant provision, has the effect of placing a positive duty on parties to negotiate in accordance with principles of 'good faith and fair dealing'. There are two points of contrast here with English law. First, the Principles treat the negotiating process as a discrete entity, with liabilities arising irrespective of whether a contract is made. In general, under English law there is no liability for wrongdoing during negotiation unless the parties end up having made a contract.[2] Second, the duty is a positive one. In English law the duties in relation to negotiation are primarily negative.[3] That is, the law intervenes when a person has behaved in a way which leads to the breach of a particular rule; it does not generally do so where a person has failed to act in a way which would have been beneficial to the other side.[4]

The notion of positive obligations of 'good faith and fair dealing' in the performance of contractual obligations are common in other systems of law,[5] including some common law systems,[6] though they do not always extend to the negotiation stage. The concept had very limited recognition, however, under the classical law of contract.[7] It is now being introduced through the influence of European directives, such as those concerned with unfair terms in consumer contracts[8] or the rights of commercial

---

2   The major exception to this is in relation to the tort of negligent misstatement, which is based on the existence of a 'duty of care' rather than the existence of a contract – see below, 10.4.4.

3   The idea of a specific obligation to negotiate in good faith was clearly rejected by the House of Lords in *Walford v Miles* [1992] 2 AC 128; [1992] 1 All ER 452 – see Chapter 2, 2.15.2.

4   There are, however, some limited circumstances where a failure to speak may amount to a misrepresentation. These are dealt with below at 10.3.3.

5   See, for example, French Civil Code, Art 1134; German BGB, Art 242.

6   For example, in the United States, ss 1–203 of the Uniform Commercial Code.

7   For example, Contracts of *uberrimae fidei* ('the utmost good faith') are the main exception, arising in relation to insurance – see below, 10.3.3.

8   As dealt with in Chapter 9, 9.8.

agents.[9] The regulations giving effect to these directives have used the language of good faith, and the English courts are therefore having to get to grips with it.[10] As yet, this has not led to any general move to develop good faith principles in areas not directly covered by such regulations. In particular, in relation to pre-contractual statements, which are the main concern of this chapter, the obligation is in general not to tell lies, rather than to tell the truth.

Why should this be the case? Why did the classical English law of contract not impose an obligation on contracting parties to be open with each other in negotiations, and to reveal all information which is relevant to their contract? There are two main answers which may be given to this question. The first is that such a positive obligation would not have sat easily with the archetype of a contract which tended to form the basis of the classical analysis. This was of two business people, of equal bargaining power, negotiating at arm's length. In such a situation, the court's attitude, based on 'freedom of contract', is that they should as far as possible be left to their own devices. If one of the parties requires information prior to a contract, then that party should ask questions of the other party. If what is then said in response turns out to be untrue, then legal liability will follow, but if no such request for information has been made, then it is not the court's business to say to the silent party 'you should have realised that this information would have been important to the other side, and you should therefore have disclosed it'.

The second answer is based on 'economic efficiency'. Information is valuable, and those in possession of it should not necessarily be required to disclose it. If, for example, a purchaser has spent money on extensive market research and is aware that there is a demand for a particular product in a particular market, it would not make economic sense (in a system based on capitalism and free trade) to require the disclosure of that information. The purchaser is enabled, by the use of the information, to buy goods at a price that is acceptable to the seller, and then resell them at a profit in the market that the purchaser has discovered. If the purchaser had to disclose the information to the seller in that situation, the point of having done the market research would be lost. In other words, disclosure would discourage entrepreneurial activity designed to increase economic activity, and thereby increase wealth.[11] There is obviously some strength in this argument, but two notes of caution should be sounded. First, it is now recognised that it is not always legitimate to make use of information which can be turned to economic advantage. In the area of share dealing, for example, the use of 'insider information' is now regarded as so undesirable that in certain circumstances to do so is treated as a criminal offence.[12]

Second, the archetypal model does not, of course, conform with the reality of

---

9 Dealt with in Chapter 6, 6.2.2.
10 See, for example, *Director General of Fair Trading v First National Bank plc* [2002] UKHL 52; [2002] 1 All ER 97, discussed in Chapter 9, 9.8.2.
11 See, for example, Kronman, 1978, pp 13–25.
12 See the Criminal Justice Act 1993, s 52.

much contractual dealing. Most obviously, many, if not the majority, of contracts are made between parties who are unequal – most obviously when the contract is business to consumer, but also in many business to business contracts. Withholding information which disadvantages the weaker party in such a situation may well be regarded as unacceptable. Moreover, even where business contractors are more or less equal partners, it does not necessarily make economic sense to conceal information from the other side. Where the contract is a long-term, 'relational' one, or where it is expected that the two contracting parties will want to do business with each other in the future, acting in a way which the other side may see as 'taking an unfair advantage' is probably not a sensible policy.[13] Even where there is no such continuing relationship, it may not be advantageous to gain a reputation for sharp dealing, since this is likely to discourage other potential contractual partners. It is likely, therefore, that business practice will in fact be more open than might be assumed from a rigid application of the 'economic efficiency' model. If that is the case, and the courts are professing to operate commercial law in a way that reflects the way in which business people actually conduct their relationships, a greater recognition of the value of openness would be justifiable.

10.2.1 Other remedies for pre-contractual statements

It should be noted that there are some situations where Parliament has intervened, generally in consumer contracts,[14] to impose an obligation of disclosure. An example is the requirement under the Consumer Credit Act 1974 that the interest charged for credit should be presented to the potential debtor in a standardised form (the 'APR') which assists in making comparisons between the terms offered by different lenders.[15] There are also some situations where, independent of any possible liability for misrepresentation, criminal liability is attached to making misleading statements to potential contractors.[16] These controls over pre-contractual statements are not discussed further here.

A further civil remedy for certain types of statement inducing a contract (that is, those which can be put into the form of a promise) may be available where the promise

---

13 See, for example, Macneil, 1978; Macaulay, 1963.
14 And often in response to the requirements of European Community law.
15 For the control of information given in advertisements, see the Consumer Credit Act (CCA) 1974, s 44 and the Consumer Credit Advertisement Regulations 1989, SI 1989/1125. Breach of the Regulations is a criminal offence: CCA 1974, s 167(2). For the control of information to be contained in credit agreements, see the CCA 1974, s 60 and the Consumer Credit (Agreements) Regulations 1983, SI 1983/1553 (as amended most recently by SI 1999/3177), implementing EC Directive 87/102. The sanction for non-compliance is that any agreement made is 'not properly executed' and therefore only enforceable by order of the court: ss 61(1) and 63.
16 See, for example, the Consumer Protection Act 1987, s 20, penalising the giving of misleading indications of price in consumer contracts, and the liability for 'false trade descriptions' under the Trade Descriptions Act 1968.

can be found to form part of a collateral unilateral contract, of the form 'If you enter into a contract with me, I promise you X'. This has been discussed in Chapters 5 and 8,[17] and is not considered further here.

10.3 DEFINITION OF MISREPRESENTATION

With the above background in mind, we can turn to the rules which are actually applied by the English courts in relation to pre-contractual statements, as encompassed in the law relating to 'misrepresentation'. The law here is based primarily on common law rules, but with statutory intervention in the form of the Misrepresentation Act 1967, mainly affecting the position as to remedies.

The law relating to misrepresentation is concerned with the situation in which a false statement leads a contracting party to enter into a contract which would otherwise not have been undertaken. It provides in certain circumstances for the party whose actions have been affected to escape from the contract or claim damages (or both). There are a number of possible actions. The contract may be rescinded under the common law. Damages may be recovered under the Misrepresentation Act 1967. The tort actions for deceit, or negligent misstatement,[18] may provide alternative bases for the recovery of damages.

The basic requirements that are necessary in order for there to be a contractual remedy for a misrepresentation are as follows. The false statement must have been made by one of the contracting parties to the other; it must be a statement of fact, not opinion or law; and the statement must have induced the other party to enter into the contract. These elements will be considered in turn.

10.3.1 Statement by one party to the other

Where a claimant is seeking to rescind a contract on the basis of a misrepresentation, or to recover damages under s 2 of the Misrepresentation Act 1967,[19] the normal rule is that the false statement must have been made by, or on behalf of,[20] the other contracting party. If a person has entered into a contract on the basis of a misrepresentation by a third party, this will have no effect on the contract, or on the person's legal relationship with the other contracting party. A person who buys shares in a company, on the basis of a third party's statement that it has just made a substantial profit, cannot undo the share purchase if the statement turns out to be untrue.

---

17 See 5.9 and 8.4.2.
18 Under the principle first stated in *Hedley Byrne & Co Ltd v Heller & Partners Ltd* [1964] AC 465; [1963] 2 All ER 575 – see below, 10.4.4.
19 Below, 10.4.6.
20 For example, by an agent. A principal may be liable for false statements made by an agent even if these were made without authority – see Chapter 6, 6.5.

This general principle has been affected, at least in certain circumstances, however, by the House of Lords' decision in *Barclays Bank v O'Brien*.[21] In this case, a husband made a misrepresentation to his wife as to the extent to which the matrimonial home was being used as security for his business debts. On the basis of this misrepresentation, the wife entered into a contract of guarantee with the bank, using the house as security. The House of Lords held that because the bank should have been aware of the risk of misrepresentation by the husband, but had taken no steps to encourage the wife to take independent legal advice, it could not enforce the contract of guarantee against her.[22] In effect, therefore, a misrepresentation made by a person who was not the other contracting party was being used to rescind the contract. This decision and subsequent case law is discussed in detail in Chapter 13.[23] There is no reason to expect it to result in a broad exception to the general principle stated above. It does open the door, however, to similar arguments in other circumstances where a party may reasonably expect a third party to make misrepresentations.[24]

If the claimant is simply seeking damages rather than rescission of the contract, the actions for deceit or negligent misstatement at common law may be available,[25] even if the statement was not made by or on behalf of the other party to the contract.

10.3.2 Statement of existing fact

In relation to the actions for rescission, deceit or under the Misrepresentation Act 1967, the statement must be one of fact, not opinion.[26] Thus, in *Bisset v Wilkinson*,[27] a farmer told the prospective purchaser of his land that it would support 2,000 sheep. It was held by the Privy Council that this was not a misrepresentation, even though it turned out to be inaccurate. The farmer had not at any point carried on sheep farming on the land, and the purchaser was aware of this. In the circumstances, therefore, the farmer's view on the matter was no more than an expression of opinion, and not a statement of fact.

FOR THOUGHT

What do you think the outcome of *Bisset v Wilkinson* would have been if the farmer had been experienced in sheep farming, though he had never farmed sheep on this particular land?

---

21 [1994] 1 AC 180; [1993] 4 All ER 417.
22 The House of Lords specifically rejected any suggestion that the husband was acting as agent for the bank when making the false statement.
23 See 13.7.3 below.
24 This is discussed further in Chapter 13 (see 13.7.1–13.7.10 below).
25 That is, under the *Hedley Byrne v Heller* principle – below, 10.4.4.
26 Under the *Hedley Byrne v Heller* type of action, a negligently given opinion can give rise to liability.
27 [1927] AC 177.

The courts have recognised three situations where a statement which appears to be one of opinion can nevertheless be treated as one of fact. First, the opinion must not be contradicted by other facts known to the person giving it. In *Smith v Land and House Property Corp*,[28] the statement that a tenant was 'most desirable', while on its face an opinion, was treated as a misrepresentation because the maker of the statement knew that the tenant had in fact been in arrears with his rent for some time. Second, where the statement of opinion comes from an 'expert', it may amount to a representation that the expert has based it on a proper consideration of all the relevant circumstances. In *Esso Petroleum Co Ltd v Mardon*,[29] a representative of Esso gave a view as to the likely throughput of petrol at a particular petrol station. In giving this estimate, however, the representative had overlooked the fact that the conditions imposed by the local planning authority meant that the petrol station would not have a frontage on the main road. The statement as to the likely throughput was clearly at one level an opinion. The Court of Appeal, however, took the view that in the circumstances it involved a representation that proper care had been taken in giving it, and that this was a statement of fact. Third, a statement of opinion which is not genuinely held can be treated as a false statement of fact in relation to the person's state of mind. This derives from the view expressed in *Edgington v Fitzmaurice*[30] that a statement of an intention to act in a particular way in the future may be interpreted as a statement of fact, if it is clear that the person making the statement did not, at that time, have any intention of so acting. In this case a company prospectus, designed to attract subscribers, contained false statements about the uses to which the money raised would be put. It was held that this statement of intention could be treated as a representation as to the directors' state of mind at the time that the prospectus was issued, and could thus be treated as a statement of fact. As Bowen LJ put it:[31]

> . . . the state of a man's mind is as much a fact as the state of his digestion. It is true that it is very difficult to prove what the state of a man's mind at a particular time is, but if it can be ascertained it is as much a fact as anything else. A misrepresentation as to the state of a man's mind is, therefore, a misstatement of fact.

A similar lack of belief in the truth of what is being said may also turn a statement of opinion into a misrepresentation. It is a false statement of the person's current state of mind.

It has traditionally been thought that a false statement of law was not to be

---

28 (1884) 28 Ch D 7.
29 [1976] QB 801; [1976] 2 All ER 5. See also Chapter 8, 8.4.2. Cf *Notts Patent Brick and Tile Co v Butler* (1866) 16 QBD 778 – a statement by a solicitor that he was 'not aware' of any restrictive covenants applying to a piece of land, when in fact he had not checked the position, was held to be a misrepresentation.
30 (1885) 29 Ch D 459.
31 Ibid, p 482.

treated as a statement of fact for the purposes of misrepresentation.[32] This point may need reconsideration, however, in the light of the House of Lords' decision in *Kleinwort Benson Ltd v Lincoln City Council*.[33] Here the House overturned the long-held view that mistakes of law could not be used as the basis for an action for restitution of money paid. It had previously been thought that this was only available in relation to mistakes of fact. If the courts have here assimilated 'law' to 'fact', it may well be argued that the same should apply to misrepresentations. This was the view taken by the High Court in *Pankhania v Hackney London Borough Council*,[34] in which the judge held that the 'misrepresentation of law' rule has not survived *Kleinwort*.[35] He took the view that:

> The distinction between fact and law in the context of relief from misrepresentation has no more underlying principle to it than it does in the context of relief from mistake. Indeed, when the principles of mistake and misrepresentation are set side by side, there is a stronger case for granting relief against a party who has induced a mistaken belief as to law in another, than against one who has merely made the same mistake himself . . . The survival of the 'misrepresentation of law' rule following the demise of the 'mistake of law' rule would be no more than a quixotic anachronism.

A misrepresentation can be made by actions as well as words. This is illustrated by the case of *Spice Girls Ltd v Aprilia World Service BV*.[36] Spice Girls Ltd, the company formed to promote the pop group, the Spice Girls, was in the process of making a contract for the promotion of Aprilia's scooters. Shortly before the contract was signed, the members of the group all took part in the filming of a commercial for Aprilia. At that time, they knew that one member of the group intended to leave, as she did shortly after the contract had been signed. The group's participation in the filming was held to amount to a representation that Spice Girls Ltd did not know and had no reasonable ground to believe that any of the existing members had at that time a declared intention to leave. This was untrue, and therefore the participation in the filming amounted to a misrepresentation by conduct.

10.3.3 Misrepresentation by silence

In general, there is no misrepresentation by silence. Even where one party is aware that the other is contracting on the basis of a misunderstanding of some fact relating to the

---

32 Unless, of course, the maker of the statement knew that the statement of law was false, in which case it would be a false representation as to the maker's state of mind about the accuracy of the statement of law (on the basis of *Edgington v Fitzmaurice*).
33 [1999] 2 AC 349. The case is discussed further in Chapter 19, 19.3.3.
34 [2002] EWHC 2441.
35 Ibid, para 55.
36 [2000] EMLR 478.

contract, there will generally be no liability. This is in line with the general approach outlined at the beginning of this chapter, that English law imposes a negative obligation not to tell falsehoods, rather than a positive obligation to tell the truth.

There are, however, some exceptions to this. First, the maker of the statement must not give only half the story on some aspect of the facts. Thus, in *Dimmock v Hallett*,[37] the statement that flats were fully let when, in fact, as the maker of the statement knew, the tenants had given notice to quit was capable of being a misrepresentation.[38] Second, if a true statement is made, but then circumstances change, making it false, a failure to disclose this will be treated as a misrepresentation. In *With v O'Flanagan*,[39] for example, a statement was made by the vendor of a medical practice that its income was £2,000 per annum. This was true at the time, but as a result of the vendor's illness the practice declined considerably over the next few months, so that by the time it was actually sold, its value had reduced significantly. The Court of Appeal held that the failure to notify the purchaser of the fact that the earlier statement was no longer true amounted to a misrepresentation.[40]

Third, certain contracts, such as those for insurance,[41] are treated as being 'of the utmost good faith' (*uberrimae fidei*), and require the contracting party to disclose all relevant facts. In an insurance contract, for example, there is an obligation to disclose material facts, even if the other party has not asked about them. Thus, in *Lambert v Co-operative Insurance Society*,[42] a woman who was renewing the insurance on her jewellery should have disclosed that her husband had recently been convicted of conspiracy to steal. The fact that she had not mentioned this meant that, when some of her jewellery was subsequently stolen, the insurance company was entitled not to compensate her under the policy. The obligation is to disclose such facts as a reasonable insurer might have treated as material.[43] The test of materiality does not always seem to be applied very strictly, however. In *Woolcutt v Sun Alliance and London Insurance Ltd*,[44] a policy for fire insurance on a house was invalidated because the insured had failed to disclose in a mortgage application, which indicated that the mortgagee would insure the

---

37 (1866) LR 2 Ch App 21.

38 This is similar to the situation where a statement of opinion can become a statement of fact because the maker is aware of facts making the opinion untrue: *Smith v Land and House Property Corp* (1884) 28 Ch D 7 – above, 10.3.2.

39 [1936] Ch 575. For discussion of this decision see Bigwood, 2005.

40 This does not apply where the statement is one of intention, and the intention later changes: *Wales v Wadham* [1977] 1 WLR 199 – wife's statement during negotiations for a divorce settlement that she did not intend to remarry.

41 In *Carter v Boehm* (1766) 3 Burr 1905, Lord Mansfield justified this approach to insurance contracts on the basis that they were based on 'speculation'.

42 [1975] 2 Lloyd's Rep 485.

43 This test was adopted by Mackenna J in *Lambert* on the basis that it was the standard applied to marine insurance by s 18 of the Marine Insurance Act 1906, and that there was no reason why a different standard should apply to other types of insurance.

44 [1978] 1 All ER 1253.

property concerned, that he had been convicted of robbery some 10 years previously. It is not immediately obvious why this fact was material. Caulfield J simply treated it as 'almost self-evident' that 'the criminal record of the assured can affect the moral hazard which the insurers have to assess'.[45]

The obligation most frequently operates to the disadvantage of the insured person, but that it can also apply to the insurer was confirmed by the House of Lords in *Banque Financière v Westgate Insurance*,[46] which concerned the failure by the insurer to disclose wrongdoing by its agent. A similar obligation applies to contracts establishing family settlements. Thus, in *Gordon v Gordon*,[47] a settlement was made on the presumption that an elder son was born outside marriage, and was therefore illegitimate. In fact, the younger son knew that his parents had been through a secret marriage ceremony prior to the birth of his elder brother. The fact that he had concealed this knowledge, which was clearly material, meant that the settlement had to be set aside.

Finally, there are some contracts which involve a fiduciary relationship, and this may entail a duty to disclose. In this category are to be found contracts between agent and principal,[48] solicitor and client, and a company and its promoters.[49] Other similar relationships which have a fiduciary character will be treated in the same way, and the list is not closed.

10.3.4 Misrepresentation must induce the contract

It is not enough to give rise to a remedy for misrepresentation for the claimant to point to some false statement of fact made by the defendant prior to a contract which they have made. It must also be shown that that statement formed some part of the reason why the claimant entered into the agreement. In *JEB Fasteners Ltd v Bloom*,[50] for example, which was concerned with this issue of reliance in the context of an action for negligent misstatement at common law, it was established that the plaintiffs took over a business having seen inaccurate accounts prepared by the defendants. Their reason for taking over the business, however, was shown to have been the wish to secure

---

45 [1978] 1 All ER 1253, p 1257. As Collins points out (2003, p 210), if the insurer was concerned about previous criminal convictions it could have asked specific questions to this effect. The position was complicated by the fact that the insurance was effected via the mortgagee (a building society) so that there were no direct dealings between the assured and the insurer. The insurer could, however, presumably have required the building society to make relevant inquiries.

46 [1991] 2 AC 249; [1990] 2 All ER 947. See also *Manifest Shipping Co Ltd v Uni-Polaris Shipping Co Ltd, The Star Sea* [2001] UKHL 1; [2001] 1 All ER 743.

47 (1816–21) 3 Swans 400; 36 ER 910.

48 For example, *Armstrong v Jackson* [1917] 2 KB 822 – see Chapter 6, 6.7.1.

49 *Boardman v Phipps* [1967] 2 AC 46; [1966] 3 All ER 721. There are also various statutory protections for prospective investors in companies, contained, for example, in the Public Offer of Securities Regulations 1995, SI 1995/1536 and the Financial Services and Markets Act 2000, ss 90 and 91 and Sched 10.

50 [1983] 1 All ER 583.

the services of two directors. The accounts had not induced their action in taking over the business. Similarly, where the claimant has not relied on the statement, but has sought independent verification, there will not be sufficient reliance to found an action.[51]

On the other hand, it is not necessary for the misrepresentation to be the sole reason why the contract was entered into. In *Edgington v Fitzmaurice*,[52] the plaintiff was influenced not only by the prospectus, but also by his own mistaken belief that he would have a charge on the assets of the company. His action based on misrepresentation was nevertheless successful. Provided the misstatement was 'actively present to his mind when he decided to advance the money', then it was material. The test is, according to Bowen LJ:[53]

> . . . what was the state of the plaintiff's mind, and if his mind was disturbed by the misstatement of the defendants, and such disturbance was in part the cause of what he did, the mere fact of his also making a mistake himself could make no difference.

Nor does it matter that the party deceived has spurned a chance to discover the truth. In *Redgrave v Hurd*,[54] false statements were made by the plaintiff about the income of his practice as a solicitor, on the strength of which the defendant had entered into a contract to buy the plaintiff's house and practice. He had been given the chance to examine documents which would have revealed the true position, but had declined to do so. This did not prevent his claim based on misrepresentation.

This principle will not be applied, however, where the true position was set out in the contract signed by the claimant. In *Peekay Intermark Ltd v Australia and New Zealand Banking Group Ltd*[55] a representative of the defendant bank had described an investment opportunity to the claimant in general terms. Some days later the representative sent to the claimant the full terms and conditions of the investment. This contract contained provisions which made the investment more risky than it appeared from the initial broad description given by the representative. The claimant looked over the documents briefly, and initialled them, but did not read them in detail, assuming that they were in line with what he had been previously told. He subsequently sought damages under s 2(1) Misrepresentation Act 1967 on the basis of the representative's negligent misrepresentation of the terms. He succeeded at first instance, but on appeal, the Court of Appeal held for the defendant. It ruled that although the documents sent to the claimant did not correspond to the investment previously outlined by the representative, the defendants had not misrepresented the documents themselves. Since the

---

51 *Atwood v Small* (1838) 6 Cl & F 232.
52 (1885) 29 Ch D 459.
53 Ibid, p 483.
54 (1881) 20 Ch D 1.
55 [2006] 2 Lloyd's Rep 511.

claimant had looked at and signed these documents it was not then open to him to claim that he was induced to sign by an earlier misrepresentation.

It seems that if the statement is one on which a reasonable person would have relied, then there is a rebuttable presumption that the claimant did in fact rely on it. This was the view of the Court of Appeal in *Barton v County NatWest Ltd*.[56] Moreover, the presumption will not disappear simply as a result of the fact that the claimant has given evidence; the burden remains on the defendant to disprove it.

The contrary position – that is, where it is claimed that the claimant did in fact rely on the statement, even though a reasonable person would not have done so – has also been given some consideration. In other words, does the reliance on the statement have to be 'reasonable' in order for it to be a material inducement to contract? This issue was considered in *Museprime Properties Ltd v Adhill Properties Ltd*.[57] Property owned by the defendant was sold by auction to the plaintiffs. There was an inaccurate statement in the auction particulars, which was reaffirmed by the auctioneer, to the effect that rent reviews of three leases to which the properties were subject had not been finalised. The plaintiffs sought to rescind the contract for misrepresentation. The defendants argued, as part of their case, that the misrepresentation was not material because no reasonable bidder would have allowed it to influence his bid. Scott J held (approving a passage to this effect in Goff and Jones, 1993)[58] that the materiality of the representation was not to be determined by whether a reasonable person would have been induced to contract. As long as the claimant was *in fact* induced, as was the case here, that was enough to entitle him to rescission. The reasonableness or otherwise of his or her behaviour was relevant only to the burden of proof: the less reasonable the inducement, the more difficult it would be for the claimant to convince the court that he or she had been affected by the misrepresentation.

It is difficult to be sure how far this principle can be taken. Suppose, for example, I am selling my car and, prior to the contract, I tell the prospective purchaser that the car is amphibious and will go across water. Can the purchaser later claim against me because this ridiculous statement turns out to be untrue, as he has discovered now that the car is at the bottom of the river? Clearly, there may be difficulties of proving that there was reliance in fact, as noted above, but assuming that it is established that the statement was believed by the purchaser (for example, by the fact that he tried to drive across a river), the *Museprime* approach would give a remedy in misrepresentation. Would the courts go this far? Or would some degree of reasonable reliance be introduced, where, for example, no reasonable person would ever have believed the statement to be true?

The answer may lie in differentiating between 'reasonableness' for the purposes of materiality, and the reasonableness of a person's believing that the statement was true.

---

56 [2002] 4 All ER 494 (note); [1999] Lloyd's Rep Bank 408, placing some reliance on the Australian case of *Australian Steel and Mining Corp Pty Ltd v Corben* [1974] 2 NSWLR 202.

57 [1990] 2 EG 196; (1990) 61 P & CR 111.

58 Page 168.

The *Museprime* test can be seen as primarily concerned with the former type of 'reasonableness'. It is dealing with the question of whether a reasonable person would have regarded a statement of this type as containing information which would be a material factor in deciding whether to enter into the contract or not. In relation to the sale of a house, for example, a statement that a garden fence had been erected three years ago (when perhaps in fact it had been erected two years ago) might be seen as immaterial to the contract, so that the 'reasonable purchaser' would have been unlikely to have been induced to contract on the basis of it. The *Museprime* approach would say, however, that provided that the court believed that it was regarded as material by the particular purchaser, then it could be treated as a misrepresentation. The unreasonableness of that view would be irrelevant. On the other hand (as with the example of the allegedly amphibious car), if the statement, while about something which if true would undoubtedly be 'material' in that it would affect the value of what was being sold, is so far-fetched that no reasonable person would believe it, it may be that the courts would be more prepared to impose a test of reasonableness on the claimant. A distinction of this kind would make sense, but it cannot be said that it comes through clearly in the judgment in *Museprime*. That case seems to suggest that whether there was reliance on the statement is always simply a matter of proof, and that reasonableness only becomes relevant as part of the evidential process.

The position is apparently different, however, in relation to insurance contracts. Where the case is one of non-disclosure in such a contract (which is a contract *uberrimae fidei* – requiring the utmost good faith), the test is whether a reasonable insurer would have relied on the misrepresentation. This was the view of the House of Lords in *Pan Atlantic Insurance Co Ltd v Pine Top Insurance Co Ltd*.[59]

10.4 REMEDIES FOR MISREPRESENTATION

The remedies available for misrepresentation depend to some extent on the state of mind of the person making the false statement. If the statement is fraudulent, the remedies may be more extensive than if it is made negligently or innocently. There are remedies available under common law and equity and also under the Misrepresentation Act 1967.

10.4.1 Rescission

The principal remedy under English law for a misrepresentation was for a long time the rescission of the ensuing contract. This view of the effect of misrepresentation makes sense if the false statement is viewed as affecting the agreement between the parties. If the agreement has been reached on a false basis, then it is appropriate that it should be

---

59 [1995] AC 501.

set aside. Moreover, once the agreement has been set aside there is then limited scope for the award of damages. This approach makes most sense if the dominant view of contractual obligations is, as it was under classical contract law, that they are based on a consensus between the parties (probably derived from the mutual exchange of promises). The growth of the idea of reliance as an important element in the definition of contractual obligations, however,[60] would suggest that the remedy for misrepresentation should be based on the extent to which reliance on the false statement has led to loss. This would mean the provision of compensatory damages playing a much more important role in the remedies available. That trend can be observed as having occurred during the latter half of the twentieth century, with both common law and statute providing for damages to be much more widely available as a remedy for misrepresentation. These developments are considered later in this chapter. This has not, however, been at the expense of the availability of rescission.

Rescission remains available in any situation where a misrepresentation has induced a contract, whether the false statement was fraudulent, negligent or wholly innocent.[61] The remedy allows the parties to be restored to their original positions. Thus, if the contract is one for the sale of goods, both the goods, and the price paid for them, must be returned. Prior to the Misrepresentation Act 1967, there could be no rescission for misrepresentation where either the false statement had become part of the contract or where the contract had been performed. This was changed by s 1 of the Misrepresentation Act 1967, which states:

> Where a person has entered into a contract after a misrepresentation has been made to him, and:
> (a)   the misrepresentation has become a term of the contract; or
> (b)   the contract has been performed;
> or both, then, if otherwise he would be entitled to rescind the contract without alleging fraud, he shall be so entitled, subject to the provisions of this Act, notwithstanding the matter mentioned in paras (a) and (b) of this section.

There are certain bars, however, to the availability of rescission. The remedy will be lost in the following situations. First, it may be lost where the party to whom the statement was made has affirmed the contract. That is, the party to whom the statement has been made, knowing or having discovered that the statement was false, nevertheless continues with the contract. In *Long v Lloyd*,[62] for example, a representation was made as to the fuel consumption of a lorry by the seller (the defendant). After buying the lorry, the plaintiff discovered that this statement was untrue, and that the lorry had various

---

60 See Chapter 3, 3.15.2.
61 Although in certain circumstances the court now has a discretion under s 2(2) of the Misrepresentation Act 1967 to award damages in lieu of rescission for an innocent misrepresentation – see below, 10.4.8.
62 [1958] 2 All ER 402.

other defects. The defendant offered to contribute towards the cost of repairs. The plaintiff accepted this offer, and later sent the lorry on a long journey during which it broke down. He then tried to rescind the contract for misrepresentation. It was held that he had affirmed the contract with full knowledge of the false statement, and had therefore lost the right to rescind. The justification for this bar is presumably that if the claimant has continued with the contract, having knowledge of the misrepresentation, the statement cannot have been as material a factor in making the contract as is being alleged.

FOR THOUGHT

Do you think that the outcome of *Long v Lloyd* would have been different if the purchaser had simply accepted the offer of contribution to the repairs, but had not sent it on the journey during which it broke down? What if there had been no discussion of paying for the repairs, but the purchaser had continued to use the lorry, knowing about the defects?

The second way in which the right to rescind may be lost is by lapse of time. In *Leaf v International Galleries*,[63] the purchaser of a picture stated to be by John Constable discovered, on trying to sell it some five years later, that this statement was false. His attempt to rescind for misrepresentation failed because of the lapse of time. This case was fairly clear. In other situations, it will be a matter for the court to consider in all the circumstances whether the lapse of time is sufficient to preclude rescission. It may be significant that in *Leaf v International Galleries,* Lord Denning drew an analogy with the rules relating to the acceptance of goods under the Sale of Goods Act 1893.[64] The case law on this issue used to suggest that a fairly short time from the contract, measured in days or weeks rather than years, would be sufficient to amount to 'acceptance' (and thereby prevent rejection for breach of contract).[65] Changes to the wording of the relevant section of the Sale of Goods Act 1979 have meant that more recent case law has adopted a more flexible approach to when a contract has been affirmed.[66] In relation to misrepresentation it is likely that the stricter approach to assessing the time at which the loss of the right to rescind for misrepresentation will occur will continue to be taken. The justification for this bar is less clear than that based on affirmation. Why should the fact that the claimant only discovers the falsity of the defendant's statement after a significant lapse of time mean that the right to rescind should be lost? If the misrepresentation was material, the claimant has still contracted on a false basis, and it is not clear why this falsity should not be regarded as allowing the claimant to say that

---

63 [1950] 2 KB 86; [1950] 1 All ER 693.
64 Now dealt with by the Sale of Goods Act 1979, s 35.
65 See, for example, *Bernstein v Pamsons Motors (Golders Green) Ltd* [1987] 2 All ER 220; *Truk (UK) Ltd v Tokmakidis GmbH* [2000] 1 Lloyd's Rep 543.
66 *Clegg v Olle Andersson* [2003] EWCA 220.

the contract would never have been made had the truth been known. Of course, in some situations, if a contract has proceeded on a satisfactory basis for some time and the discovery of the misrepresentation is unlikely to make any practical difference, it may be justifiable to say that this is a situation equivalent to affirmation and the contract should stand. Once again, the basis would be that the statement was not in fact material to the contract. Alternatively, it might be argued that after a long lapse of time it is in practice difficult to undo a contract in a way that does not cause undue hardship to the other side. But this point is largely dealt with by the next bar, that is, where restitution is impossible. The bar based simply on lapse of time can probably be justified only on the basis that there is a desirability of certainty and finality in contractual relationships, and to have the possibility of rescission remaining open for years after the making of the contract would go against this. This bar remains, however, the one for which it is most difficult to find convincing justifications.

The next bar arises where restitution is impossible. This may arise, for example, where goods have been destroyed, consumed or irretrievably mixed with others. In *Clarke v Dickson,* [67] Crompton J gave two colourful examples of this. In argument he commented that 'If you are fraudulently induced to buy a cake you may return it and get back the price; but you cannot both eat your cake and return your cake'.[68] In his judgment he gave the following example:[69]

> Take the case . . . of a butcher buying live cattle, killing them and even selling the meat to his customers. If the rule of law were as the plaintiff contends, that butcher on discovering a fraud on the part of the grazier who sold him the cattle could rescind the contract and get back the whole price: but how could that be consistent with justice?

In *Clarke v Dickson* itself, the purchaser of shares in a company was unable to rescind the contract because he had:[70]

> . . . changed the nature of the article: the shares he received were shares in a company on the cost book principle; the plaintiff offers to restore them after he has converted them into shares in a joint stock corporation.

Moreover, the company was at the time in the course of being wound up, so there was no chance of a profit being made from the shares. A simple decline in value will not, however, be sufficient to bar rescission.[71] The requirement of precise restitution has

---

67 (1858) EB & E 148; 120 ER 463.
68 Ibid, p 152; p 465.
69 Ibid, p 155, p 466.
70 Ibid, p 154; p 466, per Erle J.
71 *Armstrong v Jackson* [1917] 2 KB 822; cf *Cheese v Thomas* [1994] 1 All ER 35, discussed in Chapter 13, 13.8.1.

been applied less strictly in equity than under the common law. For example, the common law would not allow rescission where a lessee had gone into possession of the land leased, on the basis that once it had been occupied, precise restitution was impossible. Equity will allow rescission subject to rent being paid for the period of occupation.[72] In *Erlanger v New Sombrero Phosphate Co,*[73] the contract involved the purchase of a mine, which the buyer worked for a period before seeking to rescind. The court allowed rescission on the basis of a payment being made to cover the profits that the buyer had made and the deterioration in the mine. The approach of equity is to do what is 'practically just' even where precise restitution is impossible.[74]

The final bar arises where rescission would affect the rights of third parties. In some ways this is simply a further example of the bar based on impossibility of restitution. It constitutes a major limitation where goods obtained on the basis of a (probably fraudulent) misrepresentation have been sold on to an innocent third party. The courts will not, in such a situation, require the third party to disgorge the goods.[75] This has caused particular problems for claimants where there has been a misrepresentation as to the identity of a purchaser, which is relevant to creditworthiness. As a result, attempts have been made (generally unsuccessfully) to argue that such contracts are void for mistake.[76]

10.4.2 Operation of rescission

A contract is not automatically rescinded as a result of a misrepresentation, even where none of the bars noted above apply. It is 'voidable' rather than 'void'. The choice of whether or not to rescind rests with the innocent party. Until that decision is made, the contract is treated as valid and enforceable. To rescind the contract, the innocent party will generally be expected to give notice of this to the other side. There is no particular form required as long as it is made clear the contract is being rescinded. Starting legal proceedings to have the contract set aside will constitute notice of rescission.[77]

It may well be, particularly where the misrepresentation was fraudulent, that the party making the false statement is no longer easily contactable. In that circumstance, there is authority that other reasonable steps which clearly indicate an intention to rescind may be enough. In *Car and Universal Finance Co Ltd v Caldwell,*[78] C, the owner

---

72 *Hulton v Hulton* [1917] 1 KB 813.
73 (1878) App Cas 1218.
74 Ibid, p 1279, per Lord Blackburn.
75 See, for example, *Phillips v Brooks* [1919] 2 KB 243; *Lewis v Averay* [1972] 2 All ER 229. The position is also affected by s 23 of the Sale of Goods Act 1979, which allows a buyer of goods who is in possession under a voidable title (which is the position where there has been a misrepresentation) to pass a good title to a third party who buys the goods in good faith.
76 See Chapter 11, 11.6.3 to 11.6.4.
77 *Reese Silver Mining Co v Smith* (1869) LR 4 HL 64.
78 [1965] 1 QB 525; [1964] 1 All ER 290.

of a car, sold it to N in return for a cheque which was dishonoured. The giving of a cheque constitutes a representation that the drawer believes that it will be met when presented; if no such belief is held, it is a misrepresentation. As soon as the cheque was returned, C at once informed the police and the Automobile Association. It was held that this was sufficient to avoid the contract, in the circumstances. Since C had acted before N had managed to resell the car, the innocent third party who had later bought it had acquired no title. C could therefore recover the car.[79]

10.4.3 Damages at common law

At common law, damages were traditionally only available in relation to fraudulent misrepresentations, under the tort of deceit. There is now the possibility of damages being recovered for negligent misstatements under the tort of negligence, as developed in *Hedley Byrne & Co Ltd v Heller & Partners Ltd*[80] and subsequent cases. These are discussed in the next section.[81]

The leading case on deceit is *Derry v Peek*.[82] A prospectus for a tram company indicated that it had the right to use steam power. In fact, the Board of Trade refused permission, and the company failed. The plaintiff had bought shares in reliance on the statement in the prospectus, and sought damages for the tort of deceit. The House of Lords held that for an action for deceit, it was necessary to show fraud. This meant, in the words of Lord Herschell, that a false representation must be proved to have been made:[83]

> . . . (1) knowingly; or (2) without belief in its truth; or (3) recklessly, careless whether it be true or false.

On the facts, the defendants were not liable because they honestly believed the truth of their statement in the prospectus. The requirements for deceit remain, however, as set out in this case. As can be seen, mere negligence is not enough – knowledge of the falsity, or a reckless disregard for the truth is needed. In *Thomas Witter Ltd v TBP Industries Ltd*,[84] it was held that the 'recklessness' must be sufficiently serious to amount to fraud. This implies 'dishonesty' on the part of the maker of the statement,

---

79 Treitel (2003, p 373) doubts whether this rule should be extended beyond fraudulent misrepresentations, because of its harsh effect on the innocent third party. The Law Reform Committee for similar reasons recommended in 1966 that the decision in *Caldwell* should be reversed: 12th Report, Cmnd 2958, para 16. Its practical effect has, however, been reduced by the decision in *Newtons of Wembley v Williams* [1965] 1 QB 560 that a fraudulent purchaser in possession can pass a good title by virtue of the Sale of Goods Act 1979, s 25.
80 [1964] AC 465; [1963] 2 All ER 575.
81 See 10.4.4.
82 (1889) 14 App Cas 337.
83 Ibid, p 374.
84 [1996] 2 All ER 573.

though not necessarily in the sense in which that word is used in the criminal law: *Standard Chartered Bank v Pakistan National Shipping Corp (No 2)*.[85]

Once deceit is established, damages will be assessed according to the tortious measure, which aims to put the parties in the position they would have been in had the tort not occurred – that is, in this context, if the false statement had not been made.[86] This may not simply be a matter of restoring the parties to their pre-misrepresentation positions: in appropriate cases the court may also take account of benefits which the claimant has missed out on as a result of the misrepresentation.[87] Although the tortious measure is used, the damages for deceit may be more extensive than is usually the case in tort, since in *Doyle v Olby (Ironmongers) Ltd*[88] it was held that the defendant will be liable for all losses which can be shown to be the consequences of the false statement, without being limited by the normal rules of 'remoteness' (which would limit damages to those which were reasonably foreseeable by the defendant).[89] The justification for this rule seems to be a 'moral' one, based on the fact that the defendant who has deliberately or recklessly lied should not be allowed to place limits on the claimant's recovery of losses.[90] This is a clear departure from the normal approach towards damages in the civil law, which takes fair compensation for the claimant as the guiding principle. If the normal rule in tort is that fair compensation is limited by the foreseeability of the claimant's loss, why should this not apply to deceit? The state of mind of the defendant when making the statement has no effect on the claimant's losses. The wider measure of damages can only be seen as intended to punish the defendant for having acted deceitfully.[91]

The effect of this rule was demonstrated in the House of Lords decision in *Smith and New Court Securities Ltd v Scrimgeour Vickers (Asset Management) Ltd*.[92] The case concerned the sale of a parcel of shares in F Ltd, owned by the defendants. They offered them to the plaintiffs, but fraudulently claimed that other bids had been received. This fraudulent misrepresentation led the plaintiffs to increase their offer from 78p per share to 82.25p per share. This offer was accepted, and the parcel of over 28 million shares was sold to the plaintiffs for just over £23m. It then transpired that F Ltd had been the victim of another unrelated fraud, and its share price plummeted. The plaintiffs resold the shares, suffering a loss of over £11m. The plaintiffs claimed this in damages from the defendants; the defendants claimed that they should be limited to the difference between the price they would have been prepared to pay without the misrepresentation (78p per share) and the contract price (82.25p per share). The

---

85 [2000] 1 Lloyd's Rep 218.
86 The contractual measure would aim to put them in the position they would have been in had the statement been true – see Chapter 18, 18.3.
87 See, for example, *East v Maurer* [1991] 2 All ER 733, discussed below.
88 [1969] 2 QB 158; [1969] 2 All ER 119.
89 For further discussion of the rules of remoteness, see Chapter 18, 18.5.1.
90 See the comments of Lord Denning [1969] 2 QB 158, p 167; [1969] 2 All ER 119, p 122.
91 Or as enforcing 'the public policy of deterring deliberate wrongdoing': Hooley, 1991, p 550.
92 [1996] 4 All ER 769.

defendants succeeded in the Court of Appeal, but the House of Lords held that the application of *Doyle v Olby* entitled the plaintiffs to recover their full losses. The plaintiffs would not have made the contract but for the misrepresentation (the offer of 78p would not at the time have been acceptable to the defendants), and they were, therefore, as a result of the misrepresentation 'locked into the property'. Their full consequential losses were therefore recoverable.

Attempting to put claimants into the position in which they would have ended up had the misrepresentation not been made may, in some circumstances, allow the recovery of certain types of lost profit. In *East v Maurer*, [93] the false statement related to a hairdressing business which the plaintiff bought. The defendant had stated that he had no intention of opening another hairdressing shop in the area. This was untrue, and when he did open such a shop, the plaintiff sued for damages resulting from his loss of business. If the statement had been true, the plaintiff would have been likely to have made substantial profits from the business which he had bought. Such profits would only, however, be recoverable in an action for breach of contract, where 'expectation interests' are compensated.[94] On the other hand, if the statement had not been made, the plaintiff would probably have bought a different business, and would have made some (though not as extensive) profits from that. The court felt that these hypothetical profits should be recoverable. The action for fraudulent misrepresentation may thus come very close to providing the same level of damages as are available for breach of contract.

10.4.4 False statements and the tort of negligence

In certain situations, damages for the tort of negligence may be recoverable in relation to misstatements. The law governing this area derives from the House of Lords' decision in *Hedley Byrne & Co Ltd v Heller & Partners Ltd*.[95] In this case, the plaintiffs had asked their bank to give an opinion on the financial standing of another firm. The bank gave a positive report, and the plaintiffs entered into contracts with the firm. Shortly afterwards the firm went into liquidation, owing substantial sums to the plaintiffs. They sued the bank, alleging that the statements as to the financial status of the firm had been made negligently. On the facts, the House of Lords held that the bank was protected by a 'without responsibility' disclaimer which it had attached to its advice.[96] It held, however, that in the absence of this the bank would have been liable. This established the possibility, therefore, of taking action in the tort of negligence in relation to statements made without proper care which result in loss. For this to be available, however, a 'duty of care' must be shown to exist between the maker of the statement

---

93 [1991] 2 All ER 733.
94 See Chapter 18, 18.4.1.
95 [1964] AC 465; [1963] 2 All ER 575.
96 The reasonableness of such a disclaimer would now have to be considered under s 2 of the UCTA 1977. See Chapter 9, 9.7.4, and the case of *Smith v Eric S Bush* [1990] 1 AC 831; [1989] 2 All ER 514.

and the person who has acted on it. Much of the extensive subsequent case law on this area has been concerned with the question of when such a duty will arise, which, it has been suggested, depends on there being a 'special relationship' between the parties. At times, however, it seemed that all that was needed was that the maker of the statement could reasonably foresee that the person to whom the statement was made would rely on it, and would suffer loss if it turned out to be untrue.[97] The House of Lords' decision in *Caparo Industries plc v Dickman* severely restricted the circumstances in which such a duty will be found to exist, though this has been softened to some extent by the subsequent decisions in *Henderson v Merrett Syndicates Ltd*[98] and *White v Jones*.[99] The current position seems to be that, in addition to the reasonable foreseeability of reliance and harm, there must be sufficient 'proximity' between the parties, and that it must be just and reasonable for the duty to be imposed. *Henderson v Merrett* and *White v Jones* indicate that a voluntary assumption of responsibility by the maker of the statement will generally be sufficient to establish a duty.[100] The issue of proximity is the most difficult, but will normally be satisfied where the statement is made in a context in which the parties are anticipating that a contract will be made between them. It was held by the Court of Appeal in *Esso Petroleum Co Ltd v Mardon*[101] that a common law duty of care could arise in such a situation, and this has been confirmed in the more recent cases of *Gran Gelato Ltd v Richcliff (Group) Ltd*[102] and *Henderson v Merrett Syndicates Ltd*.[103]

The need for the *Hedley Byrne* action for contracting parties was reduced by the enactment of the Misrepresentation Act 1967,[104] which for the first time introduced a remedy in damages for non-fraudulent misrepresentations. Nevertheless, there are still situations where it may be useful to plead common law negligence alongside, or as an alternative to, liability under the Act. One advantage of the *Hedley Byrne* action, for example, is that it applies to all types of statement, not just statements of fact. A negligently expressed opinion may therefore give rise to the possibility of action in tort, where an action in contract would not be available (because the statement is not one of fact), unless the claimant proved that the opinion was not genuinely held, or that the expresser of the opinion was aware of facts which rendered it untenable. In general, however, an action under s 2 of the Misrepresentation Act 1967 will be the preferred choice for the claimant because it offers, as will be seen below, advantages in terms of the burden of proof and the extent of damages which are recoverable.

---

97 See, for example, *Anns v Merton London Borough Council* [1978] AC 728; [1977] 2 All ER 492.
98 [1995] 2 AC 145; [1994] 3 All ER 506. See also *Spring v Guardian Assurance plc* [1995] 2 AC 296; [1994] 3 All ER 129.
99 [1995] 3 All ER 481. This case is discussed further at 5.10.
100 This basis for a duty was recognised in *Hedley Byrne* but doubt was cast on it by *Caparo Industries plc v Dickman*.
101 [1976] QB 801; [1976] 2 All ER 5. The facts of this case have been given in Chapter 8, at 8.4.2.
102 [1992] Ch 560.
103 [1995] 2 AC 145; [1994] 3 All ER 506.
104 See below, 10.4.6 to 10.5.

10.4.5 Indemnity at common law

As has been indicated above, the primary remedy for misrepresentation at common law was rescission. There was also, however, in certain circumstances a right to claim an indemnity for expenses incurred, in addition to rescission. As is shown by *Whittington v Seale-Hayne*,[105] however, such expenses must have been directly related to the obligations of the contract. The case concerned the lease of premises for poultry breeding which the landlord had stated were in good sanitary condition. The lease included a covenant under which the tenant was obliged to effect certain repairs (in line with local authority requirements). In fact, the premises were not sanitary, and the plaintiffs decided to rescind for misrepresentation. They also claimed, in addition to a refund of the rent, compensation in relation to rates paid, repairs carried out, loss of stock, medical and removal expenses. It was held that they could only recover the cost of the rates, and of repairs carried out under the covenant. These were obligations which arose directly from the contract, and were recoverable on an 'indemnity' basis. The other items came into the category of a claim for damages, and so were not recoverable. The test is whether the expenses or losses were necessarily incurred as a result of entering into the contract. Thus, the claim for an indemnity is very limited in scope.

The availability of an action for damages under the Misrepresentation Act 1967 means that the only situation nowadays when the claimant might wish to consider claiming for an indemnity is where the contract is being rescinded for a totally innocent, non-negligent, misrepresentation.

10.4.6 Damages under s 2(1) of the Misrepresentation Act 1967

The Misrepresentation Act 1967 introduced a statutory remedy in damages (whether or not rescission is also granted) for what is commonly referred to as 'negligent misrepresentation'. In fact, s 2(1) does not use this phrase, but makes the remedy available where the person making the misrepresentation would have been liable to damages if it had been made fraudulently:

> (1) Where a person has entered into a contract after a misrepresentation has been made to him by another party thereto and as a result thereof he has suffered loss, then, if the person making the misrepresentation would be liable to damages in respect thereof had the misrepresentation been made fraudulently, that person shall be so liable notwithstanding that the misrepresentation was not made fraudulently, unless he proves that he had reasonable grounds to believe and did believe up to the time the contract was made that the facts represented were true.

---

105 (1900) 82 LT 49. See also *Newbigging v Adam* (1886) 34 Ch D 582 – rescission of a partnership; indemnity against liabilities incurred while a partner.

The test of what is a misrepresentation will be as set out earlier in this chapter. As will be noted from the final part of the section, this action is advantageous to the claimant in that, once it is established that a false statement was made, the burden of proof shifts to the defendant to establish that there were reasonable grounds for believing it to be true. Moreover, the courts seem to be prepared to be fairly strict as to what will be regarded as reasonable grounds. In *Howard Marine Dredging Co Ltd v A Ogden & Sons (Excavations) Ltd,* [106] the representation concerned the capacity of a barge. A representative of the owner told a potential charterer that the capacity was about 1,600 tonnes. This figure was based on his memory of the relevant entry in the usually authoritative *Lloyd's Register,* which stated that the capacity was 1,800 tonnes. In fact, as was made clear in the ship's documents, the correct figure was much less, at only 1,055 tonnes. The charterers subsequently sought to claim damages under s 2(1) on the basis of this misrepresentation. The Court of Appeal held that an incorrect statement did give rise to an entitlement to such damages because the defendant had failed to prove that he had reasonable grounds for belief in the truth of the statement. Reliance on the *Lloyd's Register* was insufficient when the correct figure was in documentation in the owner's possession.

FOR THOUGHT

Do you think the outcome of this case would have been any different if the representative had previously seen the correct figure, but no longer had the ship's documents available to him at the time when he relied on the *Lloyd's Register*?

10.4.7 Measure of damages under s 2(1)

One difficulty which has arisen with s 2(1) is the measure of damages – should it be contractual or tortious? In *Watts v Spence* [107] there was some suggestion that it should be contractual. The Court of Appeal, however, in *Sharneyford v Edge* [108] ruled that it should be tortious. The issue was considered further in *Royscot Trust Ltd v Rogerson.* [109] A car dealer misrepresented to the plaintiff finance company the amount of a deposit paid by a customer in connection with a hire purchase agreement. The finance company would not have been prepared to lend as much as it did had it known of the true value of the deposit. The finance company suffered a loss when the customer defaulted on his payments, after having sold the car to an innocent third party (who obtained good title under the Hire Purchase Act 1964). In an action by the plaintiff against the dealer for non-fraudulent misrepresentation, the only dispute was as to the amount of damages

106 [1978] QB 574.
107 [1976] Ch 165; [1975] 2 All ER 528.
108 [1987] Ch 305; [1987] 1 All ER 588.
109 [1991] 3 All ER 294.

payable. The measure used by the judge at first instance was supported by neither party in the appeal, so that the Court of Appeal effectively had to decide the matter *de novo*. It confirmed that in an action for misrepresentation under s 2(1) of the Misrepresentation Act 1967, the correct measure of damages is tortious rather than contractual. Moreover, since the wording of s 2(1) makes liability conditional on the situation where 'the person making the misrepresentation would be liable to damages in respect thereof had the misrepresentation been made fraudulently', damages should be assessed in the same way as for fraudulent misrepresentation. This meant that the defendant was liable for all losses flowing from the defendant's misrepresentation, as is the case with the tort of deceit,[110] and not simply for those losses which were reasonably foreseeable. Although the wording of the section itself gives rise to the so-called 'fiction of fraud' alluded to above, the weight of academic opinion, as evidenced by all the leading contract textbooks, has been in favour of applying the negligence remoteness rules, because to apply the deceit rule would operate too harshly in a situation where the defendant has been negligent rather than deliberately fraudulent. The Court of Appeal in this case, however, was not prepared to be swayed by these arguments of policy. It found that s 2(1) aligned liability under it with liability for fraud. The wording of the section was clear and the court saw no reason to depart from its literal meaning.

This is, however, a very narrow view of statutory interpretation, which ignores the policy behind both the introduction of s 2(1) and the reason for the wide scope of damages in relation to deceit. The reason for enacting s 2(1) was to allow damages to be recovered for *negligent* misrepresentations leading to a contract, in the same way that *Hedley Byrne v Heller* had allowed a remedy for negligent misstatements in other contexts.[111] The policy behind the broader damages for deceit is to punish or deter deliberate wrongdoing. These two factors taken together suggest that it was unlikely to have been Parliament's intention to enact that more extensive damages should be available under s 2(1) than under the tort of negligence. Moreover, as has been pointed out by Hooley,[112] it is by no means clear that the literal meaning of the section is as clear as was suggested by the Court of Appeal. The phrase 'so liable' in s 2(1), rather than meaning 'liable in the same way as if the statement had been made fraudulently', could just as easily be interpreted to mean simply 'liable in damages'. If there is ambiguity, the court should be free to adopt a reading which accords with overall policy concerns. Interpreting the section in the way suggested by Hooley would have enabled the Court of Appeal to have applied the law in a way which was more in keeping with the overall objectives of the section, and would have left the wider range of damages to those cases where they are much more justifiable – that is, where the maker of the statement has deliberately lied, or at least has shown a reckless disregard for the truth.

---

110 *Doyle v Olby (Ironmongers) Ltd* [1969] 2 QB 158; [1969] 2 All ER 119 – see above, 10.3.3.

111 At the time that the Misrepresentation Act 1967 was enacted it was thought that *Hedley Byrne* would not apply as between contracting parties. This has now been shown to be incorrect: *Esso Petroleum Co Ltd v Mardon* [1976] QB 801; [1976] 2 All ER 5 – see above, 10.3.2.

112 Hooley, 1991.

The approach taken by the Court of Appeal in *Royscot* appeared to be treated with some scepticism by the House of Lords in *Smith New Court Securities Ltd v Scrimgeour Vickers (Asset Management) Ltd*,[113] but the issue was not directly before it, and so no final view was expressed. For the moment, at any rate, the 'fiction of fraud' analysis, unsatisfactory as it is, remains good law.

This presumably also means that, on the basis of *East v Maurer*,[114] certain types of lost profits may be recoverable. The damages under s 2(1) may therefore be almost as extensive as for breach of contract, particularly since they are not restricted by any rule of remoteness. The result is that there seems to be little reason now why a person who enters into a contract on the basis of a misrepresentation should ever seek to establish deceit. The action under s 2(1) of the 1967 Act is much to be preferred since it places on the defendant the burden of proving not only that the statement was believed to be true, but also that there were reasonable grounds for such a belief. If no greater damages are recoverable by proving deceit, there seems little point in trying to do so.

10.4.8 Damages under s 2(2) of the Misrepresentation Act 1967

Section 2(2) of the Misrepresentation Act 1967 allows a court to award damages in lieu of rescission, whether or not they are also awarded under s 2(1). This power is to be exercised if the court is:

> . . . of the opinion that it would be equitable to do so, having regard to the nature of the misrepresentation and the loss that would be caused by it if the contract were upheld, as well as to the loss that rescission would cause to the other party.

Since the power is stated to be in lieu of rescission, it has been presumed that it will be lost if the right to rescind has been lost, for example, by lapse of time, or the intervention of third party rights.[115] This was not accepted in *Thomas Witter Ltd v TBP Industries*,[116] in which it was suggested that the power to award damages was not dependent on the continued availability of the right to rescind, since this would be too restrictive an interpretation of the section. The judges in two subsequent cases have, however, not followed this line. In both *Floods of Queensferry Ltd v Shand Construction Ltd*[117] and *Government of Zanzibar v British Aerospace (Lancaster House) Ltd*,[118] the view was expressed that the availability of damages under s 2(2) is dependent on the right to rescind not having been lost. In the latter case, Judge Raymond Jack QC saw the purpose of s 2(2) as being to allow the court to award damages where, for some

---

113 [1996] 4 All ER 769.
114 [1991] 2 All ER 733 – see above, 10.4.3.
115 See above, 10.4.1.
116 [1996] 2 All ER 573.
117 [2000] BLR 81.
118 [2000] 1 WLR 2333.

reason, this would be more equitable to the defendant than requiring or upholding rescission. Since the power was an alternative to rescission, it could not be used where rescission itself was not available. In that situation the claimant could still claim damages under s 2(1), though subject to the restriction that they were only available where the defendant had been negligent. The judge saw this as maintaining a correct balance between the remedies available for negligent and wholly innocent misrepresentation.[119]

As regards the *measure* of damages under s 2(2), there is no binding authority, but some guidance has been provided by *obiter* statements in *William Sindall plc v Cambridgeshire County Council*.[120] Hoffmann and Evans LJJ agreed that the measure must be different from that applying under s 2(1). This must be so, given that s 2(3) recognises the possibility (or even likelihood) that damages under s 2(2) will be less than under s 2(1). Where, as in this case, the contract concerned the sale of property, the measure should simply be an amount that would compensate the plaintiff for the loss he had suffered on account of the property not being that which it was represented to be. As Evans LJ put it, it should be 'the difference in value between what the plaintiff was misled into believing he was acquiring, and the value of what he in fact received'.[121] The assessment should be made at the time of the contract, and subsequent losses caused by a fall in market value should not be taken into account. There is no suggestion in these statements that any account should be taken of consequential losses, and this is surely right. To compensate for these would go beyond replacing the value of the right to rescind, and is surely better left to be dealt with under s 2(1).[122]

10.5 EXCLUSION OF LIABILITY FOR MISREPRESENTATION

Section 3 of the Misrepresentation Act 1967, as amended by s 8 of the Unfair Contract Terms Act (UCTA) 1977, restricts the possibility of exclusion of liability for misrepresentation. It states:

> If a contract contains a term which would exclude or restrict:
> (a) any liability to which a party to a contract may be subject by reason of any misrepresentation made by him before the contract was made; or
> (b) any remedy available to another party to the contract by reason of such misrepresentation,

---

119 Beale (1995a and 1995b) has argued that there *should* be a power to award damages for non-negligent misrepresentation even where rescission is lost, in order to prevent the possibility of the unjust enrichment of the defendant, but doubts whether under the present wording of s 2(2) there is such a power.

120 [1994] 3 All ER 932.

121 Ibid, p 963.

122 See also the comments on this case by Beale, 1995a, approving the approach to s 2(2) based on 'difference in value' as at the time of the contract.

that term shall be of no effect except in so far as it satisfies the requirement of reasonableness as stated in s 11(1) of the Unfair Contract Terms Act 1977; and it is for those claiming that the term satisfies that requirement to show that it does.

Thus, as regards any contract term which attempts to restrict either liability for mis-representation or any remedy available in relation to it, this will only be effective if it satisfies the requirement of reasonableness under s 11 of the UCTA 1977.[123] The fact that a clause is in common use will not prevent it from being found to be unreasonable. In *Walker v Boyle*,[124] the court considered a clause contained in a contract for the sale of property, which stated that 'no error, misstatement or omission in any preliminary answer concerning the property shall annul the sale'. Even though the clause in this case was one which was contained in the National Conditions of Sale, and commonly used by solicitors, this did not prevent the court from holding that it was unreasonable. It was also confirmed by the House of Lords in *HIH Casualty and General Insurance Ltd v Chase Manhattan Bank*[125] that a party cannot exclude liability for its own fraudulent misrepresentation (though it left open the possibility of excluding such liability where the statement was made by an agent, provided sufficiently explicit language was used).

There have been a number of cases on s 3 of the Act, in both its pre- and post-UCTA form, relating to the question of the type of clause that is caught by this provision. In particular, what is its effect in relation to a clause which states that no representations have been made, or that no reliance is to be placed on any that are made?

In *Overbrooke Estates Ltd v Glencombe Properties Ltd,*[126] the conditions of sale at an auction contained the following clause: 'The vendors do not make or give and neither the Auctioneers nor any person in the employment of the Auctioneers has any authority to make or give any representation or warranty in relation to [the property].' The auctioneers, as agents for the vendors, told the prospective purchasers that there were no local authority schemes for the area in which the property was situated. The purchasers later discovered that it was likely to be included in a slum clearance scheme, and tried to withdraw from the contract. The vendors relied on the clause set out above; the purchasers claimed that this was an unreasonable limitation clause, caught by s 3 of the 1967 Act. The court held that the clause did not operate in this situation as a limitation of liability clause, but simply defined the authority of the vendor's agent.[127] It was perfectly permissible for the vendors to do this. The purchasers were aware of the limitation of authority at the time they entered into the contract, and could not therefore use any statement by the agent to escape from it.

---

123 For which, see Chapter 9, 9.7.10.
124 [1982] 1 WLR 495.
125 [2003] UKHL 6; [2003] 2 Lloyd's Rep 61.
126 [1974] 1 WLR 1155.
127 For the law relating to the limitation of the authority of agents, see Chapter 6, 6.5.

The *Overbrooke* decision did not make it clear what the approach would have been had the representation come directly from the vendors, rather than via their agents. In *Cremdean Properties Ltd v Nash*,[128] however, the Court of Appeal took the view that the scope of the earlier decision was limited to the situation of agency. The court was considering a clause in a contract for the sale of two properties which stated that the accuracy of the particulars supplied could not be guaranteed and that 'Any intending purchaser . . . must satisfy himself by inspection or otherwise as to the correctness of each of the statements contained in these particulars'. It was suggested by the vendors that this did not amount to an attempt to exclude liability, but rather brought about a situation in which it was as if no representation had ever been made. The court firmly rejected this argument. Referring to the *Overbrooke* decision, Bridge LJ commented that:

> It is one thing to say that s 3 [of the Misrepresentation Act 1967] does not inhibit a principal from publicly giving notice limiting the ostensible authority of his agents; it is quite another thing to say that a principal can circumvent the plainly intended effect of s 3 by a clause excluding his own liability for a representation which he has undoubtedly made.

Even if the vendor had explicitly said that, notwithstanding anything in the particulars, no misrepresentations within the meaning of the Misrepresentation Act 1967 were made, this would still have been treated by the court as an attempt to exclude liability falling within the scope of s 3. The same view was taken in *Inntrepreneur Estates (CPC) Ltd v Worth*,[129] where the clause stated that the lessee acknowledged that no reliance was placed on pre-contractual statements. Although on the facts it was held that there were no pre-contractual statements on which the lessee had relied, Laddie J stated that, if there had been, the clause would have fallen within the scope of s 3 and would have been treated as unreasonable.

Subsequent cases have followed the same line as in *Cremdean v Nash*, drawing a distinction between the effect of an 'entire agreement' clause on an action for breach of the main or collateral contract, and its effect on an action for misrepresentation. In *McGrath v Shah*,[130] it was held that a clause stating simply that 'This contract constitutes the entire contract between the parties, and may be varied . . . only in writing under the hands of the parties or their solicitors' did not fall within the scope of s 3 of the Misrepresentation Act 1967. It was effective to prevent an argument that pre-contractual representations had become part of the contract. It did not, however, deal with actions for misrepresentation, and was not struck down by s 3.[131]

---

128 (1977) 244 EG 547.
129 [1996] 1 EGLR 84.
130 (1987) 57 P & CR 452.
131 The action in this case was not based on misrepresentation. The judge declined to express a view on the second half of the clause in question, which did explicitly refer to 'representations'.

A similar analysis was adopted in *Thomas Witter Ltd v TBP Industries Ltd.*[132] The entire agreement clause was again held here to be ineffective in excluding liability for an action in misrepresentation, as opposed to a contractual action based on an allegation that a representation had become part of the contract. Nor was the second part of the clause effective. This purported to limit the pre-contractual statements which could be relied on in a misrepresentation action to those referred to in a schedule to the contract.[133] The clause might cause difficulties in establishing that some other representation had in fact been relied on, but if this could be shown, then an action could be based on it. Furthermore, Jacob J held, *obiter*, that even if these provisions did attempt to exclude liability for misrepresentation, they would be unreasonable under s 3 because their scope would be too wide, potentially extending to fraudulent misrepresentation.[134]

The position as to the relationship between entire agreements and the exclusion of liability for misrepresentation was usefully summarised by Lightman J in *Inntrepreneur Pub Co (GL) v East Crown Ltd.*[135] The clause in question had two parts. Clause 14.1 was an 'entire agreement' clause. Clause 14.2 stated that the tenants 'have not relied upon any advice or statement of the Company or its solicitors'.[136] Lightman J analysed the effect of these provisions as follows:[137]

> An entire agreement provision does not preclude a claim in misrepresentation, for the denial of contractual force to a statement cannot affect the status of the statement of a misrepresentation. The same clause in an agreement may contain both an entire agreement provision and a further provision designed to exclude liability eg, for misrepresentation or breach of duty. As an example, clause 14 in this case, after setting out in clause 14.1 the entire agreement clause, in clause 14.2 sets out to exclude liability for misrepresentation and breach of duty. Whether this latter provision is legally effective for this purpose may turn on the question of its reasonableness as required by s 3 of the Misrepresentation Act 1967: see, eg, *Inntrepreneur Estates (CPC) v Worth*. But ... s 3 has no application to an entire agreement clause defining where the contractual terms between the parties are to be found: see *McGrath v Shah*.

This clear statement is helpful, but only emphasises that the law in this area now seems to be based on fairly technical distinctions as to the precise effect of each particular

---

132 [1996] 2 All ER 573.
133 This stated 'the Purchaser acknowledges that it has not been induced to enter into this Agreement by any representation or warranty other than statements contained or referred to in Schedule 6': ibid, p 595.
134 In coming to this conclusion the judge emphasised that it was the potential scope of the clause that had to be considered when assessing reasonableness, rather than its application to the facts of the case before the court: ibid, p 598.
135 [2000] 2 Lloyd's LR 611.
136 Ibid, p 614.
137 Ibid.

clause. Those wishing to avoid liability for pre-contractual statements will have to use a range of different clauses to cover all possibilities, some of which will be subject to reasonableness tests and some of which will not. Those faced with contractual provisions of this kind may well be confused as to their precise scope and what they are intended to achieve. The position is complicated by the fact that pre-contractual statements may end up being treated as misrepresentations, collateral warranties, or terms of the main contract (or more than one of these). It is unfortunate that a more straightforward way of dealing with reliance losses arising from statements which have induced a contract cannot be found. The current position, however, is the result of piecemeal historical development of the law, and there seems to be no current move towards any fundamental reconsideration of the area.

10.6 FURTHER READING

Allen, D, *Misrepresentation*, 1988, London: Sweet & Maxwell

Beale, H, 'Damages in lieu of rescission for misrepresentation' (1995a) 111 LQR 60

Beale, H, 'Points on misrepresentation' (1995b) 111 LQR 385

Bigwood, R, 'Pre-contractual misrepresentation and the limits of the principle in *With v O'Flanagan*' [2005] CLJ 94

Hooley, R, 'Damages and the Misrepresentation Act 1967' (1991) 107 LQR 547

11 MISTAKE

Contents

11.1 OVERVIEW

This chapter deals with situations where a contract is affected by a mistake on the part of one or both parties. The general approach of the English courts, the different categories of mistake, and the way in which the concept is dealt with in the Principles of European Contract Law are dealt with first. The main topics then discussed are:

■ Mistakes nullifying agreement. This deals with mistakes where the parties have

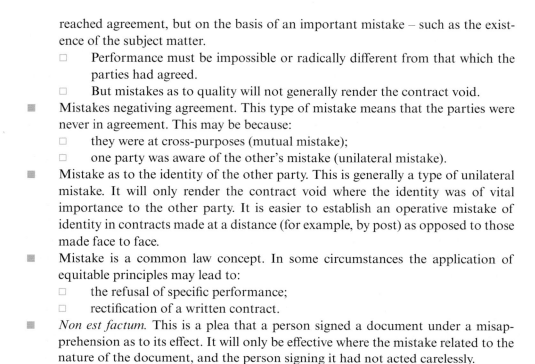

reached agreement, but on the basis of an important mistake – such as the existence of the subject matter.

□ Performance must be impossible or radically different from that which the parties had agreed.

□ But mistakes as to quality will not generally render the contract void.

■ Mistakes negativing agreement. This type of mistake means that the parties were never in agreement. This may be because:

□ they were at cross-purposes (mutual mistake);

□ one party was aware of the other's mistake (unilateral mistake).

■ Mistake as to the identity of the other party. This is generally a type of unilateral mistake. It will only render the contract void where the identity was of vital importance to the other party. It is easier to establish an operative mistake of identity in contracts made at a distance (for example, by post) as opposed to those made face to face.

■ Mistake is a common law concept. In some circumstances the application of equitable principles may lead to:

□ the refusal of specific performance;

□ rectification of a written contract.

■ *Non est factum.* This is a plea that a person signed a document under a misapprehension as to its effect. It will only be effective where the mistake related to the nature of the document, and the person signing it had not acted carelessly.

11.2 INTRODUCTION

This chapter is concerned with the situations in which a contract may be regarded as never having come into existence, or may be brought to an end, as a result of a mistake by either or both of the parties. Although the overall theme is that of 'mistake', as will be seen, the situations which fall within this traditional categorisation are varied, and do not have any necessary conceptual unity. Moreover, they may have a considerable overlap or interaction with other areas of contract law – in particular, offer and acceptance, misrepresentation and frustration.[1]

The rules developed by the courts impose fairly heavy burdens on those arguing that a mistake has been made. This is not surprising. It would not be satisfactory if a party to a contract could simply, by saying 'I'm sorry, I made a mistake', unstitch a complex agreement without any thought for the consequences for the other party, or any third parties who might be involved. To allow this to be done would be to strike at the purposes of the law of contract, which has as one of its main functions the

---

1 That is why in some texts one or more of the topics dealt with in this chapter are discussed in the context of the other rules to which they most closely relate. Smith (1994) has argued that 'there is no room for the application of a distinct doctrine of mistake, additional to the principles of the formation of the contract and of implied terms'.

provision of a structure within which people can organise their commercial relationships with a high degree of certainty. On the other hand, a fundamental principle of the English law of contract is that, as far as possible, the courts should give effect to the intentions of the parties. If either, or both, of the parties has genuinely made a mistake as to the nature of their contract, to enforce it may run counter to their intentions.[2] The courts do, therefore, recognise the possibility of mistakes affecting, or even destroying, contractual obligations which would otherwise arise. The power to intervene in this way is, however, used with considerable circumspection.

This general reluctance to allow mistakes to affect a contract does not, of course, prevent the parties themselves from agreeing that a mistake will allow the party who has made the mistake to rescind the contract. This is not unusual in relation to consumer contracts made with large chain stores. These organisations often feel able (presumably because of their volume of business and their strength of position in the market) to allow customers who have simply changed their minds to exchange or return goods even though they are in no way defective. As was noted in Chapter 2, there are also some statutory provisions which allow consumers a short period in which to change their minds about particular sorts of contract, particularly those involving 'distance contracts' or long-term credit arrangements.[3] In such a situation, the consumer who realises that he or she has made a mistake of some kind in relation to the contract will be able to escape from it, provided that action is taken within the specified time limits. These arrangements are, however, exceptions to the general position under the common law, which will only allow a party to undo the agreement in a limited range of circumstances.

11.3 CATEGORIES OF MISTAKE

As noted above, there are various ways in which a party may make a mistake in relation to the contract. It may, for example, relate to the subject matter, the identity of the other contracting party, or the specific terms of the contract. Three particular types of mistake may be identified. In the first, the parties are found to have reached agreement, but on the basis of an assumption as to the surrounding facts which turns out to be false (for example, the subject matter of the contract has at the time of the agreement ceased to exist). The mistake may, following the House of Lords' decision in *Kleinwort Benson*

---

2 The issue of how the parties' 'intentions' are determined by the courts, and in particular whether this is done by a 'subjective' or 'objective' approach, is a complex issue which is considered further below, 11.6.1. It is arguable that certain types of 'objective' approach may lead to the court deciding that what the parties 'intended' was something which in fact neither party had in mind: see, for example, Spencer, 1973.

3 See, for example, the Consumer Protection (Distance Selling) Regulations 2000, SI 2000/2334; the Consumer Credit Act 1974, s 67; the Timeshare Act 1992, ss 5 and 6; and the Consumer Protection (Cancellation of Contracts Concluded Away From Business Premises) Regulations 1987. For further discussion of this type of provision, see Chapter 2, 2.14.

Ltd v Lincoln City Council,[4] be one of law. This was confirmed by the Court of Appeal in *Brennan v Bolt Burdon*.[5] In this case a dispute had been settled on the basis of a ruling in a first instance decision which was then overturned on appeal. The claimant sought to set aside the settlement on the basis that it was based on a mistake of law. This argument succeeded in the High Court. The Court of Appeal set out the relevant approach in these terms:[6]

> (1) As with any other contracts, compromises or consent orders may be vitiated by a common mistake of law. (2) It is initially a question of construction as to whether the alleged mistake has that consequence. (3) Whilst a general release executed in a prospective or nascent dispute requires clear language to justify an inference of an intention to surrender rights of which the releasor was unaware and could not have been aware. . . , different considerations arise in relation to the compromise of litigation which the parties have agreed to settle on a give-and-take basis. . . (4) For a common mistake of fact or law to vitiate a contract of any kind, it must render the performance of the contract impossible . . .

The question was, therefore, whether the courts below were correct to find that in this case there was a sufficient mistake of law to vitiate the agreement. The Court of Appeal found that there was not. A distinction can be drawn between situations where there is an unequivocal but mistaken view of the law, and where there is a doubt as to the law. The majority of the Court of Appeal felt that this case involved a doubt as to the law of service at the time the compromise agreement was made, rather than an unequivocal mistake. Moreover, the compromise agreement remained possible to perform. As a result, the appeal was allowed and the claimant was held to her compromise agreement.

This type of mistake, whether of fact or law, is the type of mistake referred to by Lord Atkin in *Bell v Lever Bros*[7] as a mistake which 'nullifies' consent.[8] There is here, in technical terms, a valid contract (in that it is formed by a matching offer and acceptance and supported by consideration) but it would, if put into effect, operate in a way which is fundamentally different from the parties' expectations.[9] The courts will therefore sometimes intervene to set the contract aside, and treat it as if it had never existed.[10]

---

4 [1999] 2 AC 349; [1998] 4 All ER 513. This case is discussed in Chapter 19, at 19.3.3.

5 [2004] EWCA Civ 1017; [2005] QB 303.

6 Ibid, para 17.

7 [1932] AC 161.

8 It is also referred to by some writers as a 'common mistake' – see, for example, Cheshire, Fifoot and Furmston, 2001, p 254.

9 Collins (2003, p 125) suggests that this type of mistake is better analysed as involving an implied condition precedent (for example, that the subject matter of the contract is still in existence) and that the failure of this condition renders the contract unenforceable. This is an attractive analysis, but does not represent the way in which the courts say they are dealing with the relevant cases.

10 In equity it may be possible, while rescinding the contract, to do so on terms which re-arrange the obligations between the parties so as to give some effect to the agreement – see below, 11.7.

This type of mistake has close links with the doctrine of 'frustration' which applies in situations where events *after* the formation of the contract (such as the destruction of the subject matter) fundamentally affect the nature of the agreement.[11]

The second and third types of mistake arise where the court finds that there is, in fact, a disagreement between the parties as to some important element of the contract. These are mistakes which Lord Atkin, in *Bell v Lever Bros,* referred to as 'negativing consent', in that they are said to operate to prevent a contract ever existing, because of the lack of agreement between the parties. Within this general category, however, two different situations must be distinguished. First, it may be that neither party is aware of the fact that the other is contracting on the basis of different assumptions as to the nature or terms of the agreement. They are at cross-purposes, but do not realise this until after the contract has apparently been agreed.[12] This situation relates to the issues discussed in Chapter 2, in that it can be questioned whether there was ever a matching offer and acceptance. The second type of situation where there may be a mistake 'negativing' agreement is where one party is aware of the mistake being made by the other, and indeed may even have encouraged it.[13] Where such encouragement has taken place there is likely to be an overlap with misrepresentation; dissolution of the contract on the basis of mistake is then only likely to be sought where the remedies for misrepresentation would be inadequate.[14]

Although, as has been noted above, there is a lack of conceptual unity in this area, the theme which may be said to link these various situations is that of 'agreement failure'. There is an apparent agreement between the parties, but that agreement is either impossible to perform, or if performed would operate in a way which would be contrary to the expectations of at least one of the parties. Because this is the focus, there is little scope here for reliance-based remedies. If a mistake is operative,[15] then the primary remedy will be to set the agreement aside, either in its entirety[16] or on particular terms.[17] Damages are not awarded in relation to a contract which has been based on an operative mistake.[18]

---

11 See *Amalgamated Investment and Property Co Ltd v John Walker & Sons* [1976] 3 All ER 509, which was pleaded in both mistake and frustration. The doctrine of frustration is dealt with in Chapter 16.

12 Cheshire, Fifoot and Furmston call this 'mutual mistake', though this phrase is sometimes also, and confusingly, used to refer to what is here called a 'common mistake'.

13 This type of mistake is often referred to as a 'unilateral mistake'.

14 This is most likely to arise where one of the bars to rescission applies (see Chapter 10, 10.4.1) – such bars do not apply if the contract is found to be void for mistake.

15 That is, sufficiently serious to justify the court's intervention.

16 Which is the approach of the common law to a 'failed' agreement – see, for example, *Ingram v Little* [1961] 1 QB 31; [1960] 3 All ER 332 – discussed below, at 11.6.4.

17 This approach has been adopted in some cases by the courts applying the rules of equity. Alternatively, the court may use the mistake as the basis for a refusal to grant an order for specific performance.

18 Unless the mistake is the result of a misrepresentation – in which case damages may be recoverable on one of the bases outlined in Chapter 10. This will be an alternative, however, to setting the contract aside for mistake.

Before considering the detailed rules which the English courts have developed to deal with these various categories of mistake, the approach adopted in the Principles of European Contract Law should be noted, as a point of comparison.

11.4 MISTAKE IN THE PRINCIPLES OF EUROPEAN CONTRACT LAW

The Principles of European Contract Law deal with mistake in Art 4.103. This provides that:

(1) A party may avoid a contract for mistake of fact or law existing when the contract was concluded if:
    (a) (i)   the mistake was caused by information given by the other party; or
        (ii)   the other party knew or ought to have known of the mistake and it was contrary to good faith and fair dealing to leave the mistaken party in error; or
        (iii) the other party made the same mistake, and
    (b) the other party knew or ought to have known that the mistaken party, had it known the truth, would not have entered into the contract or would have done so only on fundamentally different terms.

The power to avoid a contract does not arise, however, if the party's mistake was 'inexcusable', or if the party had undertaken the risk of the mistake occurring, or should in the circumstances have undertaken it.[19] The first limitation means that a foolish mistake may not be used to avoid a contract. The second means that where the contract itself places the risk of the mistake occurring on the party wishing to avoid the contract, or should be interpreted in the circumstances as having placed the risk on that party, then again the obligations of the contract may not be avoided.[20]

There are a number of points of comparison and contrast between these suggested principles and those that currently operate in English law. First, the initial words of the Article make it clear that contracts falling within its scope are voidable, rather than void, as they would be under the common law. In other words, it is up to the party who feels affected by the mistake to take action to bring the contract to an end, and it will presumably subsist until that point.[21] In English law, if there is an operative mistake, the common law treats the contract as void *ab initio* (from the beginning), and therefore never having existed as far as the law is concerned.[22]

---

19 Article 4.103(2).

20 An example of a case which might well fall within the second limitation is the Australian decision in *McRae v Commonwealth Disposals Commission* (1951) 84 CLR 377 – discussed below, 11.5.1.

21 This is the position in English law in relation to misrepresentation, as discussed in Chapter 10, 10.4.2.

22 Some of the consequences of this approach are noted below, 11.5.4.

Second, the Article brings together two of the three types of mistake identified in the previous section of this chapter. Paragraph (1)(a)(iii) deals with a mistake nullifying consent, or 'common mistake'. Paragraphs (1)(a)(i) and (ii) deal with one type of mistake negativing consent, that is, 'unilateral mistake' where one party is, or should be, aware of the other's mistake. The Article does not, however, deal with the other type of mistake negativing consent, which arises when the parties are simply at cross-purposes and neither is aware of the fact. Presumably this type of mistake would, under the Principles, be left to be dealt with by the provisions dealing with the formation of the agreement. It is not clear, however, why unilateral mistakes could not also be dealt with by these provisions. It is just as arguable in those situations that there is no agreement. The answer is perhaps that it is felt that where there is a unilateral mistake, the party who discovers his or her mistake should have the option of continuing with the contract. If the contract was dealt with as never having come into existence, this might in some circumstances be to the advantage of the party who encouraged or was aware of the other's mistake. This is an area, however, where the Principles depart from the approach taken by the common law, which treats the effect of a mistake negativing agreement as being the same whether or not the mistake is unilateral.

11.5 MISTAKES NULLIFYING AGREEMENT ('COMMON MISTAKE')[23]

The clearest type of mistake which renders a contract fundamentally different from that which the parties thought they were agreeing to, and which will be regarded as rendering the contract void, is where the parties have made a contract about something which has ceased to exist at the time the contract is made.[24] If, for example, the contract concerns the hire of a specific boat which, unknown to either party, has been destroyed by fire the day before the contract was made, the agreement will undoubtedly be void for common mistake. The parties have reached agreement, but that agreement is nullified by the destruction of the subject matter. This type of common mistake is sometimes referred to by the Latin tag of *res extincta*. An example from the cases is *Galloway v Galloway*.[25] The parties, who thought they had been married to each other, made a separation agreement. It was then discovered that their supposed marriage was invalid because the husband's previous wife was still alive. As a result, the separation agreement was void and the 'husband' had no liability under it.

As regards contracts for the sale of goods, the common law rule is given statutory effect by s 6 of the Sale of Goods Act (SGA) 1979. This states that:

---

23 As to the history of this type of mistake, see Simpson, 1975b, pp 265–69.
24 Where the subject matter ceases to exist *after* the contract is made, the doctrine of frustration, which is dealt with in Chapter 16, applies, rather than mistake.
25 (1914) 30 TLR 531.

> Where there is a contract for the sale of specific goods, and the goods without the knowledge of the seller have perished at the time when the contract is made, the contract is void.

The word 'perished' almost certainly encompasses more than simply physical destruction, as is shown by the pre-SGA 1893 case of *Couturier v Hastie*.[26] The contract in this case was for the purchase of a cargo of corn. At the time of the contract, the cargo had, because it was starting to deteriorate, been unloaded and sold to someone else. The purchaser was held to have no liability to pay the price. There are some doubts, however, as to the true basis for the decision in this case; these are referred to in the next paragraph.[27]

11.5.1 Subject matter which never existed

The cases we have been considering deal with the situation where the subject matter *did* exist at one point, but has ceased to do so by the time of the contract. The position is more difficult where the subject matter has *never* existed. There seems no logical reason why the contract should not equally be void for mistake in such a case, but this was not the view of the High Court of Australia in *McRae v Commonwealth Disposals Commission*.[28] The Commission had invited tenders for a salvage operation in relation to an oil tanker, said to be 'lying on the Jourmand Reef'. The plaintiffs were awarded the contract, but on arrival found that neither the tanker nor the reef existed. The Commission claimed that the contract was void for mistake, and that they therefore had no liability. The court held, however, that there was a contract, in that the Commission had to be taken to have warranted the existence of the tanker. The plaintiffs were entitled to damages to compensate for their costs in putting together the abortive enterprise. In reaching this conclusion, the court did not accept that the decision in *Couturier v Hastie* was truly based on 'mistake'. It was simply that the plaintiff's claim in that case, that the price was payable on production of the shipping documents, could not be upheld as being part of the contract. It is certainly true that the House of Lords in *Couturier v Hastie* never mentioned mistake as the basis for its decision. The case is perhaps in the end best regarded as an example of the kind of situation in which an operative mistake could occur, and which would now fall within s 6 of the SGA 1979, rather than as a direct authority on the issue.

FOR THOUGHT

What do you think the outcome of *McRae* would have been if there had been a ship in the specified location, but it had already been salvaged by the time the Commission made the contract with McRae?

---

26 (1856) 5 HLC 673. Section 6 of the 1893 Act, which was in the same terms as s 6 of the 1979 Act, was intended to give statutory effect to the principles applied in *Couturier v Hastie*.
27 For a thorough survey of the possible interpretations of the case, see Atiyah, 1957.
28 (1951) 84 CLR 377.

McRae can be taken to indicate a more general principle to the effect that where one of the parties has specifically promised that the subject matter exists, then mistake has no role to play, and the other party can sue for breach of the promise. This could apply not only where the subject matter has never existed, but also where it did once exist and has been destroyed prior to the agreement. This makes particular sense where, as in *McRae,* one party can reasonably be taken to have superior knowledge about the existence of the subject matter. The other party is then *relying* on this superior knowledge in entering into the contract, and it may well be appropriate that if that reliance turns out to be unjustified, damages should be recoverable. Simply setting the agreement aside because it has failed might not be sufficient in such circumstances.

There would be a difficulty, however, in applying this to contracts for the sale of goods. This is because s 6 of the SGA 1979 states that, in such a case, the contract is void. There is no provision in the section for the parties to agree to the contrary, and it is by no means clear that the courts would imply one.[29] There is no problem where the goods never existed, because the use of the word 'perished' in s 6 implies that the goods did once exist: if they did not, then the section has no application. It would be odd, however, if the law drew such a clear distinction, simply in sale of goods cases, between the situation where the subject matter once existed and the situation where it never existed. There are several ways in which such an odd result might be avoided. First, it might be said that the *McRae* approach *only* applies where the subject matter never existed. This would produce a workable rule, but it would be difficult to see any policy behind the distinction. Second, it might be argued that the word 'perished' in s 6 encompasses the situation where the goods never existed. This interpretation would lead to all sale of goods contracts being treated in the same way, but differently from other contracts. However, it is again difficult to see any underlying policy which would justify the distinction. Third, it could be argued, as suggested by Atiyah,[30] that the courts should be prepared to interpret s 6 as not intended to apply whenever specific promises about the existence of the goods have been made. This would produce the most analytically satisfactory answer in that it would align all sale of goods contracts with the general rule. It probably also involves, however, the most adventurous statutory interpretation, and it is by no means certain that the courts would be willing to adopt it. The area therefore remains unclear. The approach adopted in *McRae*, however, seems sensible, and is in line with the modern law's recognition that disappointed reliance should generally be compensated. It makes sense for that approach to be adopted wherever possible, even if it does leave contracts for the sale of specific goods which have perished in an anomalous position.

---

29 At various points the Act states that the provisions of a section apply unless the parties agree otherwise: there is no statement of this kind in s 6. Nevertheless, Atiyah has argued that the effect of the section should be able to be overturned by a contrary intention of the parties: Atiyah, 1957, pp 348–49.

30 Ibid.

11.5.2 Impossibility of performance

An operative common mistake may also arise where, although the subject matter of the contract has not been destroyed, performance is, and always was, impossible. This may result from a physical impossibility, as in *Sheikh Bros v Ochsner*,[31] where land was not capable of growing the quantity of crop contracted for, or legal impossibility,[32] where the contract is to buy property which the purchaser already owned.[33] A contract based on a mistake of law will also fall into this category.[34] There is also one case, *Griffith v Brymer*,[35] where a contract was found void for what may be regarded as 'commercial impossibility'.[36] The contract was to hire a room to view an event which, at the time of the contract, had already been cancelled. Performance of the contract was physically and legally possible, but would have had no point.[37]

11.5.3 Mistake as to quality

Can there be an operative common mistake where the parties are mistaken as to the quality of what they have contracted about? Suppose A sells B a table, both parties being under the impression that they are dealing with a valuable antique, whereas it subsequently turns out to be a fake? Can B claim that the contract should be treated as void on the basis of a common mistake?[38] The leading House of Lords authority is *Bell v Lever Bros*.[39] The plaintiffs (Lever Bros) had reached an agreement for compensation with the defendant over the early termination of his contract of employment. This termination agreement was itself a contract, providing for the payment of £50,000. The

---

31 [1957] AC 136.

32 The case of *Cooper v Phibbs* (1867) LR 2 HL 149 is sometimes cited as an example of the application of this principle. In fact, the contract, which was to rent land in which the tenant already held a beneficial (though not legal) interest, was set aside by the House of Lords as being voidable in equity, rather than void at common law. This is indicated by the fact that terms were imposed on the rescission, which would not be possible if the contract were void at common law. As to the equitable remedies for mistake, see below, 11.7.

33 See Lord Atkin's statement to this effect in *Bell v Lever Bros Ltd* [1932] AC 161, p 218.

34 As indicate by *Brennan v Bolt Burdon* [2004] EWCA Civ 1017; [2005] QB 303 – discussed above, 11.3.

35 (1903) 19 TLR 434.

36 See Treitel, 2003, p 288.

37 There are a number of cases arising out of the same events as *Griffiths v Brymer* which, because the cancellation occurred *after* the contract had been made were dealt with as cases of 'frustration' – see Chapter 16, 16.3.3.

38 This type of situation will in practice often be dealt with by the provisions of the SGA 1979 and, in particular, the implied term under s 13 that goods should match their description, as in *Nicholson and Venn v Smith-Marriott* (1947) 177 LT 189. For discussion of s 13, see Chapter 8, 8.6.11. If A has made a statement about the nature of the table, there may also be the possibility of rescission or damages for misrepresentation.

39 [1932] AC 161. For a full discussion of the background to the case and the way in which it moved from being about the trustworthiness of managers to becoming a leading authority on 'mistake', see MacMillan, 2003.

plaintiffs then discovered that the defendant had previously behaved in a way which would have justified termination without compensation. They therefore argued that the compensation contract should be regarded as being void for mistake. The House was reluctant to allow a mistake as to the quality, or value, of what had been contracted for to be regarded as an operative mistake. As Lord Atkin put it:[40]

> In such a case, a mistake will not affect assent unless it is the mistake of both parties and is as to the existence of some quality which makes the thing without the quality essentially different from the thing as it was believed to be.

This would not be the case in an example such as that of the antique which turns out to be a fake. Lord Atkin again comments:[41]

> A buys a picture from B: both A and B believe it to be the work of an old master, and high price is paid. It turns out to be a modern copy. A has no remedy in the absence of representation or warranty.

Applying this approach to the case before the House, the conclusion was that there was no operative mistake. The plaintiffs had obtained exactly what they had bargained for, that is, the release of the contract with the defendant. The fact that the plaintiffs could have achieved the same result without paying compensation by relying on the defendant's earlier conduct was immaterial.

This conclusion has sometimes been regarded as indicating that there can never be an operative mistake as to quality.[42] However, the decision does not go quite that far, as the first quotation from Lord Atkin above shows. He specifically recognises the possibility that a mistake as to whether the subject matter of the contract has a particular quality may nullify consent provided it is a quality, the absence of which makes the subject matter 'essentially different'. The difficulty is that if, as was held in *Bell v Lever Bros*, a mistake worth £50,000 does not make a contract essentially different, then what kind of mistake will do so? The fact that *Bell* did not shut the door on operative mistakes as to quality was, however, noted by Steyn J in *Associated Japanese Bank Ltd v Credit du Nord SA*.[43] He held that a contract of guarantee which was given on the basis of the existence of certain packaging machines, was void at common law when it turned out the machines did not exist at all. B, as a means of raising capital, had entered into

---

40 [1932] AC 161, p 218.

41 Ibid, p 224.

42 The decision in *Bell v Lever Bros* has recently been described as possibly being 'the most unsatisfactory decision handed down by the House of Lords in modern times': Harris, Campbell and Halson, 2002, p 244. The criticism relates in part to the very limited scope for common mistake which was recognised by the House in this case.

43 [1988] 3 All ER 902. For a detailed analysis of the relationship between this case and *Bell v Lever Bros*, see Treitel, 1988 and Smith, 1994.

an arrangement with the plaintiff bank, under which the bank bought the four machines from B for £1,021,000. The bank then immediately leased the machines back to B. B, of course, had obligations to make payments under this lease to the plaintiff. These obligations were guaranteed by the defendant bank. B was unable to keep up the payments, and the plaintiff sought to enforce the guarantee against the defendant, by which time it had been discovered that the machines had never existed. This mistake, which had been made by both plaintiff and defendant, of course, had great significance for the guarantee. There is no doubt that the defendant would not have given the guarantee if it had known the truth. But was the guarantee rendered void by this mistake? Steyn J refused to accept that *Bell* precluded an argument based on common mistake as to quality. His view was that, on the facts, such a mistake was not operative in *Bell*, not least because it was by no means clear that Lever Bros would have acted any differently even if they had known the truth. It was open, therefore, to consider whether the mistake was operative in the case before him. It should be noted that this was not a case of *res extincta*, though it comes close. The machines were not the subject matter of the contract under consideration. The subject matter was in fact a contract in relation to the machines the performance of which had been supported by a guarantee given by the defendant. Steyn J concluded:[44]

> For both parties, the guarantee of obligations under a lease with non-existent machines was essentially different from a guarantee of a lease with four machines which both parties at the time of the contract believed to exist.

The contract of guarantee was therefore void for common mistake at common law.[45] The position would therefore seem to be that some mistakes as to the quality, or value, of the subject matter of the contract can give rise to an operative mistake provided that the mistake has a sufficiently serious effect in relation to matters which are fundamental to the contract. There are *obiter* statements in *Nicholson and Venn v Smith-Marriott*,[46] where the mistake was as to the provenance of antique table linen, which would also support such a view, though equally, in *Leaf v International Galleries*,[47] where the mistake was as to whether a picture was painted by Constable, there are *obiter* statements which envisage a very limited role for this type of mistake. The fact that there are so few reported cases where it has been held that a common mistake is operative to avoid the contract at common law suggests that the latter view may well be correct.

This view is reinforced by the most recent reconsideration of the area by the

---

44 [1988] 3 All ER 902, p 913.

45 Treitel (1988, p 507) has suggested that *Bell v Lever Bros* exemplifies the application of the policy of respect for the sanctity of contract, whereas *Associated Bank* is based on the policy of giving effect to the reasonable expectations of honest men.

46 (1947) 177 LT 189.

47 [1950] 2 KB 86; [1950] 1 All ER 693. The case is discussed further in Chapter 10 at 10.4.1.

Court of Appeal in *Great Peace Shipping Ltd v Tsavliris ('The Great Peace')*.[48] The contract concerned the charter of a ship, *The Great Peace*, to provide urgent assistance with a salvage operation. At the time of the contract both parties thought that the ship was about 35 miles from the salvage site. In fact it was about 410 miles away. When the charterer discovered this, it found another ship that was much closer and sought to avoid the contract for *The Great Peace* on the basis of common mistake. The Court of Appeal held that the mistake was not sufficiently serious to render the contract void at common law – it would still have been possible for *The Great Peace* to render assistance at the salvage, even though at a later time than anticipated. The principles set out in *Bell v Lever Bros* were confirmed as indicating the correct approach to such issues. In coming to this conclusion, the Court of Appeal took the opportunity to review the whole basis for the doctrine of common mistake. It came to the view that it was properly regarded as being based not on any theory of terms to be implied into the contract, but as a rule of law similar to that which operates in relation to the doctrine of frustration.[49] The court restated the requirements for common mistake in the following way (which it saw as consistent with *Bell v Lever Bros*):[50]

(i)   there must be a common assumption as to the existence of a state of affairs;

(ii)   there must be no warranty by either party that that state of affairs exists;

(iii)   the non-existence of the state of affairs must not be attributable to the fault of either party;

(iv)   the non-existence of the state of affairs must render performance of the contract impossible;

(v)   the state of affairs may be the existence, or a vital attribute, of the consideration to be provided or the circumstance which must subsist if performance of the contractual adventure is to be possible.

Point (ii) (and to some extent (iii)) obviously deals with the situation that arose in *McRae v Commonwealth Disposals Commission*.[51] The reference to 'impossibility' in (iv) must be read in the light of the analogies which the court was drawing with the doctrine of frustration. Under that doctrine, a contract may be discharged if performance has become impossible or 'radically different' from that which the parties intended. It would seem that such an approach should also apply in relation to mistake. That this is the view of the Court of Appeal in *The Great Peace* is confirmed by its treatment of mistakes as to quality. As will be seen, in point (v) it refers to a 'vital attribute' which may not have existence, and this clearly extends the scope of the doctrine beyond physical non-existence of the subject matter. Moreover, the court approved the analysis of Steyn J in the *Associated Japanese Bank* case, in which he

48 [2002] EWCA Civ 1407; [2002] 4 All ER 689.
49 Which is dealt with in Chapter 16.
50 [2002] EWCA Civ 1407; [2002] 4 All ER 689, para 76.
51 Above, 11.5.1.

concluded that *Bell v Lever Bros* still left open the possibility of a mistake as to quality rendering a contract void where the mistake renders 'the subject matter of the contract essentially and radically different from the subject matter which the parties believed to exist'.[52] The Court of Appeal's specific approval of this passage, and of the conclusions reached by Steyn J on the facts of the *Associated Japanese Bank* case, confirm that mistakes as to quality may render a contract void, albeit very rarely.

On the facts which arose in *The Great Peace*, the Court of Appeal agreed with the trial judge that the mistake as to the position of the vessel was not sufficiently serious to render the contract void. In particular, when the true position of the vessel was discovered, the charterers did not cancel the contract until they had located another vessel which was nearer. The implication was that if no other such vessel had been located, they would have continued with the charter concerning *The Great Peace*. If that was the case, it could not be argued that the contract for *The Great Peace* was 'impossible' or even 'radically different' from that which the parties had intended.

11.5.4 Effect of an operative common mistake

The effect of an operative common mistake at common law is to render the contract void *ab initio* (from the beginning). It is as if the contract had never existed, and therefore, as far as is possible, all concerned must be returned to the position they were in before the contract was made. This applies equally to third parties, so that the innocent purchaser of goods which have been 'sold' under a void contract will be required to disgorge them, and hand them back to the original owner. These powerful and far-reaching consequences perhaps explain why the courts have shown a reluctance to extend the scope of common mistake too far, preferring to allow the flexible application of equitable remedies to pick up the pieces in many cases. The use of equity has, however, been significantly reduced since the Court of Appeal's decision in *The Great Peace*.[53]

11.6 MISTAKES NEGATIVING AGREEMENT

As indicated above, there are two categories of mistake which may have the effect of negativing agreement – that is, where the contract fails because there never was an agreement between the parties as to some essential matter. The first category is where neither side is aware of the fact that the other is contracting on a different basis. The lack of agreement is 'mutual'. The second category is where one party is aware of the other's mistake. Here the mistake is 'unilateral'. These two categories will be considered separately.

---

52 [1988] 3 All ER 902, pp 912–13.
53 For the effect of this decision on the remedies available in equity to deal with mistake, see 11.7 below.

11.6.1 'Mutual mistake'

'Mutual mistake' refers to the situation where the parties are at cross-purposes, but neither side is aware of this when they purport to make a contract. The mistake may relate to the subject matter of the contract, or the identity of the other contracting party. If the mistake is sufficiently fundamental that it means in effect that there was no agreement between the parties, then there can be no contract, and any actions taken on the basis that there was a contract will have to be undone.

A classic example of a situation which might give rise to this kind of mistake is to be found in *Raffles v Wichelhaus*.[54] The alleged contract was for the purchase of a cargo of cotton due to arrive in England on the ship *Peerless*, from Bombay. There were two ships of this name carrying cotton from Bombay, one of which left in October, the other in December. The plaintiff offered the December cargo for delivery, but the defendant refused to accept this, claiming that he intended to buy the October cargo. The plaintiff tried to argue that the contract was simply for a certain quantity of cotton, and that the ship from which it was to be supplied was immaterial. The defendant, however, put his case in these terms:[55]

> There is nothing on the face of the contract to shew that any particular ship called the *Peerless* was meant; but the moment it appears that two ships called the *Peerless* were about to sail from Bombay there is a latent ambiguity, and parol evidence may be given for the purpose of shewing that the defendant meant one *Peerless*, and the plaintiff another. That being so, there was no *consensus ad idem*, and therefore no binding contract.

The court stopped argument at this point, and held for the defendant. There is, however, no report of any judgment, so it is impossible to be certain of the exact basis of the decision. It is perhaps significant, however, that a few years later the case was cited by Hannen J in *Smith v Hughes* as authority for the proposition that:[56]

> . . . if two persons enter into an apparent contract concerning a particular person or ship, and it turns out that each of them, misled by a similarity of name, had a different ship or person in his mind, no contract would exist between them.

Whatever the precise basis for the decision in *Raffles v Wichelhaus* itself, therefore, there seems no doubt that if the parties are at cross-purposes, the contract will be void for mutual mistake. This will, of course, only apply where there is a fundamental ambiguity in the contract, and no objective means of resolving it.

---

54 (1864) 2 H & C 906; 159 ER 375. The case has attracted much academic attention. For the historical context, see Simpson, 1989. For an argument that the commonly accepted interpretation of the case was 'invented' by Holmes, see Gilmore, 1974, pp 40–42.

55 (1864) 2 H & C 906, pp 907–08; 159 ER 375, p 376.

56 (1871) LR 6 QB 597, p 609.

This type of mistake raises a question which was discussed in Chapter 2 – that is, how do the courts decide what the parties intended? Clearly the intentions can only be inferred from the words and actions of the parties, rather than their actual states of mind. The approach is therefore primarily objective – what would a reasonable person viewing the actions and hearing the statements of the parties think that they intended? If, taking the objective view, there was agreement, then the contract will not be avoided for mutual mistake. As was noted in Chapter 2,[57] however, the objective valuation may be made from the point of view of one of the parties,[58] or from the point of view of an independent third party.[59] It seems that in the area of mutual mistake, the question of whether there is an agreement based on detached objectivity is going to be the crucial question. The facts of a mutual mistake case will often be such that both parties may be able to argue that they reasonably believed the other party to be intending on a particular basis. The outcome of the case would then depend on who was bringing the action. That was clearly not the approach taken in *Raffles v Wichelhaus*.[60] The plaintiffs there could have argued that they intended to sell the December cargo and reasonably believed that that was what they believed the defendants were intending to buy. Equally, the defendants could argue that they reasonably believed that the plaintiffs were intending to sell the October cargo. If the defendants' view had prevailed, it would have meant that there was a contract for sale of the October cargo, and the plaintiff was in breach of contract. This was not the outcome of the case, however.[61] It appears to have been the view of the court that there was no contract at all.

This will not necessarily be the outcome, however, if, from a point of view of detached objectivity, a third party would reasonably believe that the contract had been made on particular terms. Thus, in *Rose (Frederick E) (London) Ltd v William H Pim Jnr & Co Ltd,*[62] there was confusion between the parties as to whether they were contracting about 'horsebeans' or 'feveroles' (a particular type of horsebean). From the point of view of detached objectivity, however, the contract simply appeared to be for 'horsebeans', and that was how it was interpreted by the court.[63] This could not apply in *Raffles v Wichelhaus,* since a third party looking at what had passed between the parties would have been unable to determine which ship was intended. The only

---

57 See 2.4.1.

58 Promisor or promisee objectivity.

59 Detached objectivity.

60 Gilmore (1974, pp 35–40) argues that *Raffles v Wichelhaus* is in fact an example of the courts using a subjective approach to the question of whether there was agreement between the parties – there was no contract because there was no 'meeting of the minds'. He alleges that the modern 'interpretation' of the case derives solely from the writings of Holmes.

61 At least insofar as it has been understood in *Smith v Hughes* and later cases.

62 [1953] 2 QB 450; [1953] 2 All ER 739.

63 The case was concerned with the possibility of the 'rectification' of a contract (and is discussed in that context below, 11.8.2). For a further example of a court's refusal to find a mutual mistake, using an 'objective' approach, see *NBTY Europe Ltd v Nutricia International BV* [2005] EWHC 734 Comm; [2005] 2 Lloyd's Rep 350.

possibility in that case, therefore, was for the 'contract' to be treated as void, for failure of agreement.

Spencer has argued that the use of 'detached objectivity', which he labels the 'fly on the wall' approach, can lead to absurd results, as he felt that it did in *Rose v Pim*.[64] He gives the example of two people with little knowledge of English who contract for the sale and purchase of a 'bull', intending in fact to deal with a 'cow'. He suggests that the detached objectivity approach would lead to the contract being deemed to be one for a bull, which is not what either party intended. But this is to suggest that detached objectivity can be used in a way which ignores the context and the surrounding circumstances. In *Raffles v Wichelhaus*, for example, no doubt if there was evidence to show that the parties had in fact been in agreement about which ship was meant, then the contract would have been upheld, despite the fact that 'detached objectivity', applied in the absence of such additional information, would be unable to determine which ship was intended. The 'bull' and 'cow' example could surely take into account the understanding of these words as shared by the parties. In cases of mutual mistake, evidence that despite confusing language, there was agreement, will prevent the contract being avoided. In the absence of such agreement, the question to be asked is what would a reasonable third party, looking at what was said and done, think that the parties to the agreement intended. In *Raffles*, the confusion was such that it was not possible to give a definite answer to this question. A similar result occurred in *Scriven Bros v Hindley*,[65] where there was confusion as to the nature of two lots in an auction, one being 'hemp', the other being much less valuable 'tow'. The defendant who had bid an unusually high price for the tow, in the mistaken belief that it was hemp, was allowed to avoid the contract.[66]

In *Smith v Hughes*,[67] however, which again concerned an alleged mutual mistake in relation to the subject matter of the contract, a different view was taken. The plaintiff had offered to sell oats to the defendant. The defendant thought that he was buying 'old' oats. When delivered, they turned out to be 'new', and of no use to the defendant. The trial judge directed the jury that if they thought that the defendant believed that he was contracting for old oats, they should give a verdict for the defendant, which they did. On appeal, however, the Queen's Bench held that it was not enough that the defendant had made a mistake. To allow him to escape from the contract, it would be necessary to show that the defendant thought that it was a term of the contract that the oats were 'old', *and that the plaintiff was aware that the defendant thought this* (that is, a 'unilateral', rather

---

64 Spencer, 1973. His criticism of *Rose v Pim* is based on the fact that both parties intended to deal in 'feveroles'. It is by no means clear, however, that that is an accurate view of the facts, since it seems that at the time of the contract neither party understood how feveroles differed from horsebeans.

65 [1913] 3 KB 564.

66 The case might now be categorised as one of 'unilateral mistake', since there was some evidence that the auctioneer realised that the bid was made on the basis of a mistake. At the time, however, it was not dealt with on this basis, the court finding that there was no contract simply on the basis that the parties were not *ad idem*.

67 (1871) LR 6 QB 597.

than 'mutual', mistake). Looked at objectively, it appeared to be simply a contract for the sale of a specific parcel of oats, about which there was no ambiguity.

The approach here, therefore, as in general with issues as to the creation of an agreement, is to concentrate on what can be deduced objectively from what the parties have said or done, rather than to try to determine their precise state of mind at the time of the alleged agreement.

FOR THOUGHT

What do you think the outcome of *Smith v Hughes* would have been if the defendant had, during pre-contractual discussion, indicated that he was looking to buy old oats?

11.6.2 Unilateral mistake

Unilateral mistake refers to the situation where the agreement is 'negatived' (that is, prevented from coming into existence), because one party is aware that the other is mistaken about an aspect of the contract. In many situations involving unilateral mistake there will have been a misrepresentation which will provide the other party with a remedy. If there was no such misrepresentation, however, or the remedies available for misrepresentation are inadequate, there may be a remedy on the basis of a mistake. For this to be available, however, the mistake must be sufficiently important that, viewed objectively, it prevents there being an agreement. As we have seen, the court in *Smith v Hughes* thought that the result would have been different if the plaintiff had been aware that the defendant was acting on the basis of a mistake *as to a term of the contract*. For example, if the mistake, as in *Smith v Hughes*, relates to some quality of whatever constitutes the subject matter of the contract, it is not enough that A is aware that B has made some mistake about this quality; A must also realise that B regards A as having undertaken a contractual obligation that the subject matter has the quality concerned. As has been noted in the discussion of misrepresentation, the law of contract does not generally intervene simply because one party is more knowledgeable than the other.[68] Taking advantage of superior knowledge or information is seen as tending towards wealth creation in a capitalist economic context. The approach taken by English law is exemplified by the following quotation from Rimer J in *Clarion Ltd v National Provident Institution*.[69] In considering the scope for the courts to intervene where one party is aware of another's mistake, he took the example of negotiations for a compromise of a legal action (though the approach suggested is clearly intended to be of wider application):[70]

---

68 See Chapter 10, 10.2.
69 [2000] 2 All ER 265.
70 Ibid, p 281. He is commenting on issues raised by Young J in the Australian case of *EasyFind (NSW) Pty Ltd v Paterson* (1987) 11 NSWLR 98, p 106.

The compromise of litigation is a contractual exercise in which it is the common-est thing for each side to be aware of facts and matters of which it knows or at least suspects the other side is ignorant. If each side knew all that the other side knew then either no or only a very different compromise would be reached. In the negotiation of such compromises[71] the parties must be careful not to make any misrepresentations. But there is in my view no general duty imposed on them in the nature of a duty of disclosure. The negotiations are in the nature of an arm's length commercial bargain. Each party has to look after its own interests and neither owes a duty of care to the other. It would in my view be astonishing if, in the ordinary case, a defendant could later set aside a compromise merely because he had learnt. . . that he had materially overpaid a claimant who, unbeknown to him but well known to the claimant's advisers probably could not have proved his case at all.

It is, therefore, only where the party with the superior knowledge is seen as acting un-fairly towards the other (for example, by inducing the other's misunderstanding through false statements) that the courts will intervene. This basis for intervention has clear links with the concept of 'good faith', which, as we have seen, operates in many other juris-dictions and is part of the proposed Principles of European Contract Law.[72]

An example of a situation where one party was not allowed to take advantage of a mistake made by the other is to be found in *Hartog v Colin and Shields.*[73] The contract was for the sale of hare skins. The price quoted by the seller was stated to be 'per pound'. This was a mistake, since the price should have been 'per piece'. The mistake meant that the skins appeared to be being offered at a price about two-thirds lower than intended by the seller. The normal practice in the trade is for skins to be sold by the piece. The buyers accepted the seller's offer in the terms stated, but the seller refused to supply on this basis, claiming that the buyers were trying to take unfair advantage of a genuine mistake. The court was of the view that the buyers were aware that a mistake had been made.[74] On this basis there was no contract, and the sellers did not have to supply at the price stated. This case fulfils the requirements set out in *Smith v Hughes.* The mistake was as to a term of the contract (the price of the goods) and the other party was aware that a mistake as to this term had been made.

---

71 That is, in effect, 'contracts'.

72 See the discussion at 10.2.

73 [1939] 3 All ER 566; cf also *Centrovincial Estates plc v Merchant Investors Insurance Co Ltd* [1983] Com LR 158.

74 The case does not make it clear whether it is necessary to prove actual knowledge of the mistake, or simply that the party 'taking advantage' *should have been* aware of the mistake. The normal approach to deciding on issues as to the state of mind of a party would suggest that the test should be objective – that is, 'would a reasonable person in the position of this party have realised that a mistake had been made by the other side'.

11.6.3   Mistaken identity

Unilateral mistake may arise in relation to any aspect of the contract. The majority of reported cases, however, concern mistakes as to the identity of the other contracting party. The general rule is that the mistake, to be operative, must relate to the *identity* of the person with whom you are contracting, not his or her *attributes*. This is a distinction which may be easier to state than to apply. Indeed, Lord Denning suggested in *Lewis v Averay* that it was a 'distinction without a difference':[75]

> A man's name is one of his attributes. It is also a key to his identity. If, then, he gives a false name, is it a mistake as to his identity? or a mistake as to his attributes? These fine distinctions do no good to the law.

Nevertheless, it is submitted that the distinction may in some situations serve some purpose. Suppose, for example, I negotiate a contract for my shop to be opened by a particular film star, and this is advertised widely. I will not be satisfied if the agency with whom I have made the contract sends either (a) someone with the same name as the film star, but with no other similar qualities, or (b) another film star, but not the one whose presence I have advertised. In such a case, the identity of the individual is of central importance to the contract. A misunderstanding on this matter should raise the possibility of the contract being void for mistake. On the other hand, in the majority of contractual situations, the identity of the party with whom one is contracting is not important. The concern is as to whether they will perform their obligations under the contract, not who they are. In particular, there is generally no reason to allow a person to back out of a contract simply for thinking mistakenly that the other party was wealthy, and therefore creditworthy.

The courts have been more willing to treat mistakes of identity as operative where the contract has been made through the post, or via an agent, rather than in person. In *Boulton v Jones*,[76] for example, the defendant had sent an order to one 'Brocklehurst' with whom he had dealt regularly. Brocklehurst had, however, just transferred the business to his foreman, who fulfilled the order. The defendant resisted a claim for payment by the foreman on the basis that he had a 'set-off' against Brocklehurst, arising out of their previous dealings. The court accepted that the existence of this set-off made the identity of the other party of crucial importance to the defendant, and the contract was set aside.

This result may appear a little harsh to the plaintiff in *Boulton v Jones* who, while aware of the defendant's mistake, was not trying to take any unfair advantage. This was not the case, however, in *Cundy v Lindsay*.[77] A fraudulent individual named Blenkarn placed large orders for handkerchiefs with the plaintiffs. Blenkarn was trading from

---

75 [1972] 1 QB 198, p 206.
76 (1857) 27 LJ Exch 117.
77 (1878) 3 App Cas 459.

Wood Street, and the plaintiffs thought that they were dealing with a reputable firm by the name of Blenkiron & Co, which also had its business in Wood Street. Blenkarn deliberately contributed to this mistake by the manner in which he signed his order. The goods were supplied and sold on to the defendant, who was an innocent third party. The House of Lords confirmed that there was no contract between the plaintiffs and Blenkarn. As Lord Cairns put it:[78]

> Of him [Blenkarn], they [the plaintiffs] knew nothing, and of him they never thought. With him they never intended to deal. Their minds never for an instant of time rested upon him, and as between him and them there was no consensus of mind which could lead to any agreement or any contract whatever.

As will be noted, this introduces a rather more subjective element, concerned with the fact of agreement, than is usually the case in this area. Even from an objective point of view, however, the fact that the plaintiffs had addressed the orders, and other correspondence, to 'Messrs Blenkiron', indicated that they had been under a misapprehension about whom they were dealing with, and had not intended to contract with Blenkarn. The consequences of the decision, however, were serious for the innocent defendants, who had to return the handkerchiefs (for which they had paid) to the plaintiffs, and were left to seek compensation from the fraudulent Blenkarn. The continued authority of *Cundy v Lindsay* has been recently confirmed by the decision of the House of Lords in *Shogun Finance Ltd v Hudson*,[79] which is discussed below, in 11.6.4.

For the mistake as to identity to be operative, the mistaken party must be able to show who it was that was the intended contracting party. Thus, in *King's Norton Metal Co v Edridge, Merrett & Co*,[80] although once again a contract was induced by a fraudulent person (Wallis), who was pretending to be a firm called 'Hallam & Co', the contract was upheld. This was because 'Hallam & Co' was a pure invention, created by Wallis. There was no genuine firm of that name with whom the plaintiffs could have thought they were dealing. The mistake was therefore not one of identity, but of attributes. The plaintiffs thought that they were dealing with a firm, though in fact they were dealing with a private individual, Wallis.

11.6.4   Contracts made 'face to face'

It becomes much harder to argue for mistake where the contract is made face to face or, as the courts often describe it, *inter praesentes*. The courts are reluctant to accept that you did not intend to contract with the person who is standing in front of you, even

---

78 (1878) 3 App Cas 459, p 465.
79 [2003] UKHL 62; [2004] 1 All ER 215. Though it should be noted that two members of the House (Lord Nicholls and Lord Millett) were of the view that *Cundy v Lindsay* should be overruled.
80 (1897) 14 TLR 98.

though you may have been under a misapprehension as to that person's attributes or qualities. The importance of this distinction was demonstrated and reaffirmed in *Shogun Finance Ltd v Hudson*.[81] A person had pretended to be someone else for the purpose of obtaining a car on hire purchase terms. Although the negotiations relating to the transaction were with the car dealer, the written contract, in which the false name was given, was with the finance company. The majority of the House of Lords held that this was not a contract *inter praesentes*, and the finance company was allowed to avoid the contract on the basis of unilateral mistake.[82] They were clearly influenced in this conclusion by the fact that the finance company would only deal with a person whom, after carrying out checks, it deemed to be creditworthy – and this was the person named in the written contract, not the 'rogue' pretending to be that person. In addition, the contract was formed by the written documentation exchanged with the finance company, not by the dealer as agent for the finance company. By contrast, the minority in the House of Lords felt that the decision in *Cundy v Lindsay*[83] should be overruled, and that the presumption outlined below, that one intends to contract with the person with whom one is dealing, should apply to contracts made in writing as well as those made in person. The majority's decision, however, means that the law continues to apply particular rules to contracts made face to face.

The starting point for consideration of the approach of English law to contracts *inter praesentes* is *Phillips v Brooks*.[84] In this case a person went into a jeweller's shop. He selected various valuable items, including a ring. As he was writing a cheque in payment, he said 'You see who I am, I am Sir George Bullough', giving an address in St James' Square. The plaintiff checked this information in a directory, and then allowed the man to take the ring with him. The cheque was dishonoured, and the man turned out not to be Sir George at all. He had in the meantime, however, passed the ring to the defendant, who had taken it in all innocence. The court held that the contract was with the person in the shop. The plaintiff had failed to establish that the identity of that person was a crucial element in the contract.

This approach was followed in *Lewis v Averay*,[85] in which the fraudulent party pretended to be a famous television actor, and on that basis induced the plaintiff to part with his car in return for a worthless cheque. In support of his claim, the fraudulent party produced a 'pass' from Pinewood Film Studios which carried his photograph and an official stamp. By the time the cheque was dishonoured and the plaintiff had discovered the fraud, the car had been sold to the defendant, who had bought it in good

81 [2003] UKHL 62; [2004] 1 All ER 215.
82 This had the effect of preventing an innocent third party, who had bought the car from the 'rogue', from obtaining a good title. It meant that the finance company was able to avoid the protection normally given to private purchasers of cars which are sold in breach of a hire purchase agreement provided by the Hire Purchase Act 1964, s 27.
83 (1878) 3 App Cas 459.
84 [1919] 2 KB 243.
85 [1972] 2 All ER 229.

faith, innocent of any deception. The perpetrator of the fraud having disappeared from the scene, the plaintiff sued the defendant in the tort of conversion for recovery of the car, or its value plus damages. It was held that the contract, while probably voidable for misrepresentation, was not void for mistake, so that the innocent third party who was now in possession of the car was entitled to retain it. Looking at the outward appearances of the transaction, it was simply a contract under which the plaintiff sold the car to the fraudulent purchaser. The identity of the purchaser was not an important factor. Since the plaintiff had not managed to avoid the contract before the car had been sold to an innocent third party, the contract had to stand.

It is difficult, however, to reconcile with these two cases the decision in *Ingram v Little*.[86] Here, the contract was, as in *Lewis v Averay*, for the sale of a car. It was owned by three women who lived together. A man calling himself Hutchinson answered their advertisement. He offered a sum which was acceptable to the women, but then produced a cheque book. The woman who was conducting the negotiations at that point indicated that in no circumstances would they accept payment by cheque. The man then gave a full name and an address. One of the other women then left the house to visit the post office and consult a telephone directory, which confirmed that a person of that name lived at the address given. They then allowed him to take the car in exchange for the cheque. The man was not, however, Mr Hutchinson, and the cheque proved worthless. The women brought an action to recover the car from an innocent third party purchaser. The Court of Appeal confirmed the view of the trial judge that they should succeed. The response to the offer of a cheque, and the procedure of checking in the directory, indicated that the identity of the other contracting party was of the utmost importance, and the contract was therefore void for mistake.

The principle applied is the same in all three of the cases just discussed, that is, the identity of the other contracting party must be sufficiently important to form part of the basis of the contract. It is difficult to see, however, that there really was that much difference in the situation in *Ingram v Little* to justify applying the principle differently from the way in which it was applied in *Phillips v Brooks* and *Lewis v Averay*. There have been attempts to explain the differences on the basis of the precise stage in the process when the contract was made. Thus, in *Phillips v Brooks*, it might be argued that the contract was made before there was any mention of 'Sir George Bullough',[87] whereas in *Ingram v Little*, the plaintiffs were only prepared to contract once they had checked that a Mr Hutchinson did live at the address quoted. These arguments appear rather strained, however. The reality is that in all three cases the plaintiff was tricked into parting with property by the fraud of the other contracting party. They could not use the remedy of misrepresentation because the fraudulent party had already disposed of the property to an innocent third party by the time the fraud was discovered. The question was simply which of two 'innocent' parties should bear the loss caused by the fraud.

---

86 [1961] 1 QB 31; [1960] 3 All ER 332.
87 This was the view taken by Viscount Haldane in *Lake v Simmons* [1927] AC 487, p 501, but does not really fit with the reported facts – see the comments of Treitel, 2003, p 300.

The general view seems to be that the approach taken in *Lewis v Averay* is in general to be preferred. The original owner is marginally less 'innocent' than the third party, because it is the owner's actions which have 'allowed' the fraud to be perpetrated.[88] Lewis could, for example, have insisted, notwithstanding the fact that he thought he was dealing with a famous actor, that the cheque should be cleared before possession of the car was surrendered. In that situation the 'fairest' result is to allow the loss to lie with the original owner. This result is also probably suggested by adopting the approach of 'detached objectivity'. What would a third party viewing the transaction reasonably think had occurred? Would they think that the seller was intending to deal with the person standing in front of them, or only with a particular named individual? All this suggests that *Ingram v Little* is the anomalous case, and that there is probably little point in engaging in protracted analysis to fit it into a coherent doctrine. Indeed, the decision in *Ingram v Little* was not unanimous, since Lord Devlin dissented. In the course of his judgment, he expressed the view that it was unfortunate that the rules relating to mistake meant that if it was operative at common law, and the contract was void, it often meant that, as in *Ingram v Little*, one of two innocent parties had to suffer, and there was no good basis for choosing between them. He suggested that it would be better to have some system whereby the losses could be apportioned in such a case. This suggestion, which would be likely to produce a fairer result in many cases, has not, however, been taken up.[89] The current state of the law in this area was strongly criticised by the Court of Appeal and by the minority in the House of Lords in *Shogun Finance Ltd v Hudson*.[90] Lord Millett commented that:[91]

> We cannot leave the law as it is. It is neither fair nor principled, and not all of the authorities can be reconciled; some, at least, must be overruled if it is to be extricated from the present quagmire.

But the majority disagreed, and the law has been left as it was. Jackson has suggested that the judgments in *Ingram v Little* and *Lewis v Averay* reflect what is probably the general 'social evaluation' of the cases – that is, that while the plaintiffs in *Ingram v Little* were tricked out of their car, and were thereby 'defrauded', Lewis was simply 'fooled'.[92] He was the victim of his own stupidity. Jackson also suggests that this difference in approach is reflected in the language used by the judges in the two cases.

---

88 There is no reason why such an argument should not equally apply to mistaken identity cases which involve fraud between parties who are not contracting face to face – this was not the view taken by the majority of the Court of Appeal, however, in *Shogun Finance Ltd v Hudson* [2001] EWCA Civ 1001; [2002] 4 All ER 572.

89 It was considered by the Law Reform Committee in 1966, but rejected as impractical: Twelfth Report, *Transfer of Title to Chattels*, Cmnd 2958.

90 [2003] UKHL 62; [2004] 1 All ER 215

91 Ibid, para 84

92 Jackson, 1988.

FOR THOUGHT

(1) Do you think the outcome of *Ingram v Little* would have been the same had the person defrauded been a young man rather than three elderly women? (2) What steps could Lewis have taken to put himself in the same position as the women in *Ingram v Little?*

It will be easier for a claimant to convince a court that the identity of the other party is important if the claimant has sought the person out. If you advertise goods to the general public, it may be difficult then to suggest that you really wanted to contract with one person in particular. If, however, you have gone to that person's place of business, specifically to enter into a contract, then the argument that the identity of the other party was important is likely to be much more convincing. This may be illustrated by *Hardman v Booth*.[93] The plaintiffs had approached a firm, Thomas Gandell & Sons. They dealt with Edward Gandell, a member of the family who they thought was acting for the firm, though in fact he was acting on his own account. He intercepted goods sent by the plaintiffs and sold them to the defendant. It was held that the plaintiffs never intended to deal with Edward, but only with the firm, and the contract was therefore void for mistake.

It may also be possible to rebut the presumption where the fraudulent party is deemed to have been contracted with on the basis that he or she was an agent for someone else, rather than contracting in his or her own right. This situation was considered in *Lake v Simmons*.[94] A woman went to a jeweller's shop and represented that she was the wife of VB. She asked to be allowed to take two pearl necklaces, because VB was planning to purchase one for her, and he wished to see them on approval. She was allowed by the plaintiff to take the necklaces. In fact, she was not VB's wife, though she was living with him. Having received the necklaces, she absconded. The issue in the case was whether the plaintiff could recover from his insurance company. The decision turned primarily on the terms of the insurance policy, and whether in giving the necklaces to the woman, the plaintiff could be said to have 'entrusted them to a customer'. If that were the case, the insurance company would not be liable. The House of Lords held that since the transaction was entered in the plaintiff's books as being with VB, the woman was not the 'customer' and the plaintiff could recover under his insurance policy. Viscount Haldane also suggested, however, that the plaintiff was only dealing with the woman as the wife of VB. Since the plaintiff was 'entirely deceived as to the identity of the person' with whom he was dealing, there was no *consensus ad idem*, and therefore no contract.[95] Identity was significant here, since if the woman was simply VB's agent, her own creditworthiness was irrelevant, whereas if she were contracting on

93 (1863) 1 H & C 803.
94 [1927] AC 487.
95 Ibid, p 500.

her own behalf, the plaintiff might well have been more reluctant to allow her to take goods without paying for them.[96]

The argument based on agency will not apply, however, if the 'agent' is a mere 'conduit' for the performance of a transaction. This was the view taken in *Citibank NA v Brown Shipley*,[97] where a rogue obtained foreign currency from Bank A by inducing Bank B to issue a draft on a genuine account. The draft was collected by the rogue, or his associate, from Bank B and presented to Bank A. Bank A rang Bank B to check that the draft was genuine, and having been assured that it was, delivered the foreign currency to the rogue. It was held that in this case the identity of the rogue was irrelevant to the transactions as between the two banks. It had not been established that it was 'fundamental' to them that the person who collected the draft from Bank B and presented it to Bank A 'was a particular person about whom they were mistaken, as opposed to a person whose attributes did not include authority from their customer [that is, the holder of the genuine account against which the draft was drawn] as they believed'.[98] An action against Bank A for conversion of the draft therefore failed.

11.7 MISTAKE IN EQUITY

As we have seen, the common law rules for identifying an operative mistake are very restrictive. For about 50 years, at the end of the twentieth century, courts held that this restrictive approach could be mitigated by a broad equitable remedy of rescission. This would arise where a common mistake was not sufficiently fundamental for the contract to be set aside at common law, but was serious enough for equity to intervene. The starting point for this approach is generally agreed to have been Lord Denning's judgment in the Court of Appeal in *Solle v Butcher*.[99]

The mistake in this case was as to whether the rent payable in relation to a particular property was subject to control under the Rent Restriction Acts. This was held not to be sufficiently serious to render the contract void. However, as Lord Denning put it:[100]

> A contract is also liable in equity to be set aside if the parties were under a common misapprehension either as to facts or as to their relative and respective rights, provided that the misapprehension was fundamental, and that the party seeking to set it aside was not himself at fault.

---

96 A mistake which is simply as to creditworthiness would not, however, generally be sufficient to void the contract: see, for example, *Lewis v Averay*.
97 [1991] 2 All ER 690.
98 Ibid, p 702.
99 [1950] 1 KB 671; [1949] 2 All ER 1107.
100 Ibid, p 693; p 1120.

This made it clear that it was not every mistake which would give rise to equitable relief. It had to be 'fundamental' – but this seemed to be wide enough to include serious mistakes as to the quality or value of the subject matter of the contract.

The line taken by Lord Denning in *Solle v Butcher* was followed by the High Court and the Court of Appeal in a number of subsequent cases.[101] It was never really clear, however, why there should be two sets of rules dealing with the effect of mistakes. Indeed, it is not clear why, if the rules of equity allow a broader range of mistakes to lead to the setting aside of contracts, this approach was not applied in *Bell v Lever Bros*. None of the usual bars to equitable relief applied in that case, but the House of Lords in that case seemed to feel that the common law was all it was concerned with. In more recent cases, the courts have struggled to explain the difference between mistakes which take effect in equity as opposed to at common law. The issue was considered by Evans LJ in *William Sindall plc v Cambridgeshire County Council*. His conclusion was that there must be:[102]

> ... a category of mistake which is 'fundamental', so as to permit the equitable remedy of rescission, which is wider than the kind of 'serious and radical' mistake which means that the contract is void and of no effect in law.

In trying to distinguish between them, he suggested that:

> The difference may be that the common law rule is limited to mistakes with regard to the subject matter of the contract, whilst equity can have regard to a wider and perhaps unlimited category of 'fundamental' mistake.

In the case before him, the mistake related to the existence of a sewer running across a piece of land sold for development. There was no mistake about the subject matter, which was the piece of land. The mistake as to the existence of the sewer could have been sufficiently serious to give rise to a right of rescission, but on the facts it was not. The additional cost raised by the existence of the sewer was no more than £20,000, which, on a contract where the sale price was over £5m, could not be said to be 'fundamental'.

The approach suggested by Evans LJ was reconsidered by Rimer J in *Clarion Ltd v National Provident Institution*.[103] He took the view, however, that mistake would only operate, in equity as in the common law, where the mistake was as to the terms of the contract or its subject matter, or as to the identity of the other contracting party. Noting the broader approach of Evans LJ in *William Sindall plc v Cambridgeshire*

101 For example, *Grist v Bailey* [1967] Ch 532; *Magee v Pennine Insurance* [1969] 2 QB 507; *Nutt v Read* [2000] 32 HLR 761; *West Sussex Properties Ltd v Chichester DC* [2000] NPC 74.
102 [1994] 1 WLR 1016, p 1042.
103 [2000] 2 All ER 265.

County Council, he rejected this as 'at most a somewhat tentative *obiter* comment',[104] and refused to develop it further. The rejection of Evans LJ's suggestion, however, makes the distinction between common and equitable mistake even more vague. It seems to have been accepted since the decision of Steyn J in *Associated Japanese Bank (International) Ltd v Credit du Nord SA*[105] that common law mistake is not limited to cases of *res extincta*, but that other mistakes, if sufficiently fundamental, may avoid a contract. If that is so, then what type of mistake is sufficiently fundamental to allow for relief in equity, but not sufficiently fundamental to avoid the contract at common law?

The importance of this rather confused law on the scope of equitable mistake has, however, been significantly reduced by the decision of the Court of Appeal in *Great Peace Shipping Ltd v Tsavliris, The Great Peace*.[106] In this case, the facts of which have been given above,[107] the Court of Appeal reviewed the whole line of cases flowing from *Solle v Butcher*. Its conclusion was that *Solle v Butcher* was incorrectly decided. There is no general power to set aside contracts other than for a mistake which is operative at common law. As Lord Phillips put it, delivering the judgment of the court:[108]

> Our conclusion is that it is impossible to reconcile *Solle v Butcher* with *Bell v Lever Bros*. The jurisdiction asserted in the former case has not developed. It has been a fertile source of academic debate, but in practice it has given rise to a handful of cases that have merely emphasised the confusion of this area of our jurisprudence.

The result is that the broad discretion to set aside a contract on terms no longer exists: the only remedies that equity can now employ to deal with mistakes where a contract is not void at common law are the refusal of specific performance and rectification, which are considered below.

Finally, it should be noted that, even in equity, the mistake must be made at the time of the contract. In *Amalgamated Investment and Property Co v John Walker & Sons*,[109] a property was listed as a building of special interest by the Department of the Environment. This placed serious restrictions on the ways in which it could be used, and reduced its value by £1.5m. This was clearly a mistake of the kind which might allow equitable relief, but unfortunately the 'listing' of the building had taken place two days after the contract for its sale had been concluded. The mistake was not operative at the time of the contract, and so there could be no relief on this basis either under common law or in equity.

---

104 [2000] 2 All ER 265, p 280.
105 [1988] 3 All ER 902.
106 [2002] EWCA Civ 1407; [2002] 4 All ER 689.
107 Above, 11.5.3.
108 [2002] EWCA Civ 1407; [2002] 4 All ER 689, para 157.
109 [1976] 3 All ER 509.

11.8 FORMS OF EQUITABLE RELIEF

Once it is established that equity will take account of the mistake, what remedies are available? There are two: refusal of specific performance and rectification. As has been noted in the previous section, the remedy of rescission on terms, which was used for a time, has now been rejected by the Court of Appeal in *The Great Peace*. This was a very powerful remedy, in that it not only allowed the court to set a contract aside, but also empowered it to impose conditions – so that in *Solle v Butcher* (discussed above, 11.7), for example, the lease was rescinded, but on condition that the tenant could remain, provided that he paid rent at the maximum which the landlord could have asked for under the rent control legislation. Such a power was out of line with the classical reluctance of courts to intervene in the substance of contracts, and its rejection represents a return to a more traditional approach, as well as having the effect of decreasing uncertainty in this area.

11.8.1 Refusal of specific performance

As we will see in Chapter 18, the order of specific performance is a discretionary remedy. In deciding whether to order it, the court can take into account any hardship which might be caused by so doing. For example, the buyer of a painting which, between contract and performance, is discovered not to be by Constable, as had been thought, may well be able to resist specific performance (though there may still be a liability to pay compensatory damages). Thus, in *Malins v Freeman*,[110] where a buyer at an auction mistakenly bid for one lot, thinking that it was another, this mutual mistake was held to be sufficient to allow the buyer not to be made to go through with the contract. In contrast, in *Tamplin v James*,[111] where the defendant bid for an inn and shop, incorrectly thinking that a garden was included, the contract was enforced. The mistake as to the *extent* of the property was distinguishable from a case where the mistake was as to the identity of the property.

11.8.2 Rectification

Where an agreement is contained in a document which contains an inaccuracy, in the form of either an error or an omission, the equitable remedy of rectification may be granted. It is clearly available where both parties miss the error (a common mistake), or if one party knows of the other's mistake (a unilateral mistake). Thus, in *Roberts v Leicestershire County Council*,[112] a construction contract, which contained a completion date which was a year later than the contractors believed it to be, was rectified, because there was clear evidence that representatives of the other party were well aware

---

110 (1837) 2 Keen 25.
111 (1879) 15 Ch D 215.
112 [1961] Ch 555; [1961] 2 All ER 545.

of the basis on which the contractors were undertaking the project. The position was similar in *Templiss Properties Ltd v Hyams*,[113] which concerned a lease where the intention had been that the rent should be exclusive of business rates, whereas it was expressed to be inclusive of such rates. Although in this case the tenant's solicitors were not aware of the mistake, it was shown that the tenant himself was aware, and so rectification was ordered. If the mistake is simply a mutual mistake, however, the courts will not grant rectification. A sufficiently serious mistake of this kind will allow the contract to be rescinded, of course, but rectification will not be available.[114]

It follows from this that if an oral agreement, though based on a mistake, is accurately reproduced in a subsequent document, rectification is not appropriate and will not be granted. In *Rose (Frederick E) (London) Ltd v William H Pim Jnr & Co Ltd*,[115] for example, the plaintiff had been asked by a third party to supply 'horsebeans described as feveroles'. The plaintiffs entered into a contract with the defendants for the purchase of 'horsebeans'. Both plaintiffs and defendants thought that 'horsebeans' was just another name for 'feveroles'. In fact, feveroles are a higher quality horsebean. The defendants supplied ordinary horsebeans, but these were unacceptable to the third party, who wanted feveroles. The plaintiffs sought to have their written contract with the defendants rectified to refer to feveroles. They would then be able to succeed in an action for supply of goods of the wrong description. The Court of Appeal held, however, that this was not possible:[116]

> Their agreement as expressed both orally and in writing, was for 'horsebeans'. That is all the sellers committed themselves to supply, and all they should be bound to.

Although there was a misapprehension underlying the contract, a 'common mistake', in fact, this was not a reason for providing the remedy of rectification.

11.8.3 Bars to rectification

Because this remedy is equitable, it may be lost by virtue of lapse of time or the intervention of third party rights. If this is the case, the claimant will have to argue for common law mistake in order to obtain any remedy.

11.9 CONTRACTS SIGNED UNDER A MISTAKE

The courts are not inclined to be sympathetic towards people who put their names to contracts without reading or understanding them. In general, therefore, a person will be

---

113 [1999] EGCS 60.
114 *Riverlate Properties Ltd v Paul* [1975] Ch 133; [1974] 2 All ER 656.
115 [1953] 2 QB 450; [1953] 2 All ER 739.
116 Ibid, p 462.

taken to have notice of, and to be bound by, all the provisions of a contract which has been signed, whether they have been read or not.[117] There are some exceptional circumstances, however, where the courts will allow a plea of *non est factum* – 'it is not my deed'. The mistake must be such that the document as a whole is 'radically different' from that which the person thought he or she was signing. Moreover, the person must not have been 'careless' in signing the document. These principles are derived from the House of Lords 'decision in *Saunders v Anglia Building Society*.[118]

11.9.1 Availability of the plea

The result of these principles, and in particular the second one, is that the doctrine will rarely be available to literate adults of full capacity. The courts will, however, make the remedy available to those who are tricked into signing the contract, and it may also operate to protect those who from 'defective education, illness, or innate incapacity'[119] fail to understand what they are signing.

A relatively recent (and fairly rare) example of the successful use of the plea is to be found in *Lloyds Bank plc v Waterhouse*.[120] Here, the defendant, who was illiterate, signed a guarantee regarding his son's future liabilities to the plaintiff bank. The father thought that this guarantee related solely to the son's purchase of a farm, whereas in fact it covered all the son's liabilities. The trial judge found that this did not amount to a fundamental difference, and that the defendant had been careless in not having the document read to him. He gave judgment for the plaintiff. The defendant appealed.

The majority of the Court of Appeal regarded the mistake as to the extent of the guarantee as being sufficient to support the plea of *non est factum*. The evidence showed that the father would not have signed it if he had known its true nature, even though he was aware of the financial value of the guarantee. As to carelessness, although the bank was unaware of the defendant's illiteracy, and there was no suggestion of impropriety on its part, the defendant had clearly taken steps (by asking questions of the bank's officials) to ascertain his liability. The plea of *non est factum* was made out.

11.9.2 Nature of the mistake

At one time, the difference in the extent of the guarantee in the above case would not have been regarded as sufficient, as it was thought that the document had to be of a different 'character' for the defence to be available. That test was rejected, however, in *Saunders v Anglia Building Society*, in favour of the more broadly based question

---

117 See *L'Estrange v Graucob* [1934] 2 KB 394, discussed above, 9.4.

118 [1971] AC 1004. The facts are given below at 11.9.2. The case also appears in some reports under the name *Gallie v Lee*.

119 As Lord Reid put it in *Saunders v Anglia Building Society* [1971] AC 1004, p 1016.

120 [1990] Fam Law 23.

of whether the document was 'radically' or 'fundamentally' different. In this case, an elderly widow had been tricked by her nephew into signing an assignment of the lease of her house to a third party. She thought she was signing a deed of gift to her nephew. The reason why she had failed to read the document was that she had broken her reading glasses. The House of Lords regarded this as an acceptable reason for failing to read the document, and held that it did not amount to 'carelessness'. The widow failed, however, on the first test, relating to the nature of the document. Although it involved a different transaction from what she thought, the purpose of the assignment was, albeit indirectly, to provide financial assistance to her nephew. This is what she had wished to achieve by the deed of gift. The document was not, therefore, sufficiently different for the plea to succeed.

FOR THOUGHT

Do you think the outcome of this case would have been different if the woman had thought that she was signing a mortgage on the house, enabling her to raise money, rather than making a gift to her nephew? Would the document then have been 'radically different'?

If the plea is successful, the transaction is void and unenforceable.

11.10 CONCLUSIONS ON 'MISTAKE'

The lack of coherence in English contract law in dealing with the issue of 'mistake' will be evident from the above discussion. Would it be possible to devise a set of principles to deal with mistake which did not have these defects? The suggestions contained in the Principles of European Contract Law set out at the beginning of this chapter would certainly be an improvement on the current position. In particular, the treatment of mistakes as always rendering a contract 'voidable' rather than 'void' would be significant in allowing much greater flexibility in dealing with the consequences of mistake. It would be a major improvement in English law if such an approach were adopted. Moreover, it would be best if this applied to *all* categories of mistake (including 'mutual mistakes', which are not included within the scheme proposed by the Principles of European Contract Law). In other words, whenever the parties regard themselves as having made a contract,[121] but one of them subsequently raises the argument that it was founded on a mistake, the court should have the power to set the contract aside. In

---

121 Although this may appear to be a very subjective test, what is really important is whether the parties (or at least one of them) has *acted* in reliance on this supposed contract. If there has been no such reliance on either side, then there is no particular problem about setting the contract aside as if 'void' *ab initio*.

reaching the decision as to whether to do so, and if so on what terms, there are two main factors which ought to be considered. The first is whether the risk of the mistake was in fact dealt with by the contract – for example, did one party clearly agree to take the risk of the subject matter of the contract not existing?[122] The second is the extent of good faith reliance on the contract by the parties or third parties. One of the defects of the current finding that a contract is void for mistake is that, for example, in a common mistake situation, costs incurred towards performance are lost, even if these all fall on one side. A more flexible approach, based on voidability, would enable the court, if appropriate, to impose terms apportioning such losses between the parties.[123] Such a power should also be available in cases of unilateral mistake.[124] This is particularly important where the reliance of third parties on the fact that the original contract was valid needs proper consideration.[125] It may well be that in cases where a fraudulent contracting party has disappeared, the fact of the third party's reliance should in general lead to the result most commonly arrived at in English law in relation to face to face contracts – that is, that the loss should fall entirely on the party to the original contract who has been the victim of the fraud. Nevertheless, it would be advantageous in relation to both face to face contracts, and those created without such interaction,[126] to allow the court the power to distribute losses, perhaps on a similar basis to that adopted in relation to frustrated contracts.[127]

It will be seen that the above suggestions are pragmatic rather than formalistic. They are based on the approach that where an agreement has failed as the result of a mistake (of whatever kind), the precise analysis of the nature of that agreement is in general of less importance than the practical consequences of its failure. Unless it is clear that one of the parties has undertaken the risk of the mistake being made, a flexible approach based on voidability is likely to lead to the most satisfactory results for all concerned.

---

122 As, for example, in *McRae v Commonwealth Disposals Commission* (1951) 84 CLR 377 – discussed above, 11.5.1.
123 What is being suggested is something akin to the equitable power of rescission on terms used in cases such as *Solle v Butcher* [1950] 1 KB 671, but incorporating an even greater power to distribute losses.
124 The courts would, of course, still need to decide that the unilateral mistake went beyond making a 'bad bargain'. This is most likely to be demonstrated most clearly by fraudulent behaviour by the other contracting party.
125 It may be objected here that third parties in an *Ingram v Little* [1961] 1 QB 31 situation do not in fact 'rely' on the original contract. They are probably ignorant of that contract. What they are relying on is the fact that the person with whom they are dealing has good title to the property they are offering for sale. Nevertheless, this type of indirect reliance needs to be catered for.
126 The availability of more flexible powers would hopefully prevent arguments based on 'mistake' from leading to the circumvention of statutory provisions designed for the protection of consumers – as apparently happened in *Shogun Finance Ltd v Hudson*. This is surely unacceptable.
127 See the Law Reform (Frustrated Contracts) Act 1943 – discussed in Chapter 16. The precise methods used in that Act have not proved uncontroversial in their application, and a clearer formula than the one used in that Act would be needed if the power to distribute was to be granted by statute, rather than being developed by the courts as part of their equitable remedies.

11.11 FURTHER READING

Atiyah, PS, '*Couturier v Hastie* and the sale of non-existent goods', (1957) 73 LQR 340

Hare, C, 'Identity mistakes: a missed opportunity' (2004) 67 MLR 993

Jackson, B, *Law, Fact and Narrative Coherence*, 1988, Liverpool: Deborah Charles

Macmillan, C, 'How temptation led to mistake: an explanation of *Bell v Lever Bros Ltd*' (2003) 119 LQR 625

Macmillan, C, 'Mistake as to identity clarified?' (2004) 120 LQR 369

Simpson, AWB, 'Contracts for cotton to arrive: the case of the two ships *Peerless*' (1989) 11 Cardozo L Rev 287

Simpson, AWB, 'Innovation in nineteenth century contract law' (1975b) 91 LQR 247

Smith, JC, 'Contracts – mistake, frustration and implied terms' (1994) 110 LQR 400

Spencer, J, 'Signature, consent and the rule in *L'Estrange v Graucob*' (1973) 32 CLJ 104

Treitel, GH, 'Mistake in contract' (1988) 104 LQR 501

12 DURESS

CONTENTS

12.1 OVERVIEW

This chapter deals with the position where one party alleges that he or she only entered into the contract as a result of threats made by the other party. The questions that need to be considered are:

■ What type of threats will allow a party to escape from a contract? To what extent can threats other than of physical violence have this effect? The relevant question now seems to be simply whether there was illegitimate pressure being used for an improper objective.

■ In what situations may 'economic duress' be sufficient to affect the contract? It is important here, as in relation to other types of duress, that the party alleging duress had no real alternative to compliance.

■ Can there be duress where there is a threat to perform an act which involves no breach of the criminal law or civil obligation (such as breach of contract)? The answer seems to be that there can be, but only where the threat is being used for an improper purpose.

■ What are the remedies for duress? It renders a contract voidable, but does not allow the recovery of damages.

The chapter also compares the English law position with the proposals in the Principles of European Contract Law.

12.2 INTRODUCTION

This chapter is concerned with situations in which an agreement which appears to be valid on its face is challenged because it is alleged that it is the product of improper pressure of some kind. This may take the form of threats of physical coercion or 'economic' threats (such as to break a contract), which place pressure on the other party. It seems that explicit threats are needed. Suppose, for example, that a woman has been beaten by her husband in the past, and is then asked by him to sell him her share in the matrimonial home at a gross undervalue. She agrees through fear of what he might do to her, even though he has made no threat to her on this occasion. It seems that this situation cannot be treated as duress, because the threat is implied, rather than explicit.[1] English courts would deal with such a situation under the closely related, but conceptually distinct,[2] category of 'undue influence'. This basis for setting aside contracts is dealt with in Chapter 13.

One of the problems with economic duress lies in establishing the boundaries of acceptable behaviour of this kind, since economic pressure clearly has a legitimate place within business dealings, and this issue is explored below. If, however, the contract has been entered into as a result of illegitimate threats, it is rendered voidable.[3] The courts may be regarded as intervening either because there is no true agreement between the parties, or simply because a person who has been led to make a contract which otherwise he or she would not have done as a result of the exertion of illegitimate pressure should be allowed to escape from it. The latter argument is probably the one which represents the most satisfactory analysis of the situation, but there are many judicial statements which refer to duress 'vitiating' the consent of the threatened party. This is discussed further in the next section.

1 Compare, however, the Australian case of *Farmers' Co-operative Executors and Trustees Ltd v Perks* (1989) 52 SASR 399, discussed in Birks and Chin, 1995, p 66, where it seems that the judge was prepared to find duress in circumstances similar to those given in the text. There is no comparable English authority.
2 The distinction might be denied by those who argue that duress and undue influence can both be encompassed within a general doctrine of 'good faith' – see, for example, Adams and Brownsword, 1995, Chapter 7.
3 There are statements by Lord Cross in *Barton v Armstrong* [1976] AC 104, suggesting that duress renders a contract void, but the general view is that its effect is to make it voidable.

12.3 DURESS BY PHYSICAL THREATS OR OTHER COERCION

Although it is possible that a person could be physically forced to sign a contract by someone holding their arm and moving it, the most obvious form of duress is where a contract is brought about as a result of a threat of physical injury. A fairly modern example is to be found in *Barton v Armstrong*,[4] where the managing director of a company was threatened with death if he did not arrange for his company to make a payment to, and buy shares from, the defendant. The Privy Council held that the contract could be set aside for duress.

Originally, the nature of the threats which would be treated as constituting duress was very limited; for example, threats in relation to goods were at one time held to be insufficient,[5] though even this rule was apparently subject to the exception that money paid under duress of goods could be recovered.[6] With the development of the concept of 'economic duress' (discussed below, at 12.4), however, a much broader view of the type of threats that can vitiate a contract has been taken. The current approach would seem to be represented by the approach of the Privy Council in *Attorney General v R*.[7] In this case, a soldier claimed that he had signed a 'confidentiality agreement', restricting his ability to publish information about his experiences in the SAS, because if he had not he was threatened with being removed from the SAS (though remaining in the army). Such removal would normally only have taken place as a result of disciplinary action. The case originated in New Zealand, where the trial judge held in the soldier's favour. The New Zealand Court of Appeal reversed this decision. There was a further appeal to the Privy Council. The decision was delivered by Lord Hoffmann: his starting point was the decision of the House of Lords in the 'economic duress' case, *Universe Tankships Inc of Monrovia v International Transport Workers' Federation*.[8] He noted that Lord Scarman had identified two elements to duress:[9] the first was pressure amounting to compulsion of the will of the victim; the second was the illegitimacy of that pressure. The first element was not in issue in the case, since it was accepted that for the soldier to be returned to a regular army unit would have been regarded in the SAS as a public humiliation. He had no practical alternative to compliance.

As regards the second element, this could be viewed from two aspects:

(a)   the nature of the pressure; and
(b)   the nature of the demand which the pressure is applied to support.

In relation to the 'nature of the pressure', where the threat was to carry out some

---

4 [1976] AC 104.
5 *Skeate v Beale* (1840) 11 A & E 983.
6 *Astley v Reynolds* (1731) 2 Stra 915.
7 [2003] UKPC 22; [2003] EMLR 24.
8 [1983] 1 AC 366; [1982] 2 All ER 67 – discussed below, 12.4.1.
9 Ibid, para 15.

unlawful act, this would generally lead to the pressure being regarded as 'illegitimate'. It was not necessarily the case, however, that a threat of a lawful action would be legitimate. This is where the second aspect – that is, 'illegitimacy' – needs to be considered. This looks at what the person issuing the threat is trying to achieve. Was their objective a legitimate one? To illustrate the point, Lord Hoffmann quoted from Lord Atkin in *Thorne v Motor Trade Association*,[10] where he said:[11]

> The ordinary blackmailer normally threatens to do what he has a perfect right to do – namely communicate some compromising conduct to a person whose knowledge is likely to affect the person threatened . . . What he has to justify is not the threat, but the demand of money.

FOR THOUGHT

Does this mean that a person who signs a contract because the other party threatened to tell his wife about an affair can later escape from the contract on the grounds of duress?

Applying this approach to the case before it, the Privy Council took the view that the threat was in itself lawful. The power to return to a regular unit could be exercised at the discretion of the relevant officers within the army. Was, then, the objective of the threat such that it rendered this lawful threat illegitimate? The trial judge had thought that it was, in that it was effectively a military order which purported to control R's conduct after he had left the service. The Court of Appeal and the Privy Council disagreed. R had not been issued with a command which created an obligation under military law; rather, he was faced with a choice which may have constituted 'overwhelming pressure', but was not an exercise by the Ministry of Defence of its legal powers over him. Since the objective of restricting unauthorised disclosures concerning military operations was in itself a legitimate objective, the plea of duress failed.

This broad approach to defining the limits of duress must be assumed to be the one which will be adopted by English courts in future (though, of course, as a decision of the Privy Council, *Attorney General v R* is only of persuasive authority – and since duress was not found, the more general statements could be treated as *obiter*). The case does not resolve all issues as to the nature of duress, however, and some of these are worth further consideration.

For example, the cases on duress are full of references to the claimant's will being 'overborne' (and this is echoed in the Privy Council's references to 'compulsion'). In most cases this will be an inaccurate description of what has happened. The claimant

---

10 [1937] AC 797.
11 Ibid, p 806.

has not been forced to act as an automaton. The decision to make the contract has been taken as a matter of choice. It is simply that the threat which has led to that choice is regarded by the courts as illegitimate, and justifies allowing the party threatened to escape from the consequent contract.[12] The fact that this is the basis of the modern doctrine is illustrated by the fact that it was by no means certain in *Barton v Armstrong* that the threats which were made were the sole reason for the managing director's decision. The approach of the majority of the Privy Council appears in the opinion of Lord Cross. He noted that, in relation to misrepresentation, there is no need to prove that the false statement was the sole reason for entering into the contract.[13] He then commented that:[14]

> Their Lordships think that the same rule should apply in cases of duress and that if Armstrong's threats were 'a' reason for Barton's executing the deed he is entitled to relief even though he might well have entered into the contract if Armstrong had uttered no threats to influence him to do so . . .

If this is the case, then it clearly is inappropriate to talk of the will of the person subject to the threats being 'overborne'. The duress simply becomes a wrongful act of a similar kind to a misrepresentation, which, if it has influenced the other party's decision to make a contract, provides a basis for that contract being voidable.[15]

This analysis suggests that the concept of duress focuses on the wrongfulness of the behaviour of the defendant rather than its effect on the claimant.[16] Not all commentators would accept that this necessarily follows from the rejection of the 'overborne will' approach to duress. Birks and Chin have pointed out that there are authorities which make it clear that duress may be used as a reason to set aside a transaction, notwithstanding the fact that the defendant has acted in good faith.[17] If this is so, it

---

12 As Atiyah (1995, p 267) and others have pointed out, the House of Lords has specifically rejected the 'overborne will' in relation to the criminal law defence of duress: see *Lynch v DPP for Northern Ireland* [1975] AC 653, but the courts have been more reluctant to reject this language in the context of the law of contract. See also Atiyah, 1982; Halson, 1991.

13 See 10.3.4, above.

14 [1976] AC 104, p 119.

15 It seems also to be implicit in Lord Cross's opinion that there is not even any need for it to be proved that the threats were the major element in the decision. He certainly regards this as the case in relation to fraudulent misrepresentation, 'for in this field the court does not allow an examination into the relative importance of contributory causes' (ibid, p 118), and the whole tenor of his opinion is to align duress with fraud.

16 Note that in the following discussion, for ease of treatment, 'defendant' is used to indicate the party issuing the threat, and 'claimant' the party potentially affected by it, notwithstanding the fact that cases may involve the defendant seeking to prevent an action to enforce a contract on the basis that the claimant has used duress.

17 Birks and Chin, 1995, citing *Morgan v Palmer* (1824) 2 B & C 729 (money paid in order to pay a licence); *Maskell v Horner* [1915] 3 KB 106 (payment of tolls under threat of seizure of goods). Birks and Chin are mainly concerned with undue influence, rather than duress, but this does not affect the

cannot be the case that it is the defendant's 'wickedness' which is the reason for treating a contract as voidable; the availability of the remedy must depend on the effect of the defendant's behaviour on the claimant. This distinction becomes more important once the categories of behaviour which can constitute duress are broadened. When the threats are of physical violence, it is easy to see that criminality as in itself justifying the court's intervention. When 'economic' and other threats are accepted as giving rise to the possibility of duress, the borderline between what is legitimate and illegitimate is narrow, and the likelihood of the threats being made in good faith increases. This leads to the conclusion that although, as indicated in *Barton v Armstrong*, the threats do not need to be the sole reason for the claimant's agreement to the contract, they do have to be *part* of that reason. If a strong-willed claimant has shrugged off the threats, then a claim of duress will not be allowed, even if a reasonable claimant might have been affected by them.[18]

There are thus two questions to ask in relation to duress: (1) were the defendant's threats 'illegitimate', and (2) was the claimant's behaviour affected by them? Only if both are answered positively will the conditions arise for the contract to be set aside.[19] The claimant may have voluntarily entered into the contract, but would not have done so but for the threats of the defendant.[20] The suggestion in the quotation from Lord Cross, above, that duress is available even if the contract would have been made without the threats surely goes too far. Lord Cross accepts that there must be some causal link between the threats and the contract; it is difficult to understand how, if this is the case, the duress can be regarded as effective if the claimant would have made the contract even if the threats had not been made.[21] If we are to accept Lord Cross's suggestion, however, this would mean rewording the test suggested above (that is, 'The claimant may have voluntarily entered into the contract, but would not have done so but for the

---

validity of the point being made. In *Universe Tankships Inc of Monrovia v International Transport Workers' Federation* [1982] 2 All ER 67, for example, the threat was to take industrial action which the union concerned thought was lawful: see below, 12.4.1. It may be, however, that if the threat is to do something otherwise lawful, 'bad faith' *will* be needed to turn it into duress: see *CTN Cash and Carry Ltd v Gallaher* [1994] 4 All ER 714 – discussed below, 12.4.3.

18 To this extent, the approach to duress is subjective. The tests will be: (a) would a reasonable person have been affected? If not, then no duress; (b) if a reasonable person would have been affected, was this particular claimant affected? If not, then no duress.

19 Smith (1997a) has argued that, in fact, there are two separate limbs to duress, namely 'operative wrongdoing' and 'impairment of consent', and that *either* of these may provide a basis for treating a contract as voidable.

20 An analogy might be drawn with the criminal law approach to consent in sexual offences: a person who agrees to have sexual intercourse because of threats that have been made may be found to have been raped. While the act of intercourse was 'voluntary', in that it was not brought about by physical force, it was not undertaken with consent – see, for example, *R v Olugboja* [1981] 3 All ER 443.

21 This might make sense if the rules relating to duress were being applied to punish the defendant or to discourage others from using threats in the future, rather than to provide relief for the claimant. This would, however, be contrary to the normal approach in contract, which normally takes as its primary concern the protection and compensation of the claimant.

threats of the defendant') to read: 'The claimant may have voluntarily entered into the contract, but would not have done so *so readily* in the absence of the threats of the defendant.' Lord Scarman, on the other hand, has on more than one occasion emphasised that part of the test of whether duress was operative is whether the claimant had any real alternative but to submit.[22] This clearly implies that the contract would not have been made but for the threats, and this seems the more satisfactory approach.[23]

The language used in talking of duress does not assist in clarifying these issues. First, the use of the word 'threat' carries pejorative overtones, and suggests deliberate bad behaviour on the part of the defendant. The usage is understandable given the origins of duress in putting someone in fear of physical violence. What is, however, meant in the modern context is simply an indication from the defendant to the claimant that if the claimant does not enter into the contract, then the defendant will act in a particular way. The shorthand use of the word 'threat' must not be allowed to carry with it any necessary connotation of deliberate wrongdoing.

Second, 'improper' or 'illegitimate' are the adjectives most commonly used to qualify the defendant's behaviour. Once again these may carry the implication of wrongdoing by the defendant,[24] derived from the origins of duress. It would perhaps be more accurate to refer to behaviour which is 'inappropriate'. This allows account to be taken of the context in which the behaviour takes place – does it go beyond what a reasonable person would regard as acceptable in all the circumstances?

A reformulation of the test of duress using this language would be as follows. Did the claimant enter into the contract at least partly as a result of an indication of future behaviour by the defendant which put pressure on the claimant and was inappropriate in all the circumstances? No doubt, however, the more manageable formulation of 'Did the claimant enter into the contract at least partly as a result of illegitimate threats from the defendant?' will more likely, in practice, be used.

12.4 ECONOMIC DURESS

The broadening of the approach to what behaviour can constitute duress, as reflected in *Attorney General v R*,[25] perhaps means that it is no longer necessary to deal with 'economic duress' as a separate category. However, it was in this area that the courts

22 See *Pao On v Lau Yiu Long* [1980] AC 614, p 635; *Universe Tankships Inc of Monrovia v International Transport Workers' Federation, The Universe Sentinel* [1983] 1 AC 366, p 400; [1982] 2 All ER 67, p 88.
23 In *Huyton SA v Peter Cremer GmbH & Co* [1999] CLC 230, Mance J suggested that Lord Cross's approach in *Barton v Armstrong* should be limited to cases involving threats of personal violence, whereas a stricter 'but for' test of causation should apply in cases of economic duress. This provides an explanation of the different approaches, but it is unsatisfactory that duress should operate so differently depending on the type of threat involved. It is submitted that, as suggested here, the better view is that Lord Cross's statement should not be followed.
24 'Improper' probably does so to a greater extent than 'illegitimate'.
25 [2003] UKPC 22; [2003] EMLR 24 – discussed above, 12.3.

first recognised that something other than physical threats could constitute duress, and so it is worth examining the development of the concept as a means of understanding how the law has developed to its current position.

The first recognition of economic duress as a basis for allowing a party to escape from a contract is probably to be found in the *obiter* statements of Kerr J in *Occidental Worldwide Investment Corp v Skibs A/S Avanti, The Siboen and The Sibotre*.[26] The case concerned a renegotiation of charters of two vessels, under the threat that otherwise the charterers would go out of business. In other words it was a threat that the contractual obligations under the charters would be broken. It was recognised that this could in some circumstances have amounted to duress sufficient to render the agreement voidable. On the facts, however, the other party had not agreed to the renegotiation under duress, but simply as a result of ordinary commercial pressures. In *North Ocean Shipping Co v Hyundai Construction, The Atlantic Baron*,[27] the devaluation of the dollar led to a demand for an increase in the price payable under a contract for the construction of a tanker. Mocatta J held that this did amount to duress:[28]

> The Yard were adamant in insisting on the increased price without having any legal justification for so doing and the owners realised that the Yard would not accept anything other than an unqualified agreement to the increase. The owners might have claimed damages in arbitration against the Yard with all the inherent uncertainties of litigation, but in view of the position of the Yard vis à vis [the owners] relations with Shell[29] it would be unreasonable to hold that this is the course they should have taken: see *Astley v Reynolds* (1731) 2 Str 915. The owners made a very reasonable offer of arbitration coupled with security for any award in the Yard's favour that might be made, but this was refused. They then made their agreement, which can truly I think be said to have been made under compulsion . . .

There was duress, because the defendants' threat to break their contract had no legal justification, and the plaintiffs had no realistic alternative but to submit if they wished to preserve the chance of the charter to Shell. The plaintiffs had, however, delayed for eight months between the delivery of the tanker and the initiation of their claim. This delay meant that the right to rescind had been lost through lapse of time. These two cases therefore recognised the possibility of duress based on improper commercial pressure, but did not in fact apply it to the facts before them. The difficulty with this test is the requirement that the pressure should be 'improper'. In commercial dealings,

---

26 [1976] 1 Lloyd's Rep 293, pp 335–36. Kerr J saw support for such an approach in the decision in *D and C Builders v Rees* [1966] 2 QB 617; [1965] 3 All ER 837 – discussed in Chapter 3, 3.12.4.

27 [1979] QB 705; [1978] 3 All ER 1170.

28 Ibid, p 719; pp 1182–83.

29 With whom the owners were negotiating for a lucrative contract for the charter of the tanker, once constructed.

'threats' may often be made as a means of encouraging the other party to contract – for example, 'If you don't agree to this contract we will take all our other business elsewhere', or 'we will not give you any discount on orders in the future', or 'we will provide these goods to your main competitor at a substantial discount'. All of these threats may have the effect of 'encouraging' the other party to contract, but they are unlikely to be regarded as 'improper'. They are simply part of the rough and tumble of business life.[30] Where, then, is the line to be drawn?

It is suggested that, at the very least, the threat should involve the commission of a tort, or a breach of contract – in other words, a threat to do an act which is, in the broadest sense, unlawful. Thus, the threat to encourage others not to fulfil their contracts with the victim (that is, the tort of 'inducing breach of contract'), or the threat to break other agreements which the party doing the threatening has with the victim, might give rise to the possibility of a plea of 'economic duress'. This test is satisfied in virtually all the cases where economic duress has been held to have occurred. There is one recent decision of the Court of Appeal, however, *CTN Cash and Carry v Gallaher*,[31] which contains *obiter* statements to the effect that a threat to commit an entirely lawful act may nevertheless constitute duress. And, of course, in *Attorney General v R*, as we have seen,[32] the Privy Council has indicated that in its view, threats can be 'illegitimate' as a result of their context, even if they are to do something lawful. *CTN Cash and Carry v Gallaher* is discussed further below (see 12.4.3).

12.4.1 Industrial action

The cases which have subsequently developed and applied the concept of economic duress have often been concerned with industrial action. A trade union threatens to encourage its members to break their contracts with a particular employer (for example, by going on strike or refusing to do certain work) unless the employer agrees to act in a certain way. To carry out the threatened action would (subject to the applicability of any protective trade union legislation) amount to the tort of inducement of breach of contract. This may well be regarded as going beyond legitimate pressure and thus amount to duress. For example, in *Universe Tankships Inc of Monrovia v International Transport Workers' Federation, The Universe Sentinel*,[33] the union 'blacked' a ship owned by the plaintiffs, by instructing its members not to deal with it, and therefore preventing it from leaving port. In order to escape from this, the owners, *inter alia*, made a payment to the union's welfare fund. They later brought an action to recover this as a payment made under duress. It was held that the threatened industrial action was unlawful under English law, and the payment was recoverable.

Subsequent changes in English employment law, extending the scope of unlawful

---

30 See also Collins, 2003, pp 155–57.
31 [1994] 4 All ER 714.
32 Above, 12.3.
33 [1983] 1 AC 366; [1982] 2 All ER 67.

industrial action, have had the effect of extending the scope of economic duress. This is shown by *Dimskal Shipping Co SA v International Transport Workers' Federation, The Evia Luck*,[34] which also confirmed that the question whether the actions of a party amount to economic duress must be judged by English law, not the law of the country where the actions took place. The ITF had, through industrial action, persuaded the respondents to agree to contracts involving the payment of large sums of money in respect of back pay to its crew. This was to bring the respondents' terms of employment in line with those approved by the ITF. The respondents sought to have these contracts, which were expressed to be governed by English law, avoided for duress. The judge at first instance refused, since the actions of the ITF were legal where they took place (in Sweden). The Court of Appeal overturned this judgment, and the ITF appealed to the House of Lords which held, with Lord Templeman dissenting, that the issue of what amounted to duress had to be determined by English rather than Swedish law. Since the actions of the ITF would have been unlawful under English employment law, the respondents were entitled to avoid the contracts made as a result of them.

12.4.2 Breach of contract

Where the unlawful action threatened is simply a breach of contract, rather than a tort (which may well be the case outside the industrial context), it may be more difficult to identify the boundaries of legitimate pressure. Some assistance is provided by the opinion of Lord Scarman in the Privy Council case of *Pao On v Lau Yiu Long*.[35] In this case, the plaintiff had threatened not to proceed with a contract for the sale of shares, unless the other side agreed to a renegotiation of certain subsidiary arrangements. The defendant agreed, but when the plaintiff later tried to enforce these arrangements, claimed that they had been extracted by duress and were therefore voidable. Lord Scarman identified the following factors as being relevant to whether a person acted voluntarily, or not, and therefore under duress:[36]

> . . . it is material to inquire whether the person alleged to have been coerced did or did not protest; whether, at the time he was allegedly coerced into making the contract, he did or did not have an alternative course open to him such as an adequate legal remedy; whether he was independently advised; and whether after entering into the contract he took steps to avoid it.

On the facts of the case, the claim for duress failed, because the defendant had had an alternative course open: that is, he had an adequate legal remedy in an action for specific performance in relation to the original agreement. Lord Scarman referred to this test again in *Universe Tankships Inc of Monrovia v International Transport Workers'*

---

34 [1992] 2 AC 152; [1991] 4 All ER 871.
35 [1980] AC 614; [1979] 3 All ER 65.
36 [1980] AC 614, p 635; [1979] 3 All ER 65, p 78.

Federation, The Universe Sentinel, where he referred to the victim having 'no practical choice but to submit to the duress'.[37]

A clear example of a person being faced with no alternative but to comply, in a case not concerned with industrial action, is to be found in *Atlas Express Ltd v Kafco (Importers and Distributors) Ltd*.[38] The defendants, Kafco, were a small manufacturing company who had a very valuable contract with Woolworths, a store with branches throughout the country. Kafco employed Atlas, a national firm of carriers, to make deliveries to Woolworths. Atlas found that they had, through their own miscalculation of the quantities of Kafco's goods which could be carried on their lorries at one time, entered into the contract on uneconomic terms. They told Kafco that they must agree to an increase in the charge for carriage, or else Atlas would not make the deliveries. Kafco could not risk being in breach of their contract with Woolworths, and so agreed to the increased charge, under protest. When Atlas brought an action to recover the increased charges, Kafco resisted on the grounds of duress. The court accepted the argument that losing the contract with Woolworths, or being sued by them, would have been so disastrous for Kafco that they had no real alternative but to go along with Atlas's suggestion. An action for damages against Atlas for breach of the original contract would not have been able to provide compensation sufficient to counteract the effects of the destruction of their business relationship with Woolworths. Kafco were not obliged to pay the additional carriage costs.

FOR THOUGHT

What do you think the outcome of this case would have been if Kafco had had other significant outlets for their goods, apart from Woolworths?

A similar situation arose in the earlier case of *B & S Contracts and Design Ltd v Victor Green Publications Ltd*.[39] There was a contract for the erection of exhibition stands. An industrial dispute arose a week before the exhibition between the constructor of the stands and its employees. The constructor sought a contribution of £4,500 from the defendants, who had let out the stands to exhibitors, to assist in settling the dispute with the employees. This was paid and the contract was performed. The defendants then deducted the £4,500 when paying the contract price. The constructor sued to recover this sum. It was held by the Court of Appeal that the payment of £4,500 was made under duress and was not enforceable. The defendants had no other way out of what would have been a disastrous situation, because of its effect on the exhibition, and they were entitled to treat the payment as being forced out of them by economic duress. Legal action against the constructor in this situation would not have been adequate,

37 [1983] 1 AC 366, p 400; [1982] 2 All ER 67, p 88.
38 [1989] QB 833; [1989] 1 All ER 641.
39 [1984] ICR 419.

because of the time pressure. The failure of the exhibition would have had consequences for the defendants going beyond anything that would have been recoverable in damages from the constructor. A major test for the illegitimacy of the threat of economic pressure, which turns it into duress, thus seems to be that the action threatened leaves the person threatened with no realistic alternative to compliance.

Situations involving a threat to break a contract unless a further payment is made can, of course, raise issues of consideration. Under the doctrine in *Stilk v Myrick*,[40] the threatening party can be argued to be providing no consideration for a promise to make the additional payment. This indeed was regarded as an additional ground for the defendants' success in *Atlas Express v Kafco*. Tucker J, after lengthy discussion of economic duress, concluded his judgment with the terse comment:[41]

> In any event, I find that there was no consideration for the new agreement. The plaintiffs were already obliged to deliver the defendants' goods at the rates agreed under the terms of the original agreement. There was no consideration for the increased minimum charge . . .

The scope for the use of this means of dealing with cases of economic duress involving the modification of existing contracts has, of course, been significantly reduced by the Court of Appeal's decision in *Williams v Roffey Bros & Nicholls (Contractors) Ltd*.[42] The recognition that the 'practical benefit' of obtaining the timely performance of an existing obligation may amount to good consideration for a new promise means that in 'duress' situations consideration is likely to be found. The claimant will probably have agreed to make the additional payment (or whatever else is required) in order to avoid unfavourable consequences which would flow from the defendant's threatened actions. Avoiding those consequences will be likely to be regarded as a 'practical benefit' and therefore good consideration. The result is that duress becomes of increased importance in dealing with this type of situation.[43]

12.4.3 Must the threat be of an unlawful act?

The examples of duress so far considered have all involved an act which is in some respects a breach of law. It involves a crime, or a tort, or a breach of contract. Is this a necessary characteristic for duress, and in particular economic duress, to be operative? In *CTN Cash and Carry v Gallaher*,[44] the threat was to withdraw credit from the other

---

40 (1809) 2 Camp 317; 170 ER 1168; 6 Esp 129; 170 ER 851 – see Chapter 3, 3.9.6.

41 [1989] QB 833, p 841; [1989] 1 All ER 641, p 646.

42 [1991] 1 QB 1; [1990] 1 All ER 512 – see Chapter 3, 3.9.8.

43 Atiyah (1995, p 273) has suggested, however, that in a situation where the courts find that there were good commercial reasons for accepting a variation (and thus that there was consideration) it may be difficult to argue that the acceptance was forced by 'duress'.

44 [1994] 4 All ER 714.

party, and to insist on cash for goods supplied. The circumstances in which this occurred were that the plaintiffs had ordered from the defendants cigarettes to the value of £17,000. These had, as a result of the defendants' mistake, been delivered to the wrong warehouse, in a different town. It was arranged that the defendants would collect them and transport them to the right warehouse. Before this could be done, however, there was a burglary at the warehouse to which the cigarettes had been wrongly delivered, and they were stolen. The defendants believed, mistakenly as a matter of law, that the cigarettes were at the plaintiffs' risk when they were stolen. They therefore insisted that the plaintiffs should pay for them, backing this up with the threat to withdraw credit. The plaintiffs reluctantly paid, but then brought an action to recover the £17,000 on the basis that it had been paid under duress. The Court of Appeal found that, on the facts, there was no economic duress, partly because the 'threat' was issued in good faith.[45] Although the defendants might have been regarded as abusing their position as the monopoly supplier of certain very popular brands of cigarettes, they were in this case genuinely under the impression that their claim for payment was legitimate. Moreover, as Steyn LJ commented:[46]

> . . . an extension [of the categories of duress] capable of covering the present case, involving 'lawful act duress' in a commercial context in pursuit of a *bona fide* claim, would be a radical one with far-reaching implications. It would introduce a substantial and undesirable element of uncertainty in the commercial bargaining process.

The court did not accept, however, that the fact that what was threatened was perfectly lawful, and would not have involved the supplier in any breach of contract, was in itself fatal to a claim. It thought that it was possible, in appropriate circumstances, for a threat to commit an entirely lawful act to amount to duress. In coming to this conclusion, it noted with approval the opinion of Professor Birks that it ought not to be the case that 'those who devise outrageous but technically lawful means of compulsion must always escape restitution'.[47] The Court of Appeal's statements on this issue are, of course, *obiter*, but they are supported by the views (also strictly *obiter*) of the Privy Council in *Attorney General v R*.[48] As such, they indicate a possible further extension of the concept of economic duress. Whether it is a desirable or necessary extension is open to doubt. The problems of drawing the line between legitimate pressure and economic duress will become even more difficult if a requirement of 'unlawfulness' is rejected. The arguments for and against such a development in the law are very

---

45 It has been noted earlier that 'bad faith' is not generally a necessary requirement for duress – above, 12.3. Where, however, there is no other 'unlawfulness', it may well be that it becomes a much more relevant factor.

46 [1994] 4 All ER 714, p 719.

47 Birks, 1989, p 177.

48 [2003] UKPC 22; [2003] EMLR 24 – discussed above, 12.3.

similar to those which apply in relation to whether the courts should adopt a general principle that 'unconscionable' agreements are unenforceable. This is discussed in Chapter 13, 13.9.

12.5 REMEDIES FOR DURESS

The remedy that the victim of duress will be seeking is to escape from the agreement that has resulted from the duress – in other words, rescission. As has been noted in relation to mistake and misrepresentation,[49] however, rescission may be lost through affirmation of the contract, lapse of time,[50] or the intervention of third party rights. It was confirmed by the High Court in *Halpern v Halpern*[51] that, as has been assumed in previous editions of this text, the person claiming duress must be able to make restitution of any property transferred for rescission to be available. The parties had been engaged in a dispute over an inheritance. This was then settled on the basis of a compromise agreement. When the claimants sought damages for breach of this agreement, the defendants alleged that it had been entered into under duress. Certain documents had been destroyed as part of the compromise agreement. The High Court held that since these documents could not be restored to the claimants, the right to rescind the agreement for duress had been lost. The court came to this conclusion by analogy with the position at common law in relation to fraudulent misrepresentation, and in equity in relation to undue influence. In both these situations the person seeking to rescind is required to make counter-restitution, and there was no reason why the same principle should not apply in relation to duress.

Damages are not available for duress, even where the contract is not rescinded. This reflects the origins of duress in the idea that there was no binding agreement because of the lack of true consent. If that conceptual basis for duress no longer retains its dominance, however, there is little reason why damages resulting from the duress should not be recoverable, on a 'reliance' basis, as they are now for most categories of misrepresentation.

12.6 DURESS UNDER THE PRINCIPLES OF EUROPEAN CONTRACT LAW

Article 4.108 of the Principles of European Contract Law is headed 'Threats'. It is relatively short and reads, in its entirety, as follows:

---

49 See 11.8.2 and 10.4.1 above.

50 See, for example, *North Ocean Shipping Co v Hyundai Construction, The Atlantic Baron* [1979] QB 705; [1978] 3 All ER 1170; above, 12.4.

51 [2006] EWHC 1728 (Comm); [2006] 3 All ER 1139.

A party may avoid a contract when it has been led to conclude it by the other party's imminent and serious threat of an act:

(a)   which is wrongful in itself; or

(b)   which it is wrongful to use as a means to obtain the conclusion of the contract, unless in the circumstances the first party had a reasonable alternative.

As will be seen, this largely corresponds to the current approach to duress under English law. There is no indication in the Principles themselves as to what is meant by 'wrongful'. In the annotations it is made clear that it includes threats not only of physical harm to the other contracting party or a third party, but also of financial loss resulting from, for example, a breach of contract. This seems in line with the current English position that the threat must normally involve a crime, tort or breach of contract.

The type of threat intended to be covered by (b) is something which, while lawful in itself, is 'not a proper way of obtaining the benefit sought'.[52] The example given is of a threat by an employee to expose an employer's affair, unless the employer pays increased wages – in other words, blackmail.[53]

The final phrase of the Article, referring to the lack of a reasonable alternative, here applies to all types of duress; in English law it has generally been regarded as of most significance in relation to economic duress.

As to remedies for duress, in addition to the contract being voidable, where that remedy is not used or is lost,[54] Art 4.117 allows damages to be recovered for any loss caused by the threat. This is in contrast to English law, and fills the gap noted above (12.5).

12.7 FURTHER READING

Atiyah, PS, 'Economic duress and the overborne will' (1982) 98 LQR 197

Birks, P, and Chin Nyuk Yin, 'On the nature of undue influence' (1995), Chapter 3 in Beatson, J and Friedmann, D (eds), *Good Faith and Fault in Contract Law*, 1995, Oxford: Clarendon Press

Halson, R, 'Opportunism, economic duress and contractual modifications' (1991) 107 LQR 649

Smith, SA, 'Contracting under pressure: a theory of duress' (1997a) CLJ 343

Smith, SA, *Atiyah's Introduction to the Law of Contract*, 6th edn, 2006, Oxford: Clarendon Press, Chapter 11

---

52 Lando and Beale, 2000, p 258.

53 Blackmail has been recognised as a possible form of duress by Lord Scarman in *Universe Tankships Inc of Monrovia v International Transport Workers' Federation, The Universe Sentinel* [1983] 1 AC 366; [1982] 2 All ER 67.

54 Through lapse of time (Art 4.113) or confirmation of the contract (Art 4.114).

13 UNDUE INFLUENCE

CONTENTS

13.1 OVERVIEW

Undue influence is the equitable concept which supplements the common law vitiating factor of duress. It operates largely through the application of presumptions. The following aspects are discussed in this chapter:

■ The underlying principles. When does influence become 'undue'? Imbalance of power between the parties is an important element in identifying undue influence.

- Actual undue influence. If there is direct evidence that a party agreed to a contract under the influence of improper pressure at that time, this will constitute actual undue influence. Such evidence is, however, rare.
- Presumptions. A relationship of influence will be presumed where:
  - the parties are in one of a number of recognised relationships (for example, solicitor–client); the presumption is in these circumstances irrebuttable;
  - the relationship between the parties has developed in a way that leads to one party dominating the other; this type of presumption may be rebutted by evidence to the contrary.
- Disadvantageous transactions. Where a contract between parties in a relationship of presumed influence clearly operates to the disadvantage of the weaker party, then undue influence will be presumed. It will be up to the alleged influencer to demonstrate that the other party entered into the contract with a full appreciation of what was involved (for example, after receiving independent legal advice).
- Effects. A contract entered into on the basis of actual or presumed influence is voidable. The usual bars to rescission apply (for example, lapse of time, third party rights). No damages are available.
- Third parties. Where a debtor has persuaded a person to act as surety or guarantor, the creditor will be put on notice whenever the relationship between debtor and surety is non-commercial (for example, husband persuading wife to use the family home as security for business debts). In that situation:
  - the creditor will be affected by any undue influence used by the debtor; the transaction may be voidable on that basis;
  - the creditor can protect itself by insisting that the surety receives legal advice before entering into the transaction.
- Unconscionability. English law recognises no general concept of unconscionability.

  A similar approach is to be found in the Principles of European Contract Law, though the PECL do allow for a broader range of remedies.

13.2 UNDUE INFLUENCE: THE CONCEPT

Duress is essentially a common law concept. Alongside it must be placed the equitable doctrine of 'undue influence'. This operates to release parties from contracts that they have entered into,[1] not as a result of improper threats, but as a result of being 'influenced' by the other party, whether intentionally or not.[2] The precise scope of the

---

1 The concept can also be used to set aside gifts or bequests.
2 Though references to the 'abuse' of influence in the most recent House of Lords decision on the area suggest the need for some deliberation (that is, *Royal Bank of Scotland v Etridge (No 2)* [2001] UKHL 44; [2001] 4 All ER 449), the development of the concept does not seem to require this.

concept may be due for reconsideration. At present, there are authorities which are treated as being concerned with undue influence, largely because of the limited scope given to duress at the time they were decided. In *Williams v Bayley*,[3] for example, the plaintiff had agreed to give a mortgage over his colliery as security for debts incurred by his son, who had forged his father's signature on promissory notes. The creditors had threatened that the son would be prosecuted if the mortgage was not given.[4] The agreement was set aside as being obtained by undue influence. Similarly, in *Mutual Finance Ltd v John Wetton & Sons Ltd*,[5] implied, though not explicit, threats to prosecute a member of a family company in relation to a forged guarantee led to the company giving a new guarantee.[6] This was again set aside on the basis of undue influence. Both these cases involve 'pressure' being placed on a party in much the same way as occurs with duress. It is possible that the expansion in the type of threats which are now treated as potentially giving rise to duress[7] would mean that they would now be put in that category. There is still the difficulty, however, that the courts seem reluctant to extend duress to implied rather than explicit threats. There is a strong argument that all these situations, involving pressure resulting from express or implied threats, might be usefully re-categorised as 'duress', leaving 'undue influence' to deal with relationships where one party has lost autonomy because of his or her relationship with the 'influencer'.[8] At the moment, the courts have not been prepared to take such a step.

One of the main difficulties with undue influence, as with duress, is to find the limits of legitimate persuasion. If it were impermissible to seek to persuade, cajole or otherwise encourage people to enter into agreements, then sales representatives would all be out of a job. 'Influence' in itself is perfectly acceptable: it is only when it becomes 'undue' that the law will intervene. Clarity in deciding when that has occurred is not assisted by the fact that the word 'undue' has two potential meanings. It can be used to indicate some impropriety on the part of the influencer. The influence is 'undue' because an imbalance of power between the parties has been used illegitimately by the influencer. Alternatively, the word can be used simply to indicate that the level of influence is at such a level that the influenced party has lost autonomy in deciding whether to enter into a contract. This does not imply any necessary impropriety on the part of the influencer. The point has been recognised in the High Court of Australia,

---

3 (1866) LR 1 HL 200.
4 It is not clear from the facts as reported whether specific threats were ever made by the creditors, but the House of Lords took the view that all concerned must have acted on the basis that this is what they were suggesting would happen if the father did not agree to the mortgage.
5 [1937] 2 All ER 657.
6 The forgery was committed by one of the Wetton sons; the other, in agreeing that the company should give the guarantee, was also concerned about the effects on his father's precarious health if his brother were prosecuted for forgery.
7 For which, see Chapter 12.
8 This argument is fully developed by Birks and Chin (1995), who suggest that all 'pressure' cases should be dealt with as duress. By contrast, Cope (1985) has suggested that all cases of duress should be treated as undue influence.

where 'undue' has been given the second meaning, and undue influence distinguished from unconscionable conduct. As Deane J put it:[9]

> Undue influence, like common law duress, looks to the quality of the consent or assent of the weaker party ... Unconscionable dealing looks to the conduct of the stronger party in attempting to enforce, or retain the benefit of a dealing with a person under a special disability in circumstances where it is not consistent with equity or good conscience that he should do so.

English courts, however, have tended to emphasise the wrongdoing of the stronger party in undue influence cases, though it cannot be said that their approach is consistent, and there are undue influence cases which indicate that such wrongdoing is not an essential element.[10] The issue is whether the concept is 'claimant-focused' or 'defendant-focused'.[11] If it is claimant-focused, then what matters is whether the claimant acted autonomously in entering into the contract; if it is defendant-focused, then what matters is whether the defendant has deliberately taken advantage of the claimant's weaker position. As suggested above, the English courts have not consistently applied one approach or the other, and this adds to the uncertainty about the precise scope of the concept. The most recent House of Lords decision, *Royal Bank of Scotland v Etridge (No 2)*,[12] adopts what is primarily a defendant-focused analysis, based on whether there has been 'abuse' of a position of influence, and this seems to be the dominant approach.[13]

How, then, do the courts decide when influence has overstepped the limits of acceptability and become 'undue'? The basic test in English law is that it is only where there is some relationship between the parties (either continuing, or in relation to a particular transaction) which leads to an inequality between them that the law will intervene. The starting point for the law's analysis is therefore not the substance of the transaction, but the process by which it came about. Was this the result of a person who was in a position to influence the other party by abusing that relationship in some way? An initial task is therefore to identify which relationships will give rise to this inequality. Once they have been identified, then further questions will arise as to the precise scope of the doctrine.

The whole area of undue influence has twice in the last 15 years been given a thorough examination by the House of Lords – in 1993, in *Barclays Bank plc v*

---

9 *Commercial Bank of Australia Ltd v Amadio* (1983) 151 CLR 447, p 474.

10 For example, *Allcard v Skinner* (1887) 36 Ch D 145, where the defendant was the lady superior of a religious order. See also Birks and Chin, 1995, where the argument for the adoption of the approach taken in *Commercial Bank of Australia v Amadio* is strongly made.

11 The 'claimant' here being the person influenced and the 'defendant' the alleged 'influencer' – see the corresponding discussion in relation to duress, in Chapter 12, 12.3, note 16.

12 [2001] UKHL 44; [2001] 4 All ER 449.

13 See, in particular, the speech of Lord Hobhouse. See also the Court of Appeal decision in *UCB Corporate Services Ltd v Williams* [2002] EWCA Civ 555; [2002] 3 FCR 448.

O'Brien,[14] and in 2001, in *Royal Bank of Scotland v Etridge (No 2)*.[15] Between these two decisions there were many Court of Appeal decisions, mainly concerned with the situation where a bank is infected by the undue influence of a husband who has persuaded his wife to use the matrimonial home as security for a business loan. Most of this case law is, following *Etridge*, of historical interest only, but one or two of the decisions are worthy of note. The main focus in the rest of this chapter will, however, be on the views of the House of Lords as expressed in *O'Brien* and *Etridge*.

In the leading speech in *O'Brien*, Lord Browne-Wilkinson adopted the analysis of the Court of Appeal in *Bank of Credit and Commerce International SA v Aboody*[16] to the effect that there are two main categories of undue influence, the second of which must be divided into two further separate sub-categories. The categories were actual undue influence (described as 'Class 1') and presumed undue influence (described as 'Class 2'). Presumed undue influence was then sub-divided into influence arising from relationships (such as solicitor–client, doctor–patient) which will always give rise to a presumption of undue influence ('Class 2A') and influence arising from relationships which have developed in such a way that undue influence should be presumed ('Class 2B'). These divisions have subsequently been used in many cases. The House of Lords has now taken the view, however, (in *Royal Bank of Scotland v Etridge (No 2)*)[17] that, while there is a distinction between 'actual' and 'presumed' influence, it should not operate quite as suggested by the categorisation adopted in *O'Brien* and that, in particular, the concept of Class 2B influence is open to misinterpretation.[18]

The concept of 'actual undue influence' will be considered first, followed by 'presumed undue influence', and the review of this area by the House of Lords in *Etridge*.

13.3 ACTUAL UNDUE INFLUENCE

In relation to actual undue influence, the claimant must prove, on the balance of probabilities, that in relation to a particular transaction, the defendant used undue influence. There is no need here for there to be a previous history of such influence. It can operate for the first time in connection with the transaction which is disputed. An example of this type of influence is to be found in *BCCI v Aboody*.[19] Mrs Aboody was 20 years younger than her husband. She had married him when she was 17. For many years, she signed documents relating to her husband's business, of which she was nominally a director, without reading them or questioning her husband about them. On the occasion which gave rise to the litigation, she had signed a number of guarantees and charges

---

14 [1994] 1 AC 180; [1993] 4 All ER 417.
15 [2001] UKHL 44; [2001] 4 All ER 449.
16 [1990] 1 QB 923; [1992] 4 All ER 955.
17 [2001] UKHL 44; [2001] 4 All ER 449.
18 'It is not a useful forensic tool': ibid, para 107; p 483, per Lord Hobhouse.
19 [1990] 1 QB 923; [1992] 4 All ER 955.

relating to the matrimonial home, in order to support loans by the bank to the business. She had taken no independent advice, though the bank's solicitor had at one meeting attempted to encourage her to take legal advice. During that meeting, Mr Aboody, in a state of some agitation, came into the room and, through arguing with the solicitor, managed to reduce his wife to tears. It was held that although Mr Aboody had not acted with any improper motive, he had unduly influenced his wife. He had concealed relevant matters from her, and his bullying manner had led her to sign without giving proper detached consideration to her own interests, simply because she wanted peace.

The Court of Appeal in this case, following *dicta* of Lord Scarman in *National Westminster Bank plc v Morgan*,[20] held that Mrs Aboody's claim to set aside the transaction nevertheless failed, because it was not to her 'manifest disadvantage'. The loans which she was guaranteeing had, in fact, given the company a reasonably good chance of surviving, in which case the potential benefits to Mrs Aboody would have been substantial. The risks involved did not, therefore, clearly outweigh the benefits. The House of Lords, in *CIBC Mortgages plc v Pitt*,[21] subsequently indicated, however, that 'manifest disadvantage' is not a requirement in cases of actual, as opposed to presumed, undue influence. If similar facts were to recur, therefore, a person in the position of Mrs Aboody would be likely to succeed in having the transactions set aside. The concept of 'manifest disadvantage' has been the subject of further reconsideration by the House of Lords in *Etridge*, and this is discussed below. The principle that such disadvantage is not required where actual undue influence is proved remains valid, however. A person is entitled to have a contract set aside if he or she has been bullied into making it, notwithstanding that that person may receive some benefit from it.

Where actual undue influence is proved it is not necessary for the claimant to prove that the transaction would not have been entered into but for the improper influence. This was the view of the Court of Appeal in *UCB Corporate Services Ltd v Williams*.[22] The position is analogous to that applying to misrepresentation or duress: as long as the influence was a factor in making the decision to enter into the transaction, that is sufficient.[23]

13.4 PRESUMED INFLUENCE: RECOGNISED RELATIONSHIPS

Under the *O'Brien* category 2A there were certain relationships which were presumed to give rise to undue influence. The revision of this principle adopted in *Etridge* is that

---

20 [1985] AC 686; [1985] 1 All ER 821.
21 [1994] AC 200; [1993] 4 All ER 433.
22 [2002] EWCA Civ 555; [2002] 3 FCR 448, not following statements apparently to the contrary by the Court of Appeal in *BCCI v Aboody*, since these were regarded as inconsistent with the House of Lords' view of *Aboody*, as expressed in *CIBC Mortgages v Pitt*, paras 85–91.
23 For a consideration of some of the problems with this position in the context of duress which may apply equally to undue influence, see Chapter 12, 12.3.

these relationships give rise to a presumption of influence but not necessarily undue influence. They are relationships 'where one party is legally presumed to repose trust and confidence in the other'.[24] As Lord Nicholls put it:[25]

> The law has adopted a sternly protective attitude towards certain types of relationship in which one party acquires influence over another who is vulnerable and dependent . . . In these cases the law presumes, irrebuttably, that one party had influence over the other. The complainant need not prove he actually reposed trust and confidence in the other party. It is sufficient for him to prove the existence of the type of relationship.

The relationships which fall into this category include parent–child,[26] guardian–ward,[27] trustee–beneficiary,[28] doctor–patient,[29] solicitor–client[30] and religious adviser–disciple.[31] It does not include husband–wife.[32] The relationships are those where a person has placed trust and confidence in another, and so is liable to act on that other's suggestions without seeking independent advice. Other relationships (other than husband–wife) which have these characteristics could be added to the list in the future. The inclusion of parent–child in the list is surprising. It is assumed that the parent will dominate the child. This may be true where the child is a minor. Once the child has attained majority, however, the possible relationships are various. Indeed, once the parents have reached old age, the most likely relationship is that the parent will place trust and confidence in the child.[33] It is submitted that the presumption ought only to arise as between parent and child when the child is a minor.[34]

An example of this category of presumed influence is *Allcard v Skinner*.[35] The plaintiff had entered a religious order of St Mary at the Cross, and had taken vows of poverty, chastity and obedience. The defendant was the lady superior of the order. Over a period of eight years during which she was a member of the order, the plaintiff gave property to the value of £7,000 to the defendant, most of which was spent on the purposes of the order. It was held that the property was prima facie recoverable as having been given under the undue influence of membership of the order, which

---

24 [2001] UKHL 44, para 104; [2001] 4 All ER 449, p 482.
25 Ibid, para 18; p 460.
26 *Bainbrigge v Browne* (1881) Ch D 188.
27 *Hylton v Hylton* (1754) 2 Ves Sen 547.
28 *Ellis v Barker* (1871) 7 Ch App 104.
29 *Radcliffe v Price* (1902) 18 TLR 466.
30 *Wright v Carter* [1903] 1 Ch 27.
31 *Allcard v Skinner* (1887) 36 Ch D 145.
32 *National Westminster Bank plc v Morgan* [1985] AC 686; [1985] 1 All ER 821.
33 As in, for example, *Coldunell Ltd v Gallon* [1986] QB 1184; [1986] 1 All ER 429.
34 It might also be thought that the protection given to minors, on the basis of lack of capacity (for which, see Chapter 7), would be sufficient in relation to the formation of contracts.
35 (1887) 36 Ch D 145.

required obedience to the defendant. This was so even though no direct pressure had been placed on the plaintiff. The influence was presumed from the relationship itself. The plaintiff's action to recover her property did not succeed, however, as she did not initiate her action until some six years after she had left the order. This lapse of time was held to operate as a bar to recovery.

FOR THOUGHT

Assuming the time lapse had not occurred in this case, was there anything that the religious order could have done to prevent any gift being recoverable on the basis of undue influence? Doesn't this make the situation very difficult for religious groups which expect members to undertake obedience to the leaders of the group, if any property received is liable to be returned?

Once there is a relationship from which influence is presumed, in what circumstances can the court conclude that the influence was 'undue', under the approach in *Etridge*?[36] This is where the concept which was previously referred to as 'manifest disadvantage' becomes relevant. Lord Nicholls referred back to the statement by Lindley LJ in *Allcard v Skinner*, which was cited by Lord Scarman in developing the concept of 'manifest disadvantage' in *National Westminster Bank plc v Morgan*. Lindley LJ pointed out that a small gift made to a person falling within one of the presumed categories of influence would not be enough in itself to put the transaction aside:[37]

> But if the gift is so large as not to be reasonably accounted for on the ground of friendship, relationship, charity, or other ordinary motives on which ordinary men act, the burden is upon the donee to support the gift.

Following this principle, Lord Nicholls pointed out that it would be absurd if every minor transaction between those in a relationship of presumed influence was also presumed to have been brought about by the exercise of *undue* influence:[38]

> The law would be out of touch with everyday life if the presumption were to apply to every Christmas or birthday gift by a child to a parent, or to an agreement whereby a client or patient agrees to be responsible for the reasonable fees of his legal or medical advisor ... So something more is needed before the law reverses the burden of proof, something which calls for an explanation. When that

---

36 Other than by proving actual undue influence, which would defeat the point of having a presumption of confidence at all.
37 (1887) 36 Ch D 145, p 185.
38 [2001] UKHL 44, para 24; [2001] 4 All ER 449, p 461. See the similar comments of Lord Hobhouse, para 104; p 482 and Lord Scott at para 156; p 501.

something more is present, the greater the disadvantage to the vulnerable person, the more cogent must be the explanation before the presumption will be regarded as rebutted.

What is being looked for is a transaction which 'failing proof to the contrary, is explicable only on the basis that it has been procured by undue influence'.[39] In other words, it is not the sort of transaction which the vulnerable person would have entered into in the normal course of events. Lord Hobhouse gives the example of a solicitor buying a client's property at a significant undervalue.[40] The fact that a transaction provides no benefit to the vulnerable person will be evidence supporting the suggestion of undue influence. Thus, once there is a relationship falling within one of the categories of automatically presumed influence, and a transaction which is not of a kind forming one of the normal incidents of such a relationship, there will be an inference of undue influence. It will then be up to the alleged influencer to show that the other party acted without being affected by such influence. The easiest way to do this is likely to be to show that the claimant received independent legal advice before entering into the transaction, though the Privy Council in *Attorney General v R* did not think that this was necessarily conclusive.[41] It is certainly not sufficient for the alleged influencer simply to show that there had been no 'wrongdoing' on his or her part.[42]

13.5 PRESUMED INFLUENCE: OTHER RELATIONSHIPS

Even where a relationship does not fall into one of the categories listed in the previous section, it may in fact have developed in a way which indicates that one person is in a 'dominant' position over the other. The dominated person will be likely in such a situation to act on the advice, recommendation or orders of the other, without seeking any independent advice, and without properly considering the consequences of his or her actions. This is the category of case which, under the *Aboody/O'Brien* classification, was referred to as Class 2B presumed undue influence. Following the House of Lords' decision in *Etridge*, these cases should no longer be referred to in this way.[43] There is no *presumption* of undue influence in such cases. The fact that the claimant placed trust and confidence in the defendant in relation to the management of the claimant's

---

39 [2001] UKHL 44, para 30; [2001] 4 All ER 449, p 462.
40 Ibid, para 104; p 482.
41 [2003] UKPC 22; [2003] EMLR 24, para 23.
42 *Hammond v Osborn* [2002] EWCA Civ 885; [2002] WTLR 1125 – applied in *Pesticcio v Huet* [2004] EWCA Civ 372; [2004] WTLR 699.
43 The clarity of their Lordships' exposition of this area is not helped by the fact that Lord Nicholls uses as an example of this category of case *Bainbrigge v Browne* (1881) 18 Ch D 188, which involved a father taking advantage of his children – a relationship falling into the category where influence (though not necessarily undue influence) is presumed, even under the *Etridge* approach: [2001] UKHL 44, para 15; [2001] 4 All ER 449, p 459.

financial affairs will have to be proved by evidence.[44] If that is done, then any disadvantageous transaction entered into at the instigation of the dominant party will constitute *prima facie* evidence that the trust and confidence of the claimant has been abused. The burden of proof will shift to the defendant to produce evidence to counter this inference. If no such evidence is produced, the court will be entitled to conclude that the transaction was in fact brought about by the exercise of undue influence.[45] In other words, the issue is the inferences which the court is entitled to draw from the evidence before it, and where the burden of proof lies in relation to that evidence.

Probably the majority of the reported cases which have been regarded as falling under the old Class 2B, and which now involve establishing that a relationship of trust and confidence has developed outside the recognised categories, concern a dominant husband and a subservient wife. Similarly, it was held by the Court of Appeal in *Leeder v Stevens*[46] that a relevant relationship had arisen between a married man and a woman with whom he had had what the court called 'a loving relationship' over a period of 10 years. A transaction in which she had transferred to him a half share in her house, valued at £70,000, in return for a payment of £5,000 was set aside. This case emphasised the strength of the presumptions. The trial judge had found no evidence of actual coercion at the time of the transaction. The Court of Appeal held that this was irrelevant. Once the relationship was established, and there was a transaction that called for explanation, then it was up to the man to prove that the woman had entered into the transaction with full appreciation of its consequences, and having been properly advised.

Situations of trust do not only arise in the context of sexual or other intimate relationships, as is shown by *Attorney General v R*,[47] where the Privy Council recognised that a relationship between a soldier and his regiment could be such as to give rise to a presumption of influence. Another example is *Lloyds Bank Ltd v Bundy*.[48]

Mr Bundy was an elderly farmer. He had provided a guarantee and a charge over his house to support the debts of his son's business. He was visited by his son and the assistant manager of the bank. The assistant manager told Mr Bundy that the bank could not continue to support the son's business without further security. Mr Bundy then, without seeking any other advice, increased the guarantee and charge to £11,000. When the bank, in enforcing the charge, subsequently sought possession of the house, Mr Bundy pleaded undue influence. It was held that the existence of long-standing relations between the Bundy family and the bank was important. Although the visit

---

44 Lord Scott is prepared to accept, however, that little or no evidence will be needed to establish a reciprocal relationship of trust and confidence between husband and wife living together (ibid, para 159; p 502), although he also suggests that undue influence is an unlikely, though possible, explanation for a wife's agreement to act as surety for her husband's business debts (ibid, para 162; p 503).

45 See ibid, Lord Nicholls, para 14; p 459; Lord Hobhouse, paras 106–07; p 483; Lord Scott, para 161; p 503. All three suggest that an analogy with the tortious concept of *res ipsa loquitur* may be helpful.

46 [2005] EWCA Civ 50; 149 SJLB 112.

47 [2003] UKPC 22; [2003] EMLR 24.

48 [1975] QB 326; [1974] 3 All ER 757.

when the charge was increased was the first occasion on which this particular assistant manager had met Mr Bundy, he was, as Sir Eric Sachs put it in the Court of Appeal, 'the last of a relevant chain of those who over the years had earned or inherited' Mr Bundy's trust and confidence.[49] The charge over the house was obviously risky given the precarious state of the son's business. There was no evidence that the risks had been properly explained to Mr Bundy by the assistant manager, and therefore Mr Bundy could not have come to an informed judgment on his actions. The charge was set aside on the basis of undue influence.[50]

Although the period of time over which a relationship has developed is clearly relevant to deciding whether trust and confidence has arisen, it need not be all that long. In *Goldsworth v Brickell*,[51] for example, where the relationship existed between an elderly farmer and his neighbour, it had only been for a few months that the plaintiff had been relying on the defendant. Nevertheless, it was held that the relationship involved sufficient trust and confidence for a disadvantageous transaction to require explanation. In the absence of evidence that the elderly farmer had exercised an independent and informed judgment, the relevant transaction was set aside.

In *Credit Lyonnais Bank Nederland NV v Burch*,[52] it was held that a relationship of trust and confidence could arise between an employer and a junior employee. The employee had acted as babysitter for the employer, and had visited his family at weekends and on holidays abroad. She had agreed to her house being used as collateral for the employer's business overdraft. It was held by Millett LJ in the Court of Appeal, using the now discredited Class 2B category, that a presumption of undue influence between two people in a relationship which was 'easily capable of developing into a relationship of trust and confidence' could be established by the 'nature of the transaction' which had been entered into.[53] If 'the transaction is so extravagantly improvident that it is virtually inexplicable on any other basis', then 'the inference will be readily drawn'.[54] This use of the substance of the transaction as an element in establishing a presumption of undue influence was unusual. The other pre-*Etridge* cases in this area operated on the basis of establishing the presumption from the way in which the relationship has developed, before looking at the position in relation to the transaction under consideration. As will be seen below, the disadvantageous nature of the

---

49 Contrast the House of Lords' view in *National Westminster Bank plc v Morgan* [1985] 1 All ER 821, where it was held that there was no relationship of trust and confidence between a bank manager and a wife who had executed a charge over the matrimonial home. Although the manager had visited her at home to obtain her signature, the relationship did not go beyond the normal business relationship of banker and customer.

50 The judgments in this case make reference to 'presumptions' of abuse of influence which would need reconsideration in the light of *Etridge*. It is not suggested, however, that the *Etridge* approach would lead to a different conclusion on the facts.

51 [1987] 1 All ER 853.

52 [1997] 1 All ER 144.

53 Ibid, p 154.

54 Ibid, p 155.

transaction has generally been used as a basis for deciding whether or not relief should be granted, once a presumption of influence has been made. Millett LJ's approach was not specifically followed by the other members of the Court of Appeal, though Swinton Thomas LJ stated in general terms that he agreed with Millett LJ's reasons for his decision.[55] This aspect of *Burch* was not considered by the House of Lords in *Etridge*, though the outcome of the case was clearly approved by Lord Nicholls.[56] Millett LJ's analysis, however, would not seem to fit with the *Etridge* approach. This would look at the relationship between the employer and employee to see if trust and confidence had developed. If it had, then the disadvantageous and risky nature of the transaction which the employee had entered into would raise an inference that it was not under-taken on the basis of informed consent, and that the trust and confidence had been abused. The employer would then need to produce evidence to contradict that infer-ence. If, on the other hand, there was no evidence of a relationship of trust and confidence, no inferences would be drawn from the disadvantageous nature of the transaction, and the employee would need to produce specific evidence of undue influ-ence in order to have it set aside. There is no suggestion in the House of Lords' speeches in *Etridge* that the nature of the transaction can be used to establish a relationship of trust and confidence. Thus, if the employee had entered into a disadvantageous transac-tion simply because she thought it was a good way of currying favour with the boss, perhaps enhancing her prospects of promotion, there would be no scope for a finding of undue influence.

The *Burch* case raises the question of the extent to which the risky or disadvanta-geous nature of a transaction is a part of the consideration of whether there was undue influence. *Etridge* has changed the focus on this issue, but to understand where the law has got to, it will be helpful to look at a little of the history.

13.6 REQUIREMENT OF 'MANIFEST DISADVANTAGE'

The concept that a transaction must be to the 'manifest disadvantage' of the claimant in order for it to be set aside for some types of undue influence derives from the speech of Lord Scarman in *National Westminster Bank plc v Morgan*.[57] Here, Mrs Morgan had agreed to a legal charge over the matrimonial home as part of an attempt to refinance debts which had arisen from her husband's business. She had been visited at home by the bank manager and had thereupon signed the charge. Lord Scarman, with whom the rest of the House agreed, held that her attempt to have the charge set aside for undue

---

55 For an enthusiastic response to *Burch* as a welcome development in the law controlling substantively unfair transactions, as opposed to simply procedural unfairness, see Chen-Wishart, 1997. For a more sceptical reception see Tjio, 1997.

56 [2001] UKHL 44, paras 83, 89; [2001] 4 All ER 449, pp 474, 476.

57 [1985] AC 686; [1985] 1 All ER 821. Lord Scarman was adopting and adapting an approach taken by Lindley LJ in *Allcard v Skinner* (1887) 36 Ch D 145, p 185.

influence failed for two reasons. First, the bank manager's visit was very short (only about 15 minutes in total), and there was no history of reliance as in *Lloyds Bank v Bundy*. Second, for the presumption to arise, the transaction had to be to the 'manifest disadvantage' of Mrs Morgan. This was not the case here. The charge 'meant for her the rescue of her home on the terms sought by her: a short term loan at a commercial rate of interest'.[58] Thus, although any transaction which puts a person's home at risk must in one sense be regarded as 'disadvantageous', this could not be sufficient on its own to render a contract voidable. If it were, every mortgage agreement would have to be so regarded. In looking for disadvantage, it was necessary to consider the context in which the transaction took place. If it was clear, as it seemed to be in *Morgan*, that the risks involved were, as far as the claimant was concerned, worth running in order to obtain the potential benefits of the transaction, and there was no other indication of unfairness, then the courts should be quite prepared to enforce it. As has been noted above, some of Lord Scarman's comments in *Morgan* were interpreted by the Court of Appeal in *BCCI v Aboody*[59] as applying the requirement of manifest disadvantage to situations of actual, rather than presumed, influence. This interpretation was firmly rejected by the House of Lords in *CIBC Mortgages plc v Pitt*.[60] At the same time, Lord Browne-Wilkinson expressed some concern over the need for the requirement even in cases of presumed undue influence.[61] The Court of Appeal in *Etridge* reaffirmed that it was necessary,[62] but in *Barclays Bank v Coleman*[63] suggested that the disadvantage which needed to be shown did not have to be 'large or even medium-sized', provided that it was 'clear and obvious and more than *de minimis*'.[64]

Prior to the House of Lords' decision in *Etridge*, therefore, the position was that in cases of presumed undue influence, either Class 2A or 2B, there was a requirement that the transaction should be to the manifest disadvantage of the claimant before it would be set aside. No such requirement existed in relation to actual undue influence. What exactly was meant by 'manifest disadvantage' was, however, becoming increasingly obscure, with *obiter* statements in the House of Lords and in the Court of Appeal suggesting that it might not be necessary at all. The decision of the House of Lords in *Etridge* has not changed the position in relation to actual undue influence. If such influence is established, then the court should set the agreement aside irrespective of whether it was to the actual or potential benefit of the claimant. This must be based on

58 [1985] AC 686, p 703; [1985] 1 All ER 821, p 826.
59 [1990] 1 QB 923.
60 [1994] 1 AC 200; [1993] 4 All ER 433.
61 He saw it as being potentially in conflict with the approach taken in 'abuse of confidence' cases such as *Demerara Bauxite Co Ltd v Hubbard* [1923] AC 673, where, on grounds of public policy (that is, the need to protect those to whom fiduciaries owe duties as a class from exploitation), the burden is on the fiduciary to prove that a transaction was advantageous to the claimant: ibid, p 209; pp 439–40.
62 *Royal Bank of Scotland v Etridge (No 2)* [1998] 4 All ER 705. The court was, of course, bound by the House of Lords' decision in *National Westminster Bank plc v Morgan*.
63 [2001] QB 20; [2000] 1 All ER 385.
64 Ibid, p 33; p 400.

the policy view that it is unacceptable for the courts to enforce any transaction where it has been demonstrated that the actions of one party have led to it being entered into without the free, informed consent of the other. The approach is similar to that taken in relation to a totally innocent misrepresentation, where a party is allowed to rescind without showing that the misrepresentation has caused any loss.[65]

In relation to situations where there is presumed influence, either from a recognised 'special relationship' (the *O'Brien* category 2A), or because a particular relationship of trust and confidence has been established, then, as indicated above,[66] the nature of the transaction becomes relevant in considering whether the court may draw any inferences of undue influence from that relationship. The phrase 'manifest disadvantage' should not be used,[67] and it is certainly not the case that the claimant has to prove such disadvantage to establish that there was undue influence in such a case. The relevance of the nature of the transaction is evidential.[68] If it is shown to be of a kind which calls for explanation (for example, because it benefits the defendant without providing any comparable benefit for the claimant), then this will impose a burden on the defendant to show that it was not in fact obtained by undue influence, that is, an abuse of the relationship of trust and confidence.

Lord Nicholls and Lord Scott both indicated that they did not regard the fact that a wife acts as surety for her husband's business debts as in itself being sufficient to give rise to an inference that influence has been abused. As Lord Nicholls put it:[69]

> I do not think that, *in the ordinary course*, a guarantee of the character I have mentioned [that is, the guarantee by a wife of her husband's business debts] is to be regarded as a transaction which, failing proof to the contrary, is explicable only on the basis that it has been procured by the exercise of undue influence by the husband. Wives frequently enter into such transactions. There are good and sufficient reasons why they are willing to do so,[70] despite the risks involved for them and their families . . . They may be anxious, perhaps exceedingly so. But this is a far cry from saying that such transactions as a class are to be regarded as *prima facie* evidence of the exercise of undue influence by husbands.
>
> I have emphasised the phrase 'in the ordinary course'. There will be cases

---

65 See Chapter 10, 10.4.1.

66 See 13.4 to 13.5.

67 Though it was in *Leeder v Stevens* [2005] EWCA Civ 50, para 14.

68 As Lord Scott comments, 'the nature of the transaction, its inexplicability by reference to the normal motives by which people act, may, and usually will, constitute important evidential material': [2001] UKHL 44, para 155; [2001] 4 All ER 449, p 501.

69 Ibid, para 30; p 462 (emphasis in original); cf Lord Scott's comments at para 159; p 502.

70 For example, because the husband's business is the source of the family income: ibid, para 28; p 462.

where a wife's signature of a guarantee or a charge of her share in the matrimonial home does call for explanation.[71] Nothing I have said is directed at such a case.

Lord Hobhouse seems prepared to regard the fact that a wife acts as surety for her husband's business debts as more readily raising an inference calling for an explanation by the husband – for example, that he has taken account of her interests, dealt fairly with her, and made sure that she entered into the obligation freely and with knowledge of the true facts.[72] It is likely, however, that the approach taken by Lord Nicholls and Lord Scott, with whom Lord Bingham concurred, will be the one that is followed.

The conclusion of all this is that 'manifest disadvantage' is no longer a part of the law relating to undue influence; the nature of the transaction may, however, in cases where influence is presumed, provide evidence which will put the burden on the defendant to show that the influence was not abused.

13.7 UNDUE INFLUENCE AND THIRD PARTIES

The majority of reported cases on undue influence over the past 10 years have been concerned with the effect on a transaction of undue influence by a third party. Specifically, where one party to a transaction is giving to the other a guarantee of a third party's debts, what is the effect of undue influence by the debtor on the guarantor? The typical situation of this kind, as will have been discerned from the earlier discussion, is where a wife is guaranteeing a husband's business debts and using her property, most commonly her share in the matrimonial home, as security. In such a situation, if the husband's actions amount to undue influence, does this affect the wife's transaction with the creditor? The husband is not a party to that transaction, and so the standard answer under the doctrine of privity would be 'no'. Nevertheless, in some situations of this kind (not necessarily involving husband and wife), the courts have been prepared to find that the transaction with the creditor can be set aside.

The problem that faces the court, particularly in the husband and wife cases, is that small businesses regularly depend on the use of the owner's house as collateral for loans from banks and other suppliers of finance. There is a need for some protection of vulnerable parties in this situation, but the rules should not become so strict that they lead to an unwillingness on the part of the banks to lend money. That would have a deleterious effect on small businesses and on the economy. This issue is considered

---

71 It may be that the kind of situation in mind here is that referred to by Lord Hobhouse when, in the context of the actions to be taken by a creditor, he commented that 'A loan application backed by a viable business plan or to acquire a worthwhile asset is very different from a loan to postpone the collapse of an already failing business or to refinance with additional security loans which have fallen into arrears. The former would not aggravate the risk; the latter most certainly would do so': ibid, para 109; p 484.

72 Ibid, para 106; p 483.

further (see 13.7.9 and 13.7.10) in connection with the steps that a bank is now required to take in order to protect itself against the risk of undue influence or other impropriety.

Prior to the House of Lords' decision in *Barclays Bank v O'Brien,* [73] there was some uncertainty as to the way in which the 'privity' problem should be dealt with, where the debtor has influenced the guarantor to enter into the transaction with the creditor. Two main possibilities were canvassed, namely, agency and 'special equity'.

13.7.1 Agency

In some cases (for example, *Kings North Trust v Bell*)[74] the privity issue was avoided by treating the debtor (the husband) as agent for the creditor in getting the other person (his wife) to sign the agreement. If that is the case, then the creditor, as principal, would be infected with any wrongful acts of the debtor, as agent, in obtaining the agreement. A similar analysis was adopted, though not applied on the facts, in *Coldunell Ltd v Gallon,*[75] which concerned a son taking advantage of his elderly parents.

As was pointed out, however, by Scott LJ in the Court of Appeal in *Barclays Bank v O'Brien,*[76] the analysis of such cases in terms of agency is likely to be 'highly artificial'. None of the parties is really likely to have thought of the debtor acting as agent for the creditor, and this will generally look like a contrived explanation, devised after the event, to allow the guarantor an escape route.

13.7.2 Special equity

Another possible analysis, which was preferred by Scott LJ, was to treat married women as being able to take advantage of a 'special equity'. This consists of a recognition by the courts that many wives are still in a position where the husband exercises considerable influence in relation to business decisions taken for the family. In such situations, there is therefore an obligation on the creditor, where the wife is entering a transaction which puts her home at risk, to ensure that she is given full information, and is recommended to seek independent advice.

The problem with this approach, apart from the patronising attitude towards women that it would entrench,[77] is that it is difficult to see how it could then apply to analogous situations where the relationship between debtor and guarantor is not

---

73 [1994] 1 AC 180; [1993] 4 All ER 417.
74 [1986] 1 All ER 423.
75 [1986] QB 1184; [1986] 1 All ER 429.
76 [1993] QB 109; [1992] 4 All ER 983.
77 See, for example, the criticisms in Cretney, 1992, and the comments of Wheeler and Shaw, 1994, pp 539–40.

husband and wife. Would it apply to gay couples, for example, or an unmarried man and woman who bought a house jointly?

A different and more general approach was put forward and applied by the House of Lords in *Barclays Bank v O'Brien*,[78] and this remains the basis of the law in this area.

13.7.3 The *O'Brien* analysis

The House of Lords in *Barclays Bank v O'Brien* was not inclined to adopt either of the analyses identified above. The facts of the case were as follows. Mr O'Brien persuaded his wife to sign a guarantee in relation to an overdraft facility provided by a bank, using the jointly owned matrimonial home as security. He had told her that the security was limited to £60,000, whereas in fact it was for £130,000. The employee of the bank who presented the documents for the wife's signature failed to follow a superior's instructions to explain the transaction, and to suggest that the wife took independent legal advice if she had any doubts about it. The papers were presented to the wife, open at the place for signature, and she did not read them before signing. When the bank tried to enforce the security, Mrs O'Brien claimed that she was only bound, at most, up to the £60,000 which her husband had told her was the limit of the liability.

It was found by the Court of Appeal, and not disputed in the House of Lords, that Mrs O'Brien was an intelligent and independent-minded woman, who had not been unduly influenced by her husband. The case, therefore, turned on her husband's misrepresentation of the extent of the liability, and whether this affected the bank. Although the case is therefore not strictly one which is concerned with undue influence, it was accepted in both the Court of Appeal and the House of Lords that the same principles should apply irrespective of whether the wife was claiming that it was her husband's undue influence, or his misrepresentation, which had led her to enter into the transaction.[79]

Lord Browne-Wilkinson, who gave the only substantive speech in the House of Lords, found that the law in this area had been built on a rather obscure Privy Council decision, *Turnbull v Duval*.[80] The case concerned the setting aside of a wife's guarantee of her husband's debts. However, close examination of the case showed no clear

---

78 [1994] 1 AC 180; [1993] 4 All ER 417.
79 Subsequent cases have followed this treatment of undue influence and misrepresentation as distinct but analogous concepts for these purposes. There are, however, some points in the speech of Lord Hobhouse in the most recent House of Lords decision (*Royal Bank of Scotland plc v Etridge (No 2)* [2001] UKHL 44; [2001] 4 All ER 449) which appear to suggest that misrepresentation (and duress) might be treated as a species of undue influence: see para 103; p 481. The other speeches, however, maintain the traditional distinction, and it is submitted that this approach is to be preferred. It may be, however, that there is in some cases an overlap: see *UCB Services Ltd v Williams* [2002] EWCA Civ 555; [2002] 3 FCR 448, para 86.
80 [1902] AC 429.

evidence of improper pressure from the husband. Moreover, although the case had been used to support the 'agency' analysis in later decisions, the Privy Council did not actually refer to this concept. Lord Lindley had simply stated that the creditors had 'left everything to [the husband] and must abide by the consequences'.[81] The precise basis for the holding in favour of the wife was therefore not at all clear. Building on this uncertain foundation, the law had subsequently developed 'in an artificial way, giving rise to artificial distinctions and conflicting decisions'. As a result, he sought to 'restate the law in a form which is principled, reflects the current requirements of society and provides as much certainty as possible'.[82]

13.7.4 The doctrine of notice

The basis on which he felt able to do this was by a proper application of the doctrine of 'notice', which he felt lies at the heart of equity. Where, for example, it is necessary to decide between the conflicting rights of two innocent parties, the issue may well be determined by asking whether the holder of the later right had actual or constructive notice of the earlier right. Looking first at the position of wives, Lord Browne-Wilkinson felt that the fact that many wives place confidence and trust in their husbands in relation to their financial affairs, and that the informality of business dealings between spouses raises a substantial risk of misrepresentation, meant that creditors should in certain circumstances be put on inquiry. These circumstances arose where:[83]

(a)   the transaction is on its face not to the financial advantage of the wife; and
(b)   there is substantial risk in transactions of that kind that, in procuring the wife to act as surety, the husband has committed a legal or equitable wrong that entitles the wife to set aside the transaction.

The creditor who ignores the risk, and does not take steps to ensure that the wife is acting with fully informed agreement and consent, will be deemed to have constructive notice of the wife's rights, as against her husband, to set aside the transaction on the basis of misrepresentation or undue influence.

FOR THOUGHT

What would have been the outcome of *Barclay's Bank v O'Brien* if the Bank's employee had actually followed instructions as to the advice to be given to Mrs O'Brien (see above, 13.7.3)?

---

81 [1902] AC 429, p 435.
82 [1994] 1 AC 180, p 195; [1993] 4 All ER 417, p 428.
83 Ibid, p 196; p 429.

13.7.5 Relationships covered

Turning to the broader application of these principles, Lord Browne-Wilkinson saw no reason to confine them to wives. The special position of wives is not based on that status as such, but because of the emotional and sexual ties that arise from the marriage relationship. Such ties exist between all cohabitees, both heterosexual and homosexual, whether married or not. Moreover, the principles will also apply to any situation where the creditor is aware that the surety places trust and confidence in the debtor.[84] The further development of this area in *Royal Bank of Scotland v Etridge*[85] means that the creditor will be put on notice of the risk of undue influence wherever the relationship between the debtor and surety is non-commercial. This is discussed further below (13.7.10).

13.7.6 Application of the doctrine of notice

Where the creditor is put on notice of the risk of undue influence, Lord Browne-Wilkinson outlined the following factors that will lead to the obligation being unenforceable:[86]

(a)   there must be undue influence, misrepresentation or some other legal wrong by the principal debtor;

(b)   the creditor will have constructive notice of such a wrong, and the surety's right to set aside the transaction, unless the creditor has taken reasonable steps to be satisfied that the surety entered into the obligation freely and with knowledge of the true facts;

(c)   the creditor will normally be regarded as taking such steps by (1) warning the surety (not in the presence of the principal debtor) of the amount of the potential liability and the risks involved; and (2) advising the surety to take independent legal advice.

Applying these guidelines to the facts of the case (which now need to be considered alongside the further development of the area in *Royal Bank of Scotland v Etridge (No 2)* – discussed below at 13.7.10), Lord Browne-Wilkinson concluded that Mrs O'Brien, having been misled by her husband and not having received proper advice from the bank, was entitled to set aside the legal charge on the matrimonial home.

13.7.7 Application of the doctrine of notice to actual undue influence

Barclays Bank v O'Brien was, as we have seen, dealt with not as a case of undue influence, but of misrepresentation. On the same day as it gave its opinion on this case,

---

84 As in *Avon Finance Co Ltd v Bridger* [1985] 2 All ER 581 – son and elderly parents.
85 [2001] UKHL 44; [2001] 4 All ER 449.
86 [1994] 1 AC 180, pp 198–99; [1993] 4 All ER 417, pp 431–32.

the House of Lords also ruled on another husband and wife case, which was agreed to have involved actual undue influence: *CIBC Mortgages plc v Pitt*.[87] Mrs Pitt sought to set aside a mortgage over the matrimonial home granted by the plaintiffs on the basis that she had been induced to agree to it by the undue influence of her husband. She was unaware of the amount of the mortgage (which was £150,000), though she was aware that her husband was borrowing money to finance share dealings. The trial judge found that Mr Pitt had not been acting as the creditor's agent, but that he had exercised actual undue influence over Mrs Pitt in persuading her to sign the mortgage. Moreover, the judge ruled that the mortgage agreement was to Mrs Pitt's manifest disadvantage. Nevertheless, he rejected Mrs Pitt's claim, because he held that the 'special equity' applying to wives only operated where the wife was standing surety, and not to a situation where there was a joint advance to both husband and wife by way of a loan. The Court of Appeal rejected Mrs Pitt's appeal, on the basis that the transaction was not to her manifest disadvantage. Mrs Pitt appealed to the House of Lords.

Lord Browne-Wilkinson again gave the leading speech. He, of course, applied the same approach as had been taken in *Barclays Bank v O'Brien* in relation to the effect of Mr Pitt's behaviour on the contractual relationship between Mrs Pitt and the creditor – that is, an approach based on notice. Before considering this, however, Lord Browne-Wilkinson ruled that the requirement of 'manifest disadvantage' did not apply to cases of actual undue influence.[88] Mrs Pitt would, therefore, have been able to set aside the transaction as against Mr Pitt. As far as the creditor was concerned, however, it had no direct knowledge of the influence Mr Pitt had exercised. Should it be regarded as having constructive notice? The House of Lords thought not. To the creditor, it appeared to be a straightforward mortgage transaction:[89]

> There was nothing to indicate to the [creditor] that this was anything other than a normal advance to a husband and wife for their joint benefit.

The situation of a joint advance could be distinguished from one involving a surety, because in the latter case:[90]

> ... there is not only the possibility of undue influence having been exercised but there is also the increased risk of it having in fact been exercised because, at least on its face, the guarantee by a wife of her husband's debts is not for her financial benefit. It is the combination of these two factors that puts the creditor on inquiry.

87 [1994] 1 AC 200; [1993] 4 All ER 433.
88 As has been noted above, the phrase 'manifest disadvantage' has now in any case been rejected as unhelpful in any situation of undue influence: *Royal Bank of Scotland v Etridge (No 2)* [2001] UKHL 44; [2001] 4 All ER 449.
89 [1994] 1 AC 200, p 211; [1993] 4 All ER 433, p 441.
90 Ibid.

The emphasis in these cases is now on actual, or constructive, notice.

13.7.8 Relevance of disadvantageous nature of transaction

Note that the disadvantageous nature of the transaction, which we have seen is of significance in cases of presumed undue influence, still has a minor role to play in certain (probably rare) cases of actual undue influence where a third party is involved. It is not relevant in two-party situations. A party who is shown to have obtained the other's agreement to a transaction through exercising undue influence cannot claim to be able to enforce the agreement simply because it is not disadvantageous. Nor is it relevant in a three-party situation, if the creditor has actual knowledge of the undue influence, or if the relationship between the debtor and surety is non-commercial (since *Royal Bank of Scotland v Etridge (No 2)* says that in that case the creditor will always be put on notice of the risk of undue influence). If, however, in a situation where the relationship between debtor and surety is commercial, the creditor does not have actual knowledge of undue influence, then the fact that the transaction is, or is not, to the other party's disadvantage may be relevant in deciding whether or not the creditor should be regarded as having constructive notice of the influence. This is likely to be a very rare occurrence.

13.7.9 Consequences for creditors

The House of Lords' decision in *Barclays Bank v O'Brien* placed a burden on creditors to ensure that they gave proper advice to a surety in any situation where there is a risk of undue influence. In terms of the contractual principle, the case opened another fairly broad exception to the doctrine of privity, in that the actions of a third party are allowed to affect the relationship between creditor and surety. It should be noted, however, that if the bank's own procedures had been followed by its employees in this case, the requirements laid down by the House of Lords would have been fulfilled. It does not seem, then, that the House of Lords' approach placed unreasonable burdens on creditors, particularly those large organisations which will have standard procedures for dealing with such situations. The safest approach would have been to ensure that any private individual standing as surety is advised along the lines suggested by the House of Lords in *O'Brien*.

A number of Court of Appeal decisions subsequent to *O'Brien*, however, indicated that the courts might be prepared to accept something less than this. The whole area became rather uncertain, but has now been thoroughly reconsidered by the House of Lords in *Royal Bank of Scotland plc v Etridge (No 2)*, which is discussed below at 13.7.10. First, however, some of the intervening cases will be noted, to indicate how the legal principles have developed.

In both *Massey v Midland Bank plc*[91] and *Banco Exterior Internacional v Mann*,[92]

---

91 [1995] 1 All ER 929.
92 [1995] 1 All ER 936.

the Court of Appeal took the view that a creditor who reasonably believed that a wife had been advised by a solicitor was protected against any impropriety on the part of her husband as regards undue influence or misrepresentation. Although the creditor might be put on notice by the relationship between the parties and the nature of the transaction, it was entitled to assume that a solicitor would fulfil properly the professional duty to advise the wife properly. Furthermore, in *Halifax Mortgage Services Ltd v Stepsky*,[93] it was held that where the same solicitor acted for both the creditor and the debtor in relation to the mortgage of a house, the creditor could not be taken to have notice of the fact that the debtor had falsely stated the purpose for which the loan would be used, even though the solicitor was aware of this.[94]

Two subsequent Court of Appeal decisions in this area, however, both decided in the summer of 1996, demonstrated contrasting approaches to the obligation of the creditor in relation to third party impropriety. The first case, *Credit Lyonnais Bank Nederland NV v Burch*,[95] heard in June 1996, involved a relationship of presumed undue influence between an employer, the owner of a business, and a junior employee. The employee put up her own house (valued at £100,000) as collateral for the business's bank overdraft facility of £270,000. The bank's solicitors wrote to her on several occasions and told her that she should take separate legal advice before entering into the transaction, emphasising that the document she was being asked to sign was unlimited as regards amount and time. The employee wrote a letter (though this may well have been under the employer's direction) to the solicitors acknowledging their letters, and the contents of them, and confirming that she was aware of the implications of the transaction. When the business failed, and the bank tried to enforce the agreement against the employee, she pleaded undue influence. It was held by the Court of Appeal that the bank was precluded from enforcing the agreement. It was not enough in the circumstances for the bank, via its solicitors, to have stated that the employee's commitment was unlimited, and to have encouraged her to take legal advice. The transaction was so disadvantageous to the employee that the bank should not have proceeded until the employee had had explained to her the full extent of the business's borrowings and its overdraft limit. Nor should it have done so until the employee had actually received independent legal advice. The court was quite clear that this agreement was unconscionable and could not be allowed to stand.

The second case, heard by a different Court of Appeal in July 1996, was less protective of the person allegedly unduly influenced. In *Banco Exterior Internacional*

---

93 [1996] 2 All ER 277.

94 At first instance, this was said to follow from the solicitor's general duty of client confidentiality: in the Court of Appeal, the decision was based on the more specific provision contained in s 199(1) of the Law of Property Act 1925. In *Royal Bank of Scotland v Etridge (No 2)* [2001] UKHL 44; [2001] 4 All ER 449, Lord Scott confirmed that a creditor is not to be taken to have notice of matters coming to the attention of a solicitor acting for both the creditor and the guarantor, but did not seem to think that s 199 was really relevant to the issue: paras 176–77; pp 506–07. See also Lord Nicholls, paras 75–78; p 472.

95 [1997] 1 All ER 144.

SA v Thomas,[96] a woman, D, who was in difficult financial circumstances, was a close personal friend of M, who ran a second-hand car business. M persuaded D to use her house as security for the debts of his business vis à vis the plaintiff bank, up to a value of £75,000. In exchange, he apparently agreed to pay D a regular income. D was, in effect, putting her capital at risk in exchange for this income. The bank did not know of this aspect of the arrangement. It told D that she should take independent legal advice, and she consulted a solicitor nominated by the bank. In order to complete the arrangements concerning the charge over her house, the deeds needed to be received by the bank. These were held by a solicitor who had acted for D in the past. When D sought the deeds, and explained the arrangement she was entering into with M, this solicitor strongly advised her against it. He also telephoned the bank, told them of the advice that he had given D, and suggested that they should not continue with the arrangement. When M's business failed, the bank sought to enforce the charge against D's property. D died before the action came to trial, and it was continued against her executors. The trial judge held that D had been unduly influenced by M. He found against the bank on the basis that it was put on notice of this undue influence by the solicitor's phone call. He therefore held that the guarantee could not be enforced in relation to M's liabilities incurred after that date. The Court of Appeal disagreed. It was not sure, in the first place, whether any presumption of undue influence arose. Even if it did, all the bank needed to do to rebut it was to ensure that D received independent legal advice. This it had done. It was not obliged to make further inquiries into the affairs of D and M. To do so would have been an 'unwarrantable impertinence'.[97] Nor did the phone call from D's solicitor put the bank on notice. It merely showed that D had been advised against the transaction, but, despite that advice, had decided to proceed. She was entitled to reject the solicitor's advice, and it was not for the bank to refuse to allow her to enter into the arrangement.[98] The bank was therefore entitled to enforce the charge.

The reason for the difference in approach between this case and *Burch's* case seems to lie in two factors. One is that, in *Thomas*, there was little, if any, inequality in the relationship between the parties, whereas in *Burch,* the parties were employer–employee. Second, the agreement in *Burch* was viewed as much more unequivocally disadvantageous to the guarantor. The general trend of cases in this area is better represented, however, by *Thomas,* in that there has tended to be a reluctance to extend the effect of *O'Brien* in any way which might be seen as imposing unreasonable burdens on banks and other creditors. Provided that they take reasonable steps to insure that independent advice has been sought, the courts will be reluctant to intervene. That trend has been continued in the guidelines set out by the House of Lords in *Royal Bank of Scotland v Etridge (No 2)*, and discussed below.

---

96 [1997] 1 All ER 46.
97 Ibid, p 55.
98 Compare Lord Nicholls in *Royal Bank of Scotland plc v Etridge (No 2)* [2001] UKHL 44, para 61; [2001] 4 All ER 449, p 469: 'A wife is not to be precluded from entering into a financially unwise transaction if, for her own reasons, she wishes to do so.'

A final issue was left unresolved in *Thomas*. There was in that case no legal transaction to which M, the alleged influencer, was a party. He was not a party to the guarantee, nor did he sign the charge. Sir Richard Scott VC thought that this should make no difference to the application of the principles in this area. Roch LJ, however, preferred to reserve the question for later decision, and Potter LJ expressed no view. As Sir Richard Scott pointed out, however, provided that the creditor has actual or constructive notice of misrepresentation or undue influence, there seems little justification for making a difference in outcome dependent on whether or not the debtor happens to be a party to a transaction with the creditor.

13.7.10 Practical consequences: *Royal Bank of Scotland v Etridge (No 2)*

At the start of his speech, Lord Bingham (in *Etridge*) referred to the social and economic context in which cases of this type operate. The general policy of striking the balance between the protection of the guarantor on the one hand, and the creditor on the other, clearly informs the approach taken by the rest of the House to setting out the practical guidelines which should govern the practice of creditors and legal advisers. Lord Bingham put it in these terms:[99]

> The transactions which give rise to these appeals are commonplace but of great social and economic importance. It is important that a wife (or anyone in like position) should not charge her interest in the matrimonial home to secure the borrowing of her husband (or anyone in a like position) without fully understanding the nature and effect of the proposed transaction and that the decision is hers, to agree or not to agree. It is important that lenders should feel able to advance money, in run-of-the-mill cases with no abnormal features, on the security of the wife's interest in the matrimonial home in reasonable confidence that, if appropriate procedures have been followed in obtaining the security, it will be enforceable if the need for enforcement arises. The law must afford both parties a measure of protection. It cannot prescribe a code which will be proof against error, misunderstanding or mishap. But it can indicate minimum requirements which, if met, will reduce the risk of error, misunderstanding or mishap to an acceptable level. The paramount need in this field is that these minimum requirements should be clear, simple and practically operable.

The practical steps which banks should take in situations of this type in order to try to achieve Lord Bingham's objectives were considered in some detail by three members of the House of Lords in *Etridge* – Lord Nicholls, Lord Hobhouse and Lord Scott. There are some differences in their approaches, but the speech of Lord Nicholls was approved by the two other members of the court (Lord Bingham and Lord Clyde), and what follows is based on his guidelines.

---

99 [2001] UKHL 44, para 2; [2001] 4 All ER 449, p 456.

The first issue is to decide when a bank or other creditor is 'put on inquiry' that there may be a danger of undue influence or misrepresentation, so that steps need to be taken to ensure that the bank is not affected by any impropriety. There is no doubt that this will occur whenever a wife stands surety for her husband's debts. The difficulty is to decide which other relationships, assuming the bank is aware of them, will have the same effect. Should it only apply to sexual or family relationships, or those falling within the category where the law presumes influence? The Court of Appeal had already stepped outside these categories in the *Burch* case (employer–employee). Lord Nicholls considers the possibilities in paras 82–89 of his speech.[100] His conclusion is that 'there is no rational cut-off point with certain types of relationship being susceptible to the *O'Brien* principle and others not'.[101] Therefore, 'the only practical way forward is to regard banks as "put on inquiry" in every case where the relationship between the surety and the debtor is non-commercial'. The threshold is set at a low point,[102] but the burden on the bank is 'modest'.[103] It is right that the broader scope of the *O'Brien* principle indicated by the *Burch* decision should be developed into the more general principle of the bank being put on inquiry in all cases of a non-commercial surety. Such a principle is 'workable . . . simple, coherent and eminently desirable'.[104]

Once the bank is put on inquiry, what steps does it need to protect its position, so that it will not be affected by any impropriety on the part of the debtor? Lord Browne-Wilkinson in *O'Brien* had, as noted above, suggested that representatives of the bank should see the guarantor separately, and explain the transaction and its risks. Lord Nicholls recognises the understandable reluctance of banks to do this.[105] It runs the risk that there will later be allegations that oral assurances were given by the bank's representative to the effect, for example, that the bank would continue to support the business, or would not call in its loan. Lengthy litigation may well follow as to what exactly was said and when. Banks much prefer, therefore, that the transaction should be explained by an independent adviser, generally a solicitor.

Given that it is acceptable that banks should adopt this course, what steps should they take? Lord Nicholls identifies four stages in the process.[106] First, the bank must communicate directly with the wife to check who she wishes to use as a solicitor.[107] This

---

100 [2001] 4 All ER 44, pp 474–76.

101 Ibid, para 87; p 475.

102 Lord Hobhouse acknowledges this, but notes that it has the practical advantage 'that it assists banks to put in place procedures which do not require an exercise of judgment by their officials': ibid, para 108; p 484.

103 Ibid, para 87; p 476 (Lord Nicholls).

104 Ibid, para 89; p 476. Auchmuty (2005, pp 70–71) has argued that this approach tends to veil the significance of gender in the way in which undue influence arises in heterosexual relationships.

105 Ibid, para 55; p 468.

106 Ibid, para 79; p 473. As will be seen, the third stage will not apply in all cases.

107 Although these stages apply to any situation in which a creditor is put on inquiry, Lord Nicholls explains them in terms of a 'bank' and a 'wife' (the most common example), and that terminology is adopted here.

communication should indicate the reasons why the bank is encouraging her to take legal advice – that is, that she will not later be able to dispute that she is bound by the documents she has signed. She should also be told that the solicitor may be the same one as is acting for her husband in the transaction. The bank must not proceed with the transaction until the wife has responded to this communication. Second, once a solicitor has been nominated, the bank must provide that solicitor with the financial information necessary to enable the solicitor to advise the wife properly. To the extent that this involves information supplied to the bank in confidence by the husband, his permission will be required in order to disclose it. If that permission is not forthcoming, the bank should not proceed with the transaction. Third, if the bank has suspicions that the wife has been misled, or is not acting freely, these must be communicated to the wife's solicitor. Fourth, the bank will require from the wife's solicitor a written confirmation that the nature of the documents she is being asked to sign and the practical implications of them have been fully explained to her.

Three other issues need to be considered. First, why is it satisfactory for the solicitor to be acting for the husband and the wife (as indicated by stage one, above)? Second, what should the content of the solicitor's advice be? Third, if the solicitor does not carry out the responsibilities properly, what are the wife's remedies?

As to the common situation where the solicitor acts for both the husband and wife, Lord Nicholls considered the obvious arguments against this, such as the fact that the wife may be inhibited in dealing with a solicitor who is also acting for her husband, and that the wife's interests may, even unconsciously, rank lower in the solicitor's priorities than those of the husband, the 'primary' client.[108] He also considered the arguments in favour of just one solicitor being used, such as the reduction in costs, the fact that the wife may already know and be more comfortable with the 'family' solicitor as opposed to a stranger, and that a solicitor who has had previous dealings with the family may be better placed to give advice.[109] His conclusion was that 'the latter factors are more weighty than the former', and that therefore there should be no bar to the wife's legal adviser being the same person as the husband's.[110] The wife is, of course, free to choose another solicitor, and the husband's solicitor will need to think carefully as to whether there is any conflict of interest which would mean that the wife should be advised by someone else.[111] If, however, the husband's solicitor does act for the wife, then in advising her, the solicitor is acting *for her alone*. This brings us to the second question: what should be the content of the solicitor's advice?

Lord Nicholls goes into some detail on this issue, because of his view that 'the quality of the legal advice is the most disturbing feature' of some of the appeals before

108 [2001] UKHL 44, para 72; [2001] 4 All ER 449, p 471.
109 Ibid, para 73; p 471.
110 Ibid, para 74, p 471.
111 The solicitor should also withdraw if, having agreed to act for the wife, it subsequently becomes clear that there is a real risk of any advice being inhibited by a conflict of interest or duty: ibid.

the House in *Etridge*.[112] What he has to say applies whether the solicitor is acting for both husband and wife, or solely for the wife. The solicitor must initially explain why the giving of advice is necessary, that is, primarily to provide protection for the bank, and confirm that the wife wishes the solicitor to act for her.

Assuming that the wife wishes the solicitor to act for her, there must be a face to face meeting between the solicitor and the wife in the absence of the husband. The solicitor should explain the transaction and its implications in 'suitably non-technical language'.[113] The 'core minimum' of the solicitor's advice in performing this task is summarised by Lord Nicholls in four points.[114]

(a)   The nature of the documents the wife is being asked to sign must be explained, together with their consequences, such as the risk of the loss of the matrimonial home.

(b)   The seriousness of the risks must be pointed out. This will include discussion of the purpose of the proposed facility, and the sums involved, including the amount of the wife's liability. The solicitor must discuss the wife's financial means, and ensure that she understands the value of the property being made subject to charge. The possibility of the facility being increased without reference to the wife should be dealt with. The question of whether either the husband or wife has other assets which might be used to make repayments, should the business fail, should be explored. All of these factors relate to the seriousness of the risks.

(c)   The solicitor should make it clear that the decision to give the guarantee or not is the wife's and hers alone.

(d)   The solicitor should check that the wife wishes to proceed. She should be asked whether she wishes the solicitor to negotiate further on her behalf, or whether she is content for the solicitor to write to the bank confirming that he has explained the documents and their practical consequences to her. The solicitor must not give any confirmation to the bank without the wife's specific authority.

These guidelines focus on ensuring that the wife is fully informed of the nature of the transaction into which she is entering. Lord Hobhouse, however, while agreeing with Lord Nicholls' 'core minimum', emphasises that 'comprehension' does not mean the same thing as 'lack of undue influence':[115]

Comprehension is essential for any legal documents of this complexity and obscurity. But for the purpose of negativing undue influence it is necessary to be satisfied that the agreement was, also, given freely in knowledge of the true facts. It must be remembered that the equitable doctrine of undue influence has been

---

112 The case involved eight conjoined appeals.
113 [2001] UKHL 44, para 66; [2001] 4 All ER 449, p 470.
114 Ibid, para 65; p 470.
115 Ibid, para 111; p 485.

created for the protection of those who are *sui juris* and competent to undertake legal obligations but are nevertheless vulnerable and liable to have their will unduly influenced. It is their weakness that is being protected, not their inability to comprehend.

Lord Hobhouse was satisfied that Lord Nicholls' guidelines are sufficient to provide the necessary protection. He disagreed, however, with what he saw as being the view of Lord Scott, that belief on the part of a lender that the wife has understood the nature and effect of the transaction is sufficient to exonerate the lender.[116]

The final issue considered by Lord Nicholls is the position where the solicitor has failed to act in accordance with guidelines, and the wife is thereby prejudiced. Counsel for some of the wives involved in the cases in *Etridge* argued that the bank should take responsibility for the solicitor's failures, as if the solicitor were acting as an agent for the bank. Lord Nicholls rejected this. Provided that the bank has acted as outlined by Lord Nicholls, and has received a certificate from the solicitor confirming that the wife has been advised as required, this should be sufficient to protect the bank.[117] Only in the exceptional case where the bank for some reason has cause to suspect that the wife has not properly been advised will it lose its protection. Otherwise, the wife who has not been advised properly will be left to her remedy in damages against the solicitor for negligent performance of their contract, or for the tort of professional negligence.

The procedures set out in this case by which the banks can obtain protection apply to all surety transactions entered into in the future. For those which were entered into previously, the bank will ordinarily be protected if a solicitor acting for the wife has confirmed that the wife has had brought home to her the risks she was running, even if the precise steps set out in *Etridge* have not been followed.[118] In either case, it cannot be said that any onerous burden is being placed on the banks or other creditors. It is clear that the major banks have for some time had internal procedures designed to take account of the risks involved in this type of transaction, and to try to ensure that wives or other vulnerable parties are properly advised.[119] The continuing flow of cases indicates, however, either that these procedures are not being applied properly, or that they (and by implication those suggested in *Etridge*) are inadequate to deal with the social problem raised by the issue of homes being used as security for business debts.[120] The approach of the courts, despite *O'Brien* being seen as a victory for wives, is heavily balanced in favour of the creditor, as is indicated by the fact that only one of the

---

116 [2001] 4 All ER 449, p 470.

117 Ibid, paras 75–78; pp 472–73.

118 Ibid, para 80; p 474.

119 See, for example, the procedures of the National Westminster Bank set out by Lord Hobhouse in *Etridge*: ibid, paras 117–18; pp 488–89, and in use from at least 1988. As Lord Hobhouse points out, these go further than the requirements set out by Lord Nicholls.

120 For a useful discussion of these and related issues from a feminist perspective, see Auchmuty, 2005. She argues for a greater recognition of the role of gender as an element in the way in which undue influence occurs in heterosexual relationships.

appeals in *Etridge* which involved the substantive issue of whether the wife could escape the effect of the transaction went in favour of the wife.[121] It is not clear that the House of Lords has yet managed to find a satisfactory balance between the need to protect those vulnerable to undue influence, and the need to ensure that banks and other financial institutions remain willing to lend money to small businesses in situations where domestic property may provide the only realistic security.

FOR THOUGHT

Have the courts really taken on board the problem for a proposed surety, who is expecting to continue to live with the debtor, in refusing to provide a guarantee? Even if the surety has received independent advice, taking a decision which will be likely to lead to the collapse of the debtor's business will be very difficult, and will inevitably impose severe strains on the relationship. It is hard to see the decision as ever being 'free': on the other hand, it would clearly be unacceptable if all such transactions could be set aside at the choice of the surety. Where should the balance be struck? Is the law still too favourable to the creditor and debtor?

13.8 REMEDIES FOR UNDUE INFLUENCE

The primary remedy for undue influence in cases such as those discussed in the previous section is the refusal of the courts to enforce the agreement against the person influenced. In other words, that person will often be in the position of defendant, and will use the alleged influence to escape from obligations.

In some cases, however, rescission may be sought,[122] and the usual limitations on this remedy (such as lapse of time, involvement of third party rights, and impossibility of restitution) will apply.[123]

Where rescission is ordered, the whole transaction will be set aside.[124] In *TSB*

---

121 That is, *Bank of Scotland v Bennett*. In that case the appeal succeeded because the bank had failed to give the full information relevant to the transaction to the solicitor who advised the wife. Some of the appeals involved cases where the action had been struck out before trial: here the Court of Appeal was inclined to the view that there should be a full hearing, without expressing any view on the merits of the wife's claim.

122 As, for example, in *Allcard v Skinner* (1887) 36 Ch D 145.

123 As with misrepresentation – see Chapter 10, 10.4.1.

124 The position may be different where there are two distinct parts to the transaction in relation to only one of which there is a finding of undue influence: *Barclays Bank plc v Caplan* [1998] FLR 532. Here C had been properly advised in relation to an original charge and guarantee, but not in relation to a subsequent side letter extending the guarantee.

Bank plc v Camfield,[125] the creditor tried to argue that even if it had constructive notice of the debtor's misrepresentation of the extent of the transaction to his wife, the wife had been prepared to undertake some risk. In this case, she had been willing to go ahead with a transaction which put the matrimonial home at risk to the extent of £15,000, whereas in fact liability was unlimited. The bank argued that she should still be liable for £15,000. The Court of Appeal rejected this. The test was what would the wife have done, had she known the truth? The answer was clearly that she would not have entered into the transaction at all. Therefore, the right result was for the whole transaction to be rescinded.

A slightly different situation arose in *Dunbar Bank plc v Nadeem*.[126] Here, the wife had not previously had any legal interest in the matrimonial home, which was held by her husband on a long lease. As part of a loan transaction, using the home as security, however, she acquired a beneficial interest in half of the property. When the husband defaulted on the loan repayments, the bank sought to enforce its charge over the property. The wife claimed undue influence. The trial judge held in her favour, but also ruled that simply setting aside the charge would leave her unjustly enriched, as she would have acquired an interest in the property without having to contribute to the purchase. He therefore made the rescission of the charge conditional on her repaying to the bank one half of the loan plus interest. The Court of Appeal held that this was not the correct approach. In fact, the Court of Appeal decided that the transaction should not be set aside at all, because it was not manifestly disadvantageous to the wife, and the husband had not taken any unfair advantage of her. But, if there had been undue influence, it was suggested (though of course this was *obiter*) that the correct approach would have been for the wife to give up her interest in the property (which would then have reverted to her husband). She would be released from any personal liability on the loans made to her husband, but would not have acquired any unfair benefit. Of course, this would mean that she would still not have been able to resist the bank's claim for possession of the property, which was her main objective.

13.8.1 Change in value of property

Where restitution is ordered, however, but the value of property has changed, it may be difficult to find the just result as to who should get what. This problem arose in *Cheese v Thomas*.[127] C, the plaintiff, and his great-nephew, T, the defendant, had bought a house for £83,000, C contributing £43,000, and T providing £40,000, by means of a mortgage for that amount. The house was in T's name, and C accepted that it would belong to T exclusively after C's death, but, in the meantime, it was agreed that C was to be entitled to have sole use of the house for the rest of his life. C became worried that T was not

---

125 [1995] 1 All ER 951.
126 [1998] 3 All ER 876.
127 [1994] 1 All ER 35.

keeping up the mortgage repayments, and sought to withdraw from the arrangement. The trial judge ruled that the agreement could be set aside for undue influence. The issue before the Court of Appeal was the amount of money that C should receive, since the house had been sold for £55,400, that is, a loss of over £27,500. Should he recover his full £43,000 or only, as the judge held, the appropriate proportion of the selling price? The Court of Appeal upheld the judge's view. The basic principle in applying a restitutionary remedy was that the parties were to be restored as closely as possible to the position they were in before the transaction was entered into. In general, if a claimant was able to return to the defendant property which had been transferred under the transaction, it did not matter that the property had meanwhile fallen in value. This case was different, however. The plaintiff had paid the defendant £43,000 not outright, but as part of a purchase price of a house in which both would have rights. Each had contributed a sum of money to buying a house in which each was to have an interest. In that situation, the appropriate course was for the loss in the value of the house to be shared. This was even more so where, as the judge had held, the personal conduct of the defendant was not open to criticism, in that he had acted as an 'innocent fiduciary', rather than in any morally reprehensible way.

This case was clearly a difficult one in which to do justice between the parties. It is not entirely convincing, however, on the need to depart from the basic principle of full restitution of cash paid for property, which would be the normal rule. It is not clear why the fact that the parties both had a continuing interest in the property should make such a difference. If the property had increased in value, would the plaintiff have been entitled to a share in that profit? The logical answer must be 'yes'.

13.8.2 Subsequent transactions

Where a contract is found to be voidable for undue influence, then a substitute transaction, particularly if entered into as a condition of discharging the first transaction, will be similarly voidable. This was the position in *Yorkshire Bank plc v Tinsley*.[128] A mortgage used to secure a husband's business debts was held to be voidable by the wife because of her husband's undue influence, of which the bank had constructive notice. When the husband and wife divorced, a substitute mortgage was entered into by the wife in relation to a smaller property, but the bank required the security for the business debts to continue to apply to this property. When the bank sought to enforce the security, it was held that the wife was entitled to avoid the mortgage on the basis of undue influence. This decision was confirmed by the Court of Appeal.

---

128 [2004] 3 All ER 463.

13.9 UNCONSCIONABILITY AND INEQUALITY OF BARGAINING POWER[129]

Does the approach of the courts to the issues of duress and undue influence simply reflect a general reluctance to enforce transactions which are so unfair as to be regarded as 'unconscionable'? Is this the underlying principle in these cases?

In *Lloyds Bank Ltd v Bundy,*[130] Lord Denning based his decision in favour of Mr Bundy on a broader principle than that adopted by the other members of the Court of Appeal. He identified this as 'inequality of bargaining power'. By virtue of this, he claimed:

> English law gives relief to one who, without independent advice, enters into a contract on terms which are very unfair or transfers property for a consideration which is grossly inadequate, when his bargaining power is grievously impaired by his own needs or desires, or by his own ignorance or infirmity, coupled with undue influences or pressure brought to bear on him by or for the benefit of the other.

As will be seen, this identifies, alongside the unequal bargaining power, the nature of the transaction, and its substantive fairness, as an important element in the decision to set an agreement aside. In contrast, the general approach towards undue influence and duress cases is that if the influence or duress is proved, the question of whether the transaction was beneficial to the influenced party is of no particular significance. Even in cases of presumed influence, the fact that the transaction is disadvantageous is, after the House of Lords' decision in *Royal Bank of Scotland plc v Etridge (No 2)*,[131] simply a matter of evidence which may lead to the need for an explanation, rather than being a specific element in the concept of undue influence. Lord Denning's statement therefore probably comes as close as any English judge has done to recognising a general principle of 'unconscionability'. His approach has not been followed, however, and indeed was specifically disapproved by Lord Scarman in *National Westminster Bank v Morgan*,[132] who felt that the fact that Parliament had intervened to deal with many situations of unequal bargaining power (for example, by the Consumer Credit Act 1974 and the Supply of Goods and Services Act 1982) meant that the courts should be reluctant to assume the burden of formulating further restrictions. The closest that the courts have come in the plethora of cases which have followed *Barclays Bank v O'Brien* to recognising 'unconscionability' as a ground for intervention is in *Credit Lyonnais*

---

129 For a compact and useful survey of the English approach to this area, see Brownsword, 2000, Chapter 3.
130 [1975] QB 326; [1974] 3 All ER 757.
131 [2001] UKHL 44; [2001] 4 All ER 449.
132 [1985] AC 686; [1985] 1 All ER 821. He took a similar line in *Pao On v Lau Yiu Long* [1980] AC 614; [1979] 3 All ER 65.

Bank Nederland NV v Burch. [133] Though this case and, in particular, the judgment of Millett LJ can be seen as giving some support to an approach similar to that taken by Lord Denning in *Lloyds Bank v Bundy*, the case can also be fitted within the orthodox general principles applying to undue influence, and it has not led to any significant change of direction in later cases.

The English law relating to both duress and undue influence is still, therefore, primarily concerned with procedural rather than substantive fairness. [134] Unconscionability would require it to focus more directly on the nature of the contract itself, rather than the events which led to it being formed. Moreover, the intervention has been piecemeal, dealing with situations of fraud, duress and undue influence separately, rather than as part of an overall principle. [135] A further example is the principle applied in *Cresswell v Potter.* [136] In this case the court applied a power used by the Chancery courts in the nineteenth century to set aside a transaction 'where a purchase is made from a poor and ignorant man at a considerable undervalue, the vendor having no independent advice'. [137] In *Cresswell v Potter*, Megarry J took 'poor' to mean 'a member of the lower income group' and 'ignorant' to mean 'less highly educated'. The plaintiff in the case was a telephonist, with little understanding of conveyancing transactions and documentation, and was found by the judge to meet the relevant criteria. She had received no independent advice. Her conveyance to her husband, who had left her, of her half-share in the matrimonial home, in exchange for her release from liability under the mortgage, [138] was set aside. There has, however, been little use of this principle, [139] and it cannot be said to afford more than an exceptional additional ground for setting a transaction aside on grounds of unconscionability. [140]

133 [1997] 1 All ER 144, discussed above at 13.5. See, in particular, the judgment of Nourse LJ.

134 Note, however, that Atiyah disputes that a distinction of this kind can be drawn with any degree of clarity: Atiyah, 1995, pp 284–89; Atiyah, 1986, Chapter 11, pp 333–34.

135 Though it might be suggested that the comments of Lord Hobhouse in *Etridge (No 2)*, para 103; p 481, and by the Court of Appeal in *UCB Corporate Services Ltd v Williams* [2002] EWCA Civ 555; [2002] 3 FCR 448, para 86, as to the overlap between the concepts is a step towards recognising a unifying general principle.

136 [1978] 1 WLR 255.

137 *Fry v Lane* (1888) 40 Ch D 312, per Kay J.

138 Which, in practice, was of little value to her, unless the value of the house declined to below that of the mortgage. At the time this was highly unlikely – though there have been occasions since when the concept of 'negative equity' would have meant that the release would have been of more value.

139 See, for example, *Backhouse v Backhouse* [1978] 1 All ER 1158 (considered but not applied) and *Watkin v Watson-Smith* (1986) *The Times*, 3 July.

140 But note the comments of Nourse LJ in *Credit Lyonnais Bank Nederland NV v Burch* [1997] 1 All ER 144, p 151, where he suggests that the *Fry v Lane* principle, as applied in *Cresswell v Potter* and considered in *Backhouse v Backhouse*, indicates the possibility of a general equitable power to set aside unconscionable bargains.

FOR THOUGHT

If the *Cresswell v Potter* approach is to be used, what level of education will be relevant? Will it only apply, for example, to those who have left school at the earliest opportunity and without any qualifications? Or is it a subjective test of the level of understanding of the particular transaction in question which is relevant?

Other jurisdictions have adopted a broader approach. In Australia, for example, the decision of the High Court in *Commercial Bank of Australia Ltd v Amadio*[141] formulated a principle of unconscionability on very similar lines to those suggested by Lord Denning in *Lloyds Bank v Bundy*, and this has been followed in later cases.[142] A similar approach has been adopted in Canada.[143] As Harland has pointed out, however, the *Amadio* approach is at least as much concerned with procedural as substantive unconscionability.[144] By contrast, s 2–302 of the United States Universal Commercial Code states:

> If the court as a matter of law finds the contract or any clause of the contract to have been unconscionable at the time it was made the court may refuse to enforce the contract, or it may enforce the remainder of the contract without the unconscionable clause, or it may so limit the application of any unconscionable clause as to avoid any unconscionable result.

This very broadly-worded provision has been used to deal with situations of both procedural and substantive unfairness.[145] The only provisions in any way comparable in English law, allowing courts to set a contract, or part of a contract, aside because its provisions are 'unfair' or 'unconscionable' operate only in much more limited areas or situations. Under the common law, there are, for example, powers to strike down clauses which are in unreasonable restraint of trade, or 'penalty' clauses, and these are dealt with in later chapters.[146] Under statute, there are specific provisions to deal with 'extortionate credit bargains' under the Consumer Credit Act 1974.[147] There are also

---

141 (1983) 151 CLR 447 – discussed in some detail in Harland, 1999.

142 For example, *Baburin v Baburin* [1991] 2 Qd R 240; *Louth v Diprose* (1992) 175 CLR 621; *Familiar Pty Ltd v Samarkos* (1994) 115 FLR 443; *Begbie v State Bank of New South Wales* (1994) ATPR 41–288 – all cited in Harland, 1999.

143 See Enman, 1987.

144 Harland, 1999, p 259 – he also notes, however, the view of Chen-Wishart to the effect that the judges are in reality more concerned with substantive factors than they have generally articulated: Chen-Wishart, 1989, pp 104–09.

145 See, for example, the discussion in McLaughlin, 1992. The section applies only to 'transactions' in goods, but the Second Restatement, s 208, provides a model provision in similar terms for application to any contract.

146 Restraint of trade in Chapter 15, and penalty clauses in Chapter 18.

147 Sections 137–139.

the provisions of the Unfair Contract Terms Act 1977 and the Unfair Terms in Consumer Contracts Regulations 1999, which have been discussed in Chapter 9. The UCTA 1977, however, is primarily concerned with clauses limiting liability. While the UTCCR 1999 have wider scope, they only apply to consumer contracts, and do not affect situations where what is involved is a 'bad bargain' – which may have the effect of excluding many situations of possible 'unconscionability'.[148] As we have seen, for example, the principle applied in *Cresswell v Potter* was designed to deal with sales at an undervalue. That aspect of the contract would be outside the scope of the fairness provisions of the regulations.

One of the objections to any broad principle allowing contracts to be set aside on the basis of substantive 'unconscionability' is the uncertainty that might result.[149] Apart from anything else, it is not easy to determine whether a particular contract is fair or not simply by looking at its provisions.[150] The transaction will operate within a context, and perhaps a long-term relationship, which may mean that an exchange which appears lopsided may, in fact, be based on a rational balancing which takes account of other aspects of the parties' dealings with each other. Add to this the difficulty of obtaining a uniform application of standards of fairness between different judges and different courts, and it is easy to see why English law has shied away from general provisions addressing substantive unfairness in favour of rules governing procedural impropriety. Where substantive unfairness is addressed, it is generally in relation to clauses or contracts of a particular type, with the decision being taken within a limiting statutory framework.[151] It is to be expected that this will continue to be the English approach. Any more general move towards control of unconscionability based on substantive unfairness is only likely as a result of a movement in this direction by European law.

With this in mind we turn, finally, to the proposals for this area contained in the Principles of European Law.

13.10 UNDUE INFLUENCE, UNCONSCIONABILITY AND THE PRINCIPLES OF EUROPEAN CONTRACT LAW

The Article dealing with this area is 4:109, which is headed 'Excessive Benefit or Unfair Advantage'. It gives a power to avoid a contract where two conditions are satisfied. The

---

148 See reg 6(2), and the discussion in Chapter 9, 9.8.
149 This was one of the reasons for Lord Scarman's rejection of a general doctrine of inequality of bargaining power in *Pao On v Lau Yiu Long* [1980] AC 614, p 634.
150 See the comments of Collins to this effect: Collins, 1999, p 258 onwards – 'The Illusion of Unfairness'. See also Atiyah, 1986, Chapter 11.
151 Collins (1999, p 286) on the other hand, concludes his consideration of this area by expressing the view that 'The open textured rules devised by private law appear to be the most adept at handling the complex issues which [regulating substantive unfairness in contracts] raises, though there is certainly room for specific regulation in particular market sectors . . .'

first of these relates to the position of the party wishing to set the contract aside. This party must either be dependent on or have a relationship of trust with the other party; or be in economic distress; or have urgent needs; or be improvident, ignorant, inexperienced or lacking in bargaining skill. It will be seen that this covers the situations which English law deals with as giving rise to 'undue influence' and those which fall within the *Fry v Lane* principle, as applied in *Cresswell v Potter*.[152] It goes further, however, in including situations of 'economic distress' or 'urgent need'. The kind of situation intended to be covered by urgent need is where a relative of a person injured abroad pays an excessive price for the person to be taken to hospital.[153] No example is given of 'economic distress', but it would presumably apply where a person in desperate need of cash sold property at a gross undervalue.[154]

The second condition relates to the party who is alleged to have taken an unfair advantage or unfair benefit. The requirement is that that party knows, or ought to know, of the situation of the other party falling within the first condition, and takes advantage of that situation in a way which is grossly unfair, or takes an excessive benefit.

The approach is, therefore, as under English law, what was described at the start of this chapter as 'defendant-focused'. It has to be shown that there was some 'wrongdoing' by the defendant, in terms of taking advantage of the other party's situation, before the contract may be set aside. The unfairness may come from the circumstances, however, rather than from the terms of the contract itself. The example is given of a woman living with her many children in a large but dilapidated house being persuaded to sell it for its market price when it would be impossible to find somewhere else to accommodate her family for what is paid.[155] English law would only intervene in such a situation where the undue influence was very clearly established.[156]

The approach taken in the Principles is fairly similar to that under English law, and certainly does not amount to a broad general power to avoid contracts for unconscionability.

As far as remedies are concerned, however, the Principles do go beyond what is available under English law. Paragraph 2 of the Article enables the claimant to seek to have the contract modified in line with the requirements of good faith and fair dealing, as an alternative to its being set aside. Moreover, where the claimant has given notice of avoidance, para 3 gives the court a similar power to modify the contract at the request of the *defendant*, provided the request to do so is made before the claimant has acted on the notice of avoidance.

---

152 That is, protection for the 'poor and ignorant' in relation to sales at an undervalue.

153 Lando and Beale, 2000, p 262, illustration 3.

154 It might also apply in a situation such as that in *D and C Builders v Rees* [1966] 2 QB 617; [1965] 3 All ER 837 – see Chapter 3, 3.12.4.

155 Lando and Beale, 2000, p 263, illustration 5.

156 Following *CIBC Mortgages Ltd v Pitt,* the transaction does not have to be to the disadvantage of the claimant where actual undue influence is proved.

In addition, as with 'duress',[157] Art 4:117 gives the claimant the power to recover reliance interest damages in place of or in addition to rescission of the contract. The remedies provided for by the Principles are therefore much more extensive and flexible than those available under English law.

13.11 FURTHER READING

Auchmuty, R, 'The Rhetoric of Equality and the Problem of Heterosexuality', Chapter 3 in Mulcahy, L and Wheeler, S (eds), *Feminist Perspectives on Contract Law*, 2005, London: Glasshouse Press

Birks, P, and Chin Nyuk Yin, 'On the nature of undue influence' (1995), Chapter 3 in Beatson, J and Friedmann, D (eds), *Good Faith and Fault in Contract Law,* 1995, Oxford: Clarendon Press

Cope, M, *Duress, Undue Influence and Unconscientious Bargains,* 1985, North Ryde, NSW: Lawbook Co

Brownsword, R, *Contract Law: Themes for the Twenty-First Century,* 2000, London: Butterworths, Chapter 3

Chen-Wishart, M, 'The *O'Brien* principle and substantive unfairness' (1997) 56 CLJ 60

Chen-Wishart, M, *Unconscionable Bargains,* 1989, Wellington: Butterworths

Cretney, S, 'The little woman and the big bad bank' (1992) 108 LQR 534

Enman, SR, 'Doctrines of unconscionability in England, Canada and the Commonwealth' (1987) 16 Anglo-Am LR 191

Harland, D, 'Unconscionable and unfair contracts: an Australian perspective', Chapter 11 in Brownsword, R, Hird, NJ and Howells, G (eds), *Good Faith in Contract,* 1999, Aldershot: Dartmouth

McLaughlin, G, 'Unconscionability and impracticality: reflections on two UCC indeterminacy principles' (1992) Loyola Int & Comp LJ 439

O'Sullivan, D, 'Developing *O'Brien*' (2002) 118 LQR 337

Tijo, H, '*O'Brien* and unconscionability' (1997) 113 LQR 10

157 See Chapter 12, 12.6.

14 ILLEGALITY AND PUBLIC POLICY

CONTENTS

14.1 OVERVIEW

This chapter deals with situations where otherwise valid contracts are unenforceable because they are deemed to involve 'illegality', or are otherwise contrary to public policy. The following issues are discussed:

- The reasons why illegal contracts are unenforceable. 'Public policy' is the central issue – but underlying reasons involve 'deterrence' and maintaining the integrity of the legal process (that is, not allowing it to be used to enforce illegal arrangements).
- Categories of illegality:
  - Contracts to commit crimes or torts. These are always illegal.
  - Contracts contrary to professional regulations (for example, Solicitors' Practice Rules). These will not be enforceable, but a party may be able to claim for work actually done.
  - Contracts where performance involves the breach of a statute. This is the most difficult area – the act itself is legal, but the manner of performance is not. The purpose of the statute and the knowledge of the parties will be relevant to the issue of enforceability.
  - Contracts to indemnify a person for breaking the law. This is not allowed in relation to criminal liability or intentional torts, but is permitted in relation to negligence.
- Effects of illegality. Two aspects need consideration:
  - Enforcement. Specific performance will not be available, but a legal right related to an illegal transaction may be enforceable if the party does not need to rely on the illegal act to found the claim.
  - Recovery of money or property. Generally no recovery is possible, but it may be allowed where:
    - the illegal purpose has not been carried out – a party is allowed time for a change of mind in relation to the illegal transaction;
    - the contract results from 'oppression';
    - there is no reliance on the illegal transaction;
    - the claimant is a member of the class which the statute concerned is intended to protect.
- Agreements contrary to public policy (but not illegal). In this category fall:
  - Contracts related to marriage – for example:
    - for future separation (pre-nuptial agreements are currently caught by this);
    - imposing a liability if a person marries;
    - receiving payment for arranging a marriage.
  - Contracts promoting sexual immorality. There are old cases supporting this category but it may well be obsolete in the modern law.
  - Contracts to oust the jurisdiction of the courts. The parties may agree

that matters of fact may be determined by other processes (for example, arbitration) but the courts will always retain a residual jurisdiction over matters of law.

- ☐ Contracts involving a breach of human rights. It is not clear yet whether the courts will be prepared to treat contracts which conflict with Human Rights Act obligations as unenforceable on public policy grounds.
- ■ Effects of agreements contrary to public policy:
  - ☐ no specific performance;
  - ☐ property transferred can probably be recovered.
- ■ Wagering contracts. These have been unenforceable as a result of statutory controls, but the controls have been removed by the Gambling Act 2005. Wagers will now be enforceable.

14.2 INTRODUCTION

This chapter and the next one ('Contracts in Restraint of Trade') are, like the previous two, concerned with situations where the courts will intervene to prevent the enforcement of an agreement which, on its face, has all the characteristics of a binding contract. Both are often put under the general heading of 'illegality';[1] they might also be grouped as 'contracts contrary to public policy'.[2] There are, therefore, links between these areas. It is felt, however, that they are sufficiently distinct to warrant treatment in separate chapters. There will inevitably be overlaps, and some need to cross-refer, particularly in relation to remedies. The division is simply intended to clarify the discussion of the two areas; it should not be regarded as necessarily reflecting a rigid separation adopted by the courts, or as a denial that there may be significant conceptual links between topics.

The focus in this chapter is on two types of contract. First, it looks at those which are 'illegal' in the sense that they involve the commission of a legal wrong – principally, a crime or a tort. This is an area which, even under the classical law of contract, was an accepted limitation on freedom of contract. The second part of the chapter looks at contracts which, while not illegal, are held to be unenforceable because they are for other reasons contrary to public policy.

---

1 See, for example, Treitel, 2003, Chapter 11.
2 'Public policy' is, of course, a difficult concept to pin down – as recognised by Burroughs J's famous reference to its being an 'unruly horse': *Richardson v Mellish* (1824) 2 Bing 229, p 252. It is possible to argue that the whole of the law of contract is simply a reflection of 'public policy' concerns about the regulation of transactions. Even a policy of encouraging market freedom is in itself a 'public policy'.

14.3 RATIONALE FOR THE UNENFORCEABILITY OF ILLEGAL CONTRACTS

The reasons why the courts interfere to render contracts which are 'illegal' unenforceable, as opposed to simply leaving those who have committed a crime or a tort to the relevant procedures under those areas of law, are not often explicitly stated, other than to say that it is a matter of 'public policy'. It follows, however, from the fact that 'public policy' is the central focus, that the issue of illegality may be raised by the court of its own motion, without it needing to be pleaded by either party.[3] The law is not primarily concerned here with the protection of one party, as it is in the areas of duress or undue influence, for example, but with more general concerns of the proper scope of the law of contract and its associated remedies.

Two commentators, Atiyah and Enonchong, have attempted to explore the more specific policies which underlie the law in this area.[4] Both suggest that there are two main reasons for the law's intervention. The first is that of deterrence.[5] The law reaffirms the approach taken by the criminal law or tort, and does not allow a person to benefit in any way from 'illegal' behaviour.[6] As Atiyah points out, the use of unenforceability may be a greater deterrent than the threat of criminal prosecution. In the area of consumer credit, for example, to make a large company liable to relatively small fines for failing to follow correct procedures in dealing with consumers may be less coercive than making the credit contracts unenforceable. This policy does not fully explain, however, why illegal contracts are in some circumstances unenforceable even by innocent parties. A person who does not realise that he or she is infringing the law by the making or performance of a contract cannot be deterred from doing so by making the transaction unenforceable.

A second suggested policy is more general. This is described by Enonchong as protecting 'the integrity of the judicial system by ensuring that the courts are not seen by law-abiding members of the community to be lending their assistance to claimants who have defied the law'.[7] Atiyah calls it 'the undesirability of jeopardising the dignity of the courts'.[8] This means that the courts do not wish to be seen to be involved in the

---

3 *North-Western Salt Co Ltd v Electrolytic Alkali Co Ltd* [1914] AC 461 (HL); *Edler v Auerbach* [1950] 1 KB 359 (HC); *Birkett v Acorn Business Machines Ltd* (1999) *The Times*, 26 August (CA).

4 See Atiyah, 1995, pp 342–44; Enonchong, 1998, Chapter 1, especially pp 14–20; cf also Law Commission, Consultation Paper No 154, 1999, Part VI.

5 To this Atiyah links the punishment of the 'offender'.

6 Enonchong quotes the Lord Chancellor in *Amicable Insurance Society v Bolland* (1830) 4 Bligh (NS) 194, p 211, as saying that to allow the assignees of an insurance policy on the life of a forger who had been executed for his crimes to recover under the policy would 'take away one of those restraints operating on the minds of men against the commission of crimes'.

7 Enonchong, 1998, p 17.

8 Atiyah, 1995, p 343. Atiyah also identifies a third possible policy, that is 'the desirability of bringing an illegal or undesirable state of affairs to an end'. His example (a landlord wishing to evict a prostitute), however, seems more closely linked to the contracts dealt with in the second part of this chapter (14.11 onwards) and this policy will therefore be left for consideration at that point.

enforcement of transactions with an 'illegal' element, since this will bring the legal process into disrepute. This provides more of a justification for refusing to assist even 'innocent' claimants in relation to 'illegal' contracts. Nevertheless, as Enonchong points out, both of the above reasons for not enforcing illegal contracts can run into conflict with the desirability of preventing injustice to a claimant or a windfall gain by a defendant. He suggests that the law has attempted to 'steer a middle course' but that, because it has developed by a process of accretion, there have been conflicts, often unacknowledged, between the above policies. The result of this 'has been a baffling entanglement of rules which when brought together are, like the common law itself, "more a muddle than a system" '.[9]

The confusion arises most clearly in relation to the question of the consequences of illegality, to which we shall return at the end of this chapter. For the moment, it is sufficient to note that the dominant reasons for making a contract 'illegal' are those of 'deterrence' and 'maintaining the respect of the civil justice system'.[10] If the categorisation of a contract as illegal appears to serve neither of these policies, we may legitimately question whether the categorisation is justifiable.

14.4 CATEGORIES OF ILLEGALITY

There are two main categories of illegal contract. First, there are those contracts where the agreement itself is forbidden by law (because, for example, it amounts to a criminal offence). Second, there are contracts which become illegal because of the way in which they are *performed*; generally this arises where the method of performance contravenes a statute. There is a third, subsidiary category of contracts to indemnify a person for the consequences of unlawful behaviour, which will be discussed separately.

14.4.1 Contracts which constitute a criminal offence

In some circumstances, the making of the contract itself will be a criminal act. The most obvious example is an agreement to commit a crime, such as murder or theft. If A asks B to kill C for a payment of £5,000, and B agrees, then their agreement has all the characteristics of a binding contract in the form of offer, acceptance and consideration. It also amounts to the criminal offence of conspiracy to murder (under the Criminal Law Act 1977), and so will be unenforceable. Any agreement to commit any crime will also be a criminal conspiracy, and treated in the same way. In addition, the

---

9 Enonchong, 1998, p 20, quoting Simpson, 1973, p 99.

10 The Law Commission has suggested two additional policies behind the illegality rules: (1) that no person should benefit from their own wrongdoing; and (2) punishment of the wrongdoer: Consultation Paper No 154, 1999, Part VI. Neither of these, however, explains why an innocent party is not allowed to enforce an illegal contract.

Criminal Law Act 1977 preserves the common law offence of 'conspiracy to defraud'.[11] In this case the fraudulent behaviour which is agreed need not amount to a criminal offence.

Certain contracts are made illegal by statute. Under the Obscene Publications Act 1959, for example, it is illegal to sell an 'obscene article'. Here (unlike conspiracy), the offence is only committed by one party (that is, the seller), but nevertheless the contract is illegal and will be unenforceable by either party.

14.4.2 Contracts forbidden though not criminal

It has recently been confirmed in two reported cases that a contract which is forbidden by delegated legislation, in the form of the rules of a professional body, should be treated as an illegal contract, even though the behaviour amounts at most to a disciplinary offence under the rules of that body, rather than being criminal.

Both cases concerned the Solicitors' Practice Rules 1990, made by the Law Society under s 31 of the Solicitors Act 1974. In the first case, *Mohamed v Alaga*,[12] the defendant solicitor was engaged in asylum work. The claimant was a member of the Somali community who alleged that the defendant had agreed to pay him a share of the solicitor's fees in return for introducing asylum-seeking clients and assisting in translation work. The sharing of fees was prohibited by the Solicitors' Rules, and when the claimant sued to recover what he alleged he was owed, he was met by the defence that the agreement, even if made,[13] was illegal and unenforceable. This argument was accepted by the Court of Appeal.[14]

The second case was *Awwad v Geraghty & Co.*[15] In this case the agreement was one whereby the solicitor agreed to act on a 'conditional fee' basis. This meant that the solicitor would be entitled to a higher fee if the action was successful. After the action had been settled, the solicitor sent a bill calculated at the lower rate (because the action had been settled, rather than successfully litigated), but the client refused to pay even this amount. When the solicitor sued, the client claimed that the whole agreement was illegal, as being contrary to the Solicitors' Practice Rules,[16] and was therefore

---

11 Criminal Law Act 1977, s 5, which also purports to preserve the common law offences of conspiracy to corrupt public morals or outrage public decency. Subsequent case law has, however, confirmed that 'corrupting public morals' and 'outraging public decency' are themselves substantive offences: agreements to commit them therefore amount to statutory conspiracies under s 1 of the 1977 Act, without the need for the common law offence preserved by s 5. See *R v Gibson* [1991] 1 All ER 441.

12 [1999] 3 All ER 699.

13 Which the solicitor disputed.

14 The claimant was allowed, however, to recover for the translating work which had been done on a *quantum meruit* basis: this is discussed further at 14.6, below.

15 [2000] 1 All ER 608.

16 The position as regards conditional fees has now been altered as a consequence of the Access to Justice Act 1999, so that they are now lawful in certain circumstances.

unenforceable. The Court of Appeal agreed with this analysis, and held in favour of the client.[17]

14.4.3 Contract to commit a tort

A contract to commit an intentional tort, such as assault or fraud, will be illegal in the same way as a contract to commit a crime.[18] On the other hand, it seems that a contract which involves the unintentional commission of a tort will not generally be illegal.[19] If, for example, there is a contract for the sale of property which belongs to a third party, but which both the buyer and seller believe to belong to the seller, this will involve the tort of conversion, but the contract itself will not be illegal.[20] Where only one party is innocent, it is possible that that party will be allowed to enforce the contract, though the position is uncertain.[21] There are *dicta* in *Clay v Yates*[22] that can be read to suggest that this is the case, but the point was not directly in issue and was not specifically addressed.[23]

What about a contract which would involve the commission of a 'statutory tort' under the Sex Discrimination Act 1975, the Race Relations Act 1976 or the Disability Discrimination Act 1995, in that it would involve unlawful discrimination on grounds of sex, race or disability?[24] This might occur, for example, if an employer required an agency supplying temporary staff not to send candidates of a particular sex, racial group, or suffering from a disability. If the agency complied with the employer's request, would it subsequently be able to claim its fees for supplying the staff? There is no case law on this,[25] but the general principles would suggest that, at least where the parties are aware of the effect of the discriminatory nature of their agreement, it should

---

17 In coming to this conclusion, the court affirmed the view taken in *Mohamed v Alaga*, despite the fact that it felt that the court in that case had not been referred to all relevant authorities: see the comments of Schiemann LJ: [2000] 1 All ER 608, p 622.

18 *Allen v Rescous* (1676) 2 Lev 174; *Brown Jenkinson & Co Ltd v Percy Dalton (London) Ltd* [1957] 2 QB 621. Such contracts may well also involve an agreement to commit a criminal offence.

19 The Law Commission was unable to find any authority on the issue, but assumes that the position is as stated in the text: Consultation Paper No 154, para 2.23d.

20 This example is given by Treitel, 2003, p 433, noting that it is implicit in s 12 of the Sale of Goods Act 1979 that such a contract is valid.

21 See Law Commission, Consultation Paper No 154, 1999, para 2.23; Treitel, 2003, p 433.

22 (1856) 1 H & N 73, p 80, per Martin B.

23 The case concerned the publication of a book containing a libel. The printer, on discovering the defamatory nature of the passage in question, refused to print it, but was able to recover the cost of printing the rest of the book. Martin B suggests that the printer was entitled to recover for the work 'performed' and Treitel (2003, p 433) reads this as implying that he would have recovered if the libellous statement had been published unwittingly.

24 For discussion of these 'torts' see, for example, Stone, 2006, Chapter 13.

25 But it may be significant that the courts appeared to contemplate the possibility of intervention even before the statutory 'anti-discrimination' framework was put in place: see *Nagle v Feilden* [1966] 2 QB 633, p 655; *Edwards v SOGAT* [1971] Ch 354, p 382.

be unenforceable. Even if the discrimination is unintentional,[26] it may well be that the policy of not allowing the legal process to be used in a way that undermines its integrity[27] would lead a court to refuse to enforce such an agreement.

14.4.4 Performance is contrary to statute

Performance which contravenes a statute involves contracts which are prima facie legal, and which are concerned with the achievement of an objective which is legal, but which contravene a statute by the way in which they are performed. Thus, in relation to hire purchase agreements, the Consumer Credit Act 1974 provides that unless various formalities are complied with, the agreement will be unenforceable against the creditor. The aim of the law here is to provide protection for the debtor, and the penalty of unenforceability is used to encourage creditors to make sure that they follow the procedures that Parliament has laid down.[28]

An example of the application of this approach is to be found in *Re Mahmoud and Ispahani*.[29] The contract was to sell linseed oil. It was a statutory requirement that both seller and buyer should be licensed.[30] The seller was licensed, but the buyer was not. The buyer nevertheless told the seller that he was licensed. When the buyer refused to take delivery, the seller sued. It was held that the seller could not enforce the contract because of its illegality, despite its reasonable belief that the defendant was licensed.[31] The policy underlying the regulation was to prevent trading in linseed oil other than between those who were licensed, and the innocence of the seller was irrelevant to that policy.

---

26 This would be unlikely in the example as given, but might arise if the employer imposed a requirement which was *indirectly* discriminatory and unjustifiable – for example, that all candidates should have been educated in England for at least five years.

27 See above, 14.3.

28 It was argued in *Wilson v First County Trust Ltd* [2003] UKHL 40; [2003] 4 All ER 97 that some aspects of these strict rules as to enforceability were incompatible with the creditor's right to a fair trial under Art 6 of the European Convention on Human Rights, as incorporated into English law by the Human Rights Act 1998. This argument was successful in the Court of Appeal, but was rejected by the House of Lords.

29 [1921] 2 KB 716.

30 This requirement was contained in the Defence of the Realm Regulations.

31 Could the seller in such a situation sue for misrepresentation? The court in *Mahmoud and Ispahani* refused to consider this. Whether there was such an action available would depend in part on whether the contract is void, rather than simply unenforceable. If it is void (as seems to have been the view in *Mahmoud and Ispahani*), then the seller would not have been induced to make a 'contract'. If it is simply unenforceable, then an action for misrepresentation would appear to be possible, but the courts might be unwilling to allow this to enable the seller to achieve indirectly what could not be done by a direct action on the contract: cf *Awwad v Geraghty & Co* [2000] 1 All ER 608 – *quantum meruit* claim rejected on this ground. But an action based on the tort of deceit was allowed in *Saunders v Edwards* [1987] 2 All ER 651, and in *Strongman v Sincock* [1955] 2 QB 525 the Court of Appeal allowed an action based on a collateral promise that the defendant would obtain the necessary licences, even though the main contract was unenforceable. See further, 14.6, below.

In *Hughes v Asset Managers plc*,[32] by way of contrast, the Court of Appeal upheld share transactions which had been conducted by unlicensed agents. Although the Prevention of Fraud (Investments) Act 1958 imposed sanctions on those who engaged in such trading without a licence, it did not expressly, or by implication, prohibit the making of the contracts themselves. The policy of the Act could be achieved simply by penalising those who traded without a licence.

FOR THOUGHT

(1) What could the seller in *Mahmoud and Ispahani* have done to avoid making an unenforceable contract? (2) What are the practical implications of these two decisions? Is it satisfactory that parties contemplating making a contract need to consider the policy behind any legislation which may govern their transaction?

The principles which should govern this area were considered by Devlin J in *St John Shipping Corp v Joseph Rank Ltd*,[33] which concerned a shipping contract where performance had involved overloading the ship, contrary to the Merchant Shipping Regulations. He said it was necessary to ask, first, whether the statute prohibits contracts *as such*, or only penalises certain behaviour. If the answer to the first question is that it prohibits contracts, does this contract belong to the class which the statute is intended to prohibit?

In answering the first question, he suggested that it was helpful, though not conclusive, to ask whether the object of the statute was to protect the public. If so, then the contract was likely to be illegal. If, on the other hand, the purpose was to protect the revenue (as, for example, in a requirement that those who sell television sets pass the names of the purchasers to the Post Office), then it was likely to be legal. This test is difficult to apply, as was shown by the case itself where, despite the fact that the Merchant Shipping Regulations are clearly not designed simply to protect the revenue, the contract was held to be enforceable. It seems to have carried some weight with the Court of Appeal, however, in its decision in *Skilton v Sullivan*.[34] In this case, the plaintiff entered into a contract with the defendant for the sale of koi carp. The defendant paid a deposit. Subsequently, the plaintiff issued an invoice, which described the fish as 'trout'. The defendant alleged that the plaintiff was trying to avoid paying VAT, since trout were zero-rated and koi carp were not. Thus, he argued, the contract was illegal and could not be enforced against him. The Court of Appeal considered that the plaintiff's purpose was probably to defer the payment of VAT, rather than to avoid it altogether: nevertheless, this was still an illegal purpose. The court also considered, however, that the plaintiff had formed this dishonest intention after the contract had been entered into. It was therefore not necessary for the plaintiff to rely on his unlawful

---

32 [1995] 3 All ER 669.
33 [1957] 1 QB 267; [1956] 3 All ER 683.
34 (1994) *The Times*, 25 March.

act in order to establish the defendant's liability. This was the main basis for the decision, but the court also relied on the principle that illegality which has the object of protecting the revenue is less likely to render a contract unenforceable than where the object is the protection of the public.

14.4.5 Relevance of knowledge

In *Archbolds (Freightage) Ltd v S Spanglett Ltd*,[35] it was suggested that the knowledge of the parties might be important, so that if both parties know that the contract can only be performed in a way that will involve the breach of the statute, then it will be illegal. The case concerned a contract for the carriage of goods. The defendants agreed to transport a quantity of whisky from London to Leeds for the plaintiffs. The plaintiffs were unaware that the defendants held a licence which only entitled them to carry their own goods. Pearce LJ, holding on the facts that the plaintiffs could, nevertheless, enforce the contract, stated that:[36]

> . . . if both parties know that though *ex facie* legal [a contract] can only be performed by illegality, or is intended to be performed illegally, the law will not help the plaintiffs in any way that is a direct or indirect enforcement of rights under the contract.

FOR THOUGHT

Does this mean that if both parties are aware that a time limit stated as part of a contract of carriage can only be met by a vehicle exceeding the speed limit, the contract will be illegal and unenforceable?

The issue of the knowledge of the parties has been considered further in two recent cases concerned with employment contracts. In *Vakante v Addey & Stanhope School*[37] the applicant was a Croatian national who was seeking asylum in the United Kingdom. He had been in the country since 1992, but was not allowed to work in the UK without permission. He nevertheless obtained a position as a graduate trainee teacher, and was employed for eight months. He was then dismissed. He brought a claim for racial discrimination and victimisation. Mummery LJ noted the test which had been laid down in *Hall v Woolston Hall Leisure* Ltd[38], in which the Court of Appeal suggested that the proper approach in this sort of case was:

35 [1961] 1 QB 374; [1961] 1 All ER 417.
36 Ibid, p 384; p 422.
37 [2004] 4 All ER 1056
38 [2000] 4 All ER 787 (a sex discrimination case), discussed further at 14.6.

to consider whether the applicant's claim arises out of or is so clearly connected or inextricably bound up or linked with the illegal conduct of the applicant that the court could not permit the applicant to recover compensation without appearing to condone that conduct.

In this case:

> (a) [the illegal conduct] was that of Mr Vakante; (b) it was criminal; (c) it went far beyond the manner in which one party performed what was otherwise a lawful employment contract; (d) it went to the basic content of an employment situation; (e) the duty not to discriminate arises from an employment situation which, without a permit, was unlawful from top to bottom and from beginning to end.

The Court of Appeal therefore concluded that the applicant's complaints were, applying the *Hall* test, so inextricably bound with the illegality of the relevant conduct that to allow him to recover compensation for discrimination would appear to condone his illegal conduct.

By contrast, the decision in *Wheeler v Quality Deep Trading Ltd*[39] went in favour of the applicant. She was of Thai origin and had limited knowledge of English. She was employed as a cook at a restaurant run by the defendant between November 1999 and January 2003. She was dismissed and brought an application for unfair dismissal. It transpired that she had been being paid without deduction of tax or national insurance. Inaccurate payslips were produced by the employer. The tribunal held that the applicant and her husband, who was well acquainted with the need to pay tax and national insurance and had a good grasp of English, must between them have 'known something was wrong' (para 22). It concluded that the employment contract was unlawful. On appeal, the Court of Appeal held that the tribunal had failed to apply the correct test to the situation. It did not properly distinguish between 'illegality of a contract and illegality in the performance of a legal contract' (para 26). If, as it seemed, this case fell within the second category, the test to be applied was that set out in *Hall v Woolston Hall Leisure*. It followed that:

> the employment tribunal had to be satisfied that the performance of the contract was illegal, that the employee knew of the facts which made the performance illegal and actively participated in the illegal performance.

Applying this test, the Court of Appeal noted the applicant's limited English, and the fact that it appeared that her husband had not seen her payslips until shortly before the tribunal hearing, and held that it could not be said that she had actively participated in the illegal performance.

---

39 [2005] ICR 265

The difference in outcome between these two decisions can be attributed to a significant extent to the court's view of the knowledge of the parties. In *Vakante* the applicant knew that he was acting illegally, whereas the employer was innocent; in *Wheeler* the situation was reversed. Vakante was not allowed to succeed in his claim, whereas Wheeler could.

A test based on the knowledge of the parties is not conclusive, as is shown by *Ailion v Spiekermann*.[40] The contract was for the assignment of a lease, for which a premium was to be paid. This was illegal under the Rent Act 1968, and both parties were aware of this. Nevertheless, the court ordered specific performance of the contract of assignment (though without the illegal premium).[41]

In *Anderson Ltd v Daniel*,[42] both the issue of the protection of the public and the knowledge of the parties were considered relevant. The contract was for the sale of artificial manure, made up of sweepings of various fertilisers from the holds of ships. Regulations required that the seller should specify the contents of the fertiliser and the proportions of each chemical it contained. This was impractical as far as sweepings were concerned. The Court of Appeal held the contract for sale to be unenforceable by the seller, because the statute was intended to protect purchasers. As Scrutton LJ put it:[43]

> When the policy of the Act in question is to protect the general public or a class of persons by requiring that a contract shall be accompanied by certain for-malities or conditions, the contract and its performance without these formalities or conditions is illegal, and cannot be sued upon by the person liable to the penalties.

This seems to suggest that the answer might have been different if the purchaser had sued, rather than the seller.

The overriding questions are, therefore, first, does the statute prohibit contracts? In deciding this, it may be helpful to consider whether it is intended to protect the public, or a class of the public. Second, is this particular contract illegal? Here, it may be relevant to look at the knowledge of the parties, and the guilt or innocence of the party suing.

The second issue inevitably overlaps with the more general issue of the enforce-ability of illegal contracts, which is considered further below (see 14.6).

---

40 [1976] Ch 158; [1976] 1 All ER 497.

41 This is probably best explained on the basis that the illegal part of the transaction, the premium, was severable from the lease itself. The result was that the purchaser of the lease got the best of both worlds – return of the premium, and enforcement of the lease. See 14.9, below, for further consideration on the power to 'sever' illegal obligations.

42 [1924] 1 KB 138.

43 Ibid, p 147 – citing *Little v Pool* (1829) 9 B & C 192.

14.5 CONTRACT TO INDEMNIFY

The parties may wish to make a type of insurance contract, whereby if one of them commits a crime or tort, the other will pay the amount of any fine or damages imposed, or otherwise provide compensation. Is such an agreement enforceable?

14.5.1 Criminal liability

It will generally be illegal to attempt to insure against criminal liability.[44] There appears to be an exception, however, as regards strict liability offences (that is, where the prosecution does not need to prove any 'guilty mind' on the part of the defendant in order to obtain a conviction). Provided the court is satisfied that the defendant is morally innocent, then it seems the contract will be upheld. In *Osman v J Ralph Moss Ltd*,[45] the plaintiff was suing his insurance brokers who had negligently failed to keep him informed that his car insurance was no longer valid (because of the collapse of the insurance company). As a result, the plaintiff had been fined £25 for driving without insurance (an offence of strict, or absolute, liability). The Court of Appeal held that he could recover the amount of the fine from the defendants. Sachs LJ stated that:[46]

> Having examined the authorities as to cases where the person fined was under an absolute liability, it appears that such fine can be recovered in circumstances such as the present as damages unless it is shown that there was on the part of the person fined a degree of *mens rea*[47] or of culpable negligence[48] in the matter which resulted in the fine.

The burden of proof was on the defendants to prove circumstances which rendered the fine irrecoverable.

---

44 *R Leslie Ltd v Reliable Advertising Agency Ltd* [1915] 1 KB 652. Note, however, that this case involved illegality arising from the *negligence* of the defendant; the law now seems to be prepared to allow an indemnity in such cases. In *Osman v J Ralph Moss Ltd* [1970] 1 Lloyd's Rep 313, the court preferred the earlier decision in *Cointat v Myham* [1913] 2 KB 220 to *Leslie v Reliable Advertising* on this particular point.

45 [1970] 1 Lloyd's Rep 313.

46 Ibid, p 316.

47 That is, intention or recklessness.

48 The case of *Askey v Golden Wine Co Ltd* [1948] 2 All ER was distinguished on this basis – in that case (involving the sale of liquor not fit for public consumption) there had been 'gross negligence'.

14.5.2 Civil liability

A contract to indemnify will be illegal as regards torts which are committed deliberately, such as deceit, or an intentional libel.[49] It is regarded as perfectly acceptable, however, to have such an arrangement as regards the tort of negligence, or where a tort is committed innocently (such as an unintentional libel).[50]

Where civil liability arises out of a crime, a contract which would provide compensation may be unenforceable. Thus, in *Gray v Barr*,[51] Barr, who had been cleared of manslaughter by the criminal courts, was sued in tort by the widow of his victim. He admitted liability, but claimed that he was covered by his Prudential 'Hearth and Home' insurance policy, which covered sums he became liable to pay as damages in respect of injury caused by accidents. The Court of Appeal held (in effect ignoring the verdict in the criminal court) that Barr's actions did amount to the criminal offence of manslaughter, and that he therefore could not recover under the insurance policy.

A similar refusal to allow reliance on an insurance contract was shown in *Geismar v Sun Alliance*,[52] where the plaintiff was seeking compensation for the loss of goods which had been brought into the country without the required import duty having been paid. There was nothing illegal about the insurance contract itself, which provided standard protection against loss by, among other things, theft. The court held, however, that to allow the plaintiff to recover under the policy in relation to the smuggled goods would be assisting him to derive a profit from a deliberate breach of the law. In arriving at this decision, it was relevant that the failure to pay import duty rendered the goods liable to forfeiture at any time by Customs and Excise, and that the breach was deliberate. It was not suggested that the same approach would be taken in relation to unintentional importation or innocent possession of uncustomed goods.

Different considerations apparently apply, however, where the crime is one of strict liability, or where it arises from negligence. Thus, in *Tinline v White Cross Insurance Association Ltd*,[53] the plaintiff, who had knocked down three people while driving 'at excessive speed' was able to recover from the defendants, his insurers, the compensation he was required to pay to the victims. The exception will not apply, however, if the offence was deliberate.[54] The rules in the motoring area are, however, affected by the need to uphold the effectiveness of the system of compulsory insurance, so that the

---

49 *WH Smith & Sons v Clinton* (1909) 99 LT 840. The action was by the printers of a magazine to recover on an indemnity given by the publishers in relation to libel. There was evidence that the printers were aware of the risk of libel, because the passage which eventually resulted in action being taken against both printers and publishers had been discussed and 'toned down' (though not sufficiently!).

50 *Daily Mirror Newspapers Ltd v Exclusive News Agency* (1937) 81 SJ 924, where the plaintiffs recovered damages in breach of contract to cover the cost of libel damages resulting from the publication of a photograph and caption supplied by the defendant.

51 [1971] 2 QB 554; [1971] 2 All ER 949.

52 [1978] QB 383; [1977] 3 All ER 570.

53 [1921] 3 KB 327. The degree of injury caused by the negligence is irrelevant; in this case one of the victims was killed.

54 *Gardner v Moore* [1984] AC 548; [1984] 1 All ER 1100.

victims, and families of victims, of road accidents receive proper compensation. Thus, in *Gardner v Moore*, the House of Lords held that even though a car had been driven deliberately so as to cause injury,[55] and that therefore the driver would not be able to claim an indemnity under an insurance policy, the statutory provisions contained in the Road Traffic Acts, designed to ensure compensation for the victims of road accidents, allowed the victim to recover compensation directly from the driver's insurer.[56]

14.6 EFFECTS OF ILLEGALITY: ENFORCEMENT

If a contract is found to be void for illegality, then this will, in general, mean that specific performance will be refused. This is so even if neither party has pleaded illegality.[57] The reason is that if there is no contract, the court cannot order it to be performed. It may, however, in some circumstances, be prepared to award damages. This may be done by allowing the action to be framed in tort, as, for example, in *Saunders v Edwards*,[58] where the plaintiff who had been party to an illegal overvaluation of furniture (for the purpose of avoiding stamp duty) in a contract for the sale of a flat was nevertheless allowed to sue for deceit on the basis of the defendant's fraudulent misrepresentation that the flat included a roof garden. The court took account of the 'relative moral culpability' of the two parties, and this question of 'guilt' or 'innocence' has always been relevant. During the 1980s, it was transformed by a number of decisions into a rather vague test of whether enforcement would offend the 'public conscience'.[59] The House of Lords in *Tinsley v Milligan*[60] rejected this, and reasserted a test based on whether the claimant needs to rely on the illegality to found the claim. In this case, T and M had both supplied the money for the purchase of a house. It was, however, put into the name of T alone in order to facilitate the making by M of false claims to social security payments. When the parties fell out, M claimed a share of the property on the basis of a resulting trust. It was argued for T that M could not succeed because the original arrangement had been entered into in order to further an illegal purpose. The trial judge and the Court of Appeal found for M. The House of Lords also held by a majority of 3:2, that M should succeed. In doing so, the majority rejected the approach taken by the Court of Appeal that the issue should be decided by considering whether 'the public conscience would be affronted by recognising rights created by illegal transactions'. This was too 'imponderable'. The proper test to be applied was whether the plaintiff needed to rely on the illegality in order to support her claim. In this case, the

---

55 Amounting to 'grievous bodily harm' under the Offences Against the Person Act 1861, s 18.
56 In fact, in this case, the driver was uninsured, so the claim was against the Motor Insurers' Bureau.
57 See, for example, *Birkett v Acorn Business Machines* (1999) *The Times*, 25 August.
58 [1987] 2 All ER 651.
59 See, for example, *Thackwell v Barclays Bank* [1987] 1 All ER 676; *Howard v Shirlstar Container Transport* [1990] 3 All ER 366.
60 [1994] 1 AC 340; [1993] 3 All ER 65.

presumption of a resulting trust was raised simply by the fact that M had contributed to the purchase price of the house. It was T who had to raise the illegality in order to try to rebut that presumption. Therefore, M should succeed.[61]

A similar approach was taken by the High Court in *21st Century Logistic Solutions Ltd v Madysen Ltd*,[62] where the defendant resisted a claim for payment for goods delivered on the basis that the supplier had set up the transaction with the intention of carrying out a VAT fraud. The fraud was not in fact completed, because the supplier went into liquidation. The receivers sought to enforce the contract. The High Court held that the illegality was 'too remote' to prevent its enforcement. The fact that the supplier had had an illegal intention was no reason to refuse to enforce an agreement which, on its face, appeared to be a perfectly legitimate sale of goods contract.

This approach will also apply where there is illegality in performance by one side, but the illegality is ancillary to the rights being asserted by the claimant. Thus, in *Hall v Woolston Hall Leisure Ltd*,[63] the appellant was claiming compensation for sex discrimination in relation to her dismissal from employment. She was aware that the way in which the wages paid to her had been recorded by the employer was inaccurate, and that this was a deliberate attempt by the employer to defraud the Inland Revenue. Nevertheless, she was allowed to recover compensation for the fact that she had been 'dismissed' for an unlawful reason (that is, the fact that she had become pregnant). The Court of Appeal took the view that in a case of this kind:[64]

> It is the sex discrimination that is the core of the complaint, the fact of employment and dismissal being the particular factual circumstances which Parliament has prescribed for the sex discrimination complaint to be capable of being made.

The court would not, by allowing this claim, 'be seen to be condoning unlawful conduct by the employee'.[65] It might well be otherwise where the employee had been an active participant with the employer in illegal actions.[66] Here, however, there was mere passive acquiescence by the employee in what the employer was doing, and this should not preclude her discrimination action.

The same type of approach was adopted in *Mohamed v Alaga*,[67] the facts of which have been given above. Although the claimant in that case was not allowed to share in

---

61 A similar rule has been applied to the recovery of property in cases such as *Bowmakers v Barnet Instruments* [1945] KB 65; [1944] 2 All ER 579 – see below, 14.8.4.

62 [2004] EWHC 231; [2004] 2 Lloyd's Rep 92.

63 [2000] 4 All ER 787, approving *Leighton v Michael* [1996] ICR 1091 (EAT).

64 [2000] 4 All ER 787, p 799, per Peter Gibson LJ.

65 Ibid.

66 The court accepted that Scarman LJ's test of 'knowledge plus participation', as put forward in relation to a different type of contract in *Ashmore, Benson, Pease & Co Ltd v AV Dawson Ltd* [1973] 2 All ER 856, pp 862–63, was equally applicable to the employment law context.

67 [1999] 3 All ER 699.

the solicitors' fees, because this was contrary to the Solicitors' Practice Rules, he was allowed to claim on a *quantum meruit* basis for the translating work which he had done (that is, he was paid a reasonable sum for the work completed). The view was taken that, although the defendant should have been aware of the Solicitors' Practice Rules, the claimant was ignorant of them, and it would not offend public policy for him to be able to recover a reasonable amount for the work actually done.[68]

This was the basis on which *Mohamed v Alaga* was distinguished in *Awwad v Geraghty & Co*. There the claim was by the solicitor, who was taken to be aware of the rules, and a *quantum meruit* claim was rejected: 'If the court, for reasons of public policy, refuses to enforce an agreement that a solicitor should be paid, it must follow that he cannot claim on a *quantum meruit*.'[69]

A final possibility is that the court will allow the claimant to assert a 'collateral contract' which will allow for recovery without the need to rely on the illegal agreement. This approach was adopted in *Strongman (1945) Ltd v Sincock*.[70] In this case, an architect had failed to obtain the necessary licences for building work that the plaintiffs were carrying out for him. When the builders sued to recover the price of the work which had been done, they were met by a defence that the contract was illegal and that therefore they could not recover.[71] The Court of Appeal upheld the decision of the Official Referee that there was a collateral contract under which the architect had promised to obtain the licences,[72] and that the plaintiffs could recover damages under this. It was regarded as very significant that the defendants were not to blame for the fact that the work had been carried out without a licence; nor had they been negligent in leaving it to the architect to obtain the licence.[73]

FOR THOUGHT

Would this approach provide a solution for the seller in *Mahmoud v Ispahani* (above, 14.4.4)? That is, could he have said to the buyer, if you guarantee that you have a licence then I will sell to you? Could this then be treated as an enforceable collateral contract?

The court in *Strongman v Sincock* did not make it clear what it regarded as the

---

68 [2000] 1 All ER 608 (see above, 14.4.2).

69 Ibid, pp 630–31.

70 [1955] 2 QB 525; [1955] 3 All ER 90.

71 It was accepted by all involved in the appeal proceedings, including counsel for the defendant, that the defendant had 'no merit' in raising this defence – 'justice' was clearly on the side of the plaintiffs: see Denning LJ, ibid, p 533; Birkett LJ, p 538.

72 The damages awarded by the Official Referee were equivalent to what the plaintiffs were adjudged to be owed under the building contract, had it been lawful.

73 There was evidence that it was standard practice in building contracts for the architect to obtain the necessary licences.

consideration provided by the builders for the architect's promise under this collateral contract. Presumably, it was the carrying out of the building work. The objection that the builders were already obliged to do this, so that the rule in *Stilk v Myrick* (see Chapter 3, 3.9.6) would prevent recovery, would be met by the argument that since the main agreement was illegal, the builders were in fact under no obligation to do the work. However, the contract does not really look like a 'collateral contract', since there is no main contract to which it is 'collateral'. The cynic would say that the court was here simply creating a remedy to prevent the unjust enrichment of an unmeritorious defendant.

14.7 EFFECTS OF ILLEGALITY: RECOVERY OF MONEY OR PROPERTY

The general principle which applies in the area of recovery of money or property is expressed in the Latin maxim *in pari delicto potior est conditio defendentis*.

This maxim, which is generally referred to in the abbreviated form *in pari delicto*, roughly translates as 'where there is equal fault, the defendant is in the stronger position'.[74] Thus, where money or other property has been transferred under an illegal contract, which is regarded as void, the court will not in general assist the claimant to recover it.

14.7.1 General rule: no recovery

An example of the application of the rule of no recovery is to be found in the case of *Parkinson v College of Ambulance Ltd*.[75] Colonel Parkinson was approached by a third party who told him that if he made a contribution to the College (a charity), it would be able to obtain a knighthood for him. Parkinson made a contribution of £3,000, but no knighthood was forthcoming. He brought an action to recover his money. It was held that the contract was illegal, and that Parkinson could not sustain his action without disclosing this, and his own complicity. The donation was on its face a gift, and therefore irrecoverable. It could only be explained as being part of a contract by disclosing the consideration alleged to have been given for it, that is, the promise of the knighthood. The plaintiff's action could only have any force as being for breach of this contract, but since the contract was illegal, the action had to fail.

In *Al-Kishtaini v Shanshal*,[76] the rules prohibiting the recovery of property on the basis of 'illegality' were challenged as being contrary to Art 1 of the First Protocol to

---

74 See Grodecki, 1955.
75 [1925] 2 KB 1.
76 [2001] 2 All ER Comm 601 (under the name *Shanshal v Al-Kishtaini*).

the European Convention on Human Rights, as applied to English law by the Human Rights Act 1998.[77] Article 1 of the Protocol states that:

> Everyone is entitled to the peaceful enjoyment of his possessions. No one shall be deprived of his possessions except in the public interest and subject to conditions provided for by law and by the general principles of international law.
>
> The preceding provisions shall not, however, in any way impair the right of a State to enforce such laws as it deems necessary to control the use of property in accordance with the general interest or to secure the payment of taxes or other contributions or penalties.

The courts, as public authorities under the Human Rights Act 1998, are obliged to apply and interpret the law in a way which is compatible with the Convention.[78] It was suggested in *Shanshal* that the rules relating to the non-recoverability of property transferred under an illegal contract lacked the scope for the application of a test of 'proportionality' commonly applied in case law under the European Convention, by which any restriction of rights must be 'proportionate' to the objectives which the restriction is trying to achieve.[79] The Court of Appeal unanimously rejected this. It was not convinced that the principles under attack engaged Art 1 at all, but if they did it was sure that in the case before it they were justified as being in the 'public interest' within the first paragraph of Art 1 or the 'general interest' in the second paragraph.[80] The illegality in the case arose from contracts made in breach of regulations preventing trade with Iraqi citizens,[81] passed in consequence of United Nations sanctions imposed in the aftermath of Iraq's 1990 invasion of Kuwait. Mummery LJ noted that there was a very 'high degree' of public interest involved, given the background to the regulations; and that, in any case, they were not absolute, in that it was possible to obtain permission to trade with Iraqi citizens.

This decision was only concerned to deal with the Human Rights Act point as it applied to the particular situation before the court, where the illegality arose out of a particular set of regulations. It is to be expected, however, that a similar approach would be adopted in other situations involving illegal contracts – that is, that restrictions on the recovery of property would be held to be in the public interest. Moreover, the rules are not absolute, as will be seen from the range of judge-created exceptions dealt with below. It is likely that these provide for sufficient flexibility so that, in an appropriate case, a court could take account of the question whether a

---

77 The possibility of the common law rules in this area being susceptible to such a challenge had previously been noted by the Law Commission, Consultation Paper No 154, para 1.23 – though it did not appear to regard the risk as very high.

78 Human Rights Act 1998, s 6.

79 See, for example, Stone, 2006, in particular Chapters 1 and 2.

80 See [2001] 2 All ER Comm 601, paras 50–62 (Mummery LJ); paras 90–99 (Rix LJ).

81 That is, the Control of Gold, Securities, Payments and Credits (Republic of Iraq) Directions 1990, SI 1990/1616.

refusal to allow the recovery of money or other property would be 'disproportionate', and thus achieve compatibility with the requirements of Art 1 of the First Protocol.

14.8 EXCEPTIONS TO THE GENERAL RULE

The courts have developed and recognised a number of exceptions to this rule, and there are therefore several situations where recovery of money or property will be allowed despite the illegality.

14.8.1 Illegal purpose not yet carried out

If the contract is still executory, the claimant should have the chance to have a change of mind or heart, resile from the contract, and recover property transferred. This is sometimes referred to as the *locus poenitentiae* ('the space for repentance'). Thus, in *Taylor v Bowers*,[82] the plaintiff had made a fictitious assignment of his goods to A as part of a scheme to defraud his creditors. Meetings of the creditors had been held, but no composition agreement had been reached. A had, in the meantime, parted with the goods to the defendant (who knew of the fraudulent scheme). The Court of Appeal held that because no creditors had actually been defrauded, the illegal purpose had not been carried out and the plaintiff could recover his goods from the defendant. This approach was applied by the Court of Appeal in *Tribe v Tribe*,[83] where shares had been transferred by father to son as a means of keeping assets out of the hands of landlords who were expected to be seeking substantial contributions towards repairs on property rented by the father. The transfer had been put in the form of a sale, but the son had never paid any money for the shares. In the event, no demands were made by the landlords, and the Court of Appeal, applying *Taylor v Bowers* and *Tinsley v Milligan*,[84] allowed the father to recover the shares. He had withdrawn from the transaction before any part of the illegal purpose had been carried into effect, and was in those circumstances allowed to use the explanation of what had been planned as a basis for undoing the apparent sale of the shares to his son.

This exception will not operate, however, where there has been substantial performance of the contract, as in *Kearley v Thomson*.[85] The plaintiff had paid money to the defendants, a firm of solicitors, in return for their agreement not to appear at the public examination of a bankrupt friend of the plaintiff, nor to oppose the order for his discharge. After the first part of the agreement had been carried out, the plaintiff changed his mind and tried to recover his money. The Court of Appeal refused to allow

82 (1876) 1 QBD 291.
83 [1996] Ch 107; [1995] 4 All ER 236.
84 [1994] AC 340; [1993] 3 All ER 65 – see above, 14.6.
85 (1890) 24 QBD 742.

him to do so, because there had been 'a partial carrying into effect of an illegal purpose in a substantial manner'.[86]

The withdrawal must be genuine. If the purpose of the contract is simply frustrated by the refusal of the other party to play his or her part, this exception will not apply.[87]

14.8.2 Oppression

In the case of oppression, if the claimant was in a weak bargaining position, so that there was virtually no choice about entering into the agreement, recovery may be possible. Thus, in *Atkinson v Denby*,[88] a creditor refused to accept a composition agreement unless he was paid £50, so gaining an advantage over the other creditors. The debtor paid, but later brought an action to recover the money. It was held that the debtor could recover. Although the agreement was an illegal contract, the element of oppression meant that an exception to the general rule was justified.

The rationale of this exception is that the parties while both *in delicto* are not in fact *in pari delicto*, (that is, they are not *equally* at fault). As Cockburn CJ put it in *Atkinson v Denby*:[89]

> It is true that both are *in delicto*, because the act is a fraud upon the other creditors, but it is not *pari delictum*, because the one has the power to dictate, the other no alternative but to submit.

14.8.3 Fraud

If one party entered into the contract as a result of the other's fraudulent misrepresentation that it was lawful, recovery will be allowed.[90] Again, the parties are not regarded as being equally at fault.

14.8.4 No reliance on the illegal transaction

If the plaintiff can establish a right to possession of the property without relying on the illegal contract, then recovery will be allowed. In *Bowmakers v Barnet Instruments*,[91] for example, the defendants agreed to buy some machine tools on hire purchase terms from the plaintiffs. These agreements may well have been illegal, being in contravention of

---

86 (1890) 24 QBD 742, p 747.
87 *Bigos v Bousted* [1951] 1 All ER 92 – the contract was in breach of exchange control regulations. In *Tribe v Tribe*, Millett LJ regarded this case as a dubious extension of the principle: [1996] Ch 107, p 135; [1995] 4 All ER 236, p 259.
88 (1862) 7 H & N 934; 158 ER 749.
89 Ibid, p 936; p 750.
90 *Hughes v Liverpool Victoria Legal Friendly Society* [1916] 2 KB 482.
91 [1945] KB 65; [1944] 2 All ER 579.

certain statutory regulations. There were three agreements. The defendants sold the machines which were the subject of two of the agreements, but kept the others. They refused to return them, or pay the hire. The plaintiffs' action to recover damages for conversion[92] in relation to all the machines succeeded. The Court of Appeal held that they could establish their rights over the goods without needing to rely on the illegal contracts. The defendants' rights as bailees had been brought to an end by their actions, and so the plaintiffs could rely on their basic rights of ownership to found their action.

The decision in this case is not uncontroversial,[93] and is arguably inconsistent with *Taylor v Chester*,[94] where a person who had pledged a £50 bank note as security for a debauch in a brothel (an illegal contract) was held unable to recover it. The adoption, however, by the majority of the House of Lords of a similar line of argument in *Tinsley v Milligan*,[95] applying it to claims based on an equitable title (as opposed to the legal title asserted in *Bowmakers v Barnet Instruments*) indicates that it is now well established. It is likely for the future to be regarded as a clear exception to the normal rule of non-recovery.

14.8.5 Class-protecting statutes

In some situations, the purpose for which a statute makes an agreement illegal is to protect a particular class. For example, the provisions forbidding the taking of illegal premiums under the Rent Acts are designed to protect tenants. A member of that class may be able to recover property transferred under the agreement, notwithstanding the illegality. Many statutes of this kind now contain specific provisions for recovery.[96] Where they do not, however, the courts will apply the common law rule and allow recovery, as in *Kiriri Cotton Co Ltd v Dewani*.[97] This was a Privy Council decision concerning the payment of a premium by a tenant, which was illegal under Ugandan law. The tenant was allowed to recover the premium. As Lord Denning put it:[98]

> Thus, if as between the two of them [that is, the parties to the contract] the duty of observing the law is placed on the shoulders of one rather than the other – it being imposed on him specially for the protection of the other – then they are not *in pari delicto* and the money can be recovered back.

92 An action in conversion requires the claimant to prove a right to the goods concerned. The defendants argued that such a right could not be proved in this case without resort to the illegal transactions.
93 See, for example, Treitel, 2003, pp 496–97, arguing that, while there was clearly a repudiatory breach in relation to the machines which had been sold, the same is not so obviously the case in relation to those retained by the defendants. Why did their rights as bailees not subsist in relation to these machines, so as to thwart the plaintiffs' claim based on ownership?
94 (1869) LR 4 QB 309.
95 [1994] AC 340; [1993] 3 All ER 65 – see above, 14.6.
96 For example, the Rent Act 1977, s 125; the Financial Services Act 1986, s 132.
97 [1960] AC 192; [1960] 1 All ER 177.
98 Ibid, p 204; p 181.

The underlying principle is again that in this situation the parties are not regarded as being equally at fault.

14.9 SEVERANCE

It is likely to be the case in many illegal contracts that it is only part of the arrangement which is illegal. In some circumstances the courts will allow the contract to be split into its constituent parts, with the legal section being valid, and the illegal section unenforceable. This is what occurred, for example, in *Ailion v Spiekermann*,[99] where the contract to pay the illegal premium could be severed, because a precise amount could be assigned to the illegal part of the agreement.[100] Consideration of the possibility of severance most commonly arises, however, in relation to contracts in restraint of trade, which are discussed in Chapter 15. Full discussion of this topic is therefore left until that point.[101]

14.10 PROPOSALS FOR REFORM [102]

The Law Commission is considering the need for reform of this area, and in 1999 put out a Consultation Paper suggesting some possible ways in which this could be achieved.[103]

The main thrust of the proposals is that the present 'technical and complex rules'[104] should be replaced by a 'structured discretion'. Thus, in exercising its discretion to decide whether the illegality of a transaction should act as a defence to a legal action for enforcement or the recovery of property, the court should take account of:[105]

(i)   the seriousness of the illegality involved;

(ii) the knowledge and intention of the party seeking to enforce the illegal transaction, seeking the recognition of legal or equitable rights under it, or seeking to recover benefits conferred under it;

---

99   [1976] Ch 158; [1976] 1 All ER 497 – discussed above, 14.4.5.

100 Cf *Carney v Herbert* [1985] 1 All ER 438 (Privy Council), in which illegal mortgages were severed from a transaction for the purchase of shares which they were intended to guarantee.

101 See 15.7.

102 Note that the Principles of European Contract Law do not as yet cover the area of illegal or immoral contracts. The diversity of approaches to be found amongst Member States of the European Union has meant that 'further investigation is needed to determine whether it is feasible to draft European principles on these subjects': Lando and Beale, 2000, p 227.

103 Law Commission, Consultation Paper No 154, 1999. For a broadly favourable welcome to the proposals, see Buckley, 2000.

104 Ibid, para 1.18.

105 Ibid, para 1.19.

(iii) whether refusing to allow standard rights and remedies would deter illegality;

(iv) whether refusing to allow standard rights and remedies would further the purpose of the rule which renders the transaction illegal; and

(v) whether refusing to allow standard rights and remedies would be proportionate to the illegality involved.

This discretion would not apply where there is a statutory provision which sets out the consequences of illegality, as, for example, in s 105 of the Companies Act 1985, s 126 of the Rent Act 1977 or s 35 of the Trade Descriptions Act 1968.[106]

The benefits which the Law Commission sees as flowing from such an approach are summarised in para 1.21 of the Consultation Paper:

> First, a court would be able to reach its decision on the facts of a particular case using open and explicit reasoning, giving full effect to the relevance of the illegality on the transaction. Secondly, we believe that the provisional proposals would be likely to result in illegality being used less frequently to deny a plaintiff his or her usual rights or remedies. That is, under the discretion, illegality would only act as a defence where there is a clear and justifiable public interest that it should do so.

These proposals have much to recommend them, and they would clearly preclude any future possibility of a challenge under the Human Rights Act 1998.[107] They run the risk of all proposals which introduce broad judicial discretion into the area of contract law, which is that they produce uncertainty and unpredictability – characteristics generally regarded as anathema to the commercial contractor.[108] They do not go as far as the New Zealand Illegal Contracts Act 1970, however, which allows for discretion in the adjustment of losses as between the parties.[109] The Law Commission's proposed discretion would only be as to whether the normal contractual or restitutionary remedies should be precluded by the illegality of the transaction in question.

These proposals are still under consideration, and a final report from the Law Commission is awaited. Any legislative reform is therefore unlikely in the near future.

---

106 This is in contrast to the position in New Zealand under the Illegal Contracts Act 1970, as interpreted in *Harding v Coburn* [1976] 2 NZLR 577 – see Consultation Paper 154, paras 7.94–7.102.

107 See the discussion of *Al-Kishtaini v Shanshal*, below, 14.7.1.

108 Buckley, however, suggests that the operation of the discretion under the New Zealand Illegal Contracts Act has not 'led to the uncertainty which some commentators feared': Buckley, 2000, p 180.

109 For discussion of the New Zealand Act, see Furmston, 1972–73; McLaughlan, 1984; Coote, 1992; Coote, 1993; and Cooke, 1998.

14.11   AGREEMENTS CONTRARY TO PUBLIC POLICY

The second part of this chapter, like the first, is concerned with contracts which the courts refuse to enforce. In this case, however, the reason for this refusal is not that the agreements concerned amount to, or are linked to, the commission of a crime or a tort, or are forbidden by statute. Rather, they have been held to be more generally 'contrary to public policy' and, for that reason, void and unenforceable. Most of the areas dealt with here are the creation of the judges. The final section, on the other hand, deals with gaming and wagering contracts, which are governed by statute. The categories of common law public policy have been stated to be closed,[110] so that the courts will not apply this approach to a type of contract to which it has not been applied previously. Such an approach has the advantage of promoting certainty, and keeping public policy claims within limits. Whether the courts would stick to this line if faced with a novel situation which appeared to call out for intervention is another matter.[111] One area where it is possible that they might feel inclined to intervene is if a contract appeared to infringe one of the rights recognised by the Human Rights Act 1998. This possibility is considered further below (see 14.15).

One difficulty about the development of new categories of contract to be held void at common law on the basis of public policy is that there are no clear principles which seem to link the existing categories. At the most general level, it may be said that the argument from the 'integrity of the courts' (discussed at 14.3 in relation to illegality) will apply here as well. In other words, the courts will not wish to be seen to be being used to enforce an agreement the consequences of which are seen to be 'undesirable'. But this begs the question, since it simply moves the focus from what is contrary to public policy to what is 'undesirable'. The other main policy behind the control of illegal contracts noted earlier in this chapter, that of deterrence, can have little relevance here, since the agreements concerned are not 'unlawful', simply unenforceable. The only conclusion that can be drawn is that the areas which currently fall within this heading are a ragbag collection of agreements, not linked by any discernible conceptual theme. This, in turn, adds to the difficulty in extending the category, since if there is no general principle linking those agreements which are currently within the category, the basis for arguing that other agreements should be included is never likely to be clear-cut. It is, of course, always open to Parliament to add to the areas which fall within the scope of 'public policy', and rendering further categories of contract unenforceable, though not

---

110 *Printing & Numerical Registering Co v Sampson* (1875) LR 19 Eq 462, p 465; *Janson v Driefontein Consolidated Mines Ltd* [1902] AC 484, p 491; *Fender v St John Mildmay* [1938] AC 1, p 23; *Geismar v Sun Alliance and London Assurance Ltd* [1978] QB 383, p 389; [1977] 3 All ER 570, p 575.

111 In *Lancashire County Council v Municipal Mutual Insurance Ltd* [1996] 3 All ER 545, for example, a defence based on 'public policy' was rejected, but only after careful consideration: if there were really no possibility of expanding the public policy categories, the argument would surely have been rejected out of hand. See also *Multiservice Bookbinding Ltd v Marden* [1979] Ch 84; [1978] 2 All ER 489 and *Stafford AHA v South Staffordshire Waterworks Co* [1978] 3 All ER 769.

illegal; but it is difficult to see this happening in practice. Where Parliament intervenes to control agreements, it usually does so through the medium of the criminal law.

14.12 CONTRACTS CONCERNING MARRIAGE

The courts regard it as being in the interests of society to preserve the status of marriage. Certain types of contract which are regarded as threatening to the institution of marriage are therefore treated as illegal.

14.12.1 Future separation

A contract between spouses agreeing to separate at some point in the future is invalid if it is made either before the marriage or during cohabitation.[112] In *Brodie v Brodie*,[113] Mr Brodie only agreed to marry the woman who was carrying his child if a written agreement to separate was drawn up. This, among other things, precluded the woman from bringing legal proceedings against him. The agreement was held to be contrary to public policy, and so could not be enforced. The woman was free to take legal action.

This rule does not apply to an agreement which does not relate to the distant future, but is made at a time when the marriage has already broken down and in anticipation of immediate separation.[114] It is not contrary to public policy for the parties to a failed marriage to make agreements about the distribution of their property, or for the maintenance of one party or the children of the marriage by the other.[115] Nor does the rule affect arrangements made by spouses who have been separated, and are then reconciled, since in this situation the making of the agreement is likely to aid the reconciliation.[116]

One type of agreement, which, on this basis, is clearly unenforceable in English law, is the 'pre-nuptial' agreement common in the United States, particularly where one party is very wealthy. This type of agreement is made prior to marriage in order to avoid, or minimise, disputes about the distribution of property should the marriage break down. Such an agreement will, however, be regarded as contrary to public policy by the English courts, and therefore unenforceable. Whether this should continue to be the case is arguable.[117] It might be said that such agreements are supportive of the

---

112 *Wilson v Wilson* (1848) 1 HL Cas 538.

113 [1917] P 271.

114 The same exception used to apply to a promise by a married man to marry another woman: if a decree *nisi* had been issued in relation to the first marriage, the promise was enforceable: *Fender v St John-Mildmay* [1938] AC 1; [1937] 3 All ER 402. This is no longer of any practical significance, since the action for breach of promise of marriage was abolished by the Law Reform (Miscellaneous Provisions) Act 1970.

115 But agreements arrived at as part of a divorce or judicial separation are subject to the supervision of the courts, under the Family Law Act 1996.

116 *Harrison v Harrison* [1910] 1 KB 35.

117 See, for example: Sands, 1991; Trebilcock, 1993, pp 43–44; Conway, 1995.

institution of marriage, in that they discourage parties from marrying for the wrong reasons (for example, 'gold-digging') and from separating in order to obtain a share of the wealthier party's fortune. At the moment, however, there is no sign of a change in English law on this topic.

More generally, it may be questioned whether the particular status given to marriage by the common law is sustainable in a society in which increasing numbers of couples do not feel the need to give that status to their relationship.[118] Even if it is, it would, perhaps, be preferable that the control of this area should be in the hands of Parliament, and that the common law rules should fade away in the face of the framework of legislative controls which currently govern marriage and its breakdown.

14.12.2 Restraint of marriage

A contract which imposes liability on a person if he or she marries is void. Thus, a promise by A that if he marries, he will pay a sum of money to C is unenforceable.[119] Similarly, a promise by A to make a payment if he marries anyone else other than B will also be unenforceable.[120]

14.12.3 Marriage brokage

Marriage brokage concerns a contract whereby A promises to procure a marriage for B. The professional 'matchmaker' cannot make an enforceable contract for his or her services. The rule is not limited to contracts to procure marriage with a particular person. Thus, in *Hermann v Charlesworth* (discussed further below, 14.16), Miss H entered into an agreement under which, if the defendant introduced her to someone whom she married, Miss H would pay the defendant £250. She paid a deposit which, after several unsuccessful introductions, she sought to recover. The Court of Appeal held that the contract was illegal as being contrary to public policy. It is difficult to see, however, why such contracts are any more harmful than those between 'dating' or 'introduction' agencies and their clients, which have never been regarded as contrary to public policy. Such contracts do not, of course, depend on marriage between those introduced.

---

118 The House of Lords has taken note of this in other contexts: see the comments of Lord Browne-Wilkinson in *Barclays Bank v O'Brien* [1994] 1 AC 180, p 198; [1993] 4 All ER 417, p 431.
119 *Baker v White* (1690) 2 Vern 615; 23 ER 740.
120 *Lowe v Peers* (1768) 4 Burr 2225.

14.13   CONTRACTS PROMOTING SEXUAL IMMORALITY

Contracts promoting sexual immorality will include any contract for sex outside marriage, and would presumably cover otherwise lawful homosexual, as well as heterosexual activities.[121] Such activities, while not constituting criminal offences or civil wrongs, may still be regarded as immoral, and contracts which involve them will be treated as contrary to public policy.

The rule is not limited to contracts which directly concern sexual activity, as is shown by *Pearce v Brooks*.[122] Here, there was a contract under which the plaintiffs supplied the defendant with an ornamental brougham (a type of carriage), which was to be paid for by instalments. After one instalment had been paid, the brougham was returned in a damaged condition. The plaintiffs sued for £15 compensation which was payable under the agreement if the brougham was returned. The defendant, however, was a prostitute, and there was evidence that she intended to use the brougham to attract customers. Moreover, it seems that at least one partner in the plaintiffs' firm was aware of this. On this basis, the court held that this would be an illegal contract, so that the plaintiffs would be unable to recover either under the contract or for the damage.

The knowledge of the plaintiffs was relevant here, but not every contract with a known prostitute will be illegal. In *Appleton v Campbell*[123] the action was for the recovery of board and lodging in relation to a room rented from the plaintiff. The court held that the plaintiff could not recover if he knew that the defendant was a prostitute, and that she was using the room to entertain her clients. But:[124]

> . . . if the defendant had her lodgings there, and received her visitors elsewhere, the plaintiff may recover, although she be a woman of the town, because persons of that description must have a place to lay their heads.

There are thus two factors which are necessary for the contract to be unenforceable. First, there must be knowledge that the other party is a prostitute and, second, knowledge that what was supplied under the contract is to be used for the purposes of prostitution.

The same approach will presumably apply to other 'immoral' contracts. The extent to which the other contracts are likely to be treated as 'immoral', however, must now be considered in the light of the decision in *Armhouse Lee Ltd v Chappell*.[125] In this case, the publishers of a magazine sought to recover payment for advertisements which

---

121   Note that prostitution is not in itself an offence, as opposed to 'soliciting' (see the Street Offences Act 1959, s 1), advertising (Criminal Justice and Police Act 2001, s 46) or causing, inciting or controlling prostitution for gain (see Sexual Offences Act 2003, ss 52 and 53).

122   (1866) LR Ex 213.

123   (1826) 2 C & P 347; 172 ER 157.

124   Ibid.

125   (1996) *The Times*, 7 August.

had been placed by the defendants. The defendants resisted the claim on the basis that the content of the advertisements was illegal or immoral, since they related to telephone 'sex lines', offering pre-recorded messages, live conversations and sex dating. The trial judge found for the plaintiffs. On appeal, the Court of Appeal considered a range of ways in which the advertisements could be said to be illegal, including prostitution, obscenity, and conspiracy to corrupt public morals. All were rejected. In addition, the court refused to find that 'public policy' required the contracts to be treated as unenforceable. There was no evidence that any 'generally accepted moral code condemned these telephone sex lines'. Moreover, 'it was undesirable in such a case, involving an area regarded as the province of the criminal law, for individual judges exercising a civil jurisdiction to impose their own moral attitudes'. The decision of the trial judge was therefore upheld, and the contracts were enforceable by the plaintiffs. This case suggests that it is unlikely that there will be any significant extension of the range of contracts that will be struck down on the basis of sexual 'immorality'. In the light of the comments made by the Court of Appeal and its decision, it would seem likely that illegality will only operate to prevent the enforcement of a contract where the behaviour concerned amounts to, or involves, a criminal offence.

FOR THOUGHT

If the law is to strike down 'immoral' contracts, why should this be limited to the area of sexual immorality? Are there other types of immoral behaviour (such as discriminating on inappropriate, though not illegal, grounds – for example, charging more to people with red hair) which should render unenforceable any contract made?

14.14 CONTRACTS TO OUST THE JURISDICTION OF THE COURTS

The courts are very jealous of any attempt in a contract or other agreement to try to take away their powers to oversee the agreement, interpret it, and decide on its validity. They will hold any such agreement to be void as being contrary to public policy. For example, in *Baker v Jones*,[126] the rules of the British Amateur Weightlifters' Association provided that the Association's central council was to be 'the sole interpreter of the rules', and that the council's decision was to be final. It was held that although it was perfectly in order to give a tribunal or council the power to make final decisions on questions of fact, the same could not be done as regards questions of law. These provisions in the rules were to that extent contrary to public policy, and void.

There are two exceptions to this general approach. First, in commercial matters, the procedure whereby parties may agree in their contract that disputes should be

---

126 [1954] 2 All ER 553. See also *Lee v Showmen's Guild of Great Britain* [1952] 2 QB 329.

submitted to arbitration (at least as a precondition for any legal action being taken) on questions of both fact and law has been approved by the courts (*Scott v Avery*)[127] and legislation (the Arbitration Act 1996). The crucial question is the extent to which the parties may commit themselves to treat the decision of the arbitrator as binding. Under both common law and statute, the arbitrator is allowed the final say on issues of fact. As to issues of law, the common law did not allow the parties to agree to exclude the court's jurisdiction in this area. An agreement to do so was void, and a party was free to seek a ruling from the courts on the point of law at issue.[128] The statutory position is that a party may have recourse to the court on a point of law, but only with the agreement of the other side, or the leave of the court itself.[129] Such leave will only be given if the conditions set out in s 69(3) of the Arbitration Act 1996 are satisfied. These state that:

> Leave to appeal shall be given only if the court is satisfied:
> (a)   that the determination of the question will substantially affect the rights of one or more of the parties;
> (b)   that the question is one which the tribunal was asked to determine;
> (c)   that, on the basis of the findings of fact in the award:
>   (i)   the decision of the tribunal on the question is obviously wrong; or
>   (ii)   the question is one of general public importance and the decision of the tribunal is at least open to serious doubt; and
> (d)   that, despite the agreement of the parties to resolve the matter by arbitration, it is just and proper in all the circumstances for the court to determine the question.

The jurisdiction of the court is thus retained only where it is really necessary to deal with clearly incorrect applications of the law or matters of 'general public importance'. Otherwise, the finality of arbitration and its associated benefits of reduction in costs and certainty are to be maintained.

The second exception to the general rule against ousting the courts' jurisdiction applies to a clause in an agreement arrived at on the separation of husband and wife under which the wife, in return for a promise of maintenance, agrees not to apply to the courts. Such an agreement is void to the extent that the wife is still free to apply, but is enforceable as regards the husband's promise to pay.[130]

---

127 (1855) 5 HLC 811.
128 *Czarnikow v Roth Schmidt & Co* [1922] 2 KB 478.
129 Arbitration Act 1996, s 69.
130 Matrimonial Causes Act 1973, s 34.

14.15   THE HUMAN RIGHTS ACT 1998

It was suggested above (14.11), that the Human Rights Act 1998 (HRA) might provide a source of additional grounds for finding that a contract is 'contrary to public policy'. The effect of the Act is to require the courts to have regard to the rights contained in the European Convention on Human Rights, the main Articles of which appear in Sched 1 to the HRA 1998. These rights cover a range of areas from the right to life (Art 2) to the right to private life (Art 8). It is neither possible nor necessary here to consider all these provisions in detail,[131] but an illustration will serve to indicate the potential for the development in this area.

An initial point to note is that the primary focus of the Act is on the actions of 'public authorities', so that breaches of human rights as between two private individuals will *prima facie* fall outside its scope.[132] The courts themselves, however, are 'public authorities' and therefore in developing the common law must have regard to the requirements of the HRA. Thus, in relation to the common law concept of 'breach of confidence', it is clear that the courts are now interpreting this in the light of Art 8 of the European Convention, which guarantees a right of 'privacy', so as to expand the scope of 'confidentiality' into a much wider area.[133] It is certainly possible, therefore, for a court to use the HRA as a means of expanding the grounds on which a contract, or a provision in a contract, might be found to be void as being against public policy.

Suppose, for example, that a contract provides that W has written a biography of B, which is to be published by X Ltd. B (who does not like the way in which he is portrayed in the book) then makes an agreement with X Ltd that the book will only receive a very small print run (perhaps a few hundred copies) and no publicity, in exchange for a substantial payment from B to X Ltd.[134] W feels that this is a restriction on her right of freedom of expression (as guaranteed by Art 10 of the European Convention), and persuades X Ltd to break its agreement with B. If B sues X Ltd, can X argue that its contract with B was void as being contrary to public policy?[135]

---

131 For a full discussion see, for example, Stone, 2006.

132 The issue of whether the HRA has 'horizontal' effect (that is, applying to protect a private individual from an infringement of rights by another private individual) or simply 'vertical' effect (that is, applying only to protect individuals from infringements of rights by the State or State organisations (or 'public authorities')) has been the subject of considerable, inconclusive, academic debate: see, for example: Hunt, 1998; Buxton, 2000; Wade, 2000.

133 See *Campbell v MGN* [2004] UKHL 22; [2004] 2 All ER 995.

134 It is assumed for the purposes of this illustration that this does not constitute a breach of the contract between W and X Ltd.

135 B might also sue W for the tort of inducing a breach of contract – in which case the same question as to whether the contract between B and X Ltd was valid would arise.

Another possibility is a contract which has the effect of discriminating against a person on grounds of religion – perhaps by making it difficult for that person to worship as his or her faith requires. This might be subject to challenge on the basis of an infringement of Art 9 of the Convention, which guarantees the right to 'freedom of thought, conscience and religion'. Religious discrimination is unlawful in relation to employment contracts and in connection with the provision of goods and services to the public,[136] but such a provision in another type of contract might be held to be void on public policy grounds.[137]

It is very difficult to predict whether there would be a willingness by the courts to expand public policy on this basis. If there were, then it would breathe new life into an area which is currently only of limited practical significance.

14.16   EFFECT OF CONTRACTS VOID AT COMMON LAW

The main consequence of a contract being void under one of the above heads is that it will not be enforceable by either party. In general in this area, the contract as a whole is what offends against public policy. If, however, it is only part of the agreement which does so, then the possibility of severing the offending part arises. This will operate in the same way as in relation to contracts in restraint of trade, as discussed in Chapter 15.[138]

As regards the recovery of money or property transferred under the agreement, the position here seems to be different from that which applies in relation to illegal contracts. In that area, as discussed above (14.7), the courts start from the premise that no recovery is possible,[139] but that in certain situations there are exceptions, in particular where the parties are not equally 'at fault'.[140] In relation to contracts void as being contrary to public policy, the issue of fault does not arise in the same way: nor are they stigmatised as being improper through being illegal.[141] It seems, therefore, that the courts probably will allow recovery of property transferred in relation to such contracts. Authorities are few, but this was the approach adopted in the marriage brokage case, *Hermann v Charlesworth*.[142] The plaintiff had paid a deposit to the defendant, with

---

136 Employment Equality (Religion or Belief) Regulations 2003 (SI 2003/1660); Equality Act 2006, Pt 2.

137 Article 14 of the European Convention, which deals directly with discrimination and goes beyond the categories covered by English law, is limited in that it only applies to discrimination in the way in which the other rights under the Convention are applied: it does not give a free-standing right to freedom from discrimination. Protocol 12 to the Convention does contain such a right, but as yet has not been ratified by the UK.

138 See 15.7.

139 That is, under the principle of *in pari delicto potior est conditio defendentis*.

140 See 14.8.2.

141 The concept of 'impropriety' might apply to contracts prejudicial to sexual morality but as we have seen, this is probably a very narrow range of contracts under the modern law.

142 [1905] 2 KB 123 – see above, 14.12.3.

the promise of further payment in the event that one of his introductions led to her getting married. She was allowed to recover the deposit, despite the fact that the contract was regarded as void. It seems likely that this would be the general approach to contracts falling within this area.

14.17 WAGERING CONTRACTS

Section 18 of the Gaming Act 1845 provided that:

> All contracts . . . by way of gaming or wagering, shall be null and void; and no suit shall be brought or maintained in any court of law and equity for recovering any sum of money or valuable thing alleged to have been won upon any wager . . .

As from the 1 September 2007, however, s 334 of the Gambling Act 2005 repealed s 18 of the 1845 Act. This has the effect that gambling contracts entered into from that date are legally enforceable. The 1845 Act will only apply in relation to gambling contracts entered into before 1 September 2007. Its provisions are therefore not discussed further here. For the position under the 1845 Act, reference should be made to Chapter 15 of the 6th edition of this text.

14.18 FURTHER READING

Buckley, R, 'Illegal transactions: chaos or discretion' (2000) 20 LS 155

Conway, H, 'Prenuptial contracts' (1995) 145 NLJ 1290

Coote B, 'The Illegal Contracts Act 1970', Chapter 3 in *New Zealand Law Commission, Contract Statutes Review*, 1993

Enonchong, N, *Illegal Transactions*, 1998, London: Lloyd's of London Press

Grodecki, JK, '*In pari delicto potior est conditio defendentis*' (1955) 71 LQR 254

Law Commission, *Illegal Transactions: the Effect of Illegality on Contracts and Trusts*, Consultation Paper No 154, 1999

15 CONTRACTS IN RESTRAINT OF TRADE

CONTENTS

15.1 OVERVIEW

- Contracts in restraint of trade are prima facie void under the common law, but can be enforceable if:
    - the party imposing the restraint has a legitimate interest to protect; and
    - the restraint is reasonable in the context of protecting that interest; and
    - the restraint is not otherwise contrary to the public interest.
- The reasonableness of a restraint will be assessed in relation to:
    - the length of time for which it will operate;
    - the geographical area which it will cover;
    - the scope of the restraint (that is, the range of activities covered).
- The situations where these rules tend to apply are in relation to:
    - contracts of employment – in the form of restrictions on the employment that the employee can undertake once leaving the employment of the party

imposing the restraint. Such restrictions may be justified to protect trade secrets, or connections with clients;

☐ contracts for the sale of a business – the buyer of a business is entitled to impose restraints on the seller, to prevent the seller setting up in competition with the buyer.

■ Other types of restraint that need consideration are as follows:

☐ Contracts of exclusive dealing. Agreements to take all supplies of goods (for example, petrol, beer) from one supplier may be enforceable if reasonable.

☐ Restraints on songwriters and entertainers. This is another type of contract of exclusive dealing, where the artist agrees to work only for one publisher, record company, etc. Such restrictive contracts may be enforceable if they are reasonable.

☐ Trade associations. Agreements between companies not to compete in certain areas will be unenforceable at common law unless reasonable in protecting a legitimate interest. Such agreements may also be struck down by legislative controls against anti-competitive practices.

■ In some situations the courts will be prepared to 'sever' an unreasonable part of the restraint, and enforce the remainder.

15.2 INTRODUCTION

This chapter deals with an area of law which under classical contract theory brought two principles into direct conflict. On the one hand, classical theory endeavoured to promote 'freedom of contract' – it is the parties who determine their obligations, and the courts should only intervene in exceptional circumstances. On the other, underlying classical theory was an acceptance that the 'free market', in which competition takes place between those seeking to make contracts, is the ideal economic framework for the operation of exchange transactions. What happens when the freedom to contract is used to restrict competition? The answer of the common law was limited. A range of contracts or contractual provisions which were regarded as being 'in restraint of trade' were treated as being 'illegal', on grounds of public policy, and therefore unenforceable. The main use of this approach, however, as will be seen below, was in relation to restrictions contained in contracts of employment or in contracts for the sale of a business, purporting to limit the economic activity which the employee or the seller could engage in after leaving the employment or selling the business.[1] The broader problems of 'anti-competitive' practices, and in particular the problems arising from

---

1 Though, more recently, there has been increasing case law on 'exclusive dealing', where one party commits itself to take all supplies of a particular product (for example, petrol or beer) from a single supplier.

situations of monopoly or near monopoly in a particular market, were never tackled by the common law. There is now, however, extensive statutory intervention to control this area, with much of the current law being shaped by the rules applicable in the European Economic Community.

The approach taken here is to deal only with the common law rules on 'restraint of trade', since the statutory provisions (now contained in the Competition Act 1998) tend not be part of undergraduate contract courses.

15.3 RESTRAINT OF TRADE UNDER THE COMMON LAW [2]

Contractual provisions which attempt to restrict the ways in which one of the parties may do business, or earn a living, have at different times been treated by the common law as being prima facie void,[3] or prima facie valid.[4] The current position derives from the House of Lords' decision in *Nordenfelt v Maxim Nordenfelt Guns and Ammunition Co Ltd*,[5] in which Lord Macnaghten stated the House's view of the correct approach:[6]

> The public have an interest in every person's carrying on his trade freely: so has the individual. All interference with individual liberty of action in trading, and all restraints of trade of themselves, if there is nothing more, are contrary to public policy, and therefore void. That is the general rule. But there are exceptions: restraints of trade and interference with individual liberty of action may be justified by the special circumstances of a particular case. It is a sufficient justification, and indeed it is the only justification, if the restriction is reasonable – reasonable, that is, in reference to the interests of the parties concerned and reasonable in reference to the interests of the public . . .

The current presumption is, therefore, that contracts or provisions within a contract which are in restraint of trade are unenforceable. That presumption can, however, be rebutted by proving that the restraint is 'reasonable', both as between the parties and in relation to the public interest. Much of the case law in this area is concerned with deciding what is 'reasonable' in this context.

---

2 See, generally, Trebilcock, 1986.

3 *Claygate v Batchelor* (1602) Owen 143.

4 *Mitchel v Reynolds* (1711) 1 P Wms 181. Trebilcock (1986, pp 53–54) has suggested that throughout the changes of approach there is a 'thread of continuity': 'The thread is the underlying purpose of the doctrine as a whole – the protection of the individual's right to work – and the two values or principles which make that a desirable end: the value of equity or fairness with respect to the impact of a restraint on the party restrained, and the value of economic development more generally.'

5 [1894] AC 535.

6 Ibid, p 565.

15.4   CONTRACTS RELATING TO EMPLOYMENT OR THE SALE OF A BUSINESS

Examples of the kind of restraint we are dealing with would include a restriction on a sales representative from soliciting the customers of a former employer, or a restriction on the seller of a business from setting up in competition to the buyer. For such restraints to be valid, there are three requirements which must be fulfilled: (1) there must be a valid interest which the party imposing the restraint is trying to protect; (2) the restraint must be no more extensive than is reasonable to protect that interest; and (3) the restraint must not be contrary to the public interest. Each of these requirements needs to be considered separately.

15.4.1   Must have a valid interest

Looking at the first of these requirements, an employer will have a legitimate interest in restricting the activities of a departing employee, where that employee has either acquired trade secrets, or has gained influence over the employer's customers, either because they rely on the employee's skill and judgment, or because they have dealt exclusively with that employee. As was made clear by the House of Lords in *Herbert Morris Ltd v Saxelby*,[7] it is not sufficient simply that the employee may compete with the former employer, or use 'skill and knowledge acquired by the employee in his employer's business'.[8]

Examples from the cases where a restraint on an employee has been held to protect a legitimate interest include a hairdresser,[9] a sales representative[10] and a tailor.[11]

In relation to the sale of a business, the interest which the buyer is trying to protect is likely to be the 'goodwill' in the business, that is, the existing trade which has been built up by the seller. The buyer will probably have paid a substantial sum as part of the purchase price for the benefit of taking over the 'goodwill'. In that context, the buyer has a legitimate interest in preventing the seller from setting up a business which will attract all the old customers.

The courts have been prepared to recognise that the categories of legitimate interest are not closed. For example, in *Greig v Insole*,[12] which concerned restrictions placed on professional cricketers by the cricketing authorities, Slade J recognised that there might be a public interest that the game of cricket should be properly organised and administered. On the facts, however, the restraint was in any case unreasonable. In

---

7 [1916] 1 AC 688.
8 Ibid, p 710.
9 *Marion White Ltd v Francis* [1972] 1 WLR 1423.
10 *Lucas (T) & Co Ltd v Mitchell* [1974] Ch 129; [1972] 3 All ER 689.
11 *Attwood v Lamont* [1920] 3 KB 571.
12 [1978] 3 All ER 449.

Eastham v Newcastle United Football Club Ltd,[13] however, Wilberforce J was unable to find a legitimate interest in relation to restrictions on freedom of transfer for professional footballers.[14] It seems then that, although in theory the categories of interest are open, the courts are likely to be very cautious in finding new interests.

15.4.2 **Restraint must be reasonable**

The reasonableness or otherwise of the restraint must be looked at in the context of the interest which is being protected. There are three main factors to consider: (1) the geographical area covered; (2) the length of time involved; and (3) the scope of the activities covered.

For example, if a business is sold in one town, a restriction preventing the opening of a similar business anywhere in the country would be unlikely to be regarded as reasonable. In *Mason v Provident Clothing Co*,[15] a canvasser who had been employed to sell clothes in Islington was restrained from entering into similar business within 25 miles of London. This was held to be too wide.

As regards time, this will again depend on the type of contract. In many employment cases, a restraint of one or two years at most will be all that is reasonable. In *Fitch v Dewes*,[16] however, a lifelong restraint on a solicitor's managing clerk was upheld. The justification was that the business was one to which clients were likely to return over a long period.

FOR THOUGHT

How would you advise an employer who is seeking to put a restraint clause in her employees' contracts as to the length of any restraint that might be reasonable? What period would you advise for (a) a hairdresser, and (b) an accountant who handles the tax affairs of individual clients?

The type of activity restrained must also be related to the interest being protected. A clause restraining someone who had been employed as a chiropodist from working as a hairdresser would be unlikely to be regarded as reasonable.

At one time, the approach of the courts was to take clauses literally in assessing their reasonableness. Thus, if no area were specified, the restriction would be taken

---

13 [1964] Ch 413; [1963] 3 All ER 139.

14 This area (that is, football transfers) is one which has now been developed further by the influence of European Community law relating to competition and the free movement of workers: see the *Bosman* case – *Union Royale Belge des Sociétés de Football Association v Bosman* (Case C–415/93) [1995] ECR I–4921; [1996] 1 CMLR 645.

15 [1913] AC 724.

16 [1921] 2 AC 158.

to be worldwide. The cases of *Littlewoods v Harris*[17] and *Clarke v Newland*[18] have suggested a different approach, requiring the restraint to be limited by the 'factual matrix' within which it was imposed. In *Littlewoods v Harris*, an employee who had been employed solely in connection with the plaintiffs' mail order business was made subject to a restraint which, on its face, covered all aspects of the plaintiffs' wide ranging business activities. The Court of Appeal, however, held that the relevant clause should be interpreted as being intended only to apply to the mail order business in the UK. On that basis, it was reasonable. Similarly, in *Clarke v Newland*, a broad agreement by a doctor 'not to practise' was held to mean 'practise as a general medical practitioner' (rather than, for example, in a hospital) since that was the role in which the defendant had previously been employed.

15.4.3 Public interest

There is some controversy as to whether the public interest part of the rules concerning enforceable restraint of trade does in fact exist. If it does, then it means that even if a restraint satisfies the other conditions (that is, of legitimate interest and reasonableness), it may still be struck down as being contrary to the public interest. This might be the case, for example, in relation to a restraint on the work of a leading artist, playwright, doctor or scientist, whose work might well be for the public benefit. The principle was stated in *Wyatt v Kreglinger and Fernau*.[19] The plaintiff's pension was made contingent upon his not taking any part in the wool trade. The Court of Appeal held that this stipulation was void, irrespective of whether it was reasonable as between the parties, because it was contrary to the public interest. This was followed in the similar case of *Bull v Pitney Bowes*.[20] It seems difficult, however, to find later authorities that have applied the principle, though Lord Denning supported it in relation to a solicitor in *Oswald Hickson Collier & Co v Carter Ruck*.[21] In subsequent cases, such as *Deacons v Bridge*[22] and *Kerr v Morris*,[23] the courts have refused to apply the principle to the circumstances before them, while not denying its existence.

15.4.4 Effect of breach of contract

As regards employment contracts, restraints will be unenforceable if the contract has been terminated following a repudiatory breach by the employer.[24] This does not mean,

---

17 [1978] 1 All ER 1026.
18 [1991] 1 All ER 397.
19 [1933] 1 KB 793.
20 [1966] 3 All ER 384.
21 [1984] AC 720; [1984] 2 All ER 15.
22 [1984] AC 705; [1984] 2 All ER 19.
23 [1987] Ch 90; [1986] 3 All ER 217.
24 *Rock Refrigeration Ltd v Jones* [1997] 1 All ER 1, applying *General Billposting Co Ltd v Atkinson* [1909] AC 118.

however, that a restrictive covenant contained in a contract which purports to make it enforceable after a repudiatory breach is therefore automatically unreasonable.[25] Thus, if the employee simply resigns, the restraint will be enforceable, provided it is otherwise reasonable according to the tests outlined above.

15.5 CONTRACTS OF EXCLUSIVE DEALING

It was confirmed by the House of Lords in *Esso Petroleum Co Ltd v Harpers Garage (Stourport) Ltd*[26] that a contract in which one party agrees to take all supplies of a particular product from one source (sometimes known as a 'solus agreement') could amount to an unreasonable restraint on trade. Such arrangements are particularly common in relation to the supply of petrol, and in relation to the supply of beer, etc, to public houses.[27] The House of Lords recognised in *Esso v Harpers*, as had been acknowledged in a report from the Monopolies Commission published not long before its decision,[28] that solus agreements are not necessarily disadvantageous to the public.[29] It is a question of whether the restraints imposed by them are 'reasonable' overall. Such contractual arrangements may well also fall foul of the restrictions on anti-competitive agreements contained in s 2 of the Competition Act 1998, or Art 81 of the EC Treaty, but they may nevertheless be found to be unlawful at common law.[30]

Esso Petroleum v Harpers Garage in fact concerned two solus agreements in relation to two garages run by the defendant. In respect of both, there was an agreement to take all supplies of petrol from Esso, and to keep the garage open at all reasonable hours. In relation to garage A, the agreement was to last for four years and five months. In relation to garage B, the agreement was to last for 21 years, and was linked to a mortgage over the premises held by Esso, which was also irredeemable for 21 years. The defendants started to sell cut price petrol of other brands. Esso sought an injunction to prevent them doing this. The defence was based on 'restraint of trade'.

The House of Lords held that contracts of this type could be regarded as being in restraint of trade. As with the categories looked at above, the question was then whether the restraint was reasonable as between the parties, and reasonable in the public interest. In relation to garage A, the five year restraint was reasonable. The 21 years in

---

25 *Rock Refrigeration Ltd v Jones* [1997] 1 All ER 1.

26 [1968] AC 269; [1967] 1 All ER 699.

27 See, for example, *Byrne v Tibsco Ltd* [1999] UKCLR 110; *Inntrepreneur Estates (GL) Ltd v Boyes* [1993] 2 CMLR 293.

28 *Report on the Supply of Petrol to Retailers in the United Kingdom*, 1965 HC 265.

29 For example, it can lead to reductions in suppliers' costs (if they are supplying larger quantities to a smaller number of outlets) and keep down prices for the consumer. Nor is choice unduly restricted provided there are sufficient outlets so that a consumer does not have to travel far to find an alternative brand. See, for example, para 379 of the Report.

30 The statutory provisions have a minimum threshold based on the market share of the contracting parties; the common law has no such restriction.

relation to garage B, however, was unreasonable, particularly as it was linked to a mortgage.

The *Esso* case gives no indication of what period greater than five years, but less than 21 years, might have been considered reasonable. In the later case of *Alec Lobb (Garages) Ltd v Total Oil (Great Britain) Ltd*,[31] however, a 21 year restraint was held to be reasonable because it was terminable after seven or 14 years.

In *Shell UK Ltd v Lostock Garage*,[32] the Court of Appeal had to address the issue of the point in time at which a restraint should be judged. A solus agreement requiring L to take supplies of petrol exclusively from S had originally been entered into in 1955, for a period of 20 years. In 1966, however, it had been varied to become in effect a permanent arrangement, but terminable by 12 months' notice. In 1975, at the time of an intense petrol price war, S began to supply petrol at heavily subsidised rates to garages in the same locality as L. L was not included in these arrangements, and was unable to compete without making heavy losses. It therefore sought to obtain supplies of petrol elsewhere. Part of its argument was that the restraint of trade had become unreasonable, by virtue of S's discriminatory action in response to the price war. The majority of the Court of Appeal (Lord Denning dissenting) disagreed. They felt that the reasonableness of a restraint had to be judged at the time it was made, not in the light of later circumstances. Ormrod LJ thought that any other approach would create considerable difficulties:[33]

> It would introduce into the law an unprecedented discretion in the court to suspend for a time a term in a contract; the repercussions of this are quite unforeseeable and unmanageable. For example, it would at once alter the approach of the courts to covenants in restraint of trade generally, because, if the restraint could be temporarily suspended when it was operating oppressively, many more covenants would pass the normal test at the time they were entered into. Moreover, neither party will be able to know when a covenant is or is not enforceable, or if temporarily unenforceable, when it becomes enforceable again.

The agreement here, at least in the form which it had taken since 1966, was a reasonable one, and could not be struck down as being in restraint of trade. The conclusion is, therefore, that agreements have to be judged at the time they were made, and not in the context of subsequent developments.[34]

---

31 [1985] 1 All ER 303.

32 [1977] 1 All ER 481.

33 Ibid, p 492.

34 A different approach was taken in a 'beer-tie' case as to whether an agreement which is initially invalid under Art 81 of the EC Treaty can become valid if its economic effects change as a result of changed circumstances: *Passmore v Morland plc* [1999] 3 All ER 1005.

15.5.1 Restraints on songwriters and other entertainers

A particular area of difficulty has arisen in relation to contracts entered into by songwriters, or pop musicians, with music publishers or recording companies. These often require the artists to commit themselves to one company for a lengthy period of time, with no necessary obligation on the company to promote, or even publish, the artists' work. The validity of this kind of 'exclusive dealing' agreement was considered in *Schroeder Music Publishing Co Ltd v Macaulay*.[35] The plaintiff was a young and unknown songwriter who entered into a standard form agreement with music publishers (the defendants). The copyright in all the plaintiff's compositions for the next five years was assigned to the defendants, with an automatic extension for a further five years if royalties exceeded £5,000. The defendants could terminate the agreement on one month's notice, but there was no similar power for the plaintiff. The defendants were under no obligation to publish any of the plaintiff's work. The plaintiff sought a declaration that the agreement was in restraint of trade and void. The House of Lords held that, where there was unequal bargaining power, a standard form agreement has to be looked at to see if, amongst other things, the restrictions it contains only go so far as is reasonably necessary to protect legitimate interests. In this case, the contract was in unreasonable restraint of trade because, whereas the plaintiff was totally committed to the defendants, the defendants were not obliged to publish anything.

> **FOR THOUGHT**
>
> If publishers are required to make contracts which are favourable to the songwriters won't this have the effect that they will be reluctant to take on new writers? Would this be to the long-term benefit of the industry?

The decision in *Schroeder v Macaulay* was applied in the similar case of *Clifford Davis Management Ltd v WEA Records Ltd*.[36] In *Panayiotou v Sony Music Entertainment (UK) Ltd*,[37] on the other hand, a recording contract which was probably in restraint of trade when entered into had been renegotiated after the performer concerned (George Michael) had become famous. His subsequent attempt to challenge the renegotiated agreement failed because, although it contained some unfavourable conditions, the performer had received full legal advice. Moreover, the renegotiated agreement was part of a settlement of the dispute of the original contract. In this context, public policy favoured giving effect to the settlement, and therefore the revised contract. In any case, the recording company had a legitimate interest to protect, in that it wished to sell as

---

35 [1974] 3 All ER 616.
36 [1975] 1 All ER 237.
37 [1994] Ch 142; [1994] 1 All ER 755.

many records as possible, and the restrictions on the performer were not unreasonable as a means of protecting that interest.

15.6 TRADE ASSOCIATIONS

A group of manufacturers or producers may make an agreement between themselves to protect their interests. Such agreements may fall foul of legislative provisions relating to competition under domestic or European law, but they are also subject to the control of the common law and may be struck down as being in restraint of trade. The relevant principles were considered in *English Hop Growers v Dering*.[38] The defendant, in common with other hop growers, had agreed to deliver all crops produced by him to a central selling agency. The object of the agreement was to protect the producers at a time when it was feared that there might be a glut of hops on the market. The defendant sought to escape from the agreement on the basis that it was in restraint of trade. Adopting a similar approach to the other areas which we have considered, the majority of the Court of Appeal asked whether the restriction was reasonable to protect a legitimate interest. It was held that the restraint was not in this case an unreasonable one and the agreement was upheld. This perhaps reflects the fact that the agreement here had been reached between parties bargaining at arm's length.

If such an agreement affects third parties, the court will be more likely to intervene, as in *Kores Manufacturing Co Ltd v Kolok Manufacturing Co Ltd*.[39] This concerned an agreement between two companies that neither would, without the consent of the other, employ any person who had been employed by the other company within the past five years. The agreement was intended to protect trade secrets, since they were both working on similar products involving chemical processes. In addition, at the time it was thought that their factories would be adjacent, though this turned out not to be the case. One of the companies brought an action to restrain the other from employing a particular former employee. It seems clear that there was in this case a legitimate interest to protect, but the Court of Appeal held that the restraint was too wide. It had the potential to cover an unskilled labourer as much as the chief chemist. On that basis, it was unreasonable.

15.7 SEVERANCE

In many contracts that are found to be void or unenforceable for illegality, or because they are in restraint of trade, it is likely to be the case that it is only part of the arrangement which is objectionable. To what extent can the contract be split into its constituent parts, with one part being found valid, and the objectionable part unenforceable? There

---

38 [1928] 2 KB 174.
39 [1959] Ch 108; [1958] 2 All ER 65.

are two aspects to this, namely, severance of the consideration and severance of promises. Suppose, for example, A agrees to pay B £1,000 if B will fraudulently obtain a valuable painting and frame it. The first part of this contract, involving the fraud, is illegal, but the second part, for the framing, is prima facie a perfectly legal arrangement. If B does what is required, and then sues for the £1,000, the issue of the severance of the consideration will arise. B's consideration for the promise to pay the £1,000 consists of both an illegal and a legal act. Can the two be separated? In other words, can B recover the £1,000 simply for framing the picture? If the action is by A, however, in relation to B's failure to frame the picture, the question concerns the separation of the promises. These two issues will now be considered in turn.

15.7.1   Severance of consideration

For severance of consideration to be allowed, the lawful part of the consideration must be more important than the unlawful part. For example, in a contract of employment, the employee's consideration for the payment of wages may be made up of performing the required work (legal), and a promise not to compete after leaving the employment (possibly illegal). Nevertheless, even if the restraint on future employment is too wide, the employee will be allowed to sue for wages. The consideration can be severed here, because the performance of the work is the major part of the consideration, and the restraint is subsidiary.

Note that the approach will in general be 'all or nothing'. Thus, in the example of the painting, given in the previous section, B would either be able to claim the full £1,000, or nothing at all (which would be the more likely outcome). This may not apply, however, if it is possible to assign a precise value to different parts of the contract. This occurred in *Ailion v Spiekermann*,[40] where the contract to pay the illegal premium could be severed, because a precise amount could be assigned to the illegal part of the agreement.

15.7.2   Severance of promises

The attempt to sever promises occurs most frequently in relation to restraint of trade cases, where the wish is to 'edit out' from a list of restrictions those which make the restraint too wide, but to leave the rest in force. There have traditionally been two elements to the courts' approach, namely, the 'Blue Pencil Test' and the requirement that the nature of the contract must be retained.

15.7.3   The Blue Pencil Test

The Blue Pencil Test means that severance must be possible simply by cutting out the offending words. The court will not become involved in redrafting the contract. Thus, in

---

40 [1976] Ch 158; [1976] 1 All ER 497 – see Chapter 14, 14.4.5. Compare also *Carney v Herbert* [1985] 1 All ER 438.

Mason v Provident Clothing Co,[41] the court refused to substitute the phrase 'in Islington', for 'within 25 miles of London'. In *Goldsoll v Goldman*,[42] on the other hand, a covenant in the sale of a jewellery business contained a restriction on dealing in 'real or imitation jewellery' in any of a long list of countries. This was too wide both as regards scope (the business was only concerned with imitation jewellery) and geographical area (the business was limited to the UK). Both restrictions could be narrowed, however, by simple deletions, of the words 'real or', and the list of countries other than the UK, and this the court agreed to do.

The strict application of this test traditionally required that the clause as edited still made sense, but the modern approach seems more relaxed – as discussed below (see 15.7.5).

15.7.4 Nature of the contract must be retained

The requirement that the nature of the contract must be retained seems to derive from *Attwood v Lamont*,[43] but is quite difficult to apply. In *Attwood v Lamont*, the plaintiff owned a general outfitters. The defendant was employed in the tailoring department as a tailor and cutter. He found that his contract of employment bound him, after leaving his employment, not to be concerned in the trade or business of a tailor, dressmaker, general draper, milliner, hatter, haberdasher, gentlemen's, ladies' or children's outfitter. It was suggested that the clause could be made reasonable by cutting out all the trades except 'tailor'. The Court of Appeal refused to do this, treating the covenant as an entirety, intended to cover all aspects of the plaintiff's business. To sever it would be to affect its nature.

It is very difficult to reconcile this decision with the earlier decision in *Goldsoll v Goldman* (discussed in the previous section) or the later decision in *Putsman v Taylor*.[44] In the latter case, the employee worked as a tailor at one branch, but the restriction covered all three branches owned by his employer. The court agreed to sever the names of the branches where the employee had not worked.

Despite this difficulty, the principle stated in *Attwood v Lamont* has not been overturned, and we must still accept that there is, alongside the Blue Pencil Test, a further requirement that the nature of the contract is not altered. How this principle will be applied, however, is very unpredictable.

---

41 [1913] AC 724. See above, 15.4.2.
42 [1915] 1 Ch 292.
43 [1920] 3 KB 571.
44 [1927] 1 KB 637.

15.7.5   The current approach

It may well be that the tests outlined in the previous two sections will not nowadays be applied so strictly by the courts. In *Lucas (T) & Co Ltd v Mitchell*,[45] for example, the deletion left the phrase 'any such goods' in the contract. It was necessary to look at the deleted clause in order to see what 'such goods' meant, but the deletion was nevertheless allowed to stand. Moreover, the approach taken to the interpretation of restraint clauses in *Littlewoods v Harris*[46] and *Clarke v Newland*,[47] discussed above,[48] may mean that the severance of provisions may not be so necessary. As we have seen, the courts in these cases rejected the view that widely-phrased restrictions should be given their literal meaning. Instead, they had to be interpreted within the factual context in which they had been put forward. Such an interpretation is likely to lead to the restraint, as redefined, being regarded as reasonable, thus obviating the need to consider severance.

15.8   FURTHER READING

Monopolies Commission, *Report on the supply of petrol to retailers in the United Kingdom*, 1965 HC 265

Smith, SA, 'Reconstructing restraint of trade' (1995) OJLS 565

Trebilcock, MJ, *The Common Law of Restraint of Trade*, 1986, London: Sweet & Maxwell

Whish, R, *Competition Law*, 5th edn, 2003, London: Butterworths

Wilson, S and Woodley, M, 'Restraint, drafting and the rule in General Billposting', [1998] JBL 272

---

45 [1974] Ch 129; [1972] 3 All ER 689.
46 [1978] 1 All ER 1026.
47 [1991] 1 All ER 397.
48 See 15.4.2.

16 FRUSTRATION

CONTENTS

16.1 OVERVIEW[1]

The doctrine of frustration deals with the situation where circumstances change after a contract has been made, and this makes the performance impossible, or at least significantly different from what was intended. The following aspects need discussion:

■ The nature of the doctrine. Is the doctrine based on an implied term in the contract, or simply on a rule of law?
■ What sort of events will lead to the frustration of a contract? Examples include:
  □ destruction of the subject matter – this is the clearest example of frustration;

---

1 See, generally, Treitel, 1994; McKendrick, 1995a.

□ where personal performance is important, the illness of one party may frustrate the agreement;

□ where the contract presumes the occurrence of an event, its cancellation may be treated as frustration;

□ if the contract becomes illegal, or a government intervenes to prohibit it.

■ Limitations on the doctrine. It will not apply where:

□ the contract simply becomes more difficult or expensive to perform;

□ the 'frustration' is attributable to the actions of one of the parties;

□ the parties have provided for the circumstances in the contract itself.

■ Effects of the doctrine under the common law:

□ the contract is terminated automatically; but

□ all rights and liabilities which have already arisen remain in force; except that

□ if there is a total failure of consideration, money paid may be recovered.

■ The Law Reform (Frustrated Contracts) Act 1943. This Act amends the common law, so that:

□ money paid prior to frustration can generally be recovered;

□ benefits conferred, which survive the frustrating event, can be compensated for.

The chapter concludes with a consideration of the proposals contained in the Principles of European Contract Law which apply to this area.

16.2 THE NATURE OF THE DOCTRINE

This chapter is concerned with the situation where, following the formation of a valid contract, an event occurs which is not the fault of either party, but which has a significant impact on the obligations contained in the contract. English law will sometimes, but not always, consider that such an event results in the 'frustration' of the contract, with the consequence that the parties are partially or wholly relieved from further obligations, and may be able to recover money or property transferred, and compensation for work done prior to the frustrating event.

This topic, the doctrine of frustration, has links with preceding chapters, and with the one that follows. Frustration can, from one point of view, be looked at as something that vitiates a contract, and in particular has similarities with the area of 'common mistake'.[2] Whereas, however, vitiating factors generally relate to things which have happened, or states of affairs which exist, at or before the time when the contract is made, frustration deals with events which occur subsequent to the contract coming into existence. Since frustration has the characteristics of an event which discharges parties

---

2 See Chapter 11, 11.5. Both frustration and common mistake can be analysed as methods by which the determination of 'risk allocation' is taken out of the hands of the parties, and dealt with by legal rules or the discretion of a judge.

from their obligations under a contract, it also has links with the topics of performance and breach (see Chapter 17).

The situation with which the doctrine of frustration is concerned is where a contract, as a result of some event outside the control of the parties, becomes impossible to perform, at least in the way originally intended. What are the rights and liabilities of the parties?

16.2.1 Original rule

In *Paradine v Jane*,[3] the court took the line that obligations were not discharged by a 'frustrating' event, and that a party who failed to perform as a result of such an event would still be in breach of contract. The justification for this harsh approach was that the parties could, if they wished, have provided for the eventuality within the contract itself.[4] In commercial contracts this is in fact often done, and *force majeure* clauses are included so as to make clear where losses will fall on the occurrence of events which affect some fundamental aspect of the contract.[5] Disputes about whether a contract is frustrated are therefore less common in the commercial context than those about the interpretation of a *force majeure* clause.[6]

16.2.2 Subsequent mitigation

The *Paradine v Jane* approach, however, proved to be too strict and potentially unjust, even for the nineteenth century courts, which were in many respects strong supporters of the concept of 'freedom of contract', taking the view that it was not for the court to interfere to remedy perceived injustice resulting from a freely negotiated bargain. The modern law has developed from the decision in *Taylor v Caldwell*.[7] This contract involved the letting of a music hall for the purposes of concerts and other events. After the agreement, but before the first concert, the hall was destroyed by fire. It was held that since performance was impossible, this event excused the parties from any further obligations under the contract. Blackburn J justified this approach on the basis that where the parties must have known from the beginning that the contract was dependent on the continued existence of a particular thing, the contract must be construed:[8]

---

3 (1647) Aleyn 26; 82 ER 897.

4 Trebilcock (1993, p 136) has suggested that, in fact, the courts are unlikely to be very effective in achieving an appropriate allocation of risks in the business context, and that therefore there is an argument that 'a clear, albeit austere, rule of literal contract enforcement in most cases provides the clearest signal to parties to future contractual relationships as to when they might find it mutually advantageous to contract away from the rule'. This would support a return to the *Paradine v Jane* approach.

5 The parties may also include 'hardship clauses' (to provide for modification of the contract in the light of changed circumstances), which may also be supplemented by an 'intervener clause' (giving a third person the power to determine the appropriate modification). For further discussion of these devices, see McKendrick, 1995b, pp 327–29.

6 See the comments to this effect by McKendrick, 1995b, p 323.

7 (1863) 3 B & S 826; 122 ER 309.

8 Ibid, pp 833–34; p 312.

... as subject to an implied condition that the parties shall be excused in case, before breach, performance becomes impossible from the perishing of the thing without the fault of the contractor.

The doctrine at this stage, then, is based on the existence of an implied term. This enabled the decision to be squared with the prevailing approach to freedom of contract, and was adopted in subsequent cases.[9] It also tied in with classical theory that all is dependent on what the parties intended at the time of the contract.[10] In reality, of course, this is something of a fiction.[11] Some judges in more recent cases have recognised this. In particular, Lord Radcliffe in *Davis Contractors Ltd v Fareham UDC*,[12] in a passage that has often been quoted subsequently, stated that, in relation to the implied term theory:

> ... there is something of a logical difficulty in seeing how the parties could even impliedly have provided for something which, *ex hypothesi*, they neither expected nor foresaw; and the ascription of frustration to an implied term of the contract has been criticised as obscuring the true action of the court which consists in applying an objective rule of the law of contract to the contractual obligation which the parties have imposed on themselves.

In truth, however, the problem with the implied term theory is not one of logic. Although the parties will not have foreseen the particular event,[13] there is nothing illogical about agreeing that, in general terms, unforeseen events affecting the nature of the parties' obligations will result in specified consequences. Indeed, most *force majeure* clauses will include a provision to this effect. And if this can be done by an express clause, there is no reason why it cannot be done by one which is implied.

The real objection to the implied term theory here, as elsewhere in the law of

---

9 See, for example, Lord Loreburn in *FA Tamplin Steamship Co Ltd v Anglo-Mexican Petroleum Products Ltd* [1916] 2 AC 397, p 403: 'a court . . . ought to examine the contract . . . in order to see whether or not from the nature of it the parties must have made their bargain on the footing that a particular thing or state of things would continue to exist. And if they must have done so, then a term to that effect will be implied, though it be not expressed in the contract . . .'

10 Or, more accurately, what two reasonable people in the position of the parties would be taken to have intended.

11 It can be said, as is the case with all terms implied by the courts on the basis of the parties' supposed intentions, to be based on the myth of 'presentiation', exposed in particular by Macneil, which suggests that the entire future of a contract can be determined by the obligations agreed at its outset: Macneil, 1978. See also Chapter 1, 1.5.

12 [1956] 2 All ER 145, p 159.

13 This point is made by Lord Sands' example in the Scottish case of *James Scott & Sons Ltd v Del Sel* 1922 SC 592, p 597, concerning an escaped tiger and its effect on milk deliveries – concluding that the understandable exoneration of the milkman could not reasonably be attributed to a clause in the delivery contract stating 'tiger days excepted'. The example is quoted by Lord Reid in *Davis Contractors Ltd v Fareham UDC* [1956] 2 All ER 145, p 153.

contract,[14] is that it obscures what the courts are actually doing – which is, in this case, deciding that certain events have such an effect on the contract that it is unfair to hold the parties to it in the absence of fault on either side, and in the absence of any clear assumption of the relevant risk by either party. That this is the basis for intervention has been recognised by some judges. In *Hirji Mulji v Cheong Yue Steamship Co Ltd*,[15] for example, Lord Sumner commented that the doctrine 'is really a device by which the rules as to absolute contracts are reconciled with a special exception which justice demands'. This line has been supported by Lord Wright both judicially in *Denny, Mott and Dickson Ltd v James Fraser*[16] and, more explicitly, extra-judicially.[17] It thus forms one of the two other main theoretical bases, as alternatives to the implied term, put forward as explanations of the doctrine of frustration.[18] It is by no means universally accepted, however, perhaps because of its uncertainty, and the third theory, that based on 'construction', seems to be the one that is currently favoured.[19] The most frequently cited statement of this theory is that of Lord Radcliffe in *Davis Contractors Ltd v Fareham UDC*.[20] Having outlined the artificiality of the implied term approach, he commented:

> So perhaps it would be simpler to say at the outset that frustration occurs whenever the law recognises that without default of either party a contractual obligation has become incapable of being performed because the circumstance in which performance is called for would render it a thing radically different from that which was undertaken by the contract. *Non haec in foedera veni*. It was not this that I promised to do.

---

14 See Chapter 8, 8.6.

15 [1926] AC 497, p 510.

16 [1994] AC 265, pp 274–75.

17 Wright, 1939, p 258: 'The truth is that the court . . . decides the question in accordance with what seems to be just and reasonable in its eyes.' See also the comments of Denning LJ in *British Movietonews Ltd v London and District Cinemas Ltd* [1951] 1 KB 190, p 200, basing the approach on what is 'just and reasonable' in the new situation – though these comments were specifically disapproved as being too broad by Viscount Simon in the House of Lords in this case: [1952] AC 166, p 183.

18 Lord Hailsham suggested in *National Carriers Ltd v Panalpina (Northern) Ltd* [1981] AC 675, p 687, that 'at least five theories for the doctrine of frustration have been put forward at various times'. Treitel (1994, p 583) has commented that the discussion of the theoretical basis of the doctrine has no practical importance.

19 Though this terminology is confusing since the 'implied term' theory can also be described as being based on the 'construction' of the contract: see, for example, Atiyah, 1986, p 272. Atiyah (1986, p 273) also points out that it may be inaccurate to describe the various approaches as conflicting theories, since they are in fact just answers to different questions about the doctrine of frustration: the 'just solution' is the goal or objective of the doctrine; the implied term approach is a 'technique'; and what is called here the 'construction' theory (or 'change in fundamental obligation' theory) is a statement of the conditions in which the implied term approach will be applied.

20 [1956] AC 696, pp 728–29.

The approach is, therefore, to ask what the original contract required of the parties,[21] and then to decide, in the light of the alleged 'frustrating' event, whether the performance of those obligations would now be something 'radically different'. This has been subsequently endorsed as the best approach by the House of Lords in *National Carriers Ltd v Panalpina (Northern) Ltd*.[22]

The operation of this approach requires the courts to decide what situations will make performance 'radically different' – and it is to this issue that we now turn.

16.3   FRUSTRATING EVENTS

It is clear that 'radical difference' will include, but is not limited to, situations where performance has become 'impossible'. Unfortunately, neither 'impossibility' nor 'radical difference' has a self-evident meaning in this context. Both require interpretation in their application. There is, however, guidance to be obtained from looking at the cases. Although the categories can never be closed, it is possible to identify certain occurrences which have been recognised by the courts as amounting to frustration of the contract.

16.3.1   Destruction of the subject matter

In the same way that the destruction of the subject matter prior to the formation of a contract will render it void for common mistake,[23] destruction at a later stage will fall within the doctrine of frustration, as indicated by *Taylor v Caldwell*.[24] Complete destruction is not necessary. In *Taylor v Caldwell* itself, the contract related to the use of the hall and gardens, but it was only the hall which was destroyed.[25] The contract nevertheless became impossible as regards a major element (use of the hall), and was therefore frustrated. In other words, if what is destroyed is fundamental to the performance of the obligations under the contract, then the doctrine will operate.[26]

It seems that complete physical destruction may not be necessary if the subject matter has been affected in a way which renders it useless. In *Asfar v Blundell*,[27] for example, a cargo of dates was being carried on a boat which sank in the Thames. The

---

21 This is why the theory is sometimes referred to as the 'construction' theory: the contract has to be construed to determine the obligations which it placed on the parties. Collins 1999, (pp 163–65) has criticised the heavy reliance of the courts on the formal documentation rather than the 'business deal' which underlies this: he suggests that this leads the courts, while purporting to do justice between the parties, to allocate risks in ways which do not correspond with those parties' commercial expectations.

22 [1981] AC 675.

23 As in *Couturier v Hastie* (1856) 5 HLC 673: see Chapter 11, 11.5.

24 (1863) 3 B & S 826; 122 ER 309.

25 Indeed, it seems that the defendant continued to be able to use the gardens and to charge for admission to them despite the fire: see Treitel, 1994, p 808, n 31.

26 Cf Sale of Goods Act 1979, s 7: see 16.6 below.

27 [1896] 1 QB 123.

cargo was recovered, but the dates were found to be in a state of fermentation and contaminated with sewage. The judge found that they 'had been so deteriorated that they had become something which was not merchantable as dates'.[28] On that basis, there was a total loss of the dates, and the contract was frustrated.

16.3.2 Personal services – supervening incapacity

If a contract envisages performance by a particular individual, as in a contract to paint a portrait, and no substitute is likely to be satisfactory, then the contract will generally be frustrated by the incapacity of the person concerned. Thus, in *Condor v Barron Knights*,[29] the drummer with a pop group was taken ill. Medical opinion was that he would only be fit to work three or four nights a week, whereas the group had engagements for seven nights a week. It was held that his contract of employment was discharged by frustration. The drummer was incapable of performing his contract in the way intended.

In many cases, of course, the identity of the person who is to perform the contract will not be significant. Suppose, for example, a garage agrees to service a car on a particular day, but on that day, as a result of illness, it is short-staffed and cannot carry out the service. This will be treated as a breach of contract, rather than frustration. The contract is simply to carry out the service, and the car owner is unlikely to be concerned about the identity of the particular individual who performs the contract, so long as he or she is competent.[30]

FOR THOUGHT

Do you think the position would be the same if there were a flu epidemic, and the garage had no mechanics available at all?

16.3.3 Non-occurrence of an event

If the parties reach an agreement which is dependent on a particular event taking place, the cancellation of that event may well lead to the contract being frustrated. This situation arose in relation to a number of contracts surrounding the coronation of Edward VII, which was postponed owing to the King's illness.

In *Krell v Henry*,[31] the defendant had made a contract for the use of certain rooms owned by the plaintiff for the purpose of watching the coronation procession. It was held that the postponement of the procession frustrated the contract. Although literal performance was possible, in that the room could have been made available to the

---

28 [1896] 1 QB 123, p 128.
29 [1966] 1 WLR 87.
30 Cf the cases on mistaken identity – discussed above, 11.6.3–11.6.4.
31 [1903] 2 KB 740.

defendant at the appropriate time, and the defendant could have sat in it and looked out of the window, in the absence of the procession it had no point, and the whole purpose of the contract had vanished.

By contrast in another 'coronation case', *Herne Bay Steamboat Co v Hutton*,[32] the contract was not frustrated. Here, the contract was that the plaintiff's boat should be 'at the disposal of' the defendant on 25 June to take passengers from Herne Bay for the purpose of watching the naval review, which the King was to conduct, and for a day's cruise round the fleet. The King's illness led to the review being cancelled. In this case, however, the Court of Appeal held that the contract was not frustrated. The distinction from *Krell v Henry* is generally explained on the basis that the contract in *Herne Bay* was still regarded as having some purpose. The fleet was still in place (as Stirling LJ pointed out), and so the tour of it could go ahead, even if the review by the King had been cancelled. The effect on the contract was not sufficiently fundamental to lead to it being regarded as frustrated. Brownsword has argued, however, that the contract would not have been frustrated even if the fleet had sailed away.[33] In his view the distinction between the cases is that Hutton, the hirer of the boat, was engaged in a purely commercial enterprise, intending to make money out of carrying passengers around the bay, whereas Henry was in effect a 'consumer', whose only interest was in getting a good view of the coronation procession. This approach also emphasises that it is important to determine exactly what the parties had agreed. As Vaughan Williams LJ suggested in *Krell v Henry*,[34] if there was a contract to hire a taxi to take a person to Epsom on Derby Day, and the Derby was subsequently cancelled, this would not affect the contract for the hire of the taxi; the hirer would be entitled to be driven to Epsom, but would also be liable for the fare if he chose not to go.

16.3.4 Government intervention

If a contract is made, and there is then a declaration of war which turns one of the parties into an enemy alien, then the contract will be frustrated.[35] Similarly, the requisitioning of property for use by the government can have a similar effect, as in *Metropolitan Water Board v Dick Kerr*.[36] In this case, a contract for the construction of a reservoir was frustrated by an order by the Minister of Munitions, during the First World War, that the defendant should cease work, and disperse and sell the plant.

Here, as is the case in relation to the non-occurrence of an event, it must be clear

---

32 [1903] 2 KB 683.
33 Brownsword, 1993, pp 246–47.
34 [1903] 2 KB 740, pp 751–52.
35 *Fibrosa Spolka Ackyjna v Fairbairn Lawson Combe Barbour Ltd* [1943] AC 32.
36 [1918] AC 119. See also *Bank Line v Arthur Capel Ltd* [1919] AC 435 – requisition of a ship which was the subject of a 12 month time charter. When the ship was released some six months after the expected start date, an action for non-delivery (brought on the basis that the charter could have run for 12 months from that date) failed: the charter was held to be frustrated.

that the interference radically or fundamentally alters the contract. In *FA Tamplin v Anglo-Mexican Petroleum*,[37] a ship which was subject to a five year charter was requisitioned for use as a troopship. It was held by the House of Lords that the charter was not frustrated, since judging it at the time of the requisition, the interference was not sufficiently serious.[38] There might have been many months during which the ship would have been available for commercial purposes before the expiry of the contract.

Similarly, the fact that the contract has been rendered more difficult, or more expensive, does not frustrate it. The closure of the Suez Canal in 1956 forced the sellers of goods to ship them via the Cape of Good Hope, extending the time for delivery by about four weeks. The House of Lords in *Tsakiroglou & Co v Noblee and Thorl*[39] held that this was not frustration. The route for shipment had not been specified in the contract, nor was any precise delivery date agreed. The fact that the re-routing would cost more was regarded as irrelevant.

The government intervention need not relate to war or international relations. In *Gamerco SA v ICM/Fair Warning Agency*,[40] the Spanish government's closure of a stadium for safety reasons was held to frustrate a contract to hold a pop concert there.

An unsuccessful attempt was made in *Amalgamated Investment and Property Co Ltd v John Walker & Sons*[41] to base frustration on a different type of government interference, namely the 'listing' of a building as being of architectural and historic interest, and therefore subject to strict planning conditions. Despite the fact that this was estimated as having the effect of reducing the market value of the building to £200,000 (the contract price was £1,700,000), the Court of Appeal held that the contract was not frustrated. It was not part of the contract that the building should not be listed, and the change in the market value of the property could not in itself amount to frustration. The decision presumably leaves open the possibility that if the non-listing of a building was a crucial element in the contract, then frustration could follow from such a listing.

Such an outcome is perhaps less likely in the light of the Court of Appeal's later decision in the case of *Bormarin AB v IMB Investments Ltd*.[42] In this case, a contract for the purchase of the share capital of two companies had been set up with the main purpose of enabling the buyer to be able to set off losses against gains, as was at that time allowed by tax law. Subsequently, the law changed, so that such losses could no longer be set off. The seller sought to enforce the agreement but, at first instance, it was held that the contract had been frustrated by the change in the law. On appeal, however, the Court of Appeal ruled that frustration could not be used where, as a result of a change in the law, a bargain turned out to be less advantageous than that which had been hoped.

---

37 [1916] 2 AC 397.
38 This was a majority view, with two of the members of the House dissenting.
39 [1962] AC 93; [1961] 2 All ER 179.
40 [1995] 1 WLR 1126.
41 [1976] 3 All ER 509.
42 [1999] STC 301.

16.3.5   Supervening illegality

If, after a contract has been made, its purpose becomes illegal, this will be regarded as a frustrating event. In *Denny, Mott and Dickson v James Fraser*,[43] there was an agreement for the sale of timber over a number of years. It provided that the buyer should let a timber yard to the seller, and give him an option to purchase it. In 1939, further dealings in timber were made illegal. The House of Lords held that not only the trading contract, but also the option on the timber yard, was frustrated. The main object of the contract was trading in timber and, once this was frustrated, the whole agreement was radically altered.

16.3.6   Other frustrating events

Other types of event which have been held to lead to frustration include industrial action, particularly if in the form of a strike, and the effects of war. For example, in *Pioneer Shipping Ltd v BTP Tioxide Ltd*,[44] the House of Lords upheld an arbitrator's view that a time charter was frustrated when strikes meant that only two out of the anticipated six or seven voyages would be able to be made. As regards the effects of war, in *Finelvet AG v Vinava Shipping Co Ltd*,[45] a time-chartered ship was trapped by the continuing Gulf War between Iran and Iraq. Again, the court upheld the view of an arbitrator that this was sufficiently serious to mean that the contract was frustrated.

Note that in the former case, it was the *extent* of the effect of the strike that was important. In the latter case, it was made clear that the outbreak of war did not necessarily frustrate a contract on which it had a bearing; it was only when it became clear that the war would be protracted that the contract was frustrated. This again emphasises the point that, whatever the frustrating event (and the categories are never likely to be closed), it is the *effect* of that event on the contract, and what the parties have agreed, that is the most important consideration, and not the *nature* of the event itself. Only if its effect is to change fundamentally the conditions of the contract, and to make performance radically different from what the parties had agreed, will frustration take place.

16.4   LIMITATIONS ON THE DOCTRINE

The general limitations on the availability of a plea of frustration, in terms of the seriousness of the event and its effect on what the parties have agreed, have been discussed above. In this section, three more specific limitations are noted.

---

43 [1944] AC 265; [1944] 1 All ER 678.
44 [1982] AC 724; [1981] 2 All ER 1030.
45 [1983] 2 All ER 658.

16.4.1 Self-induced frustration

If it is the behaviour of one of the parties that, while not necessarily in itself amounting to a breach of contract, has brought about the circumstances which are alleged to frustrate the contract, this will be regarded as 'self-induced frustration', and the contract will not be discharged. For example, if the fire which caused the destruction of the music hall in *Taylor v Caldwell*[46] had been the result of negligence by one of the parties, the contract would not have been frustrated. This is an obvious restriction, but it may not always be easy to determine the type of behaviour that should fall within its scope. An example of its application is *Maritime National Fish Ltd v Ocean Trawlers Ltd*.[47] The appellants chartered a trawler from the respondents. The trawler was fitted with an 'otter' trawl, which it was illegal to use without a licence, as both parties were aware. The appellants applied for five licences to operate otter trawls, but were only granted three. They decided to use these for boats other than the one chartered from the respondents. They claimed that this contract was therefore frustrated, since the trawler could not legally be used. The Privy Council held that the appellants were not discharged. It was their own election to use the licences with the other boats which had led to the illegality of using the appellants' trawler.

This decision seems fair where it is the case, as it was here, that the party exercising the choice could have done so without breaking any contract (since the trawlers to which the licences were assigned all belonged to the appellants).[48] It may not be so fair, however, if a person is put in a position where there is no choice but to break one of two contracts. Nevertheless, when this situation arose in *Lauritzen (J) AS v Wijsmuller BV, The Super Servant Two*,[49] the Court of Appeal applied the concept of self-induced frustration strictly. The parties had made a contract for the transportation of a drilling rig, which, as they both knew, could only be carried out by one of two vessels owned by the defendants, namely, *Super Servant One* and *Super Servant Two*. The contract referred to both vessels, but did not specify which one would be used. The defendants, intending to use *Super Servant Two*, allocated *Super Servant One* to other contracts. *Super Servant Two* then sank. The defendants claimed that the contract was frustrated, but the plaintiffs alleged that the impossibility of performance arose from the defendants' own acts,[50] and that they should not therefore be discharged from performance. The Court of Appeal agreed that, even though the defendants were neither negligent nor in breach of contract in the way in which they had allocated the vessels, the doctrine

---

46 See above, 16.2.2.

47 [1935] AC 524.

48 Treitel (2003, pp 906–07) has argued that this element should be treated as an important part of the decision in *Maritime National Fish*.

49 [1990] 1 Lloyd's Rep 1.

50 That is, the contract was not automatically made impossible by the sinking of the *Super Servant Two*, which would have amounted to frustration, but only by the subsequent decision of the defendants not to use the *Super Servant One* for this contract.

of frustration did not operate to remove their liability under the contract with the plaintiffs.[51] Bingham LJ felt that it was:

> . . . inconsistent with the doctrine of frustration as previously understood on high authority that its application should depend on any decision, however reasonable and commercial, of the party seeking to rely on it.

It seems then that any exercise of choice by one of the parties which contributes to a situation where the contract becomes impossible, or radically different, will prevent the doctrine of frustration from applying.

The *Super Servant Two* decision has been strongly criticised by Treitel. In his view, the situation was distinguishable from that in the *Maritime National Fish* case, because there the defendant had a choice about whether any contracts were broken or not. Moreover, to the extent that the basis of the decision in *Super Servant Two* is that it was within the shipowners' control as to what contracts were made and what risks were undertaken, this 'seems to undermine the whole basis of the doctrine of frustration: it has just as much force where the promisor enters into a single contract as where he enters into two or more, with different contracting parties'.[52]

Despite these criticisms, the decision in *Super Servant Two* has not been the subject of any reported challenge over the past 17 years, so perhaps it is not such a difficult decision for the commercial world to cope with as might appear at first sight.

16.4.2   Events foreseen and provided for

One way in which the parties can avoid the situation discussed in the previous section, and its perceived unfairness, is by including specific provision in the contract to deal with that situation. Indeed, in *Super Servant Two*, it was held that the defendants could take advantage of a specific *force majeure* clause, provided that the sinking of the vessel was not due to their negligence, even though the contract was not frustrated as far as the common law was concerned. As was noted at the start of this chapter, a *force majeure* clause is one which the parties have inserted to cover various eventualities outside their control, which may affect the contract. It will provide the way in which risks and consequential losses are to be distributed in such circumstances. The existence of such a clause, covering the facts that have arisen, will often prevent the contract from

---

51 The court did hold, however, that the defendants could rely on a *force majeure* clause included in the contract, provided that the sinking of the *Super Servant Two* did not result from their negligence (or that of their employees). For discussion of this aspect of the case, see McKendrick, 1995b, pp 323–27.

52 Treitel, 2003, p 908; Treitel, 1994, pp 490–93. McKendrick (1995b, pp 323–27) considers, but rejects, an alternative argument that allowing greater scope to frustration than was the case in *Super Servant Two* would decrease transaction costs, in that it would reduce the need for the negotiation of complex *force majeure* clauses: such a move would increase uncertainty, and a wider legal rule enforced by the courts would not provide the flexible outcomes which parties can devise for themselves by specially constructed clauses.

being frustrated. It will not inevitably do so, however, as is shown by *Jackson v Union Marine Insurance Co Ltd*.[53] A ship was chartered in November 1871 to proceed with all possible dispatch 'damages and accidents of navigation excepted' from Liverpool to Newport and there to load a cargo for carriage to San Francisco. She sailed on 2 January but, before reaching Newport, ran aground off the Welsh coast. On 15 February, the charterers abandoned the charter and found another ship. On 18 February, the ship got off, but repairs were not finished until August. The shipowner brought an action against the charterers for failure to load. It was held by the Exchequer Chamber that the exception in the contract absolved the shipowner from liability in the event of delay, but did not give him the right to sue if the delay was bad enough to frustrate the contract. This was the situation here, and so the shipowner's action failed.

FOR THOUGHT

Do you think the answer in this case would have been the same if the ship had been ready to load on 18 February?

A similar conclusion was reached in *Metropolitan Water Board v Dick Kerr*,[54] where the contract contained a provision for extension of the time for performance in the event of delays 'howsoever caused'. It was held by the House of Lords that this provision was only meant to deal with temporary delays, and did not:[55]

> . . . cover the case in which the interruption is of such a character and duration that it vitally and fundamentally changes the conditions of the contract, and could not possibly have been in the contemplation of the parties to the contract when it was made.

This suggests that the parties need to be very specific if they intend a clause to deal with circumstances which would otherwise amount to frustration. It is likely, however, that in modern circumstances, the courts will have regard to the fact that *force majeure* clauses are a common feature of commercial contracts and will attempt to interpret them in the light of the purposes which such clauses are intended to fulfil.[56]

---

53 (1874) LR 10 CP 125.
54 [1918] AC 119 – see above, 16.3.4.
55 Ibid, p 126.
56 There is, however, an argument that *force majeure* clauses are in effect exclusion clauses falling within the scope of the UCTA 1977 (see Wheeler and Shaw, 1994, p 760): to the extent that they are contained in standard terms, they would therefore need to meet the requirement of reasonableness (UCTA 1977, ss 3 and 11; see Chapter 9, 9.7.6 to 9.7.9).

16.4.3   Land

A contract for the sale of land can apparently be frustrated. This must have been assumed to be the case in *Amalgamated Investment and Property Co Ltd v John Walker & Sons Ltd*,[57] since otherwise there would have been no need to consider whether the listing of a building could have such an effect. In practice, the buyer of land will virtually always insure it from the point of exchange of contracts, and so the issue of frustration will be unlikely to arise.

In relation to leases, at one time it seemed as though frustration was not possible. Although it is clear that the doctrine of frustration can apply to contracts to use property on the basis of a licence, as in *Taylor v Caldwell*[58] and *Krell v Henry*,[59] this was not necessarily the case with a lease, which involves the tenant taking an interest in the land itself. The issue was raised in *Cricklewood Property Investment Trust v Leighton's Investment Trusts Ltd*.[60] This concerned a building lease, which was expressed to last for 99 years from May 1936. Following the outbreak of the Second World War in 1939, legislation was passed which prohibited building. The tenant claimed that the lease was frustrated. Two members of the House of Lords expressed the view that a lease could never be frustrated, while two others thought that it could if, for example, the land was washed into the sea, or became subject to a permanent ban on building. The fifth member of the panel refused to express a view on this issue, but agreed with the decision that on the facts there was in any case no frustration, because there were still 90 years left on the lease once the wartime restrictions were lifted.

The matter did not arise for decision again until 1981, and the case of *National Carriers Ltd v Panalpina (Northern) Ltd*.[61] This contract concerned a 10 year lease of a warehouse. After five years, the local authority closed the street, preventing access, because of problems with another (listed) building in the street. The closure was likely to last for about 18 months. There would, therefore, have been some three years of the lease to run after the street re-opened. The tenants, however, stopped paying rent, on the basis that the contract had been frustrated. The House of Lords took the view (Lord Russell dissenting) that there was no reason in logic or law why a lease should not be frustrated in a situation where no substantial use of a kind permitted by the lease and contemplated by the parties remained possible for the lessee. Thus, even where the land itself remained available, rather than slipping into the sea or being covered by sand, the lease could be frustrated if its purpose had been frustrated. On the facts of the case, however, the interruption to the availability of the premises was not sufficient to amount to frustration, and the landlords' action for the rent therefore succeeded.

---

57 [1983] QB 84; [1981] 3 All ER 577 – see above, 16.3.4.
58 (1863) 3 B & S 826; 122 ER 309 – see above, 16.2.2.
59 [1903] 2 KB 740 – see above, 16.3.3.
60 [1945] AC 221; [1945] 1 All ER 252.
61 [1981] AC 675; [1981] 1 All ER 161.

16.5 EFFECTS OF FRUSTRATION: COMMON LAW

The effects of a frustrating event are dealt with both by common law rules and the provisions of the Law Reform (Frustrated Contracts) Act 1943. This section deals with the common law, and the next one (16.6) with the Act. It is in this context that the objectives of the doctrine become important. Why are contracts held to be 'frustrated'? Is it simply to relieve one or other of the parties of the unfair burden of continuing obligations which have become impossible? Or is it to attempt to make a fair distribution of the losses which have arisen from an unpredictable event which was not the fault of either party?[62] As will be seen, the common law tends to take the first view, while the statutory intervention may be seen as a move towards the second. A further possibility, not so far adopted by English law but put forward in the proposed Principles of European Contract Law,[63] is that the frustrating event should lead to renegotiation of the contract, to take account of the changed circumstances.

16.5.1 Automatic termination

The first point to note is that the common law regards the frustrating event as automatically bringing the contract to an end. It is not a situation such as that which arises in relation to mistake, misrepresentation, or breach of contract, where one party can decide, notwithstanding what has happened, that the contract should continue. The application of this rule can be seen in *Hirji Mulji v Cheong Yue Steamship*.[64] By a charterparty entered into in November 1916, shipowners agreed that their ship, the *Singaporean*, should be placed at the charterers' disposal on 17 March 1917 for 10 months. Shortly before this date, the ship was requisitioned by the government. The shipowners thought the ship would soon be released, and asked the charterers if they would still be willing to take up the charter when this happened. The charterers said that they would. In fact, the ship was not released until February 1919, at which point the charterers refused to accept it. The shipowners argued that the charterers had affirmed the contract after the frustrating event, and were therefore still bound. The House of Lords held that affirmation was not possible. The frustrating event automatically brought the contract to an end, and discharged both the shipowners and the charterers from their obligations.

16.5.2 Future obligations only discharged

It is important to note that frustration, unlike an operative common law mistake, does not render a contract void *ab initio*. Its effect is to bring the contract to an end

---

62 Or, to put it in other words, to decide upon the appropriate allocation of risks in relation to such an event.
63 Discussed below, 16.7.
64 [1926] AC 497.

prematurely, but all existing obligations at the time of the contract remain unaffected, as far as the common law is concerned. If money has been paid or property transferred, it cannot generally be recovered, and if valuable services have been provided, compensation cannot be claimed.

Thus, in *Krell v Henry*,[65] the hirer of the room had paid a deposit, which was irrecoverable. On the other hand, the obligation to pay the balance did not, under the terms of the contract, arise until after the date on which the coronation procession was cancelled. This, therefore, was also irrecoverable. By contrast, in *Chandler v Webster*[66] (another case on the hiring of a room to view the coronation), under the terms of the contract, the obligation to pay arose before the frustrating event occurred. In this case, it was held that not only could money paid not be recovered, but the obligation to pay money due before the event was cancelled remained. Because frustration only discharged the contract from the point when the event occurred, the court refused to regard this as a case where there was a total failure of consideration, which might have justified recovery in quasi-contract.[67]

This aspect of *Chandler v Webster* was, however, overruled by the House of Lords in *Fibrosa Spolka Ackyjna v Fairbairn Lawson Combe Barbour Ltd*,[68] in which it was held that a frustrated contract could in some situations lead to a claim for recovery of money paid, on the basis of a total failure of consideration. An English company (the respondents) had made a contract to supply machinery to a Polish company (the appellants). The appellants had paid £1,000 towards this contract. It was then frustrated by the German invasion of Poland in 1939. The appellants sought to recover the £1,000. The House of Lords held that since they had received nothing at all under the contract, there had been a total failure of consideration and recovery was therefore possible.

This decision is probably an improvement on *Chandler v Webster*, but it still leaves two areas of difficulty and potential injustice. First, it can only apply where the failure of consideration is total. If the other party has provided something, no matter how little, no recovery will be possible. Second, it takes no account of the fact that the party who has received the money may well have incurred expenses in relation to the contract, and so will end up out of pocket if the entire sum has to be refunded. Both of these difficulties are addressed by the Law Reform (Frustrated Contracts) Act 1943.[69]

This Act also attempts to tackle another limitation of the common law, which is exemplified by *Appleby v Myers*.[70] In this case, the contract was for the erection of machinery on the defendant's premises. Payment was to be made on completion of the work. When the work was nearly finished, the whole premises, including the machinery, was destroyed by fire. The contract was undoubtedly frustrated, but the question was

---

65 [1903] 2 KB 740 – see above, 16.3.3.
66 [1904] 1 KB 493.
67 The area of quasi-contract, or restitution, is considered in Chapter 19.
68 [1943] AC 32; [1942] 2 All ER 122.
69 See below, 16.6.
70 (1867) LR 2 CP 651.

whether the plaintiffs could recover any compensation for the work they had done. The answer was no. The obligation to pay had not arisen at the time the contract was frustrated, and therefore the plaintiffs were entitled to nothing.

The common law approach, based on relieving from future obligations, thus led to the injustices outlined above. More fundamentally, the result in a particular case would depend entirely on the timing of obligations under the contract. Thus, the distinction between *Krell v Henry* and *Chandler v Webster* arose purely from the fact that in the former case payment was to be paid in two instalments, while in the latter the entire payment was due at the start of the contract. It is clearly unsatisfactory, and serves no discernible policy,[71] that the same factual situation should give rise to such different results simply on this basis. The courts proved incapable, however, of developing a more satisfactory set of rules,[72] and eventually statutory reform was put in place.

16.6 EFFECTS OF FRUSTRATION: THE LAW REFORM (FRUSTRATED CONTRACTS) ACT 1943

Before considering the provisions of s 1(2) and (3), which contain the most significant provisions of the Law Reform (Frustrated Contracts) Act (LR(FC)A) 1943, it must be noted that not all contracts are within its scope. Section 2(5) indicates that the Act does not apply:

(a)   to any charterparty, except a time charterparty or a charterparty by way of demise,[73] or to any contract (other than a charterparty) for the carriage of goods by sea;[74] or

(b)   to any contract of insurance,[75] save as is provided by sub-section (5) of the foregoing section;[76] or

---

71 Other than possibly that of 'freedom of contract': but if this is to be the governing principle, then why not return to *Paradine v Jane* (1647) Aleyn 26; 82 ER 897 – above, 16.2.1?

72 Other than the relatively minor development as regards 'total failure of consideration' in the *Fibrosa* case. This occurred just before the statutory reform: it is arguable, therefore, that the courts would in time have built on the *Fibrosa* decision to produce a more flexible set of remedies for frustration.

73 The effect of this is basically that the Act does not apply to charterparties for a particular voyage (voyage charterparties), but does apply to all other charterparties.

74 This exclusion is apparently based on the fact that established rules in shipping law dealing with the loss or misdelivery of freight should be allowed to stand: see Treitel, 2003, pp 917–18.

75 This obviously complies with the normal view of an insurance contract as representing in itself the parties' decision as to the allocation of risk. Its effect is that if, for example, goods are destroyed in a way not covered by the insurance policy, the owner is not allowed to claim a return of the premiums paid.

76 Section 1(5) provides that in deciding on the distribution of losses under s 1(2) or (3) (which is discussed below at 16.6.1 and 16.6.2), the court should ignore any contract of insurance, unless there was an express obligation to insure.

> (c) to any contract to which [section 7 of the Sale of Goods Act 1979] . . .
> applies, or to any other contract for the sale, or the sale and delivery, of
> specific goods, where the contract is frustrated by reason of the fact that the
> goods have perished.

Section 7 of the Sale of Goods Act (SGA) 1979 provides that:

> . . . where there is an agreement to sell specific goods, and subsequently the goods,
> without any fault on the part of the seller or buyer, perish before the risk passes to
> the buyer, the agreement is thereby avoided.

An 'agreement to sell' is a contract under which ownership has not yet passed to the
buyer. 'Risk' will normally pass at the same time as 'ownership',[77] though the parties
may make a different agreement if they so wish. 'Specific goods' are those which are
identified at the time of the agreement, as opposed to generic goods, which are sold by
description. Thus, a contract to buy 'all the grain currently in X warehouse' would be a
contract for specific goods; a contract to buy 'five tonnes of grain' would be a contract
for generic goods. The former contract would fall within the scope of s 7 of the SGA
1979, and would therefore not be subject to the 1943 Act if X warehouse burnt down,
destroying all the grain before the risk had passed to the buyer. The contract would be
'avoided' by s 7, and the common law rules on the effects of frustration would apply.[78]
The latter contract would not generally be capable of being frustrated, since the buyer is
not concerned with where the seller obtains the grain; but if the contract specified a
particular source for the grain (for example, 'five tonnes of the 100 tonnes currently
held in X warehouse'), then the contract could be frustrated by the total destruction of
the source.[79] In that case, the 1943 Act would apply to the contract rather than the
common law rules. There seems to be no good reason for these distinctions, which seem
to serve no sensible policy. It would surely be preferable for all sale of goods contracts
to be treated in the same way.

Section 2(3) of the LR(FC)A 1943 states that:

> Where any contract to which this Act applies contains any provision which, upon
> the true construction of the contract, is intended to have effect in the event of
> circumstances arising which operate, or would but for the said provision operate,
> to frustrate the contract, or is intended to have effect whether such circumstances
> arise or not, the court shall give effect to the said provision and shall only give

---

77 Sale of Goods Act 1979, s 20.

78 Thus, if the buyer had made a payment, this would be recoverable on the basis of a total failure of
consideration on the *Fibrosa* principle.

79 See *Howell v Coupland* (1876) 1 QBD 258 – contract for 200 tons of potatoes to be grown on a
specified piece of land. Failure of the crop led to the frustration of the contract.

effect to the foregoing section of this Act to such extent, if any, as appears to the court to be consistent with the said provision.

This makes it clear that the parties may reach their own agreement as to what the effects of frustration are going to be. In this situation, again, the LR(FC)A 1943 will have no application. The parties are deemed to be best placed to decide where the risks should lie, and it is only by default that the court will intervene.

16.6.1   Section 1(2): money paid or payable prior to frustration

Section 1(2) of the LR(FC)A 1943 deals with the *Chandler v Webster*, or *Fibrosa*, type of situation – that is, where money has been paid or is owed under the contract before the frustrating event takes place. It states that:

> All sums paid or payable to any party in pursuance of the contract before the time when the parties were so discharged [that is, by frustration] . . . shall, in the case of sums so paid, be recoverable from him as money received by him for the use of the party by whom the sums were paid, and, in the case of sums so payable, cease to be so payable.

In other words, in such a situation, money paid is recoverable, and money owed ceases to be payable. To that extent the section adopts and extends the *Fibrosa* decision, in that the rule now applies even where there is not a total failure of consideration. Subject to the provisions of s 1(3),[80] concerning the conferring of valuable benefits, there can be recovery of sums paid even where there has been partial performance by the other side.

There is, however, a proviso to s 1(2) which is designed to limit the injustice in the *Fibrosa* decision,[81] that is, even where there is a total failure of consideration, the other party may have incurred expenses in getting ready to perform. The section accordingly provides that if the party to whom sums were paid or payable:

> . . . incurred expenses before the time of discharge in, or for the purposes of, the performance of the contract, the court may, if it considers it just to do so having regard to all the circumstances of the case, allow him to retain or, as the case may be, recover the whole of the sums paid or payable, not being an amount in excess of the expenses so incurred.

It is important to note two limitations on this attempt to spread the losses of frustration between the parties.[82] First, the recovery of expenses can only take place where there

---

80 See below, 16.6.2.

81 See above, 16.5.2.

82 Goff J, however, stated in *BP Exploration Co (Libya) Ltd v Hunt (No 2)* [1982] 1 All ER 925 that the purpose of the 1943 Act was not to apportion losses, but to prevent unjust enrichment.

was an obligation to pay some money prior to the frustrating event. If the contract provided for the entire payment to become due only on completion of the contract, then there will be no scope for the recovery of expenses under s 1(2). Second, even if some money was paid or payable, it is possible that the expenses will exceed this amount, and so will not be fully recoverable. For example, if on a contract worth £5,000 a deposit of £500 has been paid, but the other party has incurred expenses of £750, the maximum that can be retained under s 1(2) is £500. The remaining £250 is irrecoverable, unless s 1(3)[83] can be brought into play.[84]

Finally, even if expenses have been incurred which could be compensated by money paid or payable, this cannot be claimed as of right. It is entirely at the court's discretion to decide whether or not there should be any recovery of expenses, depending on its view as to whether this would be just in all the circumstances. In *Gamerco SA v ICM/Fair Warning Agency*,[85] the court confirmed that the use of a broad discretion, rather than any other particular formula (for example, sharing losses equally) was the correct approach to the application of the proviso under s 1(2). The plaintiffs were claiming the repayment of $412,500 paid in connection with a pop concert which could not take place because the government had, on safety grounds, closed the stadium at which it was to be held. The defendants wished to retain an amount to cover their expenses. On the facts, there were considerable difficulties in calculating the defendants' expenses, but the judge estimated that they might have amounted to $50,000. In all the circumstances, and taking account of the plaintiffs' loss (around $450,000), the judge concluded that justice would be done if the money paid by the plaintiffs (that is, the $412,500) was returned without deduction.

FOR THOUGHT

Is this the best approach, or does it leave matters too vague and uncertain? Would it be better to simply try to share the losses equally between the parties, given that the contract has come to an end without any fault on the part of either party to the contract? If the courts adopted such an approach would it encourage parties to settle rather than litigate in relation to frustrated contracts?

The decision emphasises the very broad power which the court has in relation to the proviso to s 1(2).

---

83 Below, 16.6.2.
84 Campbell has argued that the effect of the proviso contained in s 1(2) is to confuse the restitution and reliance interests, and, in effect, that the job which the proviso is intended to do would have been better left to s 1(3). In particular, the cap on the recovery of expenses is 'a limit alien to the reliance interest with no clear justification'. The result is 'a curious hybrid unknown to reliance or restitution' with 'no sound foundation in either principle': Harris, Campbell and Halson, 2002, Chapter 16, p 248.
85 [1995] 1 WLR 1126.

16.6.2   Section 1(3): compensation for a 'valuable benefit'

Section 1(3) of the LR(FC)A 1943 provides that where a party to a contract has obtained a 'valuable benefit' (other than money) before the time of discharge, the other party can obtain compensation for having provided this. Suppose, then, that D has contracted to hire C's hall for a series of 10 concerts, with the entire fee to be payable at the end of the contract. If after one concert the hall is destroyed by fire, under the common law, C would not be able to recover anything from D. By virtue of s 1(3), however, C would be entitled to seek compensation from D in relation to the use of the hall for the one concert that took place. D would have received a 'valuable benefit' in the use of the hall for one concert. As with s 1(2), recovery is not available as of right, but is in the discretion of the court, which can award what it considers just in all the circumstances, up to the value of the benefit to the party obtaining it. In particular, the court is directed to take into account, by virtue of s 1(3)(a), any expenses incurred by the party obtaining the benefit, and also, by virtue of s 1(3)(b), the effect, in relation to the benefit, of the circumstances which frustrated the contract.

This provision would seem at first sight to provide a more satisfactory outcome to the case of *Appleby v Myers*,[86] in that it might allow the supplier of the machinery to recover compensation for the work that had been done. This depends, however, on whether the 'valuable benefit' has to be judged before or after the frustrating event has occurred. If it is the former, then some compensation may be possible; if it is the latter, then the other party may well argue that no benefit has in the end been received, since the machinery was not completed, and was in any case destroyed by the fire.

These issues were considered in some detail by Goff J, as he then was, in the only reported case on s 1(3) of the LR(FC)A 1943, *BP Exploration Co (Libya) Ltd v Hunt (No 2)*.[87] The case concerned oil concessions which had been frustrated by expropriation by the Libyan government. Goff J started by stating that the underlying principle of the Act was not the apportionment of losses, but the prevention of the 'unjust enrichment' of one party to a frustrated contract at the expense of the other. He then approached s 1(3)(b) on the basis that it involves two tasks: first, the identification of the 'valuable benefit', and secondly, the determination of the 'just sum' to be awarded, the amount of which is capped by the 'valuable benefit'. In relation to the first task, he noted that s 1(3)(b) of the Act states that the court should take into account 'the effect, in relation to the said benefit, of the circumstances giving rise to the frustration of the contract'. He therefore came to the conclusion that 'benefit' means the 'end product' of what the plaintiff has provided, not the value of the work that has been done. Thus, he concluded:[88]

---

86 (1867) LR 2 CP 651 – above, 16.5.2.
87 [1982] 1 All ER 925. The Court of Appeal and the House of Lords dismissed appeals against the first instance decision, but without any detailed consideration of Goff's analysis of the 1943 Act: [1983] 2 AC 352.
88 Ibid, p 939.

Suppose that a contract for work on a building is frustrated by fire which destroys the building and which, therefore, also destroys a substantial amount of work already done by the plaintiff. Although it might be thought just to award the plaintiff a sum assessed on a *quantum meruit* basis . . . in respect of the work he has done, the effect of s 1(3)(b) will be to reduce the award to nil, because of the effect, in relation to the defendant's benefit, of the circumstances giving rise to the frustration of the contract.

In other words, he adopted the second of the approaches outlined in the previous paragraph as regards the assessment of the benefit. This is not accepted as the correct analysis by all commentators. Treitel, for example, argues that although the Act makes reference to the relevance of the effect of the frustrating circumstances, this should be interpreted as applying to the assessment of the 'just sum' to be awarded (as discussed below), rather than the valuation of the benefit itself.[89] Goff J's judgment, however, having been upheld by the Court of Appeal and the House of Lords,[90] must be taken to represent the current law on this issue. As a result, it is clear that in a case such as *Appleby v Myers*, the answer given by the LR(FC)A 1943 is the same as that under the common law, and that no compensation will be recoverable for the work that has been done, because, once the frustrating event has occurred, it is of no value to the other party.

As has been noted, Goff J's conclusion as to the effect of s 1(3) has been criticised, but much of this criticism has been directed at the poor drafting of the section rather than his analysis of it.[91] Goff himself clearly had sympathy with the argument that the provision of services should in itself be regarded as a 'benefit' even if those services lost their value as a result of the frustrating event.[92] But he felt obliged to find that the true construction of the Act led to the opposite conclusion.

The second element in the process under s 1(3), once the valuable benefit has been determined, is the calculation of the 'just sum' to be awarded. Goff J took the view that the basic measure of recovery should be:[93]

> . . . the reasonable value of the plaintiff's performance: in case of services, a *quantum meruit* or reasonable remuneration, and in the case of goods, a *quantum valebat* or reasonable price.[94]

This, however, is subject to the limitation that the amount awarded cannot exceed

---

89 Treitel, 2003, p 915.
90 Though without any detailed consideration of the operation of s 1(3).
91 But see Haycroft and Waksman, 1984 for criticism of the judgment itself.
92 [1982] 1 All ER 925, p 940.
93 Ibid, p 942.
94 Campbell argues that this approach to the just sum, equating it with the value of the services provided, effectively reduces the two-stage process to one: Harris, Campbell and Halson, 2002, p 250.

the 'valuable benefit' which the defendant has received. If, therefore, as a consequence of the frustrating event, the valuable benefit is nil, then the just sum will also, inevitably, be nil.

The facts of *BP v Hunt* were concerned with the value of the exploitation by BP of oil concessions granted to Hunt by the Libyan government. These concessions had later been withdrawn by a subsequent government, with the proceeds being expropriated. BP were seeking compensation for the work done in exploiting the concessions. Applying the approach outlined above, Goff J found that the eventual benefit to Hunt, following the frustration, consisted of the value of the oil which he had received, plus the compensation from the Libyan government.[95] This produced a 'benefit' of £85m. The 'just sum' was, on the other hand, based on the value of the services which BP had provided to Hunt, less the value of the oil which BP had itself received under the contract. This produced a figure of £35m which, being less than the 'valuable benefit', was awarded in full.

16.6.3 Conclusions on the Law Reform (Frustrated Contracts) Act 1943

The 1943 Act has been the subject of strong criticism. McKendrick has noted that it 'suffers from a number of deficiencies' and agrees with the view of the British Columbia Law Commission that it 'was not well thought out or drafted'.[96] Campbell comments that:[97]

> As there are but a handful of Acts of Parliament which affect the basic structure of remedies for breach of contract, it is rather dismal to note that this one is so poorly drafted that it has given rise to problems of interpretation out of all proportion to its short length, and has brought very limited improvement to the common law.

Some of the criticism pulls in opposite directions, however. McKendrick is unhappy that so much discretion is left to trial judges, and suggests that it is 'regrettable that the Court of Appeal [in *BP v Hunt*] did not establish guidelines to assist . . . and to ensure a measure of consistency'.[98] Campbell, on the contrary, sees this 'abhorrence of discretion' as 'misguided':[99]

> Dispute resolution in this area is, *ex hypothesi*, highly contingent upon the unforeseen empirical circumstances of each case, and therefore it is pointless to

---

95 The enhanced value of the concession resulting from BP's work could not be included as part of the benefit, because this had been lost as a result of the frustrating event.
96 McKendrick, 1995a, p 243. See also Stewart and Carter, 1992.
97 Harris, Campbell and Halson, 2002, p 252.
98 McKendrick, 1995a, p 238.
99 Harris, Campbell and Halson, 2002, pp 252–53.

regret that the law cannot develop detailed rules. The pursuit of such rules continues to hinder explicit recognition of the use of discretion which the nature of the case and not the shortcomings of the statute make necessary.

There is nothing wrong, in his view, with giving the trial judge discretion, as long as this is not 'unbridled', and is focused on achieving 'rescission'.[100]

While Campbell's criticisms of the 1943 Act may be over-harsh (it is hard to see that it is not an improvement on the common law), his view on the role of discretion is to be preferred to McKendrick's in this situation. If the parties want certainty, which is one of the reasons for having clear legal rules, then they can achieve this through a *force majeure* clause, as we have seen that commercial contractors generally do. The point where frustration becomes important is exactly where what has happened was unpredictable. There is therefore little point in suggesting that contractual planning can be made more efficient in this area by the adoption of fixed rules. A discretion which enables a judge to take account of the context of the contract, and in particular the business context (where relevant), in deciding where losses should fall, is to be preferred. The problem with the 1943 Act is not that it allows for too much discretion, but that it constrains that discretion in the wrong ways.[101]

There has been very little case law on the 1943 Act, and this might be thought to indicate that it is in practice a successful piece of legislation. Campbell, however, suggests that the more likely explanation is that 'competent commercial parties' will have included provisions in their contracts to allow for alternative dispute resolution or arbitration which will give them 'far more flexibility to apportion loss than any conceivable restitutionary recasting of the frustration rules might do'.[102] This again supports the view that a flexible rather than a rigid law on the effects of frustration would be more likely to meet the needs of the business world.

16.7 FRUSTRATION UNDER THE PRINCIPLES OF EUROPEAN CONTRACT LAW

There are two Articles in the Principles which deal with the situation where a contract is affected by a change of circumstances. Article 6.111, which is headed 'Change of Circumstances', deals with the situation where the performance of a contract has become 'excessively onerous' for one of the parties. Article 8.108, on the other hand, which is headed 'Excuse Due to an Impediment', deals with the situation where performance has become impossible.

---

100 By which Campbell means returning the parties to their positions prior to the agreement.
101 As is demonstrated by Goff J's judgment in *BP v Hunt*.
102 Harris, Campbell and Halson, 2002, p 253. Campbell cites in support of this the empirical evidence of the non-use of contract by business people provided by the work of Macaulay and others – see Macaulay, 1963; Beale and Dugdale, 1975.

16.7.1 Change of circumstances [103]

This Article starts by reaffirming that in general a change of circumstance which makes the performance of a contract more onerous will not relieve the party concerned of its obligations. This is in line with the view under English law that generally the risks of performance turning out to be more difficult are borne by the parties as part of their normal obligations under the contract. The Article then distinguishes a situation which might overlap with certain types of frustrating event,[104] but clearly includes a much wider range of circumstances. This is where the performance becomes 'excessively onerous'. This phrase is not defined, but some examples are given in the notes accompanying the Article. It would, for instance, cover the situation in the Suez Canal cases, where the closure of the Canal was held by the English courts not to amount to frustration.[105] The other example is where 'A contract is made to supply [water] for irrigation for 50 years at a fixed price but the price becomes derisory through inflation'.[106] In such circumstances, provided that the change has occurred after the conclusion of the contract, it was not one which should reasonably have been taken into account, and the risk of the change is not allocated to either party under the contract,[107] so 'the parties are bound to enter into negotiations with a view to adapting the contract or ending it'.

This Article introduces a concept which is alien to the English law of contract – that is, an obligation to negotiate.[108] As Schanze has pointed out, however:[109]

> . . . as a matter of commercial practice . . . contracts which become impracticable are frequently renegotiated by the parties, even under factual pressures which would not amount to the classical legal standard for discharge.

They may also, as noted above,[110] deal with such situations by the inclusion of *force majeure* or 'hardship' clauses. The idea of an agreement being renegotiated, or adapted,

---

103 For discussion of an earlier version of Art 6.111, see Schanze, 1997, and the response by Samuel, 1997.

104 For example, that which occurred in *Krell v Henry* [1903] 2 KB 740, where performance was physically possible, but pointless.

105 *Tsakiroglou & Co Ltd v Noblee Thorl GmbH* [1962] AC 93; [1961] 2 All ER 179 – above, 16.3.4.

106 This is clearly based on *Staffordshire Area Health Authority v South Staffordshire Waterworks Co* [1978] 3 All ER 769, where a water supply contract was made in 1929 at a price of seven old pence (roughly 2.9 p) per 1,000 gallons, without any time limit. By 1975 the normal rate for the supply of water was 45 p per 1,000 gallons. The Court of Appeal held that the agreement was terminable by reasonable notice.

107 Article 6.111(2)(a)–(c).

108 See, for example, *Walford v Miles* [1992] 2 AC 128; [1992] 1 All ER 453, discussed in Chapter 2, 2.15.2. On the other hand, *Williams v Roffey* [1991] 1 QB 1; [1990] 1 All ER 512 (see Chapter 3, 3.9.8) can, perhaps, be seen as an attempt by the courts to *facilitate* such renegotiation, by expanding the definition of 'consideration': see McKendrick, 1995a, pp 53–54.

109 Schanze, 1997, p 156. See also Macaulay, 1963; Beale and Dugdale, 1975; and Macneil, 1978.

110 See 16.2.1. An empirical study by Schanze of the mining industry found, however, that general hardship clauses were not used: Schanze, 1997, p 159.

to deal with changed circumstances is therefore by no means unpalatable to the commercial world. The difference is that here the obligation is being imposed on them. The sanction for failure to do so is provided by Art 6.111(3). If the parties have not reached an agreement within a reasonable time, the court may terminate the contract, or adapt it so as to divide 'in a just and equitable manner the losses and gains resulting from the change of circumstances'. Moreover, damages may be awarded against a party which has refused to negotiate, or broken off negotiations, contrary to good faith and fair dealing. The intention of the drafters of the Principles is, however, that these procedures should be a 'last resort': the object is to encourage the parties to renegotiate towards an amicable settlement.

As noted above, there is no parallel to this Article in English law. The generality (not to say vagueness) of its wording would be likely to cause problems for English courts. It would, nevertheless, be an improvement on the current situation, where 'frustration' operates in an 'all or nothing' way, and there is no structured means of addressing circumstances which change a contract, but not sufficiently to frustrate it. To the extent that the proposal represents a formal recognition of what is already good commercial practice, it is to be welcomed.

16.7.2 Excuse due to an impediment

Article 8:108 deals with much more familiar ground for an English contract lawyer. This allows a party to be excused for non-performance where this is due to an 'impediment' beyond that party's control. 'Impediment' is not defined, but it is clear from the notes that it is intended to refer to circumstances which make performance impossible. Where the performance is rendered 'radically different', but not impossible, it seems that it should be dealt with under Art 6.111, above. The operation of the 'excuse' under Art 8:108 is dependent on the impediment being one which the party could not reasonably be expected to have taken into account at the time of the contract. Moreover, it must be something which the party could not reasonably have avoided or overcome.

Article 8:108(2) provides for temporary impediment, which will lead to performance being excused for the period while the impediment exists. Where, however, the delay amounts to 'fundamental non-performance', the other party may treat it as such.

Article 8:108(9) requires the non-performing party to give notice of the impediment within a reasonable time. Failure to do so will entitle the other party to damages for any consequent loss.

The principles contained in this Article are generally in line with those applying under English law to contracts frustrated by impossibility, though the obligation to give notice to the other side is an additional obligation. Article 8:108 does not, however, deal with the consequences of impossibility, other than to say that performance is excused, so that an order for specific performance[111] could not be obtained. In relation to the

---

111 See Chapter 18, 18.7.

transfer of money or property, or the provision of services, the Principles leave this to be treated in the same way as with contracts which are terminated on other grounds. Discussion of this area of the Principles will therefore be left until Chapter 18.[112]

One point will be mentioned here, however, which is contained in Art 9:303(4). This states that where a party is permanently excused by Art 8:108, 'the contract is terminated automatically and without notice at the time that the impediment arises'. Thus, as with the position in relation to frustration under English law, the termination is not dependent, as it is, for example, following a breach of contract, on the election of the party not in breach. Once a contract has become impossible to perform, it is automatically at an end.

16.8 FURTHER READING

Harris, D, Campbell, D and Halson, R, *Remedies in Contract and Tort*, 2nd edn, 2002, London: Butterworths, Chapter 16

Haycroft, AM and Waksman, DM, 'Frustration and restitution' [1984] JBL 207

Hedley, S, 'Carriage by sea: frustration and *force majeure*' (1990) 49 CLJ 209

McKendrick, E (ed), *Force Majeure*, 2nd edn, 1995a, London: Lloyd's of London

McKendrick, E, 'The regulation of long-term contracts in English law', Chapter 12 in Beatson, J and Friedmann, D (eds), *Good Faith and Fault in Contract Law*, 1995b, Oxford: Clarendon Press

Stewart, A and Carter, JW, 'Frustrated contracts and statutory adjustment: the case for a re-appraisal' [1992] CLJ 66

Treitel, GH, *Frustration and Force Majeure*, 1994, London: Sweet & Maxwell

112 See 18.9.

17 DISCHARGE BY PERFORMANCE OR BREACH

Contents

17.1 OVERVIEW

This chapter looks at the termination of a contract by either completion of performance or breach. The most significant issues are:

■ Discharge by performance. The normal rule is that performance must be precise and exact to discharge the party's obligations. This has the following consequences:

- In an 'entire' contract payment only has to be made when performance is fully completed – there is no payment for partial performance, unless:
  - the other party has prevented completion of performance; or
  - the partial performance has been accepted; or
  - the court deems there to have been 'substantial performance'.
- In a 'divisible' contract a party may be entitled to payment for completion of particular stages.
- Time of performance. If performance is offered late, is the other party obliged to accept it? The general rule is that time is not 'of the essence' unless the parties have made it so. In particular:
  - time for payment is not 'of the essence' and so late payment is not a ground for rejection; but
  - in relation to all other obligations, the House of Lords has suggested that in *commercial* contracts time is always of the essence;
  Where time is of the essence, even a very short delay will entitle the other party to terminate.
- Discharge by breach. Breach, however serious, does not automatically terminate a contract – the question is whether it entitles the other party to terminate ('repudiatory' breach). The answer is that it only does so if the breach is important – 'of the essence'. The courts divide clauses into the following.
  - Conditions. Breach of a condition entitles the other party to terminate the contract (as well as claiming damages);
  - Warranties. Breach of warranty only entitles the other party to claim damages, not to terminate;
  - Innominate terms. The consequences of breach of an innominate term depend on the seriousness of the breach. If it deprives the other party of the main benefit of the contract, it will allow that party to terminate.
- Problem areas.
  - Long-term contracts. It may be difficult in a long-term contract to determine what level of breach will be repudiatory;
  - Instalment contracts. Similarly, there may be difficulties in determining how many instalments need to be defective to constitute a repudiatory breach.
- Anticipatory breach. If a party indicates in advance that it is not going to perform, the other party may elect to terminate immediately, rather than waiting for the date for performance to arrive.

17.2 INTRODUCTION

This chapter is concerned with ways in which a contract may be discharged, so that the parties no longer have any obligations under it. We have already discussed one way in which this can happen in the previous chapter, under the doctrine of frustration. Contracts may also be discharged by express agreement. If both parties decide that

neither of them wishes to carry on with a contract which contains continuing obligations, or in relation to which some parts are still executory, they may agree to bring it to
an end early. The only problems which arise here are where the executory obligations
are all on one side, so that the party who has completed performance receives no
consideration for promising not to enforce the other party's obligations. This issue has
already been dealt with in Chapter 3, in connection with the doctrine of consideration
and, in particular, the concept of promissory estoppel, and so is not discussed further
here.[1] The focus in this chapter is on discharge by performance or by breach: discharge
in this context meaning that all further obligations of either or both of the parties are at
an end.

17.3   DISCHARGE BY PERFORMANCE

Once the parties have done all that they are bound to do under a contract, all 'primary'
obligations will cease.[2] There may, of course, be some continuing 'secondary' obligations, such as the obligation to pay compensation if goods turn out to be defective at
some point after sale and delivery.

The problem that concerns us here is what constitutes satisfactory performance.
If there is some minor defect, does this negative discharge by performance? The practical importance of this relates primarily to the situation where performance by one side
gives rise to the right to demand performance from the other. Most typically, this will
occur where payment for goods or services is only to be made once the goods have been
supplied or the services have been completed. Suppose there is some minor defect
in what has been supplied – does this entitle the other party to withhold its own
performance by refusing payment?

17.3.1   Performance must be precise and exact

The general rule under the classical law of contract is that performance must be precise
and exact, and the courts have at times applied this very strictly. Consider, for example,
two cases under the Sale of Goods Act 1893. In *Re Moore & Co and Landauer & Co*,[3]
the defendants agreed to buy from the plaintiffs 3,000 tins of canned fruit. The fruit was
to be packed in cases of 30 tins. When the goods were delivered, a substantial part of
the consignment was packed in cases of 24 tins. It was held that this did not constitute
satisfactory performance, and the defendants were entitled to reject the whole consignment. Similarly, in *Arcos Ltd v EA Ronaasen & Son*,[4] the buyer had ordered timber

---

1 See 3.10.1, 3.11.
2 For the distinction between primary and secondary obligations, see Lord Diplock in *Photo Production
   Ltd v Securicor Transport Ltd* [1980] AC 827, pp 848–49; [1980] 1 All ER 556, pp 565–66.
3 [1921] 2 KB 519.
4 [1933] AC 470.

staves for the purpose of making barrels. The contract description said that they should be 1/2 inch thick. Most of the consignment consisted of staves which were in fact 9/16 inch thick. They were still perfectly usable for making barrels. Nevertheless, it was held that this did not constitute satisfactory performance, and the buyer was entitled to reject all the staves. In other words, in both these cases, the seller had not performed satisfactorily, and so had not discharged his obligations under the contract.[5]

Both of these cases turned in part on the interpretation of s 13 of the Sale of Goods Act 1893, which implied an obligation to supply goods which match their contract description. The same provision is now contained in s 13 of the Sale of Goods Act (SGA) 1979.[6] In recent years, the courts have been a little more flexible in the application of this section, and s 15A of the 1979 Act now prevents a business purchaser from unreasonably rejecting goods which are only slightly different from the contract description. A similar approach had previously been taken by the House of Lords in *Reardon Smith Line Ltd v Hansen-Tangen*,[7] where a tanker was built at a different yard to that specified in the contract, but in all other respects met the purchaser's requirements. The House of Lords refused to accept that, by analogy with s 13 of the SGA 1979, the tanker could be rejected for non-compliance with its contractual description. Lord Wilberforce commented that some of the cases on the Act were 'excessively technical and due for fresh examination'.[8]

The principle that in general each party is entitled to expect the other to perform to the letter of their agreement remains, however. This was confirmed by the Privy Council in *Union Eagle Ltd v Golden Achievement Ltd*,[9] which concerned a contract for the sale of a flat. Time for performance had been made 'of the essence', and under the contract the purchase price was to be tendered by 5 pm on a particular day. In fact, it was tendered at 5.10 pm. The Privy Council confirmed that this entitled the seller to repudiate the agreement and retain the deposit that had been paid. The interests of certainty meant that the court should, in this type of situation, strictly enforce what the parties had agreed.

This approach makes it imperative for the parties to be careful in making their contract to ensure that they allow for flexibility in their performance if that is likely to be a problem for them.[10]

---

5 Beale, Bishop and Furmston (2001, p 428) suggest that the reason for the courts' strict approach may have been that in many cases 'the goods were being bought for resale and the exact description might be important to some other buyer further down the chain'. The suspicion must be, however, that in at least some of these cases the buyer was simply trying to find a reason to escape from a bad bargain.

6 See Chapter 8, 8.6.11.

7 [1976] 3 All ER 570.

8 Ibid, p 576. He made particular reference to *Re Moore & Co and Landauer & Co* in this context.

9 [1997] AC 514; [1997] 2 All ER 215.

10 As Collins (2003, p 293) points out in relation to the courts' general refusal to grant relief for change of circumstances making a contract more onerous (for which see Chapter 17), a strict liability rule 'provides an incentive for the parties to plan for risks and contingencies'.

17.3.2 Partial provision of services

In the sale of goods cases, a failure to meet the terms of the contract prevented the seller from claiming any compensation, even in relation to any goods supplied which did match the contract description. The buyer was entitled to withhold performance (the payment of the price) because the seller had failed in its obligations. The same approach is applied to the provision of services. Here, a person may have done a certain amount of work towards a contract, and the question is whether there is any right to claim payment under the contract for what has been done if it does not amount to complete performance.

The starting point for the consideration of this issue is the case which is regarded as the classic example of the common law's insistence on complete performance: *Cutter v Powell*.[11] The defendant agreed to pay Cutter 30 guineas provided that he served as second mate on a voyage from Jamaica to Liverpool. The voyage began on 2 August. Cutter died on 20 September, when the ship was 19 days short of Liverpool. Cutter's widow brought an action to recover a proportion of the 30 guineas. This failed. The contract was interpreted as being an 'entire' contract for a lump sum, and nothing was payable until it was completed. Thus, even though the defendant had had the benefit of Cutter's labour for a substantial part of the voyage, no compensation for this was recoverable. One reason for this rather harsh decision seems to have been that the 30 guineas was about four times the normal wage for such a voyage. The court therefore looked on it as something of a gamble.[12] Cutter had agreed to take the chance of a larger lump sum at the end of the voyage, rather than to take wages paid on a weekly basis. This element of the decision was not picked up in later cases, however, and *Cutter v Powell* was taken to lay down a general rule that in 'entire' contracts (that is, where various obligations are to be performed in return for a lump sum) nothing is payable until the contract has been fully completed.

17.3.3 Divisible contracts or obligations [13]

One way to mitigate this rule, which has the potential to operate very harshly, is to find that the contract is not entire, but divisible into sections, with the completion of each section giving rise to a right to some payment. Thus, if Cutter had been engaged at a certain rate per week, instead of for a lump sum for the whole voyage, his widow would

---

11 (1785) 6 Term Rep 320; [1775–1802] All ER Rep 159. For the full background to the case, and the somewhat fortuitous route by which it has become a 'leading case', see Dockray, 2001.

12 Dockray (2001, p 673) suggests that the court may have misunderstood the factual background on this issue, in that Cutter's skill as a carpenter would be likely to have been of special value to Powell, making the rate of pay less extraordinary than it appeared.

13 It is common to refer to entire or divisible *contracts*: as Treitel (2003, pp 785–86) has pointed out, it would be more accurate to refer to entire or divisible *obligations*. See further below, 17.3.6.

probably have been able to recover for the time he had actually served.[14] This is now the standard position in relation to employment contracts: although a salary may be stated on an annual basis, a person who leaves part way through the year will expect to be paid *pro rata*, even if the contract was for a particular project which has not been completed, or for a fixed period of time which has not expired.[15]

This will also apply if there are concurrent but independent obligations. In *Bolton v Mahadeva*,[16] there was a contract to (a) install a central heating system, and (b) supply a bathroom suite. The central heating system turned out to be defective, and there was no obligation to pay for this, but the supply of the bathroom suite was severable, and an appropriate proportion of the contract price was recoverable in relation to this obligation.[17]

17.3.4 Non-performance due to other party

If one party prevents the other from completing the obligations under an entire contract, the party who has partly performed will be able to recover on a *quantum meruit* basis for the work already done. Thus, in *Planché v Colburn*,[18] the plaintiff recovered £50 towards the work which he had done in writing a book for a series which had then been cancelled by the defendants. The contract price had been £100, but the plaintiff had not completed the book at the time that the defendants brought the contract to an end. A claimant in this situation may also be able to recover damages for consequential losses.

17.3.5 Acceptance of partial performance

If a party accepts partial performance, this may be sufficient in certain circumstances to discharge the other party's further obligations under the contract, and moreover allow that party to sue on a *quantum meruit* for the work already done. For example, suppose that goods are to be transported from London to Hull, and the van breaks down en route. If the recipient of the goods agrees to take delivery at Doncaster, the carrier will be able to sue for a proportion of the carriage. In *Christy v Row*,[19] this rule was said to be based on a fresh agreement involving an implied promise to pay for the benefit received. In this case, there was a contract of carriage in relation to seven keels of coal,

---

14 See *Taylor v Laird* (1856) 25 LJ Ex 329: a plaintiff was employed to command a steamer at £50 per month for a particular voyage but subsequently abandoned the command. It was held that he could recover for the months for which he had served.

15 See also the Apportionment Act 1870, ss 2 and 5, which state that salaries shall be treated as 'accruing from day to day'.

16 [1972] 2 All ER 1322.

17 For further discussion of this case, see below, 17.3.6.

18 (1831) 8 Bing 14; [1824–34] All ER Rep 94. This case is discussed further in the context of 'restitution' in Chapter 19, 19.4.1.

19 (1808) 1 Taunt 300.

to be taken from Shields to Hamburg. Seven keels were delivered at Gluckstadt by arrangement with the consignee. It was held that the carrier was entitled to recover freight at the contract rate of £20 per keel.

This exception will not apply, however, if the party effectively has no option but to accept the performance. In *Sumpter v Hedges*,[20] the plaintiff, a builder, contracted to build two houses and stables on the defendant's land for £565. The plaintiff did work to the value of £333, and then abandoned the contract, because he had no money. The defendant finished the buildings himself, using building materials left by the plaintiff. The plaintiff brought an action to recover the value of the work he had done on the buildings. Although it might appear that the defendant had accepted the performance, the Court of Appeal held that the plaintiff could not recover. As Collins LJ pointed out, although in some circumstances an agreement to pay might be inferred from the acceptance of a benefit, nevertheless:[21]

> . . . in order that that may be done, the circumstances must be such as to give an option to the defendant to take or not to take the benefit of the work done.

It would not be reasonable to expect the defendant to keep on his land a building which was in an incomplete state, and would constitute a nuisance.

17.3.6 Substantial performance

The principle of 'substantial performance' has the potential to constitute a more general exception.[22] It is based on the idea that where there is only a minor variation from the terms of the contract, the other party cannot claim to be discharged, but must rely on an action for damages for breach. The origins of it can be traced to *Boone v Eyre*,[23] a case concerning the sale of a plantation, together with its slaves. It was suggested by Lord Mansfield CJ that the fact that the seller could not establish ownership of every single slave stated to be included in the contract would not prevent him from recovering payment from the buyer under the agreement. The principle is, however, stated most clearly in *Dakin v Lee*[24] and *Hoenig v Isaacs*.[25]

In *Dakin v Lee*, the contract was for the repair of a house. The work was not done in accordance with the contract. In particular, the concrete underpinning was only half the contract depth; the columns to support a bay window were of 4 inch diameter solid

---

20 [1898] 1 QB 673.
21 Ibid, p 676.
22 It is argued by Treitel and Campbell that the doctrine of substantial performance can only apply to a severable obligation, since the claim that there can be substantial performance of an entire obligation is contradictory: see Treitel, 2003, pp 787–88; Harris, Campbell and Halson, 2002, p 46.
23 (1779) 1 Hy Bl 273.
24 [1916] 1 KB 566.
25 [1952] 2 All ER 176.

iron, instead of 5 inch diameter hollow; and the joists over the bay window were not cleated at the angles or bolted to caps and to each other. The official referee found that the plaintiffs had not performed the contract, and therefore could not claim for any payment in respect of it. The Court of Appeal noted that there was a distinction between failing to complete[26] and completing badly. Here, the contract had been performed, though badly performed, and the plaintiff could recover for the work done, less deductions for the fact that it did not conform to the contract requirements. Similarly, in *Hoenig v Isaacs*, there were found to be defects (which would cost £55 to repair) in work done in redecorating a flat. The total contract price was £750. It was held that there was substantial performance, and that the plaintiff could recover the contract price, less the cost of repairs.[27]

FOR THOUGHT

If the repairs in *Hoenig v Isaacs* had cost £255 rather than £55, do you think this would have made a difference to the decision? If so, where would the 'tipping point' be between substantial and non-substantial performance as regards the cost of repairs?

The Court of Appeal refused to apply substantial performance in *Bolton v Mahadeva*,[28] as regards the obligation to install a central heating system. The system as fitted gave out much less heat than it should have done, and caused fumes in one of the rooms. Although the complete system had been fitted, it did not fulfil its primary function of heating the house, and so the installer was not allowed to recover.

The doctrine of substantial performance appears to be infrequently used and may not be of great significance in practice. That it is still available, however, was confirmed by the Court of Appeal in *Young v Thames Properties Ltd*.[29] The contract was for the construction of a car park. The main complaints of the defendant (the car park owner), who was resisting paying for the work, were that the sub-base consisted of limestone scalpings 30mm deep, when, according to the contract, they should have been 100mm

---

26 As in *Sumpter v Hedges*; see 17.3.5 above.
27 Treitel (2003, p 786) explains *Hoenig v Isaacs* (and by implication *Dakin v Lee*) on the basis that the obligations as to the *quantity* of work to be done were severable from the obligations as to the *quality* of the work. The obligation as to quantity was entire; the obligation as to quality was not. There was no substantial failure of this obligation, so the plaintiff was entitled to recover. This analysis has some force, but it should be noted that in *Dakin v Lee* Pickford LJ specifically included the situation where the contractor is in breach by 'omitting some small portion of' the work as amounting to possible 'substantial performance', in addition to breach through 'doing his work badly': [1916] 1 KB 566, p 580. Similarly Lord Cozens-Hardy's example of a painter putting on two coats of paint rather than the specified three could be argued to go to 'quantity' rather than 'quality': ibid, p 579.
28 [1972] 2 All ER 1322.
29 [1999] EWCA Civ 629.

deep, and that the wrong grade of tarmacadam had been used as the top surface. The judge accepted evidence that these defects made little practical difference to the quality of the car park, and that the cost of remedying them (which would have involved taking up and relaying the whole area) would have been disproportionate. He held that the plaintiff was entitled to the contract price, less the amount which he had saved through the various failures to comply with the specifications. The Court of Appeal confirmed that the doctrine of substantial performance should be applied as laid down in *Dakin v Lee*, and that, in particular, there was a difference between work which was abandoned and work which was completed and done badly. Approval was given to the following statement in the headnote to *Dakin v Lee*:[30]

> Where a builder has supplied work and labour for the creation or repair of a house under a lump sum contract, but has departed from the terms of the contract, he is entitled to recover for his services, unless: (1) the work that he has done has been of no benefit to the owner; (2) the work he has done is entirely different from the work which he has contracted to do; or (3) he has abandoned the work and left it unfinished.

In the end, however, the 'the essence of the doctrine of substantial performance is that it depends on the nature of the contract and all the circumstances which arise in the present case'. The question of whether there had been substantial performance was one of fact and degree and, therefore, essentially an issue for the trial judge. On the facts, the judge had been entitled to conclude that the various defects which had been identified did not prevent a finding that there had been substantial performance; nor was there anything wrong with his approach to the calculation of the damages.

The same approach was adopted by the Court of Appeal in *Williams v Roffey Bros & Nicholls (Contractors) Ltd*.[31] Applying *Hoenig v Isaacs*, it held that the trial judge had been entitled to find that there had been substantial completion of the work on eight flats, entitling the plaintiffs to payment.

17.3.7 Withholding performance under the Principles of European Contract Law

This issue is dealt with by the Principles in Art 9:201.[32] A party who under the contract is not obliged to perform until the other has done so may withhold the whole or part of its performance 'as may be reasonable in the circumstances' until the other has

---

30 [1916] 1 KB 566.

31 [1991] 1 QB 1; [1990] 1 All ER 512. The facts of this case are dealt with in Chapter 3, 3.9.8.

32 Note that there are provisions relating to the manner of performance (for example, time or place of performance, currency for payment, etc.) in Chapter 7 of the Principles: Arts 7:101–7:112. These are not discussed here.

performed or tendered performance.[33] The notes to this Article make it clear that it is intended to give a more flexible right to withhold performance than that which applies under the common law, and is described above. In particular, the right does not depend on the failure to perform being 'fundamental'.[34] There is no need here, therefore, for the doctrine of 'substantial performance', as discussed above. The right to withhold performance can potentially arise in relation to any shortfall in performance by the other side, but the withholding must be 'reasonable' and is subject to the general principles of 'good faith and fair dealing' set out in Art 1:201.

17.4 TENDER OF PERFORMANCE

Being ready to perform a contract ('tender of performance') is generally treated as equivalent to performance in the sense that, if it is rejected, it will lead to a discharge of the tenderer's liabilities. Thus, as s 27 of the SGA 1979 puts it, where the expectation is that goods will be paid for on delivery:

> ... the seller must be ready and willing to give possession of the goods to the buyer in exchange for the price and the buyer must be ready and willing to pay the price in exchange for the possession of the goods.

17.4.1 Definition of tender

What amounts to satisfactory 'tender', so as to bring the above principle into play? This will largely depend on the terms of the contract, but something of the approach of the courts can be seen from *Startup v Macdonald*.[35] The plaintiff agreed to sell 10 tons of oil to the defendant. Delivery was to be 'within the last 14 days of March'. Delivery was in fact tendered at 8.30 pm on 31 March, which was a Saturday. The defendant refused to accept or pay for the goods. It was held that provided that the seller had actually found the other party, and that there was time to examine the goods to check compliance with the contract, this was a satisfactory tender.

From this it will be seen that the requirements are that the tender should meet the strict terms of the contract and that it should be brought to the attention of the other party in time for any rights which might arise on tender to be exercised.

---

33 Article 9:201(1). Performance may similarly be withheld if it is clear that there will be non-performance by the other side: Art 9:201(2). For example, if an advance payment is to be made before building work is to start, the payment may be withheld if it becomes clear that the start of the work will in any case be delayed.

34 The question of what is a 'fundamental' failure in performance is dealt with by the Principles in Art 8:103 and is discussed below at 17.10.

35 (1843) 6 Man & G 593.

17.4.2 Tender of money

If a debtor tenders payment, and this is not accepted, this does not cancel the obligation to pay. The debtor, however, is not obliged to attempt to pay again, but can wait until the creditor calls for payment.

The exact amount must be tendered. There is no legal obligation to give change, though of course in the majority of situations the creditor will be quite happy to do so.

There are particular statutory rules as to the maximum amounts of particular types of coin which will constitute 'legal tender'.[36]

17.5 TIME FOR PERFORMANCE

Is the time for performance important? Is time, as the courts put it, 'of the essence'? The common law said that it was, unless the parties had expressed a contrary intention. Equity took the opposite view, so that time was not of the essence unless the parties had specifically made it so. The equitable rule was given precedence in s 21 of the Law of Property Act 1925, so that where under equity time is not of the essence, contractual provisions dealing with time should be interpreted in the same way at common law. Note also that s 10(1) of the SGA 1979 states that:

> Unless a different intention appears from the terms of the contract, stipulations as to time of payment are not of the essence of a contract of sale.[37]

The reference to the intention of the parties which appears in this section is of general application, as was confirmed by the House of Lords in *United Scientific Holdings Ltd v Burnley Borough Council*.[38] Refusing to be bound by the position as regards the common law and equitable rules prior to 1873, the House preferred to look at the nature of the contract itself. The dispute concerned the operation of a rent review clause within a 99 year lease. The House held that time was not of the essence as far as the activation of the review machinery was concerned, so that the landlord was able to put it in motion even though he had just missed the 10 year deadline specified in the lease itself. In coming to this conclusion, the House expressed approval for the following statement in *Halsbury's Laws of England*:[39]

---

36 Coinage Act 1971, s 2.

37 Note that this only specifically deals with time of payment: it says nothing about any other obligation which may arise under the contract, such as the time for delivery.

38 [1978] AC 904; [1977] 2 All ER 62.

39 Volume 9, para 481. See Viscount Dilhorne, p 937; p 78; Lord Simon, p 944; p 83. Lord Fraser also approved the third limb of the paragraph from *Halsbury*, which reads '(3) a party who has been subjected to unreasonable delay gives notice to the party in default making time of the essence': ibid, p 958; p 94.

Time will not be considered to be of the essence unless: (1) the parties expressly stipulate that conditions as to time must be strictly complied with; or (2) the nature of the subject matter of the contract or the surrounding circumstances show that time should be considered to be of the essence.

The first element of this paragraph is unproblematic. As regards the second category, however, it is unclear whether commercial contracts should be regarded as always falling within its scope. In *Bunge Corp v Tradax SA*,[40] there are statements in both the Court of Appeal and the House of Lords that, in commercial contracts, stipulations as to time are usually to be treated as being 'of the essence'.[41] This seems to suggest a prima facie rule which is contrary to the presumption in *Halsbury* that time is not usually of the essence. The statements in *Bunge v Tradax* are somewhat diffident, however, and the House at the same time gave approval to the statement in *Halsbury*.[42] The best approach is probably that the issue should be determined on the basis of the commercial context of the particular contract under consideration rather than being subject to any specific presumption. The judicial statements are sufficiently vague to allow such an approach.[43]

Where time is not initially of the essence, it seems that it may become so by one party giving notice. This is what happened in *Charles Rickards Ltd v Oppenheim*,[44] the facts of which are given in Chapter 3.[45] This possibility appears to arise as soon as the contractual date for performance has passed. This was the view taken by the Court of Appeal in *Behzadi v Shaftesbury Hotels Ltd*,[46] which was a contract for land. The court held that if the contract contained a specific date for performance, even though this was not of the essence, there was nevertheless a breach of contract as soon as that date had passed, and the party not in breach was entitled to serve a notice immediately making time of the essence. As Purchas LJ put it:[47]

> I see no reason for the imposition of any further period of delay after the breach of contract has been established by non-performance in accordance with its terms before it is open to a party to serve such a notice. The important matter is that the notice must in all the circumstances of the case give a reasonable opportunity for the other party to perform his part of the contract.

Only after that period had expired would the party who has issued the notice be entitled

---

40 [1981] 2 All ER 513.
41 Ibid, p 535, per Megaw LJ; p 542, per Lord Wilberforce.
42 Ibid, p 542.
43 Cf Treitel's comments to this effect: Treitel, 2003, pp 797–800.
44 [1950] 1 KB 616; [1950] 1 All ER 420.
45 See 3.10.2. See also the passage from *Halsbury* approved by Lord Fraser in *United Specific Holdings v Burnley*, above, note 39.
46 [1992] Ch 1; [1991] 2 All ER 477.
47 Ibid, p 24; p 496.

to treat the contract as repudiated by the other side's failure to perform. In coming to this conclusion, the court disapproved *dicta* in *British and Commonwealth Holdings plc v Quadrex Holdings Inc*,[48] which suggested that there must be an unreasonable delay before the right to give notice making time of the essence arises. Since both these cases are Court of Appeal decisions, the latter one, *Behzadi v Shaftesbury Hotels Ltd*, should be taken to prevail, pending a ruling by the House of Lords.

17.6 DISCHARGE BY BREACH

A breach of contract will have a range of consequences. It may entitle the innocent party to seek an order for performance of the contract, to claim damages, or to terminate the contract, or some combination of these. It is termination that we are concerned with in this chapter,[49] since this will also entail the discharge of future obligations. Where the innocent party terminates a contract as a result of a breach by the other side, it is in fact likely to be indicating three things: (1) that it will not perform any of its outstanding obligations under the contract; (2) that it will not expect the other party to perform any of its outstanding obligations, and will reject performance if it is tendered; and (3) that it may seek financial compensation (damages) for losses resulting from the other party's breach.[50]

17.6.1 Effect of breach

There have at various times been suggestions that a breach of contract, if sufficiently serious, amounting to what is often called a 'repudiatory' breach, might bring a contract to an end automatically, irrespective of the wishes of the parties.[51] The current view, however, is that a breach only ever has the effect of allowing the innocent party the choice of whether to terminate the agreement or allow it to continue.[52] This was confirmed by the House of Lords in *Photo Production v Securicor*.[53] In all cases,

---

48 [1989] QB 842; [1989] 3 All ER 492.

49 The other two are dealt with in Chapter 18.

50 In some cases damages will not be sought if, for example, defective goods are supplied under a sale of goods contract. The buyer may be satisfied simply by the return of any money paid, in exchange for the rejection of the goods.

51 See, for example, Lord Denning's judgment in the Court of Appeal in *Harbutt's Plasticine v Wayne Tank and Pump* [1970] 1 QB 447; [1970] 1 All ER 225 or, in the employment law context, *Hill v CA Parsons* [1972] 1 Ch 305; [1971] 3 All ER 1345 and *Sanders v Neale* [1974] 3 All ER 327.

52 In effect, the right to terminate is a kind of 'self-help' remedy – see Harris, Campbell and Halson, 2002, pp 51–57.

53 [1980] AC 827; [1980] 1 All ER 556. In the employment area it was confirmed by the Court of Appeal in *Gunton v London Borough of Richmond upon Thames* [1980] 3 All ER 577 that the general rule applied here as well. But see also *Boyo v Lambeth* LBC [1994] ICR 727 and *Cerberus Software Ltd v Rowley* [2001] IRLR 160.

therefore, the innocent party will have the possibility of electing to either treat the contract as repudiated and therefore to terminate it or to affirm it (and possibly claim damages).

Termination for repudiatory breach is not the same thing as 'rescission', though the courts do not always distinguish between them, and in certain circumstances the effects are the same. In a simple sale of goods transaction, for example, if there is a repudiatory breach in relation to the quality of the goods, the effect may well be that the buyer will return the goods and reclaim the price. This is exactly the same as if there had been rescission for misrepresentation. There are differences, however. First, there will always be a right to claim damages for a repudiatory breach, whereas rescission (for example, in relation to a totally innocent misrepresentation) may be a remedy in itself.[54] Second, in a complex or continuing contract, whereas rescission requires the whole transaction to be undone, termination may leave intact obligations which have arisen prior to the breach – although in a simple transaction the effects may be the same.

As Lord Wilberforce explained in *Johnson v Agnew*,[55] where there is reference to 'rescission' for breach of contract:[56]

> . . . this so-called 'rescission' is quite different from rescission *ab initio*, such as may arise, for example, in cases of mistake, fraud or lack of consent. In those cases, the contract is treated in law as never having come into existence . . . In the case of repudiatory breach, the contract has come into existence but has been put to an end or discharged. Whatever contrary indications may be disinterred from old authorities, it is now quite clear, under the general law of contract, that acceptance of a repudiatory breach does not bring about 'rescission *ab initio*'.

This meant that if there had been a repudiatory breach and the claimant had been granted an order of specific performance, but such performance became impossible, a court had the power to discharge the order and award damages for the original breach.

17.6.2 Nature of repudiatory breach

What types of breach of contract will give rise to the right to treat the agreement as repudiated and therefore to terminate it? There are a number of ways of approaching this issue. It could be said that this is a matter for the parties to determine, and that they should agree in their contract whether a particular type of breach is to be repudiatory or not. Second, it could be argued that the issue can only be determined when the consequences of an actual breach are known. Third, it might be thought best to have specific legal rules which state that particular contractual obligations fall into one category or the other. English law, as we shall see, uses a mixture of all three

---

54 See Chapter 10, 10.4.1.
55 [1980] AC 367; [1979] 1 All ER 883.
56 Ibid, pp 392–93; p 889.

approaches. It will be convenient, however, to start with the third, and look at a situation where a statute determines the consequences of particular breaches.

17.6.3 The Sale of Goods Act 1979: implied conditions and warranties

The implied terms under the SGA 1979 are labelled as being either 'conditions' or 'warranties'. The consequences of this are spelt out in s 11(3), which indicates that a 'condition' is a stipulation the breach of which may give rise to a right to treat the contract as repudiated, whereas a breach of 'warranty' may give rise to a claim for damages, but not to a right to reject the goods.

The SGA 1979 thus uses the terminology of condition and warranty to distinguish between repudiatory and other breaches. Only if the term broken is a condition will the breach be repudiatory. The question then arises as to which terms are conditions and which are warranties? As far as the implied terms under the SGA 1979 are concerned, the Act itself provides the answer, by labelling them as one or the other. In relation to other provisions in a sale of goods contract, however, the question is, as s 11(3) makes clear, one of the 'construction of the contract'. This is the position in relation to most other contracts as well, and so we need to consider this next.

Before doing so, however, it is important to note that both 'condition' and 'warranty' are at times used in other senses than the ones under consideration here. 'Condition' is used, for example, in relation to a 'condition precedent' or 'condition subsequent', or generally to mean the provisions of a contract, as in 'terms and conditions'. 'Warranty' on the other hand can mean simply a 'promise' or a 'guarantee'. Care is needed, therefore, in looking at discussions of contractual terms, particularly by judges, in order to be sure that the meaning which is being attached to a particular word is clear.

17.6.4 Categorisation of terms: the courts' approach

Where a term is not labelled by statute, the courts themselves have to decide whether it is a condition, breach of which will be repudiatory and give the other party the right to terminate, or a warranty, breach of which will only give rise to a right to damages. The main factor will be the importance of the term in the context of the contract. Is it of major significance in relation to the purpose of the contract, or is its role only minor?

The traditional approach of the courts under the classical law of contract can be seen in the contrasting cases of *Bettini v Gye*[57] and *Poussard v Spiers*.[58] Both cases concerned singers. In *Poussard v Spiers*, the singer was contracted to play a part in an operetta. She was unable, as a result of illness, to be present at the start of the run, and arrived a week late. By this time, a substitute had been employed, and her failure to

---

57 (1876) 1 QBD 183.
58 (1876) 1 QBD 410.

appear was treated as a repudiatory breach. In *Bettini v Gye*, the singer was required to be present for rehearsals six days before the start of the performance. Again, as a result of illness, he was delayed, and arrived three days late. On this occasion, the court treated the failure to appear for the rehearsals as a breach which was not repudiatory. As Blackburn J said, the classification of terms 'depends on the true construction of the contract as a whole'.[59] In *Poussard v Spiers*, the failure to meet the obligation to be present for a performance was treated as much more serious than Bettini's failure to meet the obligation to be present for a rehearsal. The former breach had a much more significant impact on the main purpose of the contract than the latter.

FOR THOUGHT

If Bettini had missed all the rehearsals, do you think the outcome would have been the same? If not, what precisely was the term which amounted to a condition of the contract which Bettini would have broken (in contrast to the position on the facts as they actually occurred)?

In some cases, the courts will not look so much to the interpretation of the individual contract, but to the expectations of parties who regularly include clauses of a particular type in their agreements. In *Bunge Corp v Tradax Export SA*,[60] as we have seen,[61] it was stated that time clauses in mercantile contracts should usually be treated as conditions. As Lord Wilberforce explained, to treat such terms as 'innominate'[62] would be commercially 'most undesirable':[63]

> It would expose the parties, after a breach of one, two, three, seven and other numbers of days, to an argument whether this delay would have left the seller time to provide the goods. It would make it, at the time, at least difficult, and sometimes impossible, for the supplier to know whether he could do so. It would fatally remove from a vital provision in the contract that certainty which is the most indispensable quality of mercantile contracts, and lead to a large increase in arbitrations.

Applying this approach to the facts, a four day delay in giving notice of the readiness of a vessel to receive a cargo was a breach of a condition in the shipment contract, entitling the sellers to treat the contract as repudiated.

---

59 (1876) 1 QBD 183, p 187.
60 [1981] 2 All ER 513.
61 Above, 17.5.
62 This meaning that the right to repudiate would depend on the seriousness of the breach – see below, 17.6.7.
63 [1981] 2 All ER 513, p 541.

A similar approach to a clause relating to time was taken by the Privy Council in *Union Eagle Ltd v Golden Achievement Ltd*,[64] as noted above at 17.3.1.

17.6.5 Categorisation of terms: labelling by the parties

One way in which the courts may be able to determine the parties' intentions as regards the effect of breaking particular terms is where these have been labelled. If they have gone through the contract and referred to certain terms as conditions, and the rest as warranties, then it may be presumed that this was intended to have the same significance as the labels used in the SGA 1979. The use of labels will not be conclusive, however, as is shown by *Schuler AG v Wickman Tools Sales Ltd*.[65] The defendants were under an obligation to make weekly visits to six named firms, over a period of four and a half years, in connection with a contract under which they were given the sole selling rights of the plaintiffs' panel presses. This obligation was referred to as a 'condition', and none of the other 19 clauses in the contract was described in this way. This would seem to suggest that the parties intended that any breach of it would be repudiatory. The majority of the House of Lords refused to interpret it in this way, however. Noting that the contract required in total some 1,400 visits to be made, and that it was likely that in a few cases a visit would be impossible, Lord Reid pointed out that:

> ... if Schuler's contention is right failure to make even one visit entitles them to terminate the contract, however blameless Wickman might be. This is so unreasonable that it must make me search for some other possible meaning of the contract.

This 'other possible meaning' the House found by treating a breach of the visits clause as being a 'material breach' sufficient to bring into play other termination procedures under another clause.

A similar approach is to be found in *Rice v Great Yarmouth Borough Council*.[66] In this case the 'labelling' did not refer to conditions or warranties, but directly to the circumstances in which the right to terminate for breach would arise. The contract was for provision of leisure management and grounds maintenance services to the council for a four year period. After seven months the council purported to terminate the agreement for breach of contract. The council relied on cl 23 of the contract, which stated:

> If the contractor ... commits a breach of any of its obligations under the contract ... the council may, without prejudice to any accrued right or remedies

---

64 [1997] 2 All ER 215.
65 [1974] AC 235; [1973] 2 All ER 39.
66 [2001] 3 LGLR 4.

under the contract, terminate the contractor's employment under the contract by notice in writing having immediate effect.

The trial judge held that this clause should not be applied literally, and that there should be a right to terminate only where the breach was serious enough to be treated as repudiatory. The Court of Appeal upheld this conclusion. First, in the context of a four year contract involving substantial financial obligations and 'a myriad of obligations of differing importance and varying frequency', a common sense interpretation should be placed on the strict words of the contract. Clause 23 did not characterise any term as a 'condition' or 'indicate which terms were to be considered so important that any breach would justify termination'. It was only where there was a repudiatory breach or an accumulation of breaches which could be said to be repudiatory that the right to terminate under cl 23 would arise.[67] As noted above, in contrast to *Schuler v Wickman*, the clause was not concerned with the labelling of obligations but the process for termination, but the approach is similar: the court refuses to give the words of the contract their literal meaning. In this case, the literal wording would have allowed termination for any breach, however minor, but the Court of Appeal insisted that it must be interpreted in the overall context of the contract, and in line with 'common sense'.[68]

The decisions in *Schuler v Wickman* and *Rice v Great Yarmouth BC* do not mean that the parties' own labelling of terms is to be ignored, simply that it is not conclusive of the issue. In other cases the courts have shown themselves to be willing to give effect to clearly stated provisions as to the consequences of a breach. In *Awilco A/S v Fulvia SpA di Navigazione, The Chikuma*,[69] for example, in discussing a clause giving a right to withdraw a ship for late payment of hire, Lord Bridge said that where parties bargaining at arm's length use 'common form' clauses, it is very important that their meaning and legal effect should be certain:[70]

> The ideal at which the courts should aim, in construing such clauses, is to produce a result such that in any given situation both parties seeking legal advice as to their rights and obligations can expect the same clear and confident answer from their advisers and neither will be tempted to embark on long and expensive litigation in the belief that victory depends on winning the sympathy of the court.

---

67 That is, the approach should be that adopted in *Hong Kong Fir Shipping Co v Kawasaki Kisen Kaisha* – discussed below, 17.6.7.

68 Which presumably means what the court thinks reasonable parties would be taken to have intended by the clause at the time of contracting. If so, this becomes another example of the courts' assumption that all incidents of a long term (or 'relational') contract are capable of 'presentiation' – see Macneil, 1978, and Chapter 1, 1.5.

69 [1981] 1 All ER 652.

70 Ibid, p 659.

Similarly, in *Lombard North Central plc v Butterworth*,[71] the Court of Appeal upheld the parties' own express provisions as to the consequences of breach of terms as to payment in a contract of hire, even though they were not happy about the justice of the overall result.

17.6.6 Consequences of categorisation

The categorisation of terms as either conditions or warranties implies that the actual consequence of a particular breach is not a relevant factor. Once a term is a 'condition', any breach of it will be repudiatory, no matter that it can be easily remedied, or has on this occasion caused no substantial loss to the other party. Similarly, whatever the consequences of a breach of warranty, and however great the losses it causes, it will never give rise to the right to terminate the contract. This approach is therefore rigid, and may appear to cause injustice in some cases, but it has the merit of certainty, in that the parties can be aware in advance what the legal consequences of any particular breach will be.[72]

17.6.7 Intermediate terms

There are times when the categorisation of terms in the way outlined in the previous sections does not work and, at least since 1962, the courts have recognised that it is necessary to have an intermediate category. The leading case is *Hong Kong Fir Shipping Co v Kawasaki Kisen Kaisha Ltd*,[73] though some would argue that earlier decisions were, in fact, based on the same considerations. The term that was under consideration in *Hong Kong Fir* was that of 'seaworthiness', which appeared in a time charter of a ship. Diplock LJ admitted that some terms may be classifiable as conditions or warranties, but felt that there are many contractual undertakings of a more complex nature which cannot be classified in that way. The obligation as to seaworthiness, for example, could be broken in any number of ways. For example, the failure to have the correct number of lifejackets on board could render a ship 'unseaworthy' just as much as a major defect in the hull. In such a case, it was not possible to determine beforehand the consequences of a breach, in terms of whether it would be repudiatory or not. Rather, what a judge had to do was to:[74]

> . . . look at the events which had occurred as a result of the breach at the time when the charterers purported to rescind the charterparty and to decide whether the occurrence of those events deprived the charterers of substantially the whole benefit which it was the intention of the parties as expressed in the charterparty

---

71 [1987] QB 527; [1987] 1 All ER 267.
72 Cf the comments of Lord Bridge in *The Chikuma* (see above, 17.6.5).
73 [1962] 2 QB 26; [1962] 1 All ER 474.
74 Ibid, p 72; pp 488–89.

that the charterers should obtain from the further performance of their own contractual undertakings.

So, on this analysis, the focus is not on the parties' intentions at the time of the contract, but on the effect of the actual breach which has occurred: that is, the second of the approaches outlined at the start of this section.[75] If the breach is so serious as to strike fundamentally at the purpose of the contract, then it will be treated as repudiatory, in the same way as if it was a breach of condition; if it is less serious it will give rise only to a remedy in damages, like a warranty.

17.6.8 Effects of *Hong Kong Fir*

The courts have never doubted, since the decision in *Hong Kong Fir*, that there are three categories of term, namely conditions, warranties and 'innominate' or intermediate terms.[76] An approach based on the consequences of breach has even been adopted, perhaps somewhat surprisingly, in relation to sale of goods contracts, in *Cehave NV v Bremer Handelsgesellschaft mbH, The Hansa Nord*.[77] Lord Denning, in this case, was concerned with the definition of 'merchantable quality'[78] under the SGA 1893, the obligation to supply goods of such quality being a term labelled as a 'condition' by the statute itself. In determining whether the goods are 'merchantable', however, Lord Denning suggested that:[79]

> In these circumstances, I should have thought a fair way of testing merchantability would be to ask a commercial man: was the breach such that the buyer should be able to reject the goods . . .?

In other words, the consequences of breach are to be used to determine merchantable quality, and therefore, indirectly, whether or not a breach of condition has occurred. On the facts, since the goods, though damaged, had been used for their intended purpose as animal feed, there was not a breach which should have entitled the buyer to reject, and the goods were thus 'merchantable'. This ingenious incorporation of a *Hong Kong Fir* approach into the area of the statutorily labelled implied terms was not adopted by the other members of the Court of Appeal, although they agreed that the pellets were 'merchantable', and so cannot be regarded as authoritative. It has, in any case, probably

---

75 See above, 17.6.2.
76 Reynolds (1981, pp 548–49), following the argument of Upjohn LJ in *Hong Kong Fir*, has argued that in effect there are only two types of term: those where any breach will give rise to the right to terminate, and those where the right to terminate will depend on the consequences of the breach (that is, conflating 'warranties' with 'innominate terms'). But this analysis has not found favour in subsequent cases. See also Treitel, 2003, p 796.
77 [1976] QB 44.
78 Now 'satisfactory quality' – see above, 8.6.12.
79 [1976] QB 44, p 62.

been superseded by the much more specific statutory definitions of quality to be found in the current SGA 1979.[80] The court was, however, unanimous that the *Hong Kong Fir* approach could be applied to express obligations in a sale of goods contract. In this case, the obligation that the goods should be 'shipped in good condition' was treated as an innominate term. Since the pellets had been able to be used, it could not be said that there was a breach of sufficient seriousness to justify repudiation.

In other areas, however, the attraction of the flexibility of Diplock LJ's analysis in *Hong Kong Fir* has frequently bowed to considerations of the desirability of commercial certainty, spelt out in the quotation from Lord Bridge in *The Chikuma*.[81] Thus, in *Maradelanto Cia Naviera SA v Bergbau-Handel GmbH, The Mihalis Angelos*,[82] the obligation of being 'expected ready to load' at a particular time, a clause which clearly could be broken with varying degrees of seriousness, was treated as a condition, irrespective of the consequences of the particular breach. And as we have seen, a similar view was taken of time clauses in mercantile contracts in *Bunge Corp v Tradax SA*.[83] It will continue to be important, therefore, to ask the question 'is this a condition or a warranty?', before considering the consequences of the breach of contract. The answer to that question may render such consideration unnecessary.

17.7 SOME SPECIAL TYPES OF BREACH

There are three particular situations which call for some special consideration. The first is where the contract involves the performance of services over a period of time. In what circumstances will the breach of an innominate term be regarded as repudiatory? The second situation is where the contract is divided into instalments. What is the position if the breach relates to only a small proportion of those instalments? Finally, what is the position where the consequences of the breach do not affect the possibilities of the physical performance of the contract, but its commercial viability?

17.7.1 Long-term contracts

This issue was considered by the Court of Appeal in *Rice v Great Yarmouth BC*.[84] The contract was for the provision of leisure management and grounds maintenance services to the council for a four year period. After seven months the council purported to terminate the agreement for breach of contract. The Court of Appeal, as noted above,[85]

---

80 See above, 8.6.12.
81 See above, 17.6.5.
82 [1971] 1 QB 164; [1970] 3 All ER 125.
83 [1981] 2 All ER 513 – see above, 17.4.3. A similar view was also taken by the Court of Appeal in *BS & N Ltd v Micado Shipping Ltd (Malta) (No 2)* [2001] 1 All ER Comm 240.
84 [2001] 3 LGLR 4. See also above, 17.6.5.
85 17.6.5.

held that the clause in the contract on which the council relied did not give a right to terminate for every breach. This meant that it then had to consider the question of what, in this type of long-running contract for the provision of public services, would amount to a repudiatory breach. The Court of Appeal could find no direct authority on the issue, though there were some parallels with charterparties or building contracts. It was accepted that it was relevant to look at the contractor's performance over a full year and to ask whether the council was deprived of the whole benefit of what it had contracted for over that period. As in building contracts, past breaches were relevant not only for their own sake, but also for what they showed about the future. It was right to ask whether the accumulation of breaches was such as to justify an inference that the contractor would continue to deliver a sub-standard performance, thus leading to the council being deprived of 'a substantial part of the totality of that which it had contracted for that year'.[86]

Subject to the possibility that there were some aspects of the contract which were so important 'that the parties were to be taken to have intended that depriving the council of that part of the contract would be sufficient in itself' to justify termination, this was the approach to be adopted. The judge had dealt with the issues appropriately and there was no need to interfere with his decision, which was that the council did not have the right to terminate.

This case shows that deciding what is, on the *Hong Kong Fir* approach, a repudiatory breach in a long-term contract can be tricky. Here the Court of Appeal seems to have started from the point that deprivation of at least 25 per cent of the overall benefit of the contract (that is, performance over one year out of four) would be necessary (other than in relation to breach of any terms which might be of particular importance). The decision is understandable, but it does not particularly assist parties who may be looking for certainty as to the consequences of particular actions on their part (that is, as to if and when the other party will be entitled to treat their actions as repudiatory).

FOR THOUGHT

Would it be more satisfactory in this type of situation if the courts laid down a general rule that the breach must affect 30 per cent of the contract, for example, in order for it to be considered repudiatory? What difficulties might that give rise to?

17.7.2 Instalment contracts

A similar problem to that just considered arises here. In a contract which is to be performed by instalments, will the breach of one of them ever amount to a repudiatory

---

86 Cf *Decro-Wall International SA v Practitioners in Marketing Ltd* [1971] 2 All ER 216 – regular late payment for goods received under a continuing contract did not amount to a repudiatory breach. The consequences of late payment could be adequately compensated by recovering extra interest.

breach? If so, then the contract can be brought to an end as soon as that one breach has occurred, and there will be no further obligations as regards the rest of the instalments. On the other hand, if the innocent party allows the contract to continue, that may well amount to affirmation of the contract, so that the breach could not subsequently be relied on as being repudiatory.

The resolution of these issues may, of course, be determined by what the parties have themselves agreed in the contract. This is confirmed by s 31(2) of the Sale of Goods Act 1979, which states that in cases of defective delivery, or a refusal to accept delivery:

> . . . it is a question in each case depending on the terms of the contract and the circumstances of the case whether the breach of contract is a repudiation of the whole contract or whether it is a severable breach giving rise to a claim in compensation but not to a right to treat the whole contract as repudiated.

An example of the application of this is to be seen in *Maple Flock Co Ltd v Universal Furniture Products (Wembley) Ltd*.[87] The sellers had contracted to sell 100 tons of rag flock to the buyers. Out of the first 20 loads delivered, one, the 16th, was defective. The Court of Appeal held that this was not a repudiatory breach, since it related only to one instalment, and therefore only one and a half tons out of the whole contract. In contrast, in *RA Munro & Co Ltd v Meyer*,[88] 1,500 tons of meat and bone meal were to be delivered in 12 instalments of 125 tons. After 768 tons had been delivered, it was discovered that all were adulterated, and did not match the contract description. It was held that this was sufficient to amount to a repudiatory breach.

The proportion of the instalments involved in the breach is not the only issue, however, as is shown by the House of Lords' decision in *Mersey Steel and Iron Co v Naylor, Benzon & Co*.[89] The contract was for the sale of 5,000 tons of steel, to be delivered at the rate of 1,000 tons per month, with payment within three days of receipt of the shipping documents. The sellers delivered only part of the first instalment, but delivered the second complete. Shortly before payment was due, the sellers were the subject of a petition for winding up and, as a result, the buyers (acting on inaccurate legal advice) withheld payment. The sellers sought to treat this as a repudiatory breach. The House of Lords noted that the buyers had indicated a continuing willingness to pay as soon as any legal difficulties had been resolved, and therefore held that this was not a repudiatory breach. The context was important in determining the effect of a breach in relation to one instalment.

As well as illustrating the courts' approach to instalment contracts, this case shows that the intention of the party in breach, and the reasons for the breach, may be important factors in determining whether it is repudiatory. The fact that the buyers had

---

87 [1934] 1 KB 148.
88 [1930] 2 KB 312.
89 (1884) 9 App Cas 434.

no intention to repudiate, but were acting under a bona fide mistake of law, was a very relevant consideration.

17.7.3 Commercial destruction

In most cases of repudiatory breach, there is some act or omission which means that the obligations under the contract have only partially been fulfilled. Goods do not match their description, or are supplied in insufficient quality; services are not supplied, or do not meet contractual standards; money owed is paid late or not at all. In all these situations the innocent party is being deprived of the benefit of the contract. It is possible, however, for a party to complete his or her major obligations, but for the consequences of some minor breach to be such that, although it does not affect the practical possibility of continuing with the contract, commercially it would be unreasonable to do so. This is exemplified by *Aerial Advertising Co v Batchelors Peas*.[90] The contract was for the towing of an advertising banner on daily flights by an aeroplane. The pilot was supposed to clear his flight plan each day, but on one occasion he failed to do so. He flew over Salford, and saw a large crowd assembled in the main square. He flew close to it displaying the sign 'Eat Batchelors Peas'. Unfortunately, the date was 11 November, and the crowd had assembled to keep the traditional two minutes' silence on Armistice Day. The actions of the pilot led to much criticism of Batchelors. The judge held that it was 'commercially wholly unreasonable to carry on with the contract' and that, in the circumstances, the consequences of the breach (that is, the failure to clear the flight plan) meant that Batchelors were entitled to treat the contract as repudiated.

17.8 ANTICIPATORY BREACH

While there are obligations still to be performed, one party may indicate in advance that he or she intends to break the contract. This is known as an 'anticipatory breach', and will generally give the other party the right to treat the contract as repudiated, and to sue at once for damages. For example, in *Hochster v De La Tour*,[91] the defendant engaged the plaintiff on 12 April to enter his service as a courier, and accompany him on a foreign tour. This employment was to start on 1 June. On 11 May, the defendant wrote to the plaintiff to inform him that his services would no longer be required. It was held that the plaintiff was entitled to bring an action for damages immediately, without waiting for 1 June.

The reason for allowing this type of action, rather than making the plaintiff wait until performance is due, was given by Cockburn CJ in *Frost v Knight*.[92] He held that it

---

90 [1938] 2 All ER 788.
91 (1853) 2 E & B 678; [1843–60] All ER Rep 12.
92 (1872) LR 7 Exch 111.

involves a breach of a right to have the contract kept open as a subsisting and effective contract. It, of course, also has the practical benefit of enabling the innocent party to obtain compensation for any damage speedily.

As will be seen in the next section, however, the innocent party does not have to accept the anticipatory breach as repudiating the contract. He or she may wait until performance is due, and then seek damages for non-performance at that stage. It has even been held in one case that the innocent party can legitimately incur expenses towards his or her own performance even after a clear indication of an intention to break the contract has been given by the other side. These may then be claimed as damages once the contract date for performance has passed.[93]

17.9   EFFECT OF BREACH: RIGHT OF ELECTION

In relation to all repudiatory breaches, the innocent party has the right to elect to treat the contract as discharged and claim for damages, or to affirm the contract, notwithstanding the breach. The latter course will prevent the contract from being discharged, but damages may still be recovered.

17.9.1   Need for communication

Where the innocent party elects to treat the breach as repudiatory, this decision will normally only be effective if communicated to the other party.[94] That this is not, however, universally necessary is shown by the House of Lords' decision in *Vitol SA v Norelf Ltd, The Santa Clara*.[95] V and N had entered into a contract on 11 February 1991 for the purchase of a cargo of propane. On 8 March, V sent a telex to N repudiating the contract. This was subsequently agreed to amount to an anticipatory breach which, if accepted by N, would bring the contract to an end immediately. N did not communicate with V but, on 12 March, started to try to find an alternative buyer and, on 15 March, sold the cargo to X. V challenged the arbitrator's decision that these actions by N amounted to an acceptance of the anticipatory breach. Phillips J upheld the decision of the arbitrator. The Court of Appeal, however, reversed this decision. Since the differing consequences following from acceptance of repudiation on the one hand or affirmation of the contract on the other were immediate and serious, it was essential that the choice of repudiation should be clear and unequivocal. It needed to be manifested by word or deed. As Nourse LJ put it:[96]

---

93 *White and Carter (Councils) Ltd v McGregor* [1962] AC 413; [1961] 3 All ER 1178.
94 Cf the Principles of European Contract Law, which suggest that notice of termination should be given 'within a reasonable time': Art 9:303.
95 [1996] AC 800; [1996] 3 All ER 193.
96 [1996] QB 108, p 116.

A choice, however resolute, which gains no expression outside the bosom of the chooser cannot be clear and unequivocal in the sense that the law requires. Silence and inaction, being in the generality of cases equally consistent with an affirmation of the contract, cannot constitute acceptance of a repudiation.

What if the innocent party has failed to perform his or her obligations under the contract, as had happened here? Is this sufficient to indicate acceptance of repudiation? The Court of Appeal thought not. The failure to perform was equally consistent with a misunderstanding by the innocent party of his or her rights under the contract, or indecision, or even inadvertence. The House of Lords, however, rejected the view of the Court of Appeal and restored the decision of the arbitrator and the judge at first instance. Lord Steyn set out three principles which apply to acceptance of a repudiatory breach:

(a)   Where a party has repudiated a contract the aggrieved party has an election whether to accept the repudiation or affirm the contract.

(b)   An act of acceptance of a repudiation requires no particular form: a communication does not have to be couched in the language of acceptance. It is sufficient that the communication or conduct clearly and unequivocally conveys to the repudiating party that the aggrieved party is treating the contract as at an end.

(c)   The aggrieved party need not personally, or by an agent, notify the repudiating party of his election to treat the contract as at an end. It is sufficient that the fact of the election comes to the repudiating party's attention, for example, notification by an unauthorised broker or other intermediary may be sufficient.

In applying these principles to the case, Lord Steyn noted that the specific issue before the House was 'whether non-performance of an obligation is ever *as a matter of law* capable of constituting acceptance'.[97] Their Lordships answered this question in the affirmative, stating that whether there is acceptance in a particular case 'all depends on the particular contractual relationship and the particular circumstances of the case'.[98] These were issues of fact, which the arbitrator was in the best position to decide. Lord Steyn was quite prepared to accept, however, that the failure of the seller (N) to take the next step which would have been required if the contract was to continue (that is, submitting the bill of lading to the buyer (V)), could be found to amount to an unequivocal notification to V of N's acceptance of V's repudiation. The arbitrator was entitled to come to that conclusion on the facts, and his decision should be restored.

Despite this decision, which opens up the possibility of acceptance by inaction, the safest course for a party who intends to accept a repudiatory breach, and therefore terminate the contract, is to do so specifically, by communicating this to the other party. This will remove any danger that the behaviour of the party not in breach will be deemed 'equivocal', and therefore not sufficient to constitute a valid acceptance.

---

97 [1996] AC 800, p 811 (emphasis added).
98 Ibid.

17.9.2 Risks of acceptance

There are, of course, dangers in treating an action by the other party as repudiatory, if it turns out to be viewed otherwise by the court. The party purporting to accept a repudiatory breach may well take action (as was the case in *Vitol v Norelf*) which itself involves a breach of obligations under the contract. If this turns out not to be justified by what the other party has done, then the party who thought it was acting in response to a repudiatory breach may find the tables turned, and that that party itself is now liable to damages for its own breach of the contract. In *Federal Commerce and Navigation Co Ltd v Molena Alpha Inc, The Nanfri,*[99] which concerned the operation of three time charterparties, the charterers deducted various amounts from the hire which they paid to the owners. The owners objected and issued instructions to the masters of the vessels concerned to, *inter alia*, withdraw all authority to the charterers or their agents to sign bills of lading. This action was held to amount to a repudiatory breach which entitled the charterers to terminate the charterparties.

In *Woodar Investment Development Ltd v Wimpey Construction UK Ltd,*[100] the majority of the House of Lords seemed to take the view that this consequence would not necessarily follow if the party purporting to accept the repudiation was acting as a result of a mistake made in good faith as to his or her rights. Most commentators regard this aspect of the *Woodar v Wimpey* decision as dubious, and prefer to follow the bulk of authorities which suggest that an unjustified failure to meet contractual obligations is itself a repudiatory breach, even if it is a response to action from the other party which is mistakenly thought to be repudiatory.

17.9.3 Risks of affirmation

An election to affirm the contract carries risks as well, as is shown by *Avery v Bowden.*[101] The plaintiff chartered his ship to the defendant. The ship was to sail to Odessa, and there to take a cargo from the defendant's agent, which was to be loaded within a certain number of days. The vessel reached Odessa, but the agent was unable to supply a cargo. The ship remained at Odessa, with the master continuing to demand a cargo. Before the period specified in the contract had elapsed, war broke out between England and Russia and the performance of the contract became legally impossible. The plaintiff sued for breach. It was held, however, that even if the original action of the agent constituted a repudiatory breach, the contract had been affirmed by the fact that the ship remained at Odessa awaiting a cargo. The contract was then frustrated, and it was too late at that stage for the plaintiff to claim for breach.

Similarly, in *Fercometal Sarl v Mediterranean Shipping Co SA,*[102] it was held that a

---

99 [1979] AC 757; [1979] 1 All ER 307.
100 [1980] 1 All ER 571.
101 (1855) 5 E & B 714.
102 [1989] AC 788; [1988] 2 All ER 742.

party which had affirmed a contract following an anticipatory breach could not subsequently rely on that breach to justify its own failure to fulfil its obligations under the contract.

17.10 TERMINATION UNDER THE PRINCIPLES OF EUROPEAN CONTRACT LAW

The right to terminate a contract for breach appears in Art 9:301 of the Principles.[103] Where the right exists, it 'may' be exercised by the aggrieved party. The position is thus the same as under English law, where the choice as to whether to bring a contract to an end for breach always rests with the party not in breach, and never occurs automatically. Article 9:301 states that there is a right to terminate where 'the other party's non-performance is fundamental'. Both 'non-performance' and 'fundamental' are further defined in other Articles.

Article 1:301 defines 'non-performance' to include delayed or defective performance and 'a failure to co-operate in order to give full effect to the contract'.[104] Non-performance becomes 'fundamental' if it falls within one of the three situations specified in Art 8:103, namely, if:

(a) strict compliance with the obligation is of the essence of the contract; or
(b) the non-performance substantially deprives the aggrieved party of what it was entitled to expect under the contract, unless the other party did not foresee and could not reasonably have foreseen that result; or
(c) the non-performance is intentional and gives the aggrieved party reason to believe that it cannot rely on the other party's performance.

Category (a) is clearly similar to the concept of a 'condition' under English law, while category (b) relates to the concept of a serious breach of an innominate term. The addition of a test of 'reasonable foreseeability' to category (b) is, however, not something which applies in this area in English law. The example of a situation of this type given in the notes to the Article is that of a contract for the installation of a heating system in domestic premises, where a minor breach in relation to the control system leads to the loss of the owner's valuable collection of plants which have to be kept at a specific temperature, but of which the contractor was unaware. In English law the question of 'reasonable foreseeability' is relevant to the question of what damages are recoverable,[105] but does not arise when considering whether a breach is repudiatory.

---

103 As is the case under English law, 'termination' releases parties from future obligations, but does not affect rights and liabilities that have accrued up to the time of termination: Art 9:305.

104 The inclusion of 'non-co-operation' goes beyond the English law concept of 'breach', which requires failure of performance in relation to a specific contractual obligation.

105 For which see Chapter 18.

Similarly, category (c) has no equivalent in English law. The fact that a breach is intentional or unintentional has no effect on the rights of the other party. Under the Principles, this is relevant in a continuing contract, where the intentional breach casts doubt on future performance. The Principles are here giving greater consideration to the 'relational' nature of many contracts than English law does in this context.[106]

There is also a right to terminate under the Principles where there has been delay in relation to a performance where the delay itself is not fundamental, but the aggrieved party has given notice that, following an additional period, the contract will be terminated if the other party has not performed. This provision is to be found in Art 8:106, but is also referred to in Art 9:301(2). Its effect is to incorporate into the Principles a rule similar to that which the common law has developed as regards the power to give notice that time is to become 'of the essence', as illustrated by *Rickards v Oppenheim*.[107]

Contracts which are to be performed in parts are dealt with by Art 9:302. In relation to a contract which is divisible into separate 'units' with, for example, separate payment for each unit, the aggrieved party may terminate in relation to a particular unit in relation to which there has been a fundamental non-performance. It is only if non-performance is fundamental to the contract as a whole that the whole contract can be terminated. The second part of this Principle is clearly very similar to the English law position in relation to 'instalment' contracts, giving general effect to the approach taken in relation to sale of goods contracts by s 31(2) of the Sale of Goods Act 1979;[108] the first part, however, is rather more specific in allowing the aggrieved party to reject performance in relation to one part of the contract, rather than simply claiming damages for the defective performance.

Finally, the Principles deal with the issue of 'anticipatory breach' in Art 9:304. A right to terminate is given where 'prior to the time for performance by a party it is clear that there will be a fundamental non-performance by it'. This provision is stated to be based on the common law, and in particular *Hochster v de la Tour*.[109] It is to be assumed, therefore, that the intention is that the Principles will operate in the same way as English law in relation to anticipatory breach.

17.11 FURTHER READING

Brownsword, R, 'Retrieving reasons, retrieving rationality? A new look at the right to withdraw for breach of contract' (1992) Journal of Contract Law 83

Dockray, M, '*Cutter v Powell*: a trip outside the text' (2001) 117 LQR 664

---

106 See Chapter 1, 1.5.
107 [1950] 1 KB 616; [1950] 1 All ER 420, above 17.4.3. See also Chapter 3, 3.10.2.
108 Above, 17.7.2.
109 (1853) 2 E & B 678.

Harris, D, Campbell, D and Halson, R, *Remedies in Contract and Tort*, 2nd edn, 2002, London: Butterworths

Reynolds, FMB, 'Discharge of contract by breach' (1981) 97 LQR 541

Treitel, GH, 'Affirmation after repudiatory breach' (1998a) 114 LQR 22

Treitel, GH, 'Types of contractual terms', Chapter 3 in *Some Landmarks of Twentieth Century Contract Law*, 2002, Oxford: Clarendon Press

18 REMEDIES

CONTENTS

18.1 OVERVIEW

An action for breach of contract will normally be intended to provide a remedy for the claimant. The two main remedies in English law are damages and specific performance, and these provide the focus for this chapter. The following issues are discussed:

■   Purpose of damages. The general rule is that damages are compensatory, rather than punitive, and are intended to put claimants in the position they would have been in had the contract been performed properly.

■   Measure of damages. There are several methods of calculating damages:

- Expectation interest. This is the usual measure. It allows the claimant to recover lost benefits, such as lost profits that would have been made. Problems can arise where:
  - the benefits were not certain – the claimant may be compensated for the loss of a chance to obtain the benefit;
  - the costs of providing the benefit are out of proportion to the value of the benefit itself – the court may refuse to allow full recovery in these circumstances.
- Reliance interest. The claimant may choose to seek damages on this basis – compensating for expenses incurred in relation to the contract – where the expectation interest is difficult to calculate (though not where the claimant has simply made a bad bargain).
- Restitution interest. This simply allows the claimant to recover money paid to the defendant – for example, for defective goods which have been returned. In limited circumstances a claimant has been allowed to recover the benefit that the defendant has obtained through breaking the contract, but this is exceptional.
- Non-pecuniary losses. The claimant can exceptionally recover for loss of enjoyment or mental distress caused by a breach of contract. Either the contract must be one which has the provision of non-pecuniary benefits as an important objective, or the breach must have caused physical discomfort which has led to the distress.
- Limitations on recovery. The claimant's right to damages is limited by:
  - the rule of remoteness – the claimant can recover only those losses which were normally to be expected, or, if unusual, were in the reasonable contemplation of the parties at the time of the contract;
  - mitigation – the claimant must take reasonable steps to prevent the losses increasing.
- Liquidated damages clauses are enforceable; penalty clauses, aiming to 'terrorise' the defendant into performance, are not.
- Specific performance. This equitable remedy will only be available where damages would be inadequate. The order will not be made where:
  - it would need continuous supervision;
  - it relates to personal services;
  - it would cause undue hardship to the defendant;
  - the claimant has not acted equitably.
- Injunctions. These can be used to prevent a breach of contract, but not as means of indirectly obtaining specific performance where this remedy would not be permitted.

The chapter concludes with discussion of the treatment of remedies in the Principles of European Contract Law.

18.2   INTRODUCTION[1]

At various points during the earlier chapters, remedies of one kind or another have been considered. Rescission and damages for misrepresentation were discussed in Chapter 10, for example, and rescission for mistake in Chapter 11. The 'self-help' remedies of withholding performance and terminating on the basis of repudiatory breach were dealt with in Chapter 17.[2] Here, we are considering more generally the award of damages for breach of contract, and the order of 'specific performance', which will instruct a party to perform its obligations under an agreement. Some more general references to injunctions will also be necessary.[3]

In general, as we shall see, the common law aims to put the parties into the position they would have been in had the contract been performed by ordering one party to pay money to the other. Where one of the parties has performed its side of the bargain and is awaiting payment from the other party, this can be achieved by the 'action for an agreed sum', or in sale of goods contracts the 'action for the price'.[4] In other words, the party who has promised to pay for goods or services which have been transferred or performed by the other party, can be required to make good that promise. This was, for example, the form of action taken by Mrs Carlill to compel the Carbolic Smoke Ball Co to pay her the £100,[5] and it is in practice probably the most frequently used action following a breach of contract.[6] In other situations, the normal requirement will be for the payment of compensatory damages. An order to perform part of the contract, other than paying money that is owed, is much more unusual.

We start, therefore, by considering the remedy of 'damages', and will then look at specific performance and injunctions.

18.3   DAMAGES: PURPOSE

The basic principle of contractual damages is that of *restitutio in integrum*, or full restitution, which involves putting the innocent party into the position it would have been in had the contract been performed. This principle can be traced back to *Robinson v Harman*,[7] and has recently been restated by Lord Scott in *Farley v Skinner*:[8]

---

1 See, generally, Harris, Campbell and Halson, 2002; Burrows, 2004; Beale, 1980.
2 Rescission for mistake or misrepresentation can also be regarded as 'self-help', in that there is no necessity for the court's involvement.
3 'Specific performance' is a type of injunction, which requires a person to act in a particular way; injunctions are also used to *prohibit* a person from carrying out some action.
4 See the Sale of Goods Act 1979, s 49.
5 See *Carlill v Carbolic Smoke Ball Co* [1893] 1 QB 256 – discussed in Chapter 2, 2.7.6.
6 See, for example, Harris, Campbell and Halson, 2002, p 160, n 12; Collins, 1999, pp 324–25.
7 (1848) 1 Exch 850, p 855.
8 [2001] UKHL 49, para 76; [2001] 4 All ER 801, pp 826–27.

The basic principle of damages for breach of contract is that the injured party is entitled, so far as money can do it, to be put in the position he would have been in if the contractual obligation had been properly performed. He is entitled, that is to say, to the benefit of his bargain.

The main objective of contract damages is therefore compensation, not punishment.[9] Although, of course, in some situations, a party thinking about breaking an agreement may be deterred by the prospect of having to pay damages, or a party who has broken an agreement may suffer considerably from having to pay compensation, nevertheless these consequences are not the purpose of the award. This is shown by the fact that if the party not in breach has suffered no quantifiable loss, only nominal damages will be awarded. If, for example, there is a failure to deliver goods, and the buyer is able to obtain an alternative supply without a problem, and at a price which is the same or lower than the contract price, no substantial damages will be recoverable.[10]

In relation to this aspect of contract damages, it is important to note the concept of the 'efficient breach'. Looking at the law of contract from the economic point of view, as a means of wealth maximisation,[11] it may make sense for a party to break a contract. The typical example[12] given is where a seller (S) has contracted to sell an item to a buyer (B1) for £100. Before the transaction takes place a second potential buyer (B2) offers S £200 for the item. If S sells to B2, S will receive £200, but may have to pay compensation to B1 for not fulfilling the original contract. But as long as that compensation is below £100, S will still have made a profit. All parties are in theory happy. S has sold the item at a higher price, to B2, to whom the item is obviously more valuable than it would be to B1. B1 has not received the item, but has received damages which fully compensate for any losses.

The concept of 'efficient breach' is most commonly discussed in terms of the advantage to the party breaking the contract in 'maximising gain'. As Campbell has pointed out, however, it should also be recognised as encompassing the situation where the party in breach acts to 'minimise loss'.[13] This may arise, for example, where circumstances change in a way that increases the costs of performance to an extent that the increase exceeds the damages which would be payable to the other party. Here again, the economic answer is that the efficient result is not to enforce the contract, but to allow the party whose costs have increased to escape from it by paying appropriate compensation.

---

9 See, for example, Lord Lloyd in *Ruxley Electronics and Construction Ltd v Forsyth* [1996] AC 344, p 365; [1995] 3 All ER 268, p 282: 'It is first necessary to ascertain the loss the plaintiff has suffered by reason of the breach. If he suffered no loss, as sometimes happens, he can recover no more than nominal damages. For the object of damages is always to compensate the plaintiff, not to punish the defendant.' For a contrary view, see Cunnington, 2006.

10 This is the effect of s 51(3) of the Sale of Goods Act 1979.

11 See Chapter 1.

12 See, for example, Atiyah, 1995, p 428.

13 Harris, Campbell and Halson, 2002, pp 13–21.

The concept of the efficient breach goes some way to explaining why the law of contract is generally more disposed to award damages than to insist on performance.[14] The analysis works best, however, in relation to discrete business contracts which are fully executory. Once the parties are in a long-term relationship, either in respect of the contract under consideration, or as regards a series of contracts, the economic analysis of the possible advantages of breach becomes much more complex. The risks of endangering the future relationship need to be added in to the equation. Similarly, if one party has already performed part of its obligations (particularly if these are in the form of services, rather than goods or money, thus making restitution difficult), allowing breach plus compensation may not be straightforward. Finally, in relation to consumer transactions, it may well be felt that the need to protect the consumer means that the economically efficient answer is not the one which the courts should support.[15] In addition, consumers may well place a value on what they are seeking to receive under the contract which is higher than the market value – thus giving rise to the concept of what has been called the 'consumer surplus'.[16] It is also important to remember that parties will not always act in the most economically efficient way in relation to a particular transaction: for example, being seen as a firm which honours its contracts may be more 'valuable' (though difficult to quantify) than making a bigger profit on a particular deal. Nevertheless, provided that its limitations are recognised, the concept of the efficient breach is a useful tool to apply in the analysis of the law on damages for breach of contract.[17]

This economic analysis is based on the assumption that, as stated at the beginning of this section, the purpose of contract damages is to compensate. It should be noted, however, that a possibly significant exception to the solely compensatory nature of contract damages has been opened up by the decision of the House of Lords in *Attorney General v Blake*.[18] It was held there that a defendant could, in certain circumstances, be required to hand over to the claimant a benefit acquired by breaking a

---

14 As Campbell comments, 'In this sense, the function of the law of contract is to allow breach, but on the right occasions and on the right terms': ibid, p 17.

15 See Collins, 2003, pp 401–02 for the impact of considerations of the 'social market' on the concept of 'efficient breach'.

16 The phrase was coined by Harris, Ogus and Phillips, 1979. See also Harris, Campbell and Halson, 2002, p 168. The existence of the concept has now been recognised by several members of the House of Lords – see Lord Mustill in *Ruxley Electronics and Construction Ltd v Forsyth* [1996] AC 344, p 360; [1995] 3 All ER 268, p 277, and Lords Steyn (somewhat diffidently) and Scott (in fact, though not in name) in *Farley v Skinner* [2001] UKHL 49, paras 21 and 79; [2001] 4 All ER 801, pp 810 and 828.

17 Macneil, however, suggests that, outside of 'futures' contracts, the opportunities for gain through 'efficient breach' are in reality so rare as to be almost non-existent, so that 'general propositions about remedies based on them tell singularly little about efficiency in the real world': Macneil, 1988, p 15. See also Macneil, 1980 and Macneil, 1982. These three articles are all extracted in Campbell, 2001, Chapter 7. See also Harris, Campbell and Halson, 2002, pp 19–20, for a response to some of Macneil's criticisms.

18 [2001] 1 AC 268; [2000] 4 All ER 385.

contract, even where there is no corresponding loss to the claimant. This decision and its implications are discussed fully below (see 18.4.3).

18.4 DAMAGES: MEASURE

Within the general principle of compensation, there are three basic methods by which damages may be calculated. These are conveniently labelled as 'expectation', 'reliance' and 'restitution'. Some consideration also needs to be given to consequential losses and non-pecuniary losses.

18.4.1 Expectation interest

This is the approach which most clearly relates to putting the innocent party into the position he or she would have been in had the contract been performed. It is concerned with fulfilling the expectations of that party as to the benefits that would have flowed from the successful completion of the contract.[19] In particular, where the innocent party, as will commonly be the case, was expecting to make a profit as a result of the contract, that will generally be recoverable,[20] as well as any other consequential losses flowing from the breach. Suppose, for example, A has a piece of machinery that needs repair, and he engages B to carry out the work. A tells B that the work must be done on 1 November, because A has an order for which he needs the machine on 2 November, and which he will lose if it is unavailable. If B, in breach of contract, fails to carry out the work, A will probably be able to claim the lost profit on the 2 November contract. If B had performed the contract properly, A would have made the profit, and therefore it should be recoverable.

In general, the calculation of the expectation interest is simply a matter of looking at where the claimant would have ended up if the contract had been performed properly. In making that calculation, account must of course be taken of any costs which the claimant may have saved by the defendant's non-performance. It is the claimant's *profit* on the contract that is recoverable, which will not necessarily involve the defendant in paying the full price of the missing performance. If, for example, in the situation described in the previous paragraph, the non-availability of the machine has meant that A has employed less staff and therefore has a reduced wage bill, this must be taken into account in assessing the profit which has been lost. It also follows that if A would not in fact have made any profit from the transaction, only nominal damages will be recoverable.

There are two situations which may cause particular difficulty for calculation of

---

19 In contrast to the standard measure of damages in tort, which aims to compensate for losses arising from the wrongful action by putting the claimant back into the position he or she was in prior to the tort being committed.

20 Subject to the rules of remoteness, mitigation, etc, dealt with below, 18.5.

the expectation interest, and which merit further consideration: first, where the profit was not certain and, second, where the cost of fulfilling the claimant's full expectation may be disproportionate to the eventual benefit.

In the situation where the profit was not certain to be made, there may be a partial recovery on the basis that the claimant has lost the chance to make it. In *Chaplin v Hicks*,[21] for example, the breach of contract prevented the plaintiff from taking part in an audition.[22] She was allowed to recover a proportion of what she might have earned had she been successful in the audition. Similarly, in *Simpson v London and North Western Railway Co*,[23] the defendant failed to deliver some specimens to a trade fair by the specified date. The plaintiff was allowed to recover compensation for the loss of sales he might have made had the specimens arrived on time. In these cases, it should be noted that the claimant may do better than would have been the case if the contract had not been broken. Ms Chaplin might not have been selected at the audition, and Mr Simpson might not have made any sales. The court may be said in fact to be placing a monetary value on what is essentially a non-pecuniary loss – that is, the loss of a chance. Alternatively, it might be said that in this situation the compensatory aspects of contract damages are tinged with a punitive element, in that the defendant is made to pay in order to show that his or her behaviour fell below an acceptable level.[24]

The second area of difficulty in finding the appropriate award to meet the claimant's expectations arises in connection with the situation (usually occurring in construction contracts) where the cost of providing the claimant with exactly what was bargained for may be out of all proportion to the benefit which would thereby be obtained. This problem was given full consideration by the House of Lords in *Ruxley Electronics and Construction Ltd v Forsyth*.[25]

The defendant in this case entered into a contract for the construction of a swimming pool and building to enclose it, at a cost of £70,000. The depth of this pool at one end was to be 7ft 6in. After the work was completed, the depth of the pool was discovered to be only 6ft 9in. The plaintiff sought to recover payment for the installation of the pool. The defendant counterclaimed that the pool did not meet its specification and sought compensation for this. It was not possible for the pool to be adapted, and the only way to produce a pool with a depth of 7ft 6in would have been by

---

21 [1911] 2 KB 786. See also Reece, 1996.

22 The case is often referred to as involving a 'beauty contest' (see Treitel, 2003, p 956; Harris, Campbell and Halson, 2002, p 81; Halson, 2001, p 465), but this is clearly wrong.

23 (1876) 1 QBD 274. For other examples of this type of situation, see *Manubens v Leon* [1919] 1 KB 208 (opportunity for hairdresser to earn tips); *Joseph v National Magazine Co* [1959] 1 Ch 14 (opportunity to enhance reputation by publishing a book).

24 See, for example, the comment by Vaughan Williams LJ: 'But the fact that damages cannot be assessed with certainty does not relieve the wrongdoer of the necessity of paying damages for his breach of contract': [1911] 2 KB 786, p 792. Bridge (1995, p 445) suggests that the award of damages in this area is simply a result of the courts' unwillingness to limit the claimant to nominal damages.

25 [1996] AC 344; [1995] 3 All ER 268. A very helpful analysis of this case is to be found in O'Sullivan, 1997.

total reconstruction. This would have cost over £20,000. The position under previous case law on this type of situation involving building contracts was that the court would normally allow the recovery of the 'cost of cure' – that is, putting the building into the condition it should have been in if the breach had not occurred. This is subject to the limitation that if the cost of cure is significantly greater than the reduction in value of the property concerned, then the court may refuse to allow it.[26] This limitation did not, however, normally apply to the situation where the 'cure' relates to the defendant providing something which was specifically promised in the contract. Thus, in *Radford v De Froberville*,[27] the plaintiff was allowed to recover for the cost of building a brick wall, because this is what had been contracted for, even though a cheaper fence would have served the purpose (which was simply to mark a boundary).

This aspect of the courts' approach must now be considered in the light of *Ruxley Electronics and Construction Ltd v Forsyth*.[28] The trial judge found that the pool was entirely suitable for the purpose for which the defendant wished to use it and, given the very high cost of reconstruction, held that the measure of damages should be the difference in value between the pool as supplied, and a pool which met the contract specification. He assessed this difference as nil, but awarded the defendant £2,500 for 'loss of amenity'. The defendant appealed, and the Court of Appeal held that he was entitled to have a pool which met the contract specification. It awarded him damages of over £20,000 to meet the cost of reconstruction. The plaintiff appealed. The House of Lords restored the trial judge's decision. It confirmed that in building contracts there are two principal measures of damages, namely, the difference in value and the cost of reinstatement. Where it would be unreasonable to award the cost of reinstatement (because, for example, the expense would be totally out of proportion to the benefit to be obtained), the court should award the difference in value. As Lord Jauncey put it:[29]

> Damages are designed to compensate for an established loss and not to provide a gratuitous benefit to the aggrieved party . . .

Given that the defendant had a perfectly serviceable swimming pool, 'were he to receive the cost of building a new one and retain the existing one he would have recovered not compensation for loss but a very substantial gratuitous benefit'.[30] The appropriate measure here was therefore the difference in value, which (given the judge's finding) meant that only nominal damages were recoverable under this head. The House of Lords was, however, prepared to allow the judge's award of £2,500 for 'loss of amenity' to stand. The precise nature of this award is considered further, below.

---

26 *Watts v Morrow* [1991] 4 All ER 937 – cost of repairing house £34,000, diminution in value £15,000.
27 [1978] 1 All ER 33.
28 [1996] AC 344; [1995] 3 All ER 268.
29 Ibid, p 357; p 274.
30 Ibid, p 358; p 275.

What do you think the outcome of *Ruxley Electronics v Forsyth* would have been if the swimming pool had been too shallow to allow the claimant to carry out some activity, such as diving? Would the claimant then have been able to claim the cost of having the pool re-built?

The House of Lords' decision in this case appears quite sensible on the facts. Nevertheless, it leaves open the problem that an unscrupulous contractor can apparently now play fast and loose with the contract specifications in a construction contract, provided that the final product is fit for the purposes for which the other party wishes to use it. If it is so fit, then the cost of reconstruction to meet the contract specification is likely to be considered unreasonable, and there may well be little or no difference in the market value of the building. The innocent party is effectively left without a remedy, despite the fact that what has been provided is not what he or she wanted. Comparison can be made with the position as regards sales of goods, where the purchaser may still have a remedy, even if goods are 'fit for their purpose', if they do not match the contract description. By virtue of s 13 of the Sale of Goods Act 1979, the purchaser will generally be able to reject such goods. The person who contracts for the construction of a building now seems to be in a much weaker position. Much will depend on just how far the courts are prepared to go. Suppose, for example, I contract for a house to be built with a special warm air heating system which has to be built into the walls during construction. The builder constructs a house with a conventional gas-fired central heating system and radiators. The house is perfectly fit to be lived in, and its value is not significantly different from the house with a warm air system (indeed, it may have a higher market value). Am I really to be left without any effective remedy against the builder? The principles applied by the House of Lords in *Ruxley Electronics v Forsyth* would seem to suggest so. This is a situation which might have been dealt with by the restitutionary approach suggested by the Court of Appeal in *Attorney General v Blake*.[31] The constructors of the swimming pool had delivered a 'skimped performance' and the Court of Appeal's approach would have allowed the court to award to the plaintiff the money that had been saved in not building the swimming pool to the contract specification.[32] This aspect of the Court of Appeal's judgment in *Blake* was, however, specifically rejected by the House of Lords in that case.[33]

As was noted above, the only award which the plaintiff received in *Ruxley Electronics v Forsyth* was for 'loss of amenity'. What is the precise nature of this award? There are two possible answers. One is that it is based on the concept of the 'consumer surplus' – that is, that it compensates the claimant for something which has been

---

31 [1998] Ch 439; [1998] 1 All ER 833. See below, 18.4.3.

32 Though, on the facts, the constructors do not seem to have saved any significant sum on the work.

33 [2000] 1 AC 268; [2000] 4 All ER 385.

contracted for going beyond the market value of what is to be provided. The expectation interest must therefore be increased to take account of this. The second possibility is that it is an example of one of the limited range of cases where the courts are prepared to award damages for 'distress and inconvenience' arising as a consequence of a breach of contract. This area is discussed further below (see 18.4.6). The House of Lords' decision in *Farley v Skinner*[34] has made it clear that the award in *Ruxley Electronics v Forsyth* should be put into the *first* category. *Farley v Skinner* concerned a contract for the survey of a house, where the surveyor had been specifically asked by the prospective purchaser to check on aircraft noise. The surveyor failed to do this properly, and the purchaser, having moved in, sought compensation for the fact that his enjoyment of the property was reduced, though there was no reduction in its market value. The House of Lords approved an award of £10,000 for loss of a benefit which had been contracted for, as distinct from consequential damages for 'discomfort', and in the process confirmed that this was also the correct way to view *Ruxley Electronics v Forsyth*.

This means that the award for 'loss of amenity' is a separate element in the expectation interest which, in appropriate cases, will be awarded in addition to any other elements (for example, reduction in the market value of what has been supplied).[35] The calculation of the value of a 'loss of amenity' is always going to be difficult, since it is by its nature 'non-pecuniary' loss. In both *Ruxley Electronics* and *Farley v Skinner*, the House of Lords clearly took the view that the amounts should be modest,[36] and that the awards in both cases were generous to the claimant. No satisfactory method of calculating what should be awarded is put forward, however, and it seems to be left to the virtually unfettered discretion of the trial judge as to how much should be given under this head. This is clearly unsatisfactory, as O'Sullivan has pointed out,[37] but it is difficult to find a solution. The value of the benefit lost is by definition something personal to the claimant, yet the claimant's subjective view cannot be allowed to be the determining factor. It may be that all that can be done is to wait for practice to develop (as it has done in other areas of non-pecuniary loss) so that a standard level for this type of award gradually becomes established.

Finally, it should be noted that the award for loss of amenity is most likely to arise in non-business contracts. There seems little doubt that if the swimming pool in *Ruxley Electronics* had been built for a developer who was going to sell the property once it was completed, then no damages at all would have been recoverable for the failure to build it to the specified depth.

---

34 [2001] UKHL 49; [2001] 4 All ER 801.

35 See O'Sullivan, 1997, pp 14–16. This would also seem to be implicit in Lord Scott's comment in *Farley v Skinner* to the effect that damages for discomfort (as opposed to loss of amenity) would not be recoverable in addition to a reduction in market value: [2001] UKHL 49, para 109; [2001] 4 All ER 801, p 833.

36 See also *Freeman v Niroomand* [1996] 52 Con LR 116, discussed in O'Sullivan, 1997, p 16.

37 O'Sullivan, 1997, pp 17–18. See also Harris, Ogus and Phillips, 1979.

18.4.2   Reliance interest[38]

In some situations, it may not be easy for the claimant to calculate the profits that would have been made. Here it may prove more sensible to abandon the attempt, and instead to seek recovery of the expenditure which has been incurred in anticipation of the contract. This is what is referred to as the 'reliance' interest. The result of this type of award is that the claimant is put back to the position prior to the contract being made, rather than in the position if the contract had been performed properly.[39]

An example of this type of situation is *Anglia Television Ltd v Reed*.[40] Reed was an actor who was under contract to play a leading role in a television film. At a late stage, Reed withdrew, and the project was unable to go ahead. In suing Reed for breach of contract, Anglia did not seek their lost profits. It would have been very difficult to estimate exactly what these would have been, given the uncertainties of the entertainment industry. Instead, they sought, and were awarded, compensation for all the expenses incurred towards setting up the film. This, somewhat surprisingly, included expenditure incurred *before* the contract with Reed was entered into, provided that these fell within the rule of remoteness.[41] The basis for this was that at the time the contract was entered into the defendant must have been aware of the expenditure that had already taken place, and that therefore this would be wasted if the project collapsed.

The decision as to whether to seek expectation or reliance damages will generally lie with the claimant (as was made clear in *Anglia Television Ltd v Reed*). There have been examples, however, of the court deciding that reliance is the appropriate measure. This occurred in the Australian case of *McRae v Commonwealth Disposals Commission*,[42] in relation to the contract to salvage a non-existent ship. In some situations, on the other hand, the court may say that the reliance measure should not be available. This will be the case, for instance, where the difficulty in identifying profits results primarily from the fact that the claimant has made a bad bargain. Thus, in *C and P Haulage v Middleton*,[43] some of the plaintiff's costs were in fact reduced as a result of the breach, and the plaintiff's loss of equipment (which had to be handed over to the defendant) was an integral part of the original contract. In that situation, the plaintiff was only allowed to sue for the expectation interest. The burden of proving that the bargain was 'bad' in this sense falls, however, on the defendant.[44] The claimant does not

---

38 See Fuller and Perdue, 1936 – the classic article analysing the reliance interest.

39 The measure is thus much closer to the normal tort measure of damages.

40 [1972] 1 QB 60; [1971] 3 All ER 690.

41 See below, 18.5.

42 (1951) 84 CLR 377 – loss of profits rejected as too speculative. For other aspects of this case, see Chapter 11, 11.5.1.

43 [1983] 3 All ER 94.

44 *CCC Films (London) Ltd v Impact Quadrant Films Ltd* [1985] QB 16; [1984] 3 All ER 298. See also the Australian case of *The Commonwealth of Australia v Amann Aviation Pty Ltd* [1991] 174 CLR 64, discussed in this context by Bridge, 1995, p 468.

have to prove that sufficient profit would have been made on the contract to cover the expenses incurred.

Although in general a choice must be made as to which measure of damages is being sought, in certain circumstances it may be possible to recover both expectation and reliance losses, as long as this does not lead to double recovery. Thus, in *Naughton v O'Callaghan*,[45] which concerned a racehorse which turned out not to have the pedigree contracted for, the buyer recovered the difference in value resulting from this breach (expectation loss) and the costs of training and stabling (reliance loss). Where lost profits are claimed, however, it is only if net profits are claimed that reliance damages may also be available. If *gross* profits are recovered, the claimant cannot also recover the money that would have been spent in generating these profits. In the case of *Cullinane v British 'Rema' Manufacturing Co Ltd*,[46] there appears to have been some confusion between gross and net profits, and the case is sometimes cited as authority for the proposition that expectation and reliance damages can never be recovered together.[47] It is submitted, however, that the better view is that outlined above, which distinguishes between gross and net profits.[48]

18.4.3   Restitution

'Restitution' in relation to contract damages traditionally refers to the return of money paid, such 'damages' being largely a corollary of termination following a repudiatory breach.[49] If such a breach has been accepted, and the claimant has returned any benefits received, or is willing to do so, then he or she will also be entitled to claim the restitution of anything which has been given to the defendant. The easiest example is the situation of defective goods. The buyer returns the goods and expects the refund of the price. In many situations, and in particular in relation to consumer contracts, that may be all that can be recovered by way of damages. The buyer may not have been expecting to make a profit out of the use or resale of the goods, and there may be no other losses resulting from the breach. In appropriate circumstances, however, it is possible to combine a claim for restitution with one for reliance or expectation damages. In *Millar Machinery Co Ltd v David Way & Son*,[50] the plaintiff recovered all three. The contract involved the purchase of a machine which proved to be defective on delivery and was rejected. The disappointed buyer had spent money on installation costs, and had lost

---

45 [1990] 3 All ER 191.
46 [1954] 1 QB 292; [1953] 2 All ER 1257.
47 See, for example, Lord Denning in *Anglia Television Ltd v Reed* [1972] 1 QB 60, pp 63–64; [1971] 3 All ER 690, p 692.
48 See also Harris, Campbell and Halson, 2002, pp 130–32; Beale, 1980, p 156; Beale, Bishop and Furmston, 2001, p 625; MacLeod, 1970.
49 For which, see Chapter 17, 17.6.2.
50 (1935) 40 Com Cas 204.

profits from the use of the machine. He was able to recover the price (restitution), the installation costs (reliance) and the lost profits (expectation).[51]

Restitution also has a more general role to play in relation to contracts which are void, or rescinded (for example, for mistake or misrepresentation), or where no contract has ever come into existence.[52] These situations are not ones which arise on breach, and so are not discussed further here.

There is, however, another meaning to 'restitution' (as discussed in Chapter 19), which refers to the rectification of a situation which has led to the 'unjust enrichment' of a party. Contract damages have not traditionally been awarded on this measure, and the idea that there could be recovery not only for the claimant's loss, but also for the defendant's gain, was specifically rejected by the Court of Appeal in *Surrey CC v Bredero Homes Ltd*.[53] Here a developer deliberately built more houses on a piece of land than it was entitled to under its contract with the local authority from which the land was acquired. The Court of Appeal held that the damages would only be nominal because the local authority had suffered no loss. The case of *Attorney General v Blake*[54] has, however, re-opened this issue. The case concerned the notorious spy George Blake, who had been a member of the British secret services. He was convicted in 1961 of spying for Russia and sentenced to a total of 42 years' imprisonment. In 1966, he escaped and fled to Moscow where he continues to live. While there, he wrote his autobiography, which was published in 1990. The book included descriptions of his life as a member of the secret services. He was to be paid £50,000 on the signing of the contract, £50,000 on the delivery of the manuscript and £50,000 on publication. At the time of the legal action, £90,000 remained payable by the publishers. The Attorney General brought an action to prevent Blake receiving any further benefit from the book. The Court of Appeal held that the Attorney General could succeed in that, in his role as guardian of the public interest, he could obtain an injunction to prevent a person benefiting from criminal activity (the disclosures made by Blake in the book amounting to offences under the Official Secrets Act 1989). However, the court, in addition, considered the situation as regards contract law. Blake was in breach of contract, since when he joined the secret service he undertook a lifelong contractual obligation not to disclose anything about his work. The problem was to establish any loss for which compensation could be awarded to the Crown. If no such loss existed, then the damages could only be nominal. The Court of Appeal, however, felt that although the Attorney General at that stage had declined to argue the point, this was a situation where an exception to the general compensatory rule might be made. It suggested that the law was 'now sufficiently mature to recognise a restitutionary claim for profits made from a breach of contract in appropriate circumstances'. What are the

51 Only net profits were recoverable.
52 See Chapter 19.
53 [1993] 3 All ER 705.
54 [2001] 1 AC 268; [2000] 4 All ER 385.

'appropriate circumstances'? The Court of Appeal suggested two. First, in relation to 'skimped performance':[55]

> This is where the defendant fails to provide the full extent of the services which he has contracted to provide and for which he has charged the plaintiff.

The example given is of a fire service which did not provide the contracted number of firemen, horses, or length of hosepipe.[56] The fire service had saved expenses, but had not failed to put out any fires. Nevertheless, it was suggested by Lord Woolf that it would be just to allow the other contracting party to recover damages based on the amount which the fire service had saved by this 'skimped' performance.[57]

The second situation in which the court suggested that restitutionary damages might be appropriate is where the defendant has obtained a profit 'by doing the very thing which he contracted not to do'.[58] This was exactly Blake's situation. He had promised not to disclose information about his work, but this was precisely what he had done in writing and publishing the book. It is clear that, had the Attorney General pursued this issue, the Court of Appeal would have been prepared to award damages for breach of contract on this basis. It reconciled this approach with that taken in *Surrey CC v Bredero Homes Ltd* on the basis that that decision should be regarded as allowing restitutionary damages to be available in exceptional cases.

When the case reached the House of Lords, the contractual basis of the claim was fully argued. The House reached the same effective result as the Court of Appeal by rejecting the public law claim, but allowing the Attorney General to recover the money due to Blake on the basis of breach of contract. Lord Nicholls, who delivered the main speech on behalf of the majority,[59] found support for such an approach in a first instance decision which preceded *Surrey v Bredero Homes*, but was approved in it, namely *Wrotham Park Estate Co Ltd v Parkside Homes Ltd*.[60] In this case houses had been built on land in breach of a restrictive covenant, and the plaintiff sought an injunction which would have led to their demolition. The court was reluctant, 'for social and economic reasons',[61] to grant such an injunction. Instead the judge awarded

---

55 [1998] Ch 439, p 458; [1998] 1 All ER 833, p 845.
56 As in the American case of *City of New Orleans v Firemen's Charitable Association* (1891) 9 So 486 – though no recovery was, in fact, allowed in this case.
57 A major objection to this example is, as pointed out by Campbell, that if the fire service had not failed in its duties under the contract (ie, to put out fires) in what sense could its performance be said to be 'skimped'?: Harris, Campbell and Halson, 2002, pp 277–78. Indeed, it would not appear that there was any breach of contract at all. Atiyah (1995, p 451), however, clearly regards the situation as involving a breach, and one in relation to which the law is 'seriously deficient' in not providing a remedy.
58 [1998] Ch 439, p 458; [1998] 1 All ER 833, p 846.
59 Lord Hobhouse dissented, on the basis that he could see no grounds for the Crown recovering substantial damages for Blake's breach of contract.
60 [1974] 2 All ER 321.
61 Lord Nicholls in *Attorney General v Blake* [2001] 1 AC 268, p 282; [2000] 4 All ER 385, p 395.

damages based on an estimate of the cost of obtaining a release from the restrictive covenant. This he valued at 5 per cent of the profit which the defendants had made on the development. This decision is difficult to reconcile with *Surrey v Bredero*, though it is true that in the latter case no injunction was sought, so that the earlier case may be thought to be based on the power to award damages in lieu of an injunction.[62] This analysis was not accepted by the Court of Appeal, however, in *Jaggard v Sawyer*.[63] Moreover, the House of Lords in *Johnson v Agnew*[64] has clearly held that the damages awarded in relation to a breach of contract should be the same whether awarded in equity (as would be the case if given in substitution for an equitable remedy such as an injunction) or under common law. In *Blake*, Lord Nicholls did not attempt to achieve a reconciliation of these issues. His conclusion was simply that 'in so far as the *Bredero Homes Ltd* decision is inconsistent with the approach adopted in the *Wrotham Park* case, the latter approach is to be preferred'.[65] He went on to declare that *Wrotham Park* stood as a 'solitary beacon' showing that contract damages are not always confined to the recovery of financial losses. Damages on the *Wrotham Park* basis were not, however, what the Attorney General was seeking in *Blake*. He was not asking for a sum by which Blake could have bought his release from the restrictive provision in his contract of employment; on the facts the Crown would not have agreed to such a release on any terms. The Attorney General was, therefore, seeking a full 'account of profits' made by Blake from the breach. Lord Nicholls, despite the assistance of counsel, was unable to find any cases in which the courts have made such an order in a contract case,[66] but noted that there is a 'light sprinkling' of cases in which an order to the same effect as an account of profits has been made, but not with that label.[67] From here he jumped to the somewhat surprising general conclusion that 'there seems to be no reason, in principle, why the court must in all circumstances rule out an account of profits as a remedy for breach of contract'.[68]

Having opened this box, however, the difficulty is to find a way to keep the remedy within bounds, and in particular to avoid it disrupting the normal expectations of

---

62 As now provided by the Supreme Court Act 1981, s 50. The power was originally given by the Chancery Amendment Act 1858, s 2, commonly known as Lord Cairns' Act.

63 [1995] 2 All ER 189.

64 [1980] AC 367; [1979] 1 All ER 883.

65 [2001] 1 AC 268, p 283; [2000] 4 All ER 385, p 396.

66 Though he notes that such an approach was rejected in *Tito v Waddell (No 2)* [1977] Ch 106; [1977] 3 All ER 129 by Megarry J, and even more forcefully by Kerr J in *Occidental Worldwide Investment Corp v Skibs, The Siboen and the Sibotre* [1976] 1 Lloyd's Rep 293.

67 The cases cited are *Lake v Bayliss* [1974] 2 All ER 1114; *Reid-Newfoundland Co v Anglo-American Telegraph Co Ltd* [1912] AC 555 and *British Motor Trade Association v Gilbert* [1951] 2 All ER 641.

68 [2001] 1 AC 268, p 284; [2000] 4 All ER 385, p 397. Lord Nicholls objects to the label 'restitutionary damages'; but since the point of an account of profits must be the prevention of the unjust enrichment of the defendant, which is the basis of restitutionary remedies, his objection seems to be without merit.

commercial contracts.[69] Lord Nicholls' response to this is to state that the remedy of an account of profits will only be available 'in exceptional circumstances'.[70] What then will constitute exceptional circumstances? On this question Lord Nicholls' speech is unhelpfully vague. It seems that exceptional cases will arise where normal damages are 'inadequate', and that all the circumstances must be taken into account. Beyond this, however, the only guidance given is that a relevant question is 'whether the [claimant] had a legitimate interest in preventing the defendant's profit-making activity and, hence, in depriving him of his profit'.[71] The problem with this is that it is capable of a very broad or a very narrow interpretation: in one sense the claimant will always have a 'legitimate interest' in preventing a breach of contract, and thus preventing the defendant's consequent profit-making activity; in the narrow sense, this will only arise where the claimant has a non-commercial interest in preventing the actions which constitute the breach. It is to be suspected that the latter is what Lord Nicholls means, but the language used does not make this clear. On the facts of *Blake*, the case was 'exceptional', and an account of profits appropriate, because 'the Crown had and has a legitimate interest in preventing Blake profiting from the disclosure of official information, whether classified or not, while a member of the service or thereafter'.[72] Moreover, the obligation being broken was 'closely akin to a fiduciary obligation, where an account of profits is a standard remedy in the event of breach'.[73]

FOR THOUGHT

If *Blake* is applied more generally, would it mean that a former employee who breaks a restrictive covenant in relation to future employment (for which, see 15.4) could be made to hand over the wages earned from doing so?

It remains to be seen whether *Blake* will turn out to be a major development in the law relating to damages for breach of contract, or simply an interesting, but anomalous, sidenote. The decision has been the subject of severe criticism,[74] and it is difficult not to have sympathy with Lord Hobhouse's dissenting view that the majority had departed from principle in order to stop Blake benefiting from 'his past deplorable criminal conduct'.[75] If that is true, the effect of the case should be regarded as being limited by its own particular and exceptional facts, and therefore not indicating a new path for the

---

69 It causes particular problems for the concept of the 'efficient breach' which, it has been suggested above (18.3) is an important element in the standard English law approach to contract damages.
70 [2001] 1 AC 268, p 285; [2000] 4 All ER 385, p 398.
71 Ibid.
72 [2001] 1 AC 268, p 287; [2000] 4 All ER 385, p 399.
73 Ibid, p 287; p 400.
74 See, for example, Hedley, 2000; Harris, Campbell and Halson, 2002, Chapter 17.
75 [2001] 1 AC 268, p 299; [2000] 4 All ER 385, p 411.

development of restitutionary, as opposed to compensatory, damages for breach of contract.

Subsequent case law is so far equivocal as to how far courts will find situations sufficiently 'exceptional' to justify using the *Blake* approach. In *Esso Petroleum Co Ltd v Niad Ltd*,[76] the breach of contract was committed by a petrol station which failed to pass on to its customers discounts given to it by its supplier. It would clearly be difficult for the supplier in this situation to prove its loss on an expectation measure. The judge at first instance, however, thought that there were two other bases on which the supplier might recover.

First, he suggested that there could be an account of profits derived from the defendant's breach of contract. The judge referred to the fact that in *Attorney General v Blake*, such a remedy was regarded as 'exceptional'. Nevertheless, he thought that this case was exceptional because:[77]

(a)   damages were an inadequate remedy;
(b)   the obligation to implement and maintain recommended pump prices was fundamental to the contract;
(c)   the defendant's breach was much more extensive than previously thought, and continued after it had been pointed out;
(d)   the supplier had a legitimate interest in preventing the defendant from profiting from its breach of obligation.

This appears to be adopting a very broad approach to exceptional circumstances. Many of these factors would apply to many commercial disputes, and it is difficult to see them as rendering the case 'exceptional' in the way that *Attorney General v Blake* was exceptional.

The other possible approach which the judge suggested was the 'restitutionary' remedy of requiring the defendant to pay back to the supplier the amount by which the actual prices charged to customers exceeded the recommended prices. The judge cited no authority in support of such a course, but it might be thought also to follow from *Attorney General v Blake*. Once again, however, the problem is whether this case was truly 'exceptional', thus justifying such a departure from the normal approach to compensatory damages.

It is to be hoped that this case is not an example of a trend towards extensive use of the *Blake* 'exception', which it seems unlikely that the House of Lords intended should apply to straightforward commercial disputes.[78]

The second case to consider *Blake* is a Court of Appeal decision, *Experience Hendrix LLC v PPX Enterprises*.[79] The dispute arose out of a settlement of an earlier

---

76   [2001] EWHC 458 (Ch).
77   Ibid, para 63.
78   For further criticism of this case, see Sandy, 2003.
79   [2003] EWCA Civ 323; [2003] 1 All ER Comm 830.

case between the parties, under which the defendant had agreed not to grant further licences in relation to recordings made by the guitarist, Jimi Hendrix. The defendant did issue such licences and the claimant sought compensation. The judge at first instance granted an injunction but no compensation. The Court of Appeal considered whether it would be appropriate in this case to award an account of profits, on the basis of *Blake*. It decided, however, that this was not an 'exceptional' case within the meaning of *Blake*. In particular, Mance LJ pointed out that:[80]

> We are not concerned with a subject anything like as special or sensitive as national security. The State's special interest in preventing a spy benefiting by breaches of his contractual duty of secrecy, and so removing at least part of the financial attraction of such breaches, has no parallel in this case. Secondly, the notoriety which accounted for the magnitude of Blake's royalty earning capacity derived from his prior breaches of secrecy, and that too has no present parallel. Thirdly, there is no direct analogy between [the defendant's] position and that of a fiduciary.

This approach seems much more satisfactory than that adopted in the *Niad* case (to which the Court of Appeal in *Hendrix* referred, but without expressing a view on its correctness or otherwise).

The Court of Appeal did, however, hold that damages were recoverable on a different basis. This it did by drawing on the decision in *Wrotham Park Estate Ltd v Parkside Homes Ltd*,[81] and holding that the plaintiff could recover a sum which it might have demanded from the defendant as the price of relaxing the terms of the previous settlement and allowing the defendant to issue the licences.

In terms of academic commentary on *Blake*, there is further interesting and critical discussion of the implications of this decision by Campbell and Harris (2002). They argue that the implication of the *Blake* decision is that all breaches should be penalised. This, they say, is misguided, because not all breaches are 'wrongs' which should be deterred:

> Breach has a positive, indeed essential, role in the operation of the law of contract as the legal institution regulating economic exchange and pursuit of its general prevention is inconsistent with the operation of a market economy.

A response to Campbell and Harris is to be found in Jaffey (2002), who argues that a general rule which only 'punishes' non-performance where losses are caused to the other party, and an exceptional rule punishing non-performance itself (as in *Blake*) can both be accommodated within a particular version of the 'reliance' theory of contract.

---

80 [2003] EWCA Civ 323; [2003] 1 All ER Comm 830, para 37.
81 [1974] 2 All ER 321 – see above.

Under this theory, parties contract on the basis of 'assumptions of responsibility for reliance' by the other party. Generally, such reliance, if disappointed, can be compensated by ensuring that the innocent party is not 'worse off' as a result of having entered into the contract. In exceptional cases, however, reliance can only be compensated by actual performance – for example, where the contractual obligation is not to disclose confidential information. In such cases:[82]

> Non-performance is wrongful, and performance should be compelled by order of specific performance if possible, and if not the law should respond with disgorgement or even punitive damages.

Jaffey sees his reliance-based approach as capable of accommodating both the general economic arguments of Campbell and Harris relating to 'efficient breach' and the possibility of restitutionary remedies in exceptional cases, such as *Blake*.

18.4.4 Consequential losses

There are some losses which flow from the breach, but which cannot be put into the category of 'expenses' (that is, reliance) or thwarted expectations. Provided the causal link can be established, and they are not too remote,[83] then they will be recoverable. If there is a contract for the purchase of a piece of machinery, for example, and it is defective, then the expectation interest may allow the recovery of lost profits that would have been gained by using the machine. If, however, the defect causes the machine to explode, which results in damage to the buyer's premises, or personal injury to the buyer, compensation in relation to these consequential losses can also be recovered.

18.4.5 Supervening events

The issue of the measure of damages when supervening events have increased the claimant's loss was considered by the Court of Appeal in *Beoco Ltd v Alfa Laval*.[84] The first defendants had installed a heat exchanger at the plaintiffs' works. A leak was discovered, and a repair attempted by the second defendants. The plaintiffs put the heat exchanger back in use without carrying out proper tests. In fact, the defects in the exchanger were more extensive than had been realised, and shortly afterwards it exploded. The plaintiffs sought to recover from the first defendants an amount relating to the loss of profits they would have suffered as a result of the need to further repair or replace the exchanger had it not exploded. Their action was based on the defendants' breach of contract in their initially having supplied a defective exchanger. The Court of

---

82 Jaffey, 2002, p 576.
83 See below, 18.5.
84 [1994] 4 All ER 464.

Appeal held that the measure of damages for hypothetical losses should be the same in contract as in tort.[85] Thus, where a supervening event causes greater damage than the original breach of contract, the claimant cannot recover losses which would have been suffered had the event not occurred. Since the explosion was caused by the negligence of the plaintiffs' employees, they could not recover the lost profits which they might otherwise have suffered as a result of the first defendants' breach of contract. This conclusion is out of line with the normal approach to the assessment of contractual damages, which requires the issues to be looked at in the light of the parties' knowledge *at the time of the contract*. This is the way in which the question of 'remoteness' is dealt with.[86] Taking account of later events, as in this case, means that they may well have the effect of reducing the defendants' liability. If, however, the event does not occur until after the damages have been assessed, then this will not apply. Thus, if in this case the explosion had not occurred until after trial, the plaintiffs would probably have been able to claim the lost profits they were seeking. This runs the risk of making the assessment of damages dependent on rather arbitrary factors, such as when exactly a particular event occurs.

A different approach to a particular type of supervening event was taken by the House of Lords in *South Australia Asset Management Corp v York Montague Ltd*.[87] This was concerned with cases where there has been a negligent overvaluation of a property which has been used as security for a loan. The question at issue is to what extent should the negligent valuer be liable for the fact that the property has reduced in value because of a fall in the market. Suppose, for example, that the property is valued at £15m when its true value is £10m. The lender lends £12m. When the borrower defaults, the property is sold but, because of a fall in market values, only realises £5m. Should the valuer be liable for the full loss which the lender has suffered (that is, £7m) or only the difference between the valuation and the actual value at the time of the contract (£5m)? The House of Lords took the view that the valuer should only be liable for those losses which are properly attributable to having given wrong information. It held that the lender's loss in this situation is having less security for the loan than was thought. The correct measure of damages is therefore the difference between the actual and true valuations – in the example given above, £5m. The decision, which reversed the judgment of the Court of Appeal, is not uncontroversial. There is some strength in the Court of Appeal's view that if the valuer had given correct information, the lender would not have entered into the transaction at all, and that therefore the full losses should be recoverable. The House of Lords has, however, settled this issue for the time being.

---

85 For which, see *Carslogie Steamship Co Ltd v Royal Norwegian Government* [1952] AC 292; [1952] 1 All ER 20.
86 See below, 18.5.1.
87 [1997] AC 191; [1996] 3 All ER 365.

18.4.6 Non-pecuniary losses

Contract damages are primarily concerned with economic losses of one kind or another, which are more or less quantifiable in money terms. In some situations, however, non-pecuniary losses will be caused. If, for example, a defective product results in personal injury to the purchaser, there is no reason why damages should not be recovered in relation to the pain and suffering so caused. Of course, third parties who are injured will have to rely on tortious remedies at common law or under the Consumer Protection Act 1987.

A more difficult question arises in relation to mental distress, anguish or annoyance caused by a breach of contract. The courts have tended to be wary of awarding compensation under this heading, but the whole area has recently been reconsidered in a number of House of Lords decisions.[88] The traditional view is that expressed in *Addis v Gramophone Co Ltd*.[89] The House of Lords refused to uphold an award which had been made in relation to the 'harsh and humiliating' way in which the plaintiff had been dismissed from his job in breach of contract. This line was followed in a more recent dismissal case, *Bliss v South East Thames RHA*,[90] where a surgeon had sued the health authority by which he was employed. The authority had, following a dispute between the surgeon and a colleague, required him to undergo a psychiatric examination. The surgeon refused and was suspended. The surgeon treated this as a repudiatory breach and sued for breach of contract. He succeeded at first instance, and was awarded £2,000 for mental distress. The Court of Appeal held, however, that it was bound by *Addis v Gramophone*, and held that it was not possible to recover damages for mental distress in an action for wrongful dismissal.

In coming to this conclusion, it disapproved the decision in *Cox v Phillips Industries Ltd*,[91] where damages were recovered for distress and anxiety resulting from a demotion. Some doubts about *Addis v Gramophone* were raised by the decision of the House of Lords in *Malik v BCCI*,[92] the facts of which have been given at 8.6.7. The House took the view that where there was a breach of the implied term of trust and confidence in an employment contract, *Addis* should not be regarded as precluding an award of damages for loss of reputation or difficulty in obtaining future employment. The House was not, however, dealing with the manner of dismissal in this case, and was not concerned with 'injury to feelings'. The House of Lords has subsequently confirmed in *Johnson v Unisys Ltd*[93] that *Addis* should not be regarded as having been overruled in *Malik v BCCI*. Damages for distress and injury to feelings resulting from

---

88 *Johnson v Gore Wood & Co* [2001] 1 All ER 481 *Johnson v Unisys Ltd* [2001] UKHL 13; [2001] 2 All ER 801; *Farley v Skinner* [2001] UKHL 49; [2001] 4 All ER 801.
89 [1909] AC 488.
90 [1985] IRLR 308.
91 [1976] 3 All ER 161.
92 [1998] AC 20; [1997] 3 All ER 1.
93 [2001] UKHL 13; [2001] 2 All ER 801.

the manner of a dismissal are still unavailable in an action for breach of contract.[94] Exceptionally, however, it may be possible to claim damages for non-pecuniary loss in relation to a breach of contract which is constituted by treatment leading up to a dismissal. This was the view of the House of Lords in the most recent consideration of this area, *Eastwood v Magnox Electric*.[95]

On the other hand, it has been held that where one of the purposes of the contract is to provide pleasure and enjoyment, damages for distress and disappointment caused by a breach may be recovered. Thus, in *Jarvis v Swan's Tours Ltd*,[96] such damages were awarded in relation to breach of contract in the provision of a holiday which had promised to provide 'a great time'.[97] Where, however, the contract is a purely commercial one, damages for anguish and vexation will not be allowed. Thus, in *Hayes v James and Charles Dodd*,[98] the plaintiffs were suing their solicitors for breach of contract. The solicitors had given an assurance that a right of way existed in relation to access to a property which the plaintiffs were purchasing for their business. This turned out to be untrue, and the plaintiffs' business failed as a result. The trial judge awarded damages of £1,500 to each plaintiff for anguish and vexation. The Court of Appeal, however, applied the same approach as in *Bliss v South East Thames RHA*. This meant that, as Staughton LJ held:[99]

> . . . damages for mental distress in contract are, as a matter of policy, limited to certain classes of case. I would broadly follow the classification by Dillon LJ in *Bliss v South East Thames RHA*: '. . . where the contract which has been broken was itself a contract to provide peace of mind or freedom from distress.' It may be that the class is somewhat wider than that. But it should not, in my judgment, include any case where the object of the contract was not comfort or pleasure, or the relief of discomfort, but simply carrying on a commercial activity with a view to profit.

Subsequent cases have taken a similar line. In *Watts v Morrow*, the general rule and its exceptions were restated by Bingham LJ, in a passage which has subsequently been approved by the House of Lords:[100]

---

94 Lord Hoffmann in *Johnson v Unisys* suggested that non-pecuniary losses could be recovered under the statutory regime governing 'unfair dismissal', and used this as part of the argument for rejecting a common law action. This suggestion was rejected by the House of Lords in *Dunnachie v Kingston-upon-Hull City Council* [2004] UKHL 36; [2004] 3 All ER 1011. Damages under s 123(1) of the Employment Rights Act 1996 do not extend to non-pecuniary loss.

95 [2004] UKHL 35; [2004] 3 All ER 991.

96 [1973] QB 233; [1973] 1 All ER 71.

97 A similar approach can be seen in *Jackson v Horizon Holidays* [1975] 3 All ER 92 – discussed in Chapter 5, 5.7.

98 [1990] 2 All ER 815.

99 Ibid, p 824.

100 [1991] 4 All ER 937, pp 959–60 (emphasis added). Approved in *Johnson v Gore Wood & Co* [2001] 1 All ER 481 and in *Farley v Skinner* [2001] UKHL 49; [2001] 4 All ER 801.

A contract-breaker is not in general liable for any distress, frustration, anxiety, displeasure, vexation, tension or aggravation which his breach of contract may cause to the innocent party . . . But the rule is not absolute. Where the *very object* of the contract is to provide pleasure, relaxation, peace of mind or freedom from molestation, damages will be awarded if the fruit of the contract is not provided or if the contrary result is procured instead . . . A contract to survey a house for a prospective purchaser does not fall within this exceptional category. In cases not falling within this exceptional category, damages are in my view recoverable for *physical inconvenience* and discomfort caused by the breach and mental suffering directly related to that inconvenience and discomfort.

Bingham LJ's analysis allows for two categories of case where non-pecuniary losses may be recoverable. The first is where the 'very object' of the contract is to provide pleasure, etc. This will include contracts for holidays, wedding photographs, etc.[101] It will not include cases where disappointment is an incidental consequence of a breach. Thus, in *Alexander v Rolls Royce Motor Cars Ltd*,[102] the Court of Appeal refused to award damages for disappointment, loss of enjoyment or distress resulting from a breach of a contract to repair the plaintiff's motor car. The second of Bingham's categories is where the breach of contract has caused 'physical inconvenience and discomfort'. These two categories have now been fully reviewed by the House of Lords in *Farley v Skinner*.[103]

The claimant was seeking damages from a surveyor who had inspected and reported on a house which the claimant had then bought. Specific instructions had been given to the surveyor to check and report on any problems with aircraft noise.[104] The surveyor failed to mention in his report that the house was near an aircraft navigation beacon, around which aircraft were often 'stacked' waiting to land, so that the use and enjoyment of the property was affected by aircraft noise (particularly at weekends). By the time the case reached the House of Lords, there was no dispute that the surveyor had been in breach of contract. The county court judge found that the value of the house was not affected by the breach, but awarded the claimant £10,000 for non-pecuniary damage. The Court of Appeal overturned the award on the basis that, applying the *Watts v Morrow* tests, this was not a case where the 'very object' of the contract was to provide pleasure,[105] nor could the annoyance caused by the aircraft noise be considered to amount to 'physical inconvenience'. The House of Lords restored the

---

101 See *Diesen v Samson* 1971 SLT (Sh Ct) 49 (a Scottish case dealing with wedding photographs); *Heywood v Wellers* [1976] QB 446; [1976] 1 All ER 300 (solicitor's failure to take action to protect the plaintiff from 'molestation').

102 [1996] RTR 95.

103 [2001] UKHL 49; [2001] 4 All ER 801.

104 The house was situated near to Gatwick Airport, so this was clearly likely to be an issue.

105 In this the court was influenced by the fact that *Watts v Morrow* was itself a case of a negligent survey, and damages for non-pecuniary loss had been refused.

judge's award. The four speeches delivered differ in some respects in their reasoning,[106] but there is a fair degree of similarity between the positions of Lord Steyn and Lord Scott. Since Lord Browne-Wilkinson in concurring expressed agreement with both their speeches, their conclusions will be taken as representing the *ratio* of the case.

In analysing Bingham's first category, where the 'very object' of the contract is to provide pleasure, etc, the view was taken that this should not be confined too narrowly. It did not mean that the overall contract had to be one concerned with the provision of pleasure. Lord Steyn said: 'It is sufficient if a major or important object of the contract is to give pleasure, relaxation or peace of mind.'[107] Lord Scott went even further. Relying on *Ruxley Electronics and Construction v Forsyth*,[108] he concluded that:[109]

> . . . if a party's contractual performance has failed to provide to the other contracting party something to which that other was, under the contract, entitled, and which, if provided, would have been of value to that party, then, if there is no other way of compensating the injured party, the injured party should be compensated in damages to the extent of that value.

The question for Lord Scott is therefore simply whether there is an obligation of the relevant type within the contract; it does not necessarily have to be a major part of the contract.[110]

The statements of Lord Steyn and Lord Scott clearly apply where there is a positive obligation to bring about a result – for example, to provide a holiday of the right quality, or a swimming pool of a specified depth. In *Farley v Skinner*, the obligation was not of this kind. The surveyor did not undertake to guarantee that the property was unaffected by aircraft noise, but simply to take reasonable care in checking whether it was so affected. It was partly on this basis that the Court of Appeal had distinguished *Farley v Skinner* from *Ruxley Electronics v Forsyth*. Lord Steyn, however, refused to accept that this made any difference. He could not see, for example, that there was any difference between a travel agent who guarantees that there is a golf course next to a hotel and one who negligently advises that all hotels in a particular chain have golf courses nearby. In both cases the holidaymaker's holiday may be spoilt by the breach of contract.[111] It was therefore 'difficult to see why in principle only those

---

106 For a full discussion, see McKendrick and Graham, 2002.

107 [2001] UKHL 49, para 24; [2001] 4 All ER 801, p 812 – disapproving the Court of Appeal's decision in *Knott v Bolton* (1995) 45 Con LR 127, in which non-pecuniary damages were refused for an architect's failure to provide a wide staircase for a gallery and impressive entrance hall.

108 [1996] AC 344; [1995] 3 All ER 268. The case is fully discussed above, 18.4.1.

109 [2001] UKHL 49, para 79; [2001] 4 All ER 801, p 828.

110 Campbell, however, regards the treatment of Bingham's first category in *Farley v Skinner* as 'a most regrettable muddying of a pool which had begun to clear': Harris, Campbell and Halson, 2002, p 599.

111 See, also, the similar example given by Lord Clyde at [2001] UKHL 49, para 43; [2001] 4 All ER 801, p 818.

plaintiffs [*sic*] who negotiate guarantees may recover non-pecuniary damages for a breach of contract'.[112] Any distinction between obligations of 'guarantee' and those to take reasonable care should therefore be rejected. Lord Scott did not specifically deal with this point, but it is implicit in his conclusions that he agreed with the line taken by Lord Steyn. The conclusion of the House was, therefore, that the buyer could in this case recover damages under Bingham LJ's first category, as applied in *Ruxley Electronics v Forsyth*.

Both Lord Steyn and Lord Scott, however, also took the view that there could be recovery under Bingham LJ's second category. The Court of Appeal had felt that the aircraft noise did not constitute 'physical inconvenience'. The House disagreed. Their view is most clearly stated by Lord Scott. Noting that the distinction between 'physical' and 'non-physical' may be unclear (for example, is being awoken at night by aircraft noise 'physical'?), he concludes:[113]

> In my opinion, the critical distinction to be drawn is not a distinction between the different types of inconvenience or discomfort of which complaint may be made, but a distinction based on the cause of the inconvenience or discomfort. If the cause is no more than disappointment that the contractual obligation has been broken, damages are not recoverable even if the disappointment has led to a complete mental breakdown. But, if the cause of the inconvenience or discomfort is a sensory (sight, touch, hearing, smell etc) experience, damages can, subject to the remoteness rules, be recovered.

Since in this case it was clear that the effect was 'physical' in this sense, the buyer was entitled to damages under this heading, as an alternative to those under the first category.

As to the amount that should be awarded, the House was clearly of the view that the judge's £10,000 was on the high side, but did not interfere with it, nor give any clear guidance on how judges should approach this issue in the future. The problem is the same as that which has been discussed above in relation to *Ruxley Electronics v Forsyth*,[114] and the only answer is probably to wait for case law to establish a 'going rate' for particular types of non-pecuniary loss.

In *Hamilton Jones v David Snape*,[115] the principles set out in *Farley v Skinner* were applied to a contract with a solicitor, where the solicitor had negligently failed to prevent the claimant's children being removed from the jurisdiction by their father. The High Court held that damages for the consequent distress to the claimant were recoverable in an action for breach of contract. A significant purpose of the contract was to

---

112 [2001] UKHL 49, para 25; [2001] 4 All ER 801, p 812.
113 Ibid, para 85; p 829. See also Lord Hutton, paras 57–60; pp 824–25.
114 18.4.1.
115 [2004] EWHC 241; [2004] 1 All ER 657.

ensure that the claimant retained custody of her children and the pleasure and peace of mind that would result from this. On the basis of *Watts v Morrow*, as interpreted in *Farley v Skinner*, the claimant was awarded damages of £20,000 for mental distress. This fairly substantial award suggests that the courts may be prepared to move beyond the very cautious approach to the issue of the appropriate level of damages in this area taken in *Farley v Skinner*.

Farley v Skinner has clearly expanded the scope for recovery for non-pecuniary losses. Exactly how far remains to be seen. The High Court decision in *Wiseman v Virgin Atlantic Airways Ltd*[116] suggests that the courts will remain reluctant to allow compensation in this area. The claimant had been refused access to a flight by the defendant's staff, in breach of contract. He had also been falsely accused of having a false passport, and claimed to have been ridiculed by the defendant's staff and called a criminal. The court held that there could be no recovery for any of these non-pecuniary losses (though without making any reference to *Farley v Skinner*). The court clearly did not regard a normal flight from Nigeria to England as being a contract for which enjoyment was a main objective. As regards the claimant's mental distress, there was limited medical evidence, and in any case it was not linked to 'physical inconvenience or discomfort' as required by the *Watts v Morrow* test. As this case shows, the courts are likely to continue to adopt a restrictive line towards claims for non-pecuniary loss.

FOR THOUGHT

> Do you think the outcome would have been the same if the claimant had been returning from holiday, and had booked the flight as part of that contract?

As regards the long-term influence of *Farley v Skinner*, one of the most interesting developments is Lord Scott's interpretation of *Ruxley Electronics v Forsyth* as establishing a general right to damages in relation to the 'consumer surplus',[117] as expressed in this passage:[118]

> In summary, the principle expressed in the *Ruxley Electronics* case should be used to provide damages for deprivation of a contractual benefit where it is apparent that the injured party has been deprived of something of value but the ordinary means of measuring the recoverable damages are inapplicable. The principle expressed in *Watts v Morrow* should be used to determine whether and when contractual damages for inconvenience or discomfort can be recovered.

If these categories of damages do expand as a result of this decision, this will place

---

116 [2006] EWHC 1566; 103 LSG 29.
117 See above, 18.4.1. See also the comments of Lord Steyn at [2001] UKHL 49, para 21; p 810.
118 Ibid, para 86; p 829.

more weight on the rule of remoteness, to be discussed in the next section, as a means of keeping the floodgates closed.

18.5 LIMITATIONS ON RECOVERY

There are two main limitations on the amount of damages which can be recovered for a breach of contract, namely, the rule of remoteness and the requirement of mitigation. The issue of contributory negligence will also be considered below (see 18.5.7).

18.5.1 The rule of remoteness

At various points in this chapter, it has been mentioned that the award of damages under a particular head will be subject to the rule of remoteness. This is a rule which basically prevents consequential losses from extending too far, and placing unreasonable burdens on the defendant. It should also be recalled that in Chapter 10 it was noted that, in relation to the tort of deceit and the remedy for negligent misrepresentation under s 2(1) of the Misrepresentation Act 1967, all consequential losses are recoverable without limitation.[119] This is exceptional, however, and in general, in both tort and contract, damages are only recoverable in relation to losses which are not too remote.

The type of recovery the rule is designed to prevent is as follows. Suppose that a contract for the hire of a car is broken in that the one supplied is unfit for its purpose and breaks down. The hirer may as a result fail to arrive at a sale where he would have been able to buy a valuable painting which he could have resold for a £100,000 profit. Should the hire company be liable for the £100,000? English law will normally regard this loss as too remote from the breach to be recoverable. To take a recent example from a decided case, in *Wiseman v Virgin Atlantic Airways Ltd*[120] the claimant had been delayed for some days in catching a flight as a result of the defendant's breach of contract. While he was waiting for a replacement flight he was attacked by robbers. It was held that this was too remote from the breach of contract to give rise to any compensation from the airline company. This approach ties in with the view of contract law as a mechanism by which the parties to an exchange transaction allocate the risks of their enterprise. In order to be able to do this properly, they must be aware of the risks at the time of contracting, so that they can be properly catered for in the contract price, exclusion clauses, or other terms of the contract. If unforeseen losses were recoverable, this would unbalance the contractual relationship.[121]

---

119 See 10.4.3.

120 [2006] EWHC 1566; 103 LSG 29.

121 This explanation cannot, of course, apply to the similar rule which operates in the law of tort. It may be, therefore, that the contractual rules of remoteness also have a basis in ideas of 'fairness'. For discussion of the justification of the differences between the contract and tort approaches from an economic perspective, see Bishop, 1983.

18.5.2 The rule in *Hadley v Baxendale*

In contract, the starting point for the rule of remoteness is *Hadley v Baxendale*.[122] In this case, there was delay in the transport of a broken mill-shaft which resulted in considerable losses for the mill owner, because no spare shaft was available. The court stated the rule as being that the defendant will only be liable for losses:[123]

> ... either arising naturally, that is, according to the usual course of things, from such breach of contract itself, or such as may reasonably be supposed to have been in the contemplation of both parties at the time they made the contract as the probable result of the breach of it.

Applying this to the facts of the case, the court held that in most cases of a breach of this kind, no such losses would have followed, so that it could not be said that the losses followed naturally from the breach. Nor were the defendants aware, at the time of the contract, of the circumstances which meant that the mill would not be able to function at all without this particular shaft. Therefore, the losses were not recoverable.

18.5.3 Relevance of knowledge

There are two aspects of this test which should be noted. First, it is clear that the remoteness rule has to be assessed on the basis of the parties' knowledge *at the time the contract is made*. The House of Lords in *Jackson v Royal Bank of Scotland*[124] confirmed that this was so, even if the time between formation and breach was short. The reason for this is that, as indicated above, awareness of a particular risk may affect the terms of the contract. If, to use the example given above, the firm hiring out a car is aware that the customer is using it to attend a sale in order to buy a rare painting, the firm may want to (a) increase the price, (b) insert an exclusion clause, (c) seek insurance of the risk, or (d) refuse to enter into the contract at all. Knowledge which the defendant acquired after the formation of the contract is therefore irrelevant to the rule of remoteness.

It should be noted that it seems that 'knowledge' here means more than simply 'awareness': the relevant information must be given in a context where it is clear that the information giver is expecting the other party to assume the relevant risk. The casual mention of a particular fact will not be sufficient.[125]

---

122 (1854) 9 Exch 341; 156 ER 145. For consideration of the commercial and industrial context in which the case was decided, see Danzig, 1975.

123 (1854) 9 Exch 341, p 354; 156 ER 145, p 151.

124 [2005] UKHL 3; [2005] 2 All ER 71.

125 *Kemp v Intasun Holidays* [1987] BTLC 353 – mention of the plaintiff's medical condition when booking a holiday was insufficient to make the defendant liable for losses resulting from it. For discussion of the practical problems in communicating special circumstances to large, fragmented organisations, see Danzig, 1975, pp 279–80.

18.5.4 'Reasonable contemplation' test

Second, the rule as stated in *Hadley v Baxendale* appears to have two parts, the first relating to the natural consequences of breach, and the second to the contemplation of the parties. As interpreted in the later cases of *Victoria Laundry (Windsor) Ltd v Newman Industries*[126] and *Koufos v C Czarnikow Ltd, The Heron II*,[127] however, the two limbs are really just aspects of one general principle. As Lord Walker commented in *Jackson v Royal Bank of Scotland plc*,[128] the test 'cannot be construed and applied as if it were a statutory test, nor are its two limbs mutually exclusive'. The situation must be looked at through the eyes of the reasonable defendant, who will be presumed to have in contemplation the normal types of loss which would follow from the breach. As regards anything more unusual, it will have to be established that the particular defendant had sufficient actual knowledge to be aware of the risk. The test is thus, simply, what can this defendant, bearing in mind his or her state of knowledge at the time of the contract, be reasonably presumed to have expected to be the consequence of the breach of contract which occurred?

In *Victoria Laundry (Windsor) v Newman*, the breach of contract was a lengthy delay in the delivery of a boiler which the plaintiffs (as the defendants were aware) wished to use in their laundry and dyeing business. The Court of Appeal held that the plaintiffs could recover lost profits at a level reasonably to be anticipated from a business of this type. They could not recover, however, in relation to some particularly lucrative dyeing contracts with the Ministry of Defence, of which the defendants were unaware.

18.5.5 Degree of risk

In *The Heron II*, the plaintiffs lost money when the ship they had chartered to carry a cargo of sugar deviated from its route and arrived late at the port of destination. The sugar was sold immediately, as had always been the plaintiffs' intention, but the market price had fallen significantly as compared with the date on which the ship should have arrived. The issue was whether the shipowners were liable for this loss, since they were not specifically aware of the charterers' intentions in relation to the sale of the cargo. The House of Lords therefore had to consider the degree of risk that had to be contemplated before a loss was not too remote. It is a difficult concept to pin down, and there is no clear, single phrase which is used to express it. The House agreed, however, that the test in contract was distinguishable from that in tort, which is based on 'reasonable foreseeability'. The contract test is stricter than that, and depends on the loss being contemplated as 'not unlikely', or 'liable to result'. Lord Reid put it this way:[129]

---

126 [1949] 2 KB 528; [1949] 1 All ER 997.
127 [1969] 1 AC 350; [1967] 3 All ER 686.
128 [2005] UKHL 3; [2005] 2 All ER 71, paras 46–49.
129 [1969] 1 AC 350, p 385; [1967] 3 All ER 686, p 691.

The crucial question is whether, on the information available to the defendant when the contract was made, he should, or the reasonable man in his position would, have realised that such loss was sufficiently likely to result from the breach of contract to make it proper to hold that the loss flowed naturally from the breach or that loss of that kind should have been within his contemplation.

Applying this approach, it was held that the shipowners should have known that it was not unlikely that the sugar would be sold as soon as it arrived at its destination. They must also have been aware that the price of sugar fluctuates, and that there was a risk that a delay would mean that the plaintiffs would suffer a loss on the sale.

It seems that it is the *type* of loss, rather than the precise way in which it occurs, or its extent, which must be contemplated. In *Parsons (Livestock) Ltd v Uttley Ingham & Co Ltd*,[130] the defective installation of a hopper used for storing pig food led to the death of a large number of the plaintiff's pigs, as a result of the food going mouldy. The defendants were held liable for this loss, because some harm to the pigs was within the reasonable contemplation of the parties as something which would result from a defective installation, even though the particular disease was not. As Lord Scarman put it:[131]

> While, on [the judge's] finding, nobody at the time of contract could have expected E coli to ensue from eating mouldy nuts, he is clearly, and as a matter of common sense, rightly, saying that people would contemplate . . . the serious possibility of injury and even death among the pigs.

Where a particular unusual aspect of the claimant's activity has increased the loss caused by the defendant's breach, the defendant will only be liable if he had actual knowledge. Thus, in *Balfour Beatty Construction (Scotland) Ltd v Scottish Power plc*,[132] the House of Lords held that a supplier of electricity who was in breach of contract because of an interruption in the supply was not liable for the full losses suffered by the plaintiff. The interruption had occurred while the plaintiff was in the middle of a construction project which required a 'continuous pour' of concrete. The break in supply meant that the work which had been done was worthless, and had to be demolished. There was no evidence, however, that the defendants were aware of the need for a continuous pour, and there was no presumption that a supplier of a commodity should be taken to be aware of all the techniques involved in the other party's business.

In the most recent House of Lords consideration of this area, *Jackson v Royal Bank of Scotland*, the Bank had, in connection with the supply of letters of credit, allowed a customer of the claimant to discover the amount of the claimant's mark-up on goods it was supplying. The customer therefore took its business elsewhere. The

130 [1978] QB 791; [1978] 1 All ER 525.
131 Ibid, p 812; p 541.
132 1994 SC 20.

Bank had broken its contractual duty of confidence. The House, applying the *Hadley v Baxendale* test, held that it was within the reasonable contemplation of the parties at the time of the contract that a breach of this term would lead to some loss. The contract had no cut-off point, so the only limit was when the loss became too speculative. The House was happy to accept the quantification of the loss which had been arrived at by the trial judge, based on a four-year period of lost sales. The Court of Appeal, which had limited the loss to one year, had erred in taking into account the knowledge of the parties at the time of the breach – this was not relevant to the application of the remoteness rules.

Once a breach of contract has occurred, the claimant is not entitled to sit back and do nothing while losses accumulate. There is an obligation to take reasonable steps to mitigate losses, which was laid down by the House of Lords in *British Westinghouse Electric and Manufacturing Co v Underground Electric Railways Co of London*.[133] Viscount Haldane LC explained that this obligation:[134]

> . . . imposes on a plaintiff the duty of taking all reasonable steps to mitigate the loss consequent on the breach, and debars him from claiming any part of the damage which is due to his neglect to take such steps.

Furthermore:

> . . . this . . . principle does not impose on the plaintiff an obligation to take any step which a reasonable and prudent man would not ordinarily take in the course of his business. But when in the course of his business he has taken action arising out of the transaction, which action has diminished his loss, the effect in actual diminution of the loss he has suffered may be taken into account even though there was no duty on him to act.

In other words, the court will look at what the claimant's actual losses are, rather than what they might hypothetically have been had the claimant not acted, even though the claimant's actions in reducing the loss have gone beyond what might reasonably have been required. If the claimant has done nothing, however, the court will consider what steps might reasonably have been taken to reduce the losses. The claimant will be debarred from claiming any part of the damage which is due to a failure to take such steps. So, if the seller fails to deliver in a sale of goods contract, the buyer will be expected to go into the market and attempt to obtain equivalent goods. If such are

---

133 [1912] AC 673.
134 Ibid, p 689.

available at, or below, the market price, then only nominal damages will be recoverable. If the buyer fails to enter the market until the price has risen, or pays over the odds, these increased losses will not be recoverable. Similarly, a reasonable offer of performance following a breach should not be spurned. In *Payzu Ltd v Saunders*,[135] the plaintiffs had failed to make prompt payment for an instalment of goods. The defendants had, in breach of contract, then refused to deliver unless the plaintiffs agreed to pay cash with each order. It was held that the plaintiffs should have accepted this offer, which would have reduced their loss (since the market value of the goods in question was rising above the contract price).

Mitigation only requires the claimant to act 'reasonably' in all the circumstances. In *Wroth v Tyler*,[136] the plaintiff's lack of resources was considered a reasonable ground for a failure to go into the market and make an alternative purchase. Similarly, in *Lagden v O'Connor*,[137] a claimant who was unable to pay for a hire car, and therefore had to obtain one on credit, which was more expensive, was allowed to recover the full loss. As Lord Nicholls put it:[138]

> [I]n measuring the loss suffered by an impecunious plaintiff [*sic*] by loss of use of his own car the law will recognise that, because of his lack of financial means, the timely provision of a replacement vehicle for him costs more than it does for his affluent neighbour.

The principle of mitigation raises particular problems in cases of anticipatory breach. If the claimant accepts the breach, and the contract terminates immediately, then the normal rules will apply. If, however, the claimant does not accept the breach, but elects to affirm the contract and wait for the other party to perform, it seems that in some circumstances there is not any duty at that stage to reduce losses. In *White and Carter (Councils) Ltd v McGregor*,[139] the defendants had contracted to buy advertising space on litter bins owned by the plaintiffs. This contract was wrongfully cancelled by the defendants before any work had been done. The plaintiffs refused to accept this anticipatory breach, and went ahead with the production and display of the advertisements over the full three years of the contract. They then sued for the full sum due under the contract.[140] The House of Lords, by a majority of 3:2, held that there is no obligation

---

135 [1919] 2 KB 581.
136 [1974] Ch 30; [1973] 1 All ER 897.
137 [2003] UKHL 64; [2004] 1 All ER 277. This case concerned a negligence claim in tort, but the mitigation principles are the same as for a contractual action.
138 [2003] UKHL 64, para 7. Note that two members of the House of Lords dissented from the conclusion.
139 [1962] AC 413; [1961] 3 All ER 1178.
140 In other words, this was an action for an agreed sum, rather than for compensatory damages: see above, 18.2.

on the claimant in such a situation to mitigate the losses, and full recovery is possible. The decision has been regarded as harsh on the defendant, and involving an unnecessary waste of resources. It has been widely criticised,[141] but it still stands as the leading authority on this issue. Lord Reid, however, identified two limitations, one practical and one legal, which exist in relation to the situations where a *White and Carter* response to anticipatory breach will be acceptable. The practical limitation is that the claimant will not be able to act in this way where the performance of the contractual obligations requires the co-operation of the defendant, as will often be the case.[142] As regards the legal limitation, Lord Reid suggested that:[143]

> It may well be that, if it can be shown that a person has no legitimate interest, financial or otherwise, in performing the contract rather than claiming damages, he ought not to be allowed to saddle the other party with an additional burden with no benefit to himself.

Lord Reid clearly felt that the burden of proving the absence of any such 'legitimate interest' rested on the defendants, and in this case they had not attempted to establish it.[144] Lord Reid does not specify what might constitute a 'legitimate interest', but clearly this might arise where failing to continue with the contract might involve the party in breach of other obligations owed to third parties.[145] This type of interest was found to exist by Kerr J in *Gator Shipping Corp v Trans-Asiatic Oil Ltd SA, The Odenfeld*,[146] in holding that the owners of a vessel were not obliged to accept the repudiatory breach of a time charter. In other cases, however, the 'no legitimate interest' restriction has been used to distinguish *White and Carter*. Thus, in *Attica Sea Carriers Corp v Ferrostaal Poseidon Bulk Reederei GmbH, The Puerto Buitrago*,[147] the Court of Appeal considered a case where the charterers of a ship had a repair obligation. The repairs would have cost twice the value of the ship, and the charterers tried to return it unrepaired (which involved a breach of the charter). The owners refused to accept this breach, and insisted that the charterers should continue to pay the charter hire until the ship was repaired. The Court of Appeal held for the charterers. Orr LJ (with whom Browne LJ agreed) based this in part on the fact that the charterers had here shown that the shipowners

---

141 See Furmston, 1962; Goodhart, 1962; Burrows, 2004; Harris, Campbell and Halson, 2002, pp 161–65.

142 This limitation was applied by Megarry J in *Hounslow LBC v Twickenham Garden Developments Ltd* [1971] Ch 233 – work to be done on property owned by the other party. The need for 'passive co-operation' was sufficient to exclude the *White and Carter* approach.

143 [1962] AC 413, p 481; [1961] 3 All ER 1178, p 1183.

144 Though this may surely have been because they did not realise that they needed to.

145 Friedmann (1995) has suggested that this limitation indicates that 'the right to keep the contract open, coupled with the right to claim the agreed sum, are not absolute but in fact subject to a requirement of good faith'.

146 [1978] 2 Lloyd's Rep 357.

147 [1976] 1 Lloyd's Rep 250.

had no legitimate interest in continuing the charter.[148] A similar line was taken by Lloyd J in *Clea Shipping Corp v Bulk Oil International Ltd, The Alaskan Trader*,[149] where, after 12 months of a two year charter, the charterers indicated that they did not wish to continue with the contract, following the breakdown of the ship. The owners, however, repaired the ship and kept it crewed and ready for the remainder of the charter period. It was held that the owners did not have a legitimate interest in continuing with the contract as opposed to claiming damages.

The position is, therefore, that *White and Carter (Councils) v McGregor* remains good law, but the two restrictions set out in Lord Reid's speech can generally be used to avoid its being applied in inappropriate and unreasonable circumstances.

18.5.7 Contributory negligence

In tort, it is well established that the damages recoverable may be reduced by the claimant's own, contributory, negligence.[150] Does the same principle apply in contract? The issue was considered by the Court of Appeal in *Forsikringsaktieselskapet Vesta v Butcher*,[151] which stated, *obiter*, that the Law Reform (Contributory Negligence) Act 1945 did apply where there was concurrent liability in tort and contract (that is, where the breach of contract consisted of negligent performance, in a situation where there was also a tortious duty of care). This has subsequently been accepted as correct by the House of Lords in *Platform Home Loans Ltd v Oyston Shipways*.[152] Where, on the other hand, the breach of contract is based on strict liability, there is no scope for contributory negligence, and the 1945 Act is irrelevant. This was confirmed by the Court of Appeal in *Barclays Bank plc v Fairclough Building Ltd*,[153] which concerned a breach of strict obligations arising under a building contract. The judge had held that the plaintiffs had failed to supervise the work properly, and therefore reduced the damages. The Court of Appeal reversed this decision. Where contractual liability was strict, it was inappropriate to apportion losses, even if the defendant might also be said to have been negligent. Simon Brown LJ explained his reasons for coming to this conclusion in this way:[154]

> The very imposition of a strict liability upon the defendant is to my mind inconsistent with an apportionment of the loss. And not least because of the absurdities that the contrary approach carries in its wake. Assume a defendant, clearly

---

148 Lord Denning agreed, but more generally on the basis that *White and Carter* ought not to be used as a form of disguised 'specific performance' where damages would be an adequate remedy.
149 [1984] 1 All ER 219.
150 See, in particular, the Law Reform (Contributory Negligence) Act 1945.
151 [1989] AC 852; [1988] 2 All ER 43.
152 [2000] 2 AC 190; [1999] 1 All ER 833.
153 [1995] QB 214; [1995] 1 All ER 289.
154 Ibid, p 233; p 306.

liable under a strict contractual duty. Is his position to be improved by demonstrating that besides breaching that duty he was in addition negligent?

Where, however, the contractual liability is based on 'negligence', but there is no concurrent tortious duty, there is no clear authority. There is some suggestion from the case of *De Meza v Apple*[155] that the Act does apply in such a case, but this was not supported by *dicta* in *Forsikringsaktieselskapet Vesta v Butcher*. And although losses were apportioned in *Tenant Radiant Heat Ltd v Warrington Development Corp*,[156] this was on the basis of one side having broken the contract, and the other being independently liable in tort. The area is thus in some confusion, and a clear ruling from the House of Lords would be helpful. The Law Commission has recommended that contributory negligence should always be available to apportion losses where there has been breach of a contractual duty to take reasonable care,[157] whether or not there is an overlap with tort, and this seems the most sensible solution.

One issue which has been considered by the House of Lords is the way in which contributory negligence should be dealt with in cases of overvaluation of property. The general rule for calculating damages in such cases has been established in *South Australia Asset Management Corp v York Montague Ltd*,[158] discussed above (see 18.4.5). The issue in *Platform Home Loans Ltd v Oyston Shipways Ltd*[159] was, first, whether contributory negligence applies where the claimant's 'negligence' is different from the defendant's negligence; and, second, if it does, to what sum any reduction should be applied. On the first question, the Court of Appeal held that the fact that the lender had an imprudent lending policy could operate as contributory negligence to reduce damages, even though this had nothing to do with the defendant's negligent overvaluation of the property. The analogy was used of the seat belt cases in tort: not wearing a seat belt will not contribute to the negligence of the driver, but it can be used as a reason for reducing the claimant's damages. The House of Lords upheld the Court of Appeal on this issue. It disagreed, however, on the second issue, that is, the way in which the reduction should be calculated. The Court of Appeal had held that the percentage reduction suggested by the trial judge should be applied to the lender's loss as established by the *South Australia Asset Management Corp* approach. This limited the loss to the difference between the overvaluation and the true valuation at the time of the contract. Thus, in this case, the difference in the valuations was £500,000 and the judge had found the lender to be 20 per cent contributorily negligent. The Court of Appeal therefore awarded damages of £400,000. The House of Lords, however, held that the reduction should be applied to the lender's full loss, which had been increased by the fall in market values. In this case, the property had been resold for only £435,000, and

---

155 [1975] 1 Lloyd's Rep 498.
156 [1988] EGLR 41.
157 Law Commission, 1993, para 4.7.
158 [1997] AC 191; [1996] 3 All ER 365.
159 [2000] AC 190; [1999] 1 All ER 833.

the trial judge had found that the lender's full loss was £611,748. It was to this figure that the 20 per cent reduction should be applied. Only if the resulting amount was higher than the figure arrived at on the *South Australia Asset Management Corp* calculation should it be capped at that level. In this case, the 20 per cent reduction produced a figure of £489,398. Since this was below the figure of £500,000, the lender was entitled to recover this amount, rather than the £400,000 awarded by the Court of Appeal.

18.6 LIQUIDATED DAMAGES AND PENALTY CLAUSES

The parties to a contract may decide to include provision as to the compensation which is to be paid in the event of a breach. This is known as a 'liquidated damages' clause, and is generally a perfectly acceptable arrangement to which the courts will happily give effect. It is an example of the parties deciding between themselves not only where the risks should lie, but the extent of such risks. Economic analysis is likely to conclude that such clauses are an efficient mechanism, in that they reduce the transaction costs which might otherwise follow a breach of contract in terms of negotiating compensation or, in the worst case, having to take legal action to recover it.[160]

The limitation which English law imposes on this approach is that the sum specified in the contract must be a 'genuine pre-estimate' of the claimant's loss, and not a 'penalty'. If it is the latter, then it will be unenforceable. This distinction was insisted upon by the House of Lords in *Dunlop Pneumatic Tyre Co Ltd v New Garage and Motor Co Ltd*.[161] In this case, a sum of £5 was stated to be payable 'by way of liquidated damages and not as a penalty' in relation to a wide range of breaches of contract. The House of Lords held that, despite the parties' own statement, a sum payable could constitute a penalty not only if it was excessive in comparison to the loss, but also if it was payable on the occurrence of a range of events, which would be likely to produce a range of different losses. That was the case here, but nevertheless the House felt that on balance the £5 should not be regarded as a penalty. It may therefore be acceptable to use a single figure for compensation as a type of 'averaging' of the likely losses resulting from a range of breaches, the precise effects of which may be difficult to quantify.

18.6.1 Application of the principles

The principles in this area are clear enough. The difficulty comes in applying them to particular provisions. The area was reconsidered by the Privy Council in *Philips Hong Kong Ltd v Attorney General of Hong Kong*.[162] The case concerned a claim by Philips

---

160 See Harris, Campbell and Halson, 2002, pp 139–42, and in particular the articles cited at p 142, nn 13 and 14.

161 [1915] AC 79. It has more recently been approved by the Privy Council in *Philips Hong Kong Ltd v Attorney General of Hong Kong* (1993) 61 BLR 41.

162 Ibid.

that they were not liable to pay the Hong Kong government liquidated damages for delay in completion of contract works, because these amounted to a penalty. The Court of Appeal of Hong Kong allowed an appeal from a first instance decision upholding Philips' claim. Philips appealed to the Privy Council. The Privy Council stated that in deciding whether a clause was a penalty clause, or a genuine pre-estimate of damages, the court was not helped by the use in argument of unlikely hypothetical examples of situations where the sums payable under the liquidated damages clause would be wholly out of proportion to any loss. Although the clause must be judged objectively, at the date on which the contract was made, what happened subsequently could provide valuable evidence of what could reasonably be expected to be the loss at the time the contract was made. The appeal was dismissed. In reaching its conclusions, the Privy Council accepted Lord Dunedin's statement in *Dunlop Pneumatic Tyre Co Ltd v New Garage and Motor Co* that:[163]

> The question whether a sum stipulated is penalty or liquidated damages is a question of construction to be decided upon the terms and inherent circumstances of each particular contract, judged as at the time of the contract not as at the time of the breach . . .

Nevertheless, as noted above, it was felt that what had actually happened might provide a better guide than hypothetical examples thought up by counsel. Furthermore, where the range of possible losses was broad, the better approach might be simply to say that the clause was not intended to apply to breaches where the liquidated damages would be totally out of proportion to the loss, rather than to strike the clause down in its entirety. The court was clearly influenced by the fact that this was a commercial contract where what the parties had agreed should normally be upheld. The decision suggests a flexible, but to some extent unpredictable, approach to the effect of such clauses.

In *Duffen v Fra Bo SpA*,[164] the Court of Appeal considered a term in an agency contract which provided that on termination by the agent the principal should immediately pay the agent £100,000. This was stated in the contract to be 'liquidated damages' with the sum being 'agreed by the parties to be a reasonable pre-estimate of the loss and damage which the agent will suffer on termination of the agreement'. Nevertheless, the court held that it was a penalty clause and thus unenforceable. It was not a genuine attempt to estimate the loss which the agent would suffer following breach by the principal, nor was it graduated in relation to the unexpired term of the agent's contract. Enforcing it would give the agent a substantial windfall which would be both 'extravagant and unconscionable'.

It should also be noted that a clause which imposes an obligation on a consumer

---

163 [1915] AC 79, pp 86–87.
164 [2000] 1 Lloyd's Rep 180.

to pay a 'disproportionately high sum' for failure to fulfil an obligation may well be unenforceable by virtue of the Unfair Terms in Consumer Contracts Regulations 1999.[165] These Regulations are discussed in more detail in Chapter 9.[166]

18.7 SPECIFIC PERFORMANCE

As noted at the beginning of the chapter, the only situation where the common law required performance of a contractual obligation was in relation to the action for an agreed sum, following performance by the claimant. The other aspect of what some commentators refer to as 'literal enforcement',[167] that is, the power to order a party to perform a non-monetary obligation, was left to the Chancery courts. The remedy of specific performance involves the court in issuing an order directing one of the parties to a contract to carry out his or her obligations. The sanction for a failure to comply is that the person concerned will be in contempt of court, and liable to fines and imprisonment as a consequence. Since the remedy is an equitable one, developed by the Chancery courts, it is discretionary, unlike damages, which are available as of right.[168] This means that a claimant is not entitled to the order simply as a result of proving that the other party is in breach of its obligations. Once this has been established, the court will then decide whether it is appropriate in this particular case that the order should be made. For example, as we saw in Chapter 11, one way in which the courts will allow a party to escape the consequences of a mistake concerning the terms of the contract is by refusing to order specific performance.[169] Similarly, the order may not be granted if the claimant has taken advantage of the defendant, for example, because he or she was drunk.[170]

Although this discretionary element inevitably attaches a degree of uncertainty to the remedy, in fact, the courts have developed a number of rules about its use, which mean that in many cases, it will be fairly easy to determine whether or not the order is likely to be granted. The rest of this section looks at these.

18.7.1 Adequacy of damages

One of the reasons why the remedy of specific performance developed is that, in certain situations, damages will be an inadequate remedy. If no pecuniary loss can be

---

165 See Sched 3, para 1(e).

166 See above, 9.8.

167 See, for example, Beale, Bishop and Furmston, 2001, Chapter 23; Harris, Campbell and Halson, 2002, Chapter 10.

168 That is, once the claimant has proved a breach of contract the court must award some damages, even if they are only nominal.

169 See above, 11.8.1.

170 *Malins v Freeman* (1837) 2 Keen 25.

established, or if it is impossible to quantify, this would mean that there would be no effective sanction for a breach of contract, in the absence of the order for specific performance. In *Harnett v Yielding*, for example, Lord Redesdale said:[171]

> Unquestionably, the original foundation of these decrees was simply this, that damages would not give the party the compensation to which he was entitled; that is, it would not put him in a situation as beneficial to him as if the agreement were specifically performed.

Thus, as Kindersley VC explains in *Falcke v Gray*,[172] the Courts of Equity would not allow an injustice to stand, but intervened to order performance of the obligations. Now, of course, the remedy is available in all courts, and the question to be asked is: when will damages not be regarded as an adequate remedy?

If there is a contract for the sale of goods in which there is an active market, then it is very unlikely that an order for specific performance will be granted.[173] The party not in breach can buy or sell in the market, and be compensated by way of damages for any financial loss resulting from a difference between the contract and market prices.[174] If, on the other hand, what is being sold is a valuable antique, or some other item which is not generally available, specific performance may well be the appropriate remedy. This distinction is supported by s 52 of the Sale of Goods Act 1979, which allows for specific performance in relation to 'specific' or 'ascertained' goods, but not 'generic' goods. Even where the goods are 'specific', however, the discretion to order performance will not be exercised unless they are something out of the ordinary. It is not appropriate to order performance where the goods in question are 'ordinary articles of commerce and of no special value or interest'.[175]

Similarly, it is normally the case that the order will be available to enforce contracts for the sale of land, since every piece of land is regarded as unique. This applies in favour of the seller as well as the buyer, because it is a general principle that there should be mutuality in the availability of the remedy.[176]

---

171 (1805) 2 Sch & Lef 549.
172 (1859) 4 Drew 651; 62 ER 250.
173 If the market is affected by unusual circumstances, the courts may well be more prepared to grant a remedy which effectively requires performance. See, for example, *Sky Petroleum Ltd v VIP Petroleum Ltd* [1974] 1 WLR 576, where at the time of an 'oil crisis' the court was prepared to grant an injunction restraining an oil company from withholding supplies to filling stations.
174 Insisting on performance in this situation would interfere with the concept of the 'efficient breach', which suggests that allowing a party to breach may in fact increase 'wealth'. See above, 18.3.
175 *Cohen v Roche* [1927] 1 KB 169, p 181. The goods in this case were a set of eight Hepplewhite chairs which were sold for £60 and valued by the court at £70–£80.
176 See below, 18.7.4.

FOR THOUGHT

> Is it true that every piece of land is unique? If you are buying a new house on a housing estate, on which the houses are of identical design, does it really matter which one you end up with? Or, if you are buying a terraced house to let out to students, are you concerned with precisely which property you acquire, as long as it is of an equivalent value?

In *Behnke v Bede Shipping Co Ltd*,[177] a 'unique' ship was held to be capable of being subject to an order for specific performance, but in *The Stena Nautica (No 2)*[178] the decision went the other way. The Court of Appeal accepted that as a matter of law a ship could, in appropriate circumstances, be the subject of an order for specific performance. On the facts, however, it was felt that the judge had been wrong to make such an order, relating to the plaintiffs' option to purchase a vessel. A factor that had apparently weighed heavily with the judge was that the ship concerned was a sister ship of other vessels operated by the plaintiffs. On the other hand, he had made the order subject to another charter with a third party which was to operate for the next two years. The Court of Appeal found these two elements in the judge's decision to be inconsistent. As May LJ commented:[179]

> If the sister ship point was relevant and indeed vital, in deciding whether the [plaintiffs] should be limited to their remedy in damages, it is I think somewhat surprising that the learned judge went on in effect to deprive them of the use of the sister ship over the next two years, in imposing the condition that he did on the order for specific performance which he made.

Indeed, it is always likely to raise a question as to whether such an order is necessary, on the basis that damages are inadequate, if it is made subject to a delay in its operation.

In some cases, it seems that if damages would only be nominal, then the order may be made. Thus, in *Beswick v Beswick*,[180] the fact that the deceased's estate suffered no direct loss from the failure of the nephew to pay his aunt meant that only nominal damages would be recoverable in an action by the estate. Justice clearly demanded, however, that the contract should be enforced, and so the order was granted. It will not always be the case that the fact that damages would be nominal will allow specific performance to be ordered. If that were so it would include all the cases of sale of goods where there is an available market offering a price more attractive than the

---

177 [1927] 1 KB 649.
178 [1982] 2 Lloyd's Rep 336.
179 Ibid, p 349.
180 [1968] AC 58; [1967] 2 All ER 1197. The facts of this case are given above, 5.3.1.

contract one. There must be some other factor which will persuade the court to make the order, but it is difficult to predict what this will be, or to make a list of the appropriate circumstances.

18.7.2 Need for supervision

The court will be reluctant to order specific performance where it would have to supervise the parties over a period of time to ensure compliance. In *Ryan v Mutual Tontine Westminster Chambers Association*,[181] for example, the court refused to grant specific performance of a landlord's obligation to have a resident porter 'constantly in attendance'. It appears, however, to be only where the supervision would need to concern the detail of performance that this limitation applies. In *Wolverhampton Corp v Emmons*,[182] the contract concerned a building contract for some new houses, which would obviously take time to complete. The court was prepared to order specific performance because the obligations of the defendant were clearly defined by the building plans, and so there would be no need for detailed supervision while the work was being done.

A more recent example of the application of this principle is to be found in *Cooperative Insurance Society Ltd v Argyll Stores (Holdings) Ltd*.[183] In this case, the plaintiffs were seeking specific performance of a covenant in a lease of retail premises to keep them open for business during particular hours. The defendants had closed the supermarket which had been run at the premises. The trial judge refused specific performance, but this ruling was overturned by the Court of Appeal. The House of Lords in its turn restored the ruling of the trial judge. It held that it was not usually appropriate to give an order for specific performance requiring someone to carry on a business. One of the main reasons for this was the prospect of the court having to make a series of orders over a period of time, backed up by the heavy handed remedy of contempt of court, in order to ensure compliance. This was not appropriate, not least in terms of likely cost to the parties and the resources of the judicial system. A one-off award of damages would be much more satisfactory. The trial judge's decision should therefore be restored.

18.7.3 Personal services

The courts will be reluctant to grant an order for specific performance in relation to employment or other contracts for personal services. The fact that the matter has come to court almost certainly shows that relations between the parties have broken down, and it would be undesirable to try to force them to work together. Where, however, it can be demonstrated that mutual trust and respect does still exist, then the order may be

---

181 (1893) 1 Ch 116.
182 [1901] 1 KB 515.
183 [1998] AC 1; [1997] 3 All ER 297.

available. In *Hill v CA Parsons & Co Ltd*,[184] for example, a dismissal had resulted from union pressure, rather than a dispute between employer and employee. This limitation on the general rule as regards personal services was also recognised in *Powell v Brent London Borough Council*,[185] where an injunction was granted. The problem in this case had arisen simply because the employer had appointed the employee after a process which did not comply with the requirements of its equal opportunities procedures. The subsequent dismissal of the employee was a result of this rather than any dissatisfaction with the employee's work. Of course, most disputes about employment will nowadays fall to be considered under the employment protection legislation, which specifically provides for 're-instatement' as one of the remedies for unfair dismissal.

18.7.4 Need for mutuality

A court will not order specific performance unless it would also be available against the party seeking it. Thus, a minor trying to enforce a contract for non-necessary goods would be likely to fail on the basis of this lack of mutuality. If, however, unenforceable obligations have in fact already been performed, the court may order the other side to go through with the contract. The time to assess the issue is as at the date of trial, rather than the date of contract, as is shown by *Price v Strange*.[186] In this case, the defendant had granted the plaintiff the continuation of an underlease of a flat, at an increased rent, in consideration for his agreeing to carry out certain internal and external repairs. The agreement started to operate, and the plaintiff carried out the interior repairs. At that point, the defendant purported to terminate the agreement. She then had the exterior repairs completed at her own expense. The plaintiff sought an order for specific performance, but the trial judge rejected this. His reason was that, at the time of the contract, the plaintiff's obligations to carry out the repairs would not have been specifically enforceable, so that there was a lack of mutuality. The Court of Appeal disagreed. By the time of the trial, all the repair work had been completed, and the plaintiff was not in danger of being forced to grant the underlease without being able to enforce the obligation to carry out the repairs. The court felt that the time of trial was the correct point at which to decide the issue, and therefore granted the order sought by the plaintiff.

18.7.5 Hardship

If the granting of an order, which on other grounds would seem to be available, will cause disproportionate hardship to the defendant, the court will refuse it. This is an aspect of the general 'equitable' nature of the remedy, which requires the court always

---

184 [1972] 1 Ch 305; [1971] 3 All ER 1345.
185 [1986] ICR 176.
186 [1978] Ch 337; [1977] 3 All ER 371.

to have in mind the need to achieve justice between the parties. In *Denne v Light*,[187] for example, specific performance of a contract for the sale of land would have left the defendant with a plot surrounded by land owned by others, and with no point of access. The order was not granted. Even straightforward financial hardship, if sufficiently severe, may be enough, particularly if it was unforeseeable at the time of the contract. In *Patel v Ali*,[188] the defendant had become disabled, and relied greatly on a network of support from neighbours. This network would have been lost if she had been forced to move, and it would have been very expensive to have to pay for equivalent help. The order for specific performance was not granted.

18.7.6 Claimant must have acted equitably

Since specific performance is an equitable remedy, the courts will apply the general equitable maxims that 'he who seeks equity must do equity', and 'he who comes to equity must come with clean hands'. In other words, the claimant will not be granted the remedy unless he or she, in the eyes of the court, has also acted equitably. For example, the remedy was refused in *Walters v Morgan*,[189] where the plaintiff had taken advantage of the defendant's ignorance as to the true value of property over which a mining lease had been granted. Similarly, in *Shell UK Ltd v Lostock Garage Ltd*,[190] the Court of Appeal refused to grant an injunction which would have in effect compelled the defendants to go through with a contract. The plaintiff's discriminatory pricing policy was regarded as unfair, and a basis for refusing the order.

18.8 INJUNCTIONS

In some situations, the courts will be prepared to grant an injunction restraining a person from acting in a way which will amount to a breach of contract. The injunction may be 'interlocutory', that is, temporary, pending a full trial, or permanent. One example of a situation where this may be a valuable remedy is in relation to restrictive covenants relating to the sale of a business, or competing employment.[191] In any contract in which a party promises *not* to do something, there will be potential scope for the use of an injunction. An injunction, however, like the order for specific performance, is an equitable remedy, and thus subject to the discretion of the court.

The courts will not allow an injunction to be used as an indirect means of specifically enforcing a contract for which a direct order to perform would not be granted.

---

187 (1857) 8 DM & G 774; 44 ER 588.
188 [1984] Ch 283; [1984] 1 All ER 978.
189 (1861) 3 De GF & J 718; 45 ER 1056.
190 [1977] 1 All ER 481. See also Chapter 8, 8.6.6.
191 See Chapter 15, 15.4.

Thus, in *Page One Records v Britton*,[192] the court refused an injunction which would have restrained a pop group from employing anyone as their manager other than the plaintiff, with whom they had fallen out. This was regarded as effectively forcing the group to employ the manager, and would amount to an indirect enforcement of a contract for personal services. Earlier decisions, however, had shown the courts being more willing to act in this area. In *Lumley v Wagner*,[193] for example, a singer had been restrained from singing in other theatres,[194] and in *Warner Bros v Nelson*,[195] the actress Bette Davis had been restrained from working in films or theatre for any other company. The court in this case felt that she was not being compelled to work for Warner Bros because she could have found employment other than as an actress, a conclusion which was technically correct, but practically very unrealistic. It may be that the *Page One* decision represents the more likely approach of a modern court to these issues.

18.9 REMEDIES UNDER THE PRINCIPLES OF EUROPEAN CONTRACT LAW

Remedies are dealt with in Chapter 9 of the Principles, which is one of the longest chapters. Some of the topics covered have already been dealt with elsewhere – for example, withholding performance and terminating for breach were discussed in Chapter 17. This section will look at the remaining topics in the order with which they have been dealt in this chapter.

18.9.1 Damages: measure

The right to damages for breach is recognised by Art 9.501, and is specifically stated to cover non-pecuniary losses[196] and the 'loss of a chance' (described as 'future loss').[197] The normal measure of damages is stated in Art 9:502 to be 'such sum as will put the aggrieved party as nearly as possible into the position in which it would have been if the contract had been duly performed'. In other words, it is the 'expectation interest' which will generally be awarded, taking into account both losses which the claimant party has suffered, and gains of which it has been deprived.

---

192 [1967] 3 All ER 822.
193 (1852) 1 De GM & G 604; 42 ER 687. See Waddams, 2001 for the background to this case.
194 Cf *Lumley v Gye* (1853) 2 E & B 216; 118 ER 749 – discussed in Chapter 5, 5.14.
195 [1937] 1 KB 209; [1936] 3 All ER 160.
196 There is nothing specific in the Principles to state any limit on the non-pecuniary losses that are recoverable. The issues addressed in *Addis v Gramophone*, *Watts v Morrow*, *Ruxley Electronics v Forsyth* and *Farley v Skinner* (as discussed above at 18.4.6) are therefore not dealt with. The illustration given deals with loss of enjoyment in relation to an unsatisfactory holiday – but this is one of the less problematic areas.
197 For which see above, 18.4.1.

Although this measure of damages is stated to be the 'general' measure, no other measure is mentioned in Chapter 9 of the Principles. In particular, there is no reference to the 'reliance' interest, and it seems that this would not be available as an alternative to the expectation interest, as it is under English law.

18.9.2 Remoteness

A rule of remoteness is stated in Art 9:503, under the heading 'foreseeability'. This states that in general there is only liability for losses which the party in breach 'foresaw or could reasonably have foreseen at the time of the conclusion of the contract as a likely result of its non-performance'. This is clearly in line with the English law rule of remoteness, apart from the fact that it is in terms of 'reasonable foreseeability' rather than 'reasonable contemplation'. To that extent it may cover a wider range of losses than the English rule. More significantly, the second part of the Article excludes from the rule of remoteness breaches which are 'intentional or grossly negligent'. Thus, the Principles import into the general law of contract the rule which in English law only applies in relation to misrepresentations.[198] This means that, in relation to a substantial proportion of breaches of contract, no remoteness rule will apply, and the defendant will be liable for all losses which are attributable to the breach.

18.9.3 Mitigation

Mitigation is dealt with by Art 9:505, under the heading 'reduction of loss'. This Article provides that the party in breach is not liable for losses 'to the extent that the aggrieved party could have reduced the loss by taking reasonable steps'. This is very much the same approach as under English law. As the notes to the Article make clear,[199] it is intended to apply to all breaches, including anticipatory breaches. Under the Principles, therefore, a case such as *White and Carter (Councils) v McGregor*[200] would be likely to be decided differently, with the claimant being expected to minimise losses by not continuing with performance once the other party has indicated that it is not going to honour the contract.[201]

18.9.4 Contributory negligence

As was noted above, English law takes a restrictive view of the impact of the claimant's behaviour as a factor in reducing damages. The Principles, in Art 9:504, allow for a

---

198 See Chapter 10, 10.4.3 and 10.4.6.
199 Lando and Beale, 2000, p 446.
200 [1962] AC 413; [1961] 3 All ER 1178. See above, 18.5.6.
201 See also Art 9:101 – performance which the other side has indicated it is unwilling to receive followed by action for the agreed sum will not be allowed if 'performance would be unreasonable in the circumstances'.

more general principle of this kind, so that wherever the claimant's behaviour has contributed to the breach or its effects, this can be taken into account in assessing damages. Two illustrations are given.[202] The first is where the claimant is supplied with a computer system which does not do the job for which the claimant required it, partly because of an inherent design defect, and partly because the claimant gave inadequate instructions as to its requirements. This situation would be likely to be dealt with by English law as a question of causation rather than damages. The second illustration is, however, a true 'contributory negligence' case. This is where the claimant is supplied with a computer which has been set to the wrong voltage, but the claimant fails to follow clear instructions to check this before switching it on. In such a situation, Art 9:504 would allow the court to reduce the claimant's damages to take account of the contributory conduct.

18.9.5 Liquidated damages and penalty clauses

The Principles do not adopt the 'all or nothing' English law approach to clauses which state the compensation to be paid in the event of breach – that is, that they are either a genuine pre-estimate of loss, and enforceable, or a penalty, and unenforceable.[203] Instead Art 9:509, while recognising the general enforceability of agreements to pay a 'specified sum' in the event of breach, also provides that the sum can 'be reduced to a reasonable amount where it is grossly excessive in relation to the loss resulting from the non-performance and the other circumstances'.[204] As the notes to the Article make clear, it is not necessarily the case that the 'reasonable amount' will be the claimant's actual loss:[205] an intermediate figure may well be appropriate as a means of respecting the parties' intention that the clause was inserted to deter default.[206]

18.9.6 Specific performance

The right to performance is dealt with first in Chapter 9 of the Principles, and this reflects the fact that in civil law jurisdictions this remedy is regarded as being available as of right, rather than, as under English law,[207] simply at the discretion of the court. In practice, Lando and Beale comment that there is little difference in the approaches, because:[208]

---

202 Lando and Beale, 2000, p 444.
203 Above, 18.6.
204 Article 9:509(2).
205 Which is what in effect happens when English courts find that a clause is unenforceable as a 'penalty'.
206 Lando and Beale, 2000, p 454.
207 Other than in relation to the action for an agreed sum.
208 Lando and Beale, 2000, p 400.

Even in civil law countries an aggrieved party will pursue an action for performance, in general, only if he has a special interest in performance which would not be satisfied by damages.

Article 9:101 deals with what in English law would be the action for an agreed sum. There is little to be said about this, except that, in line with the approach taken to mitigation, above, it is made clear that the action is not available in relation to performance following an anticipatory breach, unless the performance is 'reasonable'.[209]

Specific performance of non-monetary obligations is dealt with by Art 9:102. There is a right to such performance, but this is limited by considerations which are similar to those limiting the exercise of the discretion to make the relevant order under English law. Thus, specific performance cannot be obtained where performance would be unlawful or impossible, or would cause the other party unreasonable effort or expense, or consists in the provision of work involving personal services. Nor can it be obtained where the other party can reasonably obtain performance from another source. This final exception clearly precludes the requirement of performance in a sale of goods contract where there is an available market for the goods in question. It does not, however, go as far as the English rule which only allows specific performance where damages would be an inadequate remedy.[210] In practice, however, 'termination and damages will often satisfy [the claimant's] requirements faster and more easily than enforcement of performance'.[211]

The right to performance under Art 9:101 is intended to cover negative obligations, as well as positive ones[212] – so that it will cover the area dealt with by injunctions under English law, that is, where a party is ordered *not* to act in a way which is precluded by their contractual obligations.

The right to seek specific performance will be lost after a 'reasonable time'.[213]

18.10 FURTHER READING

Bridge, MG, 'Expectation damages and uncertain future losses', Chapter 17 in Beatson, J and Friedmann, D (eds), *Good Faith and Fault in Contract Law*, 1995, Oxford: Clarendon Press

Burrows, AS, *Remedies for Torts and Breach of Contract*, 3rd edn, 2004, Oxford: Oxford University Press

Cunnington, R, 'Should punitive damages be part of the judicial arsenal in contract cases?' (2006) 26 LS 369

Friedmann, D, 'Good faith and remedies for breach of contract', Chapter 16 in Beatson, J and Friedmann, D (eds), *Good Faith and Fault in Contract Law*, 1995, Oxford: Clarendon Press

209 Thus taking a different approach to that adopted in *White and Carter (Councils) v McGregor* [1962] AC 413; [1961] 3 All ER 1178 – above, 18.5.6.
210 Lando and Beale, 2000, p 398.
211 Ibid.
212 Ibid, p 394.
213 Article 9:102(3).

Fuller, L and Perdue, W, 'The reliance interest in contract damages' (1936) 46 Yale LJ 52

Harris, D, Campbell, D and Halson, R, *Remedies in Contract and Tort*, 2nd edn, 2002, London: Butterworths

Harris, D, Ogus, A and Phillips, J, 'Contract remedies and the consumer surplus' (1979) 95 LQR 581

Hedley, S, ' "Very much the wrong people": the House of Lords and publication of spy memoirs' [2000] Web JCLI

McKendrick, E and Graham, M, 'The sky's the limit: contractual damages for non-pecuniary loss' [2002] LMCLQ 161

O'Sullivan, J, 'Loss and gain at greater depth: the implications of the *Ruxley* decision', Chapter 1 in Rose, F (ed), *Failure of Contracts, Contractual Restitutionary and Proprietary Consequences*, 1997, Oxford: Hart Publishing

Reece, H, 'Loss of chances in the law' (1996) 59 MLR 188

Sandy, D, 'Spies, rock stars and restitutionary damages' (2003) 153 NLJ 723

19 RESTITUTION

CONTENTS

19.1 OVERVIEW

This chapter is concerned with situations where a contract has failed for some reason, and one of the parties seeks to recover (hence 'restitution') either money paid or compensation for a benefit transferred. The order of treatment is:

- Recovery of money. The situations where money may be recoverable include:
  - where there has been a total failure of consideration (for example, a party paying money has received no part of what was bargained for);
  - payment made on the basis of mistake of fact (for example, where a contract is void for a common mistake);
  - under the principle approved in *Kleinwort Benson Ltd v Lincoln City Council*, where a payment was made under a mistake of law;
  - where money has been paid to a third party for the benefit of the defendant.
- Recovery of compensation for a benefit. The payment will be on a *quantum meruit* basis. This may arise, for example:
  - where a contract has been broken, and the claimant would otherwise be without a remedy;

- □ where the contract was void;
- □ where the parties have failed to finalise their agreement (for example, as a result of exchanging inconsistent terms).

19.2 THE NATURE OF THE CONCEPT

The topics to be covered in this chapter have close links with those dealt with Chapter 18. We are concerned again with ways in which a person can seek compensation for losses or, perhaps more accurately, avoid suffering a loss. In this case, however, we are dealing with situations which have a close connection with contract, but where the standard contract remedies are unavailable because the agreement has failed in some way, other than as a result of breach by one of the parties. This might be because their attempt to make a binding agreement has been deemed to be void *ab initio* (for example, as a result of a common mistake),[1] or because their negotiations have never succeeded in reaching the stage of a mutually acceptable contract. We are therefore concerned with situations which have some relationship with contract (which is the reason why in the past this area has been know as 'quasi-contract') but which, strictly speaking, fall outside its remit. This area can be regarded as part of a more general area of law, which has come to be known as 'restitution'.[2] We have looked at this concept in Chapter 18 in respect of the award of damages on a 'restitutionary basis' for breach of contract. Here we are concerned with the areas where restitution may be awarded to parties where there is no breach of contract. Central to this more general concept is the idea of 'unjust enrichment'. Restitution comprises a body of rules for recovery of money or property in order to prevent a person becoming 'unjustly enriched'. As Lord Wright put it in *Fibrosa Spolka Ackyjna v Fairbairn Lawson Combe Barbour Ltd*:[3]

> It is clear that any civilised system of law is bound to provide remedies for what has been called unjust enrichment, or unjust benefit, that is, to prevent a man from retaining the money of, or some benefit derived from, another which it is against his conscience he should keep.

It is English law's response to this requirement in situations which are closely related to contract that we are concerned with in the rest of this chapter. There are two main topics to consider: the recovery of money, and the payment for work which has been done.

---

1 For which, see Chapter 11, 11.5.
2 The seminal work on this area is Goff and Jones, 1993. See also Birks, 1989; Burrows, 1993; Rose, 1997. The treatment in this chapter is only an outline of the relevant principles: for more detailed consideration, the reader is referred to one of the specialist restitution texts.
3 [1943] AC 32; [1942] 2 All ER 122.

19.3 RECOVERY OF MONEY

The transfer of money outside a contractual relationship raises particular problems. If I give you possession of my car in connection with a contract which turns out to be void, I can maintain an action for the recovery of it relying on my continuing rights of ownership, but with the transfer of money the position is more complicated. There will not be any possibility of identifying the particular notes or coins which have been transferred, or of 'unmixing' funds from a bank account into which they have been paid. In other words, the money itself has become the property of the person to whom it has been transferred, and the most that is left is the obligation to repay an equivalent sum. There are four situations where the possibility of such recovery is clearly recognised: (1) where there is a total failure of consideration; (2) where the money was transferred under a mistake of fact; (3) where the money was transferred under a mistake of law; and (4) where money has been paid to a third party for the benefit of the defendant.

19.3.1 Total failure of consideration

One example of this situation has already been discussed in Chapter 16, in relation to the doctrine of frustration. As we saw there, the House of Lords, in *Fibrosa Spolka Ackyjna v Fairbairn Lawson Combe Barbour Ltd*,[4] accepted that if a party who had paid money under a frustrated contract had received nothing in return, the money could be recovered. The rule is thus that the claimant must have received nothing of what had been contracted for or, rather, that the defendant has not performed any part of the contractual duties in respect of which payment is due.[5] If there has been partial performance of any kind, this remedy will not be available.

As we saw in the *Fibrosa* case itself, this rule has the potential to cause a certain amount of injustice, in that the defendant who has used the money to prepare for performance may lose out. It was in part for this reason that the procedure for a rather more equitable distribution of losses was introduced in the frustration area by the Law Reform (Frustrated Contracts) Act 1943.[6]

The action based on a total failure of consideration has also been used, not without controversy, in the sale of goods area. In the cases of *Rowland v Divall*[7] and *Butterworth v Kingsway Motors*,[8] discussed in Chapter 8,[9] it was used to allow the recovery of the full purchase price from the sellers of cars who, unwittingly, did not have the right to sell at the relevant time, even though the buyer had had some use of the

---

4 [1943] AC 32; [1942] 2 All ER 122. See 16.5.2.
5 See the comments of Lord Goff in *Stocznia Gdanska SA v Latvian Shipping Co* [1998] 1 All ER 882.
6 See 16.6.
7 [1923] 2 KB 500.
8 [1954] 1 WLR 1286.
9 See 8.6.10.

car. The fact that transfer of ownership, the main object of a contract for the sale of goods, had not taken place meant that there was a 'total failure of consideration'.

In a contract to design and construct an object, and then to transfer it to the buyer, as opposed to simply a contract of sale, the failure to transfer ownership will not amount to a total failure of consideration. This was confirmed by the House of Lords in *Stocznia Gdanska SA v Latvian Shipping Co*,[10] applying *Hyundai Heavy Industries Co Ltd v Papadopoulos*.[11] The contract was for the construction and supply of a number of ships, and payments were made in instalments. The ships were never completed or transferred, but it was held by the House of Lords that the shipyard was entitled to resist a claim by the buyers, based on a total failure of consideration, for recovery of the instalment payments.

In cases outside the sale of goods area, the fact that property has been used by the claimant (for example, by his or her going into residence under a tenancy) may well prevent a claim based on a total failure of consideration.[12]

19.3.2 Mistake of fact

Money paid under a mistake of fact will be recoverable, provided that the mistake is as to a fact which, if true, would have legally,[13] or morally,[14] obliged the claimant to pay the money or, at least, is sufficiently serious to justify the requirement of repayment. Where a contract is void as a result of being based on a common mistake of fact (such as a false belief in the existence of the subject matter), then recovery will certainly be possible. Other situations where recovery has been held to be possible include mistaken payments under insurance policies. Thus, in *Norwich Union Fire Insurance Society Ltd v Price Ltd*,[15] payment was made on the basis that a cargo of fruit had been destroyed, whereas in fact it had been resold because it was becoming overripe. Recovery of the payment was allowed. Similarly, in *Kelly v Solari*,[16] payment was made on a life insurance policy as a result of the company failing to realise that the final premium had not been paid. Although it might be argued that this was something of which the company should have been aware, recovery of the payment was allowed.

Lord Goff has suggested that recovery under this head will not be possible if the payer intended the payee to benefit in any event; or there is good consideration from the payee (such as the discharge of a debt); or the payee has changed his or her position in good faith as a result of the payment.[17] As far as payment to discharge an existing debt

---

10 [1998] 1 All ER 882.
11 [1980] 2 All ER 29.
12 *Hunt v Silk* (1804) 5 East 449; 102 ER 1142.
13 *Aiken v Short* (1856) 1 H & N 210; 156 ER 1180.
14 *Larner v LCC* [1949] 2 KB 683.
15 [1934] AC 455.
16 (1841) 9 M & W 54; 152 ER 24.
17 *Barclays Bank Ltd v Simms and Cooke (Southern) Ltd* [1980] QB 677; [1979] 3 All ER 522.

is concerned, it was confirmed by the Court of Appeal in *Lloyds Bank plc v Independent Insurance Co Ltd*[18] that such a change of position would constitute a good defence to a claim for restitution based on a mistake of fact.

19.3.3 Mistake of law

Until 1998, it was accepted that it was not possible to reclaim money paid under a mistake of law. This was based on the maxim that 'ignorance of the law is no excuse', as applied in this situation in *Bilbie v Lumley*.[19] However, in *Kleinwort Benson Ltd v Lincoln City Council*,[20] the House of Lords overturned this rule, and held that in certain circumstances money paid under a mistake of law could be recovered. In coming to this conclusion, it was following developments which had taken place in other parts of the common law world, and recommendations for change from the Law Commission.[21] The factual background to this decision was 'interest rate swap' agreements entered into by various local authorities during the 1980s as a means of raising money. The agreements involved the advance of a capital sum by the lending bank, coupled with an agreement for mutual payment of interest on a notional sum, one side paying at a fixed rate, the other at a market rate. A balancing of liabilities was to take place at various points. Clearly, the arrangement involved a prediction (almost a 'gamble') as to how market rates would change vis à vis the fixed rate. In *Hazell v Hammersmith and Fulham LBC*,[22] it was held by the House of Lords that agreements of this kind were *ultra vires* as regards the local authorities, and therefore unlawful and void. The question then arose as to whether the bank could recover the money that it had lent. The local authorities denied any liability to repay, on the basis that the money had been paid under a mistake of law and was therefore irrecoverable.

The House of Lords in *Kleinwort Benson*, with Lord Goff delivering the main speech, held that it was time to recognise that there could be recovery of money paid under a mistake of law, where this would otherwise lead to the unjust enrichment of the recipient. The recipient's honest belief in his entitlement to the money would not in itself provide a defence. The fact that the recipient had changed his position in reliance on the payment might do so. The test is whether it would be unjust to allow the recipient to retain the benefit of the money paid.

The House also confirmed that this new principle would apply where the payments were made 'under a settled understanding of the law which is subsequently departed from by judicial decision'.[23] Thus, the fact that at the time of the payment the law appeared to be clear provides no defence to an action for recovery if a court

---

18 [1999] 2 WLR 986.
19 (1802) 2 East 469; 102 ER 448.
20 [1999] 2 AC 349; [1998] 4 All ER 513.
21 Law Commission, 1994.
22 [1992] 2 AC 1; [1991] 1 All ER 545.
23 [1999] 2 AC 349, p 389; [1998] 4 All ER 513, p 544.

subsequently rules that the understanding amounted to an incorrect view of the law. Given that judicial decisions have a declaratory and retrospective effect (unlike statutes), there was no need to limit the principle in this way. The House in *Hazell,* having ruled that interest swap agreements were *ultra vires* local authorities, held that all such agreements which had been entered into up to that time had therefore been made on the basis of a mistake of law. Finally, the House held that it was irrelevant to the application of the principle that the transaction concerned had been fully performed.

The decision in *Kleinwort Benson* is clearly a very significant addition to the law of restitution. The precise way in which it will operate in practice remains to be seen. The House of Lords was only concerned with the preliminary issue of whether an action for recovery based on mistake of law was possible, not with how this should apply to the particular transactions entered into by the local authorities. There has been one reported case in which the principle has been applied: *Nurdin and Peacock plc v DB Ramsden & Co Ltd.*[24] This concerned overpayments made under a lease. After these had been made for some months, the plaintiffs discovered that they had been paying too much. Up to that point, the payments were made under a mistake of fact. The final payment, however, was made with full knowledge of the situation, but on the basis of incorrect legal advice to the effect that it would automatically be repayable if proceedings being taken against the defendant were successful. This was therefore made under a mistake of law. The court held that recovery for mistake of law did not depend on a belief on the part of the payer that there was a liability to make the payment. The final payment was recoverable as having been made on the basis of a mistake of law.

19.3.4 Payment to a third party

What is the position in respect of money which has been paid by the claimant to a third party, but which benefits the defendant? Can the claimant recover this money from the defendant? One major limitation on this is that the claimant must have been acting not purely as a volunteer, but under some constraint. A mother who decides, out of the goodness of her heart, to settle her son's debts, cannot then claim restitution from the son.

This rule was applied in a commercial context in *Macclesfield Corp v Great Central Railway,*[25] where the plaintiffs carried out repairs on a bridge which the defendants were legally obliged (but had refused) to maintain. The plaintiffs were regarded as acting purely as volunteers, and so could not recover from the defendants the money spent on the work. An example of a situation where recovery was allowed is *Exall v Partridge.*[26] The plaintiff in this case paid off arrears of rent owed by the defendant. The reason for doing this was to avoid the seizure by bailiffs of a carriage belonging

---

24 [1999] 1 All ER 941.
25 [1911] 2 KB 528.
26 (1799) 8 TR 308; 101 ER 1405.

to the plaintiff which had been left on the defendant's premises. The plaintiff was thus acting under a constraint, and not simply as a volunteer, and could recover his money.

A second limitation is that the *defendant* must have been under a legal obligation to pay the money. In *Exall v Partridge*, for example, the obligation on the defendant was to pay his rent. In *Metropolitan Police District Receiver v Croydon Corp*,[27] however, the plaintiff failed to satisfy this requirement. A policeman had been injured and could not work, but the plaintiffs, the police authority, were obliged to continue to pay his wages. The policeman sued the defendants for negligence and recovered compensation. This did not, however, contain any element for loss of wages, since the policeman was still being paid by the plaintiffs. The plaintiffs sought to recover the cost of the policeman's wages from the defendants. Their argument was that they had made payments to the policeman which were the responsibility of the defendants, since it was their negligence which had caused the policeman to be off work. Their payment of the policeman's wages was thus a benefit to the defendants. The court, however, took the view that the defendants had no legal obligation to pay the policeman's wages. Their only obligation was to compensate him for his losses. Since he had lost no wages, there was no legal obligation in this respect, and therefore the plaintiffs could not recover.

FOR THOUGHT

Would the outcome of this case have been different if the police authority had not been obliged to continue to pay the wages, but had done so as a gesture of good will to a valued employee?

19.4 RECOVERY OF COMPENSATION FOR A BENEFIT

The claimant, rather than paying money to the defendant, may have done work, or provided some other benefit. Since, by definition, any compensation for such a benefit is not defined by any agreement between the parties (because we are concerned with the situation where there is no contract), the plaintiff will be seeking compensation on a *quantum meruit* basis.[28] An analogy may be drawn with the remedy under s 1(3) of the Law Reform (Frustrated Contracts) Act 1943,[29] which empowers the court to award a sum that is just and reasonable in all the circumstances on the basis of the benefit received by the other party. There are three situations to consider, namely: where a contract has been broken; where it is void; and where agreement is never reached.

---

27 [1957] 2 QB 154; [1957] 1 All ER 78.
28 That is, the payment of an amount equivalent to the value of the benefit conferred.
29 See 16.6.2.

19.4.1 Contract broken

A broken contract will not usually give rise to consideration of a *quantum meruit* remedy, but an example of how it can be appropriate can be seen in *Planché v Colburn*.[30] The plaintiff had been engaged to write a book on Costume and Ancient Armour. He carried out research and did some of the writing. The defendants then abandoned the project. There were some further negotiations to try to renew the contract, but these failed, and the plaintiff then sued for breach of contract, and for a *quantum meruit*. The action for breach of contract would have been unlikely to succeed, because it appears that the original contract was 'entire',[31] with a specific sum payable on completion of the book. The court held that, nevertheless, the plaintiff could recover on a *quantum meruit* basis, and awarded him 50 guineas.

This type of action is likely to be unusual, but is clearly available in appropriate circumstances where a contract has come to an end, and the claimant would otherwise be without a remedy. It is difficult to see, however, that in *Planché v Colburn*, the defendant had received any benefit from the plaintiff's work, since a half-finished book was of no use to him. This also makes it difficult to fit this case within the general principle of 'unjust enrichment', since the defendant had not in fact been 'enriched'.[32]

19.4.2 Contract void

We have seen that money paid under a void contract is recoverable. Equally, work which has been done may be compensated on a *quantum meruit* basis. In *Craven-Ellis v Canons Ltd*,[33] for example, the proper procedures were not followed in appointing the plaintiff as managing director. As a result, his appointment was a nullity. Before this was discovered, however, the plaintiff rendered services for the company in accordance with the agreement which he thought had been entered into. Since the company had benefited from this work, he was allowed to recover on a *quantum meruit* claim. This enabled him to claim reasonable remuneration for the work which he had done. Similarly, in *Mohammed v Alaga*,[34] the Court of Appeal held that a person who had provided translation services under an illegal, and therefore void, fee sharing agreement with a firm of solicitors could claim on a *quantum meruit* basis for the work actually done.[35]

19.4.3 Agreement never reached

It is not uncommon in relation to complex contracts, such as those entered into in the building or engineering industries, for work to be done on a project prior to the

---

30 (1831) 8 Bing 14; 131 ER 305.
31 See 17.3.4, above.
32 See the criticism of this case in Harris, Campbell and Halson, 2002, pp 236–37.
33 [1936] 2 KB 403.
34 [1999] 3 All ER 699.
35 See further Chapter 14, 14.6.

formalisation of a contract. Although an 'agreement to agree' will not be enforced,[36] no particular problem arises with this as long as a contract does materialise at some point. The Court of Appeal's decision in *Trentham Ltd v Archital Luxfer*[37] confirms that in such a situation the courts will be happy to allow the eventual contract to act retrospectively, and govern the work that has been done. Moreover, that decision has also relaxed to some extent the rules concerning formation, making it more likely that a binding contract will be found. Nevertheless, there will still be situations where no contract exists, and it becomes necessary to decide whether, and if so on what basis, compensation can be recovered for work that has been done.[38]

Two principles seem to govern this area. First, recovery will be allowed where the work has been requested by the defendant. Second, if the work has been done without a request, but has been 'freely accepted', it seems likely that the defendant will be expected to pay something for it. In *William Lacey (Hounslow) Ltd v Davis*,[39] the plaintiffs had submitted the lowest tender for a building contract, and had been led to believe that they would be awarded it. At the defendant's request, they then prepared various plans and estimates. The defendants then decided not to proceed. The court argued by analogy from *Craven-Ellis v Canons*.[40] If it was possible to recover in relation to work done on a void contract, Barry J thought that the same should be true of:[41]

> . . . work done which was to be paid for out of the proceeds of a contract which both parties erroneously believed was about to be made. In neither case was the work done gratuitously, and in both cases the party from whom the payment was sought requested the work and obtained the benefit of it.

The plaintiffs were therefore allowed to recover a reasonable sum for the work done.

This line was followed in *British Steel Corp v Cleveland Bridge and Engineering Co Ltd*.[42] The project in this case was for the construction and delivery of a set of cast steel nodes. A 'letter of intent' was issued by the defendants, indicating that they intended to enter into the contract with the plaintiffs. The defendants then requested the plaintiffs to start work on the construction of the nodes. It proved impossible to reach agreement, however, on a number of major terms, including the price. Despite this, all the nodes were eventually constructed and delivered, though some were delivered late. The plaintiffs claimed for the value of the nodes. It was clear that there was no contract. On the other hand, the defendants had requested the work to be done, and had freely accepted the nodes when they were delivered. As a result, the plaintiffs were able to succeed in a

36 *Courtney and Fairbairn v Tolaini Bros (Hotels) Ltd* [1975] 1 WLR 297.
37 [1993] 1 Lloyd's Rep 25 – discussed above, 2.11.5.
38 The position as regards money paid will be governed by the rules discussed above, 19.3.
39 [1957] 2 All ER 712.
40 [1936] 2 KB 403 – see above, 19.4.2.
41 [1957] 2 All ER 712, p 719.
42 [1984] 1 All ER 504.

restitutionary claim for the value of what had been supplied. It should be noted, however, that the defendants' counterclaim for compensation for late delivery failed. Since there was no contract, there could be no obligation concerning the date for delivery, and therefore there was no basis on which such a claim could succeed. This indicates that although the remedy of restitution does allow the courts to avoid unjust enrichment, it is not sufficiently flexible as yet to allow the courts to take into consideration all the circumstances, and distribute losses and benefits between the parties accordingly.

19.5 FURTHER READING

Birks, P, *An Introduction to the Law of Restitution*, 1989, Oxford: Clarendon Press

Burrows, AS, *The Law of Restitution*, 1993, London: Butterworths

Goff, R and Jones, G, *The Law of Restitution*, 4th edn, 1993, London: Sweet & Maxwell

Law Commission, *Restitution: Mistakes of Law and* Ultra Vires *Public Authority Receipts and Payments*, Report No 227, 1994

Rose, F (ed), *Failure of Contracts, Contractual Restitutionary and Proprietary Consequences*, 1997, Oxford: Hart Publishing

BIBLIOGRAPHY

Adams, J, Beyleveld, D and Brownsword, R, 'Privity of contract – the benefits and burdens of law reform' (1997) 60 MLR 238

Adams, J and Brownsword, R, 'The Unfair Contract Terms Act: a decade of discretion' (1988) 104 LQR 94

Adams, J and Brownsword, R, 'Contract, consideration and the critical path' (1990a) 53 MLR 536

Adams, J and Brownsword, R, 'Privity and the concept of a network contract' (1990b) 10 Legal Studies 12

Adams, J and Brownsword, R, *Key Issues in Contract*, 1995, London: Butterworths

Adams, J and Brownsword, R, *Understanding Contract Law*, 4th edn, 2004, London: Sweet & Maxwell

Allen, D, *Misrepresentation*, 1988, London: Sweet & Maxwell

Allen, D, 'The gentleman's agreement in legal theory and in modern practice' [2000] Anglo-American Law Review 204

Atiyah, PS, '*Couturier v Hastie* and the sale of non-existent goods' (1957) 73 LQR 340

Atiyah, PS, 'Contracts, promises and the law of obligations' (1978) 94 LQR 193

Atiyah, PS, *The Rise and Fall of Freedom of Contract*, 1979, Oxford: Clarendon Press

Atiyah, PS, 'Economic duress and the overborne will' (1982) 98 LQR 197

Atiyah, PS, *Essays on Contract*, 1986, Oxford: Clarendon Press

Atiyah, PS, *An Introduction to the Law of Contract*, 5th edn, 1995, Oxford: Clarendon Press

Atiyah, PS, Adams, JN and MacQueen, H, *The Sale of Goods*, 11th edn, 2005, Harlow: Pearson Education

Auchmuty, R, 'The Rhetoric of Equality and the Problem of Heterosexuality', Chapter 3 in Mulcahy, L and Wheeler, S (eds), *Feminist Perspectives on Contract Law*, 2005, London: Glasshouse Press

Baker, JH, 'From sanctity of contract to reasonable expectation' [1979] 32 Current Legal Problems 17

Barendt, E, 'Exclusion clauses: incorporation and interpretation' (1972) 35 MLR 644

Beale, H, *Remedies for Breach of Contract*, 1980, London: Sweet & Maxwell

Beale, H, 'Penalties in termination provisions' (1988) 104 LQR 355

Beale, H, 'Unfair contracts in Britain and Europe' [1989] Current Legal Problems 197

Beale, H, 'Damages in lieu of rescission for misrepresentation' (1995a) 111 LQR 60

Beale, H, 'Points on misrepresentation' (1995b) 111 LQR 385

Beale, H, Bishop, W and Furmston, M, *Contract Cases and Materials*, 4th edn, 2001, London: Butterworths

Beale, H and Dugdale, T, 'Contracts between businessmen' (1975) 2 Brit J Law & Society 45

Beatson, J, 'Reforming the law of contracts for the benefit of third parties: a second bite at the cherry' [1992] Current Legal Problems 1

Beatson, J and Friedmann, D (eds), *Good Faith and Fault in Contract Law*, 1995, Oxford: Clarendon Press

Bennett, HN, 'Statements of fact and statements of belief in insurance contract law and general contract law' (1998) 61 MLR 886

Beyleveld, D and Brownsword, R, 'Privity, transitivity and rationality' (1991) 54 MLR 48

Bigwood, R, 'Pre-contractual misrepresentation and the limits of the principle in *With v O'Flanagan*' [2005] CLJ 94

Birks, P, *An Introduction to the Law of Restitution*, 1989, Oxford: Clarendon Press

Birks, P and Chin Nyuk Yin, 'On the nature of undue influence', Chapter 3 in Beatson, J and Friedmann, D (eds), *Good Faith and Fault in Contract Law*, 1995, Oxford: Clarendon Press

Bishop, WD, 'The contract-tort boundary and the economics of insurance' (1983) 12 JLS 241

Bowstead – see Reynolds, 2005

Bradgate, R, 'Unreasonable standard terms' (1997) 60 MLR 582

Bridge, MG, 'Expectation damages and uncertain future losses', Chapter 17 in Beatson, J and Friedmann, D (eds), *Good Faith and Fault in Contract Law*, 1995, Oxford: Clarendon Press

Bridge, MG, *The Sale of Goods*, 1998, Oxford: Oxford University Press

Bridge, MG, 'Good faith in commercial contracts', Chapter 7 in Brownsword, R, Hird, NJ and Howells, G (eds), *Good Faith in Contract*, 1999, Aldershot: Dartmouth

Bright, S, 'Winning the battle against unfair contract terms' (2000) 20 LS 331

Brown, I, 'The letter of comfort: placebo or promise?' [1990] JBL 281

Brown, I, 'The contract to negotiate: a thing writ in water?' [1992] JBL 353

Brown, I, 'The agent's apparent authority: paradigm or paradox?' [1995] JBL 360

Brownsword, R, 'Retrieving reasons, retrieving rationality? A new look at the right to withdraw for breach of contract' (1992) Journal of Contract Law 83

Brownsword, R, 'Towards a rational law of contract', in Willhelmson, T (ed), *Perspectives of Critical Contract Law*, 1993, Aldershot: Dartmouth

Brownsword, R, *Contract Law: Themes for the Twenty-First Century*, 2000, London: Butterworths

Brownsword, R, 'Individualism, cooperativism, and an ethic for European contract law' (2001) 64 MLR 628

Brownsword, R, 'After *Investors*: interpretation, expectation and the implicit dimension of the "new contextualism" ', Chapter 4 in Campbell, D, Collins, H and Wightman, J (eds), *Implicit Dimensions of Contract*, 2003, Oxford: Hart Publishing

Brownsword, R, Hird, NJ and Howells, G (eds), *Good Faith in Contract*, 1999, Aldershot: Dartmouth

Buckley, R, '*Walford v Miles*: false certainty about uncertainty – an Australian perspective' (1993) JCL 58

Buckley, R, 'Illegal transactions: chaos or discretion' (2000) 20 LS 155

Burrows, AS, 'Specific performance at the crossroads' (1984) 4 LS 102

Burrows, AS, *The Law of Restitution*, 1993, London: Butterworths

Burrows, AS, *Understanding the Law of Obligations*, 1998, Oxford: Hart Publishing

Burrows, AS, 'The Contracts (Rights of Third Parties) Act and its implications for commercial contracts' [2000] LMCLQ 540

Burrows, AS, *Remedies for Torts and Breach of Contract*, 3rd edn, 2004, Oxford: Oxford University Press

Buxton, R, 'The HRA and private law' (2000) 116 LQR 48

Campbell, D, 'The relational constitution of the discrete contract', Chapter 3 in Campbell, D and Vincent-Jones, P (eds), *Contract and Economic Organisation*, 1996, Aldershot: Dartmouth

Campbell, D (ed), *The Relational Theory of Contract: Selected Works of Ian Macneil*, 2001, London: Sweet & Maxwell

Campbell, D, Collins, H and Wightman, J (eds), *Implicit Dimensions of Contract*, 2003, Oxford: Hart Publishing

Campbell, D and Harris, D, 'Flexibility in long term contractual relationships: the role of cooperation' (1993) 20 J of Law and Soc 166

Campbell, D and Harris, D, 'In defence of breach: a critique of restitution and the performance interest' (2002) 22 LS 208

Campbell, D and Vincent-Jones, P (eds), *Contract and Economic Organisation*, 1996, Aldershot: Dartmouth

Cartwright, J, 'Damages for misrepresentation' [1987a] Conv 423

Cartwright, J, '*Solle v Butcher* and the doctrine of mistake in contract' (1987b) 103 LQR 584

Cartwright, J, *Unequal Bargaining*, 1991, Oxford: Oxford University Press

Cartwright, J, 'Remoteness of damage in contract and tort: a reconsideration' (1996) 55 CLJ 488

Chandler, A, 'Self-induced frustration, foreseeability and risk' [1990] NILQ 362

Chen-Wishart, M, *Unconscionable Bargains*, 1989, Wellington: Butterworths

Chen-Wishart, M, 'The *O'Brien* principle and substantive unfairness' (1997) 56 CLJ 60

Cheshire, Fifoot and Furmston's Law of Contract, by Furmston, M, 14th edn, 2001, London: Butterworths

Chitty on Contracts, Beale, H (ed), 29th edn, 2004, London: Sweet & Maxwell

Collins, H, *The Law of Contract*, 1st edn, 1986, London: Weidenfeld & Nicolson

Collins, H, 'Good faith in European contract law' (1994) 14 OJLS 229

Collins, H, 'Competing norms of contractual behaviour', Chapter 4 in Campbell, D and Vincent-Jones, P (eds), *Contract and Economic Organisation*, 1996, Aldershot: Dartmouth

Collins, H, *Regulating Contracts*, 1999, Oxford: Oxford University Press

Collins, H, *The Law of Contract*, 4th edn, 2003, London: Butterworths

Conway, H, 'Prenuptial contracts' (1995) 145 NLJ 1290

Cooke, R, review of *Consensus ad Idem: Essays in the Law of Contract in Honour of Guenter Treitel* (1998) 114 LQR 505

Coote, B, *Exception Clauses*, 1964, London: Sweet & Maxwell

Coote, B, 'Validation under the Illegal Contracts Act' (1992) 15 NZULR 80

Coote, B, 'The Illegal Contracts Act 1970', Chapter 3 in *New Zealand Law Commission, Contract Statutes Review*, 1993

Coote, B, '*Dunlop v Lambert*: the search for a rationale' (1998) JCL 91

Coote, B, 'Consideration and variations: a different solution' (2004) 120 LQR 19

Cope, M, *Duress, Undue Influence and Unconscientious Bargains*, 1985, North Ryde, NSW: Lawbook Co

Cretney, S, 'The little woman and the big bad bank' (1992) 108 LQR 534

Cumberbatch, J, 'In freedom's cause: the contract to negotiate' (1992) 12 OJLS 586

Cunnington, R, 'Should punitive damages be part of the judicial arsenal in contract cases?' (2006) 26 LS 369

Dalton, C, 'An essay in the deconstruction of contract doctrine' (1985) 94 Yale LJ 997

Danzig, R, '*Hadley v Baxendale*: a study of the industrialisation of the law' (1975) 4 J Leg St 249

Dean, M, 'Unfair contract terms: the European approach' (1993) 56 MLR 581

Denning, A, *The Discipline of Law*, 1979, London: Butterworths

Dockray, M, '*Cutter v Powell*: a trip outside the text' (2001) 117 LQR 664

Eisenberg, MA, 'Relational contracts', Chapter 11 in Beatson, J and Friedmann, D (eds), *Good Faith and Fault in Contract Law*, 1995, Oxford: Clarendon Press

Enman, SR, 'Doctrines of unconscionability in England, Canada and the Commonwealth' (1987) 16 Anglo-Am LR 191

Enonchong, N, *Illegal Transactions*, 1998, London: Lloyd's of London Press

Evans, DM, 'The Anglo-American mailing rule' (1966) 15 ICLQ 553

Fehlberg, B, 'The husband, the bank, the wife and her signature' (1994) 57 MLR 467

Flannigan, R, 'Privity – the end of an era (error)' (1987) LQR 564

Freeman, M, 'Contracting in the haven: *Balfour v Balfour* revisited', in Halson, R (ed), *Exploring the Boundaries of Contract*, 1996, London: Dartmouth

Fried, C, *Contract as Promise*, 1981, Cambridge, Mass: Harvard University Press

Friedmann, D, 'Good faith and remedies for breach of contract', Chapter 16 in Beatson, J and Friedmann, D (eds), *Good Faith and Fault in Contract Law*, 1995, Oxford: Clarendon Press

Fuller, L and Perdue, W, 'The reliance interest in contract damages' (1936) 46 Yale LJ 52

Furmston, MP, 'The case of the insistent performer' (1962) 25 MLR 364

Furmston, MP, 'The analysis of illegal contracts' (1966) 16 Univ of Toronto LJ 267

Furmston, MP, 'The Illegal Contracts Act 1970 – an English view' (1972–73) 5 NZULR 151

Gardner, S, 'Trashing with *Trollope*: a deconstruction of the postal rules' (1992) 12 OJLS 170

Gee, S, 'The interpretation of commercial contracts' (2001) 117 LQR 358

Gilmore, G, *The Death of Contract*, 1974, Columbus: Ohio State University Press

Goff, R and Jones, G, *The Law of Restitution*, 4th edn, 1993, London: Sweet & Maxwell

Goodhart, AL, 'Measure of damages when a contract is repudiated' (1962) 78 LQR 263

Goodrich, P, 'The posthumous life of the postal rule: requiem and revival of *Adams v Lindsell*', Chapter 4 in Mulcahy, L and Wheeler, S, *Feminist Perspectives on Contract Law*, 2005, London: Glasshouse Press

Griffith, JAG, *Politics of the Judiciary*, 5th edn, 1997, London: Fontana

Grodecki, JK, '*In pari delicto potior est conditio defendentis*' (1955) 71 LQR 254

Halson, R, 'Sailors, sub-contractors and consideration' (1990) 106 LQR 183

Halson, R, 'Opportunism, economic duress and contractual modifications' (1991) 107 LQR 649

Halson, R, 'The offensive limits of promissory estoppel' [1999] LMCLQ 256

Halson, R, *Contract Law*, 2001, Harlow: Pearson Education

Hamson, CJ, 'The reform of consideration' (1938) 54 LQR 233

Handley, KR, 'Exclusion clauses for fraud' (2003) 119 LQR 537

Hare, C, 'Identity mistakes: a missed opportunity' (2004) 67 MLR 993

Harland, D, 'Unconscionable and unfair contracts: an Australian perspective', Chapter 11 in Brownsword, R, Hird, NJ and Howells, G (eds), *Good Faith in Contract*, 1999, Aldershot: Dartmouth

Harris, D, 'Penalties and forfeiture: contractual remedies specified by the parties' [1990] LCMLQ 158

Harris, D, 'Incentives to perform, or break contracts' [1992] Current Legal Problems 29

Harris, D, Ogus, A and Phillips, J, 'Contract remedies and the consumer surplus' (1979) 95 LQR 581

Harris, D, Campbell, D and Halson, R, *Remedies in Contract and Tort*, 2nd edn, 2002, London: Butterworths

Haycroft, AM and Waksman, DM, 'Frustration and restitution' [1984] JBL 207

Hedley, S, 'Keeping contract in its place: *Balfour v Balfour* and the enforceability of informal agreements' (1985) 5 OJLS 391

Hedley, S, 'Carriage by sea: frustration and *force majeure*' (1990) 49 CLJ 209

Hedley, S, ' "Very much the wrong people": the House of Lords and publication of spy memoirs' [2000] 4 Web JCLI

Hepple, B, 'Intention to create legal relations' (1970) CLJ 122

Hird, NJ and Blair, A, 'Minding your own business – *Williams v Roffey* revisited' [1996] JBL 254

Hooley, R, 'Damages and the Misrepresentation Act 1967' (1991) 107 LQR 547

Horwitz, M, 'The historical foundations of modern contract law' (1974) 87 Harv LR 917

Howarth, W, 'The meaning of objectivity in contract' (1984) 100 LQR 205

Hudson, AH, 'Retraction of letters of acceptance' (1966) 82 LQR 169

Hudson, AH, 'Mental incapacity revisited' [1986] Conveyancer and Property Lawyer 178

Hunt, M, 'The horizontal effect of the HRA' [1998] PL 423

Jackson, B, *Law, Fact and Narrative Coherence*, 1988, Liverpool: Deborah Charles

Jaffey, P, 'Efficiency, disgorgement and reliance in contract: a comment on Campbell and Harris' (2002) 22 LS 570

Kronman, A, 'Mistake disclosure, information and the law of contracts' (1978) 7 J Leg Stud 1

Kronman, A, 'Paternalism and the law of contract' (1983) Yale LJ 763

Kronman, A and Posner, R, *The Economics of Contract Law*, 1979, Boston: Little, Brown

Lando, O and Beale, H (eds), *The Principles of European Contract Law*, Parts I and II, 2000, The Hague: Kluwer Law International

Law Commission, *Transfer of Land: Formalities for Deeds and Escrows*, Working Paper No 93, 1985

Law Commission, *Law of Contract: the Parol Evidence Rule*, Report No 154, Cmnd 9700, 1986

Law Commission, *Deeds and Escrows*, Report No 163, HC1, 1987

Law Commission, *Privity of Contract: Contracts for the benefit of third parties*, Consultation Paper No 121, 1991

Law Commission, *Contributory Negligence as a Defence in Contract Law*, Report No 219, 1993

Law Commission, *Restitution: Mistakes of Law and* Ultra Vires *Public Authority Receipts and Payments*, Report No 227, 1994

Law Commission, *Illegal Transactions: the Effect of Illegality on Contracts and Trusts*, Consultation Paper No 154, 1999

Law Commission, *Unfair Terms in Contracts*, Law Com No 292, Scot Law Com No 199, Cm 6464, 2005

Law Reform Committee, *Transfer of Title to Chattels*, Twelfth Report, Cmnd 2958, 1966

Law Revision Committee, Sixth Interim Report, Cmd 5449, 1937

Leff, A, 'Economic analysis of law: some realism about nominalism' (1974) 60 Virginia LR 451

Lewis, R, 'Contracts between businessmen: reform of the law of firm offers' (1982) 9 Brit J Law & Society 153

Luther, P, 'Campbell, Espinasse and the sailors: text and context in the common law' (1999) 19 LS 526

Macaulay, S, 'Non-contractual relations in business' (1963) 28 Am Sociological Rev 35

Macdonald, E, 'Incorporation of contract terms by a consistent course of dealing' (1988) 8 LS 48

Macdonald, E, 'Exclusion clauses: the ambit of s 13(1) of the Unfair Contract Terms Act 1977' (1992) 12 LS 277

MacLeod, JK, 'Damages: reliance or expectancy interest' [1970] JBL 19

MacMillan, C, 'The end of the exception in *Dunlop v Lambert*?' [2001] LMCLQ 338

MacMillan, C, 'How temptation led to mistake: an explanation of *Bell v Lever Bros Ltd*' (2003) 119 LQR 625

MacMillan, C, 'Mistake as to identity clarified?' (2004) 120 LQR 369

Macneil, IR, 'Restatement (Second) of Contracts and Presentation' (1974) 60 Virginia LR 589

Macneil, IR, 'Contracts: adjustments of long term economic relations under classical, neo classical and relational contract law' (1978) 72 Northwestern UL Rev 854

Macneil, IR, 'Essays on the nature of contract' (1980) 10 South Carolina Central LJ 159

Macneil, IR, 'Efficient breach: circles in the sky' (1982) 68 Virginia LR 947

Macneil, IR, 'Relational contract theory as sociology: a reply to Professors Lindenberg and de Vos' (1987) 143 Journal of Institutional and Theoretical Economics 272

Macneil, IR, 'Contract remedies: a need for a better efficiency analysis' (1988) 144 Journal of Institutional and Theoretical Economics 6

Macneil, IR, 'Relational contract theory: challenges and queries' (2000) 94 Northwestern UL Rev 877

McClintock, R, 'Objectivity in contract' (1988–91) 6 Auckland UL Rev 317

McKendrick, E, 'The battle of the forms and the law of restitution' (1988) 8 OJLS 197

McKendrick, E (ed), *Force Majeure*, 2nd edn, 1995a, London: Lloyd's of London Press

McKendrick, E, 'The regulation of long term contracts in English law' (1995b), Chapter 12 in Beatson, J and Friedmann, D (eds), *Good Faith and Fault in Contract Law*, 1995b, Oxford: Clarendon Press

McKendrick, E, 'The interpretation of contracts: Lord Hoffman's re-statement' in Worthington, S (ed), *Commercial Law and Commercial Practice*, 2003, Oxford: Hart, 139

McKendrick, E and Graham, M, 'The sky's the limit: contractual damages for non-pecuniary loss' [2002] LMCLQ 161

McLaughlan, DW, 'Contract and commercial law reform in New Zealand' (1984–85) 11 NZULR 36

McLaughlin, G, 'Unconscionability and impracticality: reflections on two UCC indeterminacy principles' (1992) 14 Loyola Int & Comp LJ 439

McMeel, G, 'The rise of commercial construction in contract law' [1998] LMCLQ 382

Miller, CJ, '*Felthouse v Bindley* re-visited' (1972) 35 MLR 489

Mitchell, C, 'Leading a life of its own? The roles of reasonable expectation in contract law' (2003) 23 OJLS 639

Mitchell, P and Phillips, J, 'The contractual nexus: is reliance essential?' (2002) 22 OJLS 115

Monopolies Commission, *Report on the supply of petrol to retailers in the United Kingdom*, HC 265, 1965

Montrose, JL, 'The contract of sale in self-service stores' (1955) 4 Am J Comp Law 235

Mulcahy, L and Wheeler, S, *Feminist Perspectives on Contract Law*, 2005, London: Glasshhouse Press

Murdoch, JR, 'The nature of estate agency' (1975) 91 LQR 357

Neill, P, 'A key to lock-out agreements?' (1992) 108 LQR 405

Ogus, A, *The Law of Damages*, 1973, London: Butterworths

O'Sullivan, J, 'In defence of *Foakes v Beer*' (1996) 55 CLJ 219

O'Sullivan, J, 'Loss and gain at greater depth: the implications of the *Ruxley* decision', Chapter 1 in Rose, F (ed), *Failure of Contracts, Contractual Restitutionary and Proprietary Consequences*, 1997, Oxford: Hart Publishing

O'Sullivan, D, 'Developing *O'Brien*' (2002) 118 LQR 337

Peden, E, and Carter, JW, 'Incorporation of terms by signature: L'Estrange Rules!' (2005) 21 JCL 96

Phang, A, 'Common mistake in English law: the proposed merger of common law and equity' (1989) 9 LS 291

Phang, A, 'Implied terms revisited' [1990] JBL 394

Phang, A, 'Implied terms in English law: some recent developments' [1993] JBL 242

Phang, A, 'Specific performance – exploring the roots of settled practice' (1998a) 61 MLR 421

Phang, A, 'Implied terms, business efficacy and the officious bystander – a modern history' [1998b] JBL 1

Phang, A and Tjio, H, 'The uncertain boundaries of undue influence' [2002] LMCLQ 231

Pollock, F, *Principles of Contract Law*, 7th edn, 1902, London: Stevens

Poole, J, 'Damages for breach of contract – compensation and personal preferences: *Ruxley Electronics and Construction Ltd v Forsyth*' (1996) 59 MLR 272

Posner, R, 'Gratuitous promises in economics and law' (1977) 6 J Leg St 411

Posner, R, *The Economic Analysis of Law*, 4th edn, 1992, Boston: Little, Brown

Powell, J, *Essay upon the Law of Contracts and Agreements*, 1790, London: details unknown

Rawlings, R, 'The battle of the forms' (1979) 42 MLR 715

Reece, H, 'Loss of chances in the law' (1996) 59 MLR 188

Reynolds, FMB, 'Discharge of contract by breach' (1981) 97 LQR 541

Reynolds, FMB, 'Unfair contract terms' (1994) 110 LQR 3

Reynolds, FMB (ed), *Bowstead and Reynolds on Agency*, 18th edn, 2005, London: Sweet & Maxwell

Robertson, A (ed), *The Law of Obligations: Connections and Boundaries*, 2004, London: UCL Press

Rose, F (ed), *Failure of Contracts, Contractual Restitutionary and Proprietary Consequences*, 1997, Oxford: Hart Publishing

Ross, J, 'Setting the standards' (2001) 145 Sol Jo 650

Saintier, S, 'New developments in agency law' [1997] JBL 77

Samuel, G, 'Failure of long term contracts and the duty to re-negotiate – a comment', Chapter 11 in Rose, F (ed), *Failure of Contracts, Contractual Restitutionary and Proprietary Consequences*, 1997, Oxford: Hart Publishing

Sands, D, 'With this contract I thee wed' [1991] LSG 15 May, p 2

Sandy, D, 'Spies, rock stars and restitutionary damages' (2003) 153 NLJ 723

Schanze, E, 'Failure of long term contracts and the duty to re-negotiate', Chapter 10 in Rose, F (ed), *Failure of Contracts, Contractual Restitutionary and Proprietary Consequences*, 1997, Oxford: Hart Publishing

Shea, A, 'Discharge from performance of contracts by failure of condition' (1979) 42 MLR 623

Simpson, AWB (ed), *Oxford Essays in Jurisprudence*, 1973, Oxford: Oxford University Press

Simpson, AWB, *A History of the Common Law of Contract*, 1975a, Oxford: Clarendon Press

Simpson, AWB, 'Innovation in nineteenth century contract law' (1975b) 91 LQR 247

Simpson, AWB, 'The Horwitz thesis and the history of contracts' (1979) 46 U Chic LR 533

Simpson, AWB, 'The rise and fall of the legal treatise: legal principles and the forms of legal literature' (1981) 48 U Chic LR 632

Simpson, AWB, 'Quackery and contract law: the case of the Carbolic Smoke Ball' (1985) 14 J Leg St 345

Simpson, AWB, 'Contracts for cotton to arrive: the case of the two ships Peerless' (1989) 11 Cardozo L Rev 287

Smith, JC, 'Civil concepts in the criminal law' [1972] CLJ 197

Smith, JC, 'Contracts – mistake, frustration and implied terms' (1994) 110 LQR 400

Smith, SA, 'Reconstructing restraint of trade' (1995) OJLS 565

Smith, SA, 'In defence of substantive fairness' (1996) 112 LQR 138

Smith, SA, 'Contracting under pressure: a theory of duress' [1997a] CLJ 343

Smith, SA, 'Performance, punishment and the nature of contractual obligations' (1997b) 60 MLR 360

Smith, SA, 'Contracts for the benefit of third parties: in defence of the Third-Party Rule' (1997c) OJLS 643

Smith, SA, *Contract Theory*, 2004, Oxford: Clarendon Press

Smith, SA, *Atiyah's Introduction to the Law of Contract*, 6th edn, 2006, Oxford: Clarendon Press

Spencer, J, 'Signature, consent and the rule in *L'Estrange v Graucob*' (1973) 32 CLJ 104

Staughton, C, 'How do the courts interpret commercial contracts?' [1999] CLJ 303

Stevens, R 'The Contracts (Rights of Third Parties) Act 1999' (2004) 120 LQR 292

Stewart, A and Carter, JW, 'Frustrated contracts and statutory adjustment: the case for a reappraisal' [1992] CLJ 66

Steyn, J, 'Contract law: fulfilling the reasonable expectations of honest men' (1997) 113 LQR 433

Stone, R, 'Usual or ostensible authority: one concept or two?' [1993] JBL 325

Stone, R, *Law of Agency*, 1996, London: Cavendish Publishing

Stone, R, 'Withdrawal of offer to settle – Pt 36 of the Civil Procedure Rules 1998' (2001) 33 SLR 23

Stone, R, *Textbook on Civil Liberties and Human Rights*, 6th edn, 2006, Oxford: Oxford University Press

Tan, Cheng-Han 'Undisclosed principals and contract' (2004) 120 LQR 480

Thompson, MP, 'Representation to expectation: estoppel as a cause of action' (1983) 42 CLJ 257

Tiplady, M, 'The limits of undue influence' (1985) 48 MLR 579

Tjio, H, '*O'Brien* and unconscionability' (1997) 113 LQR 10

Trakman, L, 'Frustrated contracts and legal fictions' (1983) 46 MLR 39

Trebilcock, MJ, *The Common Law of Restraint of Trade*, 1986, London: Sweet & Maxwell

Trebilcock, MJ, *The Limits of Freedom of Contract*, 1993, Cambridge, Mass: Harvard University Press

Treitel, GH, 'Consideration: a critical analysis of Professor Atiyah's fundamental restatement' (1976) 50 Australian LJ 439

Treitel, GH, 'Damages on rescission for breach of contract' [1987] LCMLQ 143

Treitel, GH, 'Mistake in contract' (1988) 104 LQR 501

Treitel, GH, *Frustration and Force Majeure*, 1994, London: Sweet & Maxwell

Treitel, GH, 'Affirmation after repudiatory breach' (1998a) 114 LQR 22

Treitel, GH, 'Damages in respect of a third party's loss' (1998b) 114 LQR 527

Treitel, GH, 'Types of contractual terms', Chapter 3 in *Some Landmarks of Twentieth Century Contract Law*, 2002, Oxford: Clarendon Press

Treitel, GH, *The Law of Contract*, 11th edn, 2003, London: Sweet & Maxwell

Unberath, H, 'Third party losses and black holes: another view' (1999) 115 LQR 535

Unger, J, 'Self-service shops and the law of contract' (1953) 16 MLR 369

Unger, R, *The Critical Legal Studies Movement*, 1983, Cambridge, Mass: Harvard University Press

Vincent-Jones, P, 'The reception of Ian Macneil's work on contract in the UK', Chapter 3 in Campbell, D (ed), *The Relational Theory of Contract: Selected Works of Ian Macneil*, 2001, London: Sweet & Maxwell

Vogenauer, S and Weatherill, S, *The Harmonisation of European Contract Law*, 2006, Oxford: Hart Publishing

von Mehren, A, 'General limits on the use of contract', Vol vii, *International Encyclopaedia of Comparative Law*, 1982, The Hague: Mohr/Nijhoff

Waddams, S, 'Johanna Wagner and the rival opera houses' (2001) 117 LQR 431

Wade, HRW, 'Horizons of horizontality' (2000) 116 LQR 217

Wallace, D, 'Third party damage: no legal black hole' (1999) 115 LQR 394

Warwick, M, 'Misuse of the matrix' (2003) 153 NLJ 1579

Wedderburn, KW, 'Collateral contracts' [1959] CLJ 58

Wheeler, S and Shaw, J, *Contract Law Cases, Materials and Commentary*, 1994, Oxford: Clarendon Press

Whish, R, *Competition Law*, 5th edn, 2003, London: Butterworths

Wightman, J, *Contract: A Critical Commentary*, 1996, London: Pluto Press

Wightman, J, 'Negligent valuations and a drop in the property market: the limits of the expectation loss principle' (1998) 61 MLR 68

Wilhelmsson, T (ed), *Perspectives of Critical Contract Law*, 1993, Aldershot: Dartmouth

Wilkinson, HW, 'Unfair contract terms – not again?' (2000) 150 NLJ 1778

Williams, DC, 'A survey of recent case law' (1953) 10 NILQ 117

Williston, S, *Williston on Contracts*, 4th edn (edited by Lord, RA), 1990, New York: Lawyers Co-operative Publishing

Wilson, S and Woodley, M, 'Restraint, drafting and the rule in General Billposting' [1998] JBL 272

Wright, RA, *Legal Essays and Addresses*, 1939, Cambridge: Cambridge University Press

Yates, D, *Exclusion Clauses in Contracts*, 2nd edn, 1982, London: Sweet & Maxwell

Yates, D, 'Drafting *force majeure* and related clauses' (1991) 3 J of Cont L 186

INDEX

acceptance of offers 30, 52–3; auctions 50–2; battle of the forms 30, 55–6, 60; certainty and 30, 89–94; by conduct 61; distinction from counter-offer 53–4; by electronic communication 69–76; in ignorance of offer 81; inertia selling 63–4; internet transactions 74–6; postal 30, 65–9; recent developments 58–60; request for information 54–5; retraction of 85–9; by silence 62–5; termination of offers and 83–5; time of acceptance 72–3; traditional view 56–8; unilateral contracts 61, 76–83
actual undue influence 422, 425–6, 439–41
adjudication costs 19
advertisements 43–7
affirmation: risks of 561–2
agency 207–8; commercial agents 210, 220, 221; creation 208, 211–12; definition 207, 208–10; duties of agent 208, 217–20; duties of principal 208, 220–1; powers of agent 208, 212–15; privity and 208, 210–11; ratification 208, 215–17; relevance of labels 209–10; termination 208, 226–8; third party and agent 208, 223–6; third party and principal 208, 221–3; undue influence and 436
agreement: enforcement of see enforcement; formation of see formation of agreement; incomplete 91–3; unilateral contracts 81–2
ambiguity: construction of terms and 261
anticipatory breach of contract 536, 558–9
apparent authority of agent 214
apprenticeships 235–6
arbitration 488
authority of agent 208, 212–15; breach of implied warranty of 225–6

battle of the forms 30, 55–6, 60

Blue Pencil test 503–4
breach of contract 536, 547–55; anticipatory 536, 558–9; commercial destruction 558; economic duress and 414–16; effect 547–8, 559–62; instalment contracts 536, 556–8; long-term contracts 536, 555–6; Principles of European Contract Law (PECL) and 562–3; repudiatory 536, 548–58, 559–62; restraint of trade and 498–9; right of election 559–62
bribes 220

capacity 231–2; effects of entering into contract with minor 232, 238–40; intoxication and 232, 243; mental disability 232, 242–3; minors' contracts 233–8; minors' liability in tort 232, 240–2; reasons for limitations on 232–3
care: agents' duty of 218; modification of duty of care 201–2
categorisation of terms of contracts 549–53
certainty: offer/acceptance and 30, 89–94
children/minors: effects of entering into contract with minor 232, 238–40; employment 235–7; fostering of 11; liability in tort 232, 240–2; minors' contracts 233–8; necessaries 234–5; reasons for limitations on capacity 232
classical law of contract 1, 3–5, 12
class-protecting statutes 480–1
coercion 407–11
cohabitation: agency from 212
collateral contracts 343–4; agency and 225; pre-contractual statements 254–5; privity of contract and 168, 192–3
collective agreements: intention to create legal relations 162–4
commercial agents 210, 220, 221
Common Frame of Reference (CFR) project 26–7

unconscionability and inequality of
bargaining power 422, 452–5
undue influence 18, 406, 421–5; actual 422,
425–6, 439–41; 'manifest disadvantage'
requirement 422, 432–5; presumed 422,
426–32; Principles of European Contract
Law (PECL) and 422, 455–7; remedies
449–51; third parties and 422, 435–49;
unconscionability and inequality of
bargaining power 422, 452–5
unfair terms: consumer contracts 329–35
unilateral contracts 30, 47; acceptance of
offers and 61, 76–83; agreement 81–2
unilateral mistake 372, 388–9
unjust enrichment 14
unsolicited goods 63–4
usual authority of agent 213
utmost good faith 348–9, 352

variation of contracts: consideration and
124–7; Contracts Rights of (Third Parties)
Act 1999 and 180–1; need for accord and
satisfaction 125; waiver concept 125–7
vicarious immunity 199–201
voluntary transactions 10–11

wagering contracts 461, 491
waiver concept 125–7
warranties 267–8; implied 536, 549
wartime: frustration and 514–15
wealth maximisation 20
will theory of contract 4
written contracts *see* formalities
wrongful interference with contractual rights
168, 204–5

young people *see* children/minors